H2

INTERNATIONAL MEDICAL GUIDE FOR SHIPS

Including the ship's medicine chest

Second edition

World Health Organization
Geneva
1988

The World Health Organization was established in 1948 as a specialized agency of the United Nations serving as the directing and coordinating authority for international health matters and public health. One of WHO's constitutional functions is to provide objective and reliable information and advice in the field of human health, a responsibility that it fulfils in part through its extensive programme of publications.

The Organization seeks through its publications to support national health strategies and address the most pressing public health concerns of populations around the world. To respond to the needs of Member States at all levels of development, WHO publishes practical manuals, handbooks and training material for specific categories of health workers; internationally applicable guidelines and standards; reviews and analyses of health policies, programmes and research; and state-of-the-art consensus reports that offer technical advice and recommendations for decision-makers.

These books are closely tied to the Organization's priority activities, encompassing disease prevention and control, the development of equitable health systems based on primary health care, and health promotion for individuals and communities. Progress towards better health for all also demands the global dissemination and exchange of information that draws on the knowledge and experience of all WHO's Member countries and the collaboration of world leaders in public health and the biomedical sciences.

To ensure the widest possible availability of authoritative information and guidance on health matters, WHO secures the broad international distribution of its publications and encourages their translation and adaptation. By helping to promote and protect health and prevent and control disease throughout the world, WHO's books contribute to achieving the Organization's principal objective – the attainment by all people of the highest possible level of health.

Illustrations by Shaun Smyth.

ISBN 92 4 154231 4

© World Health Organization 1988
Reprinted 1992, 1994, 1996, 1997

PRINTED IN SWITZERLAND
85/6641 – 92/9137 – 93/9866 – 96/10834 – 23 000
97/11547 – Schüler SA – 4000

Contents

Preface

Over 20 years have passed since the first edition of the *International Medical Guide for Ships* (IMGS) was published by the World Health Organization. During this time, it has served the international seafaring community well.

Scientific progress and developments in seafaring during the last decade have made it necessary to revise and update the guide. In September 1981, the Joint ILO/WHO Committee on the Health of Seafarers met in Geneva to review its technical content in detail and discuss the necessary changes. The Committee included representatives of the Inter-Governmental Maritime Consultative Organization (now the International Maritime Organization), of seafarers and of shipowners, experts on maritime medicine, and staff members of ILO and WHO. A list of the participants will be found in Annex 6.

Because it was important to have the revised version of the guide as soon as possible, it was decided to base it on recently published and updated national medical guides for ships.

The publishers of those guides have kindly made texts and illustrations available to WHO thus greatly reducing the time required to prepare the revised text. Thanks are due particularly to the United Kingdom Department of Trade and the United States Department of Health and Human Services, Public Health Service, for their contributions. Crown copyright material from the 1983 edition of *The ship captain's medical guide*[1] is used with the permission of the Controller of Her Britannic Majesty's Stationery Office. Material from *The ship's medicine chest and medical aid at sea*[2] was made available to WHO by the Office of the Surgeon General, United States Department of Health and Human Services, Public Health Service.

The updating of the guide began shortly after the joint ILO/WHO Committee meeting. The draft sections of the updated text were later reviewed by the relevant units and divisions at WHO Headquarters.

The general layout of the guide has been changed from that of the first edition, to make it easier for non-medical persons responsible for the health of people on board ship to find advice on how to deal with emergencies without delay.

Conditions requiring immediate first aid are dealt with in Chapter 1, the pages of which are colour marked.

This chapter is followed by one on the toxic hazards of chemicals carried on board ship, in which there are cross-references to the *Medical first aid guide for use in accidents involving dangerous goods*[3] published by the International Maritime Organization (IMO) on behalf of ILO, IMO, and WHO. This is the Chemicals Supplement to the present guide and must be available on board all ships that carry, or might carry, dangerous cargo.

The approach, used in the first edition, of grouping diseases in chapters based on systems: respiratory, digestive, nervous, etc. (as in a medical textbook) has been changed. For easy reference, about 60 diseases and medical problems have been selected (e.g., abdominal pain, chest pain, colds, cough, headache, and high temperature), arranged in alphabetical order, and described in a single chapter (Chapter 8).

Because of the increased employment of women on ships, a chapter on pregnancy and women's medical problems has been added. Other new chapters included in the revised guide deal with the medical care of castaways and rescued

---

[1] DEPARTMENT OF TRADE. *The ship captain's medical guide*. London, Her Majesty's Stationery Office, 1983.

[2] DEPARTMENT OF HEALTH AND HUMAN SERVICES, PUBLIC HEALTH SERVICE, OFFICE OF THE SURGEON GENERAL. *The ship's medicine chest and medical aid at sea*. Washington, DC, US Government Printing Office, 1984 (DHHS Publication No. (PHS) 84-2024).

[3] *Medical first aid guide for use in accidents involving dangerous goods*. London, International Maritime Organization, 1985.

persons, external assistance to be obtained in case of serious health problems at sea, and diseases of fishermen. The diseases described in the last-mentioned chapter have been selected mainly on the basis of experience among fishermen in the North Atlantic and North Sea. Contributions by doctors from fishing vessels operating in tropical waters are invited, so that a wider range of fishermen's diseases may be covered in the next edition.

It was decided that the section on the International Code of Signals in the first edition of the guide served no useful purpose, and it has been dropped. Coded messages on such important matters as health emergencies on board ship may give rise to misunderstanding and should be avoided as far as possible. Plain language should be used in communicating with doctors on shore or on board other ships.

Advice on the prevention of diseases has been included in the sections dealing with them, and also in a brief separate chapter (Chapter 16).

---

[1] WHO Technical Report Series, No. 770, 1988 (*The use of essential drugs:* third report of the WHO Expert Committee).

A list of medicines recommended for use on board ships follows the chapter giving general advice on medicines. It is based on the WHO list of essential drugs,[1] and generic names are used.

Both the list of medicines and the list of recommended surgical equipment, instruments, and supplies given in the guide should be reviewed once every two years by the national health authorities of the maritime countries and the necessary changes, deletions, and additions made, in order to keep up with scientific progress and the requirements of maritime practice.

The number of illustrations in the guide has been more than doubled and new tables have been added. These will make the book more useful for the training of non-medical personnel in dealing with health problems on board ship.

At the September 1981 meeting of the Joint ILO/WHO Committee, references were made to the modern telemetric system of sending health information from ship to a hospital on shore and back. Since the equipment and the necessary shore units are not yet available in most maritime countries, this subject has not been dealt with in the present edition.

Introduction.
How to use the guide

The three functions of this guide are:
- to enable users to diagnose and treat injured and sick seafarers;
- to serve as a textbook on medical problems for those studying for a certificate in medical training;
- to help in giving crews some training on first aid, and on the prevention of diseases.

The guide should be kept in the ship's medical cabinet.

Those seeing this revised, second edition of the guide for the first time, should familiarize themselves with its contents. This will not only refresh and update their knowledge of medical problems, but will also help them to find *quickly*, in the relevant chapter and page, all the necessary information and advice, when there is a case of injury or illness on board.

First aid

First aid treatment for casualties is presented in Chapter 1 and, as regards toxic hazards, in Chapter 2. The pages of Chapter 1 have coloured corners to make it quickly and easily identifiable. Normally, there will also be on board a copy of the IMO publication *Medical first aid guide for use in accidents involving dangerous goods* (the Chemicals Supplement to the present guide),[1] in which more information on the subject of poisoning may be found.

Chapter 4 describes such further treatment for wounds and other injuries as may be necessary, following first aid and removal of a casualty to the ship's hospital or cabin.

In an emergency, there will probably be no time to find and consult the relevant sections of the guide concerning first aid and the application of

---

[1] *Medical first aid guide for use in accidents involving dangerous goods.* London, International Maritime Organization, 1985.

artificial respiration to a casualty, since one or two minutes may mean the difference between life and death. All seafarers should therefore receive training in the basic first aid skills, and their training and retraining in this area should be continued on every voyage. The most important life-saving skills are: artificial respiration, heart compression, and the control of severe bleeding.

It is necessary that on board all ships not carrying a doctor there should be at least one crew member, but preferably more, not only with a good practical knowledge of first aid skills, but also with training in nursing patients, administering oxygen and drugs from the ship's medicine chest, giving injections, etc. These skills cannot be learned simply by reading sections of this guide. They must be demonstrated and practised under supervision before the need arises to employ them at sea.

Illness

When a person falls sick, the first step is diagnosis. Some diseases and medical problems are relatively easy to diagnose; the diagnosis of others may be much more difficult.

Chapter 3 (Examination of the patient) describes how to take a patient's history, how to conduct a physical examination, how to note and record symptoms and signs of disease systematically, and also how to draw conclusions leading to a probable diagnosis.

The tables and figures in the text will be helpful, particularly in cases of abdominal or chest pain.

Diagnosis of the common diseases need not always be difficult if the person responsible is methodical and makes plenty of legible notes.

Once the initial diagnosis is made, find the relevant section in the guide, read the description of the disease, and give the recommended treatment.

Monitor and record the patient's progress carefully. If other symptoms arise, check again to see whether the initial diagnosis was correct. If you are unsure of the diagnosis and the patient does not appear to be very ill, treat the symptoms only: for instance, relieve pain by giving acetylsalicylic acid or paracetamol tablets and allow the patient to rest in bed. See how the illness progresses. If the symptoms disappear you are on safe ground. If they do not, you will normally find that by the second or third day of the illness, the symptoms and signs are sufficient to permit a diagnosis. If the patient's condition worsens and you are still unable to make a diagnosis, seek RADIO MEDICAL ADVICE.

General advice on nursing the patient while he has to remain in bed, on treatment procedures, and on administering medicaments, is given in Chapter 5 (General nursing care).

Communicable diseases are described in Chapter 6, sexually transmitted diseases in Chapter 7, and other diseases and medical problems, including such general signs and symptoms as high temperature, cough, oedema, and abdominal and chest pain, in Chapter 8.

Women patients

Many ships carry women as passengers or crew members; some of their specific medical problems, and also pregnancy and childbirth, are described in Chapters 10 and 11.

Fishermen, castaways, radio medical advice

Also covered are diseases of fishermen (Chapter 9), and medical care of castaways and rescued persons (Chapter 12); advice is also given on what to do in the event of death at sea (Chapter 13).

Chapter 14 describes how to prepare and present information on a case of disease to the doctor on shore (or on board another ship), when requesting radio medical advice, and also how to arrange for the transport of a patient by helicopter.

Prevention

Prevention is always better than cure. Many diseases occurring among seafarers can easily be prevented. The chapters on environmental control aboard ship (Chapter 15) and disease prevention (Chapter 16) should be read by the person responsible for the health of the crew, seafarers should be advised accordingly, and appropriate measures aimed at controlling diseases should be taken, such as: conducting regular sanitary inspections of the ship and maintaining cleanliness in the crew's living quarters and the galley, controlling disease vectors on board, chemoprophylaxis of malaria, immunization, etc.

Medicines

Chapters 17 and 18 of the guide contain information on the procurement and storage of medicines for the ship's medicine chest and on their use. All the medicines are listed in alphabetical order, and also according to the site and nature of their action. Advice is given for each of them as regards use, dosage in adults, and specific precautions to be taken when administering them.

The Annexes

Annex 1 contains notes on anatomy and physiology, while the different regions of the body are named in Annex 2. These two annexes will help in the examination of patients, in diagnosis, and in the preparation of notes for a doctor on shore before requesting his advice by radio. Annex 5 describes a procedure for the disinfection of potable water with chlorine.

Chapter 1

First aid

First aid is the emergency treatment given to the ill or injured before professional medical services can be obtained. It is given to prevent death or further injury, to counteract shock, and to relieve pain. Certain conditions, such as severe bleeding or asphyxiation, require *immediate* treatment if the patient is to survive. In such cases, even a few seconds' delay might mean the difference between life and death. However, the treatment of most injuries or other medical emergencies may be safely postponed for the few minutes required to locate a crew-member skilled in first aid, or to locate suitable medical supplies and equipment.

All crew-members should be prepared to administer first aid. They should have sufficient knowledge of first aid to be able to apply true emergency measures and decide when treatment can be safely delayed until more skilled personnel arrive. Those not properly trained must recognize their limitations. Procedures and techniques beyond the rescuer's ability should *not* be attempted. More harm than good might result.

Contents

Priorities

On finding a casualty:

- look to your own safety: do not become the next casualty;
- if necessary, remove the casualty from danger or remove danger from the casualty (but see observation below on a casualty in an enclosed space). If there is only one unconscious or bleeding casualty (irrespective of the total number of casualties), give immediate treatment to that casualty only, and then send for help.

If there is more than one unconscious or bleeding casualty:

- send for help;
- then start giving appropriate treatment to the worst casualty in the following order of priority: severe bleeding; stopped breathing/heart; unconsciousness.

If the casualty is in an enclosed space, do not enter the enclosed space unless you are a trained

1

member of a rescue team acting under instructions. Send for help and inform the master.

It must be assumed that the atmosphere in the space is hostile. The rescue team MUST NOT enter unless wearing breathing apparatus which must also be fitted to the casualty as soon as possible. The casualty must be removed quickly to the nearest safe adjacent area outside the enclosed space unless his injuries and the likely time of evacuation make some treatment essential before he can be moved.

General principles of first aid aboard ship

First aid must be administered *immediately* to:

- restore breathing and heart-beat;
- control bleeding;
- remove poisons;
- prevent further injury to the patient (for instance, his removal from a room containing carbon monoxide or smoke).

A rapid, emergency evaluation of the patient should be made immediately at the scene of the injury to determine the type and extent of the trauma. Because every second may count, only the essential pieces of the patient's clothing should be removed.

In the case of an injured limb, get the sound limb out of the clothing first, and then peel the clothes off the injured limb. If necessary, cut clothes to expose the injured part.

Keep workers from crowding round.

The patient's pulse should be taken. If it cannot be felt at the wrist, it should be felt at the carotid artery at the side of the neck (see Fig. 2). If there is no pulse, heart compression and artificial respiration must be started (see Basic life support, page 6). The patient should be treated for shock if the pulse is weak and rapid, or the skin pale, cold, and possibly moist, with an increased rate of shallow, irregular breathing. Remember that shock can be a great danger to life, and its prevention is one of the main objectives of first aid (see Shock, page 17).

The patient should be kept in the position that best provides relief from his injuries. Usually this is a lying-down position, which increases circulation of the blood to the head.

The patient should be observed for type of breathing and possible bleeding. If he is not breathing, mouth-to-mouth or mouth-to-nose artificial respiration must be given (see pages 8–9).

Severe bleeding must be controlled.

During this time, the patient, if conscious, should be reassured and told that all possible help is being given. The rescuer should ask about the location of any painful areas.

The patient should be kept in a lying-down position and moved only when absolutely necessary. The general appearance of the patient should be observed, including any signs and symptoms that may indicate a specific injury or illness.

The patient should *not* be moved if injuries of the neck or spine are suspected. Fractures should be splinted before moving a patient (see pages 19–22). No attempt should be made to set a fracture.

Wounds and most burns should be covered to prevent infection. The treatment of specific injuries will be discussed more fully in the rest of this chapter, and in the next chapter.

Once life-saving measures have been started or deemed not necessary, the patient should be examined more thoroughly for other injuries.

The patient should be covered to prevent loss of body heat.

If necessary, protect him also from heat, remembering that in the tropics, the open steel deck on which he may be lying will usually be very hot.

The patient should not be given alcohol in any form.

Never underestimate and do not treat as minor injuries:

- unconsciousness (page 3);
- suspected internal bleeding (page 40);

2

- stab or puncture wounds (page 68);
- wounds near joints (see Fractures, page 19);
- possible fractures (page 19);
- eye injuries (page 76).

Note. Never consider anyone to be dead, until you and others agree that:

- no pulse can be felt, and no sounds are heard when the examiner's ear is put to the chest;
- breathing has stopped;
- the eyes are glazed and sunken;
- there is progressive cooling of the body (this may not apply if the surrounding air temperature is close to normal body temperature).

Unconscious casualties

(See also: Basic life support: artificial respiration and heart compression, page 6; General nursing care, Unconscious patients, page 104.)

The causes of unconsciousness are many and are often difficult to determine (see Table 1). Treatment varies with the cause, but in first aid it is usually not possible to make a diagnosis of the cause, let alone undertake treatment.

The immediate threat to life may be:

- breathing obstructed by the tongue falling back and blocking the throat;
- stopped heart.

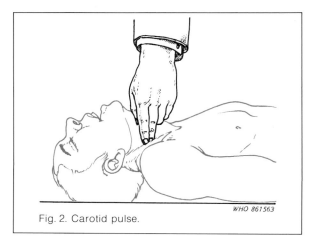

Fig. 2. Carotid pulse.

WHO 861563

Breathing

With an unconscious patient, first listen for breathing. To relieve obstructed breathing, tilt the head firmly backwards as far as it will go (see Fig. 1).

Listen and feel for any movement of air, because the chest and abdomen may move in the presence of an obstructed airway, without moving air. The rescuer's face should be placed within 2–3 cm of the patient's nose and mouth so that any exhaled air may be felt against his cheek. Also, the rise and fall of the chest can be observed and the exhaled breath heard (see Fig. 1).

Remove patient's dentures, if any.

Heart

Next, listen for heart sounds. Feel pulse at wrist (see page 94) and neck (carotid pulse, see Fig. 2).

Quickly check the carotid (neck) pulse by placing the tips of the two fingers of one hand into the groove between the windpipe and the large muscle at the side of the neck.

The carotid pulse is normally a strong one; if it cannot be felt or is feeble, there is insufficient circulation.

Check the pupils of the eyes to see if they are dilated or constricted. When the heart stops

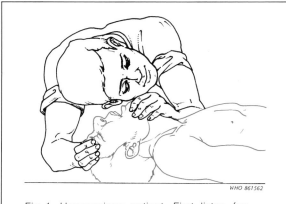

Fig. 1. Unconscious patient. First listen for breathing.

WHO 861562

3

Table 1. Diagnostic signs in unconsciousness

	1 Fainting (p. 199)	2 Concussion (p. 74)	3 Brain com- pression (p. 74)	4 Epilepsy (p. 195)	5 Stroke (p. 231)	6 Alcohol (p. 164)	7 Opium and morphine (p. 191)
Onset	usually sudden	sudden	usually gradual	sudden	sudden as a rule	gradual	gradual
Mental condition	complete unconsciousness	unconsciousness but sometimes confusion only	unconsciousness deepening	complete unconsciousness	complete or partial unconsciousness	stupor, later unconsciousness	unconsciousness deepening
Pulse	feeble and fast	feeble and irregular	gradually slower	fast	slow and full	full and fast, later fast and feeble	feeble and slow
Respiration	quick and shallow	shallow and irregular	slow and noisy	noisy, later deep and slow	slow and noisy	deep, slow, and noisy	slow, may be deep
Skin	pale, cold, and clammy	pale and cold	hot and flushed	livid, later pale	hot and flushed	flushed, later cold and clammy	pale, cold, and clammy
Pupils	equal and dilated	equal	unequal	equal and dilated	unequal	dilated, later may contract; eyes bloodshot	equal, very contracted
Paralysis	none	none	present (of leg or arm)	none	present in leg, arm, or face, or all three, on one side	none	none
Convulsions	none	none	present in some cases	present	present in some cases	none	none
Breath	–	–	–	–	–	smells of alcohol	with opium, musty smell
Special points	often giddiness and swaying before collapse	often signs of head injury; vomiting on recovery	often signs of head injury; remember delayed onset of symptoms	tongue often bitten; urine or faeces may be voided; sometimes injury in falling	over middle age; eyes may look to one side; sometimes loss of speech	absence of the smell of alcohol excludes it as cause, but its presence does not prove that alcohol is the cause	look for source of supply

8 Barbiturate (sedative tablets) (p. 57)	9 Uraemic coma (p. 236)	10 Sunstroke and heat-stroke (p. 205)	11 Electric shock (p. 19)	12 Cyanide (prussic acid) (p. 57)	13 Diabetic coma (p. 187)	14 Shock (p. 17)	
gradual	gradual	gradual or sudden	sudden	very rapid	gradual	gradual	Onset
stupor, later deepening uncon-sciousness	very drowsy, later un-conscious-ness	delirium or uncon-sciousness	unconscious-ness	confusion, later un-conscious-ness	drowsiness, later un-conscious-ness	listlessness, later un-conscious-ness	Mental condition
feeble and fast	full	fast and feeble	fast and feeble	fast and feeble, later stops	fast and feeble	fast and very feeble	Pulse
slow, noisy, and irregular	noisy and difficult	difficult	shallow and may cease	slow, gasping, and spas-modic	deep and sighing	rapid and shallow with occa-sional deep sigh	Respiration
cold and clammy	shallow, cold and dry	very hot and dry	pale, may be burnt	cold	livid, later pale	pale, cold and clammy	Skin
equal, some-what con-tracted	equal and contracted	equal	eyes may squint	equal, staring eyes	equal	equal, dilated	Pupils
none	none	none	may be pre-sent	none	none	none	Paralysis
none	present in some cases	present in some cases	present in some cases	present	none	none	Convulsions
–	sometimes smells of urine	–	–	smells of bit-ter almonds	smells of acetone	–	Breath
look for source of supply	vomiting in some cases	vomiting in some cases	muscular spasm often causes tight gripping of the electri-fied object	rapid de-terioration; breathing may stop	in early stages headache, restless-ness, and nausea; test urine for sugar	may vomit; in early stages, shivering, thirst, defec-tive vision, and ear noises	Special points

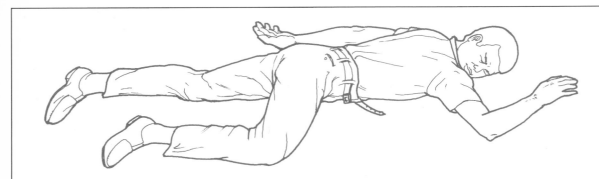

Fig. 3. The position for an unconscious patient: turn him face down, head to one side; no pillows should be used under the head. Pull up the leg and the arm on the side to which the head is facing, pull up the chin. Stretch other arm out, as shown. His clothes should be loosened at the neck and waist, and any artificial teeth removed.

beating, the pupils will begin to dilate within 45–60 seconds. They will stay dilated and will not react to light (see Physical examination (eyes), p. 63).

The examination for breathing and heart action should be done as quickly as possible. The rescuer must immediately establish if the casualty

- is not breathing and the heart has stopped, or
- is not breathing but the heart has not stopped.

Not breathing, heart stopped

A trained first-aider must begin heart compression at once. Unless circulation is restored, the brain will be without oxygen and the person will die within 4–6 minutes.

- Lay casualty on a hard surface.
- Start heart compression at once (see page 9).
- Give artificial respiration (see page 8), since breathing stops when the heart stops.

The necessary aid can be given by one person alternately compressing the heart and then filling the lungs with air, or — better still — by two people working together (see page 11–12).

Not breathing, heart not stopped

- Open mouth and ensure the airway is clear (see Airway, page 7).
- Begin ARTIFICIAL RESPIRATION at once (see page 8).

If the heart is beating and breathing restored, and the casualty is still unconscious, place the casualty in the UNCONSCIOUS POSITION (see Fig. 3).

Turn casualty face down, head to one side or the other (Fig. 3). *No pillows should be used under the head.* Now pull up the leg and the arm on the side to which the head is facing. Then pull up the chin. Stretch the other arm out as shown. The subsequent treatment of an unconscious person is described in Chapter 5 (page 104).

Follow other general principles of first aid (see page 2).

Basic life support: artificial respiration and heart compression

Basic life support is an emergency life-saving procedure that consists of recognizing and correcting failure of the respiratory or cardiovascular systems.

Oxygen, which is present in the atmosphere in a concentration of about 21%, is essential for the life of all cells. The brain, the principal organ for conscious life, starts to die if deprived of oxygen for as little as four minutes. In the delivery of oxygen from the atmosphere to the brain cells, there are two necessary actions: breathing (taking in oxygen through the body's air passages) and the circulation of oxygen-enriched blood. Any profound disturbance of the airway, the breathing, or the circulation can promptly produce brain death.

Basic life support comprises the "**ABC**" steps, which concern the airway, breathing, and circulation respectively.

Its prompt application is indicated for:

A. Airway obstruction
B. Breathing (respiratory) arrest
C. Circulatory or Cardiac (heart) arrest.

Basic life support requires no instruments or supplies, and the correct application of the steps for dealing with the above three problems can maintain life until the patient recovers sufficiently to be transported to a hospital, where he can be provided with *advanced* life support. The latter consists of the use of certain equipment, cardiac monitoring, defibrillation, the maintenance of an intravenous lifeline, and the infusion of appropriate drugs.

Basic life support must be undertaken with the maximum sense of urgency.

Ideally, only seconds should intervene between recognizing the need and starting the treatment. Any inadequacy or absence of breathing or circulation must be determined immediately.

If breathing alone is inadequate or absent, all that is necessary is either to open the AIRWAY or to apply ARTIFICIAL RESPIRATION.

If circulation is also absent, artificial circulation must be instituted through HEART COMPRESSION, in combination with artificial respiration.

If breathing stops before the heart stops, enough oxygen will be available in the lungs to maintain life for several minutes. However, if heart arrest occurs first, delivery of oxygen to the brain ceases immediately. Brain damage is possible if the brain is deprived of oxygen for 4–6 minutes. Beyond 6 minutes without oxygen, brain damage is very likely.

It is thus clear why speed is essential in determining the need for basic life support and instituting the necessary measures.

Once you have started basic life support, do not interrupt it for more than 5 seconds for any reason, except when it is necessary to move the patient; even in that case, interruptions should not exceed 15 seconds each.

Airway (Step A)

ESTABLISHING AN OPEN AIRWAY IS THE MOST IMPORTANT STEP IN ARTIFICIAL RESPIRATION. Spontaneous breathing may occur as a result of this simple measure. Place the patient in a face-up position on a hard surface. Put one hand beneath the patient's neck and the other hand on his forehead. Lift the neck with the one hand, and apply pressure to the forehead with the other to tilt the head backward (see Fig. 4). This extends the neck and moves the base of the tongue away from the back of the throat. *The head should be maintained in this position during the entire artificial respiration and heart compression procedure.* If the airway is still obstructed, any foreign material in the mouth or throat should be removed immediately with the fingers.

Once the airway has been opened, the patient may or may not start to breathe again. To assess whether breathing has returned, the person providing the basic life support must place his ear about 2–3 cm above the nose and mouth of the patient. If the rescuer can feel and hear the movement of air, and can see the patient's chest and abdomen move, breathing has returned. Feeling and hearing are far more important than seeing.

With airway obstruction, it is possible that there will be no air movement even though the chest and abdomen rise and fall with the patient's attempts to breathe. Also, observing chest and abdominal movement is difficult when the patient is fully clothed.

Breathing (Step B)

If the patient does not resume adequate, spontaneous breathing promptly after his head has

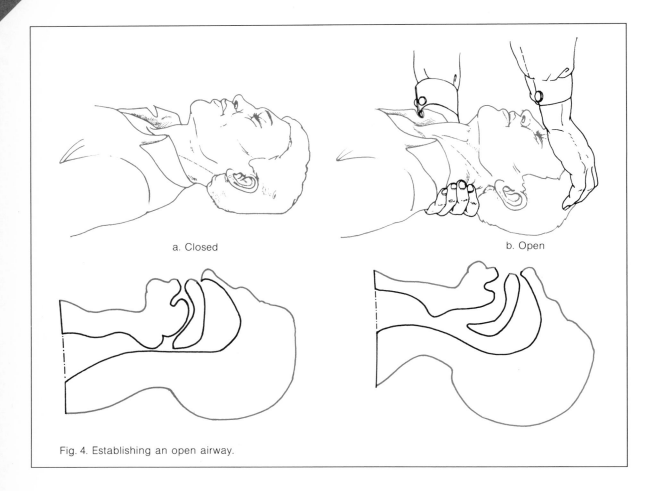

a. Closed

b. Open

Fig. 4. Establishing an open airway.

been tilted backward, artificial respiration should be given by the mouth-to-mouth or mouth-to-nose method or other techniques. Regardless of the method used, preservation of an open airway is essential.

Mouth-to-mouth respiration

- Keep the patient's head at a maximum backward tilt with one hand under the neck (see Fig. 4b).
- Place the heel of *the other hand* on the forehead, with the thumb and index finger toward the nose. Pinch together the patient's nostrils with the thumb and index finger to prevent air from escaping.

Continue to exert pressure on the forehead with the palm of the hand to maintain the backward tilt of the head.
- Take a deep breath, then form a tight seal with your mouth over and around the patient's mouth (see Fig. 5).
- Blow four quick, full breaths in first without allowing the lungs to deflate fully.
- Watch the patient's chest while inflating the lungs. If adequate respiration is taking place, the chest should rise and fall.
- Remove your mouth and allow the patient to exhale passively. If you are in the right position, the patient's exhalation will be felt on your cheek (see Fig. 6).

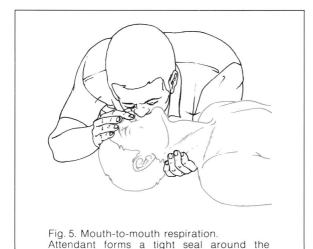

Fig. 5. Mouth-to-mouth respiration. Attendant forms a tight seal around the patient's mouth with his own mouth and blows forcefully.

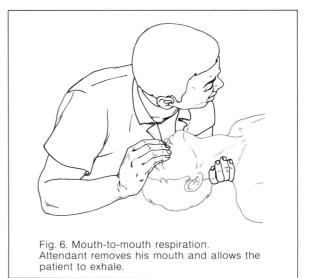

Fig. 6. Mouth-to-mouth respiration. Attendant removes his mouth and allows the patient to exhale.

- Take another deep breath, form a tight seal around the patient's mouth, and blow into the mouth again. Repeat this procedure 10–12 times a minute (once every five seconds) for adults and children over four years of age.
- If there is no air exchange and an airway obstruction exists, reach into the patient's mouth and throat to remove any foreign matter with your fingers, then resume artificial respiration. A foreign body should be suspected if you are unable to inflate the lungs despite proper positioning and a tight air-seal round the mouth or nose.

Mouth-to-nose respiration

The mouth-to-nose technique should be used when it is impossible to open the patient's mouth, when the mouth is severely injured, or when a tight seal round the lips cannot be obtained (see Fig. 7).

- Keep the patient's head tilted back with one hand. Use the other hand to lift up the patient's lower jaw to seal the lips.
- Take a deep breath, seal your lips round the patient's nose, and blow in forcefully and smoothly until the patient's chest rises. Repeat quickly four times.

- Remove your mouth and allow the patient to exhale passively.
- Repeat the cycle 10–12 times per minute.

Alternative method of artificial respiration (Silvester method)

In some instances, mouth-to-mouth respiration cannot be used. For instance, certain toxic and caustic materials constitute a hazard for the rescuer, or facial injuries may prohibit the use of the mouth-to-mouth or mouth-to-nose technique. An alternative method of artificial respiration (shown in Fig. 8) should then be applied. However, this method is much less effective than those previously described and it should be used only when the mouth-to-mouth technique cannot be used.

Artificial respiration should be continued as long as there are signs of life; it may be necessary to carry on for up to two hours, or longer.

Heart compression (Step C)

In attempting to bring back to life a non-breathing person whose heart has stopped beating, heart compression (external cardiac compression) should be applied along with artificial respiration.

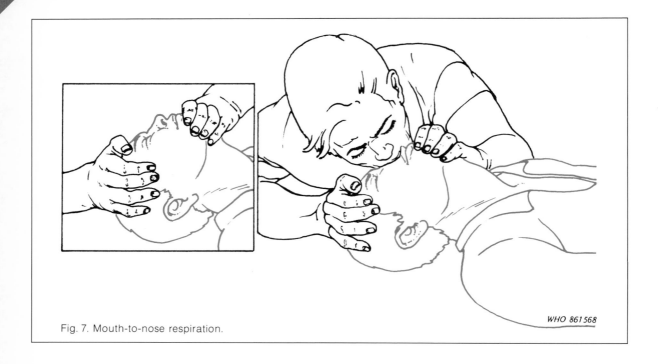

Fig. 7. Mouth-to-nose respiration.

WHO 861568

Artificial respiration will bring oxygen-containing air to the lungs of the victim. From there, oxygen is transported with circulating blood to the brain and to other organs. Effective heart compression will — for some time — artificially restore the blood circulation, until the heart starts beating.

Technique for heart compression

Compression of the sternum produces some artificial ventilation, but not enough for adequate oxygenation of the blood. For this reason, artificial respiration is always required whenever heart compression is used.

Effective heart compression requires sufficient pressure to depress the patient's lower sternum about 4–5 cm (in an adult). *For chest compression to be effective, the patient must be on a firm surface. If he is in bed, a board or improvised support should be placed under his back. However, chest compression must not be delayed by a search for a firmer support.*

Kneel close to the side of the patient and place the heel of one hand over the lower half of the sternum. Avoid placing the hand over the tip (xiphoid process) of the breastbone, which extends down over the upper abdomen. Pressure on the xiphoid process may tear the liver and lead to severe internal bleeding.

Feel the tip of the sternum and place the heel of the hand about 4 cm nearer the head of the patient (see Fig. 9). Your fingers must never rest on the patient's ribs during compression, since this increases the possibility of rib fractures.

- Place the heel of the other hand on top of the first one.
- Rock forward so that your shoulders are almost directly above the patient's chest.
- Keep your arms straight and exert adequate pressure almost directly downwards to depress an adult's lower sternum 4–5 cm.
- Depress the sternum 60 times per minute for an adult (if someone else is available to give artificial respiration). This is usually enough to maintain blood flow, and slow enough to allow the heart to fill with blood. The com-

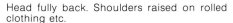

Head fully back. Shoulders raised on rolled clothing etc.

Hard surface

WHO 861569

A. Lay the patient on his back on a firm surface.
   Raise his shoulders on a cushion or folded jacket, or in some other way.

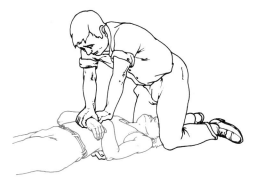

B. Kneel astride the patient's head. If necessary, turn his head to one side to clear out the mouth.
   Grasp his wrists and cross them over the lower part of his chest.

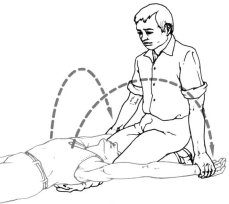

C. Rock your body forward and press down on the patient's chest. Release the pressure and, with a sweeping movement, draw the patient's arms backwards and outwards as far as possible. Repeat this procedure rhythmically (twelve times per minute). Keep the mouth clear.

Fig. 8. The Silvester method: an alternative method of artificial respiration.
It is particularly recommended for patients who have swallowed poison.

pression should be regular, smooth, and uninterrupted, compression and relaxation being of equal duration. **Under no circumstances should compression be interrupted for more than five seconds** (see page 7).

It is preferable to have two rescuers because artificial circulation must be combined with artificial respiration (see Fig. 10). The most effective artificial respiration and heart compression are achieved by giving one lung inflation quickly after each five heart compressions (5:1 ratio). *The compression rate should be 60 per minute if two rescuers are operating.* One rescuer performs heart compression, while the other remains at the patient's head, keeps it tilted back, and

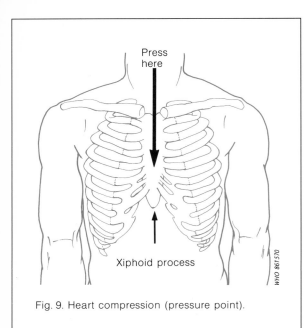

Fig. 9. Heart compression (pressure point).

Press here

Xiphoid process

WHO 861570

continues rescue breathing (artificial respiration). **It is important to supply the breaths without any pauses in heart compression, because every interruption in this compression results in a drop of blood flow and blood pressure to zero.**

A single rescuer must perform both artificial respiration and artificial circulation using a 15:2 ratio (see Fig. 11). Two very quick lung inflations should be delivered after each 15 chest compressions, without waiting for full exhalation of the patient's breath. A rate equivalent to 80 chest compressions per minute must be maintained by a single rescuer in order to achieve 50–60 actual compressions per minute, because of the interruptions for the lung inflations.

Checking effectiveness of heart compression: pupils and pulse

Check the reaction of the pupils. If the pupils contract when exposed to light, this is a sign that

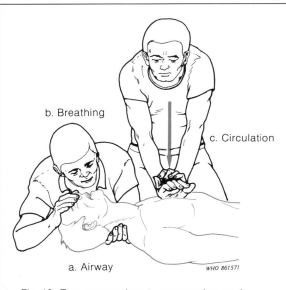

b. Breathing

c. Circulation

a. Airway

WHO 861571

Fig. 10. Two-rescuer heart compression and artificial respiration.

Five chest compressions:
– at a rate of 60 per minute
– no pause for ventilation.

One respiration:
– after each 5 compressions
– interposed between compressions.

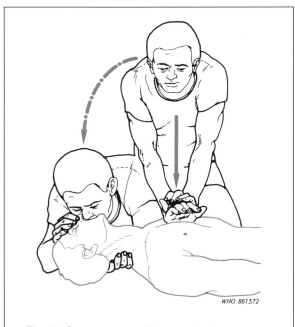

WHO 861572

Fig. 11. One-rescuer artificial respiration and heart compression.

Fifteen chest compressions:
– at a rate of 80 per minute.

Two quick lung inflations.

the brain is receiving adequate oxygen and blood. If the pupils remain widely dilated and do not react to light, serious brain damage is likely to occur soon or has occurred already. Dilated but reactive pupils are a less serious sign.

The carotid (neck) pulse (see Fig. 2, page 3) should be felt after the first minute of heart compression and artificial respiration, and every five minutes thereafter. The pulse will indicate the effectiveness of the heart compression or the return of a spontaneous effective heartbeat.

Other indicators of this effectiveness are:
- expansion of the chest each time the operator blows air into the lungs;
- a pulse that can be felt each time the chest is compressed;
- return of colour to the skin;
- a spontaneous gasp for breath;
- return of a spontaneous heartbeat.

Summary of points to be remembered when applying artificial respiration and heart compression

Don't delay   Place victim on his back on a hard surface.

Step A. **Airway** – If patient is unconscious, open the airway; thereafter make sure it stays open.

- Lift up neck.
- Push forehead back.
- Clear out mouth with fingers.

Step B. **Breathing** – If patient is *not* breathing, begin artificial respiration. Mouth-to-mouth or mouth-to-nose respiration.

- Before beginning artificial respiration, check *carotid pulse* in neck. It should be felt again after the first minute and checked every five minutes thereafter.
- Give four quick breaths and continue at a rate of 12 inflations per minute.
- Chest should rise and fall. If it does not, check to make sure the victim's head is tilted as far back as possible.
- If necessary, use fingers to clear the airway.

Step C. **Circulation** – If pulse is absent, begin heart compression. If possible, use two rescuers. *Don't delay*. One rescuer can do the job.

- Locate pressure point (lower half of sternum).
- Depress sternum 4–5 cm, 60 to 80 times per minute.
- If *one rescuer* – 15 compressions and two quick inflations.
- If *two rescuers* – 5 compressions and one inflation.

Pupils of eyes should be checked during heart compression. Constriction of a pupil on exposure to light shows that the brain is getting adequate blood and oxygen.

Terminating heart compression

Deep unconsciousness, the absence of spontaneous respiration, and fixed, dilated pupils for 15–30 minutes indicate cerebral death of the victim, and further efforts to restore circulation and breathing are usually futile.

In the absence of a physician, artificial respiration and heart compression should be continued until:

- the heart of the victim starts beating again and breathing is restored;
  or
- the victim is transferred to the care of a doctor or of other health personnel responsible for emergency care;
  or
- the rescuer is unable to continue because of fatigue.

Severe bleeding

The human body contains approximately 5 litres of blood. A healthy adult can lose up to half a litre of blood without harmful effects, but the loss of more than this can be threatening to life.

Haemorrhage from major blood vessels of the arms, neck, and thighs may occur so rapidly and extensively that death occurs in a few minutes. Haemorrhage must be controlled immediately to prevent excessive loss of blood.

Bleeding may occur externally following an injury to the outside of the body, or internally from an injury in which blood escapes into tissue spaces or the body cavity.

The signs and symptoms of excessive loss of blood are: weakness or fainting; dizziness; pale, moist, and clammy skin; nausea; thirst; fast, weak, and irregular pulse; shortness of breath; dilated pupils; ringing in the ears; restlessness; and apprehension. The patient may lose consciousness and stop breathing. The number of symptoms and their severity are generally related to how fast the blood is lost and in what amount.

Once the bleeding has been controlled, the patient should be placed in a reclining position,

encouraged to lie quietly, and treated for shock (see page 17).

Fluids should not be given by mouth when internal injury is suspected.

Control

Bleeding may be controlled by direct pressure, elevation, and pressure at pressure points. A tourniquet should be applied *only* when every other method fails to control the excessive bleeding.

Direct pressure

The simplest and preferred method of controlling severe bleeding is to place a dressing over the wound and apply pressure directly to the bleeding site with the palm of the hand (see Fig. 12). Ideally a sterile dressing should be applied; otherwise, the cleanest cloth available should be used. In the absence of a dressing or cloth, the bare hand may be used until a dressing is available. If the dressing becomes soaked with blood, another dressing should be applied over the first one with firmer hand pressure. The initial dressing should not be removed because this will disturb the clotting process.

A pressure bandage can be applied over the dressing area to hold the dressing in place (see Fig. 13). The bandage should be tied over the dressing to provide additional pressure.

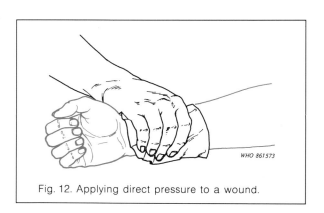

WHO 861573

Fig. 12. Applying direct pressure to a wound.

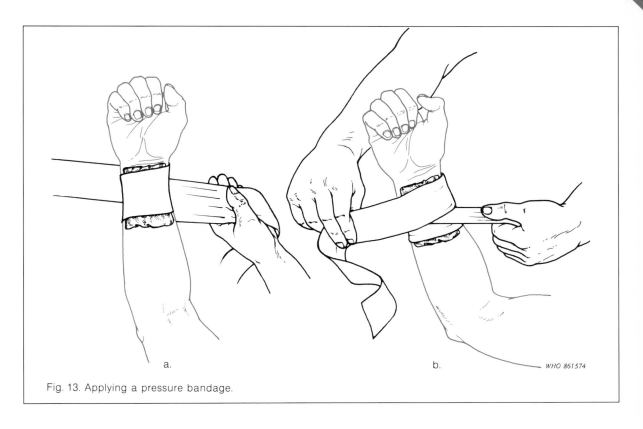

a. b. WHO 861574

Fig. 13. Applying a pressure bandage.

Do *not* cut off the circulation. A pulse should be felt on the side of the injured part away from the heart. If the bandage has been applied properly, it should be allowed to remain in place undisturbed for at least 24 hours. If the dressings are not soaked with blood and the circulation beyond the pressure dressing is adequate, they need not be changed for several days.

Elevation

When there is a severely bleeding wound of an extremity or the head, direct pressure should be applied on a dressing over the wound with the affected part elevated. This elevation lowers the blood pressure in the affected part and the flow of blood is lessened.

Pressure points

When direct pressure and elevation cannot control severe bleeding, pressure should be applied to the artery that supplies the area. Because this technique reduces the circulation to the wounded part below the pressure point, it should be applied only when absolutely necessary and only until the severe bleeding has lessened. There are a large number of sites where the fingers may be applied to help control bleeding (see Fig. 14). However, the brachial artery in the upper arm and the femoral artery in the groin are those where pressure can be most effective.

The pressure point for the brachial artery is located midway between the elbow and the armpit on the inner arm between the large muscles. To apply pressure, one hand should be round the patient's arm with the thumb on the outside of the arm and the fingers on the inside. Pressure is applied by moving the flattened fingers and the thumb towards one another. The pressure point for the femoral artery is located on the front of the upper leg just below the middle of the crease of the groin. Before pressure is applied, the patient should be turned on his back. Pressure

15

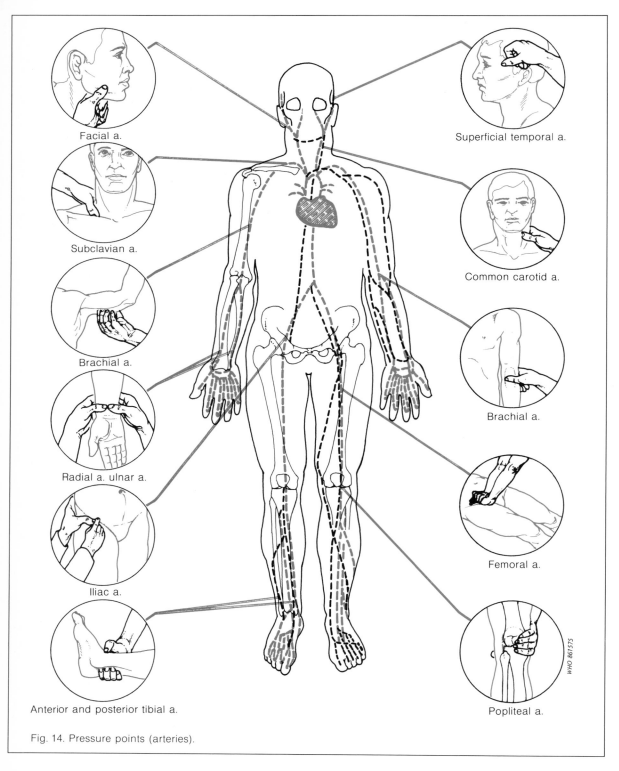

Facial a.

Superficial temporal a.

Subclavian a.

Common carotid a.

Brachial a.

Brachial a.

Radial a. ulnar a.

Femoral a.

Iliac a.

Popliteal a.

Anterior and posterior tibial a.

Fig. 14. Pressure points (arteries).

WHO 861575

should be applied with the heel of the hand while keeping the arm straight.

Tourniquet

A tourniquet should be applied to control bleeding *only* when all other means have failed. Unlike direct hand pressure, a tourniquet shuts off all normal blood circulation beyond the site of application. Lack of oxygen and blood may lead to the destruction of tissue, possibly requiring amputation of a limb. Releasing the tourniquet periodically will result in loss of blood and danger of shock. If the tourniquet is too tight or too narrow, it will damage the muscles, nerves, and blood vessels; if too loose, it may increase blood loss. Also, there have been cases where tourniquets have been applied and forgotten. **If a tourniquet is applied to save a life, immediate RADIO MEDICAL ADVICE must be obtained.**

A tourniquet must be improvised from a *wide* band of cloth. An improvised tourniquet may be made from folded triangular bandages, clothing, or similar material.

Fig. 15 shows how to apply a tourniquet, and how to secure it with a piece of wood. Record the time the tourniquet was applied. If you are sending the casualty to hospital, attach a sheet of paper to his clothing or an extremity, indicating this time.

Note
- Never cover the tourniquet with clothing or bandages, or hide it in any way.
- Never loosen the tourniquet, unless a physician advises it.

Shock

Shock following an injury is the result of a decrease in the vital functions of the various organs of the body. These functions are depressed because of inadequate circulation of blood or an oxygen deficiency.

Shock usually follows severe injuries such as extensive burns, major crushing injuries (particularly of the chest and abdomen), fractures of large bones, and other extensive or extremely

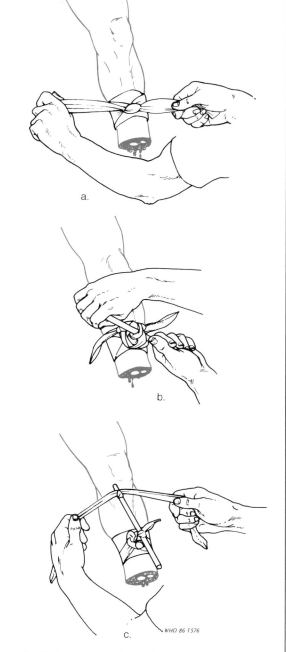

Fig. 15. Applying and securing a tourniquet.

Note
- Never cover the tourniquet with clothing or bandages, or hide it in any way.
- Never loosen the tourniquet, unless a physician advises it.

painful injuries. Shock follows the loss of large quantities of blood; allergic reactions; poisoning from drugs, gases, and other chemicals; alcohol intoxication; and the rupture of a stomach ulcer. It also may be associated with many severe illnesses such as infections, strokes, and heart attacks.

In some individuals the emotional response to trivial injuries or even to the mere sight of blood is so great that they feel weak and nauseated and may faint. This reaction may be considered to be an extremely mild form of shock which is not serious and will disappear quickly if the patient lies down.

Severe shock seriously threatens the life of the patient.

Signs and symptoms of shock are:

- *Paleness*. The skin is pale, cold, and often moist. Later it may develop a bluish, ashen colour. If the patient has dark skin, the colour of mucous membranes and nail beds should be examined.
- *Rapid and shallow respirations*. Alternatively breathing could be irregular and deep.
- *Thirst, nausea, and vomiting*. These frequently occur in a haemorrhaging patient in shock.
- *Weak and rapid pulse*. Usually the pulse rate is over 100.
- *Restlessness, excitement, and anxiety*. These occur early, later giving way to mental dullness, and still later to unconsciousness. In this late stage the pupils are dilated, giving the patient a vacant, glassy stare.

Although these symptoms may not be evident, all seriously injured persons should be treated for shock to prevent its possible development.

Treatment

- *Eliminate the causes of shock*. This includes controlling bleeding, restoring breathing, and relieving severe pain.

- *Have the injured person lie down*. The patient should be placed in a horizontal position. The patient's legs may be elevated approximately 30 cm to assist the flow of blood to the heart and head. The legs should not be elevated if there is injury to the head, pelvis, spine, or chest, or difficulty in breathing.

- *Keep the patient warm, but not hot*. Too much heat raises the surface temperature of the body and diverts the blood supply away from vital organs to the skin.

- *Relieve pain as quickly as possible*. If pain is severe, 10 mg of morphine sulfate may be given by intramuscular injection. If the blood pressure is low, morphine sulfate should *not* be given because it may cause an additional drop in the pressure. Also, it should not be given to injured patients unless pain is severe. The dosage should be repeated only after obtaining RADIO MEDICAL ADVICE.

- *Administer fluids*. Liquids should not be given by mouth if the patient is unconscious, drowsy, convulsing, or about to have surgery. Also, fluids should *not* be given if there is a puncture or crush wound to the abdomen, or a brain injury. If none of the above conditions is present, give the patient a solution of oral rehydration salts (half a glass every 15 minutes).
Alcohol should NEVER be given.

The intravenous administration of fluids is preferable in the treatment of shock, if a person trained to administer them is available (see page 117). Dextran (60 g/litre, 6%) and sodium chloride (9 g/litre, 0.9%) solution (injection) may be given intravenously.

In a case of suspected shock, get RADIO MEDICAL ADVICE.

Clothing on fire

If someone's clothing is on fire, by far the best way to put the fire out is to use a dry-powder fire extinguisher *at once*. If a dry-powder extinguisher is not available, then lay the person down and smother the flames by wrapping him in any available material, or throw bucketfuls of water over him, or use a hose, if available. Make sure that all smouldering clothing is extinguished.

First aid

Note. The powder from a fire extinguisher will not cause much, if any, eye damage. Most people shut their eyes tightly if sprayed with powder. Any powder in the eye should be washed out immediately after the fire has been extinguished and while burns are being cooled.

Heat burns and scalds

All heat burns should be *cooled as quickly as possible* with running cold water (sea or fresh), applied for *at least ten minutes,* or by immersion in basins of cold water. If it is not possible to cool a burn on the spot, the casualty should be taken to a place where cooling can be carried out. Try to remove clothing gently but do not tear off any that adheres to the skin. Then cover the burned areas with a dry, non-fluffy dressing larger than the burns, and bandage in place.

For further advice on classification, treatment, and prognosis in burns, see Burns and scalds (page 80).

In cases of severe burns followed by shock (see page 17), obtain RADIO MEDICAL ADVICE as soon as possible.

Electrical burns and electrocution

Make sure you do not become the next casualty when approaching any person who is in contact with electricity. If possible, switch off the current. Otherwise insulate yourself before approaching and touching the casualty, by using rubber gloves, wearing rubber boots, or standing on an insulating rubber mat.

Electrical lines may be removed from the casualty with a wooden pole, a chair, an insulated cord, or other non-metal object.

Then check casualty immediately for breathing and heartbeat.

If casualty is not breathing, give artificial respiration (see page 8).

If heart has stopped, apply heart compression (see page 9).

Send for help.

When the casualty is breathing, cool any burnt areas with cold water and apply a clean, dry, non-fluffy covering to these areas.

The treatment for electrical burns is the same as for thermal burns (see page 80). It includes relief of pain, prevention and treatment of shock, and control of infection.

Electrical burns may be followed by paralysis of the respiratory centre, unconsciousness, and instant death.

Chemical splashes

Remove contaminated clothing. Drench casualty with water to wash the chemical from the eyes and skin. *Give priority to washing the eyes* which are particularly vulnerable to chemical splashes. If only one eye is affected, incline the head to the side of the affected eye to prevent the chemical from running across into the other eye.

For further advice on treatment, see Skin contact and Eye contact (page 56) in Chapter 2, Toxic hazards of chemicals.

Fractures

A fracture is a broken bone. The bone may be broken into two or more pieces or it may have a linear crack. Fractures are described as closed if the skin remains unbroken. If there is a wound at or near the break, it is said to be an open fracture (see Fig. 16).

Careless handling of a patient may change a simple fracture into a compound one, by forcing jagged bone-ends through intact overlying skin. Compound fractures accompanied by serious bleeding are likely to give rise to shock (see page 17), especially if a large bone is involved.

The following are indications that a bone is very probably broken:

- The fact that a heavy blow or other force has been applied to the body or limbs.
- The casualty himself, or other people, may have heard the bone break.
- *Intense pain,* especially on pressure or movement at the site.

19

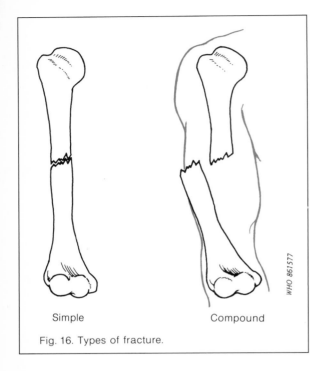

Simple   Compound

WHO 861577

Fig. 16. Types of fracture.

- *Distortion.* Compare good with injured limb or side of the body to see if the affected part is swollen, bent, twisted, or shortened.
- *Irregularity.* The irregular edges of a broken bone can sometimes be seen in an open fracture. They may be seen or felt under the skin in a closed fracture.
- *Loss of use.* The casualty may be unable or unwilling to use the injured part because of the pain. He may also experience severe pain if an attempt, even a very gentle one, is made to help him move it. Watch his face for signs of pain. Occasionally, if the broken ends of a bone are impacted together, the patient may be able to use the affected part but usually only with a fair amount of pain.
- *Unnatural movement and grating of bone-ends.* Neither of these symptoms should be sought deliberately. A limb may feel limp and wobbly, and grating may be felt when an attempt is made to apply support to the limb. Either of these indicates that the bone is certainly broken.
- *Swelling.* The site may be swollen and/or bruised. This may be due to internal bleeding.

Swelling almost always occurs immediately, and discoloration of the skin may follow.

General treatment

RADIO MEDICAL ADVICE should be sought early in the case of a compound fracture or a severe type of fracture (skull, femur, pelvis, spine) because it might be necessary to evacuate the patient from the ship.

Unless there is an immediate danger of further injury, the patient should not be moved until bleeding is controlled and all fractures are immobilized by splinting.

Bleeding

Bleeding from open fractures should be stopped in the normal way by pressing the area the blood comes from and applying a dressing. Blood will not come from the broken bone-end but from around the break. Care must be exercised in lifting up the affected part if it is broken, but it should always be elevated if bleeding is severe. People can die from loss of blood; they will not die from a broken bone, although moving it may be painful. Rest is very important to prevent further bleeding, to prevent further damage, and to relieve pain.

If bleeding is well controlled, the wound can be treated. The area round it should be cleansed thoroughly with soap and water and then disinfected with 1% (10 g/litre) cetrimide solution. Surface washings should not be allowed to spill into the wound. The wound itself should not be washed. It should be covered with a sterile dressing. Particles of dirt and pieces of clothing, wood, etc. should be gently removed from the wound with sterilized forceps. Blood clots should not be disturbed, as this may cause fresh bleeding. The wound should not be sutured. Dressings on it should be allowed to remain in place 4–5 days (if there is no wound infection).

Pain

If the patient is in severe pain, 10 mg of morphine sulfate may be given by intramuscular injection. Before repeating the dosage, RADIO MEDICAL ADVICE should be obtained.

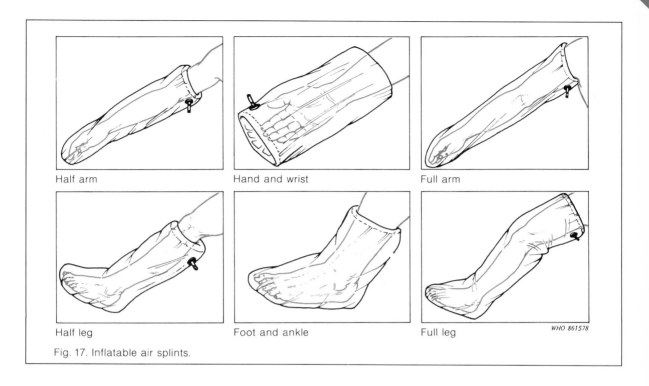

Half arm

Hand and wrist

Full arm

Half leg

Foot and ankle

Full leg

WHO 861578

Fig. 17. Inflatable air splints.

Care should be taken not to aggravate pain by moving or roughly handling the injured part.

Immobilization

Inflatable splints are a useful method for temporarily immobilizing limb fractures but are unsuitable for fractures that are more than a short distance above the knee or elbow, as they cannot provide sufficient immobilization in these places. The splint is applied to the limb and inflated by mouth (see Fig. 17). Other methods of inflation can make the splint too tight and thus slow down or stop the circulation. Inflatable splints can be applied over wound dressings.

The splints are made of clear plastic through which any bleeding from the wound can easily be seen. All sharp objects and sharp edges must be kept well clear of inflatable splints to avoid puncture.

To provide adequate stability, the splint should be long enough to extend beyond the joints at the end of the fractured bone.

Inflatable splints may be used when a patient is being transported about the ship or during removal to hospital. **They should not be left in place for more than a few hours.** Other means of immobilizing the fracture should be used after that period.

Immobilize a limb in the position in which it is found, if it is comfortable. If it does become necessary to move an injured limb because of poor circulation or for any other reason, first apply traction by pulling the limb gently and firmly away from the body before attempting to move it.

If a long bone in the arm or leg has been fractured, it should be straightened carefully. Traction should be applied on the hand or the foot, and the limb moved back into position (see Fig. 18). Compound fractures of joints, such as the elbow or knee, should not be manipulated. They should be placed gently into a proper position for splinting. The knee should be splinted straight. The elbow should be splinted at a right angle.

21

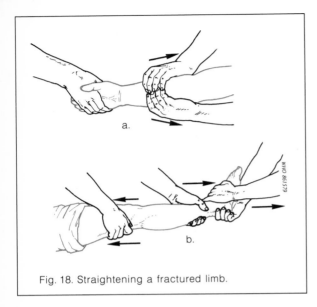

Fig. 18. Straightening a fractured limb.

Circulation of the blood

Check and re-check the circulation of blood in a fractured limb by pressing on a nail. When circulation is normal, the nail becomes white when pressed and pink when released. Continue until you are satsified that all is well. Danger signs are:

- blueness or whiteness of fingers and toes;
- coldness of the parts below the fracture;
- loss of feeling below the injury (test for this by touching casualty lightly on fingers or toes and asking him if he can feel anything);
- absence of pulse.

If there is any doubt at all about the circulation, loosen all tight and limb-encircling dressings at once and straighten out the limb, remembering to use traction when doing so. **Check the circulation again.** If the limb does not become pink and warm and you cannot detect a pulse, then medical help is probably urgently necessary if amputation is to be avoided. Get RADIO MEDICAL ADVICE.

Remember that fractures may cause serious blood loss internally. Check and take the appropriate action (see Internal bleeding, page 40, and Severe bleeding, page 14).

Fractures of specific body areas

Skull

A fracture of the skull may be caused by a fall, a direct blow, a crushing injury, or a penetrating injury such as a bullet wound. The patient may be conscious, unconscious, or dizzy, and have a headache or nausea. Bleeding from the nose, ears, or mouth may be present; and there may be paralysis and signs of shock.

Treatment. The patient with a head injury should receive immediate attention to prevent additional damage to the brain. The patient should be kept lying down. If the face is flushed, the head and shoulders should be elevated slightly. If the face is pale, the head should be kept level with the body or slightly lower. Bleeding can be controlled by direct pressure on the temporal or carotid arteries. The patient should be moved carefully with the head supported on each side with a sandbag.

Morphine sulfate should never be given.

Upper jaw

In all injuries of the face, ensuring an adequate airway must be the first consideration (see Airway, page 7).

Treatment. If there are wounds, bleeding should be controlled. Loose teeth should not be removed without RADIO MEDICAL ADVICE, unless it is feared that they will be swallowed or block the airway.

Lower jaw

A fracture may cause a deformity of the jaw, missing or uneven teeth, bleeding from the gums, swelling, and difficulty in swallowing.

Treatment. The injured jaw may interfere with breathing. If this occurs, the jaw and tongue should be pulled forward and maintained in that position. A problem arises when *both* sides of the jaw are broken. In this case the jaw and tongue may move backwards and obstruct the air passages. Hook a finger — yours or the casualty's — over and behind the lower front teeth and pull the jaw, and with it the tongue, forward. Then, if possible, arrange for the casualty to sit up with his head forward. Clenching the teeth may also stop further slippage. If the casualty cannot be put in a sitting position on account of other injuries, he must be placed in the unconscious position and another person must stay with him, keeping the jaw pulled forward, if necessary, and watching carefully for any sign of obstructed breathing. Normally, jaw fractures give little trouble because the casualty sits with the teeth clenched, often refusing to speak much on account of pain. The spasm in the jaw muscles which is caused by pain keeps the teeth clenched and the jaw immobilized.

Application of cold compresses may reduce the swelling and pain. The patient's jaw must be immobilized not only by closing his mouth as much as possible but also by applying a bandage (see Fig. 19). If the patient is unconscious or bleeding from the mouth, or if there is danger of vomiting, an attendant must be present at all times to loosen the bandage if necessary.

Treat for pain (see page 20).

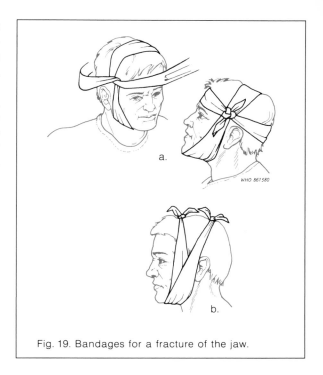

Fig. 19. Bandages for a fracture of the jaw.

Collar bone, shoulder blade, and shoulder

Fractures in these areas are often the result either of a fall on the outstretched hand or a fall on the shoulder. Direct violence to the affected parts is a less common cause. Place loose padding about the size of a fist into the armpit. Then tie the arm to the body. A convenient way of doing this is to use a triangular sling (see Fig. 20). Keep the casualty sitting up as he will be most comfortable in this position.

Upper arm (humerus) and the elbow

Complications may occur in fractures of the humerus because of the closeness of the nerves and blood vessels to the bone. There is pain and tenderness at the fracture site, and an obvious deformity may be present. The patient may be unable to lift his arm or to bend his elbow.

Treatment. A full-arm, inflatable air splint should be applied to the fracture (see Fig. 17). If inflatable splints are not available, the arm should be placed in a sling, with the sling and arm secured to the body by a wide cravat bandage (see Fig. 20). A short padded splint, applied to the outer surface of the arm, may also be used (see Fig. 21). The elbow should not be bent, if it does not bend easily. Long, padded splints should be applied, one to the outer surface and another to the inner surface of the arm. If there is any possibility that the elbow is involved in the fracture, the joint should be immobilized with a splint (see Fig. 22).

Treat for pain (see page 20).

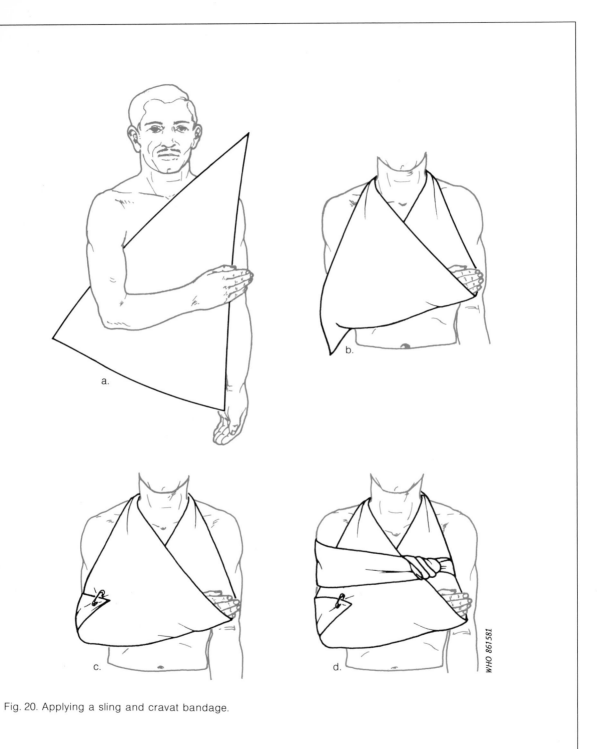

Fig. 20. Applying a sling and cravat bandage.

WHO 861581

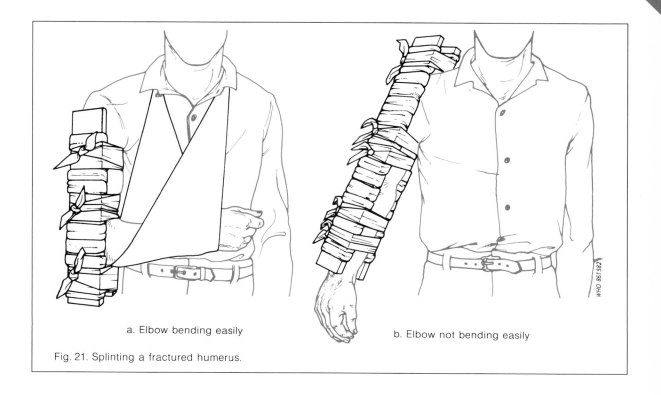

a. Elbow bending easily

b. Elbow not bending easily

Fig. 21. Splinting a fractured humerus.

Lower arm (radius and ulna) or forearm

There are two large bones in the forearm, and either one or both of these may be broken. When only one bone is broken, the other acts as a splint and there may be little or no deformity. However, a marked deformity may be present in a fracture near the wrist. When both bones are broken, the arm usually appears deformed.

Treatment. The fracture should be straightened carefully by applying traction on the hand (see Fig. 18, page 22).

A half-arm, inflatable air splint should be applied to the fracture (see Fig. 17). If inflatable splints are not available, two well-padded splints should be applied to the forearm, one at the top and one at the bottom (see Fig. 23). The splints should be long enough to extend from beyond the elbow to the middle of the fingers. The hand should be raised about 10 cm higher than the elbow, and the arm supported in a sling (see Fig. 23). If necessary, a splint may be improvised using, e.g., a magazine.

Treat for pain (see page 20).

Wrist and hand

A broken wrist is usually the result of a fall with the hand outstretched. Usually there is a lump-like deformity on the back of the wrist, along with pain, tenderness, and swelling.

A fracture of the wrist should *not* be manipulated or straightened. In general, it should be managed like a fracture of the forearm.

The hand may be fractured by a direct blow or may receive a crushing injury. There may be pain, swelling, loss of motion, open wounds, and broken bones. The hand should be placed on a padded splint which extends from the middle of the lower arm to beyond the tips of the fingers. A firm ball of gauze should be placed under the fingers to hold the hand in a cupped position.

25

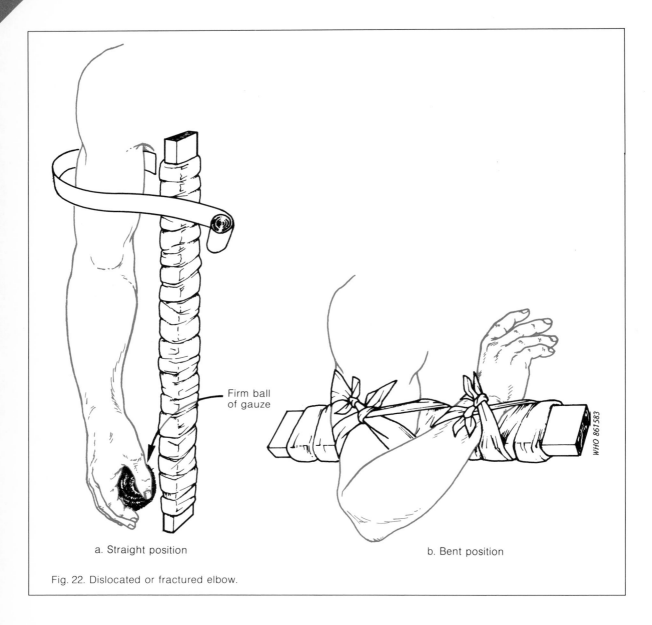

Firm ball
of gauze

WHO 861583

a. Straight position

b. Bent position

Fig. 22. Dislocated or fractured elbow.

Roller gauze or elastic bandage may be used to secure the hand to the splint (see Fig. 24). The arm and hand should be supported in a sling (see Fig. 20). Often, further treatment is urgent, regardless of the severity of the injury, to preserve as much of the function of the hand as possible. RADIO MEDICAL ADVICE should be obtained.

Treat for pain (see page 20).

Finger

Only the fractured finger should be immobilized, and the mobility of the other fingers should be maintained. The finger should be straightened by grasping the wrist with one hand and applying traction to the fingertip with the other. The finger should be immobilized with a splint (see Fig. 25). The patient should be examined by a physician as soon as possible.

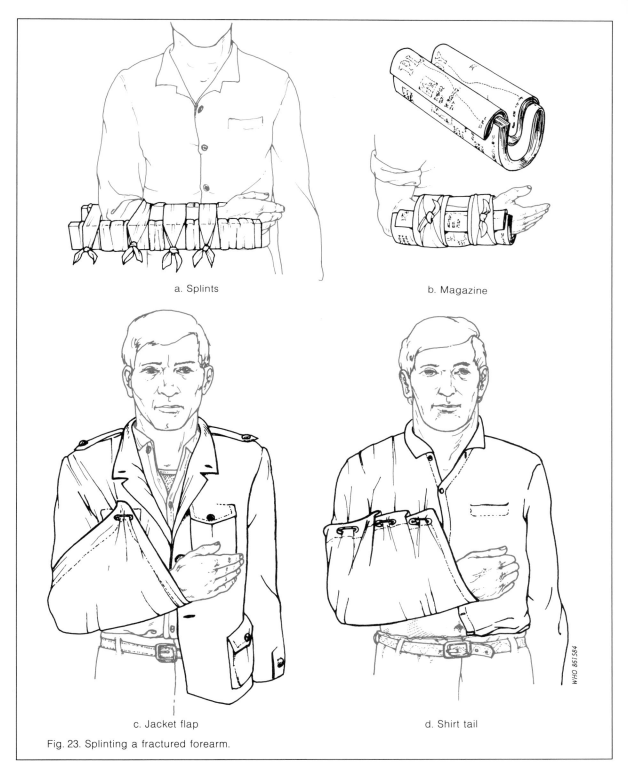

a. Splints

b. Magazine

c. Jacket flap

d. Shirt tail

Fig. 23. Splinting a fractured forearm.

WHO 861584

27

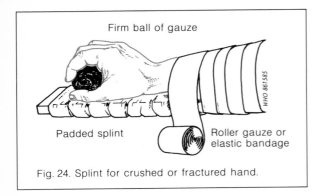

Firm ball of gauze

Padded splint

Roller gauze or elastic bandage

WHO 861585

Fig. 24. Splint for crushed or fractured hand.

Spine

A FRACTURED SPINE IS POTENTIALLY A VERY SERIOUS INJURY. IF YOU SUSPECT A FRACTURED SPINE TELL THE CASUALTY TO LIE STILL AND DO NOT ALLOW ANYONE TO MOVE HIM UNTIL HE IS SUPPORTED ON A HARD FLAT SURFACE. Any careless movement of a casualty with a fractured spine could damage or sever the spinal cord, resulting in permanent paralysis and loss of feeling in the legs and double incontinence for life.

Falls from a height are the likeliest cause of spinal injury at sea. *Always* suspect a fracture of the spine if a person has fallen a distance of over two metres. Ask if there is any pain in the back. Most people with fractures of the spine have pain, but a very few *do not*. So, check carefully how the injury happened and, if in doubt, treat it as a fractured spine. First ask the casualty to move his toes to check whether or not he has paralysis and check also that he can feel you touching his toes.

A casualty who has a fractured spine must be kept still and straight. *He must never be bent or jackknifed by being picked up under the knees and armpits*. He can, however, be safely rolled over (see Fig. 26) on to one side or the other, because, if this is done gently, there is very little movement of the spine. The aim in first aid will be to place the casualty on a hard flat surface where his spine will be fully supported and to keep him like that until X-rays can be taken.

Tell the casualty to lie still immediately you suspect a fractured spine. If you drag him about or move him unskilfully you could cause permanent paralysis.

Tie the feet and ankles together with a figure-of-eight bandage and get the casualty lying still and

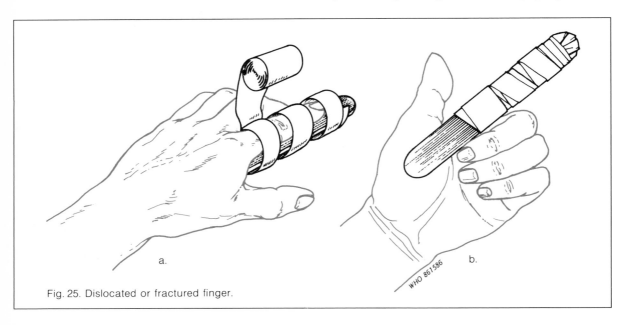

a.

b.

WHO 861586

Fig. 25. Dislocated or fractured finger.

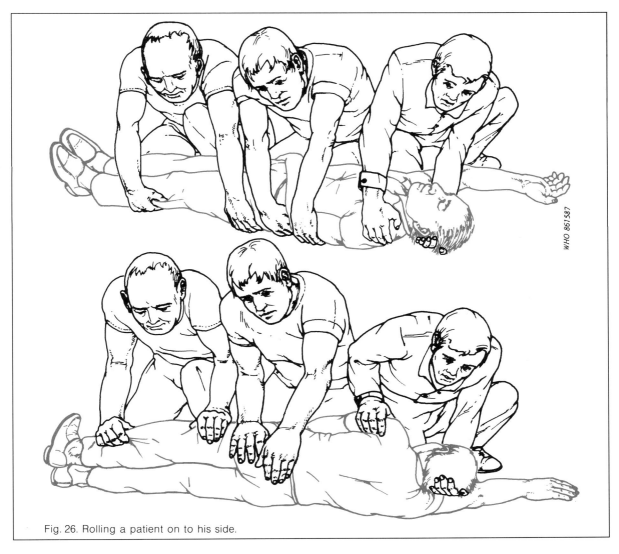

Fig. 26. Rolling a patient on to his side.

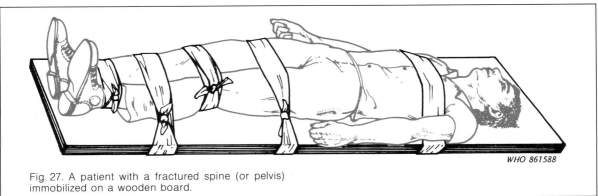

Fig. 27. A patient with a fractured spine (or pelvis)
immobilized on a wooden board.

29

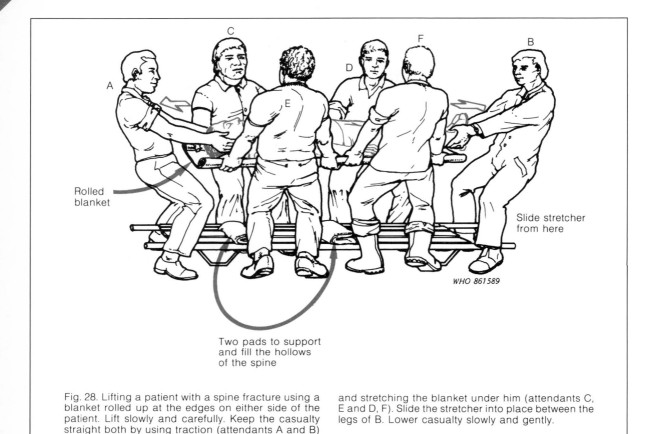

Rolled
blanket

Slide stretcher
from here

WHO 861589

Two pads to support
and fill the hollows
of the spine

Fig. 28. Lifting a patient with a spine fracture using a blanket rolled up at the edges on either side of the patient. Lift slowly and carefully. Keep the casualty straight both by using traction (attendants A and B) and stretching the blanket under him (attendants C, E and D, F). Slide the stretcher into place between the legs of B. Lower casualty slowly and gently.

straight. Use traction on the head and on the feet to straighten him out. Do not fold him. Take your time. He can now lie safely in this position for as long as is necessary. So do not be in a hurry to move him. Prepare a stiff supporting stretcher. A Neil-Robertson or basket stretcher will do. A canvas stretcher will *not* do unless it has stiff wooden boards laid transversely over the canvas to provide a rigid support for the back. There may be a need to stiffen some models of the Neil-Robertson stretcher.

If a Neil-Robertson stretcher is not available, a wide wooden board may be used for immobilization of the patient, as shown in Fig. 27. This improvised method of immobilization may also be used in a case of suspected pelvic fracture.

Another method of lifting a patient with a spine injury is shown in Fig. 28. First, roll the casualty

very carefully (see Fig. 26) on to a blanket spread out flat. Then roll up both edges of the blanket very tightly and as close as possible to the casualty. Prepare a stretcher, stiffened with wooden boards. Two pads must be provided to support and fill the hollows of the spine, which are in the small of the back and behind the neck. The back pad should be larger than the neck pad (see Fig. 28).

Now prepare to lift the casualty. Have *at least* two people grasping each side of the blanket, and one person at the head and one at the feet to apply traction. Those lifting the blanket should be spaced so that more lifting power is available at the body end which is heavy compared with the end bearing the legs. A further person is required to push the prepared stretcher under the casualty when he is lifted.

Begin by applying traction to the head and feet. Pull under the jaw, under the back of the head, and around the ankles. When *firm* traction is being applied, lifting can commence slowly.

Lift the casualty very slowly and carefully to a height of about half a metre, i.e., just enough to slip the stretcher under the casualty. Be careful, take time, and keep the casualty straight.

Slide the stretcher between the legs of the person who is applying traction to the ankles. Then move the stretcher in the direction of the head, continuing until it is *exactly* underneath the casualty. Adjust the position of the pads to fit exactly under the curves in the small of the back and neck.

Now lower the casualty very, very slowly on to the stretcher. Maintain traction until he is resting firmly on the stretcher.

The casualty is now ready for removal. If he has to be placed on any other surface, that surface must be hard and firm and removal precautions must be as described above, with plenty of people to help and with traction on the head and feet during removal.

As there will be so many people helping and it is important to handle the casualty with great care, it may be useful to have someone read out the relevant instructions before each operation is carried out.

See Stroke and paralysis (page 231) for further advice on how to treat a patient with an injury to the spinal cord.

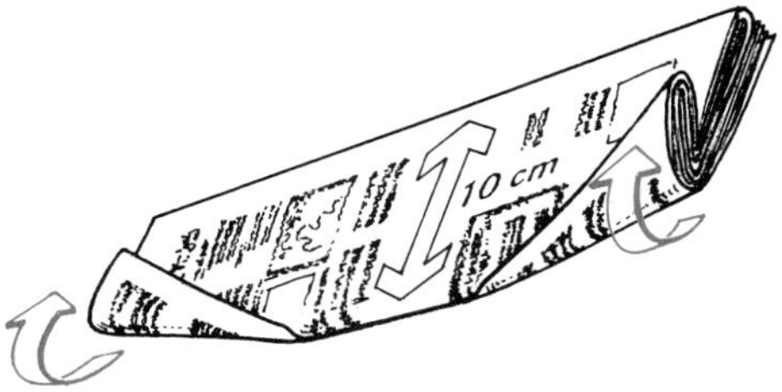

A. Fold a newspaper so that the height is the distance from the chin to the top of the collar-bones (about 10 cm). Tuck in the corners.

B. Put the newspaper collar around the neck, with the centre of the paper to the front of the neck.

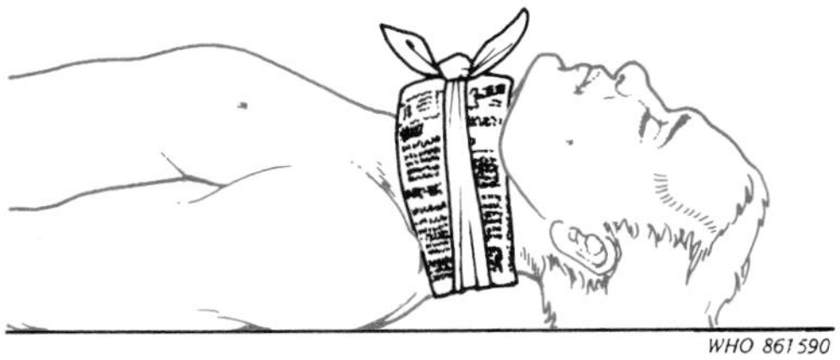

WHO 861590

C. Fix the newspaper collar with an encircling tie.

Fig. 29. An improvised neck collar.

Neck

Injuries to the neck are often in the form of compression fractures of the vertebrae, due for example to the victim standing up suddenly and bumping his head violently or to something falling on his head. Falls from a height can also produce neck injuries. Treatment is similar to that described above for fractures of the spine, because the neck is the upper part of the spine.

The casualty should be laid flat, if not already in this position, and should be kept still and straight. A neck collar should then be applied gently to stop movement of the neck while an assistant steadies the head. An improvised neck collar can be made quite easily from a newspaper. Fold the newspaper so that the width is about 10 cm at the front. Fold the top edge over to produce a slightly narrower back. Then tie this around the neck with the top edge under the chin and the bottom edge over the top of the collar bones. Tie a bandage, scarf, or necktie over the newspaper to hold it in place. This will keep the neck still (Fig. 29).

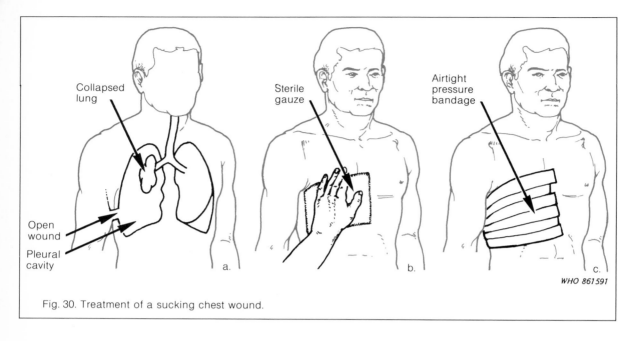

Fig. 30. Treatment of a sucking chest wound.

Chest

Injuries to the ribs are often the result of falling against a sharp or angled edge. Serious injuries can result from heavy blows on the chest or from falls from a height.

Sharp pain due to broken ribs may be felt, the pain becoming stronger in time with the movements of breathing. The lung may be damaged; this may be shown by the casualty coughing up bright red blood that is usually frothy.

If there is an open wound (a sucking wound) of the chest, this must be sealed *immediately,* otherwise air is drawn into the chest cavity and the lungs cannot inflate as the vacuum inside the chest is destroyed. A large dressing should be applied over the sucking wound, and the dressing and the whole area should be covered with wide sticking plaster to provide an *airtight seal* (see Fig. 30). A useful dressing for a sucking wound can be made from petroleum jelly on gauze, which is placed over the wound with a layer of aluminium foil or polythene outside. The hole is then covered, and the dressing bound tightly with a wide sticking plaster. A wet dressing may also be used to provide an airtight seal.

If nothing else is available, use the casualty's own bloodstained clothing to plug the wound temporarily.

The usual rules about stopping bleeding by pressing the point where the blood comes from also apply. In all cases of chest injury, a pulse chart should be started at an early stage in order to check on possible internal bleeding. The respiratory rate should also be recorded.

Conscious chest-injury casualties should be placed in a seated position because this makes breathing easier. If the casualty cannot sit up, he should be placed in a half-sitting position, either supported by a pillow at the back or leaning forward against a pillow over the knees (see Fig. 31). If possible the casualty should also *lean on the injured side* to cut down movement on that side — this will ease pain and help to decrease any internal bleeding in the chest (Fig. 32).

Unconscious chest-injury casualties should be placed in the unconscious position, *lying on the injured side.* This will cut down movement and so help to prevent bleeding inside the chest. A head-down tip should also be applied, if possible, to help to keep the air passage clear by drainage. If there is frothy blood from the

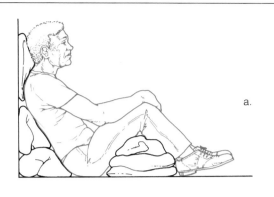

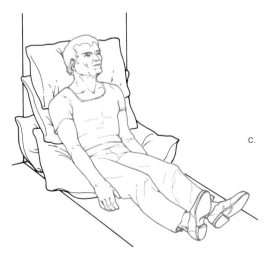

Fig. 31. Anyone who has difficulty in breathing should be kept in a half-sitting position leaning back (**a**) or leaning forward (**b**), or in the high sitting-up position (**c**). It is particularly important that a casualty showing signs of pulmonary oedema should be placed in position **c**.

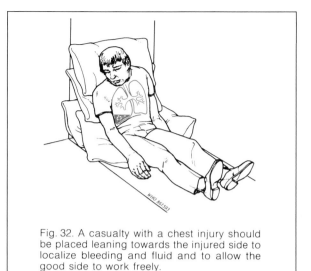

Fig. 32. A casualty with a chest injury should be placed leaning towards the injured side to localize bleeding and fluid and to allow the good side to work freely.

mouth or nose, use a sucker, if possible, or mop out the blood to keep the air passages clear.

Pelvis

A fracture of the pelvis is usually due either to a fall from a height or to direct violence in the pelvic area. The casualty will complain of pain in the hip, groin, and pelvic areas and perhaps also of pain in the lower back and buttock areas.

The ring compression test is useful. Press *gently* on the front of both hip bones in a downward and inward direction so as to compress the pelvic ring. This will give rise to sharp pain if the pelvis is broken. Some movement of the pelvic bones may also be felt if there is a fracture.

If you think that the pelvis may be fractured, tell the casualty not to pass urine. If he has to pass urine, keep the specimen and examine it for the presence of blood (page 107).

If the bladder or urethra (the channel from the bladder to the tip of the penis) is damaged, urine can leak into the tissues.

Pelvic fractures can cause severe and even life-threatening bleeding into the pelvic and lower abdominal cavities. So, start a pulse chart (Fig. 41, page 41) immediately and check for concealed internal bleeding (page 40).

33

a.

b.

c.

WHO 861594

Fig. 33. Three people lifting a casualty with a fracture of the pelvis.

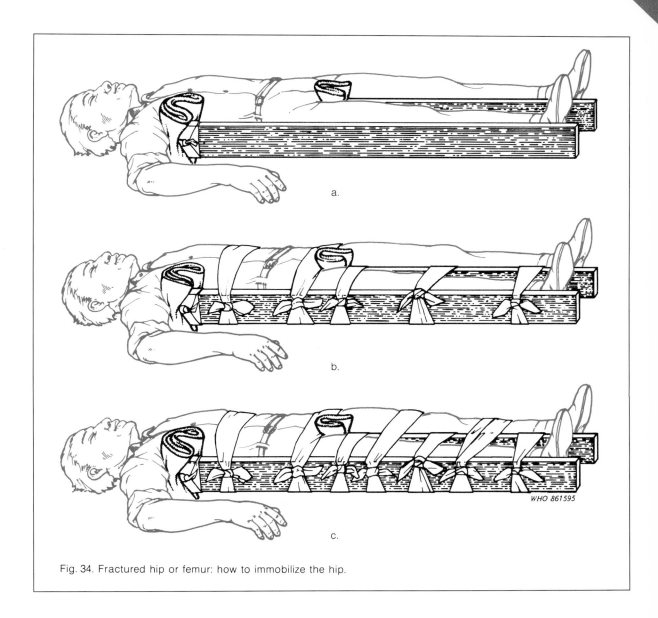

a.

b.

WHO 861595

c.

Fig. 34. Fractured hip or femur: how to immobilize the hip.

Casualties with a fractured pelvis should be lifted with great care (see Fig. 33). If the patient has a lot of pain, use the same technique as for a fractured spine (Fig. 28) before putting the casualty on a stretcher or on a wooden board (Fig. 27). Keep the casualty lying in whatever position is most comfortable to him — on the back, on one side, or face downwards. Remember to *keep checking* for concealed internal bleeding (page 40).

A patient with a fractured pelvis may be in shock (see page 17). If necessary, treat him for shock, but do not place him in a shock position.

A long wooden board (see Fig. 27) or rigid stretcher will provide the necessary support

35

during transportation. The patient should not be rolled, because this may cause additional internal damage. A pad should be placed between the patient's thighs, and the knees and ankles bandaged together, as shown in Fig. 27.

Treat for pain (see page 20).

Hip to knee

A broken thigh bone is a potentially serious injury and will cause significant blood loss. If it is combined with other fractures and/or injuries, then the loss may easily reach a level at which blood replacement will become necessary.

There is severe pain in the groin area, and the patient may not be able to lift the injured leg. The leg may appear shortened and be rotated, causing the toes to point abnormally outward.

Shock will generally accompany this type of fracture.

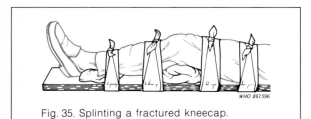

Fig. 35. Splinting a fractured kneecap.

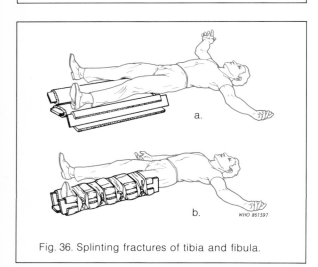

Fig. 36. Splinting fractures of tibia and fibula.

Get RADIO MEDICAL ADVICE.

A fracture of the *neck of the thigh bone* will produce shortening of the injured leg and cause the casualty to lie with the whole lower limb and foot flopped outwards.

Fractures of the *shaft of the thigh bone* are usually fairly easy to diagnose.

If you think that the thigh is broken, first pad between the thighs, knees, legs, and ankles with folded blankets or any other suitable soft material. Then bring the good leg to the broken leg. Do this slowly and carefully. Next, bring the feet together. If the attempt to do this causes pain, apply traction gently and slowly and then bring the feet together. Now tie a figure-of-eight bandage around the feet and ankles to keep the feet together. Next, prepare the splints to immobilize the hip.

A well-padded board splint should be placed from the armpit to beyond the foot. Another well-padded splint should be placed on the inner side of the leg from the groin to beyond the foot. The splints should be secured in place with an adequate number of ties, and both legs tied together to provide additional support (see Fig. 34). The patient should be transported on a stretcher or a long board to a bed in his quarters or sick-bay.

Treat for pain (see page 20).

Knee

A fracture of the knee is generally the result of a fall or a direct blow. Besides the usual signs of a fracture, a groove in the kneecap may be felt. There will be inability to kick the leg forward, and the leg will drag if an attempt is made to walk.

Treatment. The leg should be straightened carefully (see Fig. 18). A full-leg, inflatable air splint should be applied. If other types of splint are used, a well-padded board splint should be applied, with padding under the knee and below the ankle. The splint should be secured in place with ties (see Fig. 35).

Treat for pain (see page 20).

Lower leg (tibia and fibula)

Fractures of the lower leg are common and occur as a result of various accidents. There is a marked deformity of the leg when both bones are broken. When only one bone is broken, the other acts as a splint and little deformity may be present. When the tibia (the bone in the front of the leg) is broken, a compound fracture is likely to occur. Swelling may be present, and the pain is usually severe enough to require administration of morphine sulfate.

Treatment. The leg should be straightened carefully, using slight traction (see Fig. 18). A full-leg, inflatable air splint may be applied, if available (see Fig. 17). The air splint will assist in controlling the bleeding, if there is a compound fracture. If other types of splint are used, a well-padded splint should be applied to each side of the leg, and another should be placed under the leg. The splints should extend from the middle of the thigh to beyond the heel (see Fig. 36).

Treat for pain (see page 20).

Both legs

There may be considerable blood loss if both legs are broken. Look for signs of shock (see page 17), and if necessary, give appropriate treatment.

Prepare well-padded stiffish supports reaching from the thigh to the ankles for below-the-knee fractures, and from the armpit to the ankles for above-the-knee fractures. Pad between the thighs, knees, legs, and ankles. Then bring both feet together as gently as you can, using traction if necessary (page 21).

Now tie a figure-of-eight bandage round the feet and ankles to keep the feet together.

The padded splints should now be applied to the outside of both legs. Tie with enough encircling bandages to keep the splints and the legs secured firmly together. Avoid making any ties over the site of any break. Then check circulation and feeling in the toes as described on page 22. The casualty should be moved while remaining straight and flat on a stretcher (Fig. 37).

Treat for pain (page 20).

Ankle and foot

A fracture of the ankle or foot is usually caused by a fall, a twist, or a blow. Pain and swelling will be present, along with marked disability.

Treatment. If available, a half-leg, inflatable air splint should be applied. If conventional splints are applied, the ankle should be well-padded with dressings or a pillow. The splints, applied to each side of the leg, should extend from mid-calf to beyond the foot (see Fig. 38).

Treat for pain (page 20).

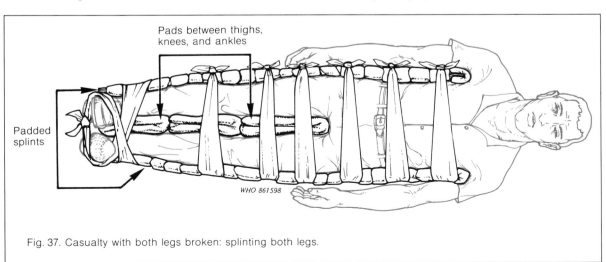

Pads between thighs, knees, and ankles

Padded splints

WHO 861598

Fig. 37. Casualty with both legs broken: splinting both legs.

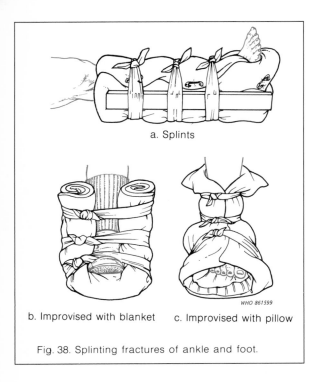

a. Splints

b. Improvised with blanket   c. Improvised with pillow

WHO 861599

Fig. 38. Splinting fractures of ankle and foot.

Dislocations

A dislocation is present when a bone has been displaced from its normal position at a joint (Fig. 39). It may be diagnosed when an injury occurs at or near a joint and the joint cannot be used normally. Movement is limited. There is pain, often quite severe. The pain is made worse by attempts to move the joint. The affected area is misshapen both by the dislocation and by swelling (bleeding) which occurs around the dislocation. Except that there is no grating of bone-ends, the evidence for a dislocation is very similar to that for a fracture (page 19). Always remember that fractures and dislocations can occur together.

First aid

Dislocations can be closed or open. If a wound is present at or near a dislocation, the wound should be covered both to stop bleeding and to help prevent infection. Do not attempt to reduce a dislocation. A fracture may also be present, in

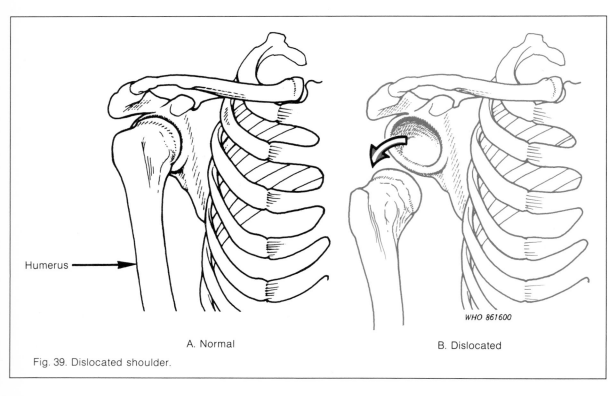

Humerus

A. Normal

B. Dislocated

WHO 861600

Fig. 39. Dislocated shoulder.

which case attempted manipulation to reduce the dislocation can make matters worse.

Prevent movement in the affected area by suitable immobilization. The techniques for immobilization are exactly the same as for fractures of the same area(s) (pages 19–37). Look out for impaired circulation and loss of feeling (see page 22). If these are present, and if you cannot feel a pulse at the wrist or ankle, try to move the limb gently into a position in which circulation can return, and keep the limb in this position. Look then for a change in colour of the fingers or toes, from white or blue to pink.

Transport the casualty in the most comfortable position. This is usually sitting up for upper-limb injuries and lying down for lower-limb injuries.

For further treatment of dislocations, see Chapter 4, page 82.

Head injuries

Head injuries commonly result from blows to the head and from falls, often from a height.

Most preventable deaths from serious head injuries are the result of obstructed breathing and breathing difficulties, not brain damage. Apart from covering serious head wounds, **your attention should be concentrated on the life-saving measures that support normal breathing and prevent obstructed breathing** (see Airway, page 7). This will ensure that the brain gets sufficient oxygen. In this way, you have a good chance of keeping the casualty alive until he can have skilled medical aid in a hospital. Get RADIO MEDICAL ADVICE.

See the section on assessing the significance of a head injury (page 73) for a fuller discussion of the subject.

In the case of some head injuries or where a foreign body or a fracture is directly below an open wound, it may not be possible to control bleeding by pressure. In such circumstances a *ring-pad* should be used. A paraffin gauze dressing is placed over the wound, a suitably sized ring-pad is placed around the wound and over

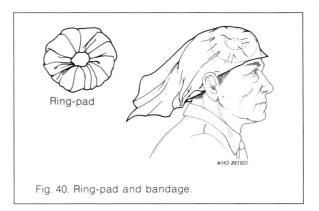

Fig. 40. Ring-pad and bandage.

the edge of the dressing, and the pad is held in place by a bandage. The pad should press on the blood vessels but not on the foreign body or the fracture.

A ring-pad can be made by passing a narrow bandage twice around the fingers of one hand to form a ring and then wrapping the remainder of the bandage around the ring to form a doughnut-shaped pad (Fig. 40).

Blast injuries

Explosions produce sudden and violent disturbances of the air. As a result men may be thrown down or injured by falling wreckage. In addition, the blast of air itself may strike the body with such violence as to cause severe or fatal internal injuries. There may be blast injuries to more than one part of the body; any combination of injuries to the following sites may be found.

Lungs

Blast can damage the small blood vessels of the lungs so that bleeding takes place inside the lungs. The patient will be shocked and he will have difficulty in getting his breath, together with a feeling of tightness or pain in the chest; his face will usually be blue, and there may be blood-stained froth in his mouth. Carry the patient into the fresh air, if this is reasonably possible. Support him in a half-sitting position (see Fig. 31, page 33). Loosen tight clothing.

39

Keep him warm. Encourage him to cough and spit out any phlegm. **Morphine must not be given.** Artificial respiration by the mouth-to-mouth method should be given if breathing fails.

Head

Blast injuries to the head are rather like concussion (page 74). In some cases there may be paralysis of the limbs due to damage to the spinal cord. The patient may be completely unconscious or extremely dazed. In the latter case people may be found sitting about, incapable of moving and taking no notice of what is going on. Although often to all outward appearances uninjured, they have no energy or will to move. They are momentarily "knocked silly" and may behave very foolishly. For example, although there may be an easy way of escape from a sinking ship, they may be too dazed to take it, or, if one of them should fall, he might drown from immersion in only 20 cm of oil or water because he has not the sense to get up.

If patients are unconscious, treat them accordingly (page 3).

If they are dazed, take them by the hand and lead them to safety. Tell them firmly everything that they must do. Think of them as very small children. By acting in this manner you may save many lives. For example, you may prevent men going down with the ship when they have not the sense to abandon it.

Abdomen

Bleeding is caused inside the abdomen by blast damage to the organs there. Such damage is usually due to the effects of underwater explosions on men in the sea. Shock and pain in the abdomen are the chief signs; they may appear some time after the explosion. For treatment, see Injury to the abdomen (Internal injuries, page 73) and Internal bleeding (below).

Internal bleeding

Internal bleeding may result from a direct blow to the body, from strains, and from diseases such as peptic ulcer.

Internal bleeding can be concealed or visible. Bleeding round a broken limb may be concealed but may be detectable because it causes a swelling, the size of which shows the amount of the bleeding. Bleeding into the chest or abdominal cavities may be revealed if blood is coughed up or is vomited. Stab and puncture wounds can cause serious internal bleeding.

The casualty will be shocked. At first he will be pale, giddy, faint, and sweating. His pulse rate and respiration rate will rise. Later his skin will become cold and his extremities will become slightly blue. The pulse will become difficult to feel and very rapid (Fig. 41). The breathing will be very shallow. He will complain of thirst and nausea, become restless, and complain that he cannot breathe properly ("air hunger"). These three signs show that bleeding is still occurring. Later he will cease to complain, lose interest in his surroundings, and become unconscious.

The most important indication of continuing bleeding is a *rising pulse* and falling blood pressure. Anyone in whom internal bleeding is suspected must therefore have his pulse rate and blood pressure recorded at fixed and frequent intervals, say, every 5–10 minutes. After about an hour of such recording it should be clear whether or not he is bleeding internally. If the patient's blood pressure remains about normal, and the pulse rate falls or remains steady, he is not bleeding.

People who have concealed internal bleeding may need a blood transfusion. Get RADIO MEDICAL ADVICE.

It is important to keep what blood is available circulating around the lungs and brain. Lay the casualty down with a slight head-down tilt. Raise the legs to divert the blood out of the legs towards the brain and lungs. Maintain this position when transporting the casualty to the ship's hospital or to a cabin. If he is restless or in severe pain, morphine may be given (page 305).

Bleeding from the nose

Pinch the soft part of the nose firmly for 10 minutes while keeping the head well forward

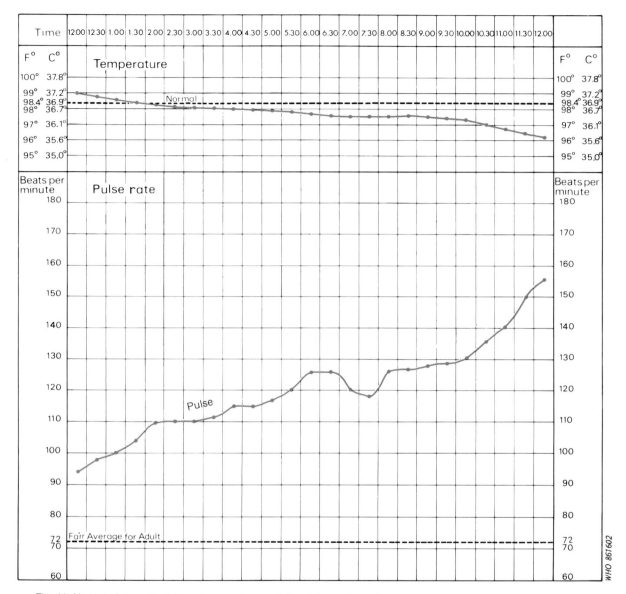

Fig. 41. Haemorrhage: the falling temperature and the rising pulse rate.

WHO 861602

over a basin or bowl. The pinching is most easily done by the casualty himself. At the end of 10 minutes, slowly release the pressure and look for drips of blood in the basin or bowl. Absence of drips will show that bleeding has stopped (Fig. 42).

Instruct the casualty not to blow his nose for the next four hours and to refrain from violent nose-blowing over the next two days.

If bleeding has not stopped, continue pressure on the soft part of the nose for a further 10

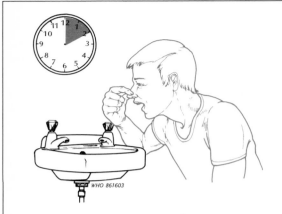

Fig. 42. Bleeding from the nose. Pinch the soft part of the nose firmly for 10 minutes.

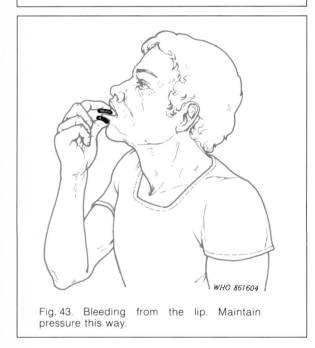

Fig. 43. Bleeding from the lip. Maintain pressure this way.

minutes and release slowly again. If bleeding has not stopped after 20 minutes, it may be necessary to pack the affected side of the nose with strip-gauze.

Bleeding from the lip, cheek, and tongue

Press on *both* sides of the lip, cheek, or tongue to stop bleeding. Use a piece of gauze or a swab on

each side to help maintain pressure and stop the fingers slipping. Pressing is usually most easily done by the casualty himself under the direction of another person or with the aid of a mirror (Fig. 43).

Bleeding from a tooth socket

See Dental emergencies, page 184.

Bleeding from the ear passage

This is usually caused by a head injury or by blast. Place a large pad over the ear and bandage it in position. Keep the affected ear *downwards*. If the casualty is unconscious, place him in the unconscious position (see Fig. 3, page 6) with the affected ear downwards. Never plug the ear passage with cotton wool or other material. Get RADIO MEDICAL ADVICE.

Choking

Choking is usually caused by a large lump of food that sticks at the back of the throat and thus stops the person concerned from breathing. The person then becomes unconscious very quickly and will die in 4–6 minutes unless the obstruction is removed.

Choking can be mistaken for a heart attack. The distinguishing features are:

- the person who is choking may have been seen to be eating;
- the person who is choking usually cannot speak or breathe; this is not the case if the person is having a heart attack;
- the person who is choking will turn blue and lose consciousness quickly because of lack of oxygen;
- the victim of a choking incident can signal his distress (he cannot speak) by grasping his neck between finger and thumb. This is known as the "Heimlich sign" and if it is understood by all personnel the risks involved in choking should be reduced.

If the casualty is conscious, stand behind him, place your closed fist (thumb side) against the place in the upper abdomen where the ribs divide. Grasp the fist with your other hand. Press suddenly and sharply into the casualty's abdomen with a hard quick upward thrust. Repeat several times if necessary (Fig. 44).

For self-treatment, try to cough forcibly while using your own fist as described above; alternatively, use the back of a chair, the corner of a table or sink, or any other projection that can be used to produce a quick upward thrust to the upper abdomen.

If the casualty is unconscious, place him on his back and turn the face to one side. Kneel astride him and place one hand over the other with the heel of the lower hand at the place where the ribs divide. Press suddenly and sharply into the abdomen with a hard quick upward thrust. Repeat several times if necessary (Fig. 45). When the food is dislodged, remove it from the mouth and place the casualty in the unconscious position (see Fig. 3, page 6).

Suffocation

(See also: Ventilation, Chapter 15, page 283.)

Suffocation is usually caused by gases or smoke. Remember that dangerous gases may have no smell to warn you of their presence. Do not enter enclosed spaces without the proper precautions. Do not forget the risks of fire and/or explosion when dealing with inflammable gases or vapours.

First aid

Get the casualty into the fresh air. If necessary, give artificial respiration and heart compression and place in the unconscious position (see Fig. 3, page 6).

Administer oxygen (see page 51).

Strangulation

Hanging is one form of strangulation and is fortunately rare on board ship. It is not always deliberate, but can be an accident. It is important to have a clear mental picture of the scene, so that your evidence is helpful at any later inquiry. The face in hanging is dark blue from interference with blood supply to the head, the eyes protrude, and the face and the neck are swollen.

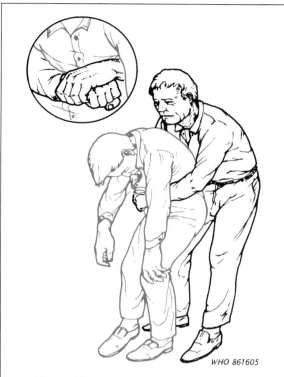

Fig. 44. Heimlich manoeuvre (rescuer standing and victim standing or sitting). Standing behind the victim, wrap your arms around his waist. Grasp your fist with your other hand and place the fist against the victim's abdomen. Press the abdomen with a quick upward thrust.

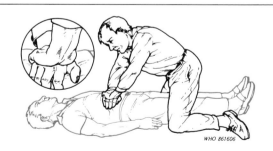

Fig. 45. Heimlich manoeuvre (rescuer kneeling and victim lying on his back). Kneel astride the victim's hips. Put one hand on top of the other and place the heel of the bottom hand on the abdomen. Press in with a quick upward thrust. Repeat, if necessary.

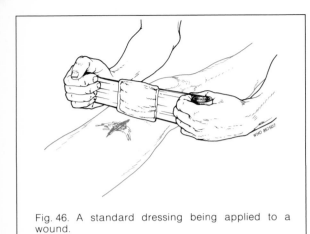

Fig. 46. A standard dressing being applied to a wound.

First aid

1. Cut and remove the noose, while supporting the body. Loosen all constricting clothing. Give treatment for unconscious casualty (see page 3).

2. If breathing has ceased, start artificial respiration and, if the heart is not beating, carry out heart compression (page 9). When breathing is restored, administer oxygen (see page 51).

3. Maintain a constant watch on the patient until you are able to hand him over to the care of the doctor. This is necessary, partly for medical reasons, partly because a suicide attempt might be repeated.

Standard dressing

This consists of a pad of sterilized gauze attached to a bandage. The pad is near one end of the bandage. It is sterile, i.e., free from germs, so do not allow it to touch anything (including your own fingers) before placing it on the wound, as shown in Fig. 46.

Note
- Always select a dressing with a pad larger than the wound to be covered.
- Hold the bandage taut as you put it round the limb, head, or body, so as to secure the pad widely and firmly.

Transporting a casualty

The removal of a sick or injured person either from the site of an accident or ashore is a matter of importance, since his life may depend on the arrangements made, particularly if he has spinal injuries, a heart condition, or a severe fracture, with any of which he is likely to be suffering from shock. So use the utmost gentleness, reassure your patient, try to have a clear picture in your mind of the nature of the disability you are dealing with, and exercise common sense.

Unless there is danger from fire, explosion, or toxic substances, do not move a casualty until:
- suspected fractures have been immobilized; and
- severe bleeding has been stopped.

Then check out the best route for transport, lift the casualty gently and carry him smoothly — remember that every jolt causes him unnecessary pain.

The method of transport will depend on the situation of the casualty and the nature of the injury.

If the ship is in port, it is usually best to await the arrival of an ambulance because the attendants will be expert in handling casualties. You can assist them and give them the benefit of your knowledge. For instance, if a patient has fallen to the bottom of a hold, the best procedure is to take down a stretcher, give first-aid treatment, then place the stretcher on a hatch cover or similar flat platform and have the patient lifted by ship's crane over the side. This lift can be a frightening experience for a helpless and shocked person, and he will be reassured if the person in charge stands on the hatch cover with legs astride the stretcher, maintaining balance by holding on to the guy wires. Similarly, if the patient is on deck and the gangway is narrow or unsteady, it may be far less unnerving for him if he is lowered over the side on a hatch cover or something similar.

Manhandling

Ordinary manhandling may be possible, in which case two helpers carry a casualty, with each one using an arm to support the casualty's back and

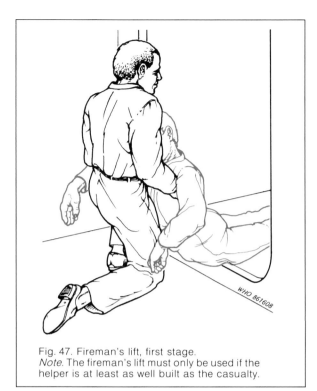

Fig. 47. Fireman's lift, first stage.
Note. The fireman's lift must only be used if the helper is at least as well built as the casualty.

Fig. 48. Fireman's lift, second stage.
The helper's left arm under and around the casualty's left thigh.

Fig. 49. Fireman's lift, third stage.
The helper stretches himself, stands upright, and shifts the casualty so that his weight is well balanced across the helper's shoulders.

shoulders and his spare hand to hold the casualty's thighs. If conscious, the casualty may help to support himself with his hands on the shoulders of the helpers.

The simple *pick-a-back* method is useful only where the casualty is conscious and able to hold on by putting his arms round the carrier's neck.

In a narrow space, the simple *fore-and-aft* carry may be best. One helper supports the patient under his arms, and the other under his knees.

Other methods of manhandling are demonstrated in Fig. 47–55.

One advantage of the *three-handed seat* (Fig. 50 and 51) is that one of the helpers has a free arm and hand that can be used either to support an injured limb or as a back support for the casualty. Which of the two helpers has the free arm will depend on the nature of the injury.

As a last resort, the *drag-carry* method may have to be used in narrow spaces, particularly where there is wreckage following an explosion and where it may be possible for only one man to reach a trapped patient and rescue him. After

45

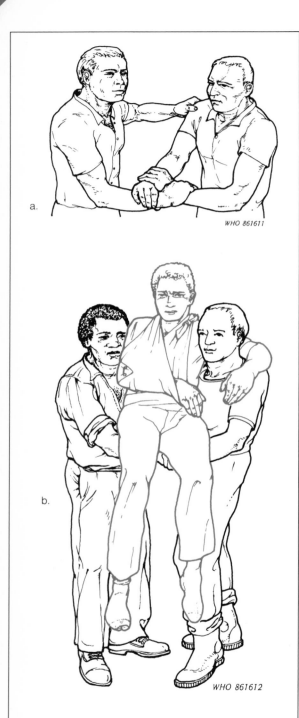

Fig. 50. Three-handed seat.
a How the wrists are held.
b Carrying the casualty, his uninjured arm round the shoulder of one of the helpers.

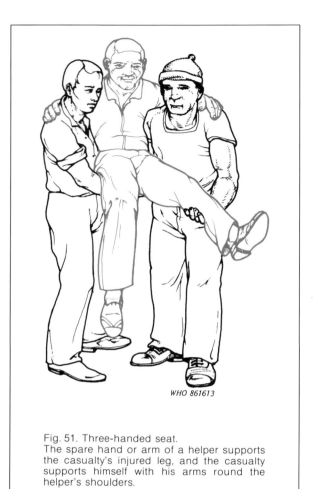

Fig. 51. Three-handed seat.
The spare hand or arm of a helper supports the casualty's injured leg, and the casualty supports himself with his arms round the helper's shoulders.

the initial rescue, two men may be able to undertake further movement through a narrow space. The method is demonstrated in Fig. 53 and Fig. 54. Ensure that the tied wrists do not interfere with any breathing apparatus the rescuer may be wearing.

Neil-Robertson stretcher
(Fig. 56)

A number of modifications of this type of stretcher exist under various names.

A good general-purpose stretcher for use on board ship, it is easily carried, gives firm support to the patient, and is particularly useful in narrow spaces, when difficult corners have to be negotiated, or when the patient has to be hoisted.

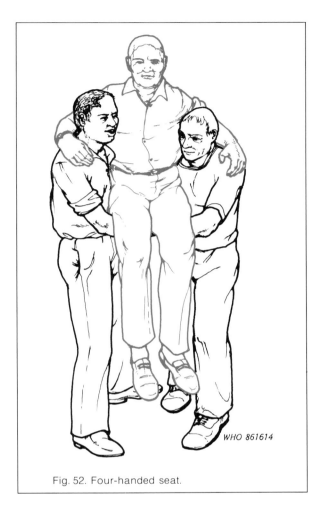

Fig. 52. Four-handed seat.

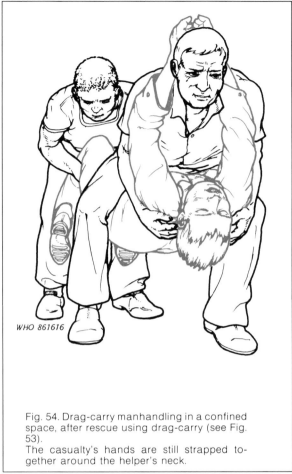

Fig. 54. Drag-carry manhandling in a confined space, after rescue using drag-carry (see Fig. 53).
The casualty's hands are still strapped to-gether around the helper's neck.

Fig. 53. Drag-carry.
The helper crawls along carrying the casualty between his legs; the casualty's hands are strapped together around the helper's neck.

The stretcher is made of stout canvas stiffened by sewn-on bamboo slats. The upper portion takes the head and neck, which are steadied by a canvas strap passing over the forehead. The middle portion is wrapped round the chest and has notches on which the armpits rest. This part has three canvas straps which are used for fastening the stretcher round the chest. The lower portion folds round the hips and legs down to the ankles.

If the patient is unconscious, place him on his back and tie his ankles and feet together with a figure-of-eight bandage, and his knees with a broad-fold bandage; also his wrists (Fig. 57).

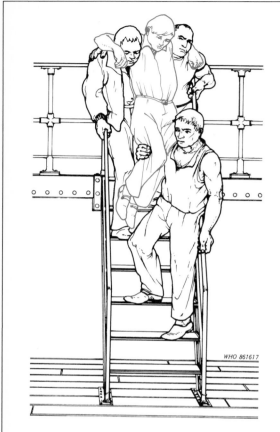

Fig. 55. Manhandling to the deck below.
The weight of the casualty's thighs is taken by
the third helper.

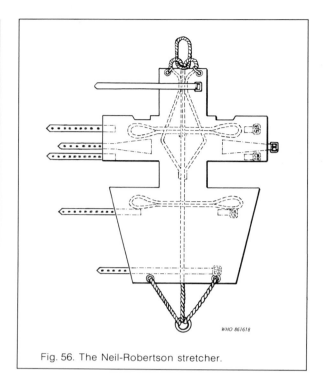

Fig. 56. The Neil-Robertson stretcher.

Three persons are required to carry out the lift.
No. 1 takes charge; he stands astride the
patient's legs, with his right hand under the left
calf and his left hand under the right thigh
(Fig. 57). No. 2 stands astride the chest and
clasps his hands underneath the patient. No. 3
places the patient's wrists (tied together) round
No. 2's neck. If the patient is conscious he may
himself be able to clasp his hands round the neck
of No. 2. The stretcher, with all straps unfas-
tened, should be positioned close to the head of
the patient. If spinal injury is suspected, extreme
care should be exercised in moving the casualty
(see page 28).

No. 1 now gives the order to lift, while No. 3
supports the head of the unconscious patient

with one hand and, with the other, slides the
stretcher under the patient, at the same time
opening out the flaps. When the stretcher is in
position, No. 1 gives the order to lower and all
lower together.

The stretcher is now strapped up and the patient
is ready for removal (Fig. 59); this can be done
most conveniently with four bearers (Fig. 60).

The Neil-Robertson stretcher can also be used to
remove casualties vertically (Fig. 61).

First aid satchels or boxes

These should contain iodine solution, a large
standard dressing, 2 medium standard dressings,
4 small standard dressings, 8 triangular bandages, some cotton wool, safety pins, sticking
plaster, scissors, and a pencil and paper.

One box should be included in the ship's medicine locker for swift transfer to the site of an
accident. Others placed at strategic positions,
particularly in a large ship, can be an aid to
prompt action if the crew are made aware of

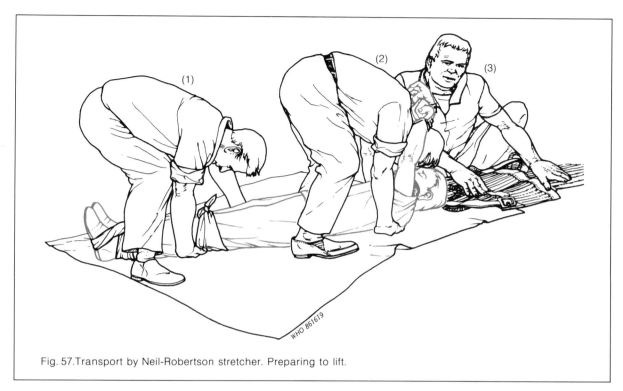

Fig. 57.Transport by Neil-Robertson stretcher. Preparing to lift.

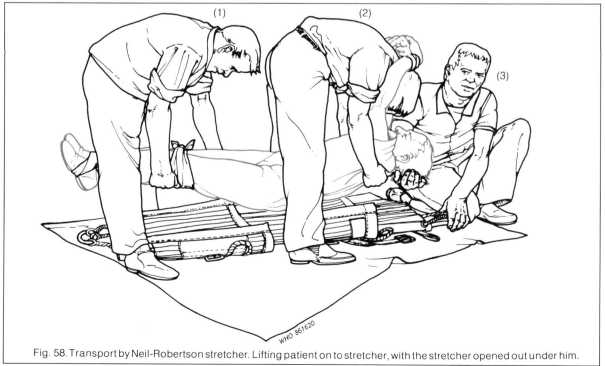

Fig. 58. Transport by Neil-Robertson stretcher. Lifting patient on to stretcher, with the stretcher opened out under him.

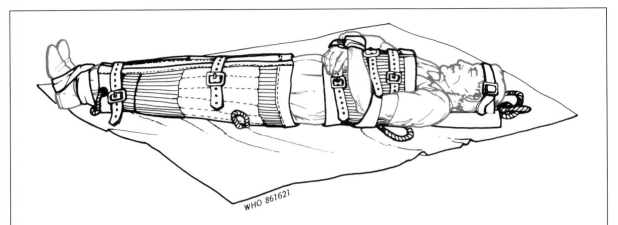

Fig. 59. Transport by Neil-Robertson stretcher. The stretcher is strapped up and the patient is ready for removal. The arms can be strapped inside or outside the chest section of the stretcher, depending on the injuries.

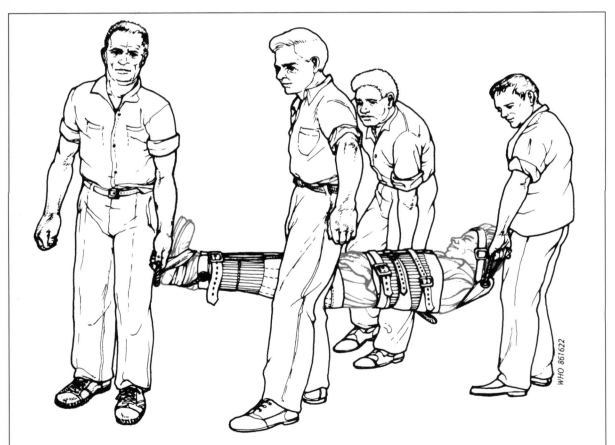

Fig. 60. Transport by Neil-Robertson stretcher. Patient strapped into stretcher and ready. If neck may be hurt, take great care not to bend it.

their location and contents. These extra boxes are, however, liable to be thoughtlessly used for minor unreported casualties and, in some instances, are subject to pilfering. Routine checking of their contents is therefore essential.

Emergency medical outfits

There is a special need on merchant vessels, and on medium-sized and large fishing vessels with crews numbering over 20, for an emergency medical outfit readily accessible for use if the medical cabinet should be destroyed or made inaccessible by fire. The emergency outfit should be sited well away from the ship's medical cabinet or the ship's hospital.

Oxygen administration (oxygen therapy)

Oxygen is essential to life. It is given for treatment when the body is unable to get enough oxygen from the air because of damage to the lungs or for other reasons, such as suffocation (see page 43) or carbon monoxide poisoning (page 58).

Oxygen must be given with care since it can be dangerous to patients who have had breathing difficulties for a number of years due to lung disease, particularly chronic bronchitis.

Oxygen should be given only where advised in this guide. Usually, it is given to a patient who is breathing without assistance but is unconscious or cyanotic (has bluish skin); also, oxygen should be given to all patients suffering from carbon monoxide or other toxic gas poisoning even when they are conscious.

There are two stages at which a patient may require oxygen: (1) during rescue from the place of an accident, and (2) when the patient is in the ship's sick-bay.

During rescue from the place of an accident

During this time the patient should be connected to the portable oxygen apparatus through a

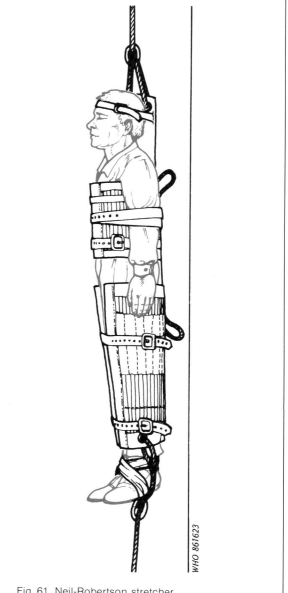

WHO 861623

Fig. 61. Neil-Robertson stretcher.
Moving a casualty vertically.
Note. To steady the stretcher's movements, a rope goes from the foot of the stretcher to a helper below.

mask placed over his face. The oxygen valve should be turned on and oxygen administered until the patient is transferred to the ship's sick-bay.

When the patient is in the ship's sick-bay

The procedure set out below should be followed.

The unconscious patient

1. Ensure that a clear airway has been established (see page 7) and an airway (see page 104) has been inserted.
2. Place over the nose and mouth a disposable mask designed to give 35% oxygen to the patient. Ensure that it remains securely in place. Check that the equipment is correctly assembled according to the manufacturer's instructions and that the cylinder contains sufficient oxygen.
3. Connect the mask to the flowmeter, using the tubing provided, and set the flowmeter to 4 litres per minute. Administration of oxygen should continue until the patient no longer has difficulty in breathing and has a healthy colour.

The conscious patient

1. Ask the patient whether he usually suffers from severe difficulty in breathing and a chronic cough, i.e., chronic bronchitis (see page 178).
    If the patient has severe chronic bronchitis, then he should be given only 24% oxygen, using an appropriately designed mask, with the flowmeter set at 4 litres per minute.
2. All other patients should be given 35% oxygen, using an appropriately designed mask, with the flowmeter set at 4 litres per minute.
3. The mask should be placed over the patient's mouth and nose and secured in place.
4. The patient should be placed in the high sitting-up position (see Fig. 31, page 33).
5. Check that the equipment is correctly assembled according to the manufacturer's instructions and that the cylinder contains sufficient oxygen.
6. Turn on the oxygen flowmeter at 4 litres per minute.

Oxygen therapy should be continued until the patient no longer has difficulty in breathing and has a healthy colour.

If the patient has difficulty in breathing, or the face, hands, and lips remain blue for longer than 15–20 minutes, he probably has one of the following complications: bronchitis (see page 177), pneumonia (see page 221), circulatory collapse in congestive heart failure (see page 205), or pulmonary oedema. In such a case, seek RADIO MEDICAL ADVICE.

WARNING. Smoking, naked lights, or fires must not be allowed in a room where oxygen is being administered, because of the risk of fire.

Chapter 2

Toxic hazards of chemicals, including poisoning

Ships carry a number of substances in addition to cargo that are potentially toxic. For instance, medicines are not generally poisonous but can become so if taken other than as prescribed. Then there are substances like cleaners, degreasers, and disinfectants that can give rise to toxic hazards through misuse. For instance, emptying a bucket of bleaching solution into a lavatory bowl containing a proprietary caustic cleaner may result in the release of poisonous gas in a confined space. Notes on specific toxic substances are given at the end of this chapter (pages 57–59).

Toxic substances can affect the body in various ways:

- through the lungs by inhalation of toxic gases and fumes;
- through the mouth and digestive system, if swallowed;
- through skin contact;
- through eye contact.

Breathing in is the most common route of poisoning in the shipping industry and the toxic substance may consist of vapour, gas, mist, spray, dust, or fumes. Swallowing of a poison occurs less frequently and is usually the result of an accident. Absorption through the skin and by inhalation may have a delayed effect. The substances that cause harm do so by burning, or causing local damage to, the skin, eyes, or other tissue, or by general poisoning after absorption. Allergic reactions are also possible. The effects may be sudden and dramatic, or gradual and cumulative. The damage may be temporary or permanent. Suspect every chemical to be dangerous until you know otherwise. Whatever the cause of the poisoning, treatment must be prompt. Complications of poisoning can be avoided by rapid emergency treatment.

Contents

Note. More detailed information on the treatment of the effects of specific chemicals is given in the Chemicals Supplement to the present guide, i.e., the *Medical first aid guide for use in accidents involving dangerous goods.*[1]

[1] *Medical first aid guide for use in accidents involving dangerous goods.* London, International Maritime Organization, 1985.

53

Diagnosis of poisoning

General principles

The diagnosis of poisoning may be simplified if one or more of the following factors point to the probable cause:
- the circumstances of the incident, e.g., a leakage of chemicals;
- the nature of the illness, and its relationship in time to recent exposure to chemicals;
- the epidemiological aspects, e.g., if more than one person is involved and all develop a similar illness.

It must be realized however that:
- the effects of some poisons resemble those of natural illness, e.g., vomiting and diarrhoea, or collapse;
- because a ship is carrying a cargo of chemicals it does not follow that the cargo is responsible for the illness (this is, in fact, unlikely unless there is evidence of a leakage);
- different individuals may be exposed to the poison at different times, or to a different extent during a single episode, and they may as a result become ill at different times or to differing degrees;
- individuals react differently to poisons according to their health, their constitution, and the extent of their exposure to the poison.

In a typical case of poisoning, *three stages* of illness may be distinguished, namely latent, active, and late.

The latent stage

This is the interval between the moment of entry of a poison into the body and the appearance of the first symptoms (feelings) or signs. These usually occur rapidly after exposure, but in some cases there may be a delay of several hours before they develop.

The active stage

This is the stage at which the signs and symptoms of the poisoning are apparent. Often there are a great many different chemicals that could produce these signs and symptoms and they therefore have to be treated in a general way.

The general symptoms of poisoning include:
- headache
- nausea and vomiting
- drowsiness
- changes in mental behaviour
- unconsciousness
- convulsions
- pain.

Signs of severe poisoning are:
- a rapid and weak pulse
- grey or blue colour of the skin
- severe difficulty in breathing
- a prolonged period of unconsciousness.

The late stage

The signs and symptoms usually resolve after a few hours in the majority of incidents, particularly if the degree of exposure is small. If a greater amount of chemical has been absorbed, or the period of exposure prolonged, or the chemical is very toxic, symptoms may persist for some hours or even days. The patient's condition may deteriorate as a result of complications, the most common of which are: suffocation (page 43), bronchitis (page 177), pneumonia (page 221), pulmonary oedema, heart failure, circulatory collapse, liver failure, and kidney failure.

For details regarding various toxins, the signs and symptoms of poisoning by them, and the appropriate first aid and follow-up treatment, refer to *Medical first aid guide for use in accidents involving dangerous goods,*[1] the Chemicals Supplement to the present guide.

Inhaled poisons

Many chemicals produce fumes that can irritate the lungs and cause difficulty in breathing. They also produce such symptoms as cough and burning sensation in the chest.

---

[1] *Medical first aid guide for use in accidents involving dangerous goods.* London, International Maritime Organization, 1985.

Gases such as carbon dioxide (page 57) and carbon monoxide (page 58) may also be poisonous, particularly in a confined space, because they replace oxygen in the air and blood.

The main symptoms are:

- difficulty in breathing
- headache, dizziness, and nausea
- unconsciousness in some cases.

Always remember that some poisonous gases, such as carbon dioxide, carbon monoxide, and some refrigerant gases, have no smell to warn you of their presence (see Ventilation, page 283, for rescue from an enclosed contaminated space).

Remember that the presence of certain gases, e.g., hydrogen, may make it necessary to take precautions against fire and explosion.

Treatment

- Remove the casualty at once into the fresh air. Loosen tight clothing and ensure a free airway (page 7).
- Start artificial respiration by the mouth-to-mouth method if breathing is absent.
- Start heart compression if the heart has stopped (page 9). In cases of carbon monoxide and toxic gas poisoning, give oxygen (see Oxygen administration, page 51) as soon as the spontaneous respiration has been restored.
- Keep the patient at rest in bed for at least 24 hours or until he has fully recovered.
- Complications may occur after this type of poisoning. They are: severe difficulty in breathing, with frothy sputum (pulmonary oedema[1]) and pneumonia and bronchitis (pages 221 and 177).

Do not give morphine to a casualty who has been gassed.

Swallowed poisons

Most of these exert their dangerous effects on the stomach and intestines causing retching,

vomiting (sometimes the vomit is blood-stained), abdominal pain, colic, and later diarrhoea. Examples of such poisons are arsenic, lead, poisonous fungi, berries, and contaminated or decomposed food (see Food-borne diseases, page 199). Particularly severe symptoms are caused by corrosives, strong acid, alkalis, or disinfectants, which burn the lips and mouth and cause intense pain.

Other poisons produce general toxic effects without irritation of the gastrointestinal tract. After ingestion, the onset will be gradual, following their absorption into the blood stream and their effect on the nervous system, which may cause unconsciousness and death. Examples are the various types of sedative tablets or medicines for pain relief, when taken in excessive amounts. Alcohol taken to excess may likewise act as an acute poison (see page 164).

Treatment

Identify the nature of the poison, if possible. If the victim is conscious and in pain, he will usually cooperate. If he is unconscious, there may be a bottle or container nearby which will provide the answer. Do not, however, waste time over identification. Prompt treatment is more important.

Do not make the casualty vomit.

If the casualty is conscious, give one sachet of activated charcoal in 500 ml (half a litre) of water.

If the casualty is unconscious, put him in the unconscious position (page 6) and:

- give artificial respiration if breathing has stopped;
- give heart compression if the heart has stopped;
- DO NOT give anything by mouth;
- seek RADIO MEDICAL ADVICE if the casualty remains unconscious.

In cases of hydrogen cyanide (prussic acid) poisoning (page 57) where breathing and pulse

---

[1] *See: Medical first aid guide for use in accidents involving dangerous goods.* London, International Maritime Organization, 1985, p. 25.

are present, break an ampoule of amyl nitrite[1] into a clean handkerchief or cloth and hold it under the patient's nose so that he inhales the vapour.

All patients should be kept warm in bed until they have recovered.

Skin contact

Toxic substances can affect the skin in two ways:

- by direct contact, causing redness and irritation and, in severe cases, burns of the skin;
- by absorption through the intact skin, producing general symptoms such as drowsiness, weakness, and in rare cases unconsciousness.

Treatment

- The contaminated clothing and shoes should be removed immediately.
- Wash off the chemical with copious amounts of lukewarm water for at least 10 minutes. Continue for a further 10 minutes if there is any evidence of chemicals still on the skin.
- If a burn has occurred, treat as on page 80.
- If burns are severe and extensive, obtain RADIO MEDICAL ADVICE.

Eye contact

Many substances, notably chemical liquids, and the fumes of certain chemicals will produce redness and irritation if the eyes are accidentally splashed by, or exposed to, them. Treatment should be immediate.

Wash the substance out of the eye with copious amounts of fresh water as quickly as possible, keeping the eyelids wide open (Fig. 62). This must be done thoroughly for 10 minutes. If there is any doubt whether the chemical has been completely removed, repeat washing for a further 10 minutes. If severe pain is experienced, physical restraint of the patient may be neces-

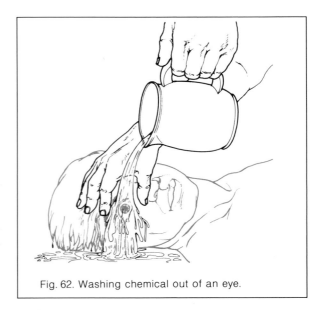

Fig. 62. Washing chemical out of an eye.

sary in order to be certain of effective treatment. Read pages 76–79 about identifying and treating damage to the eye.

For pain, give two paracetamol tablets by mouth every four hours until the pain subsides. If there is very severe pain refer to page 305.

Get RADIO MEDICAL ADVICE.

Special considerations

If you are dealing with a suicide attempt, it is your duty to do everything you can to save the victim's life and to guard against further attempts.

Important: the patient should not be left without an attendant.

You should save any remains of poison that you may find in a glass, cup, bottle, or package. Also collect any vomited matter in a bowl and seal it in a bottle. These items may be helpful for identifying the toxic substance and deciding on further treatment after the patient has been seen by a doctor or taken ashore.

---

[1] Amyl nitrite inhalant, 0.3-ml crushable ampoules, should be included in the medicines carried by the ship, if the crew may be exposed to hydrogen cyanide poisoning.

Specific toxic substances

(For treatment, see under Inhaled poisons, Swallowed poisons, etc. above.)

Drugs

Many drugs can be taken accidentally or in an attempt at suicide. The most common are sedatives (sleeping tablets) and tranquillizers. These include the barbiturates and such drugs as diazepam. They usually cause a gradual onset of unconsciousness, which may be prolonged. The breathing may slow down and become shallow. In severe cases it may stop. In barbiturate poisoning unconsciousness may be present for several days, but the majority of patients recover.

Simple pain-killers such as acetylsalicylic acid and paracetamol may also be taken in overdose. Acetylsalicylic acid causes vomiting, ringing in the ears, and deep rapid breathing. In a severe overdose, this drug can cause bleeding in the gut and the patient may vomit up bright red blood. Paracetamol does not usually cause any immediate symptoms except occasional vomiting. It can, however, cause liver damage 2 or 3 days after being swallowed if more than 20–30 tablets are taken. Neither of these drugs causes unconsciousness.

Disinfectants

Many types of disinfectant such as carbolic acid, cresol, and bleaching solutions are toxic.

Carbolic acid (phenol) and cresols cause a severe rash on contact with the skin in dilute solutions. Strong concentrated solutions will produce painless white burns of the skin. If they are swallowed, burns of the mouth will occur, and there may be severe vomiting, followed by collapse and unconsciousness. Convulsions may occur (page 195).

Bleaches (e.g., lavatory cleaners, etc.) are usually solutions of sodium hypochlorite in water. They cause irritation of the skin and are poisonous if swallowed. The patient may complain of burning in the mouth and stomach and feel generally unwell.

On contact with acids, these substances release fumes that are irritating to the lungs, causing a cough, a feeling of breathlessness, and burning in the throat. However, the fumes are not severely toxic, and the symptoms usually subside rapidly.

Solvents, petroleum products, and fuel oils.

These substances usually cause symptoms after the vapours have been accidentally inhaled. The symptoms are drowsiness, dizziness, nausea, and occasionally vomiting. If severe exposure occurs, the patient may become unconscious. If the substances are swallowed, they usually produce the same symptoms, but the nausea and vomiting are worse.

Cyanide

Hydrogen cyanide (prussic acid) gas is used in fumigating ships. Both the solid cyanide and the gas are extremely poisonous, and symptoms and signs may develop very rapidly. They are slightly corrosive, if swallowed, and cause a burning feeling in the mouth and in the abdomen. However, the main danger is general poisoning. There will be shortness of breath, anxiety, and rapid loss of consciousness. Convulsions can occur (page 195). Death may result within a few minutes.

Carbon dioxide (carbonic acid gas)

Suffocation by this odourless gas may occur when its concentration in the air is so high that it replaces a substantial part of the oxygen. This may happen while crew-members are dealing with a fire in a hold. The gas is also produced if grain in the hold ferments, and it may be generated by refrigerated cargoes of certain foods; it is also used as a refrigerant. The gas is heavier than air and collects in the lower parts of holds and compartments. A person exposed to it experiences giddiness, difficulty in breathing, and headache. Later he may fall down and lose consciousness.

Carbon monoxide

This odourless inflammable gas also occurs in hold fires, as the product of an explosion, in the waste gases of petrol- and oil-driven engines, and when refrigerated meat cargoes decompose. It is lighter than air and highly poisonous, even in very low concentrations.

A person suffering from the effects of this gas feels giddy, often with muscular weakness; he may become unconscious quickly. In severe cases, the lips may be bright red, and the skin of the face and body pink in colour.

Oxygen inhalation is a treatment of choice in this type of poisoning, and it should be given as soon as possible (see page 51).

Refrigerant gases

Inhalation of *ammonia vapour* will cause intense irritation, ranging from a catching of the breath with smarting and watering of the eyes (in the case of low concentrations) to intense irritation and corrosion of the whole air passages, gasping for breath, collapse, and death (when concentrations are high).

Carbon dioxide is also present in refrigerants. If a person becomes faint or loses consciousness in a refrigerating plant where there is no evidence of escaping ammonia, he is probably suffering from the effects of carbon dioxide.

Methyl chloride is a colourless gas, smelling like ether. It may cause drowsiness, mental confusion, coma, nausea, vomiting, convulsions, and death. It is also dangerous in low concentrations because of its explosive nature. On no account should any naked light be exposed in the presence of the vapour; electric motors should be stopped to avoid the risk of sparking. A heavy-duty electric torch, switched on before approaching the leak, is the only safe light to use.

Freon is an odourless gas, which is generally harmless, except when present in a concentra-tion high enough to deprive a person of sufficient oxygen. The signs of oxygen deficiency are faintness, staggering gait, collapse, and unconsciousness.

Poisonous gases from refrigerated cargoes

Certain refrigerated cargoes, including fruit, vegetables, and cheese, generate carbon dioxide during normal storage. With any failure of a refrigerating plant, food cargoes (especially meat) may generate poisonous and inflammable gases. This can be particularly dangerous if the cargo space is flooded. Carbon monoxide, ammonia, hydrogen sulfide, and hydrogen may be generated in addition to carbon dioxide. In any great concentration these gases are extremely poisonous and some are explosive. Full precautions against fire and explosion must be taken in addition to those against suffocation and poisoning.

Other gases

Trichloroethene — usually called trilene or "trike" — is a volatile anaesthetic gas which causes drowsiness, mental confusion, nausea, vomiting, and coma. It can also result in death. It is used medically in obstetrics and dentistry because it acts quickly. In the impure form it is used as a dry-cleaning agent. Some people are addicted to "sniffing" it (see Drug abuse, page 189).

Prevention of poisoning

(See also: Ventilation, page 283; Control of disease vectors, page 290.)

Remember: prevention is better than cure

Knowledge of the basic safety precautions and strict adherence to them by people working with dangerous goods, and also knowledge of the conventional labelling of these goods, play an important part in the prevention of poisoning.

For the handling of some dangerous goods, protective clothing (e.g., rubber or plastic gloves, aprons, boots) and breathing apparatus (compressed air system, smoke helmet) may be required and should be provided. They should be kept on board ship and be available at the workplace, regularly inspected, and cleaned or replaced. Adequate washing and shower facilities for the workmen should be provided nearby.

In the event of a leakage or spillage involving dangerous gas or fumes, the use of a gas detector is advised before a space is declared to be free. Gas masks will not provide complete protection, but may be used to aid escape. The place where a leakage has occurred should be immediately treated with an appropriate neutralizing substance and then covered with sand, which should afterwards be removed in a special container to a safe place.

Holds and closed spaces in which toxic vapours and gases could accumulate should be thoroughly ventilated, and a gas detector (not an explosimeter) used, before people are allowed to enter and also during cargo-handling operations. Places used for the storage of dangerous goods should be decontaminated, if necessary, after use and/or before reuse.

Dangerous goods should not be carried or stored in proximity to other materials (particularly foodstuffs) that, as a result of contact with the dangerous goods, could cause illness or accidents (poisoning).

Special measures relating to the prevention of poisoning in particular cases are given in the sections pertaining to each individual group of substances in the IMO publication mentioned at the beginning of this chapter (see page 53).

Chapter 3

Examination of the patient

Contents

A systematic and complete examination of the patient is essential to evaluate the extent of an illness. Such an examination is composed of two basic parts: (1) the history, i.e., a chronological story of the patient's illness from the first symptoms to the present time; and (2) the physical examination, in which the patient is examined for physical evidence of disease. The findings should be recorded accurately, concisely, and completely.

Many patients reporting to the sick-bay may have a minor illness or injury, such as a splinter or blister, that often requires only a brief examination prior to treatment for the specific complaint. Patients who appear quite ill will require a thorough evaluation and a more detailed examination.

An accurate record should be made of all phases of every illness, beginning with the history and physical examination. Daily records should be kept during the course of the illness. Often the diagnosis will not be evident when the patient is first seen; but, as complaints and delayed physical signs appear in the next several days, the symptom complex may become clearer. Many infectious diseases first manifest themselves only as fever and general malaise, but in several days a rash may appear (as in measles), or jaundice (as in hepatitis), or a stiff neck and coma (as in meningitis). These signs and symptoms help to establish a definitive diagnosis.

A clear, concise recording of the signs and symptoms of the patient's illness is important in communication by radio, or when a patient is transferred to a physician's care.

History-taking

Taking the history is an important part of the examination and often a diagnosis may be made from the history alone. All possible information should be obtained and organized logically to tell the story of the patient's illness.

Recording the history

The recorded history should begin with the time the patient first noted any symptoms of sickness,

61

body changes, or a departure from good health. Symptoms and events up to the present time should be included. The dates or times at which various symptoms appeared should be noted as precisely as possible. The patient should be encouraged to talk freely, without interruption. Specific leading questions should be asked.

Some questions that will help the patient to give the history are:

- "How did your illness start?"
- "What was the first symptom you noticed?"
- "How long have you had this?"
- "How and where does it affect you?"
- "What followed?"

It is important to be specific about the main symptom or symptoms, such as pain in the abdomen (see Table 5, page 162) or severe headache. Time should not be wasted on vague symptoms such as tiredness, weakness, and loss of appetite. These non-specific symptoms are a part of almost every illness. The patient should be asked if he has ever experienced similar symptoms or had the condition or problem before. He should be asked for the diagnosis of any similar situation in the past, the treatment that was prescribed, and the medicaments he had taken. Also, any medicaments that the patient is currently taking should be noted, because his present illness might be a reaction to medication (for instance, allergy to penicillin or another drug).

Pain

Pain is one of the most common bodily symptoms. These are questions that should be asked:

- "How did the pain start?" "What were you doing at the time?"
- "Where is the pain located?" (Ask the patient to point to the area of pain so you can be specific in your notes. See Annex 2 for the names of the various parts of the body.)
- "How severe is the pain?" "Does it make you double up?" "What is the pain like?" (e.g., cramping, sharp, dull, or aching). "Is it constant or intermittent?"

- "Does the pain radiate to any other body area?"
- "Has it ever moved from one area to another?"
- "Is there a way you can bring on the pain or relieve it?"
- "Is there anything that makes the pain worse?"
- "Does medication help to relieve it?"

Past illnesses

Next, the patient should be asked to describe any past illness, injuries, or operations. This will help rule out certain conditions. For example, if he has had an appendectomy (surgical removal of the vermiform appendix), then pain in the right lower quadrant of the abdomen cannot be acute appendicitis. Or an illness may be a recurrence. If he had been hospitalized in the past for a duodenal ulcer and now comes in with burning mid-upper abdominal pain that is relieved by antacids and milk, then he is probably having pain from a recurrent ulcer. Previous diagnoses should be kept in mind, such as diabetes or high blood pressure; these conditions may get worse during an illness and cause complications. The patient should be asked if he is allergic to any drugs, or if any drugs have ever made him ill.

Review of body systems

When the diagnosis is not obvious or complete and if time permits, a general review of the various body systems and associated symptoms may be helpful.

The patient should be asked if he now has any of the following things to report.

Head	- History of wounds (trauma), severe headaches.
Eyes	- Blurred vision, double vision, pain, yellow colour of the sclera (white part of the eye), pain on looking at light.
Ears	- Loss of hearing, severe dizziness, pain, or drainage.

Nose	■ Bleeding, runny, or stuffy.
Mouth	■ Sores, pain, trouble swallowing.
Neck	■ Stiffness, enlarged glands, tenderness.
Respiratory	■ Cough and character of material coughed up, coughing up blood, chest pain when breathing, shortness of breath.
Cardiac	■ Pain in middle of chest, swelling of both legs, shortness of breath on exercising or when sleeping flat in bed, forceful or rapid heart beat, history of high blood pressure, heart attack, history of rheumatic fever.
Gastro-intestinal	■ Poor appetite, indigestion, nausea, vomiting, diarrhoea, constipation, jaundice, pain in stomach, blood in stool or in vomit.
Genito-urinary	■ Pain when urinating, pain in middle of back, frequent urination, straining to urinate, blood or pus in urine, discharge from penis.
Neurological	■ Paralysis or severe weakness of a part of the body (an arm or legs), convulsion, or seizure.
Family and social history	■ The patient should be asked if other members of his family have ever suffered from diabetes, tuberculosis, heart disease, cancer, or other diseases that may now be appearing in the patient. Also ask about the amount of alcohol and tobacco the patient uses. The date of his last drink should be noted if chronic alcoholism is suspected, because delirium tremens may start 5–7 days after a patient stops drinking.

Physical examination

This is the second basic part of the evaluation of the patient. By this time, some observations will have been made on such factors as the patient's speech, general appearance, and mental status. Now, another system of collecting information, based on observation of definitive signs of disease, must be used.

To carry out a basic examination, it is necessary to have a clock or watch with a second hand, blood pressure apparatus, a stethoscope, a thermometer, and a quiet room.

Vital signs	■ What is the blood pressure? ■ What is the pulse rate? ■ What is the patient's temperature?
General appearance	■ Note the position of the patient's body and his facial expression. ■ Is he tense, restless, or in an unusual posture? Note his general ability to move and respond.
Skin	■ Note location of rashes or sores. ■ Is the rash red, made up of small or large spots? Are the spots separated, or do they run together? Do they itch? Are they elevated or flat? ■ Is the skin hot and dry, or cold and wet? ■ What is the colour of the skin? Is there evidence of jaundice (yellowness)? ■ Are the lips and nailbeds a dusky blue colour, or are they pale and white?
Head	■ Is there evidence of trauma, such as a cut, bruise, or swelling?
Eyes	■ Is there evidence of jaundice or inflammation in the sclera (white part of the eye)? (Check for jaundice in the sunlight, if possible; in many normal

63

people, there is a slight yellow cast of the sclerae in artificial light.)

- Can he move both eyes together up and down, and to each side?
- Are the pupils the same size? Do they get smaller when a light is shone into the eyes? (This is a normal reaction.)

Ears
- Check for blood in the ear canal, especially if a blow to the head is known or suspected.

Nose
- Look for bleeding or abnormal discharge.

Mouth and throat
- Are the gums swollen or extremely red?
- Are the colour and movement of the tongue unusual?
- Does the throat have abnormal redness, swelling, or ulcerated patches?
- Observe the patient swallow. Does he have difficulty swallowing?
- Note any abnormal odour to the breath.

Neck
- The patient should be asked to lie down and the examiner's hands placed behind the patient's head. When he is relaxed, the head should be lifted gently, bending the neck so that his chin will touch his chest. Observe for (1) an unnatural stiffness of the neck, or (2) discomfort when the legs are lifted from the table with the knees straight.
- Check for any enlarged glands on the side of his neck. Note if they are tender, movable, soft, or hard.

Chest
- The patient's breathing should be observed. Note if it is painful and if both sides of the chest move together.

- Note if he has to sit up to breathe.
- A stethoscope should be used to listen to all areas in the front and back and compare each side (see Fig. 125, page 179, and Table 6, pages 180–181).

Abdomen
- Look at the contour. Is it symmetrical?
- Ask about any scars. They may indicate previous surgery and rule out certain diseases of the gall-bladder or appendix, if these organs have been removed.
- Feel the abdomen, noting tender areas. Is the abdomen soft or rigid? (See Fig. 122, page 161, and Table 5, pages 162–163.)

Genitalia
- Check for sores, as in syphilis, being careful not to touch any.
- Is there any discharge from the penis?
- Check the testicles for swelling and tenderness.
- Check the groin for swollen glands and for hernia (rupture).

Arms and legs
- Check for movement and strength of all parts. Is there any weakness or paralysis? (If the patient is unable to move his leg, for example, find out if it is due to pain, or if it truly is paralysis, which usually causes no pain.)
- Check for swelling and for tenderness. Is one leg or arm affected, or are both?

Back
- Is there tenderness or deformity?
- The kidney area should be tapped gently with the fist to check for tenderness. This area lies in the back on either side of the spine and between the top of the pelvic bone and last rib.

Nervous system
- Does the patient show abnormal concern about his illness?
- Note general mental status. Is he rational? Is his behaviour abnormal? Can he remember today's date and do simple arithmetic?
- Are his coordination and gait normal? As a test, have the patient take a few steps and pick up with each hand an object from a table or chair. If the patient is too ill to walk, note how he moves, turns over, and picks up objects in bed.

Symptoms and signs

The preceding section of this chapter described how to obtain useful information on a patient. The approach included questions about symptoms and things that the patient can feel and describe, plus an examination of the patient for signs or things that can be seen without relying on the patient's cooperation. The examiner's observation of the patient should begin at the head and proceed systematically to the feet.

After the examiner has obtained all the required information, it must be sorted and rearranged in different ways if it is to make sense. Related things must be brought together. A recommended way of organizing the information when asking for medical advice by radio is described in Chapter 14, External assistance, page 277.

Drawing conclusions

Write down the main complaints, note the body systems that might be involved, and ask more detailed questions about the symptoms. The physical examination may be performed again, and note taken of the body systems affected by the abnormal findings. If necessary, ask further questions or reexamine areas that will help to clarify the findings. Often by a process of elimination, the problem will be reduced to a few possible diagnoses. Next, turn to the chapters of this book that describe the diseases or conditions possibly involved, and decide which one comes closest to explaining all the signs and symptoms observed. The material in these chapters might suggest other special tests or additional questions that should be asked.

At this point, if a definitive diagnosis cannot be made, knowledge of the case will be sufficient for presentation by radio to a physician.

Body discharges such as vomit, faeces, sputum, and urine should be examined carefully for abnormal colour, consistency, and above all presence of blood. Blood in the faeces may be bright red, dark brown, or the colour of tar. Blood in the urine is usually red in colour; but the urine may have to settle for several hours before blood can be seen. If the patient appears jaundiced, his urine will usually be dark yellow in colour. To confirm a jaundiced condition, the urine should be put into a small bottle and shaken vigorously. In jaundice the foam will be yellow; normally it is white. Comparison can be made with a normal urine specimen.

Two important final points: First, when in doubt, always compare the physical findings on a patient with those for a normal person; or compare corresponding left and right parts, e.g., the eyes or ears, in the same patient. Second, continue to observe and recheck the patient for things that may have been missed. Avoid a quick decision or diagnosis! Snap decisions might be wrong.

Note on malingering

Malingering is feigning illness to avoid work or to gain some personal advantage. The malingerer either has no disability or, if he has one, deliberately exaggerates its symptoms. In any suspect case, take a careful history and make a careful routine examination, which should include the temperature and pulse rate.

Treatment

If the diagnosis is not absolutely certain, as is likely, give the patient the benefit of the doubt and leave him till a doctor sees him. In the meantime, keep him strictly in bed on a light diet, see that he passes faeces regularly, and prohibit smoking and alcoholic drinks.

Chapter 4
Care of the injured

This chapter is about the care and treatment, after first aid, of a casualty who has been moved to the ship's hospital or to his own cabin for the definitive treatment of injuries sustained on board.

Cleanliness and sterilizing

To prevent infection in wounds, burns, and other injuries, all dressings and instruments should be sterile.

Dressings should be supplied prepacked and sterilized.

There are two ways of obtaining sterile instruments:

- The instruments or equipment can be obtained in prepacked sterilized containers. Such instruments are for once-only use and are disposable. Disposable equipment is very convenient to use.
- Instruments that are not disposable should be sterilized prior to use by placing in boiling water for not less than 20 minutes. The "patient end" of an instrument must not touch anything before use, and the operator should touch only those parts of the instrument he has to handle in using it.

The attendant should similarly guard against infecting the wound by:

- rolling up sleeves;
- thoroughly washing hands, wrists, and forearms, first with soap and running water and then with 1% cetrimide solution.

General care of wounds

Types of wound

Wounds may be divided into six types: abrasions, avulsions, contusions, incisions, lacerations, and puncture or stab wounds.

Abrasions are open wounds caused by the skin being rubbed or scraped. They can be quite painful if large areas of skin have been scraped off. Usually an abrasion is not very deep and bleeding is limited to an oozing from damaged

Contents

capillaries and small veins. There is a danger of infection from bacteria ground into the wound with dirt, grease, and other foreign matter.

Avulsions are open wounds that may be caused by explosions, accidents involving vehicles or heavy machinery, and animal bites. Tissue is separated forcibly or torn, with loss of skin and soft tissue. Heavy bleeding usually follows immediately.

A *contusion* (*bruise, blood blister*) is a closed superficial wound, usually caused by a blow from a blunt object, a bump against a stationary object, or crushing. Blood seeping into soft tissues from injured vessels and capillaries causes swelling and pain that may be severe at the site of the injury. If the injury is over a bone, the possibility of a fracture should be considered.

Incisions are open wounds caused by sharp objects such as knives, broken glass, and sharp metal edges. These wounds are smooth-edged and bleed freely. The amount of bleeding depends upon the depth, location, and size of the wound. There may be severe damage to muscles, nerves, and tendons if the wound is deep.

Lacerations are open wounds caused by objects such as dull knives, broken glass, stones, and moving parts of machinery, or by direct blows. The edges are usually jagged and irregular, and pieces of tissue may be partly or wholly pulled away. Contamination with dirt, grease, or other foreign matter increases the likelihood of infection.

Punctures are open wounds caused by such objects as wooden or metal splinters, knives, nails, fish-hooks, ice-picks, and bullets. Although the opening of a puncture wound may be small and the external bleeding minor, the object may have penetrated deep into the body, causing internal haemorrhage and injury to organs. *Stab wounds* are especially dangerous because the underlying structures will have been penetrated and infection will have been carried into the deep tissues. Because the wound is not cleansed by external bleeding, the possibility of infection is increased and there is a danger of tetanus (lockjaw) or gas gangrene.

Wounds vary enormously in extent and depth, depending on how they are caused. The types just described fall into two groups:

- simple cuts or wounds
- deep and gaping wounds.

A *simple cut or wound* involves the skin, the subcutaneous layer, and the superficial layers under the skin, but *not the muscle*.

A *deep and gaping wound* is usually the result of crushing, of an explosion, or of being caught in machinery. There is always serious skin damage, with associated damage to underlying tissue and muscle and inevitable infection. Not infrequently, blood will ooze from the first-aid dressing and sometimes blood will be seen to be spurting from an artery.

Natural healing

Simple wounds will heal quickly and with insignificant scarring, provided the skin edges can be kept in contact with very little movement and infection is not present.

The healing of deep and gaping wounds involves the growth of new flesh to close the gap. This process is necessarily accompanied by some discharge. It is slow and painful. A scar remains which is unsightly and possibly disabling.

Treatment

Before starting any further treatment:

- Prepare materials and equipment required to cleanse, stitch (if necessary), and re-dress the wound.
- Consider whether antibiotic therapy is necessary. Simple sutured wounds and superficial packed wounds should not require antibiotics. In other cases, and especially with deep wounds involving damage to muscles, start the standard antibiotic treatment (page 308). When in doubt, give antibiotics.
- Treat for pain if necessary (page 305).
- Check whether the casualty has been immunized against tetanus, and whether he has received a "booster" tetanus toxoid injection within the last 5 years.

If yes, do not give him either globulin or toxoid. If not, give him 250 units of tetanus immune globulin as an intramuscular injection. Also give him one dose of tetanus toxoid intramuscularly in a different extremity and with a separate syringe.

Generally, the decision whether to give tetanus immune globulin in a particular case will depend not only on the casualty's history of previous immunization against the disease, but also on the type of injury (small or large, deep or superficial) and on the risk of tetanus infection. All people on board a ship transporting horses, cows, and other animals, or hides would be at high risk.

If in doubt whether to give globulin to your patient, get **RADIO MEDICAL ADVICE**.

Tetanus toxoid and tetanus globulin injections should be noted in the casualty's records, and it is important to ensure that the casualty understands that he has been given tetanus toxoid and/or tetanus globulin injection(s).

Next, ensure that the casualty has recovered from shock (see page 17). Then:

- Sterilize a kidney bowl to receive the sterilized instruments.
- Sterilize a pair of haemostat forceps, two pairs of tissue forceps, and scissors by boiling them for at least 20 minutes; allow the instruments to cool.
- Put out a sterile dressing, cotton wool, bandages, safety pins, and adhesive plaster.
- Prepare a bowl of 1% cetrimide solution for cleansing the surrounding skin and the wound, if necessary.
- Put within reach a dish in which to place dirty dressings or swabs.
- Put out a razor to shave, if necessary, the area around the wound. Clean the razor well in 1% cetrimide solution.

The dishes and unopened dressings should be assembled on a clean towel spread over a conveniently situated table.

When you are ready to proceed, wash your hands again, inspect the wound and remove with

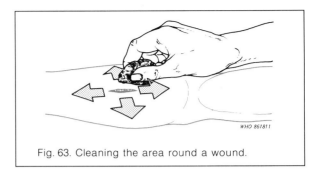

Fig. 63. Cleaning the area round a wound.

forceps any foreign bodies (dirt, wood, metal, etc.) that may be present. Next cover the wound with a dressing and cleanse the surrounding skin with swabs soaked in 1% cetrimide solution, working from the wound outward (Fig. 63).

After cleansing the surrounding skin, and, if necessary, shaving the surrounding hair to a distance of 6 cm around the wound, again inspect the wound, dabbing with gauze swabs soaked in 1% cetrimide solution. Do not use *dry* cotton wool or other fluffy materials.

Gentle pressure will usually stop any oozing blood. If there is blood spurting from a blood vessel and gentle pressure has not been successful in stemming it, it will be necessary to tie the blood vessel. Grasp it with the pointed ends of the haemostat forceps and make sure the bleeding is controlled. Next take a ligature of catgut (suture, absorbable) and, holding the forceps up, slip the ligature under the forceps and tie it off with a surgeon's knot (Fig. 64) so as to encircle the end of the artery and any tissues caught up in the tip of the forceps. Now cut the ligature-ends short, leaving only enough to ensure that the knot does not slip. Remove the forceps and inspect to see that bleeding has ceased.

Closure of wounds without stitching, using adhesive skin closures

In the case of simple cuts or wounds that nevertheless require closing, it may be possible to bring the edges together with strips of adhesive surgical plaster alone, strapped across a surgical gauze dressing.

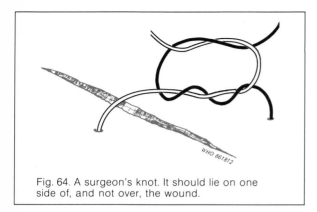

Fig. 64. A surgeon's knot. It should lie on one side of, and not over, the wound.

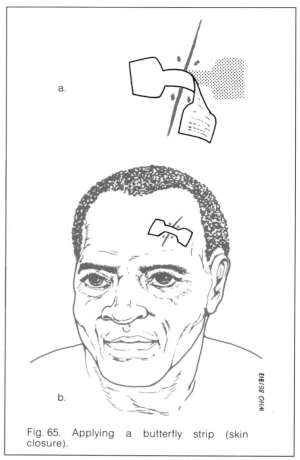

Fig. 65. Applying a butterfly strip (skin closure).

Alternatively, "butterfly closures" can be used. These consist of two adhesive patches joined by a narrow non-adhesive bridge. After removing the "butterfly closure" from its envelope and stripping off the protective backing, the edges of the wound are brought together by fixing the closure with one patch on either side of the wound and with the non-adhesive bridge across it (see Fig. 65).

Make sure that the wound edges are dry before application, or the closure will not adhere.

Larger wounds must first be covered with a sterile gauze dressing. Then two broad strips of surgical adhesive plaster are fixed to the skin, one on either side of the wound. The edges nearest to the wound are folded under to form a non-adhesive hem. Using sharp pointed scissors, a series of small holes is pierced in the folded hems opposite to each other. When laced with tape or string, the edges of the plaster can be drawn together, and this will draw the edges of the underlying wound together (see Fig. 66).

Closure of wounds by suture

Deep and gaping wounds cannot be closed effectively with adhesive plaster or "butterfly closures" alone. For these wounds you will have to consider whether suturing is appropriate.

DO NOT suture unless you can bring together not only the skin but also the deeper tissue. A

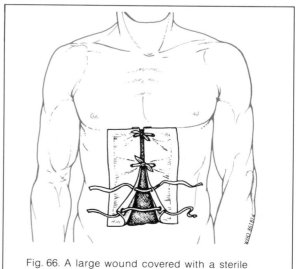

Fig. 66. A large wound covered with a sterile gauze dressing and adhesive plaster.

dead space will become infected and delay recovery, and may lead to the loss of the limb or even death. **Do not suture a wound that is over six hours old. When in doubt do not suture.**

When you decide that suturing is appropriate, you will require the following items, in addition to those listed on page 69:

- A length of silk or thread already attached to a surgical needle (these are supplied in sterile dry packs, which should not be opened until you are ready to start stitching).
- A needle-holder (Hegar-Mayo) and scissors, previously sterilized by boiling in water for 20 minutes.

The sterilized needle-holder and scissors should be placed in the sterilized kidney dish. Then decide exactly what kind of repair should be made. If the cut is linear, for example, how many stitches will be needed? If the cut is star-shaped, will one stitch to include the apices of each skin flap be adequate?

Having decided on the nature of the repair, wash your hands again, open the sterile pack, extract the needle with forceps and place it in the sterilized kidney dish.

Pick up the needle with the needle-holder. Grasp the edge of the wound nearest to you with the toothed tissue forceps, then with a firm sharp stab drive the needle through the whole thickness of the skin about 0.6 cm from its edge. Then, with the toothed tissue forceps, grasp the skin on the side of the wound immediately opposite and drive the needle upwards through the whole thickness of the skin so that it emerges about 0.6 cm from the wound edge (see Fig. 67). If the wound is deep and clean, insert the needle deeply into the underlying fatty tissue so as to draw it and the skin together. Now cut sufficient thread off the main length to tie a knot, and tie a surgeon's knot, with sufficient tension exerted (and no more) to bring the cut edges of the skin together. Insert further stitches as required at intervals of not less than 1 cm. After tying, cut off the ends of the knots, leaving about 1 cm of thread free to facilitate later removal of the

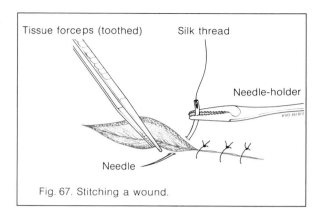
Fig. 67. Stitching a wound.

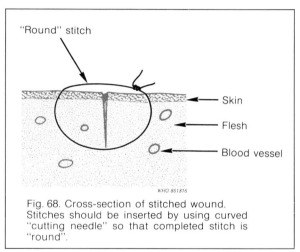
Fig. 68. Cross-section of stitched wound. Stitches should be inserted by using curved "cutting needle" so that completed stitch is "round".

stitches (Fig. 68). If the cut edges of the skin tend to curve inwards into the wound, pull them out with toothed forceps. As soon as the stitching is completed, paint the whole area with 1% cetrimide solution. Next apply sterile gauze and complete the dressing as for superficial wounds.

Stitches should be inserted using a curved "cutting" needle so that the completed stitch is "round" (see Fig. 68).

If you have a difficult, deep, and tense wound to close, use a mattress suture (Fig. 69). A mattress suture ensures that the edges of the wound are brought together not just on the surface but throughout its depth and length.

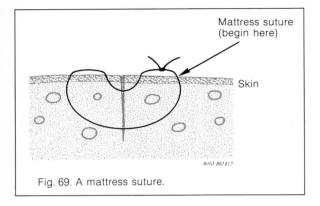

Fig. 69. A mattress suture.

indicating the formation of pus within the wound. If there is, remove the stitch and allow the wound to drain freely.

On the seventh day the stitches can be removed and a simple dressing worn until healing is complete. Remember that leg wounds take longer to heal than arm wounds. Stitches on the scalp can be removed after 6 days.

The removal of stitches is a simple and painless operation if carried out gently. Swab the area with 1% cetrimide solution. Grasp one of the ends of the stitch with sterile forceps and lift it up, so as to be able to insert the pointed blade of sterile scissors immediately under the knot (see Fig. 70a). Cut the stitch and, by gently pulling with the forceps, withdraw it (Fig. 70b).

The procedure for stitching a lip is shown in Fig. 71.

Deep and gaping wounds that cannot be sutured

If the wound is to be allowed to heal without suturing, lightly pack it with sterile petrolatum gauze. Then place about three layers of surgical gauze over this and make fast with bandages or elastic adhesive plaster. Re-dress the wound daily until it is healed. If the wound is on a limb, the limb should be elevated to encourage draining and reduce swelling.

Note. A local anaesthetic should not be necessary for the insertion of one or two simple stitches; indeed the application of the anaesthetic may in such cases be more painful than the suturing. In more complicated cases it may be desirable to infiltrate 1% lidocaine hydrochloride (see Fig. 124, page 175).

A greater or lesser degree of infection of the wound is inevitable after injury. This means that a certain amount of fluid will be produced in the damaged and inflamed tissues, and this should be allowed to escape. Remember this when inserting stitches; do not put them so close together that it is impossible for pus to discharge if it forms. Also, when inspecting a wound after stitching, look closely to see if there is swelling or tension on a stitch in any part of the wound,

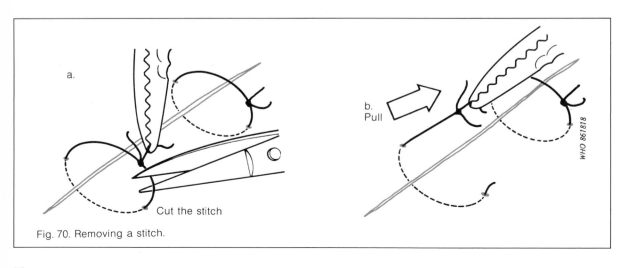

Fig. 70. Removing a stitch.

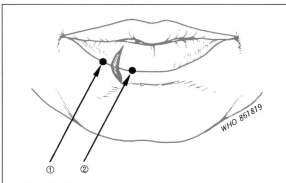

Fig. 71. Stitching a lip.
To ensure that the lip margin heals in a "straight" line, the first stitch should go in at point "1" and come out at point "2".

Internal injuries

The site of each major internal organ is shown in Annex 1 (Fig. 151). If you suspect any organ is damaged, *always* start a 10-minute pulse chart (see page 41, Fig. 41), so that internal bleeding can be recognized as soon as possible by a rising pulse rate. If the pulse rate is or becomes high, get RADIO MEDICAL ADVICE.

Restlessness is often a sign of internal bleeding, so all patients who are restless after injury need careful watching.

If the patient is restless because of great pain, and other injuries permit (i.e., there are no head or chest injuries), give morphine (page 305). This will control the pain and help to keep the patient calm and quiet, thus diminishing bleeding.

Injury to the abdomen with protrusion of gut

Get RADIO MEDICAL ADVICE. This injury requires hospital treatment ashore at the earliest moment. Until then, put the patient to bed lying on his back with his knees drawn up to relax the abdomen. No attempt should be made to push intestines back into the abdomen. Exposed intestines (gut) should be covered with clean, non-fluffy, *very damp* linen. The covering should be kept damp with cooled boiled water and should

be held on loosely by a binder. Nothing should be given by mouth. If the patient cannot be taken off the ship within about 12 hours, fluid should be given intravenously (page 117).

Give morphine (page 305) to keep the patient pain-free and at rest until he can be taken off the ship.

Head injuries

Examination

All but the most superficial head injuries are potentially dangerous. Careful examination is therefore essential.

Small wounds should be carefully examined to ensure that they are not over a fracture of the skull.

Examine the ears, nose, and throat for blood or cerebrospinal fluid (CSF), which surrounds and cushions the brain and spinal cord.

It should be assumed that the casualty has sustained *serious injuries,* if:

- he suffers from unconsciousness, other than very short-term;
- blood, blood-stained fluid, or a sticky clear fluid (CSF) is seen to be coming from the ears, the nose, or the throat;
- there is a suspected open fracture of the vault of the skull;
- brain damage is suspected, i.e., paralysis is noted;
- vomiting occurs or headache increases;
- he appears to be confused or drowsy, acts abnormally, or becomes unconscious again; or
- the pulse rate slows to below 65 per minute.

Types of head injury

Bruising will occur if a moderate force is applied. Because the head is well supplied with blood, a collection of blood (haematoma) will form in the tissues under the scalp. It may be sharply defined, hard, and tense, or it may be a fairly diffuse soggy swelling (Fig. 72).

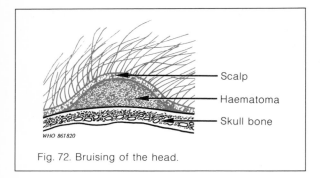

Fig. 72. Bruising of the head.

A *wound* will result from most blows to the head because there is little tissue between the skull and the scalp. The wound will bleed freely and often out of proportion to its size. Surrounding tissues may be swollen and soggy with blood that has leaked into them. The scalp edges will be ragged, not clean-cut.

Concussion of the brain can occur when the skull receives a heavy blow. It occurs because the brain is fairly soft and its function can be subject to widespread disturbance when shock waves pass through its substance. Suspect this condition if the casualty loses consciousness for only a few minutes. It is characterized by loss of memory for events before or after the injury, headache, and sometimes nausea and vomiting.

There are three types of *fracture* of the skull:

- *Linear fractures* occur in the top and sides of the skull (the vault). They are the result of direct force and are normally diagnosed only after X-ray.
- *Fractures of the base of the skull* are the result of indirect force transmitted to the base of the skull from a heavy blow to the vault, from blows to the face or jaw, or when the casualty falls from a height and lands on his feet. They can be diagnosed by *deduction,* from the manner in which the injury occurred *and* because blood or CSF will be found to be leaking into the ear, nose, or throat.
- *Depressed fractures* are the result of a heavy blow to the vault from some blunt object (for instance, a hammer). The skull fragments on impact and the pieces of bone are driven

downwards causing severe bruising and laceration of the brain tissue. Bleeding within the skull will cause compression of the brain. There is usually associated bruising and splitting of the scalp, and, when the bleeding stops, CSF may leak into the wound. The depressed area can often be felt on *gentle* examination, and sometimes pieces of bone may be found in the wound (Fig. 73).

Remember that fractures of the base of the skull are open fractures, and that depressed fractures may be open or closed. In all open fractures of the skull, infection may get into the brain and the meninges and cause serious complications.

Compression of the brain occurs when bleeding takes place within the skull, pressure builds up, and the brain function is progressively disrupted (Fig. 74).

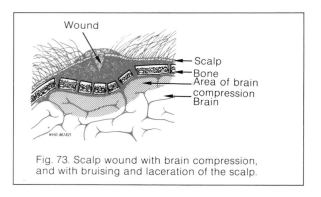

Fig. 73. Scalp wound with brain compression, and with bruising and laceration of the scalp.

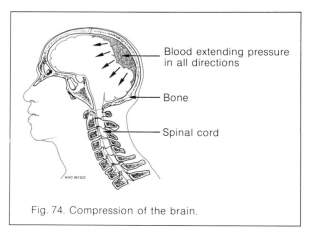

Fig. 74. Compression of the brain.

The condition is often associated with depressed fractures but can occur with injuries that appear at first sight to be comparatively minor. The usual history is a blow on the head, often just above an ear, loss of consciousness for a short period, and apparent recovery followed shortly by deepening coma. During this sequence of events any of the following may occur:

- there may be twitching of the limbs, or fits due to irritation of the brain;
- breathing may become noisy;
- the pulse may be slow and tend to become even slower;
- the pupils may become unequal or may both dilate;
- paralysis may be present on one side of the body;
- the body temperature may rise to dangerous levels (40.5 °C and above).

Treatment

Bruising (haematoma)
No specific treatment is required. An ice-bag held over the area may control the bleeding.

Superficial wounds (without fracture)
Control the bleeding by pressure. If necessary, stitch the wound.

Concussion of the brain
The casualty should be put to bed and allowed to rest for 48 hours. There may be troublesome headaches, and acetylsalicylic acid or paracetamol may be required (page 305). These headaches may continue for many weeks after an accident. The casualty should be warned to report immediately if he notices increasing headaches or drowsiness or if he vomits. He should be sent to see a doctor at the next port.

Serious injuries (fractures and compression of the brain)
If in port, such casualties should be transferred immediately to hospital. If at sea, seek RADIO MEDICAL ADVICE.

In the meantime, if the casualty is unconscious he should be kept in the unconscious position (page 6) until he regains consciousness or is transferred to medical care. He must be kept constantly under observation in case he should vomit, have fits, or become restless and move out of the unconscious position. The observation should be maintained when consciousness returns in case he lapses into coma once again.

If you suspect a depressed fracture, bleeding should be controlled by using a ring-pad (page 39).

In cases of *open fracture:*

- DO NOT poke round in scalp wounds;
- DO NOT press over wounds;
- DO NOT try to remove fragments of bone from scalp wounds.

Infection must be prevented from entering the wound and causing meningitis and inflammation of the brain tissues. Using scissors, cut any hair to as near the skin as possible for a distance of at least 5 cm around the wound. Holding a dressing gently over the wound, swab the skin with 1% cetrimide solution and dry with a sterile swab. Place a petrolatum-gauze burn-and-wound dressing over the wound and on the surrounding skin. Cover this with sterile swabs and put a ring-pad over this dressing before bandaging. Hair and cetrimide solution should not be allowed to enter the wound.

Give 600 000 units of procaine benzylpenicillin intramuscularly, followed by standard antibiotic treatment (page 308) or, if the casualty is unconscious, continue to give the same dose of procaine benzylpenicillin intramuscularly every 6 hours. If allergy develops (see Allergic reactions, page 167) give chlorphenamine, 10 mg, by intramuscular injection.

Morphine should NOT be given unless the head injury is trivial and the casualty has serious and painful major injuries elsewhere.

Longer-term management of serious head injuries

If a casualty with a serious head injury has to remain on board for more than a few hours, it will be necessary:

- to watch for changes in his condition;
- to record as much information as possible to help those to whom the casualty will eventually be transferred; and
- possibly to deal with certain complications.

Include in your records:

- date and time of the accident;
- a detailed account of how the accident happened;
- the casualty's condition when first seen;
- the condition of the casualty subsequently;
- details of the treatment you have carried out.

The *essential observations* in order of importance are:

- *Level of consciousness.* Record if the person is fully conscious, speaking normally, and responding to questions. If not, can he be roused by pinching or pricking with a pin? If the eye is touched gently with a finger, does it move?

  Deterioration of the level of consciousness and responsiveness indicates an urgent need for transfer to hospital.

- *State of the pupils.* The pupils should be compared one with the other:
  - Are they large or small?
  - Do they react to light? (When a bright light is shone on the eye, the pupil normally becomes smaller.)
  - Over the period of observation, is there any change in the size of either or both pupils?

  Enlargement of one pupil indicates an urgent need for transfer to hospital

- *Paralysis.* Can the patient move *both* arms and legs or only *one* arm and *one* leg on the same side? A deeply unconscious casualty may not respond to any form of stimulus. Move the limbs on both sides gently, and you may find that the muscles are slack on the affected side.

- *Unusual movements.* Movements such as jerking, twitching, rhythmic tremor, or throwing limbs about may be seen. These are caused by a special type of epileptic fit that occurs with some head injuries and indicate that urgent transfer to hospital is necessary.

- *Temperature, pulse and respiration rates.* The temperature should be normal and remain so. If there is damage to the heat-regulating centre of the brain, the temperature may, however, rise to very high levels. In that event, take the temperature every half hour and be prepared to carry out cooling (page 109).

The pulse rate may be slow if there is a rise of pressure inside the skull due to bleeding. A slow pulse that tends to slow down further is an indication for urgent admission to hospital.

The respiration may be slower than normal, and the breathing may be noisy. A clear airway must be maintained at all times and, if necessary, oxygen (page 51) or artificial respiration (page 8) should be given.

- *Other observations.*
  - Is there bleeding from the nose, ears, or back of throat?
  - Is there any clear fluid (cerebrospinal fluid) from nose, ears, or back of throat?
  - Note the presence of "black eyes" (a "black eye" can indicate a serious fracture of the skull).
  - Are there any injuries elsewhere in the body?

Fits may occur after a head injury. If the movements are violent, do not attempt to restrain the casualty by the use of excessive force. It is only necessary to prevent him from causing further injury to himself. If immediate transfer to hospital is not possible, give 10 mg of diazepam by intramuscular injection. Repeat every 12 hours until the patient can be put under medical care.

Obtain RADIO MEDICAL ADVICE.

Eye injuries

(See also: Eye diseases, page 196 and Fig. 128, Human eye, page 197.)

Eye injuries can be due to various causes including foreign bodies, direct blows as in a fight, lacerations, chemicals, and burns. The eye is a very sensitive organ and any injury to it must be treated competently.

Examination

The first stage in treating an eye injury is to record a full account of the injury, including the circumstances and details of the symptoms. It will then be necessary to carry out a careful examination. It helps if the casualty is lying down, with head supported and held slightly back, during the examination.

The *basic requirements* are:

- good illumination (overhead light, lamp, hand-held torch, or strong daylight);
- magnifying glass (preferably x8 loupe);
- soft paper tissues;
- moist cotton wool swabs or moist cotton buds;
- fluorescein strips (stain);
- anaesthetic eye drops (0.5% solution of tetracaine hydrochloride);
- basic eye ointment (1% tetracycline hydrochloride ointment).

Note. No opened tube of ointment should be used for treating more than one patient or for more than one course of treatment.

First, record the general appearance of the tissues around the eye(s), looking for swelling, bruising, or obvious abnormality; then examine the affected eye(s), starting with the sclera, the conjunctiva (covering both the sclera and the backs of the eyelids), and the cornea. Comparing one eye with the other is helpful and a diagram is the best method of recording the findings.

The sclera can be viewed by gently holding apart the eyelids with the fingers and asking the patient to look in four different directions. Make sure you can see well into each "corner" of the eyelids. The inside of the lower lid can be inspected by gently pulling down the lower lid with the eyes looking upwards. The upper lid must be rolled back (everted) before the underlying conjunctiva can be inspected. There are two methods of doing this. Both require the casualty to keep looking down towards the feet while they are being performed.

To evert the upper lid, ask the casualty to look downwards, then place the index finger of one hand across the upper lid while grasping the eyelashes firmly but gently between the index finger and thumb of the other hand. Pull gently downwards on the eyelashes and then, with a downward pressure of the index finger, fold the eyelid back over it. The index finger is then withdrawn and the everted lid can be held back by pressing the eyelashes against the bony margin of the socket, under the eyebrow. The underneath surface of the lid can now be examined. The eyelid will return to its normal position if the casualty looks upwards and then closes the eyelids together.

Instead of the index finger, the alternative method uses a matchstick or similar object laid across the upper lid. The same procedure is followed, with the casualty looking downwards and the eyelid being folded upwards over the matchstick, which is then withdrawn. These procedures ensure that the whole area of the conjunctiva is inspected for damage or foreign bodies (see Fig. 75).

The cornea and surrounding area should be inspected next; it is helpful to slant the light across the surface in order to show up any abnormality. A magnifying glass is valuable for this examination. The cornea should be clear and any area of cloudiness or opacity, or the presence of foreign bodies, should be noted. The surrounding sclera may be reddish in colour, which can signify corneal irritation. Any obvious loose foreign body should be removed at this stage (page 78).

Staining the eye with fluorescein will highlight any area of corneal or conjunctival damage. The fluorescein paper strip, which contains the dye, should be drawn gently across the everted lower lid with the casualty looking upwards. This wipes the dye off the strip onto the lid and, when the casualty blinks a couple of times, the dye spreads over the eye. Wipe away any excess dye from the eyelids. Any area of corneal or conjunctival damage will attract the dye and be stained green. Any such area should be clearly shown on the diagram in the notes on the casualty.

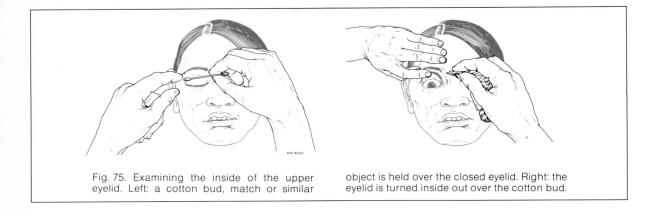

Fig. 75. Examining the inside of the upper eyelid. Left: a cotton bud, match or similar object is held over the closed eyelid. Right: the eyelid is turned inside out over the cotton bud.

The more common injuries affecting the eyes and the relevant treatments are described in the following paragraphs. Treatment for the relief of pain should be appropriate to the degree of discomfort being experienced (page 305).

Blows on, or adjacent to, the eye ("black eye")

Such blows may result either in the complete or partial detachment of the retina or in bleeding into the eyeball. If a patient with a "black eye" shows any marked deterioration in eyesight, he should be put to bed and seen by a doctor as soon as possible. Get RADIO MEDICAL ADVICE. Even if there is no discernible deterioration in eyesight, the casualty should be advised to visit a doctor at the next port.

Corneal abrasions

A scratch or abrasion on the cornea can be caused, for example, by a foreign body under the eyelids or by a fingernail touching the eye. Pain is felt immediately, and the casualty thinks there is something in the eye. Corneal abrasions can be identified by staining the eye with fluorescein (page 77). Eye ointment should be placed along the inside of the lower lid, and blinking the eyelids will smear the ointment across the eye (see Fig. 113, page 120). An eye-pad, held in place by strapping, should be applied for 24 hours. Next day re-examine the eye, using the fluorescein stain. If there is no sign of staining after careful examination, the treatment can be stopped. If the cornea still stains, repeat the treatment every 24 hours until the staining ceases or the casualty visits a doctor.

Loose foreign bodies

These can often be removed from under the lids or over the conjunctiva without the use of eye-wash solution. Use *moistened* cotton wool on a stick or a *moistened* cotton bud. Be very gentle. After you have removed the foreign body or bodies, stain the eye with fluorescein and mark any areas of staining on an eye diagram. If there is any staining, treat as for corneal abrasion.

The eyes of some persons are so sensitive that it is impossible to examine them thoroughly or remove a foreign body from them unless anaesthetic eye drops have been used.

If the foreign body is lying on the cornea, one attempt should be made to remove it, taking great care not to damage the cornea. Anaesthetic eye drops must be instilled into the eye beforehand (put three drops inside eyelids and repeat this three times at two-minute intervals). After a few minutes, an attempt to remove the foreign body should be made, using a moistened cotton bud to pick it up. Contact with the corneal surface should be minimal. If the foreign body does not move readily, no further attempt at its removal should be made. Treat as for corneal abrasion and advise the patient to see a doctor at the next port of call. The eye should be lightly covered with a dressing until the anaesthetic effect has worn off.

Foreign bodies embedded in (or completely inside) the eye

When very small pieces of metal, grit, etc. become embedded in the cornea or the sclera, it may be very difficult to see either the wound or the object, even with the help of fluorescein, and the patient may not have felt any pain when the accident occurred. However, you should suspect such an accident if, on being questioned, the patient reveals that he has been hammering, chipping, milling, boring, or striking metal with a tool, or standing near someone who was doing so, or has rubbed his eyes after getting dirt in them.

If you believe an injury of this kind has occurred, or you are in any doubt about it, treat the eye as for a corneal abrasion (page 78). However, the application of the eye ointment should be repeated often enough to keep the eye comfortable, and at least once every six hours. The casualty should see an eye specialist as soon as possible. Do not attempt to remove the foreign body yourself.

Wounds of the eyelids and eyeball

Get RADIO MEDICAL ADVICE at once, if the eyeball is cut and if the eye leaks fluid or jelly. In the meantime, close the eyelids or bring them as close together as possible. Cover the eyelid with one or two layers of sterile petroleum-jelly gauze to keep it shut. Then place an eye-pad over this. Stick the eye-pad in place with strips of adhesive tape or sticking plaster.

Chemical burns

If this has not already been done, wash the chemical out of the eye with copious amounts of water (page 56) for as long as is necessary to ensure that none remains (usually at least 10 minutes).

Then stain the eye with fluorescein. If there is marked staining of the eye, eye ointment should be applied copiously to prevent the lids sticking to the eyeball. Apply the ointment every four hours, and cover the eye with petroleum-jelly gauze and an eye-pad. The casualty should be seen by a doctor as soon as possible.

Less severe damage should be treated by 4-hourly applications of tetracycline eye ointment with an eye cover of petroleum-jelly gauze and a pad. Re-examine the eye each day, using fluorescein. Treatment should be continued for 24 hours after the eye is no longer stained by fluorescein and is white.

Arc eyes ("Welder's flash")

The ultra-violet (UV) in an electric arc can cause "sunburn" of the surface of unprotected eyes. In arc eyes, both eyes feel gritty within 24 hours and look red. Bright light hurts the eyes. The eyes should be carefully searched for foreign bodies and be stained with fluorescein. If one eye only is affected, it is probably *not* an arc eye. Its condition may be due to an embedded corneal foreign body or an area of corneal damage, which will show on staining with fluorescein.

Bathing the eyes with cold water and applying cold compresses to the lids will give some relief of symptoms. Dark glasses help the discomfort caused by light. If the eyes feel very gritty, apply tetracycline eye ointment to the eyes every 4 hours. The condition will usually clear up spontaneously within about 48 hours if no further exposure to UV occurs. Further exposure to welding should be avoided, and dark glasses should be worn in bright sunlight until the eyes are fully recovered.

Ear injuries

Foreign bodies

Sand, an insect, or some other small object in the ear may cause irritation, discomfort, or pain. If it is *clearly visible,* it may be possible to remove it with tweezers. If this cannot be done easily, NO other effort should be made to extract it by any means. The ear-drum can be pierced in attempts to remove objects that are not visible or that are stuck in the ear passage; also the object may be pushed further in.

If nothing is visible, flood the ear passage with tepid peanut, olive, or sunflower oil, which may float the object out or bring it out when the casualty drains his ear by lying down on the affected side. If these measures are unsuccessful, send the casualty to a doctor at the first available opportunity.

Injuries to the internal ear

If the ear-drum has been perforated as the result of a skull fracture, there may be a flow of cerebrospinal fluid (see page 73). This should not be stopped by inserting anything into the ear. The casualty should be placed on his injured side, with his shoulders and head propped up; this will allow the fluid to drain freely. For other injuries, put a dressing over the ear and apply a bandage. Do not put cotton wool in the ear passage. In all cases, get RADIO MEDICAL ADVICE.

Nose injuries

Foreign bodies

Sometimes, when a foreign body is stuck in a nostril, the casualty can blow it out by compressing the other nostril and blowing down the blocked one. Otherwise, if the object can be seen and is loose, it may be removed using forceps. Unless this is clearly feasible, no attempt should be made to remove the object and the casualty must be seen by a doctor.

Injuries inside the nose

If bleeding cannot be controlled by the method described on page 40, then it may be necessary to pack the nose. This is done by lubricating ribbon gauze thoroughly with petroleum jelly and inserting it as high as possible in the nostril with the aid of forceps. Put in sufficient gauze to fill the nostril without stretching it unduly. Leave the gauze in place for 48 hours, and then gently pull it out.

Fractures

A fracture of the nose cannot be dealt with on board ship and the only treatment will be to stop any persistent bleeding. Any distortion of the nose will have to be corrected in hospital.

Mouth and dental injuries

When there has been a severe blow to a jaw, especially if the jaw is broken (see Fractures, Upper jaw, Lower jaw, pages 22–23), there may be complications due to broken dentures, loss of teeth, and wounds to the gums, the lips, the tongue, and the inside and outside of the mouth.

Treatment for *external wounds* to the cheek and lips is standard.

For *wounds inside the mouth* the casualty should first rinse his mouth well with a water mouthwash to remove any loose fragments. Do *not* try to extract pieces of tooth from the gum. If the casualty is in pain, consult the section on analgesics (page 305).

Treatment for a *lost tooth* is described in Dental emergencies (page 184).

No attempt should be made to stitch *deep wounds* in the cheek and tongue. *Serious bleeding* should be controlled by pressure.

If a jaw is or may be broken, the upper and lower jaws should be held together by a bandage (page 22) with, as far as possible, the upper and lower teeth fitting together as they normally do. If the patient has dentures which still fit adequately, he should wear them; they will help to act as a splint.

If the wounds on the face or inside the mouth are other than very slight, give standard antibiotic treatment. If the casualty is unable to take tablets by mouth, give 600 000 units of procaine benzylpenicillin intramuscularly every 12 hours for five days.

Burns and scalds

The treatment of burns and scalds is the same, whether they are caused by dry or by wet heat.

Classification

Skin has an outer layer (epidermis) and a deep layer (dermis). The latter contains the sweat glands, hair follicles, and nerves relaying sensation and pain to the skin.

First-degree burns affect only the outer skin layer, causing redness, mild swelling, tenderness, and pain.

Second-degree burns extend into the deeper skin layer (dermis):

- *Superficial second-degree burns* cause deep reddening, blister formation, considerable swelling, and weeping of fluid.
- *Deep second-degree burns* may not be easy to distinguish from third-degree burns immediately after the injury. Pain may be severe because of damage to the nerve endings.

Third-degree burns involve the whole thickness of skin, and may extend to the underlying fat, muscle, and bone. The skin may be charred, black or dark brown, leathery or white, according to the cause of the burn. Pain *may* be absent owing to destruction of the nerve endings.

Fluid loss

The fluid lost in burns is the colourless liquid part of the blood (plasma). The degree of fluid loss may be determined more by the area of the burn than by its depth. *The greater the plasma loss, the more severe the degree of shock* (see Shock, page 17). Further, owing to loss of plasma, the remaining blood is "thicker" and more difficult to pump round the body, throwing extra strain on the heart.

Area of burn: the rule of nines

A recognised method of calculating the surface area of the body is the "rule of nines" (Fig. 76). In *children* (not babies), the percentage for the head should be doubled and 1% taken off the other areas.

Treatment

Try to remove patient to hospital within 6 hours, otherwise seek RADIO MEDICAL ADVICE in the case of:

- third-degree burns;
- babies;

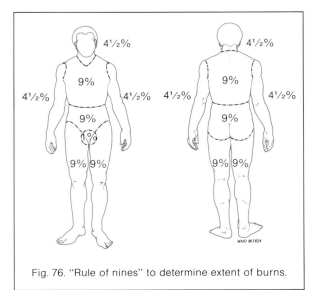

Fig. 76. "Rule of nines" to determine extent of burns.

- burns of face and genitalia, and large burns around joints;
- burns of over 18% of the body surface in adults, or 10% in children or older persons (Fig. 76).

Pending his removal to hospital, put the patient to bed and seek to restore the fluid balance by encouraging him to drink as much as possible. Give him oral rehydration salts solution to drink. If vomiting occurs and persists, intravenous infusion of 0.9% (9 g/litre) sodium chloride may be necessary, after receiving RADIO MEDICAL ADVICE. Relieve pain (page 305) and start the standard antibiotic treatment (page 308). Anxiety may be relieved by giving 5 mg of diazepam, repeated every four hours.

Less serious cases can be treated aboard ship. First assemble:

- a plentiful supply of soap, boiled warm water, and cotton swabs;
- at least two sets of sterile scissors and forceps;
- sufficient petrolatum-gauze burn-and-wound dressing to cover and overlap the cleansed burned areas;
- sterile gauze and cotton wool to go on top of the dressings as padding;

- elastic net bandages or tubular dressings;
- a face mask for each attendant.

Wash your hands and forearms thoroughly and put on a face mask. Remove the first-aid dressing to expose either a single burned area (in multiple burns) or a portion of a single burn, that is, a hand and forearm, or a quarter of the back. The aim is to limit the areas of burned skin exposed at any one time to lessen both the risk of infection and the seepage of fluid. Clean the skin round the edges of the burn with soap, water, and swabs. Clean away from the burn in every direction. DO NOT use cotton wool or other linty material for cleaning, as bits of it are likely to be left in the burn.

Leave blisters intact, but clip off all the dead skin if blisters have burst. Flood the area with clean warm boiled water from a clean receptacle to remove debris. With a swab soaked in boiled warm water, dab gently at any remaining dirt or foreign matter in the burned area. *Be gentle* as this will inevitably cause pain.

Next cover the burn with neomycin and bacitracin ointment, or the petrolatum-gauze dressing, overlapping the burn or scald by 5–10 cm, according to its size. Now apply a covering of absorbent material to absorb any fluid leaking from the burn, i.e., a layer of sterile gauze covered with a layer of sterile cotton wool. Hold this in place with a suitable bandage—tubular dressings or crepe bandages are useful for limbs, and elastic net dressings for other areas.

Thoroughly wash hands and arms before proceeding to deal as above with the remainder of a large burn, or with another burn in the case of multiple burns. In more serious cases, start the standard antibiotic treatment (page 308).

Dressings should be left undisturbed for a week unless they become smelly or very dirty, or the temperature is raised. Re-dress areas as above. First-degree burns will usually heal in a week to ten days without scarring. Second-degree burns should heal with little scarring in about three weeks.

Special burns

Severe *sunburn* with blistering should be treated as a first-degree burn according to the area of the body involved. In mild cases, keep the patient out of the sun and apply calamine lotion or zinc ointment to the painful areas.

In cases of *scalds and burns of the mouth and throat,* wash out with water and give patient ice to suck.

Respiratory burns are caused by the inhalation of hot gases and air particles and of smoke. Burns round the mouth, nose, face, hair, and neck indicate the possibility of respiratory burns. Heat from a flash fire may also cause a burn-related swelling of the top of the throat, even though there is no sign of burns on the face.

A patient with a mild injury to the respiratory passage may have only a cough, hoarseness, or a sore throat. In more severe cases the patient may suffer from marked shortness of breath, persistent coughing, wheezing, and hoarseness. In very severe cases, the respiratory passages may be blocked by a swollen throat and the lungs may partially collapse.

If the patient has difficulty in breathing, insert an airway (page 104). In any event, get RADIO MEDICAL ADVICE.

Dislocations

The commonest dislocations are of the shoulder and the finger joints. Try to deal with (that is, reduce) these dislocations if a doctor cannot see the casualty within about six hours.

All other dislocations should be left for treatment by a doctor. Until this is possible, place the patient in a comfortable position and relieve pain (page 305).

Note. In some cases a dislocation may be accompanied by a fracture of the same part or a related one, so be careful.

Dislocated shoulder

The shoulder will be painful and the patient will be unable to move it. Undress the patient to the waist and note the outline of the good shoulder, comparing it with the affected one. Usually in a shoulder dislocation the outward curve of the muscle just below the shoulder is replaced by an inward dent, and the distance from the tip of the shoulder to the elbow is longer on the injured side. This is because the head of the arm-bone usually dislocates inwards and downwards. If you think that the shoulder is dislocated, give the casualty 15 mg of morphine sulfate (1½ ampoules) intramuscularly. When the pain is relieved (in about 15–20 minutes), the casualty should lie face downwards on a bunk, couch, or table, the height of which should be sufficient for the arm to hang down without touching the deck. As the casualty lies down, hold his dislocated arm until you have placed a small pillow or big pad under the affected shoulder. Then lower the arm slowly until it is hanging straight down the side of the bunk and leave it to hang freely. The patient should remain in this position for about one hour, letting the weight of the arm overcome the muscle spasm caused by the dislocation. If after this time the dislocation is not reduced, a bucket containing a weight of 5–7 kg should be attached to a broad bandage, previously applied to the wrist, as shown in Fig. 77. If the dislocation is reduced, the patient should roll onto his good side and use the injured arm by bending the elbow and then touching the good shoulder with the fingers. Afterwards he should be helped to sit up and the arm should be kept in a sling until the shoulder is fairly comfortable (see Fig. 20, page 24). This might take up to 48 hours. When the sling is removed, the patient should exercise the joint slowly and carefully. A check X-ray should be taken at the next port. If the above treatment does *not* reduce the dislocation, get RADIO MEDICAL ADVICE.

Dislocated fingers

A finger dislocation can usually be reduced by pulling firmly on the finger. It is often a good idea to begin by bending the patient's elbow to a right angle. Pull firmly on the finger for about one minute while a helper is pulling in the opposite direction at the elbow. Keeping the ends

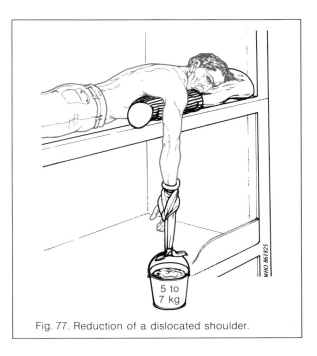

Fig. 77. Reduction of a dislocated shoulder.

of the bones apart by pulling, gently ease the joint back into its normal position. The affected finger should be immobilized by strapping it to an adjacent finger. After 24 hours, the strapping should be removed and the patient should exercise the finger slowly and carefully. A check X-ray should be taken at the next port.

Sprains and strains

These injuries are usually the result of twisting, turning, or tripping. Pain is usually felt at once, and swelling at the site of injury will occur later as a result of bleeding.

With sprains and strains, there is no sure *clinical* method of excluding associated fractures, except by X-ray. When there is doubt, it is therefore safer to assume the possibility of fracture and to treat accordingly.

Whether the injury is seen immediately or later on when much swelling may have occurred, put the casualty in his bunk and elevate the injured part, if this is possible. Cold-water compresses kept in place by a crepe bandage should be applied. An ice-pack may also help to minimize or reduce swelling. This treatment should be given for 3–4 hours.

Rest and elevation may be necessary for 2–3 days (or sometimes longer according to the severity of the injury). Continue support with a crepe bandage. Pain relief may be necessary (page 305).

If an associated fracture is not present, gentle movement of the injured part should be encouraged. Sprains and strains do much better with early movement than with too long a period of rest. The casualty can usually judge when he can use the injured part either fully or in a restricted manner.

If the casualty has not fully recovered, have an X-ray taken at the first port of call.

Bandaging

Roller bandage

A roller bandage is intended to hold a dressing securely in place over a wound. For this reason, it should be applied snugly, but not so tightly as to interfere with the circulation. Fingers and toes should be checked periodically for coldness, swelling, blueness, and numbness. If any of these symptoms occur, the bandage should be loosened immediately.

Anchoring a roller bandage

- Hold the roll of bandage in the right hand with the loose end on the bottom. The left hand may be used, if the person applying the bandage is left-handed.
- Place the outside surface of the loose end at an angle on the affected part of the body (see Fig. 78a).
- Roll the bandage round bringing it under and then over the affected part and turn down the uncovered triangle on the end (see Fig. 78b).
- Roll the bandage over the end two more times to anchor it and begin circling the affected part with it (see Fig. 78c).

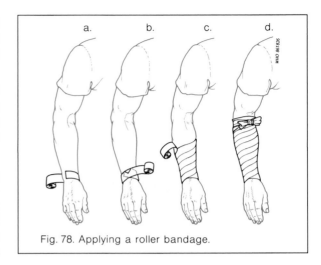

Fig. 78. Applying a roller bandage.

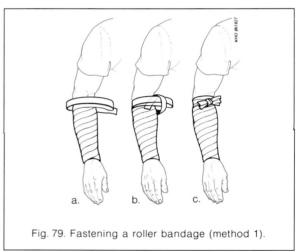

Fig. 79. Fastening a roller bandage (method 1).

Applying a roller bandage

- Continue to circle the affected part of the body with the bandage, using spiral turns (see Fig. 78d).
- Space the turns so that they overlap and completely cover the skin.

Fastening a roller bandage

Roller bandages may be fastened with clips, safety pins, or tape. Alternatively, they may be tied, as follows.

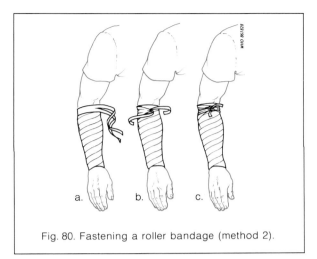

Fig. 80. Fastening a roller bandage (method 2).

Method 1

- Fold the bandage back upon itself (see Fig. 79).
- Pass the loose end around the loop formed by folding the bandage backwards and tie (see Fig. 79).

Method 2

- Split the end of the bandage lengthwise for approximately 25 cm and tie a knot to prevent further splitting (see Fig. 80).

- Pass the ends in opposite directions round the affected part and tie.

Chest or back bandage

A triangular bandage may be used to secure large dressings on wounds and burns on the chest or back. The following description applies to wounds of the chest.

- Place the point of the bandage over the shoulder. Let the rest of the bandage drop down over the chest with the middle of the base under the point (see Fig. 81a).
- Fold the base of the bandage up far enough to secure the dressing and tie the ends in the back below the shoulder blade. One long and one short end will be left (see Fig. 81b).
- Bring the long end up to the shoulder and tie it to the point of the triangle (see Fig. 81c).

Chest or abdomen bandage

This bandage may be used to secure large, bulky dressings in place on the abdomen or chest. It may be improvised from a piece of cloth, a bedsheet, or a large bath-towel. The bandage should be placed under the patient and pinned

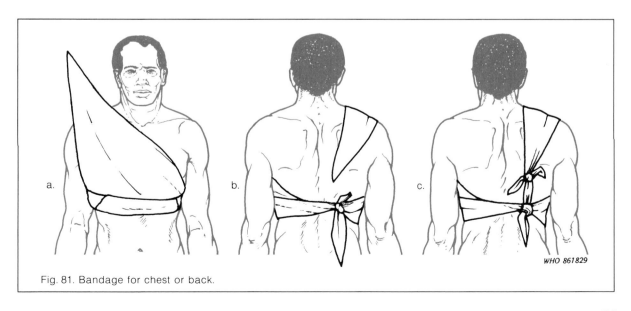

Fig. 81. Bandage for chest or back.

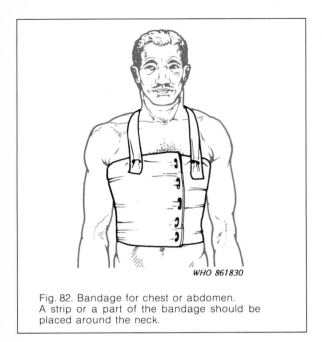

Fig. 82. Bandage for chest or abdomen. A strip or a part of the bandage should be placed around the neck.

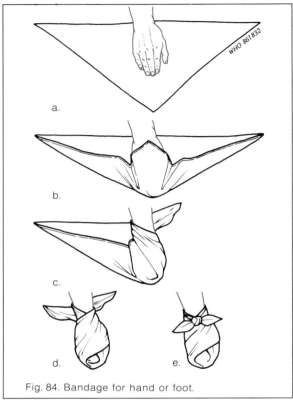

Fig. 84. Bandage for hand or foot.

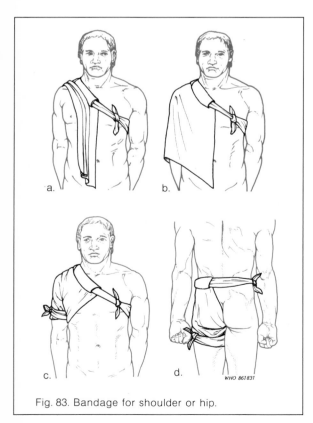

Fig. 83. Bandage for shoulder or hip.

securely in the front. A strip or a part of the bandage should be placed around the neck to hold the bandage in position (Fig. 82).

Shoulder or hip bandage

This type of bandage is used to secure a dressing in place over a wound or burn on the shoulder or hip. A triangular bandage and a cravat bandage should be used together. The cravat bandage may be made by folding a triangular bandage into a narrow band; or it may be improvised from such items as a roller bandage, a tie, or a belt.

- Place the cravat bandage on the point of the triangular bandage and roll them together several times. Fold the remainder of the triangular bandage and place it on top of the cravat (see Fig. 83).

- Place the centre of the cravat over the injured shoulder. Bring the back end of the cravat under the opposite armpit and tie slightly in front of it.
- Bring the base of the folded triangular bandage down and over the dressing on the shoulder.
- Fold up the base of the triangular bandage. Wrap the ends round the arm and tie in front.
- A view of the bandage applied to the hip is shown in Fig. 83d.

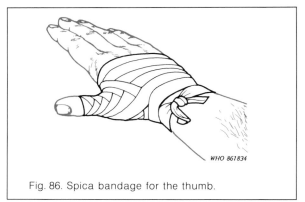

Fig. 86. Spica bandage for the thumb.

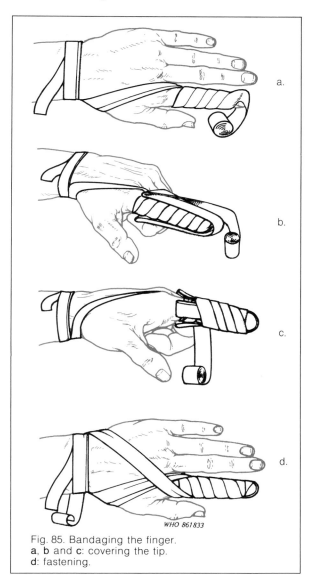

Fig. 85. Bandaging the finger.
a, b and **c**: covering the tip.
d: fastening.

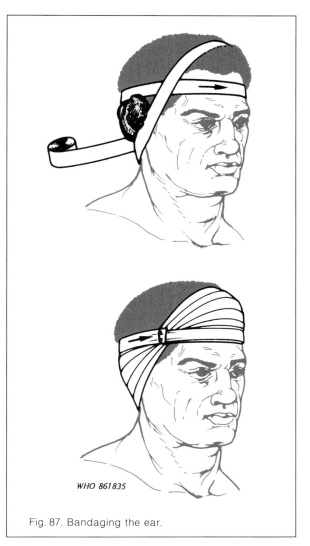

Fig. 87. Bandaging the ear.

Hand or foot bandage

One large triangular bandage may be used to secure large dressings in place on the hand or foot.

- Place the wrist or heel in the centre of a triangular bandage with the finger or toes pointing toward the point (see Fig. 84a).
- Fold the point of the bandage up and over the fingers or toes (see Fig. 84b).
- Wrap the ends of the bandage across the hand or foot to the opposite side and round the wrist or ankle (see Fig. 84c and d).
- Bring the ends of the bandage to the front of the wrist or ankle and tie (see Fig. 84e).

Finger, thumb, and ear bandages

The methods of bandaging are shown in Fig. 85, Fig. 86, and Fig. 87. Fig. 88 shows how to put a tubular rolled bandage on a finger.

Head bandage

Fig. 89 shows how to put a triangular bandage on the head.

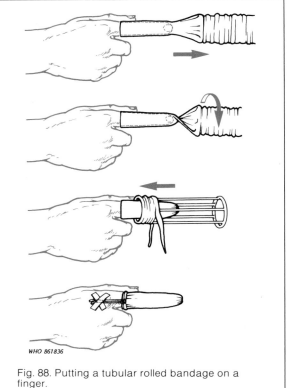

WHO 861836

Fig. 88. Putting a tubular rolled bandage on a finger.

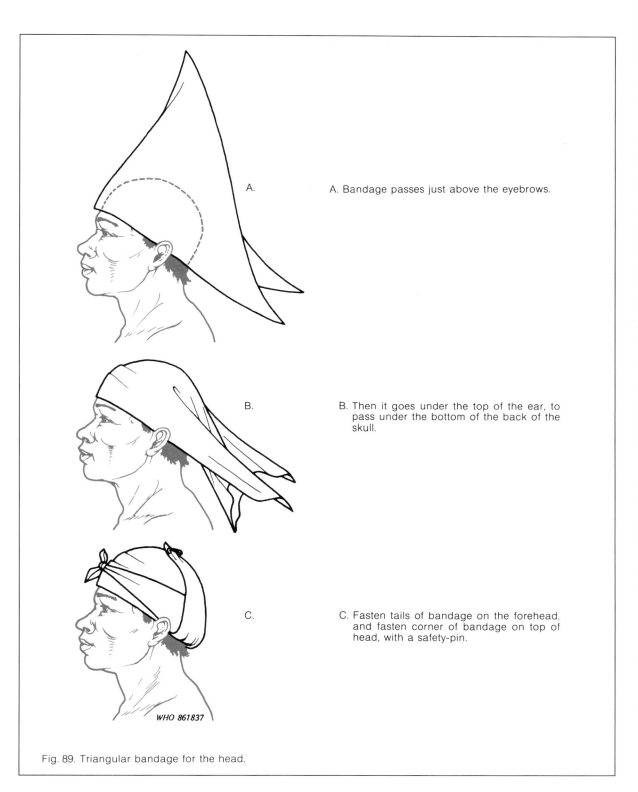

A. Bandage passes just above the eyebrows.

B. Then it goes under the top of the ear, to pass under the bottom of the back of the skull.

C. Fasten tails of bandage on the forehead, and fasten corner of bandage on top of head, with a safety-pin.

WHO 861837

Fig. 89. Triangular bandage for the head.

Chapter 5
General nursing care

Contents

This section of the guide is concerned with the care and treatment of bed patients until they recover or are sent to hospital for professional attention.

Good nursing is vital to the ease and speed of recovery from any condition. Attention to detail and comfort may make the lot of the sick or injured person much more bearable. Morale is also a vital factor in any illness. Cheerful, helpful, and intelligent nursing can do much to encourage the patient to take a positive attitude towards his illness or injury; the reverse is also true.

A sick person needs to have confidence in his attendants, who accordingly should understand his requirements. Stewards or those most keen to undertake the task are not necessarily the most suitable choice. The person to look after the patient should be selected with care, and the master or a senior officer should keep a check on his performance.

Sick-quarters

Wherever possible, a patient sufficiently ill to require nursing should be put in the ship's hospital or in a cabin away from others. In this way he will benefit from quiet, and the risk of spreading any unsuspected infection will be minimized.

Superfluous fittings and all pictures and carpets should be removed from the sick-quarters. This will lessen the accumulation of dust and facilitate cleaning. The deck should be washed daily and scrubbed twice a week. Fittings should be dusted daily with a wet cloth to clean them and then polished with a dry duster.

Adequate ventilation of the sick-quarters is of great importance and it is equally important that changes of temperature, and also draughts, should be avoided as much as possible. The ideal temperature for the sick-room is between 16 °C and 19 °C. If possible, direct sunlight should be admitted to the cabin. If the weather is warm and the portholes will admit fresh air they should be left open.

In hot weather there is a great tendency to have the patient lie in a position exposed to a cooling draught. This must not be allowed because of the risk of causing chills. Equally, if the sick-quarters are ventilated by a system of forced draught, the current of air from the outlet must not be allowed to play directly on the patient; it should be directed onto an adjacent bulkhead from which it will be deflected as a gentle current of air.

Arrival of the patient

It may be necessary to assist the patient to undress and get into bed. An unconscious or helpless patient will have to be undressed. Take off boots or shoes first, then socks, trousers, jacket, and shirt in that order.

In the case of severe leg injuries, you may have to remove the trousers by cutting down the seam of the injured leg first. In the case of arm injuries, remove the sound arm from its shirt sleeve first, then slip the shirt over the head, and lastly withdraw the injured arm carefully from its sleeve.

In cold climates the patient should always wear pyjamas. With helpless or unconscious patients the pyjama trousers should be omitted. The common tendency for the sick person to wish to add one or two sweaters should be resisted. In the tropics a cotton singlet and cotton shorts are better than pyjamas.

Blankets are unnecessary in the tropics but the patient should have some covering—either a sheet spread over him, or a sheet folded once lengthwise and wrapped round his middle.

If your patient has a chest condition accompanied by cough and spitting, he should be provided with a receptacle, either a sputum pot or an improvised jar or tin. The receptacle provided should be fitted with a cover or alternatively be covered with a piece of lint so as to distinguish it from a drinking receptacle. If the sputum pot is not of the disposable variety add a little disinfectant (see Table 3, Disinfection and sterilization, page 121). It should be thoroughly cleaned out twice daily with boiling water and a disinfectant.

Other duties may make it impossible for the attendant to give uninterrupted attention to the patient, and a urine bottle should therefore be left handy for the patient on a chair, stool, or locker, and covered with a cloth.

Food, plates, cups, knives, forks, and spoons should be removed from the sick-quarters immediately after a meal, and in no circumstances should they be left there unless the patient is infectious. In that case they should be washed up in the cabin in a basin or bucket and then be stacked neatly away and covered with a cloth.

The patient should be protected from long and tiring visits from well-meaning shipmates. Visits to patients who are ill and running a temperature should be restricted to 15 minutes.

The following check-list will make it easier to remember all important points in nursing a patient on board ship.

Check-list

- Ensure that the patient is comfortable in bed.
- Check temperature, pulse, and respiration twice daily (morning and evening), or more often if not in the normal range. A four-hourly check is usual in any serious illness. Record results.
- In appropriate cases test a specimen of urine.
- Keep a written record of the illness.
- Arrange for soft drinks to be easily available unless fluids are to be restricted.
- Specify normal diet or any dietary restrictions.
- Ensure that the person knows to ask for a bottle or a bedpan as needed—some patients do not ask unless told to.
- Check and record each day whether the patient has emptied his bowels or not.
- Check fluid intake and loss by questioning the patient about drinking and passing urine. In certain illnesses an intake–loss fluid chart must be kept (page 102).
- Check that the patient is eating and record appetite.
- Remake the bed at least twice a day, or more often if this is necessary for the patient's comfort. Look out for crumbs and creases, both of which can be uncomfortable.

- Try to prevent boredom by providing suitable reading and hobby material. A radio will also help to provide interest for the patient.
- A means of summoning other people, such as a bell, telephone, or intercom should be available if the patient cannot call out and be heard or if he is not so seriously ill as to require somebody to be with him at all times.
- Fit bunkboards at all times for seriously ill patients, and at night or in heavy weather for others. Release retaining catches of swinging beds when the ship is rolling.

Vital signs

After the patient's arrival in the sick-quarters, it will be necessary to note his vital signs. These indicate how effectively the body is carrying out the essential activities of living. They include:

- temperature;
- pulse;
- respiration;
- blood pressure;
- level of consciousness.

The body temperature

The temperature, pulse rate (page 94), and respiration (page 95) should be recorded. You should make use of temperature charts (Fig. 41) or, if charts are not available, write down your findings, indicating the hour at which they were noted. Readings should be taken twice a day and always at the same hours, say, 7 h and 19 h (7 a.m. and 7 p.m.) and more frequently if the severity of the symptoms warrants it.

It will rarely be necessary to record the temperature more frequently than every four hours. The only exceptions to this rule are in cases of severe head injury, acute abdominal conditions, and heat-stroke (pages 73, 160, and 205), when more frequent temperature recordings are required.

The body temperature is measured using a *clinical* thermometer (see Fig. 90), except in hypothermia when a low-reading thermometer must be used. To take the patient's temperature, first shake down the mercury in a clinical ther-

mometer to about 35 °C. Then place the thermometer in the patient's mouth, under the tongue. The thermometer should remain in the patient's mouth (lips closed, no speaking) for at least one minute. After one minute, read the thermometer, then replace it in the patient's mouth for a further minute. Check the reading and if it is the same as before, *record* the temperature on the chart. If it is different, repeat the process. Then disinfect the thermometer (see Table 3, page 121).

Sometimes it will be necessary to take the temperature *per rectum,* for instance in hypothermia. A thermometer used for taking a rectal temperature has a short, blunt bip to prevent injury to the rectum. First lubricate the ther-

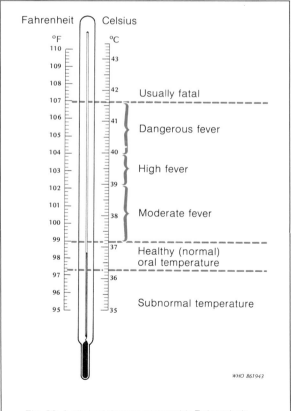

Fig. 90. A clinical thermometer with Fahrenheit and Celsius scales: comparable temperature readings and fever classification.

mometer with petroleum jelly. Then, with the patient lying on his side, push the thermometer gently into the rectum for a distance of 5 cm and leave it there for two minutes before reading it. Then disinfect the thermometer.

People who are *unconscious, restless, or possibly drunk* should not have mouth temperatures taken in case they chew the thermometer. Their temperature should be taken by placing the thermometer in the armpit and holding the arm against the side of the body for five minutes before the thermometer is read.

The normal body temperature (oral) is about 37° Celsius (centigrade); temperatures outside the range 36.3–37.2 °C are abnormal. Temperature taken in the armpit (or groin) is ½ °C lower, and in the rectum ½ °C higher. Body temperature is slightly lower in the morning and slightly higher at the end of the day. In those enjoying good health, variations in temperature are slight.

Body temperature is *low* in conditions that cause fluid loss (dehydration) such as severe bleeding and some severe illnesses of a noninfectious kind.

Body temperature is *raised,* and *fever* is said to be present, in infectious conditions and in a few disorders that affect the heat-regulating mechanism in the brain.

In feverish illnesses, the body temperature rises and then falls to normal. At first the patient may feel cold and shivery. Then he looks and feels hot, the skin is red, dry, and warm, and he becomes thirsty. He may suffer from headache and may be very restless. The temperature may still continue to rise. Finally the temperature falls and the patient may sweat profusely, becoming wet through. When this happens, he may need a change of clothing and may feel cold if left in the wet clothing or bedding.

During the cold stage, the patient should have one or two warm blankets put round him to keep him warm, but too many blankets may help to *increase* his temperature. As he reaches the hot stage, he should be given cool drinks.

If the temperature rises above 40 °C, sponging (see Cool or tepid sponge bath, page 109) or even a cool bath may be required to prevent further rise in temperature (see Heat-stroke, page 205). In the sweating stage, the clothing and bedding should be changed as necessary.

The pulse rate

The pulse rate is the number of heartbeats per minute. The pulse is felt at the wrist, or the heart rate is counted by listening to the heartbeat over the nipple on the left side of the chest. The pulse rate varies according to age, sex, and activity. It is increased by exercise and excitement; it is decreased by sleep and, to a lesser extent, by relaxation.

Pulse rates of 120 and above can be counted more easily by listening over the heart.

Normal pulse rate (number of heartbeats per minute)

age 2–5 years	about 100
age 5–10 years	about 90
adults, male	65–80
adults, female	75–85

The pulse rate will usually rise along with the temperature, about 10 beats per minute for every 0.5 °C over 38 °C. In heart disease, a high pulse rate may be found with a normal temperature.

Note and record also whether the pulse beat is *regular* or *irregular,* i.e., whether there are the same number of beats in each 15 seconds and whether the strength of each beat is about the same.

If the rhythm is very irregular, count the pulse at the wrist and *also* by listening over the heart. The rates may be different because weak heartbeats will be heard, but the resulting pulse wave may not be strong enough to be felt at the wrist. Count for a full minute in each case, and record both results.

To take the pulse rate at the wrist, the procedure is as follows:

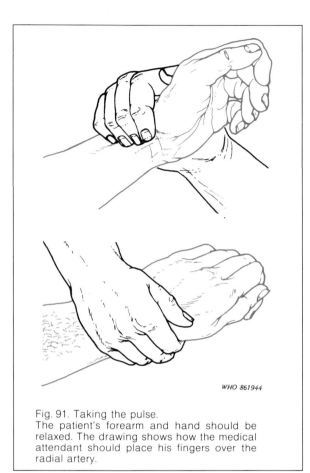

Fig. 91. Taking the pulse.
The patient's forearm and hand should be relaxed. The drawing shows how the medical attendant should place his fingers over the radial artery.

WHO 861944

The rate is the number of times per minute that the patient breathes in. It is ascertained by watching the patient and counting his inspirations. The person making the count should do so without the patient's knowledge by continuing to hold his wrist as if taking the pulse. If the patient is conscious of what you are doing, the rate is liable to be irregular. A good plan is to take the respiration rate immediately after taking the pulse.

The respiration rate varies according to age, sex, and activity. It is increased by exercise, excitement, and emotion; it is decreased by sleep and rest.

Normal respiration rate (number of breaths per minute)

age 2–5 years	24–28
5 years – adult	progressively less
adult, male	16–18
adult, female	18–20

Always count respirations for a full minute, noting any discomfort in breathing in or breathing out.

The pulse rate will usually rise about four beats per minute for every rise of one respiration per minute. This 4:1 ratio will be altered in the case of chest diseases such as pneumonia which can cause a great increase in the respiration rate.

- The patient's forearm and hand should be relaxed. Place your fingers over the radial artery, on the thumb side of the patient's wrist, as indicated in Fig. 91.
- Move your fingers until the pulse beat is located and exert enough pressure to make the pulse distinct, but not blotted out.
- When the pulse is felt plainly, count the beats for one minute. Record the result.

The respiration rate

The respiration rate will often give you a clue to the diagnosis of the case.

Blood pressure

Blood pressure readings are obtained using a sphygmomanometer (see Fig. 92 and Fig. 93) and a stethoscope to measure the force exerted by the blood in an artery in the arm. This procedure is one requiring accuracy and skill, which have to be acquired through practice.

Blood pressure varies in the healthy person as a result of many factors. Emotional and physical activity have an effect on the blood pressure. During periods of physical rest and freedom from emotional excitement, the pressure will be lowered. Age in itself is a factor in elevating blood pressure.

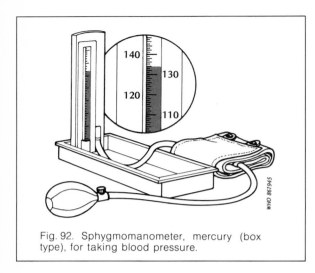

Fig. 92. Sphygmomanometer, mercury (box type), for taking blood pressure.

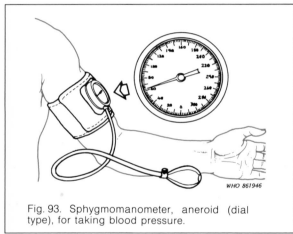

Fig. 93. Sphygmomanometer, aneroid (dial type), for taking blood pressure.

An injury or internal bleeding can result in a great loss of blood, which causes lowered blood pressure. Shock is marked by a dangerous drop in pressure.

Blood pressure is usually expressed in millimetres of mercury. Two pressures are recorded: the *systolic pressure,* as the heart beats or contracts and the *diastolic pressure,* as the heart rests. In the blood pressure recording 120/80, the *systolic pressure* is 120 mm Hg and the *diastolic pressure* is 80 mm Hg. These are within the normal range. A slight variation from these values is insignificant.

When blood pressure is being taken, the patient should lie or sit, and the arm that is to be used should be supported. Measurements may be made in either arm. In taking blood pressure, this procedure should be followed:

- Place the cuff around the patient's arm, above the elbow (see Fig. 94). Check to see that the valve on the bulb is fully closed (turned clockwise).
- Before inflating the cuff with air, find the arterial pulse on the inner side of the bend of the elbow.
- Keep fingers on this pulse and inflate the cuff by pumping on the rubber bulb until the pulse disappears.
- Place the earpieces of the stethoscope in your ears (the earpieces should be directed upwards) and position the disc of the stethoscope over the space where the pulse was felt (see Fig. 94).
- Hold the disc of the stethoscope snugly in position over the pulse with one hand, while pumping the cuff with the other.
- Pump the cuff until the mercury on the scale of the mercury apparatus, or the needle on the gauge of the aneroid apparatus, is about 30 points above the systolic pressure that was obtained previously, i.e., when the arterial pulse was felt to disappear.
- Loosen the valve slightly and permit the pressure to drop *slowly* while listening carefully for the sound of the pulse. Soon a definite beat will be heard, but it will be quite faint. If this beat is missed or if there is a question as to the pressure when it started, tighten the valve again, pump once more, and listen for the sound. The number at which the first sound is heard is the *systolic pressure.* This number should be recorded.
- Continue to deflate the cuff slowly until the sound disappears. The reading at which the last sound is heard is the *diastolic pressure.*
- Open the valve completely and allow the cuff to deflate.

Difficulty in obtaining the blood pressure reading may be due to the valve being opened too much, causing the pressure to drop too rapidly, or to the attendant having expected a louder sound through the stethoscope.

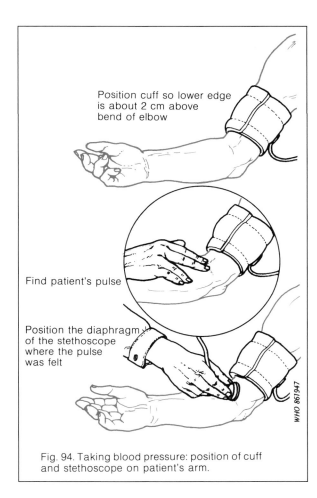

Position cuff so lower edge is about 2 cm above bend of elbow

Find patient's pulse

Position the diaphragm of the stethoscope where the pulse was felt

WHO 861947

Fig. 94. Taking blood pressure: position of cuff and stethoscope on patient's arm.

Such a patient may scream with moderate pain. He wants constant attention, moves about in bed continuously, and thrashes from side to side.

The stuporous patient lies quietly in bed, seems to be sleeping, and requests nothing. Even when awakened, he quickly returns to a sleeplike state that makes feeding difficult. The patient may be incontinent, exhibiting involuntary loss of urine or faeces.

The degree of stupor is determined by the stimuli required to awaken the patient. If he can be awakened by a voice, the level of consciousness would be described as light stupor. If he can be awakened only by pressure, e.g., by light tapping on the side of the face, the level would be described as deep stupor.

The patient in a coma lies quietly in bed, appears to be sleeping, and cannot be awakened. The patient will not ask for a drink or urinal, he cannot swallow, and may be incontinent or retain urine. Strong sensations or calling by name will not awaken the patient.

What levels of consciousness mean

The alert patient is one whose brain is functioning adequately.

The restless patient's brain is extremely active in its attempt to meet the body's needs. Restlessness is often observed in the following patients:

- those frightened, worried, or in pain;
- those haemorrhaging; the restlessness results because the brain is receiving a reduced or inadequate blood supply;
- those with a head injury or brain tumour, if the increased pressure on the brain is cutting off the blood supply to a part of the brain;
- those who have suffered a heart attack; the weakened heart cannot pump enough blood to the brain;
- those in shock, when blood pressure is so low that there is insufficient force to pump blood to the brain.

Restlessness may be an early sign of these conditions.

Levels of consciousness

Consciousness is controlled by the brain and the involuntary nervous system. There are four levels of consciousness: alertness, restlessness, stupor, and coma.

The alert patient is well aware of what is going on and reacts appropriately to factors in the environment. Facilities to supply his body needs will be requested, such as a urinal or bedpan, medication for pain, or a drink of water.

The restless patient is extremely sensitive to factors in the environment and exaggerates them.

Care of the bed patient

The bed

The bed should be made up and the linen changed at regular intervals. Remember that creases under a patient can be most uncomfortable and can cause bedsores. If the patient is gravely ill, incontinent, or likely to sweat excessively, use a waterproof sheet covered by a draw-sheet across the bottom sheet.

If the patient has a fracture or if the weight of his bedding makes him uncomfortable, the bedding can be supported by a bed cradle (or cradles). This can be improvised from a topless wooden box by removing two facing sides and then inverting it over the affected part of the patient; the bedding rests on top of the cradle.

If a patient cannot get up, his bed linen may be changed by rolling him gently to one side of the bed and untucking the used linen on the unoccupied side. This is then rolled up and placed against the patient. Clean linen is tucked under the mattress and its outer edge rolled up and placed beside the roll of used linen. The patient can then be very gently rolled over to the clean side of the bed and the job completed. The same technique can be applied, but on an end-to-end basis, for patients who have to be nursed in a seated position. If the patient is told what you are doing as you do it, he will know what to expect and will probably cooperate as far as he can. A freshened bed is a comfort to most sick people. Bed-making and changing an occupied bed is a two-person job and should not be attempted single-handed. It is easier if it is possible to position the bed in the centre of the cabin.

Fig. 95 shows how to move a patient in bed.

Bed baths

Patients who are confined to bed should be washed all over at least every other day. If they are hot, sticky, and feverish, they should be washed at least once a day. Collect all the necessary equipment, such as basin with water, sponge, etc.

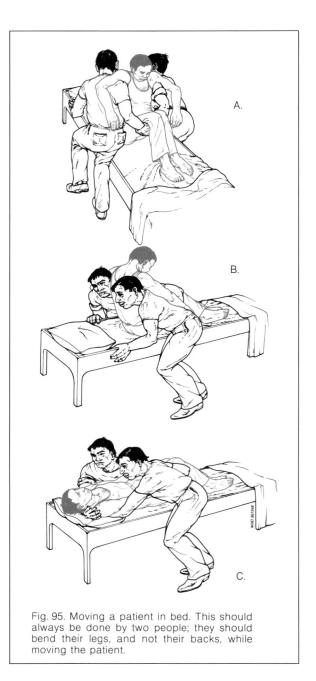

Fig. 95. Moving a patient in bed. This should always be done by two people; they should bend their legs, and not their backs, while moving the patient.

Wash the patient, beginning with the face. If the patient is well enough, he should wash his own face and genital area; otherwise the attendants should do it. Wash and dry one part of the body at a time so that the patient is not uncovered all at once.

When you have finished washing the patient, dust pressure areas and skin creases with talc.

The bed linen should be changed as frequently as necessary.

Feeding patients in bed

People who are ill or injured may not feel much like eating or may be unable to enjoy food. They may also need to be encouraged to have plenty to drink in order to prevent dehydration (see Fluid balance, page 101). Always try to find out what the patient would like to eat or drink and give him what he wants if you possibly can. Food should be presented as attractively as possible on a suitable tray. Special diets, when they are prescribed, must be strictly followed. If a weak patient spills food or drink, use towels or sheeting to keep patient and bedding as clean as possible.

Mouth care

Make sure that plenty of drinks are available and that facilities for brushing teeth and dentures are made available twice a day.

Very ill patients or unconscious patients should have their dentures removed. The inside of the cheeks, the gums, the teeth, and the tongue should be swabbed with water on a piece of cotton wool, cotton buds, or other suitable materials. If the lips are dry, apply petroleum jelly thinly. This procedure should be repeated as often as necessary.

Bedsores

Anyone in bed is constantly prone to bedsores (pressure sores) unless preventive action is taken. Unconscious patients (page 104) and the incontinent (whether of urine or faeces) are at special risk of bedsores. Frequent changes of posture, day and night, with thorough washing and drying in the case of the incontinent, will be required.

Prevention of pressure sores begins by making the patient comfortable in bed. Choose a good mattress, and keep the sheets taut and smooth. Keep the skin clean and dry. Turning should be done by two or preferably more people. Begin by

lifting the patient up a little from the bed. Then roll him over slowly and gently.

Fig. 96 shows the sites on the body where pressure sores may occur. Pillows, rubber rings, and other padding can be used to relieve pressure as indicated in the figure. Massage pressure areas gently with surgical spirit and, when they are dry, dust them lightly with talcum powder.

Bodily functions of bed patients

If the toilet or a suitable commode is available, it is always better to use these facilities where the condition of the patient permits it. Privacy is important and some people will have difficulty in performing before a witness, but the nurse or attendant should remain within hearing. Very ill patients may require support or assistance with the bedpan. Appliances *must* be emptied immediately and thoroughly cleaned and disinfected. Voided matter—faeces, urine, vomit, or sputum—should be inspected and a record kept of the amount, colour, consistency, and smell; in some instances it may be necessary to retain samples or to make tests (page 106).

Bowel movement in illness

This often worries people. There is no need for the bowels to move every day, not is it necessarily unhealthy if the bowels do not move for a week and the person feels perfectly well. In illness, food intake is often restricted and—on the basis of "less in, less out"—bowel motions cannot be expected to follow their normal pattern and will probably become less frequent.

Incontinence

Incontinence (urinary or faecal) may occur with conscious or unconscious patients. It is acutely embarrassing to conscious patients, and they should be reassured that their problem is understood and not resented. They must be kept clean. Check the patient frequently.

Collect together all the things that will be necessary to restore the patient to a clean, dry condition—that is:

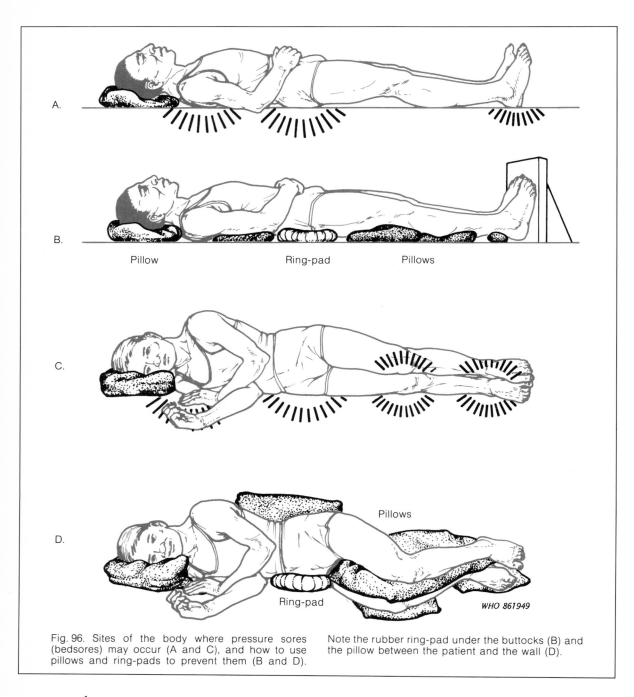

Fig. 96. Sites of the body where pressure sores (bedsores) may occur (A and C), and how to use pillows and ring-pads to prevent them (B and D). Note the rubber ring-pad under the buttocks (B) and the pillow between the patient and the wall (D).

- soap and warm water;
- toilet paper;
- cotton wool;
- towels;
- talcum powder;
- clean bed-linen;
- change of clothing/pyjamas;
- bag for soiled tissues;
- plastic bag for dirty linen/clothing.

Clean up with toilet paper. Then wash the soiled areas with cotton wool, soap, and water. When the patient has been cleaned, dry him thoroughly by patting, not rubbing, because scuffing can easily damage soiled skin. Then apply plenty of talcum powder and remake the bed with clean linen.

If the patient can walk about, it may help to get him into a bath or shower for cleaning up.

A simple device for use in urinary incontinence. Make a small cut in the teat of a condom. Stretch the teat over the end of a suitable length of flexible tubing and secure it firmly. Insert the penis into the open end of the condom. Ensure that there is at least 3–4 cm between the tip of the penis and the teat–tube junction (see Fig. 97), to prevent the tube chafing the penis. The condom should be kept correctly positioned by lengths of sticky tape attached to the abdominal skin after shaving the pubic hair.

Do not use encircling bands round the penis.

Prevent tension on the tubing by fixing it to the patient or the bed. The free end of tubing should drain into a suitable container which should be emptied at appropriate intervals.

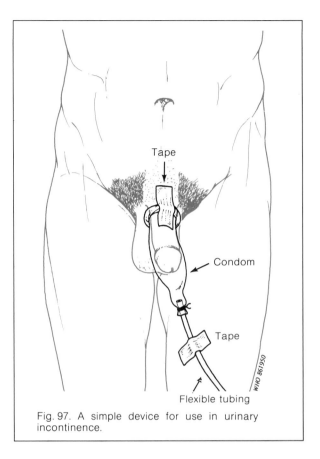

Fig. 97. A simple device for use in urinary incontinence.

Fluid balance

The body has self-regulating mechanisms to maintain a normal balance between fluid intake and fluid loss.

Fluid intake

An average daily intake of fluids from food and drink is about 2.5 litres. In temperate climates it is possible to manage for a short time on as little as one litre. In hot climates where there is a large fluid loss through sweating, an intake of 6 litres per day may be necessary.

Fluid loss

Body fluid is lost through unseen perspiration, obvious sweating, the breath, urine, and the faeces. At least 2.5 litres of fluid will be lost each day as follows:

	litres
unseen perspiration	0.5
breath	0.4
urine	1.5
faeces	0.1
Total	2.5

To this amount must be added any loss through obvious sweating. This can be high in hot climates.

Measuring fluid intake and fluid loss

In any illness where fluid balance is likely to be a problem, a *fluid chart* recording *fluid intake* and *fluid loss* should be started at once as an aid to the attendant and to the doctor or radio medical service. The amounts of "fluid in" and "fluid out" should be added up separately every

Table 2. Fluid intake and output: sample chart record in millilitres (ml)

Date and time	Type of fluid	In	Out		
		Mouth	Urine	Vomit	Other
12/8/82					
11.00	Clear soup	250			
11.15				200	very sweaty for 1 hour
12.00			500	60	
12.30	Milk	125			runny
13.00				120	diarrhoea
14.00	oral rehydration salt (ORS) solution	180			
17.00	ORS solution	200			
20.00	ORS solution	200			
20.15			20		
23.00	ORS solution	200			
12–hourly			520 + 380		?
balance		1155	900		?

difference: plus 255 ml   (but the patient lost fluid by sweating and diarrhoea, probably more than 225 ml)

1 litre = 1000 millilitres (ml).

12 hours and the totals compared (see Table 2). The information in the final column of the record should be as full as possible, including, where relevant, the duration and the intensity of the fluid loss (for instance: very sweaty for one hour). It will normally be translatable into specific quantities only by a doctor, to whom it will be useful.

During the first 12-hour period the fluid intake should normally be 0.5–0.75 litres *more* than the fluid loss. After the next 12 hours, the intake and loss over the day should balance out. A normal fluid balance can generally be assumed if the fluid intake is 1–1½ litres more than the loss by way of urine and vomit.

Imbalances

When the fluid intake exceeds the fluid loss, restrict the intake and examine the patient for oedema (page 216). When the fluid loss exceeds the fluid intake, give the patient more fluid.

Excessive loss of fluid (dehydration). Dehydration may occur in any patient sweating profusely or suffering from diarrhoea, vomiting, blood loss, or burns of areas exceeding about 10% of the body surface. Uncontrolled diabetes (see page 186) can also be a cause of dehydration. Diarrhoea and vomit both have a high fluid content which should be measured or assessed as regards the amount and the extent to which it is liquid. Anyone who suffers from either or both will require a high fluid intake to maintain fluid balance.

In illnesses where the fluid taken by mouth is vomited back it may be necessary to give fluids intravenously (page 117); this may also be necessary with certain unconscious patients. In these cases a fluid intake and output chart *must* be used. Signs of dehydration include excessive thirst, high temperature for a long time, dry skin, lacklustre eyes, dry mouth and tongue, and dark concentrated urine passed infrequently, especially if the quantities are small. Ask a dehydrated patient what he would like to drink and grant him any reasonable request. Alcohol should not be given. Cool citric fruit juices, sweetened with sugar, are nourishing.

In conditions such as *heat illnesses* (see page 205), when salt is lost with the sweat, and *cholera,* in which profuse diarrhoea occurs and salts are lost from the bowel, salt replacement is necessary. Give oral rehydration salts (ORS) in solution. If ORS are not available, give one teaspoonful of common salt (or four 1-g sodium chloride tablets) and 8 level teaspoons of sugar in a litre of water, at first in small quantities, repeated frequently.

Excessive fluid retention. See Oedema (page 216) and Catheterization of the urinary bladder (page 110).

Breathing difficulties

Patients who have difficulty in breathing will be most comfortable in a half-seated position, either lying back or leaning forward with their forearms and elbows supported on a bed-table with pillows (page 33, Fig. 31).

Care of mentally disturbed patients

Certain guiding principles must be borne in mind when dealing with any patient who, in the opinion of the ship's master, is of unsound mind.

Every such case should be considered to be *actually or potentially suicidal or homicidal.* All possible steps must therefore be taken to have a constant watch kept on the patient.

Should the master deem it necessary to place the patient under restraint, then the patient should, if possible, be housed in a single-berth cabin. Before the patient enters this accommodation, it must be carefully examined to ensure that it contains no object that the patient might use to injure himself or another, i.e., mirrors, stools or chairs, unperforated plastic bags, or electric bulbs unprotected by a strong shield.

Knives and forks should not be allowed: a spoon only should be supplied. A soft plastic or paper mug and plate should be substituted for ordinary crockery. Razors and matches should be removed from the patient's possession.

If water is laid on to the cabin, steps should be taken to control the flow from an outside point to prevent the risk of flooding.

Great care must be taken to see that the patient has not concealed in his pockets any weapon such as a knife. It may not be easy to find this out when dealing with a truculent patient, but he must be persuaded to undress, which provides an opportunity to remove and search the clothes. Braces, belts, and cords should also be removed.

The cabin door must always be firmly secured. If possible, this should be done without the knowledge of the patient. The state of a mentally disturbed patient is likely to worsen if he knows that he is locked in. Any port must be firmly screwed home and the port key removed. Care should also be taken to see that the patient cannot lock himself into the cabin. It will be an advantage if the cabin the patient is using has a port opening onto a deck or a ventilator in the door, so that the attendant can observe the patient's behaviour before entering the cabin.

As a rule only the attendant should enter the cabin, but a second person should be standing by in case assistance is required.

Patients should not be allowed out on deck while the ship is at sea, unless accompanied by two people. Remember the ship's side is always very near, and if the patient does go over the side, the lives of others will be put at risk during the rescue attempt.

Many of these patients may have delusions of persecution by their shipmates. Politeness, combined with firmness, must be exercised by the person responsible for nursing such a patient, in order to gain the patient's cooperation and trust.

A severely excited (suicidal, violent, or homicidal) patient can be immobilized on a berth or a stretcher by tying him down with two folded bedsheets, one across the chest, and the other across the legs. This should only be done as a last resort. Usually, medication and friendly but firm persuasion are effective in subduing excitement, but the patient should always be kept under observation.

Force should only be used as a last resort. If it becomes necessary, then action should be taken coolly, very firmly, and in such a way that it cannot be resisted. It is worth while remembering that a Neil-Robertson stretcher could act as a useful instrument of restraint when dealing with a mentally disturbed patient.

Unconscious patients

The careful nursing of unconscious people is a demanding, difficult, and very important task. Their survival and eventual condition will depend greatly on the care, skill, and attention given while they are unconscious.

Three MUSTS. An unconscious patient:

- MUST have a clear airway;
- MUST be kept in the unconscious position;
- MUST NEVER be left alone.

The maintenance of a clear airway is essential and requires the patient to be kept in the unconscious position (see Fig. 3, page 6). An airway (Fig. 98) can be used. Any blood, vomit, or other secretions from the mouth must be mopped out or removed by the use of a sucker. An unconscious patient must never be left unwatched in case he moves, vomits, has a fit, or falls out of his bunk.

Airway insertion

An airway (Fig. 98) should be inserted if a patient is breathing on his own but is doing so with great difficulty. The function of the airway is to ensure a clear passage between the lips and the back of the throat. Use appropriate sizes for adults and children.

First remove any dentures and suck or swab out any blood or vomit that is in the mouth to get a clear airway. Then, with the patient's head fully back, slide the airway gently into the mouth with the outer curve of the airway towards the tongue. This operation will be facilitated if the airway is wetted.

If you notice any attempt by the patient to gag, retch, or vomit, it is better *not* to proceed with the insertion of the airway. If necessary, try again later to insert it.

Continue to slide the airway in until the flange of the airway reaches the lips. Now rotate the airway through 180° so that the outer curve is turned upwards towards the roof of the mouth (Fig. 98d).

Bring the jaw upwards and push the airway in until the flange at the end of the airway is outside the teeth (or gums) and inside the lips. If necessary tape one or both lips so that the end of the airway is not covered by them.

Check now that the casualty's breath is coming through the airway. Continue to keep the jaws upwards and the head fully back, and the airway will be held in place by the teeth or gums and by its shape.

As the patient regains consciousness, he will spit out the airway. Make sure it is retained until he is fully conscious.

General management

Make sure that an unconscious patient cannot injure himself further. Some unconscious and semiconscious patients may be quite violent, or move about suddenly, so ensure that they cannot fall onto the floor or hit themselves against any hard edge or surface. A cot with sides will probably be the safest place. Do not put pillows or other padding where the patient might put his face.

The person must be turned from one side to the other at least every three hours to prevent bedsores (see page 99). Turn the patient gently and roll him smoothly from one side to the other. **The head must always be kept back with a chin-up position when actually turning, and at no time must the head be allowed to bend forwards with the chin sagging.** This is both to help to keep a clear airway and to prevent neck injuries. If you suspect that the jaw is broken or that the person has fallen from a height and may have a neck or spine injury, you should be especially careful during turning (page 28).

Check the breathing and make sure that the airway is securely in place as soon as you have turned the person.

Make sure that all joints are neither fully straight nor fully bent. Ideally they should all be kept in mid-position. Place pillows under and

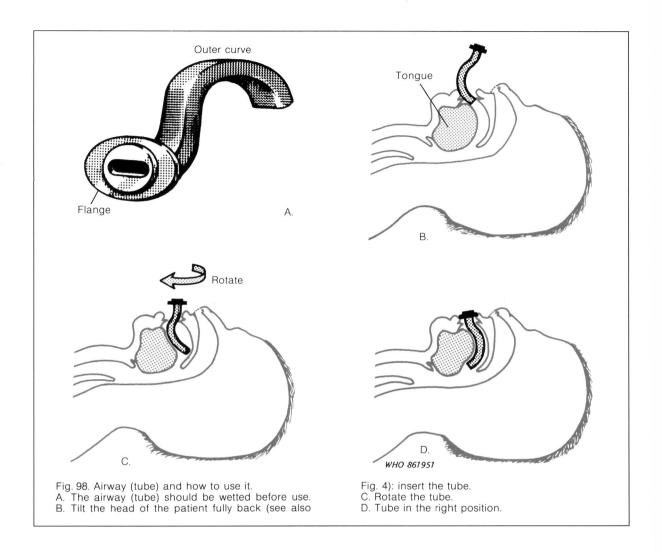

Fig. 98. Airway (tube) and how to use it.
A. The airway (tube) should be wetted before use.
B. Tilt the head of the patient fully back (see also
Fig. 4): insert the tube.
C. Rotate the tube.
D. Tube in the right position.

WHO 861951

between the bent knees and between the feet and ankles. Use a bed-cage (a large stiff cardboard box will make a good improvised cage) to keep the bedclothes from pressing on the feet and ankles. Check that elbows, wrists, and fingers are in a relaxed mid-position after turning. Do not pull, strain, or stretch any joint at any time. Make quite sure that the eyelids are closed and that they remain closed at all times, otherwise damage to the eyeball can easily occur. Irrigate the eyes every 2 hours by opening the lids slightly and pouring some saline solution gently into the corner of each eye in such a way that the saline will run across each eye and drain from the other corner. A saline solution can be made by dissolving one level teaspoonful of salt in half a litre of boiled water which has been allowed to cool.

After 12 hours of unconsciousness further problems will arise. Unconscious people must be given nothing by mouth in case it chokes them and they suffer from obstructed breathing. However, after 12 hours of unconsciousness fluid will have to be given, particularly in hot climates and/or if the patient is obviously sweating. Because the fluid cannot be given by mouth, it should be given intravenously (page 117), after obtaining RADIO MEDICAL ADVICE. An input–output chart will be necessary and the instructions given in the section on fluid balance (page 101) should be followed. An incontinence container with a condom over the penis (Fig. 97) should be used to collect the urine. The mouth, cheeks, tongue, and teeth should be moistened every 20 minutes with a small swab moistened with water. Carry out mouth care every time the person is turned.

After 48 hours of unconsciousness, move the joints at least once a day. All the joints in all the limbs should be moved very gently in such a way as to put each joint through a *full range* of movement, provided other considerations such as fracture do not prevent this. Watch that the exercise of the arms does not interfere unduly with the patient's breathing. Do the job systematically. Begin on the side of the patient that is most accessible. Start with the fingers and thumb, then move the wrist, the elbow, and the shoulder. Now move the toes, the foot, and the ankle. Then bend the knee and move the hip around. Next, turn the patient—if necessary, with the help of another person—and move the joints on the other side.

Remember that unconscious patients may be very relaxed and floppy, so do not let go of a limb until you have placed it safely back on the bed. Hold the limbs firmly but not tightly, and do everything slowly and with the utmost gentleness. Take your time, moving each joint fully before going on to the next.

Examination of faeces, urine, sputum, and vomited matter

Faeces

The bowel movements of patients vary in frequency and character so it is important to establish what is normal for each patient before drawing conclusions from an inspection of the faeces.

Common abnormalities to be looked for are blood, pus, slime (mucus), increased or diminished bile-pigment content, and worms.

Blood. Black, tarry faeces, either formed or fluid but always of offensive odour, indicate bleeding from the stomach or high up in the intestines. The blood has been altered by the digestive process (page 218).

Bright red blood suggests an abnormal condition of the lower bowel, rectum, or anus. Haemorrhoids (piles) are the most common cause of this type of bleeding (page 201) but cases should be referred to a doctor, when convenient, to exclude more serious causes.

Faeces containing *pus* are found in severe dysentery or ulceration of the intestines or when an internal abscess has discharged into the intestine.

Slimy faeces occur mainly in acute or chronic infections of the large bowel, but irritation of the bowel lining from any cause can also produce excess mucus. In infections, the mucus is often streaked with blood.

Bile pigment. Pale, putty-coloured faeces caused by a diminished bile content are associated with some liver, pancreas, or gall-bladder diseases.

Threadworms have the appearance of white threads 0.5–1 cm in length and can often be seen wriggling about in recently passed faeces (page 240).

Roundworms resemble earthworms, measure 15–20 cm in length, and can similarly be seen in recently passed faeces.

Tapeworms, the longest of the different varieties of worm, can measure 10 or more metres in length. The body is segmented and flat. Short segments may break off and be passed in the faeces. The full length is seen only when they are passed after treatment, which should be carried out under medical supervision.

Effect of certain diseases on the faeces

Acute bacillary dysentery. In severe cases, up to 30 bowel actions in 24 hours may occur with much slime and blood in the faeces (page 188).

Amoebic dysentery. There is often a long history of passing bulky, offensive faeces streaked with blood and mucus (page 189).

Cholera. Diarrhoea is frequent and profuse. In severe cases large amounts of odourless, watery fluid containing shreds of mucus, the so-called rice-water motion, are passed daily (page 128).

Typhoid. Constipation during the first week may be followed by frequent diarrhoea resembling pea soup (page 130).

Urine

In certain illnesses, the urine is found to have abnormal constituents when the appropriate tests are performed. The tests that are described in this section may help you to differentiate between one illness and another if you are in doubt about the diagnosis.

The urine should *always* be tested:

- if any person is ill enough to be confined to bed;
- if the symptoms are suggestive of an abdominal complaint;
- if the symptoms are suggestive of disease of the urinary system, i.e., the patient has pain on passing water; or
- if there is some trouble of the genital area.

All tests must be made on an uncontaminated specimen. In males, if there is any discharge from the penis or from behind the foreskin, or in females if there is a vaginal discharge, the genitalia should be washed with soap and water and dried with a paper towel or tissue before passing urine.

Urine glasses or other collecting vessels should be washed with detergent solution or with soap and water and *must* be rinsed at least three times in fresh water to remove all traces of detergent or of soap. **False positive results to the tests will be given if these precautions are not taken.**

Examine and test the urine *immediately after it has been passed,* as false results may occur if stale urine is tested.

First, examine the appearance of the urine. Hold the urine glass towards a source of light so that the light shines through it. Note the *colour* and whether the urine is crystal *clear,* slightly *cloudy,* or definitely *hazy* (turbid). Look also for *threads* floating in the urine or at the bottom of the glass. Deposits may appear as the urine cools and may be slight or heavy in amount. Note the colour and appearance of any deposit. Last, note any *odour* present such as acetone or ammonia. A fishy smell is often found in urinary infections.

Normal urine varies from a pale straw to quite a dark yellow colour. If concentrated, it becomes brownish in colour. Orange or "smoky" urine is usually due to the presence of blood in small amounts. With greater quantities of blood, the urine turns red and cloudy and small clots may be seen. The urine may be the colour of strong tea, or even slightly greenish, in persons who are jaundiced. Cloudiness that clears when acid is added to the urine is due to the presence of phosphates. These are sometimes present in normal urine. Persistent cloudiness is usually due to protein in the urine and can be found in urinary infections. Threads are usually associated with infections of the bladder or urethra, most commonly of the latter.

Test strips and tablets are supplied in the ship's medical stores, for testing urine for protein, urinary blood, glucose, ketone, pH, and bilirubin. In performing tests, the producer's instructions attached to the kit should be closely followed.

Note. Urine should normally be free of sugar and protein. However, protein may occur in the urine of some young people during the day, though not when they are in bed at night. This may happen in the absence of other signs of disease of the urinary tract. Where protein is found in a young person's urine, the patient should empty the bladder before he goes to bed and pass a specimen immediately on rising in the morning. If there is no protein in this specimen, the presence of protein in other specimens taken during the day is of no significance. A similar condition can arise with sugar, but there is no test available for use on board ship that can differentiate this from diabetes. If sugar is present in the urine, the patient should be treated as a diabetic until there is proof to the contrary (page 186).

Sputum

The quantity and type of any sputum should be noted, and in particular, the presence of any blood in it should always be recorded.

Sputum may vary in appearance, as follows:

- it may be clear and slimy, suggesting chronic bronchitis;
- thick yellow or green sputum may be coughed up in acute or chronic respiratory illnesses;
- rust-coloured sputum may be coughed up in cases of pneumonia and is due to the presence of small quantities of blood in process of decomposition;
- blood-stained sputum may be coughed up, or pure blood without sputum (see note below);
- frothy sputum, characteristic of pulmonary oedema, is always copious, and may be white or pink.

Note. If the patient appears to be spitting blood (or vomiting blood), always remember to inspect the mouth and throat carefully in a good light and make the patient blow his nose. Coughing and vomiting blood are not common conditions, whereas slight bleeding from the gums and nose is, and an anxious and nervous patient may easily mislead the inexperienced medical attendant.

Vomited matter

Always inspect any vomited matter, because it may be helpful in arriving at a diagnosis. Note its colour, consistency, and odour.

In cases of suspected poisoning, vomited matter should be collected in a suitable receptacle and covered with an airtight lid. It should then be labelled and stored in a cool place to be available for any subsequent investigation.

Possible contents of vomit are listed below.

- Partly digested food.

- Bile, causing the vomit to be yellow or yellow-green in colour. This may be indicative of a number of conditions.
- Blood. This may indicate the presence of a gastric ulcer or growth in the stomach, but it may also occur after severe straining from retching, as in seasickness, or as a complication of enlargement of the liver. The blood may be dark in colour, and resemble coffee grounds if it has been retained in the stomach for any length of time. This is due to the action of the gastric juice. (See also the note in the section on sputum above.)
- Faecal material. A watery brown fluid with the odour of faeces may be found in advanced cases of intestinal obstruction (see page 210) when there is a reverse flow of the intestinal contents.

Treatment and procedures

Application of cold

Cold should be applied to any part of the body that is injured and may bleed, in order to narrow the blood vessels and prevent haemorrhage.

Cold applications are also indicated in persons with certain infections (such as an infected appendix or abscessed tooth) to prevent swelling and further damage that swelling could cause. Thus, ice-packs are frequently used when bleeding is likely, after an injury (such as a blow to the mouth or a sprained ankle), or in treating an infected area to prevent it from filling with blood.

Prolonged application of cold, or exposure to excessive cold, may cause death of the body cells. Cold narrows the blood vessels so that the blood supply to the affected part of the body is cut off. Therefore a part receiving a cold application must be watched as carefully as one receiving a hot application. If paleness or blueness of the skin appears, the application of cold should be stopped for 15 minutes, and then resumed.

Cold eye compresses

Cold, in the form of cold compresses, is often applied to an inflamed (reddened) eye to lower the blood flow to the eye. This reduces the bloodshot appearance of the eye and eases the pain caused by swelling.

The procedure for applying cold eye compresses is as follows:

- Take sterile compresses or eye-pads.
- Place several large pieces of ice in a basin, and add tap water.
- Dip a compress into the cold solution, wring it out, and place it over the eye.
- Prepare the next compress; remove the one on the eye and replace it with the fresh compress.
- Apply cold compresses for a period of 15–30 minutes.

Cold moist compresses

These may be applied to affected parts of the body for 15–30 minutes.

Ice-bag (dry cold)

The procedure for applying an ice-bag is as follows:

- Fill the ice-bag about half full of ice.
- Expel the air before closing the bag (air increases the rapidity with which the ice melts and decreases the flexibility of the bag).
- Test the bag for leakage.
- Cover the bag with a soft absorbent material.
- Apply the bag for to the affected part (if the bag has a metal top, keep it turned away from the patient's body).
- Apply the bag for 30 minutes and discontinue for one hour; then reapply. Remove it if the patient complains of numbness, or if the affected part shows any sign of extreme whiteness or blueness.
- Refill bag as the ice melts.

Cool or tepid sponge bath

This is usually given to patients with fever over 39 °C. The patient must be watched for any adverse reaction to the cool sponge.

The procedure for giving a cool or tepid sponge bath is as follows.

- Assemble equipment:
  - thermometers;
  - basin with cool water, temperature about 15 °C;
  - washcloths (2) or a sponge;
  - large waterproof sheet;
  - cotton blankets (2);
  - towels.
- Keep the patient covered with a cotton blanket during the procedure. Remove pillows and pyjamas.
- Place the waterproof sheet covered with a cotton blanket under the patient to protect the bedding.
- Check the patient's pulse rate and rectal temperature (pages 93 and 94) and record them.
- Sponge the body in orderly fashion, uncovering one part at a time. Proceed so that no part is missed, doing arms, chest, abdomen, front part of legs, back, buttocks, and back part of legs. Alternate wash cloths as necessary.
- Watch the patient's colour and check his pulse. If the pulse becomes weak or the lips turn blue, discontinue the treatment.
- Continue the treatment for 20 minutes, if no complications occur. Check rectal temperature. If it has decreased, the cool bath was effective.

The water used for tepid sponging will tend to warm up from the heat of the person being sponged so make sure that it remains noticeably cooler than the body temperature (15–17 °C) by adding ice.

- Have a fan blowing over the patient (take care not to touch the fan with wet hands).
- Check the patient's temperature frequently as you cool him. Because this treatment causes rapid cooling of only parts of the body, it is important that the thermometer should remain in position for four minutes so that the temperature recorded is that of the body as a whole.
- After tepid sponging, when the patient's temperature is down to at least 39 °C, the skin may be dried and powdered with talc.
- If the patient complains of cold and starts to shiver and his temperature has fallen sufficiently, cover him with a thin sheet.

- As the temperature may well rise again, check the temperature *by mouth* every 30 minutes with another thermometer until it has been below 39 °C for at least an hour; thereafter check the temperature hourly until the fever has disappeared.

Note. Tepid sponging will not be a useful cooling method in the tropics, when the temperature is high and the air humid in the cabin or the ship's hospital in which the patient is being nursed (in a ship without air-conditioning). The patient's body should be cooled with cold packs, or he should be placed in a tub of cold water.

Application of heat

Heat should be applied to a patient's body when an infection is present, to increase circulation to a given part of the body, to help reduce congestion and inflammation, and to relieve pain. In cases of *abdominal pain* or *suspected appendicitis,* NEVER APPLY HEAT—contact a physician for directions.

When heat is applied to a patient's body, the following safety measures should be observed.

- Test the water to be sure it is the exact temperature required. The following temperatures are guides only:
  - hot bath   — 43 °C
  - warm bath   — 35 °C
  - foot soak   — 43 °C
  - hot wet dressing — 43 °C
  - hot-water bottle — 50 °C.
- Watch carefully for excessive redness on the patient's skin since this may indicate a burn.
- To prolong the effects of the treatment, keep the treated part warm after the heat application is removed.
- When the soak solution used on an arm or leg has to be reheated, *remove the patient's limb from the container before adding the hot water* required to raise the solution to the desired temperature.

Dry heat

Hot-water bottle. The procedure for applying a hot-water bottle is as follows.

- Fill the hot-water bottle (half or three-quarters full) with water at about 50 °C.
- Expel the air until the water comes to the top; test for leakage.
- Cover the bottle with a towel.
- Apply the bottle to the specified area of the body.
- Return to the patient in 15 minutes and check his skin for excessive redness or possible burning.
- Refill the bottle as necessary (at least every hour), to keep the water at the desired temperature.

Heating-pad. A heating-pad can also be used to supply dry heat. However, care must be taken to ensure that the temperature of the pad is not increased accidentally. Also, to avoid possible injury to the patient, electrical wiring and connections should be checked for flaws.

The area of application to the body should be checked at least every hour to offset possible burning of the patient's skin.

Catheterization of the urinary bladder

Catheterization is the insertion of a catheter (tube) through the urethra into the bladder to remove urine. When performed in a hospital by skilled persons, this procedure is relatively safe. When it is improperly performed, there is danger of infection or perforation of the bladder. **Therefore, catheterization should be done only by skilled persons.** Aboard ship, it should be carried out only when absolutely necessary, usually because of urinary tract obstruction.

A patient who has been consuming a normal amount of fluid but has not urinated in 24 hours, probably needs catheterization. Before performing it, attempt to induce a normal flow of urine by the following means:

- Provide privacy and the sound of running water.
- Let the patient stand, sit, or kneel.
- Apply a hot-water bottle to the lower abdominal area; or have the patient pour warm water (temperature about 38–40 °C) over the area.

- The patient may also lie in a hot bath, where he should try to relax and to pass urine. If he has severe discomfort give him 15 mg of morphine intramuscularly before he gets into the bath. Give him nothing to drink. Keep the bath water really hot.

If, in spite of all these efforts, the patient has still not passed urine, and catheterization is considered necessary, get RADIO MEDICAL ADVICE.

Then prepare the equipment and the patient. If morphine has not been given, give 10 mg of diazepam by mouth while the patient is still in the bath. This will take effect while preparations are being made.

Explain the procedure to the patient and state that there will be only slight discomfort. Fear and worry will stimulate the patient's muscles to tighten, making it difficult to pass the catheter into the bladder.

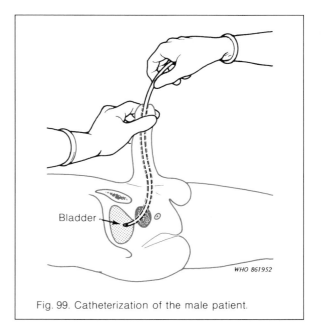

Fig. 99. Catheterization of the male patient.

Equipment needed

A sterile disposable catheterization tray which contains a 14 French (5-mm) straight catheter, sterile gloves, small forceps, cotton balls, lubricant, antiseptic solution, underpad and drape, specimen container, and label. (If a disposable catheterization set is not available, the rubber catheter and the forceps should be sterilized by boiling (see page 121).)

Preparation of the male patient

Assemble the equipment. Before opening the catheterization tray, the patient should be prepared, as follows:

- Fold the top covers to the foot of the bed, while covering the patient with a sheet or light blanket.
- Have the patient lie on his back with knees bent.
- Expose his penis, keeping the rest of the body covered; this can be done by pushing the bath blanket in from the side.

After the patient is prepared, the attendant's hands should be scrubbed thoroughly, especially under the fingernails.

Procedure

For catheterization of a male patient, the following procedure should be used:

- Follow the directions for opening the catheter and catheter tray, as written on the wrapper.
- Put on sterile gloves.
- Hold the penis with the left hand and stand at the patient's right side. With the right hand swab the end of the penis, using cotton balls and the antiseptic solution provided in the disposable catheterization tray.
- Pick up the catheter, holding it at least 20 cm from the tip. Do not touch the part of the catheter that is to be inserted inside the patient.
- Apply the lubricant to at least 15 cm of the catheter. **Thorough lubrication is essential.**
- Hold the penis straight with the left hand while inserting the catheter (see Fig. 99). This position straightens out the urethra.
- Use gentle but steady pressure to insert the catheter. A slight resistance may be felt upon approaching the bladder's sphincter muscle, but gentle pressure should push the catheter past it. If the catheter cannot be inserted

with gentle pressure, and a firm resistance is felt — **then stop!** Get RADIO MEDICAL ADVICE. **Never force the catheter as it may seriously damage the bladder or urethra.**

- Position the basin under the catheter.
- Insert the catheter (usually 15–20 cm) until urine begins to flow.
- Withdraw the catheter when the steady stream of urine starts to diminish. *Never empty the bladder completely.*
- Record the date and time of day for the procedure, and the amount and colour of the urine obtained.

Preparation of the female patient

Assemble the necessary equipment (see page 111). A floor lamp will be useful for illuminating the area of the urinary meatus. Before opening the catheterization tray, the patient should be prepared as follows:

- Fold the top covers to the foot of the bed, while covering the patient with a sheet or light blanket.
- Have the patient lie on her back with knees bent, thighs separated, and feet flat on the mattress. Drape her thighs and legs with the right and left corners of the sheet and tuck the free edges under her feet.
- Do not fold back the bottom corner of the sheet to expose the vulva until ready to start catheterization.
- Place the lamp on the far side of the bed and adjust the light to shine on the perineal area.

The attendant's hands should now be scrubbed thoroughly, especially under the fingernails.

Procedure

For routine catheterization of a female patient, the following procedure should be used:

- Follow the directions for opening the catheter and catheter tray, as written on the wrapper.
- Fold back the drape sheet to expose the vulva. Encourage the patient to relax and tell her to breathe regularly and slowly to lessen tension.
- Put on sterile gloves.

- Pour the antiseptic solution over four cotton balls in a sterile container.
- Squeeze the lubricant on to a gauze sponge.
- Place the sterile towel between the patient's thighs and pull the top edge just under the buttocks. When doing this, fold about three inches of the towel over the gloved hands to avoid possible contamination of the gloves; be careful to protect exposed sterile surfaces.
- With the gloved left hand, separate the labia to expose the urinary meatus (see Fig. 100). It should be visible as a small opening about half a centimetre above the vagina.
- Keep the left hand in position, holding the labia apart, until the catheter has been inserted. **Remember:** the gloved left hand is no longer sterile.
- With the gloved right hand, pick up one cotton ball saturated with the antiseptic solution. Without going over the same area twice, clean the meatus and vestibule from above downwards. Repeat the procedure with the remaining cotton balls. Try not to touch the meatus with the right hand. Discard the used cotton balls.
- With the gloved right hand, pick up the sterile basin and place it on the sterile towel, close to the buttocks and below the labia.

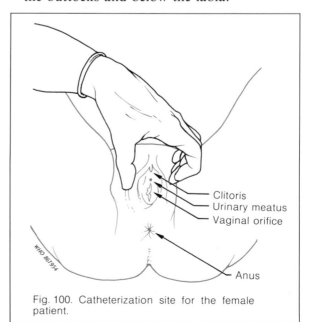

Clitoris
Urinary meatus
Vaginal orifice

Anus

Fig. 100. Catheterization site for the female patient.

- With the gloved right hand, pick up the catheter, holding it about 8 cm from the tip. Lubricate the catheter by passing it gently over the gauze sponge containing the lubricant.
- Insert the catheter into the meatus about 5 cm or until urine starts to flow. **Do not use force** if there is resistance. Do not insert the catheter more than 5 cm.
- When the flow of urine decreases, pinch off the catheter and gently withdraw it.
- Leave the patient dry, covered and comfortable.
- Record the date and time of day for the procedure, and the amount and colour of the urine obtained.

Surgical dressings

To change a dressing, a procedure should be used that will remove the old dressing without contaminating the wound or the fingers of the person removing it. Equipment (sterile dressing forceps, fresh sterile dressing, paper bag, tape) will be needed to cleanse the wound, dress it adequately, and secure it. **Sterile instruments must be used for removing the dressings adhering to the wound and for treating it.**

The size, number, and types of dressings used will depend on the nature of the wound.

To apply a surgical dressing, proceed as follows:

- Wash hands thoroughly.
- Undo materials securing the dressing; lift the dressing off, touching the outside portion only. If it is soiled, use forceps.
- Drop the soiled dressing into a waxed paper bag; later staple the bag shut and discard it into a refuse container.
- Open the gauze-dressing pack.
- Using sterile forceps, remove the gauze dressing from its wrapper and place it on the wound, taking care not to touch the portion of the dressing that is going to be placed in contact with the wound.
- Apply tape to keep the dressing in place.

(See also the first two sections of Chapter 4, Care of the injured, page 67.)

Administering medicaments

The following points should be remembered when administering medicines:

- Always give medicine on time.
- Read the label three times before giving medication.

Record the date and time of day, the name of the medicine, the amount given, and the route of administration. Do not record these until the medicine has actually been taken.

Medicaments to be given more than once a day should be spaced at a reasonable interval. For example, four times a day: at 08h 00, 12h 00, 16h 00, and 20h 00 (8 a.m., 12 noon, 4 p.m., and 8 p.m.). Antibiotics, if required to be taken four times a day, should be administered every six hours: at 24h 00, 06h 00, 12h 00, and 18h 00 (midnight, 6 a.m., noon, and 6 p.m.). The aim is to help maintain an adequate level of the antibiotic in the system at all times.

Medicaments that have to be taken before a meal should be given half an hour before it.

Routes of administration

Oral

The easiest and generally the safest and most desirable way to administer a medicament is by the oral route. Generally, absorption into the bloodstream begins to reach a therapeutic level in about 30–90 minutes and lasts 4–6 hours, depending on the characteristics of the drug and the formulation. A medicament taken on an empty stomach will usually be more rapidly absorbed than one taken after a meal.

Tablets or capsules are swallowed more easily by most persons, if placed on the back of the tongue, then washed down with water.

Sublingual

Substances that may be destroyed by the digestive juices, or certain medicaments for self-administration in an emergency, such as glyceryl trinitrate tablets, may be placed under the tongue.

Rectal

Drugs may be given by rectum as liquids or suppositories. Generally, drugs administered rectally are absorbed erratically, and this route should be used for a systemic effect only as an alternative.

Intranasal

Drugs may be given intranasally for either local or systemic action. Nose drops or sprays are usually applied to the nasal mucosa for their vasoconstrictive effect.

Subcutaneous (under the skin)

The usual sites for subcutaneous injections are the extensor surfaces of the upper arms, the back, and the lateral aspects of the thighs. The injection usually has its maximum effect in about 30 minutes.

When giving a subcutaneous injection, this procedure should be followed.

- Assemble the equipment:
  - disposable syringe;[1]
  - disposable 0.5-mm, 16-mm needle;
  - medicament (see note below);
  - alcohol sponges.

Note. Drugs for injection are supplied either in rubber-capped vials or in glass ampoules (Fig. 101). The name and strength of the drug are always marked on them. Check this carefully, using a magnifying glass, if necessary. If no name is visible, or if the name is indecipherable, the vial or ampoule should be discarded. Glass ampoules may have a coloured band round the neck at which the top of the ampoule will break off cleanly. The rubber cap of the vial is held on by a metal cap with a small tear-off seal. This seal should not be removed before the drug is required.

- If the medicament is in a multiple-dose vial, clean the rubber diaphragm on the vial with alcohol.
- If the medicament is in an ampoule, ensure that all the liquid in it is below the neck by gently tapping the neck with a finger. Then file the neck of the ampoule and break off the top.
- Remove the guard from the needle without touching the needle. If the medicament is in a vial, inject into the vial an amount of air equal to the amount of drug to be withdrawn, to help facilitate its withdrawal. Withdraw the correct amount of medicament (Fig. 102). Point the needle up and expel any air in the syringe (Fig. 103).

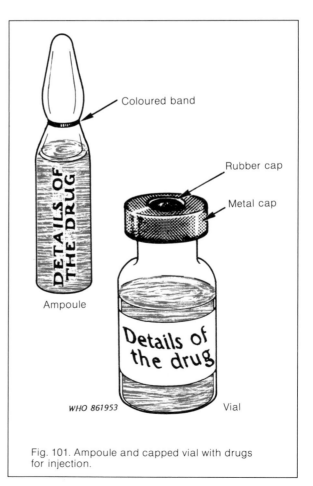

Coloured band

Rubber cap

Metal cap

DETAILS OF THE DRUG

Ampoule

Details of the drug

WHO 861953

Vial

Fig. 101. Ampoule and capped vial with drugs for injection.

---

[1] If disposable syringes are not available, glass syringes and needles, plus forceps, should be sterilized by boiling (see page 122).

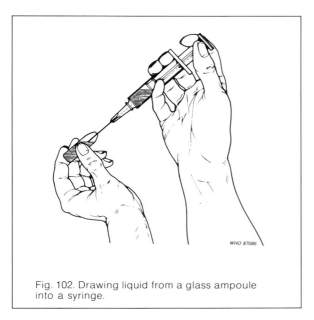

Fig. 102. Drawing liquid from a glass ampoule into a syringe.

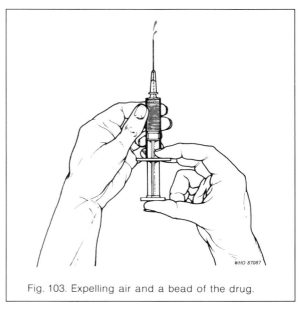

Fig. 103. Expelling air and a bead of the drug.

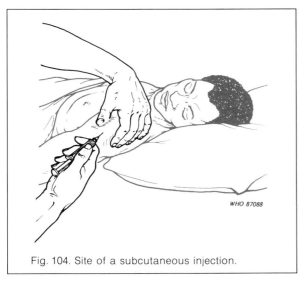

Fig. 104. Site of a subcutaneous injection.

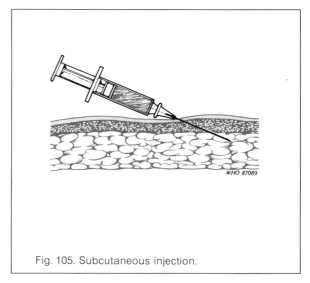

Fig. 105. Subcutaneous injection.

- Select an area on either arm, just below the shoulder on the outer aspect, and cleanse the skin with an alcohol sponge.
- Grasp the skin between the thumb and forefinger (Fig. 104), and firmly and quickly insert the needle at the prescribed angle (see Fig. 105). Draw back gently on the plunger. If no blood appears in the syringe, inject the medicament and withdraw the needle. If blood appears, repeat the procedure at a new site with sterile equipment.

- Rub the site of injection with alcohol.

- Replace the needle in the needle guard, and break the needle and the tip of the syringe (if disposable equipment is used).

Note. Plastic syringes are supplied either with needles attached, or with needles in separate plastic containers. The presterilized syringes and needles are disposable and MUST BE USED ONCE ONLY.

Intramuscular (into a muscle)

This route may be used when a medicament irritates the subcutaneous tissue, or to obtain prolonged action as in the injection of aqueous procaine benzylpenicillin.

When giving an intramuscular injection, this procedure should be followed.

- Assemble the equipment:
  - disposable syringe;
  - disposable intramuscular needle, 1 mm, 5 cm (if no disposable equipment is available, use sterilized glass syringe and needle);
  - medicament;
  - alcohol sponges.
- If the medicament is in a multidose vial, clean the rubber diaphragm on the vial with an alcohol sponge. If the medicament is in an ampoule, score the ampoule with a file and break off the top.
- Remove the guard from the needle without touching the needle. If the medicament is in a vial, inject into the vial an amount of air equal to the amount of drug to be withdrawn, to help facilitate its withdrawal. Withdraw the correct amount of medicament. Expel any air from the syringe.
- Select a site for the injection. The preferred site is in the outer upper quadrant of either buttock (see Fig. 106).
- If the buttock is to be the injection site, stretch the skin with the thumb and forefinger and insert the needle at a right angle to the skin, deeply enough to penetrate the subcutaneous fat and enter the muscle (see Fig. 107).
- Draw back on the plunger of the syringe. If no blood appears, insert the medicament and withdraw the needle. If blood appears, repeat the procedure at another site, using new sterile equipment.
- Rub the site of the injection with an alcohol sponge.

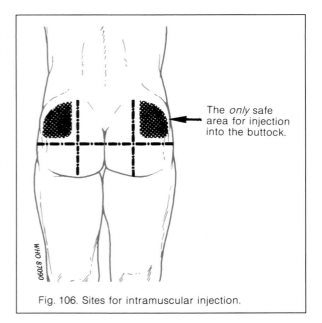

The *only* safe area for injection into the buttock.

WHO 87090

Fig. 106. Sites for intramuscular injection.

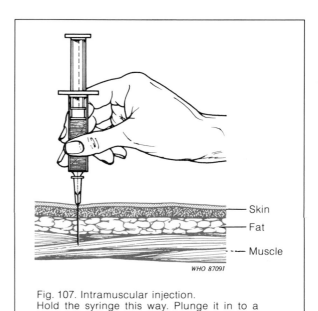

Skin

Fat

Muscle

WHO 87091

Fig. 107. Intramuscular injection.
Hold the syringe this way. Plunge it in to a depth of 2 cm (or more, if the fat layer under the skin is thick).

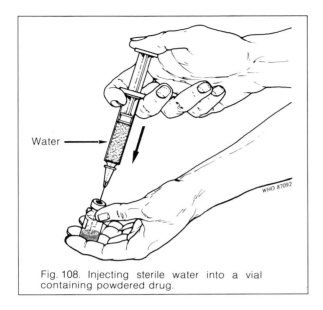

Fig. 108. Injecting sterile water into a vial containing powdered drug.

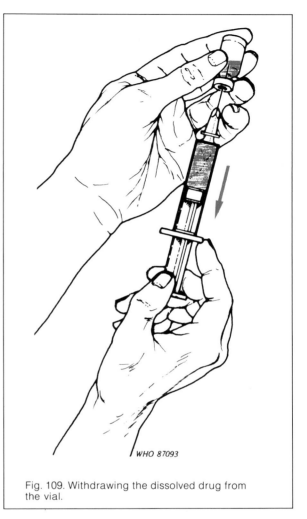

Fig. 109. Withdrawing the dissolved drug from the vial.

Penicillin in powder form. (See note on the use of penicillin, page 308.)

When making up penicillin in powder form for intramuscular injection, open an ampoule of sterile water and prepare the syringe and needle as above *but retaining the needle cover.* Draw up the required volume of water into the syringe in accordance with the instructions on the vial of penicillin. Swab the rubber cap of the penicillin vial with a swab moistened with surgical spirit. Allow the spirit to dry before inserting the needle through the rubber cap. This must be done because spirit inactivates the penicillin. Depress the plunger to inject the water into the vial (Fig. 108).

Withdraw the needle, replace the needle-cover over it, and lay the syringe and needle on the clean towel in a safe place.

Gently shake the vial so that the penicillin is thoroughly dissolved in the water. Reswab the rubber cap, allow the spirit to dry, insert the needle just through the rubber cap, and invert the vial. The penicillin can now be withdrawn from the vial into the syringe (Fig. 109). Then go through the procedure described earlier to get rid of the air before proceeding with the injection (Fig. 103).

Intravenous

The occurence of a case requiring intravenous injections or infusions of fluid on board ship would normally be extremely rare. The use of this technique on board ship by nonmedical personnel could be very hazardous. The main danger is the introduction of air bubbles into the vein.

Only when intravenous fluid infusion is recommended, as a life-saving measure, by a doctor from shore or from another ship, may this technique be used, and then only by somebody properly trained.

Prepare the following equipment:

- sterile, disposable intravenous administration set, with needle;
- tourniquet;
- surgical adhesive tape;
- dextran injection 6%, and sodium chloride, 0.9%, in a sterile bottle or plastic container;
- surgical alcohol, rubbing;
- cotton swabs;
- arm-board (to immobilize the arm).

Then proceed as follows.

- Remove the protective covering and the rubber diaphragm from the bottle of solution.
- Remove the administration set from the package. Remove the protective cover from the spike and insert the spike into the administration site of the bottle.
- Remove the protective cover from the end of the administration set. Invert the bottle so that the solution flows into the drip-chamber and through the tubing.
- When the tubing is completely full of solution, close the slide clamp.
- Attach the needle to the end of the tubing, being careful to maintain asepsis (some administration sets come with the needle already attached).
- Place the stand for the fluid container in a convenient position near the bed.
- Cut several pieces of 5-cm tape.
- Place the patient's arm on a board with a tourniquet under the arm, about 5 cm above the intended site of entry. Secure the arm to the board with a bandage. Apply the tourniquet about 5 cm above the site of the infusion and direct the ends away from the site of the injection.
- Ask the patient to open and close his fist. Observe and palpate for a suitable vein.
- Cleanse the skin thoroughly with an alcohol sponge at and around the site of the injection.
- Use the thumb to exert retractive pressure on the vein and the soft tissue about 5 cm below the intended site of injection.
- Hold the needle at a 45° angle with the bevel up in line with the vein and directly alongside the wall of the vein at a point about 1.5 cm

away from the intended site of venepuncture (see Fig. 110 and Fig. 111). Allow the fluid to enter the needle and drip out. *(This will remove all the air from the tubing, thus preventing an air embolism).* Then clamp the tube and proceed.

- Insert the needle through the skin, lower the angle of the needle until it is nearly parallel with the skin, following the same course as the vein, and insert it into the vein (Fig. 110).
- When blood comes back through the needle, open the pinch clamp and insert the needle 2–2.5 cm further into the vein.
- Release the tourniquet.
- Open the clamp on the infusion tube.
- Tape the needle securely in place (see Fig. 112).
- *Regulate the rate of flow (drops per minute) carefully.* Observe at frequent intervals to prevent variation in flow and to see that flow is stopped before all the solution is administered *(to prevent air from entering the vein).* The number of drops per ml will vary with the administration set, but will be indicated on the packaging. For example, if a set delivers 15 drops per ml and it is desired to administer 1000 ml of solution in a five-hour period, the rate of flow would be about 50 drops per minute.
- Anchor the arm on an arm-board.
- Frequently observe the site of the infusion to detect puffiness of tissue (indicating swelling from infiltration of the solution into the tissues). **If this is present, discontinue the intravenous infusion and restart in another vein, using another sterile needle.**

Eye medication

The eye is a delicate organ, highly susceptible to infection and injury. Although the eye is never free of microorganisms, the secretions of the conjunctiva have a protective action against many that cause disease. For the maximum safety of the patient, solutions and ointments introduced into the conjunctival sac (inside of eyelids) should be sterile, as should the equipment used to introduce them.

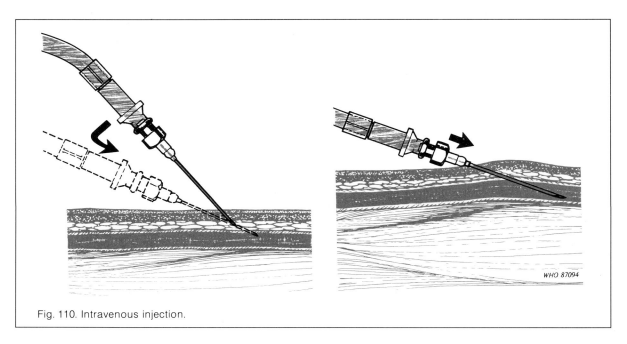

Fig. 110. Intravenous injection.

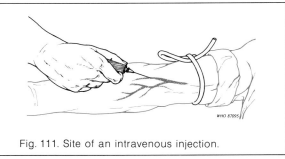

Fig. 111. Site of an intravenous injection.

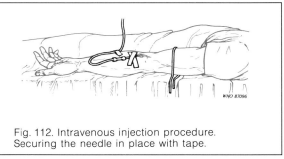

Fig. 112. Intravenous injection procedure. Securing the needle in place with tape.

Because they should not be applied directly to the sensitive cornea, medicaments intended to act upon the eye or the eyelids should be instilled on the lower conjunctival sac (see Fig. 113).

Exposing lower conjunctival sac

To expose the conjunctival sac for administration of eye medication, follow the procedure below.

- Have the patient look up.
- Place a thumb near the margin of the lower lid, immediately below the eyelashes.
- Exert pressure downwards over the bony prominence of the cheek.

- As the lower lid is pulled down and away from the eyeball, the conjunctival sac is exposed.

Instilling eye-drops

Sterile eye-drops are supplied, either in a plastic bottle fitted with a device that will dispense drops when inverted and squeezed or in a bottle fitted with a sterile dropper.

- The person administering the drops should wash his hands prior to instillation of the eye-drops. If the patient's eyes are discharging, sterile cotton balls moistened with sterile 0.9% sodium chloride solution should be in readiness.

- Cleanse the discharge, using moist cotton balls, by wiping the eyelids from the inner to the outer side. Use a new cotton ball for each stroke. If no discharge is present, this step (and the cotton balls) may be omitted.
CAUTION. **Never use dry cotton on the eye.**
- Be sure that the patient is looking up.
- Drop the prescribed number of drops into the pocket formed by the lower lid. Do not allow the dropping device to touch any part of the eye.
- Instruct the patient to close his eye gently and rotate the eyeball to spread the medicament evenly.
CAUTION. **Use only a sterile medicament prepared for eye use.**

Application of eye ointment

Before application of an ointment, the eyelids and the eyelashes should be cleansed of any discharge, as described above (Instilling eye-drops). In applying ointment to the eye, follow the procedure below.

- Hold the tube of eye ointment in an almost horizontal position to control the quantity of ointment applied and to minimize the chance of touching the eyeball or the conjunctiva with the tip (see Fig. 113). About 1–1½ cm of ointment should be extruded from the tube and distributed in the lower conjunctival sac, after exposing the inner surface of the lower lid (by applying two fingers to the cheek).
- Following the application, instruct the patient to close the eyelids and move the eyes. This will spread the ointment under the lid and over the surface of the eyeball.

Conjunctival irrigation

A sterile ophthalmic isotonic irrigating solution in a disposable "squeeze" bottle should be used for irrigation. The procedure is as follows:

- Cleanse any discharge from the eye as described above (Instilling eye-drops).
- Separate the eyelids and, gently squeezing the bottle of irrigating solution, direct the flow from the inner to the outer corner of the eye.

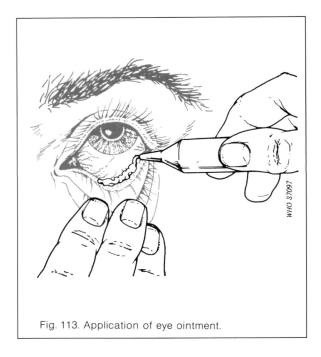

Fig. 113. Application of eye ointment.

Use only sufficient force to produce a continuous flow of the solution.
- Wipe the cheeks with a towel or absorbent tissue.

Ear medication

To prevent discomfort, medicaments for the ear should be warmed before instillation. Do *not* overheat. Ear-drops can best be instilled if the patient lies on his side with the ear to be treated uppermost. Before instilling ear-drops, it may be necessary to use a cotton-tipped applicator to remove secretions from the external ear.

In administering ear-drops, follow the procedure below.

- Straighten the ear canal by gently pulling the ear-lobe upwards and backwards for adults, downwards and backwards for infants and small children.
- Hold the tip of the dropper or inverted dropper-bottle at the opening of the ear and instil a few drops of the medication. Do not insert the dropper or the dropper-bottle into the ear canal.

• Tell the patient to remain in the same position for a few minutes to allow the medicament to remain in contact with the surfaces of the canal and to prevent leakage of drops from the ear.

Infection control

(See also Isolation, page 297)

Asepsis

Asepsis is the absence of disease-producing microorganisms and is generally considered as being of two kinds: *medical asepsis* and *surgical asepsis*. The concepts of medical and surgical asepsis used in this book are defined below.

Medical asepsis

Medical asepsis comprises those practices that attempt to reduce the number of disease-producing microorganisms and hinder their transfer from one person or place to another.

To maintain medical asepsis, the following measures are necessary:

• Wash your hands after every contact with the patient and with the equipment and supplies used in caring for him.

• Provide disposable wipes. When the patient coughs or sneezes, instruct him to cover his mouth and nose, and to turn his head away from others.

• Provide the patient with the necessary material for washing his hands after using the urinal or bedpan.

• All disposable articles taken from an infected patient's room should be sealed in a bag, and that bag in turn sealed in a second bag, using a strong adhesive tape. Infectious articles should be autoclaved or burned.

Surgical asepsis

The term surgical asepsis is used to describe the techniques that protect the patient against infection. These range from the complex technical ritual that is essential in the operating room to the use of sterile dressings in minor wounds.

In the handling of any wound (any break in the skin), the use of a sterile technique is mandatory. Hands should be washed and scrubbed thoroughly. When minor wounds are being dressed, sterile pick-up forceps should be used to handle the sterile dressings.

Do not allow sterile instruments or dressings to come into contact with anything but the wound.

Table 3. Disinfection and sterilization

Item	Means of disinfection or sterilization	Exposure time
smooth, hard-surfaced objects (non-dietary area)	2% cetrimide solution, or 3% aqueous phenolic solution	30 minutes
dietary area: cutlery, dishes, plates, glasses	sodium hypochlorite, 100 mg/litre (100 parts per million) available chlorine (see Annex 5)	30 minutes
	boiling	20 minutes
instruments [a]	3% aqueous phenolic solution, boiling	30 minutes 20 minutes
thermometers [a]	3% aqueous phenolic solution, or 2% cetrimide solution (rinse thoroughly before use)	30 minutes
items entering skin or mucous membranes [b]	autoclaving (sterilization by steam under pressure)	30 minutes at 121°C
environmental surfaces: walls, floors, etc.	3% aqueous phenolic solution, or 2% cetrimide solution	

[a] Must be cleansed with soap and water before disinfection.
[b] It is strongly recommended that all items that will have to enter the skin or be in direct contact with mucous membranes (i.e., injection needles, urinary catheters, suction catheters, etc.) be single-use, disposable items.

Avoid undue talking when treating wounds. Germs in the spray from the nose and throat can contaminate the materials and the wound itself. Presterilized plastic syringes and needles (disposable) are usually supplied for ships. But there may be situations in which only glass syringes are available; these must be sterilized by boiling before use. This will be done in the electric sterilizer. First, the metal plungers should be removed from the glass syringes. Then all parts, along with the injection needles and forceps, should be put into the sterilizer. An ample amount of distilled water is poured into it (if this is not available, previously boiled water can also be used). The syringes should be boiled for not less than 20 minutes; then the water is decanted, special care being taken to see that the glass parts are not broken. Other instruments may also be sterilized in this way, but sterilization by autoclaving is always to be preferred.

Chapter 6
Communicable diseases

Contents

(See also: Trachoma, page 199; Diarrhoea and dysentery, page 188; Food-borne diseases, page 199; Prevention of communicable diseases, page 297; Immunization, page 298.)

Communicable diseases are those that can be transmitted from one person (or animal) to another. There may be direct or indirect transmission to a well person from an infected person or animal — at times through an intermediate animal host, a vector (a mosquito), or the inanimate environment. Illnesses result when an infectious agent invades and multiplies in the host.

The occurrence and spread of disease are determined by an interplay of factors specific to the causative agent, the environment, and the individuals or groups in whom the disease occurs. An epidemic (if many were to fall ill at the same time) could endanger the operation and the safety of the ship. Thus, it is important to know how various diseases are spread, and what measures should be taken to ensure their prevention and control.

Infectious agents

Organisms that produce disease in man range in size from the submicroscopic viruses to the tapeworm, which may attain a length of several metres.

Various groups of infectious agents are listed below, together with some of the diseases they cause.

Bacteria	Sore throat, pneumonia, tuberculosis, syphilis, bacillary dysentery, cholera
Viruses	Common cold, influenza, yellow fever, poliomyelitis, rabies, measles, and viral pneumonia
Rickettsiae	Typhus fever
Protozoa	Malaria, amoebic dysentery
Metazoa	Filariasis, trichinosis, hookworm and tapeworm infections
Fungi	Ringworm and tinea pedis (athlete's foot)

Infectious agents are usually specific in their disease-producing capabilities. Several different organisms can produce diseases that resemble each other clinically (in symptoms and course) and pathologically (in the anatomical changes they cause). For example, the meningococci, tubercle bacilli, and the mumps virus can produce meningitis, which is an inflammation of the membrane that envelops the brain and spinal cord. However, a specific disease, such as tuberculosis, can be caused only by a specific agent — in this case the tubercle bacillus.

Modes of transmission

The spread of disease depends upon the ability of the infecting organism to survive outside its reservoir (source). Transmission of the agent may be either direct or indirect.

Direct transmission

Modes of direct transmission include:

- *Direct contact* with the infected person, as in kissing or sexual intercourse.
- *Droplet spread,* in which an infected person, through sneezing, coughing, or talking, sprays the face of a non-infected person with droplets containing the disease-causing agent.
- *Faecal–oral spread,* in which faecal material from an infected person is transferred to the mouth of a non-infected person, usually by the hands. The hands may be contaminated by touching such things as soiled clothing, bedding, and towels.

Indirect transmission

Indirect transmission of infectious organisms involves vehicles and vectors which carry disease agents from the source to the host.

Vehicles are inanimate or non-living means of transmission of infectious organisms. They include:

- *Water.* If polluted, specifically by contaminated sewage, water is the vehicle for such enteric (intestinal) diseases as typhoid fever, cholera, and amoebic and bacillary dysentery.
- *Milk* is the vehicle for diseases of cattle transmissible to man, including bovine tuberculosis, undulant fever, and streptococcal infections from infected udders. Diseases in which milk serves as the link between man and man include typhoid fever and scarlet fever. Milk also serves as a growth medium for some agents of bacterial diseases.
- *Food* is the vehicle for typhoid and paratyphoid fevers, amoebic dysentery, food infections, and poisoning. To serve as a vehicle, food must be moist, bland (not too acid or alkaline), raw or inadequately cooked, or improperly refrigerated after cooking, as well as having been in intimate contact with an infected source. Virtually any food meeting these requirements may be a vehicle for transmitting organisms that cause disease (see Foodborne diseases, page 199).
- *Air* is the vehicle for the common cold, pneumonia, tuberculosis, influenza, whooping cough, measles, and chickenpox. Discharges from the mouth, nose, throat, or lungs take the form of droplets which remain suspended in the air, from which they may be inhaled. When the moisture in these droplets evaporates, bacteria and viruses form "droplet nuclei" which linger on for a long time to contaminate air, dust, and clothing. The suspended nuclei are sometimes called aerosols. Although such disease agents are usually airborne and enter their hosts by way of the respiratory tract, direct contact by kissing, eating contaminated food, or using contaminated drinking-glasses enables them to enter through the gastrointestinal tract.
- *Soil* can be the vehicle for tetanus, anthrax, hookworm, and some wound infections.
- *Fomites.* This term embraces all inanimate objects, other than water, milk, food, air, and soil, that might play a role in the transmission of disease. Fomites include bedding, clothing, books, even door-knobs and drinking-fountains.

Vectors are animate or living vehicles which transmit infections in the following ways:

- *Mechanical transfer.* The contaminated mouth-parts or feet of some insect vectors mechanically transfer the infectious organisms to a bite-wound or to food. For example, flies may transmit bacillary dysentery, typhoid fever, or other intestinal infections by walking over the faeces of the typhoid or dysentery host and later leaving the disease-producing germs on food.

- *Intestinal harbourage.* Certain insects harbour pathogenic (disease-causing) organisms in their intestinal tracts. The organisms are passed in the faeces or are regurgitated by the vector, and the bite-wounds or food are contaminated. (Examples: plague, typhus fever.)
- *Biological transmission.* This term refers to a vital change (multiplication) in the infectious agent during its stay in the body of the vector. The vector takes in the organism along with a blood meal but is not able to transmit infection until after a definite period, during which the pathogen changes. The parasite that causes malaria is an example of an organism that completes the sexual stages of its life cycle within its vector, the mosquito. The virus of yellow fever also multiplies in the bodies of mosquitos.

Terms used in connection with communicable diseases

A *carrier* is a person who is liable to infect others, either without developing the disease himself or following an attack of it.

A *contact* is a person who may or may not have contracted a communicable disease following either proximity to, or contact with, an infected person.

The *incubation period* is the interval of time that elapses between a person being infected with any communicable disease and the appearance in him of the symptoms and signs of that disease. This period may vary in length from a few hours up to 21 days or longer.

The *isolation period* signifies the time during which a patient suffering from an infectious disease should be isolated from others.

The *segregation period* is the time during which a patient who may be incubating an infectious disease following contact should be segregated from others. The segregation may take the form

of isolation from others in the case of more dangerous infectious diseases, or medical supervision for minor maladies during the incubation period.

The *quarantine period* means the time during which port authorities may require a ship to be isolated from contact with the shore. Quarantine of this kind is seldom carried out except when serious epidemic diseases, such as, for instance, plague, cholera, or yellow fever are present or have recently occurred on board.

Symptoms and signs

Onset

Almost all communicable diseases begin with the patient feeling out of sorts, with a headache and perhaps a slight rise in temperature. This period may be very short, lasting only a few hours (scarlet fever), or more prolonged (diphtheria). In some diseases the onset is mild and there is not much general disturbance of health, whereas in others (e.g., typhus) it is severe and prostrating. During the onset it is often not possible to make a diagnosis.

The rash

The diagnosis of many, but not all, communicable diseases is made easier by the presence of a characteristic rash. In certain diseases (e.g., scarlet fever) the rash is spread evenly over the body, in others it is limited to definite areas. When examining an individual suspected to be suffering from a communicable disease, it is therefore of great importance to strip him completely in order to get a full picture of any rash and its distribution. Many a case has been wrongly diagnosed through failure to do this.

General rules for the management of communicable diseases

Isolation

The principles of isolation are described in Chapter 16 (page 297) and it is only necessary, therefore, to repeat the warning that, if there is the slightest suspicion that someone is suffering from a communicable disease, he should be isolated.

Treatment

Many infectious diseases do not respond to medicines. The essential element in treatment is, therefore, maintaining the patient's strength to fight the infection. This is achieved through good general nursing, and it is important to ensure that the patient does not become dehydrated.

Advice on the specific medical treatment of infectious diseases that respond to treatment is given in the sections on individual diseases. It may also be advisable to administer drugs to offset lowered resistance resulting from the primary infection and thereby prevent the occurrence of secondary infection.

See the sections on nursing a patient in bed (page 98) and on how to reduce a high fever (page 109).

Diet

Diet will very much depend on the type of disease and the severity of the fever. Serious fever is invariably accompanied by nausea, and this will automatically tend to restrict diet to beverages such as water flavoured with lemon juice and a little sugar, weak tea, or any similar alternative that is attractive to the patient. Certainly, nothing richer than diluted milk should be offered until the fever subsides and appetite begins to return. It is then important not to serve rich food immediately, but gradually to progress from bland meals such as steamed fish and boiled potatoes through soups, white meat, and eggs back eventually to a normal diet.

Essential basic rules

- *Isolate* (page 297). If anyone suffers from a temperature without obvious cause it is best to isolate him until a diagnosis has been made.
- *Strip the patient* and make a thorough examination, looking for any signs of a rash, in order to try to establish the diagnosis (page 125).

- *Put the patient to bed,* and appoint someone to look after and nurse him and organize the control of his eating and drinking utensils and their sterilization after use (page 121).
- Give *fluids* in the first instance.
- If the patient's temperature exceeds 39.5 °C make arrangements for *tepid sponging* (page 109).
- Arrange for the use of a bedpan and urine bottle if the patient shows any sign of prostration or if his temperature is high (page 298).
- If the patient is seriously ill and if there is any doubt as to diagnosis, seek RADIO MEDICAL ADVICE, failing which you should consider making for port.
- Treat symptoms as they arise.
- Do not attempt to get the patient up during convalescence if he is feeble, but keep him in bed until the next port is reached.
- *When approaching port,* send a radio message giving details of the case to enable the port health authorities to make arrangements for the isolation of the case and any contacts on arrival.

For the methods used in the prevention and control of communicable diseases on board ship, refer to Chapter 16, page 297.

Anthrax

Incubation period.	1 to 7 days, usually 3
Isolation period.	Until malignant pustule heals and temperature drops to normal

Anthrax is a serious communicable disease common to men and animals. It occurs in man as an infection of the skin (malignant pustule), or as an attack on the lungs or intestines, or as an infection widely spread throughout the body by means of the blood circulation.

Anthrax in man is usually contracted by handling infected animals, skins, hides, or furs. It can also be conveyed by the consumption of infected or insufficiently cooked meat, or by the inhalation of dust containing the bacillus.

Primarily a disease of sheep, cattle, and horses, anthrax occurs most commonly among woolsorters, felt-makers, tanners, and others who work with animals or their products. If cattle or hides are shipped by sea, exposure of crew to anthrax is a possibility.

Symptoms and signs

In most cases anthrax is accompanied by severe symptoms such as fever and prostration. When it appears as a skin infection, it begins as a red itching pimple which soon changes into a blister and, within the next 36 hours, progresses into a large boil with a sloughing centre surrounded by a ring of pimples. Alternatively it may take the form of a painless widespread swelling of the skin which shortly breaks down to form pus in the affected area.

The gastrointestinal form of anthrax resembles food poisoning (see page 199) with diarrhoea and bloody faeces. The lung form develops into a rapidly fatal pneumonia.

Treatment

The patient must be isolated since the discharges from the pustule are infectious and, in pulmonary or intestinal anthrax, aerosols produced by coughing and the discharge from the bowels are extremely infectious.

Should a case of anthrax occur at sea (which is unlikely unless as a result of handling animals, hides, skins, etc.), all dressings or other materials that come into contact with the discharge must be burnt or disposed of in some other way.

The person who is nursing the case should be very careful not to touch with the fingers any of the dressings or sores. Instruments must be used to handle dressings as far as possible, and they must subsequently be sterilized by vigorous boiling for not less than 30 minutes, since the spores of the anthrax bacillus are difficult to kill.

Treatment is not easy on board and the patient should be put ashore as soon as possible. In the meantime the standard antibiotic treatment should be given (page 308).

No attempt at surgical treatment (incision or lancing of the sore) should be made, as it is likely to spread the infection and does no good. Cover the sore with a burn and wound dressing.

Seek advice from a port health authority about the treatment of cargo.

Chickenpox (varicella)

Incubation period.   14 to 21 days
Isolation period.   Until scabs are no longer present

This highly infectious viral disease starts with fever and the patient feeling unwell. Within a day or two the rash appears on the trunk, soon spreading to the face and elsewhere, even sometimes to the throat and palate.

The rash starts as red pimples which quickly change into small blisters (vesicles) filled with clear fluid which may become slightly coloured and sticky during the second day. Within a day or two the blisters burst or shrivel up and become covered with a brownish scab. Successive crops of spots appear for up to 5 days. Although chickenpox is usually a mild disease, the rash is sometimes more severe and secondary infections such as boils or pneumonia occur. Chickenpox is a disease of childhood, but it may also — although rarely — affect adult people.

Treatment

A member of the crew who has had chickenpox, and therefore has immunity, could make a suitable nurse. The patient need not be confined to bed unless his temperature is high but he should be kept in one room. He should be told not to scratch, especially not to scratch his face, otherwise pock marks may remain for life. Calamine lotion dabbed onto the spots will ease the itching.

For fever, acetylsalicylic acid, 600 mg, should be given by mouth, every 3–4 hours (adult patient).

Cholera

Incubation period. 1 to 5 days

Isolation period. 4 to 6 weeks until patient declared free from infection by bacteriological examination (strict isolation necessary)

Cholera is a severe bacterial infection of the bowel which prevails in areas with a low level of environmental sanitation. The disease produces intense purging, muscular cramps, vomiting, and rapid collapse.

Infection occurs principally through drinking contaminated water or eating contaminated food such as uncooked vegetables, fruit, shellfish, or ice cream. Undetected carrier contacts may spread the infection.

Symptoms and signs

Most cases are mild and cannot be differentiated from diarrhoeas of other origin without laboratory help. In a typical severe case the onset is abrupt, the vomiting and purging extreme with the faeces at first bright yellow and later pale and watery, containing little white shreds resembling rice grains. The temperature is below normal, and the pulse rapid and feeble, possibly imperceptible.

The frequent copious watery faeces rapidly produce dehydration. Vomiting is profuse, first of food but soon changing to a thin fluid similar to the water passed by the bowel. Cramps of an agonising character attack the limbs and abdomen, and the patient rapidly passes into a state of collapse.

As the result of loss of fluid, the cheeks fall in, the eyes become shrunken, the nose pinched and thin, and the skin of the face shrivelled.

The body becomes cold and covered with a clammy sweat, the urine is scanty, the breathing rapid and shallow, and the voice is sunk to a whisper. The patient is now restless, throwing his arms about from side to side, racked with muscle cramps induced by loss of salt, and feebly complaining of intense thirst. If high fever is present, the patient suspected of having cholera may actually have malignant malaria (page 135), which can present a similar picture.

This stage may rapidly terminate in death or equally rapidly turn to convalescence, which will be heralded by the cessation of vomiting and purging and the return of warmth to the skin.

Treatment

If there is a suspected case of cholera on board, RADIO MEDICAL ADVICE on treatment should be obtained promptly.

The patient should be isolated and put to bed at once. Every effort should be made to replace fluid and salt loss. Keep a fluid balance chart (page 102). **The patient should be told that his life depends on drinking enough** and he should be encouraged and, if necessary, almost forced to drink sufficient oral rehydration salts (ORS) solution (see Diarrhoea, page 188) until signs of dehydration disappear (in 4–6 hours). Thereafter the patient should drink a glassful of the solution after every stool to replace loss, until diarrhoea stops. If ORS are not available, give fluid either in the form of two 1-g salt tablets dissolved in half a litre of water; or make a mixture of 20 g of sugar, a pinch of salt, a pinch of sodium bicarbonate, and juice from an orange (or from a bottle of fruit juice) in half a litre of water.

Give tetracycline, 500 mg, every 6 hours for 2 days. Give food as soon as the patient feels hungry.

If the patient is severely dehydrated and cannot drink, intravenous 0.9% sodium chloride solution (injection) may prove life-saving. Get RADIO MEDICAL ADVICE before giving this treatment. As a general rule, the amount of fluids given intravenously should equal that already lost through diarrhoea. Start oral rehydration with ORS as soon as possible.

Caution. Cholera is a disease that is transmitted through water and food. If cholera is suspected, the ship's water supply must be thoroughly treated (see Annex 5, page 354) to make sure that it is safe.

Stools and vomited matter should be flushed into the ship's sewage treatment system or retention tank. All articles used by the patient such as dishes, other eating-utensils, bedpans, urinals, bed linen, and towels, must be soaked in a disinfecting solution or boiled (see page 121). All attendants must wear gowns while in the sick-room and their hands must be washed and rinsed in a disinfectant solution (see page 121) after each contact with the patient. Medical attendants must not eat or drink anything while in the patient's room.

The patient's room and his personal effects should be disinfected following the illness. Also any part of the ship that may have been contaminated through contact with the patient, his body excretions, clothing, or other personal effects should be disinfected very carefully.

Cholera is an officially notifiable disease. Regulations require the ship's master, as soon as practicable, to notify local health authorities at the next port of call, station, or stop. The master shall then take such measures as the local health authorities direct to prevent the spread of disease.

Dengue fever

Incubation period.   3 to 15 days, usually 5 to 6 days
Isolation period.   6 days if mosquitos are prevalent

This is an acute viral fever of about 7 days' duration conveyed by a mosquito. It is sometimes called "break-bone fever". It is an incapacitating, painful disease, but is seldom, if ever, fatal. A feature of the disease is its sudden onset with a high temperature, severe headache and aching behind the eyeballs, and intense pain in the joints and muscles, especially in the small of the back. The face may swell up and the eyes suffuse, but no rash appears. Occasionally an itchy rash resembling that of measles, but bright red in colour, appears on the 4th or 5th day of the illness. It starts on the hands and feet from which it spreads to other parts of the body, but remains most dense on the limbs. After the rash fades, the skin dries and the surface flakes.

After about the 4th day the fever subsides, but it may recur some 3 days later before subsiding again by the 10th day.

General treatment

There is no specific treatment for this complaint, but acetylsalicylic acid will relieve some of the pain, and calamine lotion may ease the itching of the rash.

Diphtheria

Incubation period.   2 to 5 days
Isolation period.   2 weeks, provided the antibiotic treatment (see below) is given; sometimes this period may be longer, if the bacteriological examination shows that the patient continues to shed virulent bacilli

Diphtheria is an acute infectious disease caused by bacteria and characterized by the formation of a membrane in the throat and nose. The onset is gradual and starts with a sore throat and fever accompanied by shivering. The throat symptoms increase, swallowing being painful and difficult, and whitish-grey patches of membrane become visible on the back of the throat, the tonsils, and the palate. The patches look like wash-leather and bleed on being touched. The neck glands swell, and the breath is foul. The fever may last for two weeks with severe prostration. Bacterial toxins may lead to fatal heart failure and muscle paralysis.

General treatment

Immediate isolation is essential, as diphtheria is very infectious. Care must be taken to avoid contacts with the patient, who spreads the infection by coughing, sneezing, etc. Eating-utensils and all other articles in contact with the patient should be destroyed (magazines, books, etc.) or sterilized by boiling immediately after use (plates, glasses, etc.). The person who has handled them should wash his hands extremely thoroughly.

Specific treatment

Specific treatment is with diphtheria antitoxin, which should be given at the earliest possible opportunity if the patient can get to medical attention. Standard antibiotic treatment (page 308) should be given to all cases to limit the spread of infection, but it will not neutralize toxin that has already been produced.

Enteric fever (typhoid and paratyphoid fevers)

Incubation period. 7 to 14 days
Isolation period. Variable, i.e., until shown to be free from infection by bacteriological examination (strict isolation recommended)

The term enteric fever covers typhoid and paratyphoid fevers. Enteric fever is contracted by drinking water or eating food that has been contaminated with typhoid germs. Seamen are advised to be very careful where they eat and drink on shore, particularly in ports in the tropics. Inoculation (immunization) gives some protection against typhoid, but not against paratyphoid fever.

The following paragraphs deal in particular with typhoid fever (the paratyphoids are milder and have a shorter course).

The disease may have a wide variety of symptoms depending on the severity of attack. Nevertheless, typhoid fever, however mild, is a disease that must be treated seriously, not only because of its possible effect upon the patient, but also to prevent it spreading to others who may not have been inoculated. Strict attention must be given to hygiene and cleanliness and all clothing and soiled linen must be scrupulously disinfected.

During the first week the patient has fever, feels tired, listless, and apathetic, and may have a persistent headache, poor appetite, and sometimes nose-bleeding. There is some abdominal discomfort and usually constipation. These symptoms increase until he is forced to go to bed. At this stage his temperature begins to rise *in steps* reaching about 39–40 °C in the evenings. For about two weeks it never drops back to normal even in the mornings (see Fig. 114). Any person who is found with a persistent temperature of this kind should always be suspected of having typhoid, especially if his pulse rate remains basically normal (while he has fever). During the second week the lips become crusted,

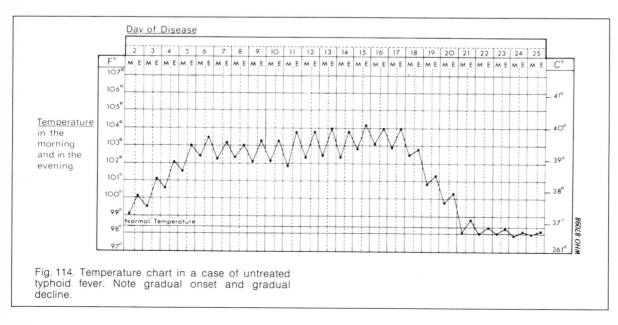

Fig. 114. Temperature chart in a case of untreated typhoid fever. Note gradual onset and gradual decline.

the tongue becomes brown, dry, and sometimes fissured, and the abdomen becomes distended. In 10–20% of cases, from about the seventh day, characteristic rose-pink spots may appear on the lower chest, abdomen, and back; these spots will disappear if pressed with the finger and return when pressure is released. Each spot lasts about 3–4 days and they continue to appear in crops until the end of the second week or later. Search for them in a good light, especially in people with dark skin. The faeces at this time may be loose, foul-smelling, and of a pea-soup colour and consistency. During the second week, mental apathy, confusion, and delirium may occur. In the more favourable cases recovery will then commence; otherwise the patient's condition will continue to deteriorate and may terminate in deep coma and death. Even when the patient appears to be recovering, he may suffer a relapse. There are a variety of complications, but the most dangerous are haemorrhage from, or perforation of, the bowel. If the faeces are found to contain blood at any stage of the disease, the patient must be kept as immobile as possible and put on a milk-and-water diet. If the bowel is perforated, peritonitis (page 220) will set in.

General treatment

Anyone suspected of having typhoid or paratyphoid fever should be kept in bed in strict isolation (page 298), until seen by a doctor. The patient's urine and faeces are highly infectious, as may be his vomit. These should all be disposed of (page 298), and the patient should scrub his hands after using the bedpan. The attendants and others coming into the room should wash and scrub their hands after handling the bedpan or washing the patient, and before leaving the room.

The patient's eating utensils should preferably be disposable, otherwise they should be reserved for him and be sterilized by boiling for at least 10 minutes after use.

The patient should be encouraged to drink as much as possible and a fluid input/output chart should be maintained (see Table 2, page 102). He can eat as much as he wants, but it is best if the food is light and free from items that might irritate the bowel.

Specific treatment

If you suspect somebody has enteric fever, get RADIO MEDICAL ADVICE. Give ampicillin, 500 mg every six hours, for two weeks. With this treatment, the fever and all symptoms should respond within 4–5 days. However, the bacilli may still be present in the bowel and cause ulcerations, so the full course of treatment should be completed.

All cases should be seen by a doctor at the first opportunity. The case notes, including details of the amount of medicine given, should be sent with the patient.

Prevention

Except for regular immunization against typhoid fever (see Immunization, page 298), the most effective means of protection against this disease and other enteric infections, including cholera (see page 128), amoebic dysentery (see page 189), and diarrhoea (see page 188), is avoiding food and drinks that may be contaminated. This is particularly important in many ports in the tropics. When eating on shore in these areas, it may be wise to take boiled meat and rice, and drink tea or coffee; and to avoid taking undercooked seafood, salads prepared from fresh vegetables and fruit, ice cream, and cold drinks, especially if they are served with ice (which may be contaminated).

Erysipelas

Incubation period.   1 to 7 days
Isolation period.   Until temperature and skin are normal

This disease is an acute inflammatory condition of the skin caused by bacteria entering the body through a scratch or abrasion. It commonly occurs on the face, but can arise anywhere.

The onset is sudden with headache, shivering, and a general feeling of malaise. The temperature rises rapidly and may reach 39.5–40.0 °C. The affected area becomes acutely inflamed and red on the 1st or 2nd day of the infection, and the inflammation spreads rapidly outwards with a well-marked, raised, and advancing edge. As the disease advances, the portions of the skin first attacked become less inflamed and exhibit a yellowish appearance. Blisters may appear on the inflamed area, which can be very painful.

General treatment

The patient must be isolated and kept in bed during the acute stage.

Specific treatment

Give the patient procaine benzylpenicillin, 600 000 units, in an intramuscular injection (see precautions regarding giving this medication, page 308), followed by standard antibiotic treatment (page 308).

Acetylsalicylic acid or paracetamol tablets can be given to ease the pain (see page 305 for dosage).

German measles (rubella)

Incubation period.   14 to 21 days, usually 18
Isolation period.   Until 7 days after the appearance of the rash

Although it is always a mild disease, German measles is highly infectious. It has features similar to those of mild attacks of ordinary measles (page 139) or of scarlet fever (page 144).

Usually the first sign of the disease is a rash of spots, though sometimes there will be headache, stiffness and soreness of the muscles, and some slight fever preceding or accompanying the rash.

The rash is quite different from that of measles. In many ways it is like the rash of scarlet fever, but the disease can usually be distinguished at once from the latter, since in scarlet fever the throat is severely inflamed, whereas this is not the case in German measles. The rash lasts from 1 to 3 days and is occasionally followed by peeling of the skin, though this depends to some extent on the intensity of the attack.

The glands towards the back of the neck are swollen and can easily be felt. This is an important distinguishing sign.

General treatment

The patient should be put to bed and kept in isolation until 7 days after the first appearance of the rash.

There is no specific therapy for rubella. Treatment should be symptomatic, the same as for measles (see page 139).

Note. Particular care should be taken to isolate patients with German measles from pregnant women: any pregnant woman on board with a fetus under 17 weeks should see a doctor ashore as soon as possible. If a patient has seen his wife in the last week he should be asked whether his wife might be pregnant. If so, she should be advised to see her doctor.

Glandular fever (gammaherpesviral mononucleosis)

Incubation period.   4–6 weeks
Isolation period.   Until arrival at port

This malady is an acute viral infection which is most likely to affect the young members of the crew. Convalescence may take up to 2 or 3 months.

The disease starts with a gradual increase in temperature and a sore throat; a white covering often develops later over the tonsils. At this stage it is likely to be diagnosed as tonsillitis and treated as such. However it tends not to respond to such treatment and a generalized enlargement of glands occurs. The glands of the neck, armpits, and groin start to swell, and become tender — those in the neck to a considerable extent. The patient may have difficulty in eating or swallowing. His temperature may soar and he may sweat profusely. Occasionally there is jaundice between the 5th and 14th day. Commonly there is a blotchy skin rash on the upper trunk and arms at the end of the first week. Vague abdominal pain is sometimes a feature. A diagnosis of diphtheria may be considered owing to the appearance of the tonsils (page 129), but the generalized glandular enlargement is typical of glandular fever (see Lymphatic inflammation, page 211).

General treatment

The patient should be confined in isolation; he should stay in bed until his temperature has settled and he feels fit to get up. Acetylsalicylic acid or paracetamol should be given to relieve pain and to moderate the temperature. Any antibiotics that have been prescribed to treat the tonsillitis should be discontinued at the end of the treatment period.

There is no specific treatment. If complications arise, get RADIO MEDICAL ADVICE.

Hepatitis, viral

Viral hepatitis is an acute infection that destroys liver cells. There are two forms of the disease presumed to be caused by different viral agents that produce more or less identical symptoms: *viral hepatitis A* (infectious hepatitis) whose virus has a short incubation period (often it can be prevented by injections of immune serum globulin), and *viral hepatitis B* (serum hepatitis) which has a longer incubation period.

Viral hepatitis A (infectious hepatitis, epidemic hepatitis, epidemic jaundice)

Incubation period.	10 to 50 days, commonly about 30 to 35 days
Isolation period.	First 14 days of illness and for at least 7 days after jaundice shows up

Hepatitis A in some patients may be so mild that a correct diagnosis is never made. Most recognized cases last about 2–3 weeks, followed by a prolonged convalescence. Transmission of infection is mainly through close person-to-person contact, via the faecal-oral route. Sudden explosive epidemics usually result from faecal contamination of a single source (e.g., drinking-water, food, milk).

The disease has an abrupt onset with a fever of 37.5–38 °C, severe headache, loss of appetite, vomiting, and abdominal discomfort. The virus is carried to the liver where it multiplies rapidly with widespread destruction of cells. The liver becomes swollen and tender with aching in the centre and upper right abdominal areas, plus acute pain from pressure just below the ribs. At this stage the patient may think he has a touch of intestinal flu that can be ignored. On the contrary, he is suffering from a very infectious acute illness, and 3–7 days after onset he shows a yellowish (jaundiced) colour in the eyes and skin due to an excess of liver bile in the blood. The colour of the urine becomes dark brown because of excess bile in the kidneys, the stools are a pale greyish-white colour, and the breath has a foul sweetish odour.

In some cases the onset resembles an acute attack of influenza, and the patient feels generally ill with severe abdominal pain, prostration, and a temperature that reaches 40.5 °C. The illness will last about 3–4 weeks, after which there will be a slow convalescence during which the patient will be listless and depressed and show little interest in food.

About 50–75% of adults who acquire hepatitis A infection develop jaundice. About 0.5% die during the acute phase.

Early detection and diagnosis of hepatitis A are important. There are no specific diagnostic measures that can be applied on board ship. Differential diagnosis depends on clinical and epidemiological evidence that will exclude other causes of jaundice coupled with fever. Acute hepatitis can be diagnosed in laboratory tests for the presence of antibody to the virus in the infected person's blood.

Treatment

RADIO MEDICAL ADVICE should be obtained. Because hepatitis A may be transmitted through the stools and urine, all excretions must be disinfected. The patient must be isolated and instructed to apply good hygienic procedures after using the bathroom. The virus is excreted in faeces and urine 14–21 days before the appearance of jaundice and for 7–14 days thereafter. The patient's blood is also infectious. There is no specific treatment.

Diet and activity should be adjusted to the clinical condition of the patient. He should be given plenty of fluids. Headache may be relieved by acetylsalicylic acid tablets. A mild laxative such as magnesium hydroxide suspension may be given. A hot-water bottle applied to the sensitive liver area may provide relief. Alcoholic drinks should not be consumed by the patient during the course of the disease and for many months after recovery.

When a member of the crew is known to have hepatitis A, others who have not had the disease should receive immune human serum globulin injections as soon as possible. RADIO MEDICAL ADVICE should be sought on whether this medication can be made available at the next port of call. Those who have been in contact with the infection will receive protection from the globulin for a period of 6–8 weeks. However, its effectiveness depends on how soon after exposure the injection is administered. Disposable inoculation equipment should be used whenever possible.

Viral hepatitis B (serum hepatitis)

Incubation period.	50 to 180 days, usually 80 to 100 days; in post-transfusion hepatitis, it may range from 10 to more than 180 days
Isolation period.	As for viral hepatitis A (see page 133)

Unlike the virus of hepatitis A, the hepatitis B virus is not transmitted through contaminated water or food. Instead it is usually spread from person to person by the use of contaminated hypodermic needles, or medical or surgical instruments, or by the transfusion of blood or blood products from a donor who is a carrier of the virus. Cases have been traced to tattoo parlours.

Transmission can also occur in the family setting and tends to be related to the degree of crowding in the household and the closeness of relationships between individuals. It may occur following the use of shared razors, toothbrushes or towels, or through close personal contact. Hepatitis B virus has been detected in various body fluids, including saliva, semen, and vaginal fluids, so that infection may be spread by kissing or by sexual intercourse, especially homosexual contact.

Hepatitis B is practically identical with hepatitis A except that its incubation period is longer. There are blood tests that can distinguish between the two infections. Symptoms may not occur for 6 months after inoculation. Its onset develops quickly with vague abdominal discomfort, loss of appetite, nausea, and vomiting often leading to jaundice. Severity varies widely from inapparent cases detected only by liver-function tests to cases of extremely rapid development with liver-cell destruction that causes death. Among the patients who develop jaundice, the mortality rate is 1–3%. Approximately 10% of cases develop chronic infection. One-third of carriers of the virus have chronic active hepatitis, which may progress to cirrhosis or cancer of the liver.

Many cases of hepatitis B have been found among drug addicts, teenagers, and young adults who share contaminated hypodermic equipment when they experiment with drugs. The use of illicit drugs and narcotics is extremely perilous and few users are aware of the additional threat of death from serum hepatitis transmitted by inadequately sterilized needles and syringes.

Safe and effective vaccines against hepatitis B have recently become available, and vaccination is recommended for certain high-risk groups and for individuals who have been exposed to the disease through sexual contact with an infected person or through accidental percutaneous exposure. Anyone who has been exposed in these ways should see a doctor at the next port of call.

Treatment

RADIO MEDICAL ADVICE should be obtained.

Disposable inoculation equipment should be used whenever possible. If this is not available, syringes and needles used for the patient should be destroyed and discarded after being autoclaved for 30 minutes.

Influenza

Incubation period.   1–3 days

This is an acute infectious disease caused by a virus inhaled through the nose or mouth. It often occurs in epidemics. The onset is sudden and the symptoms are, at first, the same as those of the common cold. Later the patient feels much worse with fits of shivering, and severe aching of the limbs and back. Depression, shortness of breath, palpitations, and headaches are common, and there may be vomiting and/or diarrhoea.

Influenza may vary in severity. Commonly a sharp unpleasant feverish attack is followed by a prompt fall in temperature and a short convalescence. Pneumonia is a possible complication (page 221).

General treatment

The patient should be watched for signs of pneumonia such as pains in the chest, rapid breathing, and a bluish tinge to the lips. He should be given plenty to drink and a light and nutritious diet if he can manage to eat.

Specific treatment

There is no specific treatment for the uncomplicated case, but the patient may be given 2 tablets of acetylsalicylic acid every 4 hours until his temperature is normal.

Malaria

Incubation period.   Usually 9 to 30 days; with some strains of the parasite there may be a protracted incubation period of 8 to 10 months

Isolation period.   None

Malaria is a dangerous tropical disease manifested by fever, debility, and sometimes coma and death. It is caused by a parasite introduced into the body by the bite of the *Anopheles* mosquito. The malaria-carrying mosquito is highly prevalent in a variety of environments where it breeds by laying eggs in water.

Ports infected with malaria

Ports between latitudes 25°N and 25°S should be regarded as infected or potentially infected with malaria, unless the ship's master has reliable recent information to the contrary. Inquiry should be made of the port authorities immediately on arrival to find out if conditions in the port are such that preventive malaria treatment should be given without delay.

Information on the malaria situation, by country, is published by WHO in *Vaccination certificate requirements and health advice for international travel* (updated and published annually).

Suppression of malaria

The risks of contracting malaria can be very greatly reduced if proper precautions are taken, and the disease can be cured if proper treatment is given. Despite this, there have been instances of several members of a ship's crew suffering attacks of malaria during a single voyage, with severe and even fatal results.

The precautions to take are:

- avoidance of mosquito bites;
- suppression of infection.

Avoidance of mosquito bites

The best way to prevent malarial infection is to take measures to avoid being bitten by mosquitos. For example, while the ship is in a malarious port, the following measures should be taken.

- Persons going on deck or ashore after dusk should wear long-sleeved shirts and trousers to avoid exposing their arms and legs. Insect repellent may be smeared on body areas not covered by clothing.

- Living accommodation should be either protected by mosquito screening or air-conditioned. Doors should be kept closed after dusk.
- Additional protection for living or working accommodation may be provided by the use of commercially available electric insecticide dispensers, using plaques of synthetic pyrethroid insecticide.
- Where surrounding spaces cannot be made mosquito-proof, mosquito nets should be fixed over beds. Impregnation of the bed-nets with synthetic pyrethroid insecticide increases their effectiveness; the impregnation remains effective for six months.
- To prevent mosquitos breeding on board, no pools of stagnant water should be allowed to develop on deck or in life-boats.

Suppression of infection (drug prophylaxis)[1]

The fewer the bites, the smaller the risk of infection, but even when the greatest care is exercised it will seldom be possible entirely to prevent mosquito bites either on shore or in the ship. For this reason, in all cases when a ship is bound for a malarial port, masters (in addition to taking all possible measures to prevent mosquito bites) should control infection by giving antimalarial drugs systematically to all the ship's company.

Suppressive treatment (drug prophylaxis) does not necessarily prevent a person from contracting a malarial infection. Attacks will, however, be held in abeyance, malaria fever should not develop, and deaths from malaria should not occur. Suppressive treatment is highly recommended when exposure to malaria is likely, as it is able to prevent attacks of malignant tertian malaria, which may threaten life if specific treatment is not started very early in the attack. Suppressive treatment should begin at the latest on the day of arrival in the malarious area. It would be preferable, however, to start one week earlier, in order to assess the individual's tolerance to the drug. The drug must be taken with unfailing regularity to be effective; even one

single omission of the weekly dose interrupts the protective effect. Suppressive treatment should be continued for 6 weeks after leaving the malarious area; this will prevent both emergence of the disease in the individual and reintroduction of falciparum malaria into areas freed from the disease. In benign tertian malaria, which is a relapsing type and much less dangerous, the antimalarial drug suppresses the disease by killing the parasites in the circulating blood that are responsible for the fever; unfortunately it does not destroy latent parasites residing in the liver. These may give rise to relapses many weeks or months after treatment has been discontinued.

All crew-members should therefore be warned that they have been exposed to possible malaria infection and that, if they fall ill at a later date, they should inform their doctor without delay that they may be suffering from malaria contracted abroad.

The recommended choice of drugs to be used for suppressive treatment is likely to change with:
- changes in the response of the parasites to drugs;
- availability of new drugs; and
- new information concerning the toxicity of drugs.

WHO publishes annually updated recommendations concerning drug protection against malaria in the booklet *Vaccination certificate requirements and health advice for international travel*; the booklet also contains information on the risk of malaria and on the occurrence of drug resistance. It is recommended that the latest edition be carried on board. It is obtainable at the addresses given on page 371 of this book. The following recommendations are based upon the 1988 edition, which should be consulted for further information.

In countries where there is a risk of malaria but no chloroquine resistance, the recommended regimen for adults is 300 mg of chloroquine (base) weekly (i.e., 2 tablets of chloroquine phosphate, 250 mg) always on the same day of the week.

In countries where there is chloroquine resistance, the following is recommended for adults:

---

[1] See also Dispensing medicines, page 305.

chloroquine, as above, *plus* proguanil 200 mg daily.

Antimalarial tablets, especially chloroquine, should be taken after food and washed down by a glass of water.

Babies and children, as well as adults, need to be protected from malaria. Tablets and syrup are available for children. Alternatively, an adult's tablet can be broken and the required amount may be administered crushed and mixed with honey or jam or milk. Chloroquine, proguanil, and their association, can be given safely to infants, young children, and pregnant women. The recommended doses for children can be expressed in fractions of the adult dose, as follows:

Age (years)	Fraction of adult dose
<1	1/8
1–4	1/4
5–8	3/8
9–11	1/2
12–14	3/4
>15	1

Precise accuracy in dividing the tablet is not essential, but the fragment of the tablet given should not be less than the amount specified.

Chloroquine phosphate or sulfate should not be used on a regular basis for years at a time without medical advice, as prolonged use may cause serious eye defects.

Persons weighing more than 70 kg should receive a weekly dose of 5 mg of chloroquine (base) per kg of body weight.

Features of the illness

Malaria mainly occurs either as a relatively mild, benign or *intermittent* fever, or as a severe, malignant, or *remittent* fever. A fever is intermittent when the temperature rises above and falls to the normal, or below it, every 24 hours or less frequently; a remittent fever is one in which the temperature goes well above the normal and then drops more than 2 °C but does not return to normal before rising again.

Mild, benign, or intermittent fever

The patient may experience slight fever, headache, generalized aching and chilliness for several days before the onset of attacks of severe fever at regular intervals. Typically, an attack in a person not protected by drugs and who has never before been exposed to malaria is marked by three distinct stages.

- *A brief cold or shivering stage lasting for up to an hour.* The patient feels cold and shivers excessively. General aching, nausea, and vomiting are frequent. The skin is cold to the touch. The temperature rises rapidly, and it may be as high as 40 °C, accompanied by a rapid weak pulse.
- *A hot or fever stage lasting for two hours or longer.* The skin becomes hot and dry, although the temperature usually does not rise further. Nausea and vomiting continue with marked thirst. A severe headache develops. The pulse is rapid and strong, and the breathing rate increases.
- *A sweating stage usually lasting for two hours.* A profuse drenching sweat begins, and with it the symptoms ease, then disappear, and the temperature falls to normal. The patient often falls into a deep sleep, after which he may feel quite well again until the next attack.

An attack may occur regularly either once each day or once every 2–3 days.

Severe, malignant, or remittent fever

The disease pattern in this more dangerous form of malaria is similar to that in the milder benign, intermittent type but is much less clear cut. Usually, the patient is ill throughout with no intervals of well-being. The following differences are to be found in the three stages of each attack.

- The *cold stage* may be very short and without much shivering. The temperature rises quickly from the start.
- The *hot stage* is considerably prolonged (6–12 hours or more).

- The *sweating stage* is not marked. The skin may be moist throughout.
- The interval between attacks is shorter (2–12 hours).
- Each attack may last from 12 to 24 hours.
- The temperature is remittent, or may remain continuously high, and it rarely comes down to normal even temporarily.

Compared with the milder benign form of malaria, there is a marked tendency in this severe malignant type towards the sudden development of one or other of the following dangerous complications, which may kill the patient with great suddenness.

- The temperature may suddenly become excessively high, rising to 42 °C, or even 43 °C.
- The patient may fall into a coma or experience mental confusion followed by coma.
- There may be kidney failure, indicated by a decreasing urine output despite normal fluid intake.
- There may be severe abdominal symptoms such as generalized abdominal discomfort, incessant vomiting, or frequent bowel actions resembling dysentery or cholera. Collapse may follow, sometimes with a low temperature.
- Fever may be accompanied by progressively increasing anaemia.
- Pulmonary oedema may be present.

Indications for antimalarial treatment

Malaria cannot be diagnosed with certainty without laboratory facilities. However, on board ship, the following should be treated as if they had the disease:

- anyone who has visited a potentially malarious area between 9 and 30 days previously and develops *either* a fever that passes through the cold, hot, and sweating stages (as described above) *or* a fever that cannot be explained otherwise;
- anyone known to be subject to attacks of malaria who develops a fever that cannot be explained otherwise.

These indications for treatment apply even if the patient has been taking regular drug prophylaxis, because, as already stated, no drug prophylaxis is 100% effective.

If the illness is not malaria, little or no harm will result from the treatment. However, failure to treat a person who has malaria can result in a death which could have been prevented by early treatment. If in doubt get RADIO MEDICAL ADVICE. If the ship is in port, a doctor should *always* be consulted.

General treatment

The patient should be put to bed in a cool place and his temperature, pulse, and respiration taken every 4 hours. If the body temperature rises to 41 °C or over, cooling should be carried out (page 109). The temperature should be taken and recorded at 15-minute intervals until it has been normal for some time. Thereafter, four-hourly recording should be resumed until the attack has definitely passed.

A simple fluid balance chart should be maintained (see Table 2, page 102), and urine specimens examined daily for haemoglobin (see Urine, page 107).

Conscious patients should be given ample fluid by mouth.

If the symptoms are severe or the patient is unconscious, obtain RADIO MEDICAL ADVICE on treatment.

Specific treatment

When malaria is strongly suspected, a blood film should be made for later examination and treatment started immediately.

Taking a blood slide

1. Obtain a sterile disposable lancet or, if one is not available, a sterile disposable syringe needle.
2. Take two microscope slides and clean them by polishing with a clean cloth.
3. Wash the patient's left thumb, dry it, swab it with surgical spirit and allow to dry.

4. Wrap a small length of bandage round the base of the thumb so as to congest the blood vessels.
5. Wash your own hands and then lightly stab the ball of the patient's thumb with the lancet or needle. A drop of blood will ooze out.
6. Take one of the microscope slides and *lightly* bring it into contact with the drop of blood near one end of the slide. Remove the bandage from the base of the thumb.
7. Place the slide on a flat surface and hold it steady with your left hand. Take the other slide, inclined at an angle of 45°, in your right hand (Fig. 115) and place the edge in the centre of the drop of blood, allowing the blood to spread along the width of the slide.
8. With a steady continuous movement draw the inclined slide along the length of the other slide to make a fine smear.
9. Allow the smeared slide to dry, then place it in an envelope labelled with the date and the patient's name.

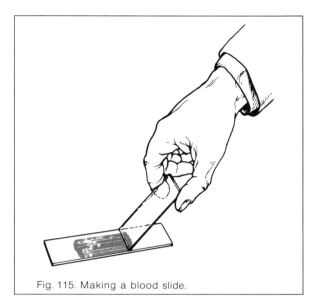
Fig. 115. Making a blood slide.

Medication

In view of the fact that malaria resistant to chloroquine occurs in most malarious areas, it is advisable to begin treatment with a drug that will reliably reduce the number of parasites in the blood, and improve the clinical condition of the patient. The only universally available drug for this purpose is quinine. The use of quinine is associated with a number of side-effects, which are not dangerous, but may be annoying to the patient. These include ringing in the ears, dizziness, blurred vision, and occasionally, nausea and vomiting. The severity of these side-effects varies from patient to patient, but is generally not sufficient to indicate a need to stop treatment.

The patient should be given two 300-mg quinine tablets, three times daily for 7 days. If he is unable to take the tablets because of persistent vomiting or loss of consciousness, quinine may be given by intramuscular injection at the same dosage used for oral administration, i.e., 600 mg, three times daily. As soon as the patient is able to swallow and retain oral drug, the dose should be given by mouth rather than by injection. For intramuscular injection, the upper outer quadrant of the buttock is preferred (see p. 116). Pain at the injection site is usual. Sterile abscess is an uncommon complication of intramuscular quinine administration.

Note. All patients who have been treated for malaria or suspected malaria must see a doctor at the next port for examination of the blood film collected earlier, and because further medical treatment may be necessary. It must be noted that malaria acquired in certain parts of the world may not be fully cured by the administration of quinine alone, and that another drug may have to be administered subsequently in order to prevent recurrence of the infection.

Measles

Incubation period. 8–13 days
Isolation period. 7 days after disappearance of rash

Measles, an acute viral disease, rarely occurs in adults. Individuals who are undernourished and have a low degree of natural or acquired immunity usually suffer more seriously from any attack. (See also the sections on German measles (page 132) and scarlet fever (page 144).)

The disease starts like a cold in the head, with sneezing, a running nose and eyes, headache, cough and a slight fever (37.5 °C–39 °C). During the next two days the catarrh extends to the throat, causing hoarseness and a cough. A careful examination of the mouth during this period may reveal minute white or bluish white spots the size of a pin's head on the inner side of the cheeks. These are known as "Koplik spots" and are not found in German measles or scarlet fever.

The rash appears on the 4th day when the temperature increases to 39–40 °C. Pale rose-coloured spots appear first on the face and spread down to cover the rest of the body. The spots run together, taking on a mottled blotched appearance. The rash deepens in colour as time goes on. After 4 or 5 days the rash begins to fade, starting to do so at the place where it first appeared. The skin may peel.

The main danger of measles is that the patient may get bronchitis (page 177), pneumonia, (page 221) or middle ear infection (page 194).

General treatment

This highly infectious disease is conveyed to others when the patient coughs or sneezes. The attendant should be careful in disposing of the patient's sputum and paper tissues. Used handkerchiefs should be boiled.

The patient should be isolated for 7 days after the rash has gone and he should be kept in bed until his cough has completely cleared.

There is no specific treatment, but the patient may be given acetylsalicylic acid tablets or paracetamol. Calamine lotion may be applied to soothe the rash.

Meningococcal meningitis (cerebrospinal fever)

Incubation period. 2 to 10 days, usually 4
Isolation period. If penicillin (or another antibiotic) given, 24 hours; if not, until patient is declared free from infection by bacteriological examination

This acute infectious fever inflames the membranes surrounding the brain and spinal cord, which may be damaged in consequence. Unless treatment is prompt and effective, the outcome is often fatal. The disease occurs in epidemics which often affect closed communities such as ships. The infection enters by the nose and mouth.

The disease starts suddenly with fever, considerable headache, and vomiting. Within the first day the temperature increases rapidly to 39 °C or more, and the headache becomes agonizing. Vomiting increases, and there is general backache with pain and stiffness in the neck. Intolerance of light (photophobia) is usually present. Sometimes a rash resembling flea-bites appears on the trunk. The patient may be intensely irritable and resent all interference, or may even be delirious.

As the meningitis develops the patient adopts a characteristic posture in bed, lying on the side with the back to the light, knees drawn up, and neck bent backwards. Unconsciousness accompanied by incontinence may develop.

Individual cases may vary in the speed of onset, severity, and clinical features.

If meningitis is suspected, get RADIO MEDICAL ADVICE. It will help the doctor if the results of the two following tests are available.

The neck-bending test

Ask the patient to attempt to put his chin on his chest. If he has meningitis, he will be unable to do so, because forward neck movement will be greatly restricted by muscle contraction. Try to increase the range of forward movement by pushing gently on the back of his head. The neck muscles will contract even more to prevent the movement, and the headache and backache will be increased.

The knee-straightening test

1. Bend one leg until the heel is close to the buttock.
2. Move the bent leg to lie over the abdomen.
3. Keeping the thigh as in 2, try to straighten the lower leg.

If the patient has meningitis, it will be impossible to straighten the knee beyond a right angle and attempts to force movement will increase the backache.

General treatment

The patient should be nursed in a quiet, well-ventilated room with shaded lights, in strict isolation (page 298). He should be accompanied at all times by an attendant who should wear a face mask to cover his nose and mouth. Tepid sponging (page 109) may be necessary and pressure points should be treated to prevent bedsores (see page 99). Usually the patient has no appetite, but he should be encouraged to drink plenty of fluid. Ice-packs may help to relieve the headache.

Specific treatment

Give 2.4 million units of procaine benzylpenicillin sterile suspension at once, followed by the same dose of this drug at six-hourly intervals. After 3 days, again get RADIO MEDICAL ADVICE regarding further treatment (whether oral penicillin may be given).

The headache should be treated with acetylsalicylic acid tablets.

The patient should be placed under the care of a doctor as soon as possible.

Mumps (epidemic parotitis)

Incubation period. 12–26 days, usually 18
Isolation period. 10 days after swelling of the glands

Mumps is a viral disease which causes swelling of the salivary glands in front of the ears and around the angle of the jaw. The swelling usually affects both sides of the face, though it may affect only one side, and it may make it difficult for the patient to open his mouth. The onset is usually sudden and may be accompanied by a slight fever. The swelling gradually diminishes and should disappear entirely in about 3 weeks.

About 20% of men with mumps get *orchitis,* which is the swelling of one or both testicles; when this occurs it usually happens on the 10th day. While very painful, orchitis does not usually result in infertility, and never causes impotence.

General treatment

The patient should be put in standard isolation for 10 days after the swelling of the glands, and stay in bed for 4–5 days or until the fever is no longer present. He can be given acetylsalicylic acid tablets or paracetamol to relieve the symptoms, but there is no specific treatment.

If he develops painful swollen testicles (orchitis) he should stay in bed. The scrotum should be supported on a pad or small pillow. The testicles should also be supported if the patient gets out of bed for any reason.

Plague

Incubation period. 2 to 6 days
Isolation period. Until declared free from infection by a doctor (strict isolation is necessary)

Plague is an extremely serious bacterial disease transmitted to man by the bite of fleas that normally live on rats. There are three types of plague, each with different manifestations:

- *bubonic,* in which buboes—swollen lymph glands—are one of the predominant signs; the involved nodes are swollen and tender and may suppurate;
- *pneumonic,* in which bronchopneumonia is the predominant symptom; this type of plague is very virulent and dangerous to people around the patient; airborne particles of sputum containing plague bacteria will infect contacts and cause localized outbreaks or devastating epidemics, with high mortality;
- *septicaemic,* which is generally rapidly fatal.

The attack of plague begins suddenly, with severe malaise, shivering, pains in the back, and sometimes vomiting. The patient becomes prostrated and suffers mental confusion; delirium and convulsions may follow. His temperature reaches about 38 °C.

About the 2nd or 3rd day, the characteristic buboes develop, most commonly in the groins. A bubo may be as large as a hen's egg. It may soften, discharge pus, and form an abscess.

In a case of suspected plague on board ship, RADIO MEDICAL ADVICE must be sought at once.

General treatment

The patient should be isolated. He should rest in bed, be encouraged to drink as much fluid as possible and have a very light diet. If the abscesses burst they should be dressed with a simple dressing, **but they must not be lanced.** Soiled linen and bed clothes should be boiled for 10 minutes or destroyed.

Specific treatment

Give tetracycline, 500 mg, every six hours for 5 days, or longer, according to RADIO MEDICAL ADVICE. Ice-packs applied to the enlarged glands may be comforting. The patient should remain on complete bed rest to avoid strain on the heart during convalescence.

Prevention of spread

Plague is a disease subject to the International Health Regulations, and should be notified as soon as possible, by the ship's master, to the local health authorities at the next port of call, station, or stop. Measures should be taken to prevent the spread of the disease as the local health authority directs.

The patient should be sent to a medical facility ashore at the first opportunity after consultation with the port health authorities.

The quarters in which the patient is nursed, as well as those occupied by the rest of the crew, should be treated with insecticide powder and dust so as to ensure the destruction of any fleas.

The pus in bubonic plague and the sputum in pneumonic plague are both highly infectious, and in pneumonic plague infection can be spread by coughing and sneezing. The nursing attendant should therefore wear a mask and protective clothing in the sick-room.

Warning. Dead rats found aboard ship should be picked up with tongs and placed in a plastic bag, which should be sealed with string, weighted, and thrown overboard; if the ship is in port, the dead rats should be disposed of in the manner required by the port health authorities.

Poliomyelitis (infantile paralysis)

Incubation period.	Commonly 7 to 12 days, with a range of from 3 to 21 days
Isolation period.	Not more than 7 days in hospital conditions; isolation is of little value in home or ship conditions because the spread of infection is greatest when symptoms first appear

Poliomyelitis is an acute viral disease that occurs chiefly in children, most cases occurring in the first three years of life. Adults are usually immune. Today the disease is wholly preventable by immunization (see page 298).

Poliomyelitis may start with no recognizable symptoms, or it may resemble a head cold with fever, vomiting, and irritability. These symptoms last about 3 days, and the temperature may rise to 40 °C. From the 4th to the 10th day, the condition will seem to be clearing. However, the symptoms return with headache, stiff neck and back, and deep muscle pains. Varying degrees of paralysis follow. The parts most commonly affected by paralysis are the limbs, shoulders, diaphragm, and chest muscles, but any muscle or group of muscles may be affected, in a process that is completed within a day or two. Thereafter improvement is gradual, either with complete recovery or some degree of paralysis.

Treatment

No specific treatment is effective. When polio-myelitis is suspected, RADIO MEDICAL ADVICE should be obtained. The patient should be put to bed, and isolation nursing technique observed. In paralysis of body parts, hot moist heat may be applied, coupled with gentle, active or passive motion as soon as the patient can tolerate it.

If urine is retained, a catheter should be inserted (see page 110). Stools and urine are infectious, so bedpans and urinals should be disinfected (see page 121).

Rabies (hydrophobia)

Incubation period.	10 days to 12 months (usually under 4 months), though the period will be shorter for patients bitten about the head and those with extensive bites
Isolation period.	Duration of the illness

Rabies is an acute infectious viral disease that is almost always fatal. When a rabid mammal bites humans or other animals, its saliva transmits the infection into the wound, from where it spreads to the central nervous system. Rabies is primarily an infection of wild animals such as skunks, coyotes, foxes, wolves, raccoons, bats, squirrels, rabbits, and chipmunks. The most common domestic animals reported to have rabies are dogs, cats, cattle, horses, mules, sheep, goats, and swine. It is possible for rabies to be transmitted if infective saliva enters a scratch or fresh break in the skin.

The development of the disease in a bitten person can be prevented by immediate and proper treatment. Once symptoms of rabies develop, death is virtually certain to result. Thus prevention of this disease is of the utmost importance.

Domestic animals that bite a person should be captured and observed for symptoms of rabies for 10 days. If symptoms do not develop, the animal may be assumed to be non-rabid. If the animal dies or is killed, its head, undamaged,

should be sent promptly, under refrigeration but not frozen, to a public health laboratory. Any wild animal that bites or scratches a person should be killed at once and the head kept under refrigeration during transportation to a public health laboratory.

Rubber gloves should be worn by the attendant for protection against infective saliva when the head is being prepared for laboratory examination. Then the gloves should be washed thoroughly with disinfectant solution and boiled in the sterilizer for five minutes before discarding. Finally the attendant's hands should be washed with disinfectant solution.

Treatment

As soon as an individual aboard ship is known to have been bitten by a dog or other possibly rabid animal, RADIO MEDICAL ADVICE should be obtained at once. Usually suspected cases are sent ashore to obtain the expert treatment and nursing care needed to prevent the disease. If it is determined that rabies prevention measures will be started aboard ship, it must be decided how the necessary medicaments will be put aboard.

Immediate local care should be given. Vigorous treatment to remove rabies virus from the bites or other exposures to the animal's saliva may be as important as specific antirabies treatment. Free bleeding from the wound should be encouraged. Other local care should consist of:

- thorough irrigation of the wounds with soap or detergent water solution;
- cleansing with 1% cetrimide solution;
- if recommended by radio, giving an antibiotic to prevent infection;
- administering adsorbed tetanus toxoid, if indicated.

Suturing of bite wounds should be avoided.

Prevention

When abroad, seamen should keep away from warm-blooded animals especially cats, dogs, and other carnivores. It is strongly advised that pets should not be carried on board ship as these may become infected unnoticed, through contact with rabid animals in ports.

Scarlet fever

Incubation period.   1 to 3 days
Isolation period.   Until all throat and nasal symptoms have disappeared, 14 days in uncomplicated cases

Scarlet fever is not often contracted by adults. It has features similar to those of measles (page 139) and German measles (page 132).

The onset is generally sudden and the temperature may rise rapidly to 40 °C on the first day. With the fever, the main early symptom is a sore throat, which in most cases is very severe. The skin is hot and burning to the touch. The rash appears on the second day and consists of tiny bright red spots so close together that the skin assumes a scarlet or boiled lobster-like colour. It usually appears first on the neck, spreading very rapidly to the upper part of the chest and then to the rest of the body. An area around the mouth may be clear of the rash. The tongue is at first covered with white fur and, when this goes, it becomes a very bright red (strawberry colour). The high fever usually lasts about a week. As the rash fades, the skin peels in circular patches.

The danger of scarlet fever arises from the complications associated with it, such as inflammation of the kidneys (test the urine for protein once a day, page 107), inflammation of the ear due to the spread of infection from the throat (page 192), rheumatism (page 222), and heart disease (page 203). These complications can be avoided by careful treatment of the disease.

General treatment

The patient must stay in bed and be kept as quiet as possible. He should be isolated, as the disease is very infectious—the infection coming from the inflamed throat and nose. The patient can be given acetylsalicylic acid tablets to relieve the pain in the throat, which may also be helped if he takes plenty of cold drinks. He can take such food as he wishes.

Specific treatment

Give the patient 600 000 units of procaine benzylpenicillin in an intramuscular injection (see the precautions regarding giving penicillin, page 308), followed after 12 hours by standard antibiotic treatment (see page 308).

Tetanus (lockjaw)

Incubation period.   4–21 days, usually 10
Isolation period.   Until landed

Tetanus is caused by the infection of a wound by the tetanus germ which secretes a powerful poison (toxin). The germ is very widespread in nature, and the source of the wound infection may not always be easy to trace. Puncture wounds are particularly liable to be dangerous and overlooked as a point of entry. In most countries inoculation against the disease usually begins in childhood, but it is necessary to have further periodic inoculations to maintain effective immunity. Fortunately the disease is very rare on board ship.

The first signs of the disease may be spasms or stiffening of the jaw muscles and, sometimes, other muscles of the face, leading to difficulty in opening the mouth and swallowing. The spasms tend to become more frequent and spread to the neck and back, causing the patient's body to become arched. The patient remains fully conscious during the spasms, which are extremely painful and brought on by external stimuli such as touch, noise, or bright light. The patient is progressively exhausted until heart and lung failure prove fatal. Alternatively, the contractions may become less frequent and the patient recovers.

Treatment

The patient should be isolated in a darkened room as far as possible from all disturbances.

If a case of tetanus should develop aboard ship, prompt evacuation to an appropriate medical facility is indicated. The patient must have constant nursing care, and the utmost quiet is essential to prevent the exhausting painful spasms.

There will be a need for treatment with sedative and muscle-relaxant drugs such as diazepam injection, 5 mg. RADIO MEDICAL ADVICE should be obtained for specific drugs and dosage, both aboard ship and during evacuation to a medical facility.

During a convulsion, the jaws should be separated with a pencil wrapped in gauze to keep the patient from biting his tongue. A liberal fluid diet should be given, if tolerated; otherwise no attempt should be made to give fluids or food by mouth.

Prevention

A person can be protected (immunized) against tetanus by injections of adsorbed tetanus toxoid. Every seaman should obtain his primary immunizations and booster shots as required (see also Immunization, page 298, and General care of wounds, page 67). All seafarers employed on board a ship carrying horses, cattle, or hides must have their tetanus immunity status checked (whether they were fully immunized in childhood and when they received the last booster dose of the vaccine). If necessary, a booster dose of tetanus toxoid must be given to any crew-member not yet protected against the disease.

Tuberculosis (TB, consumption)

This infectious disease is caused by the tubercle bacillus. Although the lung (pulmonary) disease is the most common, TB bacteria may attack other tissues in the body: bones, joints, glands, or kidneys. Unlike most contagious diseases, tuberculosis usually takes a considerable time to develop, often appearing only after repeated, close, and prolonged exposures to a patient with the active disease. A healthy body is usually able to control the tubercle bacilli, unless the invasion is overwhelming or resistance is low because of chronic alcoholism, poor nutrition, or some other weakening condition.

The pulmonary form of the disease is spread most often by coughing and sneezing.

A person may have tuberculosis for a long time before it is detected. Symptoms may consist of nothing more than a persistent cough, slight loss of weight, night sweats, and a continual "all-in" or "tired-out" feeling that persists when there is no good reason for it. More definitive signs pointing to tuberculosis are a cough that persists for more than a month, raising sputum with each cough, persistent or recurring pains in the chest, and afternoon rises in temperature.

When he reaches a convenient port, a seaman with one or more of these warning signs should see a physician.

Treatment

Every effort should be made to prevent a man who has active tuberculosis from going to sea, since this would present a risk to the crew's health as well as his own.

The treatment of tuberculosis by medication will not usually be started at sea, since the disease does not constitute an emergency.

To prevent the spread of tuberculosis, every patient with a cough, irrespective of its cause, should hold disposable tissues over his mouth and nose when coughing or sneezing and place the used tissues in a paper bag, which should be disposed of by burning.

The medical attendant should follow good nursing isolation techniques (see Isolation, page 297). No special precautions are necessary for handling the patient's bedclothes, eating utensils, and personal clothing.

Tuberculosis control

A tuberculosis control programme has three objectives: (1) to keep individuals with the disease from signing on as crew-members; (2) to locate those who may have developed the disease while aboard ship and initiate treatment; and (3) to give preventive treatment to persons at high risk of developing the active disease. The first objective can be achieved by periodic, thorough physical examinations including chest X-rays and bacteriological examination of sputum.

To identify those who might have developed active tuberculosis, a chest X-ray should be taken and a medical evaluation including bacteriological examination of sputum requested when in port, if a crew-member develops symptoms of a chest cold that persist for more than two weeks.

Also, when any active disease is discovered, survey should be made of close associates of the patient and others in prolonged contact with him. Such persons are regarded as contacts and are considered at risk for the disease; they should be given a tuberculin test and chest X-ray when next in port. If they develop symptoms, full medical examination, including bacteriological examination of sputum, should be requested.

Yellow fever

Incubation period. 3 to 6 days
Isolation period. 12 days, only if the mosquito vectors (*Aedes aegypti*) are present in the port or on board

This is a serious and often fatal disease caused by a virus that is transmitted to humans by a mosquito. The disease is endemic in Africa from coast to coast between the south of the Sahara and Zimbabwe, and in parts of Central and South America.

Symptoms and signs

The severity of the disease differs between patients. In general, from 3 to 6 days after being bitten the patient fluctuates between being shivery and being too hot. He may have a fever as high as 41 °C, headache, backache, and severe nausea and tenderness in the pit of the stomach. He may seem to get slightly better, but then, usually about the 4th day, he becomes very weak and produces vomit tinged with bile and blood

(the so-called "black vomit"). The stomach pains increase and the patient is constipated. The faeces, if any, are coloured black by digested blood. Bleeding may occur from gums and nostrils. The eyes becomes yellow (jaundice) and the mind may wander. After the 5th or 6th day the symptoms may subside and the temperature may fall. The pulse can drop from about 120 per minute to 40 or 50. This period is critical, leading to recovery or death. Increasing jaundice and extreme scantiness, or lack, of urine are unfavourable signs. Protein in the urine occurs soon after the start of the illness, and the urine should be tested for it (page 107).

General treatment

The patient must go to bed and stay in a room free from mosquitos.

The patient must be encouraged to drink as much as possible; fruit juices are recommended.

If there is a case of suspected yellow fever on board ship, RADIO MEDICAL ADVICE should be obtained. As soon as practicable, the ship's master should notify the local health authorities at the next port of call that there is a suspected case of yellow fever on board. He should then take such measures for prevention of spread of the disease as the authorities direct.

Prevention

Travellers to yellow fever areas should be inoculated against the disease. Many countries require a valid International Certificate of Vaccination against Yellow Fever for those who are going to, or have been in or passed through, such areas. See also the note on avoidance of mosquito bites in the section dealing with malaria (page 135), and the section on immunization (page 298).

CHAPTER 7

Sexually transmitted diseases

Contents

(See also: Viral hepatitis B, page 134)

The following diseases are, or can be, transmitted by sexual contact: gonorrhoea, chlamydial infections, chancroid, genital herpes, syphilis, chlamydial lymphogranuloma, granuloma inguinale, genital warts, pubic lice, scabies, viral hepatitis B (see page 134), acquired immunodeficiency syndrome, trichomoniasis, candidiasis, and bacterial vaginosis.

Sexually transmitted diseases in sailors are generally acquired through unprotected casual and promiscuous sexual contacts, often with prostitutes.

The most common symptoms of sexually transmitted diseases include discharge, redness and swelling of the genitalia, genital ulcers, lymph node enlargement, warts, and the presence of lice or mites on or in the skin. In some sexually transmitted diseases a single organ is affected, while in others the infection spreads throughout the body.

Clinical and laboratory facilities are necessary for accurate diagnosis of sexually transmitted diseases. Since such facilities are not likely to be available on board ship, the medical attendant can make only a presumptive diagnosis, based on rough clinical criteria. If the ship is more than one day from port, the medical attendant should start antibiotic treatment immediately when a sailor is thought to be suffering from a sexually transmitted disease. The subjective and objective symptoms, treatment, and response to treatment should be carefully recorded.

On arrival in port, the patient should be referred as soon as possible to a specialist who can perform the appropriate diagnostic tests and, if necessary, give additional treatment.

If possible, all sexual contacts of the patient should be traced and told to seek medical advice.

In case of any doubt concerning diagnosis or treatment, RADIO MEDICAL ADVICE should be obtained.

Urethritis and urethral discharge

Urethritis is characterized by a discharge from the orifice of the urethra, a burning sensation and pain on urination, or an itch at the end of the urethra. Urethritis may be caused by the gonococcus (gonorrhoea) or by various other organisms, as described below.

Gonococcal urethritis tends to produce more severe symptoms than non-gonococcal urethritis. The incubation time of gonococcal urethritis can range from 1 to 14 days, but is usually 2–5 days. The discharge is generally abundant, yellow, creamy and purulent (see Fig. 116).

Non-gonococcal urethritis can be caused by a variety of bacteria; in some cases, no causative organism can be found. The discharge in non-gonococcal urethritis is usually scanty, watery, mucoid or serous.

In men, a careful distinction must be made between urethritis and balanitis or posthitis, in which there are secretions from the glans penis and the prepuce (see p. 149). Wearing disposable gloves, carefully retract the prepuce to determine the origin of the discharge or secretions.

In women, the same organisms that cause urethritis can cause infection of the cervix of the uterus and the urethra. In more than 60% of women with such infections, there are no visible symptoms. In the remaining cases, the principal sign is an increase in the vaginal discharge (see also Vaginal discharge, page 154).

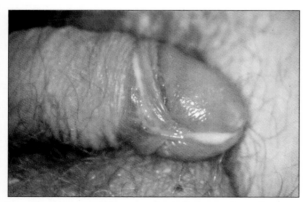

Fig. 116. Creamy, yellow, purulent discharge from the urethra, as seen in gonococcal urethritis.

Associated infections

Rectal infection

The organisms that cause urethritis can also infect the rectum. These infections are seen in women and homosexual men, and result from secondary infection from vaginal discharge or from rectal intercourse with an infected partner. The main symptoms are a discharge of pus, sometimes mixed with blood, and itching around the anus.

Conjunctivitis

Male and female patients with urethritis may also develop an infection of the conjunctivae of the eye.

Treatment

It is not generally possible to make a definitive diagnosis of the cause of urethritis without laboratory facilities. Treatment must therefore be effective for both gonococcal and non-gonococcal infections, and must take account of the facts that the patient may be infected with more than one type of organism, and that some strains of gonococcus are resistant to penicillin.

Patients should be given *either* an intramuscular injection of 2 g of spectinomycin hydrochloride *or* 10 sulfamethoxazole/trimethoprim tablets (400 mg/80 mg) in one dose daily, for 3 days. Either treatment should be followed by a course of doxycycline, one 100-mg capsule or tablet twice daily for 7 days.

This treatment should be effective for all urethral and rectal infections. If the patient also has conjunctivitis, 1% tetracycline ointment should be applied to the eye 3 times daily for one week. About one week after completion of treatment, the patient should attend a specialist clinic to verify that he is no longer infected.

All patients should be advised to have blood tests for syphilis once a month for four months.

Swollen scrotum

A swollen scrotum can be defined as an increase in volume of the scrotal sac, accompanied by oedema and redness. It is sometimes associated with pain (or a history of pain), urethral discharge, and a burning sensation on urination (see Urethritis and urethral discharge, page 148). The swelling of the scrotum is usually confined to one side.

Among ships' crews most cases of swollen scrotum are caused by inflammation of the epididymis, produced by sexually transmitted organisms. Such a cause should be strongly suspected in patients with urethral discharge or a recent history of it. The onset of epididymitis is often acute, but in some cases, it may develop over 24–48 hours. There may initially be an "unusual sensation" in the scrotum, which is rapidly followed by pain and swelling. The pain is of a dragging, aching nature.

This condition must be distinguished from testicular twisting (see p. 232). In the latter case, the testis can become non-viable within 4–6 hours of onset of vascular obstruction. This condition occurs most frequently in children and is very rarely observed in adults over the age of 25. The presence of a history of urethritis would exclude the diagnosis. In cases of testicular twisting the testicle is often slightly retracted and elevation of the scrotum does not decrease the pain. This condition needs urgent referral. Other conditions that may lead to scrotal swelling include trauma (injury), incarcerated or strangulated inguinal hernia, tumours, tuberculosis, and mumps.

Balanitis and posthitis

Balanitis is an inflammation of the glans of the penis, and posthitis is an inflammation of the prepuce. The two conditions may occur simultaneously (balanoposthitis). Lack of good hygiene, in particular in uncircumcised males, is a predisposing factor, as is diabetes mellitus.

In balanitis and balanoposthitis, a mild to profuse superficial secretion may be present. This must be carefully distinguished from urethral discharge. Wearing disposable gloves, retract the prepuce in order to determine the origin of the secretion.

Other signs include itching and irritation, causing considerable discomfort. Sometimes, the penis is swollen and retraction of the prepuce may be painful. Redness, erosion (superficial defects), desquamation of the skin of the prepuce, and secretions of varying aspects and consistency can be observed.

Treatment

The glans of the penis and the prepuce should be washed thoroughly with water three times daily. After washing, the penis should be bathed in warm potassium permanganate solution (the solution should have a faint pink colour). Dry carefully and apply 2% miconazole nitrate cream. If there is no improvement within one week, the patient should be referred to a specialist ashore. Patients with recurrent balanitis or balanoposthitis should be tested for diabetes.

Genital ulcers

Genital ulcers are a common reason for consultation, in particular in tropical countries. If not treated appropriately serious complications may arise from some of these conditions. Ulcers may be present in a variety of sexually transmitted diseases, including chancroid, genital herpes, syphilis, chlamydial lymphogranuloma, and granuloma inguinale.

The prevalence of these diseases varies according to geographical area. In Africa and South-East Asia, for instance, chancroid is the most common cause of genital ulcers, whereas in Europe and the USA, herpes genitalis is most common. Chlamydial lymphogranuloma and granuloma inguinale are much less common, and occur mainly in specific areas of the tropics. Chlamydial lymphogranuloma is endemic in West Africa and South-East Asia, while granuloma inguinale is prevalent in east Africa, India, certain parts of Indonesia, Papua New Guinea, and Suriname. Each of these diseases is described in more detail in the following pages.

Patients with one of these diseases usually complain of one or more sores on the genitals or the adjacent area. If the ulcer is located on the glans penis or on the inside of the prepuce, uncircumcised males may complain of penile discharge or of inability to retract the prepuce. In females, ulcers may be situated on the vulva, in which case the patient may complain of a burning sensation on urination.

Disposable gloves should be worn when examining the ulcers. The medical attendant should note the number and the characteristics of the lesions and the presence of lymph node swellings in the groin. Painless, indurated lesions can generally be attributed to syphilis; painful sores that bleed easily are attributable to chancroid; vesicular lesions that develop into superficial erosions or small ulcerations probably indicate herpes infection. Double infections are not uncommon. However, the clinical symptoms are often not sufficiently discriminatory to enable a definite diagnosis to be made without the help of laboratory tests. Knowledge of the relative importance of each disease in the area is crucial for a specific therapeutical approach. The recommended regimen is therefore aimed at curing the most frequently encountered diseases, chancroid and syphilis. (There is as yet no cure for genital herpes.)

Treatment

Give simultaneously: 2.4 million units of benzathine benzylpenicillin, in one dose, intramuscularly, and 2.0 g of spectinomycin hydrochloride, in one dose, intramuscularly. If the patient is allergic to penicillin, give 2.0 g of spectinomycin hydrochloride, in one dose, intramuscularly, followed by tetracycline hydrochloride, 500 mg, by mouth, 4 times a day for at least 2 weeks.

When patients with syphilis are treated with penicillin, the so-called Jarisch-Herxheimer reaction may occur (see Syphilis, pages 152–153). Fluctuating buboes should be aspirated. Bedrest should be advised for patients suffering from very painful genital ulcerations and lymph node swelling, and for those feeling severely ill.

As soon as treatment has started, patients should no longer be regarded as infectious and no special hygienic measures need to be applied. On arrival at the next port patients should be referred to a specialist together with all relevant information concerning their medical history.

Chancroid

Chancroid, almost always acquired during sexual intercourse, is caused by a bacillus. The incubation period (the time following the infecting contact to the initial appearance of symptoms) is short, usually averaging 3–5 days. The lesions are usually only seen in men; in women, clinical lesions are rare, but ulcers may be located in the vagina. The first lesion usually appears as a small inflamed bump, soon forming a blister or pustule, which breaks down within 2–3 days to become a very painful ulcer.

The classic chancroid ulcer (primary lesion) is superficial and shallow, ranging from a few millimetres to 2 cm in diameter. The edge usually appears ragged and is surrounded by a red zone. The base of the ulcer is covered by a necrotic exudate (see Fig. 117) and bleeds easily. In contrast to the syphilitic chancre, the lesion is soft, and extremely painful and tender.

In males the most frequent sites of infection are the inner and outer side of the prepuce and the groove separating the head from the shaft of the penis.

About 1–2 weeks after the appearance of the primary lesion, the glands in the groin become

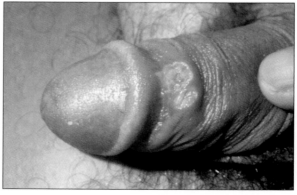

Fig. 117. Chancroid ulcer: necrotic, ragged, coalescent penile ulcer with a red border.

enlarged, painful, and tender (buboes—see Lymphatic inflammation, p. 211). At first, the swellings appear hard and matted together, but they soon become painful and red. Some time later, the lymph nodes may enlarge, become fluctuant, and discharge pus.

Treatment

Give the patient *either* an intramuscular injection of spectinomycin hydrochloride, 2.0 g, *or* two tablets of sulfamethoxazole/trimethoprim (400 mg/80 mg) twice a day for 5 days *or* two 250-mg tablets of erythromycin, 4 times daily for 7 days. If the buboes persist or become fluctuant, **RADIO MEDICAL ADVICE** should be sought.

Genital herpes

Genital herpes is caused by a virus; there are two types of this virus, type 1 and type 2. Type 1 causes herpes of the face. Genital herpes is caused by type 2 in more than 80% of cases and by type 1 in the remaining cases.

The disease can follow an asymptomatic course, the virus being harboured in the urethra without producing symptoms. Usually, however, genital herpes in men appears as a number of small vesicles on the penis (see Fig. 118), scrotum, thighs, or buttocks. The fluid-filled blisters are usually painful, but sometimes produce only a tingling sensation. Within a day or two the blisters break, leaving tiny open sores (see Fig. 119) which take 1–3 weeks to heal. Regional lymph glands near the site of infection may react by becoming swollen and tender.

In most cases, a clinical diagnosis can be made on the basis of the appearance of the lesions, in particular at the blister stage. At specialized clinics, laboratory tests may be used to confirm the diagnosis.

After the sores are healed, the virus remains dormant in the body. Weeks or months later, there may be recurrence of the active infection. These recurrent attacks tend to become less fre-

quent with time and to be less severe than the inital attack, and the lesions tend to heal more quickly.

Treatment

A definite cure for genital herpes is not yet available. Lesions should be kept clean by washing the affected sites with soap and water, followed by careful drying. Analgesics may be given to reduce discomfort.

If you are in any doubt about whether the diagnosis of genital herpes is correct, the patient should be managed as described under Genital ulcers, page 149.

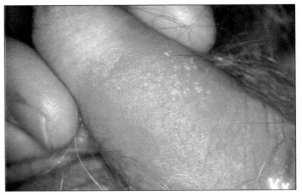

Fig. 118. Genital herpes: redness and small blisters on the shaft of the penis.

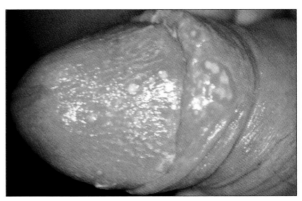

Fig. 119. Genital herpes: multiple erosions with a necrotic exudate on the head of the penis and prepuce.

Syphilis

Syphilis is caused by a spirochaete which enters the body through the mucous membranes of the genitals, rectum, or mouth, or through small cuts or abrasions in ordinary skin.

The clinical course of syphilis is usually divided into three stages. The lesions of the primary and secondary stages are usually painless and cause little disability. They may heal without treatment, and the disease can lie dormant in the body for several years. In the late stages syphilis can cause serious damage to the brain, spinal cord, heart, and other organs.

The first stage, primary syphilis, is characterized by the presence of a chancre at the point where the spirochaetes enter the body. There is a delay of 10–90 days (average 3 weeks) after contact before the onset of any visible sign of infection. Following the appearance of the initial chancre, there can be an additional delay of a few weeks before the serological (blood) tests for syphilis will become positive. The typical chancre occurs in the groove separating the head from the shaft of the penis (see Fig. 120). However, a chancre may occur anywhere on the body where there has been contact with an infected lesion. Such lesions are usually single, but there may be more than one. The primary chancres are often smooth and clean-looking on the surface. Sometimes the lesion ulcerates and leave a reddish sore with the base of the ulcer covered by a yellow or greyish exudate. Unless there is a concomitant infection with other bacteria or with herpesvirus, the ulcer will be painless. The lesion has a characteristic firmness (like cartilage) when felt between the thumb and forefinger (gloves must be worn).

Often there will be one or more rubbery, hard, painless, enlarged lymph nodes in one or both groins, or in other regions if the chancre is extragenital (see Lymphatic inflammation, page 211). In the presence of a secondary infection, the nodes may be tender. Usually these lesions will heal spontaneously within 6 weeks. At the chancre stage, the patient is highly contagious.

The secondary stage of syphilis usually develops about 6–8 weeks after appearance of the pri-

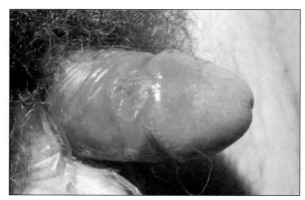

Fig. 120. Primary syphilis: hard chancre with clear base in the coronal groove of the penis.

mary chancre. In fact, the primary syphilitic chancre may still be present at the time of onset of the secondary stage. However, the secondary stage may be the first manifestation, occurring some 10–14 weeks after the infected contact. The most consistent feature of secondary syphilis is a non-itching skin rash, which may be generalized in the form of small, flat or slightly elevated pink spots, which gradually darken to become dark red in colour. They may be particularly localized on the palms, soles, or genital areas. A less frequently encountered sign is patchy loss of scalp hair. Patients with secondary syphilis may complain of malaise (not feeling well), headache, sore throat, and a low-grade fever (38.5 °C). The presence of these symptoms plus a generalized rash and/or a rash involving the palms and the soles, which does not itch, and is associated with enlarged small lymph nodes in the neck, armpits and groins, should arouse suspicion of secondary syphilis. Other signs of the secondary stage may be the occurrence of moist sores, particularly in the genital area, or of flat, moist warts in the anogenital region. It should be noted that moist lesions of secondary syphilis are teeming with spirochaetes and are thus highly infectious. In the untreated patient the diagnosis is confirmed by dark-field microscopic examination of the lesions and by a blood test for syphilis.

The symptoms of the secondary stage will eventually disappear without treatment. The disease then enters the latent (hiding) phase, before reappearing as tertiary syphilis many years later.

Treatment

Patients with suspected syphilis should be given 2.4 million units of benzathine benzylpenicillin in a single dose, administered intramuscularly. If the patient is allergic to penicillin, give *either* 500 mg of tetracycline hydrochloride by mouth, 4 times a day for 15 days *or* 500 mg of erythromycin by mouth, 4 times a day for 15 days. The patient should be referred to a specialist clinic at the next port of call.

Caution. When treated with penicillin, about 50% of patients with primary or secondary syphilis will develop the so-called Jarisch-Herxheimer reaction, which usually appears 6–12 hours after the injection. This reaction is characterized by fever, chills, joint pain, increased swelling of the primary lesions, or increased prominence of the secondary rash. It is caused by the sudden destruction of a great number of spirochaetes and should not give rise to alarm. Analgesics may help to reduce the symptoms.

Chlamydial lymphogranuloma

Chlamydial lymphogranuloma is a systemic disease of venereal origin. The incubation time ranges from 4 to 21 days. The primary lesion is usually an ulcer, a vesicle, a papule or a pustule, not more than 5–6 mm in size and often located on the groove on the head of the penis in the male patient. Commonly single, the lesion is painless, transient, and heals in a few days without scar formation. In most cases, the patient does not even notice this primary ulcerative lesion. After the lesion has healed, the commonest symptom in heterosexual men is acute swelling of the lymph nodes in the groin, often on one side only. The swelling starts as a firm hard mass, which is not very painful, and usually involves several groups of lymph nodes. Within 1–2 weeks, the glandular mass (bubo) becomes attached to the skin and subcutaneous tissue and painful fluctuation occurs, followed by formation of pus. Not all buboes become fluctuant, some evolving into firm masses. The inguinal ligament sometimes divides the matted glands into an upper and a lower part, which is the characteristic "sign of the groove". Perforation of a bubo may occur, whereupon pus of varying aspect and consistency will be discharged. Ultimately scarring will occur.

If not treated, chlamydial lymphogranuloma can produce severe anatomical changes in the urogenital and rectal regions.

Treatment

Rest in bed is essential for patients with chlamydial lymphogranuloma, because continued activity will prolong the inflammatory process, discomfort, and period of recovery. An ice-bag should be applied to the inguinal region for the first two or three days of treatment to help relieve local discomfort and tenderness. Thereafter, local application of continuous heat from a hot-water bottle will get rid of the inflammation.

The patient should be given *either* 500 mg of tetracycline hydrochloride, 4 times a day, for at least 2 weeks, *or* 100 mg of doxycycline by mouth, twice daily for at least 2 weeks *or* 500 mg of erythromycin by mouth, 4 times daily, for at least 2 weeks. Fluctuating buboes require aspiration. If the bubo persists, RADIO MEDICAL ADVICE should be sought.

Granuloma inguinale

Granuloma inguinale is an infectious bacterial disease, with insidious onset. The sites usually affected are the genitals, the groin, the upper legs next to the groin, and the perianal and oral regions. The incubation period ranges from 17 to 50 days.

The earliest cutaneous lesion may be a papule or a nodule, which ulcerates, producing a single, enlarging, beef-like, velvety ulcer, or a coalescence of several ulcers. The typical ulcer in this disease is a raised mass, looking more like a growth than an ulcer. It has a smooth, elevated edge, sharply demarcated from the surrounding skin. There is no lymph node swelling and the general health of the patient is good. If not treated, the lesions may extend to adjacent areas of the body.

The diagnosis can usually be made on the basis of the typical clinical picture. At specialized clinics microscopic examination of crushed tissue smears is used to confirm the diagnosis in the untreated patient.

Treatment

The patient should be given *either* 2 tablets of sulfamethoxazole/trimethoprim (400 mg/80 mg) twice a day, by mouth, for at least 2 weeks, *or* tetracycline hydrochloride, 500 mg, 4 times a day for at least 2 weeks. The patient should be referred to a specialist clinic at the next port of call.

Lymph node swelling

Lymph node swelling is the enlargement of already existing lymph nodes. It is unusual for lymph node swelling to be the sole manifestation of a sexually transmitted disease. In most cases, inguinal lymph gland swelling is accompanied by genital ulcers, infection of the lower limbs, or, in a minority of cases, severe urethritis. The swelling may be accompanied by pain and may be on one or both sides. Pain and/or fluctuation can sometimes be evoked by palpation. The lymph node swelling may be regional (for instance in the groin in the presence of genital ulcers, etc.) or may involve more than one region (for instance in the case of secondary syphilis or acquired immunodeficiency syndrome).

The prepuce of patients suffering from lymph node swelling should always be retracted during examination in order to detect genital ulcers or scars of genital ulcers.

The sexually transmitted diseases that cause lymph node swelling, and the corresponding clinical characteristics of the swelling, are shown in Table 4.

Treatment

The patient should be treated as described under Genital ulcers, page 149. If no improvement is noted within one week, RADIO MEDICAL ADVICE should be obtained.

Table 4. Sexually transmitted diseases causing lymph node swelling

Disease	Characteristics of swelling
Chancroid	Painful, tender, sometimes suppurating
Genital herpes	Tender
Primary syphilis	Rubbery, hard, painless, regional
Secondary syphilis	Rubbery, hard, painless, generalized
Chlamydial lymphogranuloma	Matted, sometimes painful, sometimes suppurating, often divided by inguinal ligament
Acquired immunodeficiency syndrome	In general painless, generalized

Vaginal discharge

Sexually transmitted diseases in women often produce an increase in the amount, or a change in the colour or odour of, vaginal secretions. Vaginal discharge is probably the most common gynaecological complaint. It may be accompanied by itching, genital swelling, a burning sensation on urination, and lower abdominal or back pain.

Various infections can produce such symptoms.

Trichomoniasis is a very common disease, particularly in tropical areas. It is characterized by a sometimes foul-smelling, yellow, or green foamy discharge.

Vaginal candidiasis is also a very common disease throughout the world. It is characterized by a white, curd-like discharge, vulvar itching, and sometimes a red and swollen vulva and vagina.

Bacterial vaginosis is very common, particularly in promiscuous women. In general, there is no itch. The typical discharge is a grey, sometimes foamy, fishy-smelling paste.

Other infections, e.g., gonorrhoea, may produce a white or yellow, watery or purulent discharge.

Infection with herpesvirus usually produces painful lesions (redness, blisters, ulcers) on the vulva.

It should be remembered that more than one infection may be present at a time.

Treatment

In a situation without gynaecological examination facilities and in the absence of laboratory equipment the following practical approach should be followed. First the patient should be treated for trichomoniasis and/or bacterial vaginosis (treatment A). If the condition does not improve, this treatment should be followed by an anti-gonococcal and anti-chlamydial treatment regimen (treatment B). If the symptoms still persist, an anti-candidiasis treatment (treatment C) should follow, or the patient should be referred to a specialist at the next port of call.

Treatment A

Give 2.0 g of metronidazole, by mouth, in a single dose, followed by 500 mg of metronidazole by mouth, twice daily for the next 6 days.

Caution. Metronidazole should not be given to pregnant women. Patients should abstain from alcohol during treatment.

Treatment B

Give one of the treatments described under Urethritis and urethral discharge, page 148.

Treatment C

Miconazole nitrate 2% vaginal cream should be inserted high up in the vagina, using an applicator, once daily (preferably just before the patient goes to bed) for 1 week.

Pelvic inflammatory disease

Pelvic inflammatory disease is a general expression covering various pelvic infections in women, caused by microorganisms, which generally ascend from the lower genital tract (vagina, cervix) and invade the mucosal surface of the uterus, the fallopian tubes, and the peritoneum.

Pelvic inflammatory disease, caused by sexually transmitted pathogens, is a major cause of infertility and chronic abdominal pain, and may result in ectopic pregnancy. A vigorous approach to treatment is therefore justified.

The symptoms include mild to severe lower abdominal pain on one or both sides associated with fever and vaginal discharge (see Vaginal discharge, page 154).

The use of an intrauterine device often promotes the development of pelvic inflammatory disease. It should be noted that it is difficult to diagnose pelvic inflammatory disease without appropriate gynaecological and laboratory investigations; moreover, it is difficult to differentiate this disease from other causes of acute abdominal pain, e.g., appendicitis (see Fig. 122, p. 161).

Treatment

In a case of suspected pelvic inflammatory disease, RADIO MEDICAL ADVICE should be obtained.

Drugs regimens of choice are *either* spectinomycin hydrochloride, 2.0 g, administered intramuscularly, *or* sulfamethoxazole/trimethoprim (400 mg/80 mg), 10 tablets daily in one dose, by mouth, for three days. Either treatment should be followed by a course of doxycycline, one 100-mg capsule or tablet twice daily for 10 days in combination with metronidazole, 1.0 g, by mouth, twice daily, for 10 days.

Caution. Metronidazole should not be given to pregnant women. Patients should abstain from alcohol during treatment.

Genital warts

Genital warts are caused by a virus, and occur most frequently in young adults. In male patients, warts may be present on the penis, around the anus, and in the rectum. In females, the usual sites of infection are the vulva, the area surrounding the anus, and the vagina. Warts are soft, flesh-coloured, broad-based or pedunculated lesions of variable size. They may occur singly, or several may coalesce to form a large mass, often with a cauliflower-like appearance. Small warts cause little discomfort, but large genital or anal warts are embarassing and uncomfortable to the patient and are liable to ulcerate; secondary infection and bleeding may then occur. Diagnosis is usually made on clinical grounds.

Treatment

There is no appropriate treatment that can be given on board ship. The patient should be referred to a specialized clinic at the next port of call.

Pubic lice

Pubic lice are nearly always sexually transmitted. The infection has become endemic in many countries, usually affecting young adults. The main symptom is moderate to severe itching, leading to scratching, redness, irritation and inflammation. The lice may be observed as small brown spots in the groin and around the genitals and anus (see Fig. 121). The nits attached to the hairs may be seen with the aid of a magnifying glass.

Treatment

Lindane cream, 1%, should be applied to the affected areas (pubic area, groin, and perianal region) at 8-hour intervals over a period of 24 hours. The patient should take a shower immediately before each application. At the end of the 24-hour period, the patient should again shower, and put on clean clothes.

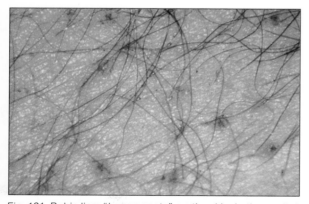

Fig. 121. Pubic lice: "brown spots" on the skin, in the genital area.

Scabies

Scabies, caused by a mite, is now recognized as a sexually transmitted disease in industrialized countries. The most common symptom is itching, particularly at night. The lesions are roughly symmetrical.

The usual sites of infection are the fingerwebs, sides of the fingers, wrists, elbows, axillary folds, around the female breasts, around the umbilicus, the penis, the scrotum, buttocks and the upper part of the back of the thighs.

With the naked eye, only papules, excoriations and crusts may be seen. Using a magnifying glass, it is possible to detect the burrows of the mites.

Diagnosis is usually made on the basis of the clinical picture. At specialized clinics microscopic examination of skin samples can be performed, to detect the female scabies mite and her eggs.

Treatment

A thin layer of lindane cream, 1%, should be applied to the entire trunk and extremities and left for 8–12 hours. At the end of this period, the patient should take a shower or a bath, and change his clothes and bed linen.

Acquired immunodeficiency syndrome

The acquired immunodeficiency syndrome (AIDS), recognized as a disease in 1981, has become a major public health concern throughout the world. In western Europe and north America, the disease has been observed mainly in male homosexuals, while in central, eastern and southern Africa and in some countries in the Caribbean, it is seen primarily in heterosexuals. Other groups at risk are recipients of blood or blood products, (e.g., people with haemophilia), intravenous drug abusers, and partners or offspring of infected persons.

This condition is caused by the human immunodeficiency virus (HIV), which has been found in various body fluids of infected persons. Nearly all infections appear to result from contact with semen, vaginal and cervical secretions, blood, or blood products of a person infected with the virus. There is no evidence that the virus is transmitted through casual contact with an infected individual, e.g., at the workplace. The risk of infection to health workers is very low.

The virus specifically attacks certain white blood cells that play a central role in the body's immune defence. The virus may remain in a state of latency in the white blood cells or may multiply without causing any symptoms in the infected individual. Whether or not they develop clinical symptoms, infected individuals should be regarded as potentially infectious to others.

Following a latency period of between 6 and 60 months, about 20–25% of infected individuals may develop a nonspecific condition known as AIDS-related complex, which is characterized by vague symptoms such as fatigue, low-grade fever, night sweats, generalized enlargement of the lymph nodes, persistent diarrhoea, and a weight loss of more than 10%. The lymph nodes are hard and not painful, and the enlargement often involves more than one site and is usually symmetrical.

Some 25–50% of infected patients may develop the full clinical picture of acquired immunodeficiency syndrome within 5–10 years after infection, either directly after the period of latency or after passing through the stage of AIDS-related complex.

The clinical manifestations may be directly attributable to infection with the virus or a direct consequence of the breakdown of cellular immunity, which can lead to a variety of opportunistic infections, autoimmune and neurological disorders, and several types of malignancy. In addition to severe weight loss or diarrhoea lasting for more than a month, patients may suffer from pneumonias caused by various organisms, skin ulcerations, meningitis and other severe infections, as well as malignant vascular tumours in the skin. AIDS is fatal in the large majority of cases, because patients have so little ability to restore cellular immune functions after they have been destroyed by HIV.

White patches of yeast infection on the mucosal surface of the mouth (thrush), usually extending into the pharynx, are a common sign of breakdown of the body's resistance to infection, and should raise suspicion of the presence of an AIDS virus infection in people with behaviour that places them at high risk. These symptoms can also be associated with other infectious diseases, and an accurate diagnosis cannot be made without specialized clinical and laboratory assistance.

Treatment

To date, there is no therapy that can restore the immune functions of a patient with AIDS. Treatment of AIDS patients consists of specific therapy for the opportunistic diseases occurring in the individual case. Patients suspected to be suffering from AIDS or AIDS-related complex should be referred to a specialist at the next port of call (see also Instructions for medical attendants, p. 158, Instructions for patients, p. 158, and Prevention of sexually transmitted disease, p. 158.

Proctitis

Proctitis is an infection of the rectum, often caused by sexually transmitted pathogens. In symptomatic infections, a discharge of pus from the anus, sometimes mixed with blood, can be observed. Itching around the anus may be present.

In females, proctitis is usually due to a secondary infection with vaginal discharge containing gonococci (see Vaginal discharge, p. 154, and Rectal infection, p. 148). In male homosexuals, proctitis is caused by anal sexual contact with an infected person.

Treatment

Patients should be treated according to the regimens outlined for urethritis and urethral discharge, page 148. If there is no response to treatment within one week, RADIO MEDICAL ADVICE should be obtained.

157

Treatment centres at ports

Many ports have one or more specialist centres, where seafarers can obtain treatment for sexually transmitted diseases. Where they exist, these centres should be used in preference to the services of a general practitioner, since they have ready access to the necessary laboratory facilities, and experience of dealing with a large number of cases of sexually transmitted disease.

The clinic staff will advise on any further treatment and tests that may be necessary. A personal booklet is given to the seaman, in which is recorded the diagnosis (in code) and the treatment given, and which he should take with him if he visits a clinic in another port.

Instructions for medical attendants

The medical attendant should wear disposable gloves when examining any infected site in patients suspected of suffering from sexually transmitted disease. If the attendant accidentally touches any genital ulcer or discharge, or any material contaminated with pus from ulcers or discharge, he should immediately wash his hands thoroughly with soap and water.

If there is a sore on the penis or discharge from the urethra, a clean gauze dressing should be kept on the penis. This dressing should be changed frequently. In female patients suffering from genital ulcers or vaginal discharge, gauze or sanitary pads should be used.

Contaminated materials should be discarded in plastic bags, so that they will not be touched or handled by others.

Instructions for patients

The patient should avoid all sexual contact until a medical specialist confirms that he is free from infection. He should also make a special effort to practise good personal hygiene; for instance, he should use only his own toilet articles (toothbrush, razor, towels, washcloth etc.) and his own clothes and linen.

During the examination and treatment, the opportunity should be taken to inform the patient about his condition, sexually transmitted diseases in general, and the precautions to be taken to minimize the risk of acquiring them (see below).

Prevention of sexually transmitted disease

Being outside their normal environment and often in circumstances that allow for promiscuity, sailors are at special risk of contracting sexually transmitted diseases.

Avoidance of casual and promiscuous sexual contacts is the best way of minimizing the risk of infection. Failing this, a mechanical barrier, such as a condom, can give both heterosexual and homosexual men and women a certain degree of protection against a number of sexually transmitted diseases. A supply of condoms should be available on board ship. The condom, or rubber, is a thin elastic covering that forms a protective sheath over the penis. If properly used, it should prevent infection during intercourse, unless the point of contact with an infected lesion is beyond the area covered by the condom. The condom comes rolled before use. It must be placed over the penis before sexual contact. The tip of the condom should be held to form a pocket to receive the ejaculate and the rest of the condom unrolled to cover the entire penis. As soon as the male has had an orgasm, the penis should be withdrawn from the vagina before it softens, because loosening of the condom may expose the penis to infection. The condom is removed by grasping the open end with the fingers and pulling it down quickly so that it comes off inside out. The condom should be discarded without further handling in case it contains infectious material.

In women, the use of a diaphragm in combination with a spermicide cream offers some protection against the acquisition of some sexually transmitted diseases; however, condoms offer better protection. In risk situations, the male partner should urinate at once after possible exposure. Each partner should subsequently wash his or her genitals and other possible infected areas.

Chapter 8

Other diseases and medical problems

Contents

Abdominal pain

Minor abdominal conditions

This group of conditions includes indigestion, "wind", flatulence, mild abdominal colic (spasmodic abdominal pain without diarrhoea and fever), and the effects of overindulgence in food or alcohol. The patient can often tell quite a lot about the possible causes of his minor abdominal conditions or upsets, so always encourage him to tell you all he can. Ask about intolerance to certain foods, such as fried foods, onions, sauces, and other spicy foods, any tendency to looseness, diarrhoea, or constipation, and any regularly felt type of indigestion and any known reasons for it. Mild abdominal pain will usually cure itself if the cause(s) can be understood and removed.

Guard against total acceptance of the patient's explanation of the causes of his pain until you have satisfied yourself, by examining his abdomen, that he is not suffering from a serious condition (Fig. 122 and Table 5). Note that a peptic ulcer may sometimes start with symptoms of slight pain (page 217).

General management

The patient should be put on a simple diet for 1–2 days, and given 2 aluminium hydroxide tablets three times a day. Repeat these at night, if the patient is in pain. If the condition does not resolve itself within two days of starting this regime, get RADIO MEDICAL ADVICE. Anyone who has *persistent or unexplained* mild abdominal symptoms should be seen by a doctor at the next port.

Abdominal emergencies

Abdominal emergencies such as appendicitis and perforated gastric or duodenal ulcer are high on the list of conditions that, ashore, would be sent to hospital for surgical treatment. While there is no doubt that early surgical treatment is usually best, this does not mean that other forms of treatment are unsuitable or ineffective. In most abdominal emergencies on board a ship at sea, surgical treatment is usually neither advisable nor possible, Note that in the *very early stages* of abdominal conditions such as appendicitis or perforated ulcers, diarrhoea, vomiting, headaches, or fevers are seldom present other than in a mild form. If these symptoms are present, the illness is much more likely to be a diarrhoea and vomiting type of illness (see page 188).

Examination of the abdomen

The abdomen should be thoroughly examined. The first thing to do is to lay the patient down comfortably in a warm, well-lit place. He should be uncovered from his nipples to the thigh and the groin should be inspected (see Hernia, page 207). Look at the abdomen and watch if it moves with the patient's breathing. Get the patient to take a deep breath and to cough; ask him if either action causes him pain and, if so, where he felt it and what it was like. Probably, if the pain is sharp he will point with his finger to the spot, but if it is dull he will indicate the area with the flat of his hand.

Look for any movement of the abdominal contents and note if these movements are accompanied by pain and/or by loud gurgling noises. Note if the patient lies very still and appears to be afraid to move or cough on account of pain or if he writhes about and cries out when the pain is at its height. Spasmodic pain accompanied by loud gurgling noises usually indicates abdominal colic or bowel obstruction. When the patient lies still with the abdomen rigid, think in terms of perforated appendix or perforation of a peptic ulcer.

Bowel sounds

When you have completed your inspection, listen to the bowel sounds for at least two minutes by placing your ear on the abdomen just to the right of the navel.

- *Normal bowel sounds* occur as the process of normal digestion proceeds. Gurgling sounds will be heard at intervals, often accompanied by watery noises. There will be short intervals of silence and then more sounds will be heard

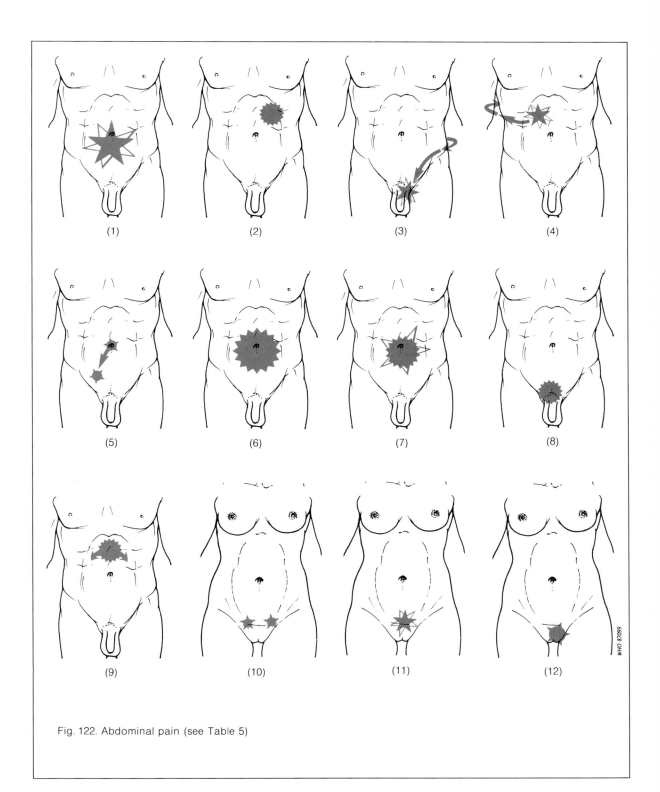

Fig. 122. Abdominal pain (see Table 5)

Table 5. Severe abdominal pain: associated symptoms and signs

Diagram[a]	Position and type of pain	Associated symptoms		
		Vomiting	Diarrhoea	General condition of patient
	A. All patients			
1	all over abdomen, or mainly about navel and lower half; sharp, coming and going in spasms	none	usually not at first, but sometimes coming on later	not ill; usually walks about, even if doubled up
2	in upper part and under left ribs, a steady burning pain	present, and usually repeated	not at first; it may follow 24–48 hours later	wretched, because of nausea, vomiting, and weakness, but soon improving
3	shooting from loin to groin and testicle; very severe agonizing spasms	may be present, but only with the spasms	none	severe distress
4	shooting from the upper part of the right side of abdomen to the back or right shoulder; agonizing spasms	may be present, but only with the spasms	none	severe distress
5	around navel at first, settling later in the lower part of the right side of abdomen; usually continuous and sharp; not always severe	soon after onset of pain, usually only once or twice	sometimes once at commencement of attack; constipation then ensues	an ill patient, tends to lie still
6	all over the abdomen; usually severe and continuous	present, becoming more and more frequent	usually none	an extremely ill patient with wasted appearance; afraid to move because of pain
7	spasmodic at first, but later continuous	increasing in frequency and amount of brown fluid	none; complete constipation	very ill
8	in the groin, a continuous and severe pain	not at first, but later as with obstruction	none; as with obstruction	very ill
9	severe and continuous pain, worst in the upper part of the abdomen	rare	none	severe shock at first, then very ill; afraid to move because of the pain
	B. Female patients			
10	lower abdominal pain—one or both sides just above midline of groin	sometimes with onset of pain	usually none	an ill patient; there may be vaginal discharge or bleeding
10	sudden onset of lower abdominal pain which may be severe	sometimes with onset of pain	none	an ill patient; may collapse if internal bleeding and pain are severe; there may be vaginal bleeding
11	lower abdominal pain; spasms like labour pains	none	none	anxious and distressed; may show some collapse if vaginal bleeding is severe
12	continuous discomfort in pit of the abdomen and the crotch; scalding pain on frequent urination	none	none	made miserable by frequent painful urination

[a] Numbers refer to Fig. 122.

Associated signs			
Temperature	Pulse rate	Abdominal tenderness	Probable cause of the pain
normal	normal	none; on the contrary, pressure eases the pain	intestinal colic (page 210)
usually normal; may be raised up to 38°C in severe cases	slightly raised, up to 80–90	sometimes, but not severe and confined to upper part of abdomen	acute indigestion (page 209)
normal, or below normal	rapid, as with shock	over the loin	renal colic (kidney stones) (page 236)
normal, or below normal	rapid, as with shock	just below the right ribs	gallstones (biliary colic) (page 172)
normal at first, but always rising later up to 38°C; it may be raised more	raised all the time (over 85), and tending to increase in rate hour by hour	definitely present in the right side of the lower part of the abdomen	appendicitis (page 169)
up to 39.5°C or more, except in final stage near death	rapid (over 110) and feeble	very tender, usually all over; wall of abdomen tense	peritonitis (page 220)
normal	rising steadily, feeble	slightly, all over; wall of abdomen not hard but distended	intestinal obstruction (page 210)
normal	rising steadily, feeble	over the painful lump in the groin	strangulated hernia (rupture) (page 208)
normal or below normal at first; rising about 24 hours later	normal at first, rising steadily a few hours later	all over; worst over site of pain; wall of abdomen hard	perforated ulcer of stomach (page 218)
tends to be high	raised all the time	lower abdomen, one or both sides	salpingitis (page 251)
normal at first; may show slight rise later	moderately raised but may be rapid and weak if internal bleeding continues	tenderness in the lower abdomen	ectopic pregnancy (page 250)
normal	normal or moderately raised; rapid if vaginal bleeding	tenderness in the lower abdomen	abortion/miscarriage (page 250)
normal but can be raised in severe infection	normal or slightly increased	moderate tenderness in central lower abdomen	cystitis (page 237)

—at least one gurgle should be heard every minute.

- *Frequent loud sounds with little or no interval* occur when the bowels are "working overtime", as in food poisoning and diarrhoea to try to get rid of the "poison", and in intestinal obstruction (total or partial, page 210) to try move the bowel contents. The sounds will be loud and frequent and there may be no quiet intervals. The general impression may be one of churning and activity. At the height of the noise and churning, the patient will usually experience colicky pain which, if severe, may cause him to move and groan.

- *Absence of bowel sounds* means that the bowel is paralysed. This condition is found with peritonitis following perforation of an ulcer or of the appendix, or serious abdominal injuries. The outlook is always serious. RADIO MEDICAL ADVICE is required, and the patient should go to a hospital ashore as soon as possible.

When you have learned all that you can by looking and listening—and this takes time—you should then feel the abdomen with a *warm hand.* Before you start, ask the patient not to speak, but to relax, to rest quietly, and to breathe gently through his open mouth so that his abdominal muscles will be as relaxed as possible. Then begin your examination by laying your hand flat on the abdomen away from the areas where the patient feels pain or complains of discomfort. If you examine the pain-free areas first, you will get a better idea of what the patient's abdomen feels like in a part that is normal. Then, with your palm flat and your fingers straightened and kept together, press lightly downwards by bending at the knuckle joints. Never prod with the fingertips. Feel systematically all over the abdomen, leaving until last those areas that may be "bad" ones. Watch the patient's face as you feel. His expression is likely to tell you at once if you are touching a tender area. In addition you may feel the abdominal muscles tensing as he tries to protect the tender part. When you have finished your examination, ask him about the pain and tenderness he may have felt. Then make a written note of all that you have discovered.

The urine of any patient suffering from abdominal pain or discomfort should always be examined and tested (page 107).

When you have completed the examination of the abdomen and recorded the temperature and pulse rate, use Table 5 and Fig. 122 to diagnose the condition or to confirm your diagnosis.

More information about each condition and the treatments are given separately under the various illnesses.

Alcohol abuse

Warning

Breath smelling of alcohol means that a drink has been taken; it does *not* tell how much has been consumed, *nor* does it mean that the condition of the patient is due to alcoholic intoxication. Head injuries, certain drugs such as sleeping tablets, and some illnesses can make a patient behave as if he were drunk. Therefore, *always* assume that the person may have other injuries, or may be ill, until you have examined him carefully.

Every year, a number of seamen die as a direct result of the excessive drinking of liquor or from accidents, such as falling from wharves and gangways, while under the influence of drink. In addition there have been cases in which men, brought on board in a semi-comatose condition, have been simply put to bed and have been found dead some hours later, as a result either of absorbing a fatal quantity of alcohol from their stomachs or of being choked by their own vomit. Being extremely drunk may therefore place a man in a critical condition. Accordingly, drunkenness, common though it may be, should never be ignored or regarded as merely funny. On the contrary, men returning on board in a severely drunken state should be treated as sick persons requiring close watching and careful nursing, if their lives are not to be further jeopardized.

Ordinary drunkenness

A description of this is scarcely necessary except for the sake of comparison with other forms of drunkenness. The man has poor control of his muscles, finding it difficult to walk or talk properly, and is unable to perform commonplace actions. His face is flushed and the whites of his eyes may be "bloodshot". He may vomit. He may be in a happy, excited mood, or want to fight, or he may cry and be very depressed owing to the loss of his normal controlling powers of reason and judgement.

"Dead drunk"

Alcohol in any form is a poison; when a large amount has been taken during a short time, especially on an empty stomach, serious poisoning or intoxication may develop. This may prove fatal as a result of respiratory or heart failure. The poisonous spirit of illicit origin offered to seamen in some ports is especially dangerous. A man who is "dead drunk" lies unconscious with slow noisy breathing, dilated pupils, a rapid pulse, and some blueness of the lips. His breath will smell of alcohol, but remember that his stupor or coma may not always be solely due to drink. The signs of a drunken stupor are much like those of other conditions causing unconsciousness. The man must be examined carefully to make as sure as possible that it really is a case of alcoholic poisoning.

Treatment

People who are drunk but conscious should be encouraged to drink 1–2 glasses of water to prevent a hangover caused by alcoholic dehydration, and to go to bed. If they are seriously drunk, they should not eat anything until they have recovered. It is advisable for someone to stay with a person who is seriously drunk, because he may inhale his vomit while asleep.

If in port, a person unconscious from alcohol should be sent to hospital. If the patient has to be kept on board, he should be put to bed and managed as in the routine for unconscious patients (page 104). Remember that he should *never* be left alone in case he moves out of the unconscious position and then dies from inhaling vomit.

Hangover

A hangover is usually made up of a headache, a general feeling of being unwell, and a stomach upset. The patient should not take further alcohol. He should take plenty of non-alcoholic fluids to combat the dehydration caused by the alcohol, paracetamol tablets, and, if necessary, an antacid (magnesium hydroxide suspension, a 5-ml teaspoonful in half a glass of water, three times a day).

The stomach upset and other complaints will usually settle within 24–36 hours if the patient takes no more alcohol, very little food, if any, and plenty of fluid.

The shakes

The shakes are a sign of withdrawal of alcohol in a person who has, over a long period of time, become dependent on alcohol. Trembling of the hands, shaking of the body, and sweating will appear in the morning when a person has not had alcohol since the previous evening. The alcohol-dependent person usually prescribes his own cure by taking a further drink. On board ship during a voyage it is reasonable to allow a small dose of alcohol in such circumstances, provided that the patient is not showing any sign of mental or emotional imbalance. The patient should be referred for treatment for alcohol dependence at the earliest opportunity.

Delirium tremens (DTs)

An attack of the DTs can be a serious medical emergency. It occurs only in people who have been regular heavy drinkers for many years. Attacks do not follow a single bout of heavy drinking by a person who normally takes only a small or moderate amount of alcohol. On the other hand, it is often a bout of drinking (such as a seaman who is alcohol-dependent may indulge in after a prolonged voyage) that leads to an attack, or it may be brought on when a heavy drinker has an injury or illness that results in the sudden cessation of his excessive "normal" intake.

The patient with delirium tremens is at first irritable and restless, and will not eat. These early signs are followed by shaking all over, especially of the hands. He is confused and may not know where he is and may not recognize those around him. He perspires freely, the body temperature may rise to 39 °C, the face is flushed, and the tongue is furred. He may be extremely disturbed, or even raving; this is usually worse at night when he is unable to sleep and sees imaginary creatures like snakes, rats, and insects, which frighten him and which he may try to pursue. He may deteriorate to a state of delirium in which there is a danger of his committing suicide or even homicide. This condition usually lasts for 3 or 4 days, after which the patient either improves and begins to acquire natural sleep, or else passes into coma, complete exhaustion, and death.

It is the severe mental and emotional disturbance that differentiates the DTs from the shakes.

General treatment

The patient should be confined and nursed as described for the mentally ill (page 103). There should be subdued lighting by day and by night to reduce as far as possible the imaginary visions he is likely to see. He should be encouraged to drink plenty of sweetened fluid and, if he will eat, should be given food. The attack may end with the patient sleeping for up to 24 hours.

Specific treatment

First try to calm the patient with a glass (50 ml) of whisky. If this proves unsuccessful, physical restraint will be necessary. In either event, give 50 mg of chlorpromazine by intramuscular injection. This may be repeated after 6 hours, if the patient is still uncontrolled. In addition, give 10 mg of diazepam by intramuscular injection and then give one 10-mg tablet of diazepam, every 4 hours until the patient is calm. Once treatment is started, it is essential that no more alcohol is given.

If in any doubt about diagnosis or treatment get RADIO MEDICAL ADVICE. In any event, refer the patient for treatment for alcohol dependence at the earliest opportunity.

Subsequent management

When a person has got over an attack of DTs, it is vital to make sure that no further access to alcohol is possible. Alcohol-dependent people are often very cunning and devious. They frequently have bottles hidden in their cabin and work areas and may try to get to these bottles or may trick other people into fetching them their bottle of "medicine".

It should be remembered that delirium related to alcohol abuse is only one type of delirium.

Other types of delirium

Delirium may be due to mental disease; to poisons that accumulate from certain systemic infections such as kidney diseases; or to drug and poison intoxication caused by a variety of agents such as lead, carbon monoxide, narcotics, and some medicaments. It may also accompany exhaustion, chronic illness, or high fever, and follow severe injury. Delirium may take the form of a fairly quiet restlessness in which the patient fidgets and mutters to himself for hours on end; or it may take the form of wild, noisy, and violent actions.

The characteristics of the *low muttering type of delirium* are: constant or occasionally disconnected and irrational speech, restless impulses, disturbing dreams, attacks of weeping or excitement, impaired mental and muscular power, involuntary urination and defecation, and, frequently, plucking at the bedclothes. When restlessness is present, the patient continually tries to get out of bed and not infrequently attempts to escape. This type of delirium may be present in all acute infectious fevers, especially in typhoid fever.

In the *violent type of delirium* usually associated with toxic conditions due to uraemia, alcohol dependence, and poisoning by drugs, there is wild maniacal excitement. At different times, the patient may be noisy or quiet, violent or calm. He is always difficult to control and is usually insensible to his surroundings. His speech is rapid and incoherent or irrelevant, eyes open and staring with pupils usually dilated, and face flushed. Homicidal mania may develop suddenly.

Remember that the onset of delirium of any type is a serious danger signal, and that special attention should be paid to identifying the underlying cause or condition which must be treated or controlled.

Allergic reactions

(See also: Dermatitis, page 225; and Urticaria, page 229.)

Certain individuals may develop an allergy or hypersensitivity to substances that are harmless to most people. An allergic individual is sensitive to allergens, which are substances that enter the body by being inhaled, swallowed, or injected, or through contact with the skin. They may come from bacterial or fungal infections in the body. A manifested allergy may be relatively mild, for example, a light attack of hay fever or a brief episode of urticaria; or it may be severe and very serious, for example, an acute attack of asthma, a stubborn or uncomfortable skin rash, or sudden collapse.

When an allergen reaches a sensitive area of the body, the tissues react irritably or even violently to produce symptoms of allergy. The allergic reactions may occur in almost any organ or tissue of the body, with symptoms determined by the location. When the nose and throat are involved, an individual may have sneezing, stuffiness, running nose, and itching of the throat and eyes. The symptoms represent hay fever (allergic rhinitis). If bronchial tissues are affected, there is wheezing, coughing, and difficult breathing (asthma). When the skin is affected, dermatitis or urticaria appears. If the digestive tract is involved, there may be nausea, vomiting, indigestion, abdominal pain, diarrhoea, or cramping. An allergic reaction may also affect the brain, causing headache.

Countless substances can cause allergic reactions. Penicillin is a common cause of drug allergy, and may be manifested by urticaria, anaphylactic shock (see this page), skin rash, or swelling of various body parts; alternatively, a reaction characterized by malaise, fever, and possibly arthritis, may occur about 10 days after penicillin is given. Drugs that may be associated with allergic reactions include antibiotics, acetylsalicylic acid, laxatives, sedatives, and tranquillizers. Eczematous dermatitis may result from contact of the skin with metals, dyes, fabrics, resins, drugs, insecticides, industrial chemicals, perfumes, rubber, plastics, and the components of certain plants.

Serious allergic reactions may occur following bee, wasp, yellow jacket, and hornet stings. Airborne substances that may produce allergy include pollens from weeds, grasses, trees, and plants; house and industrial dusts; mould spores; animal danders (skin and hair shed by domestic or wild animals); feathers found in pillows; kapok; and insecticide sprays or other vapours. In some instances, foods (such as eggs, milk, nuts, wheat, shellfish, chocolate, and fruits) may cause acute or chronic symptoms. There are many other possible factors inducing allergy, including sunlight, heat, cold, and parasites.

Avoidance of the allergenic substance or substances offers the greatest hope of permanent relief from an allergic disease. In drug allergy, once the diagnosis is suspected or established, the allergenic agent should be stopped and another drug substituted. In allergic contact dermatitis from substances such as cashew shell oil, fuel oil, paints, and tar, the patient should try to protect his skin from direct and indirect contact with the agents, even if he has to change his occupation. Patients allergic to an inhaled substance (such as feathers or animal danders) may be unable to avoid them. Airborne pollens are difficult to avoid. A physician may be able to desensitize the patient by a series of injections.

Anaphylactic shock

(See also: Shock, page 17.)

Anaphylactic shock is a severe allergic reaction and can often be fatal. It commonly occurs after an injection of a medicament such as penicillin. It may occur within seconds or minutes of contact with the incompatible substance, which may have been taken by mouth or inhalation or introduced by injection, bite, or sting. In the very worst type of allergic attack, the patient may suddenly begin to wheeze, become pale, sweat, and feel dizzy. The heart beat may become so feeble that he may lose consciousness and, unless treated promptly, he may die. This reaction can occur after contact with almost any allergen. Prevention is best. **Before giving injections or administering any medication, the patient should be asked if he has ever had an allergic reaction in the past.** If he has, RADIO MEDICAL ADVICE should be obtained before any drug is administered to him. A skin rash or other unusual side-effect following treatment is a warning to avoid the same medicine in the future.

Treatment

For anaphylactic shock, the patient should be placed in a prone position. The following medicaments should be administered intramuscularly, immediately: 1:1000 epinephrine hydrochloride injection, 1 ml; chlorphenamine maleate, 10 mg; and hydrocortisone sodium succinate, 100 mg. The three medicines should be given from separate syringes and at different body sites. The epinephrine hydrochloride injection may be repeated in 20 minutes, if the patient's condition remains serious or becomes worse. Obtain RADIO MEDICAL ADVICE.

Note. Make very sure that you do not inject epinephrine into a blood vessel. When the needle is inserted under the skin, pull the piston back and ensure that blood does not enter the syringe before epinephrine is injected.

Note. Hydrocortisone should be injected very slowly; the duration time of the intramuscular injection should be about 30 seconds.

Asthma

Asthma is a disease in which the patient suffers from periodic attacks of difficulty in breathing out, during which time he wheezes and feels as if he were suffocating. Many cases of asthma are allergic manifestations in sensitized persons. For diagnosis and treatment, see section on Asthma, page 171.

Hay fever

Hay fever is a common allergy that affects the upper respiratory tract. Generally caused by pollen, it is a seasonal disease that is prevalent in the spring, late summer, and autumn. Symptoms resemble those of an aggravated head cold, i.e., congestion of nose and eyes, sneezing, and asthma (see Asthma, page 171). An attack may last from 4 to 6 weeks, during which the patient may lose a lot of weight.

Treatment

At sea, the treatment is entirely symptomatic. Patients with hay fever are usually familiar with the symptoms and with the effects of their various remedies. Usually they do not have to go to bed or stop their regular work. Give ephedrine sulfate capsules, 25 mg, three to four times a day. More severe symptoms may be treated with chlorphenamine, one 4-mg tablet four times a day. Because the medication may induce drowsiness as a side-effect, all precision work, potentially hazardous work, or standing watch should be curtailed for the patient.

Anaemia

Anaemia is a condition caused by a reduction in the number of red cells circulating in the body or a reduction in the iron content of these cells.

It can result from haemorrhage of a large volume of blood or from constant loss of small amounts of blood, from destruction of the red cells in certain diseases (such as malaria), or from deficient or defective formation of red cells, but usually it is due to lack of available iron or certain vitamins in the diet.

Moderate anaemia is difficult to diagnose without laboratory facilities, but you may notice when you are carrying out your examination of a patient that the conjunctivae and membranes of the mouth are very pale compared with those of a healthy person. The colour of the cheeks is no guide, as such things as fever and excitement will redden them, while natural sallowness of the complexion may simulate extreme pallor.

The symptoms of severe anaemia vary, but they are best summarized as those of physical weakness and rapid fatigue, together with palpitations.

Anaemia is generally a chronic condition that requires no emergency treatment except when it is severe and of recent development. In that case the patient should be referred to a doctor at the next port of call so that a blood examination can be undertaken, the type of anaemia diagnosed, and the correct treatment prescribed.

Anal fissure

An anal fissure is an ulcer that extends into the back passage from the skin at the anal margin. The fissure is usually narrow, elongated, and purple-coloured. When passing faeces intense pain is experienced, which may continue for half an hour or more. A little slime and blood may be noticed.

Place the patient in the position described under haemorrhoids (page 201). Put on polythene gloves before examining the anus. With one finger gently open out a small segment of the anal edge. Continue until the whole circumference has been inspected. This may give rise to intense pain and make a complete examination impossible.

Thrombosed external piles (page 201) or an abscess in the anal region are the only other likely reasons for such pain.

Treatment

Relieve pain with acetylsalicylic acid or paracetamol. The area should be washed with soap and water, then carefully dried after each bowel action. Calamine lotion may be applied locally.

This treatment should be continued until the patient is seen by a doctor at the next port.

Anal itching (anal pruritus)

Localized itching around the anus is commonly caused by excessive sweating, faecal soiling, or a discharge from haemorrhoids.

The skin has a white, sodden appearance and the area is bordered by a red inflamed zone. The skin surface is typically abraded by frequent scratching, which prolongs and worsens the condition.

Threadworm infestation should be excluded as a cause (page 240).

Treatment

Any haemorrhoids should be treated (page 201).

After the bowels have moved, the area round the anus should be washed gently with soap and warm water, then patted dry with a towel before applying zinc oxide paste. Calamine lotion may also be applied. Loose-fitting cotton boxer trunks should be worn. Scratching must be strongly discouraged. If the impulse to scratch becomes irresistible, the knuckles or back of the hand, never the fingers, should be used. Consult a doctor at the next port.

Appendicitis

Appendicitis is the commonest abdominal emergency, occurring mostly in people under 30 years old, though it can appear in people of any age. When considering appendicitis as a diagnosis, always ask the patient if he knows whether his appendix has already been removed, and look for the operation scar in the right lower abdomen area.

The illness usually begins with a combination of colicky abdominal pain, nausea, and perhaps mild vomiting. The pain is usually felt in the midline just above the navel or around the navel. Later, as the illness progresses, *the pain moves from the centre of the abdomen to the right lower quarter of the abdomen (see Fig. 123). The character of the pain changes:* from being colicky, diffuse, and not well localized when it is around the navel, it becomes sharp, distinctly felt, and localized at the junction of the outer and middle thirds of a line between the navel and the front of the right hipbone.

The patient usually loses his appetite and often feels ill. The bowels are often sluggish and the breath is often rather bad, even foul.

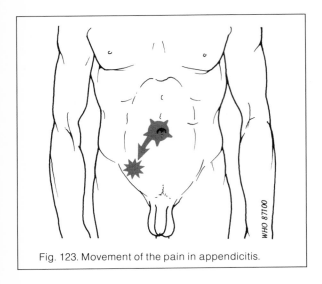

Fig. 123. Movement of the pain in appendicitis.

Examine the patient (page 160). If he complains of sharp stabbing pain when you press gently over the right lower quarter of his abdomen, and especially if you feel his abdominal muscles tightening involuntarily when you try to press gently, you can be fairly sure that the appendix is inflamed. The temperature and the pulse rate will rise as the inflammation increases.

Treatment

Once you suspect a patient has appendicitis get RADIO MEDICAL ADVICE and GET THE PATIENT TO HOSPITAL AS SOON AS POSSIBLE. Do not give a purgative.

If the patient can reach hospital within 4 to 6 hours, give him no food or liquid and no drugs as he will probably require a general anaesthetic. Keep him in bed until he is taken off the ship. Keep a record of the patient's temperature, pulse, and respiration, and send these and your case-notes to the hospital with the patient.

If the patient cannot get to hospital within 4–6 hours, put him to bed and take temperature, pulse rate, and respiration rate hourly. The patient should have no food, but can have drinks. You should start a fluid input/output chart and follow the instructions about fluid balance (page 101).

Specific treatment

Give 600 000 units of procaine benzylpenicillin intramuscularly *and* one 200-mg tablet of metronidazole at once. Then give orally 2 phenoxymethyl penicillin potassium tablets (250 mg each) and 100 mg (half a tablet) of metronidazole every 6 hours for 5 days. For patients allergic to penicillin, substitute erythromycin (500 mg first and 250 mg subsequently) for the penicillin. Treat severe pain according to RADIO MEDICAL ADVICE.

Subsequent management

If the patient is still on board after 48 hours, he should be given some fluids such as milk, sweet tea, and soup until he can be put ashore.

Anyone who was thought to have appendicitis but seems to have improved should be seen by a doctor at the next port. Improvement is shown by diminution of pain and fall in temperature.

Diagnoses that may be confused with appendicitis

In both men and women

Urinary infection (page 235). Always test the urine for protein in any case of suspected appendicitis and look for the presence or absence of urinary infection.

A perforated duodenal ulcer (page 217). This may cause sharp abdominal pain to be felt on the right, but the pain is usually all over the abdomen, which is held rigid. The onset of the pain is usually more sudden, and there is normally a past history of indigestion after eating.

Other causes of colicky abdominal pain. Renal colic (page 236), biliary colic (page 172), and cholecystitis (page 179). These can cause severe colicky pain, but usually show other features that are unlike those of appendicitis.

In women

In addition to the above-mentioned diseases, *ectopic pregnancy* should also be considered (page 250). Always ask the date of the last menstrual period and whether the periods are regular or irregular. If the sexual history allows for the possibility of pregnancy, always consider that the case may be one of ectopic pregnancy.

Salpingitis (page 251). Salpingitis is infection of the Fallopian tubes. Always inquire about evidence of infection such as recent history of sex contacts, pain on urinating, and vaginal discharge and bleeding. The fever is usually higher than in the case of appendicitis.

Asthma

Asthma is a disease in which the patient suffers from periodic attacks of difficulty in breathing out and a feeling of tightness in the chest, during which time he wheezes and feels as if he were suffocating.

The causes of asthma are usually:

- exposure to irritants to which the sufferer is sensitive—these may be either inhaled (e.g., dust, acrid fumes, or simply cold air) or ingested (e.g., shellfish or eggs);
- mental stress in highly strung and overconscientious persons;
- certain chest diseases, such as chronic bronchitis.

Asthma may begin at any age. There is often a previous history of attacks from time to time in the patient's life.

The onset of an attack may be slow and preceded by a feeling of tightness in the chest, or it may occur suddenly. Sometimes the attack occurs at night when the patient has been lying flat.

In the event of a severe attack, the patient is in a state of alarm and distress, unable to breathe properly, and with a sense of weight and tightness around the chest. He can fill up his chest with air but finds great difficulty in breathing out, and his efforts are accompanied by coughing and wheezing noises due to narrowing of the air tubes within his lungs. His distress increases rapidly in severe cases, and he sits or stands as near as possible to a source of fresh air, with his head thrown back and his whole body heaving with desperate efforts to breathe. His lips and face, at first pale, may take on a blue tinge and be covered with sweat, while his hands and feet become cold. His pulse is rapid and weak, and may be irregular. Fortunately, less severe attacks, without such great distress, are more common.

An attack may last only a short while, but it may be prolonged for many hours. Eventually, however, the breathing gradually becomes easier, and coughing may then produce some sputum. After an attack, the patient may be exhausted, but very often he appears to be, and feels, comparatively well. Unfortunately this relief may only be temporary and attacks may recur at varying intervals.

Asthma must not be confused with choking due to a patient having inhaled something, for instance food, into his windpipe. In choking symptoms occur immediately (see page 42).

Treatment

General treatment

The patient should be put to bed in a position he finds most comfortable, which is usually half sitting up. If he is emotionally distressed, try to calm him.

In severe cases of asthma, RADIO MEDICAL ADVICE should be obtained.

Specific treatment

A person who knows that he is liable to attacks has usually had medical advice and been supplied with a remedy. In such cases the patient probably knows what suits him best, and it is then wise merely to help him as he desires and to interfere as little as possible. He should be allowed to select the position easiest for himself.

A bedside vaporizer or turned-on hot shower should be used to humidify the air that is inhaled by the patient with asthma. To offset possible dehydration, the patient should be encouraged to drink plenty of fluids, especially water. More palatable liquids such as fruit juices and hot tea may be helpful.

Medicaments to enlarge the air passageways (bronchodilators), such as ephedrine sulfate, 25 mg, should be given by mouth every 4–6 hours. If the patient is unduly nervous or unable to sleep, 15–30 mg of phenobarbital should be given by mouth every 4–6 hours.

For acute asthmatic episodes, 0.3 ml to 0.5 ml of aqueous epinephrine hydrochloride injection 1:1000 should be given *subcutaneously* and, if necessary, repeated after 60 minutes.

After obtaining RADIO MEDICAL ADVICE on treatment, a 500-mg aminophylline suppository may be used. The use of a suppository should be restricted to only one or two occasions because repeated usage might cause severe rectal irritation.

Antibiotics may be given in acute asthma, because most adult asthma patients will have a bronchial infection that may or may not be apparent. RADIO MEDICAL ADVICE should be obtained as to whether antibiotics are indicated.

If all or some of the above procedures are used, most acute asthma attacks can be treated adequately (see Bronchitis, page 177).

Backache

Pain in the small of the back is a symptom of many conditions that affect the spine, spinal ligaments, back muscles, and nerves. Pain is usually the only symptom, and the general health remains normal. However, backache can be an indication of more serious underlying disease, especially kidney disease (see Urinary problems, page 235), so in every case the urine should be tested for protein (page 107) and the temperature and pulse rate taken.

Simple backache

This is usually of sudden onset; it may follow a period of heavy work or some quick movement of the back, but it can appear for no known reason. The pain may vary from a dull ache to a severe disabling pain. Some degree of spasm of the back muscles, which is made worse by movement, is always present. With rest and appropri-

ate treatment (see Muscular rheumatism, page 222) the pain will settle down within several days. The patient may then be allowed to be more active, but heavy work is inadvisable.

Some patients have severe backache from the onset and, occasionally, the main leg nerve becomes affected, resulting in sciatica (see Neuritis and neuralgia, page 215). The patient will then experience a sensation of numbness and tingling or a burning pain travelling down the leg.

Treatment

It is essential that the patient should keep the spine straight at all times. If a board to lie on can be fitted to the bed, he should remain in bed in the position that is most comfortable. Otherwise, he should lie on a hard, flat surface with minimal padding until the pain eases. Whenever possible, he should eat meals standing up with a straight back. He should be washed in bed, but allowed to go to a lavatory rather than use a bedpan. Local application of heat to the back (using a hot-water bottle) will help to relieve muscle spasm and pain. If pain is severe, give acetylsalicylic acid tablets. If pain continues it should be controlled (see Use of analgesics, page 305). Treatment should be continued and the patient kept at rest until a doctor can be consulted at the next port.

Biliary colic (gallstone colic)

Biliary colic is usually caused by a gallstone stuck in the neck of the gall-bladder or in a bile duct. There is usually a history of vague indigestion and intolerance to fat. An attack starts very suddenly without warning symptoms and may cease just as abruptly.

The bouts of colic, often very severe, are felt in the right upper abdomen just below the lowest rib, but occasionally at the same level, only more towards the mid-line. Sometimes pain is also felt passing inwards through the body to the angle of the shoulder blade. The patient feels cold, sweats profusely, and is extremely restless. Nausea is always present, and vomiting may occur. The abdomen feels bloated, and the bowel is constipated. The pulse is rapid, and the temperature is normal or slightly raised. A moderately raised temperature may indicate that the gall-bladder is also inflamed.

Examine the abdomen, look for jaundice (page 210), record the temperature, pulse rate, and respiration rate, note the colour of the urine and test it for protein (page 107), and examine the faeces. Rigid abdominal muscles prevent examination during an acute spasm of pain. Between spasms, feel for tenderness in the gall-bladder area. When the outflow of bile is blocked, the faeces become pale or putty-coloured because bile pigment is deficient. However, the urine, containing excess bile pigment, becomes much darker in colour. Look for jaundice each day. If protein is present in the urine, consider renal colic (page 236).

Treatment

General treatment

Put the patient to bed. Record the temperature, pulse rate, and respiration rate every four hours. If feverish, give only fluids for the first 48 hours. A fat-free diet should be provided thereafter.

Specific treatment

As soon as possible, mix 15 mg of morphine with 0.6 mg of atropine in one syringe and inject the mixture intramuscularly. The morphine will relieve the pain, and the atropine the spasm. Reassure the patient that the injection will act in about 15 minutes. If the pain returns, the injection should be repeated after four hours and RADIO MEDICAL ADVICE should be sought.

If gall-bladder inflammation (cholecystitis, page 179) is also present, treat it accordingly. Get RADIO MEDICAL ADVICE.

Subsequent management

Isolate any jaundiced patient (page 297) and get RADIO MEDICAL ADVICE. All cases should see a doctor at the next port.

Bites and stings

Animal bites

Animal bites may cause abrasions, lacerations, and punctures. There is a danger of bacterial infection, including tetanus, from these wounds, and rabies is also a threat.

All animal bites should be treated by thorough washing (not scrubbing) with soap and water and swabbing with 1% cetrimide solution. All traces of soap should be removed before using the cetrimide solution. The wound should then be covered with a dressing. You should check that the patient is protected against tetanus (page 145). If an hour or more later the wound is throbbing, the patient should be given the standard antibiotic treatment (p. 308). Then read the section on rabies (page 143).

Rat bites

Anyone bitten by a rat should be given the standard antibiotic treatment (page 308). The wound should be cleansed with soap and water and covered with a sterile dressing.

Snake bites

Many snakes are harmless but there are three poisonous types:

- cobras, mambas, African spitting cobras, etc;
- vipers and adders; and
- the highly poisonous sea snakes of the Pacific and Indian Oceans.

Snake bites are likely to occur ashore or from cargo. Unprovoked bites of humans seldom occur. Even if a snake is disturbed and bites, shoes will usually give complete protection against fang penetration.

There is usually local pain and swelling around a snake bite, except for sea-snake bites, which cause no local reaction but produce generalized muscle pains.

If large amounts of venom have been injected, shock (see page 17) occurs, with heart palpitations, difficulty in breathing, collapse, and sometimes convulsions. Delayed blood clotting may occur. These symptoms can present between 15 minutes and 1 hour after the bite.

General management. The common symptoms in snake bite are fright and fear of sudden death. Research has shown that serious poisoning is rare in humans and death is highly exceptional. **Reassurance is therefore most important.** Acetylsalicylic acid tablets may be given to relieve the pain.

If vomiting occurs, guard against inhalation, if necessary by putting the patient in the unconscious position (page 6).

If the snake has been killed, it should be lifted with a stick into a container and retained for identification. Do not attempt to find or kill a snake, as this might result in further bites. Do not handle a dead snake as head reactions can persist for up to one hour after death.

Treatment. If the bite occurs ashore or in port, **transport the patient to hospital immediately.** In other cases, seek RADIO MEDICAL ADVICE, giving, where possible, a description of the snake and the nature of the bite.

If the bite is on the hand, arm, foot, or leg, the best immediate treatment is to cleanse the wound with soap and water, cover it with a sterile dressing, and apply a broad, firm, but not tight, crepe bandage above the bite (see note regarding tourniquet application, page 17). Alternatively, immobilize the whole limb by the same means. The bitten limb should be moved as little as possible because movement spreads the venom.

Sucking the venom out of a bite is not generally recommended, because of the danger of aggravating bleeding, introducing infection, and poisoning the person giving the treatment. Vigorous sucking at frequent intervals may, however, be used for bites on the face and body where immobilization is not possible. The person sucking should spit out the venom extracted.

If venom from a spitting cobra enters the eye, bathe the eye thoroughly with water.

Jellyfish

It is sensible not to swim in waters where jellyfish abound. If someone has a part of a jellyfish stuck to him, this could contain sting cysts. Alcohol should be applied to the affected part to kill the undischarged sting cysts. The tentacles and slime should then be scraped off. **Do not rub the sting with wet hands or a wet cloth** as this will aggravate the sting.

In severe cases with rapid collapse, artificial respiration and heart compression may have to be carried out (page 6).

Poisonous fish

These exist in most tropical waters, especially round the islands of the Pacific and Indian Oceans. They have long spines covered by venom-secreting tissues. The stings cause an intense and often agonizing local pain.

If possible, immerse the affected part in the hottest water the patient can bear. The pain is then relieved within seconds. Remove the limb quickly from the water to avoid blistering. Reimmerse as pain recurs (usually after about 30 minutes). If the affected part of the body cannot be immersed in hot water (face or trunk), the puncture wound should be infiltrated with lidocaine as follows.

Prepare a syringe containing 1% lidocaine hydrochloride. Sterilize the skin with spirit, and push the point of the needle just under the skin. Inject sufficient lidocaine to raise a small blob under the skin. Wait for a few minutes to allow the anaesthetic to act. Lower the barrel of the syringe so that the needle is kept just under the skin, push it forward, and inject a further small amount of lidocaine. Pull the needle back, move the barrel round through about 60 degrees, push the needle forward, and inject again. By repeating this process, an area of about 3–4 cm in diameter can be anaesthetized (see Fig. 124).

Sea urchins

The spines of sea urchins can produce painful injuries when they pierce the skin. This is par-

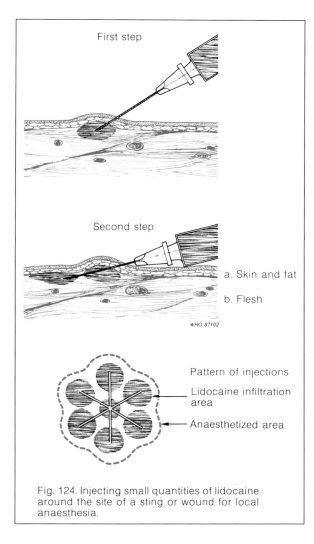

First step

Second step

a. Skin and fat

b. Flesh

WHO 87102

Pattern of injections

Lidocaine infiltration area

Anaesthetized area

Fig. 124. Injecting small quantities of lidocaine around the site of a sting or wound for local anaesthesia.

After removal of the spines, swab the skin with 1% cetrimide solution and apply a dry dressing. If you think that you have left part of the spine in the skin, refer the patient to a doctor at the next port, as small cysts may develop which, when burst, can cause a recurrence of the severe burning pain.

Scorpions, centipedes, and spiders

Local pain and fright are the commonest, and often the only, results of bites by these insects. Stings and bites by a few varieties can, however, be painful, particularly in children. In such cases, apply pressure above the bite and suck the wound vigorously for five minutes, frequently spitting out anything sucked out of the bite. Wash the wound well with soapy water, and apply a dressing to the wound. If the pain remains severe the area should be infiltrated with 1% lidocaine hydrochloride.

Bee, wasp, hornet, and ant stings

These are often painful and may be followed by considerable swelling. A sting in the throat may obstruct breathing. If you are in port and the swelling looks likely to be severe or the sting is in the throat, send the patient to hospital.

If the sting is still in the wound, try to remove it. If part of the sting is above the skin surface, try to express any remaining poison by running your thumb-nail along the length of the sting starting from its base. Wash with a cupful of water in which a teaspoonful of sodium bicarbonate (baking-soda) has been dissolved. A person who has been stung in the mouth or throat should be given the sodium bicarbonate solution to drink and an ice cube to suck.

Some patients are very susceptible to stings. Allergic symptoms can start very quickly, including rapid collapse (see Anaphylactic shock, page 167).

Human bites

A severe infection may develop in a wound caused by human teeth because the mouth

ticularly true of the sea urchin found in the Mediterranean, and off the coasts of France, Spain, and the south of England. This sea urchin has a black body 30 mm or more in diameter which is covered with sharp purple spines about 25 mm long. Parts of the spines are left in or under the skin. Remove these, using 1% lidocaine hydrochloride as local anaesthetic, if necessary. Wait for at least 5 minutes after the injection before you start to cut the skin. If the patient complains of pain in any part, give a further injection. Try to use the smallest possible amount to gain the maximum effect.

abounds with potentially harmful bacteria. However, self-inflicted bites of the tongue and lip are tolerated well.

The bite should be treated in the same way as other wounds (see page 67) and observed carefully for any infection. Treatment for tetanus is not needed because the causative organism is not found in the human mouth.

Boils, abscesses, and carbuncles

(See also Cellulitis, page 178)

Boils

A boil is an area of inflammation that begins at the root of a hair. It commences as a hard, raised, red, tender spot which enlarges. It may subside in two or three days, but more often it softens on the top and forms a yellow "head". The top breaks and the pus drains out, after which the boil heals. Normally the boil does not cause an increase in body temperature but lymphangitis (page 212) may occur.

Carbuncles

A carbuncle is a collection of small boils very close together. The boils cause a large swelling which is very painful. The temperature may rise to 38 °C and the patient will feel ill.

Abscesses

An abscess is a localized collection of pus which gives rise to a painful throbbing swelling. At first the swelling is red, hot, hard, and very tender, and after a day or two it becomes distended with pus and increasingly painful. At this stage, the skin over it becomes thinned and purplish in colour and it "gives" slightly when it is lightly touched. There is usually a rise in temperature to 38–40 °C. There may also be considerable swelling around the area, and the glands draining the area may be enlarged and painful (see Lymphatic inflammation, page 211).

The commonest sites for abscesses are on the arm, in the armpit, on the neck, in the groin, and beside the anus.

Treatment

General treatment

Where there is a small boil with localized inflammation and no rise in temperature, there is no need to give antibiotics. The area round the boil should be swabbed with 1% cetrimide solution and, when it has been dried, a light dry dressing should be applied. Where there is a large boil, a carbuncle, or an abscess, any hair round the area should be clipped short before swabbing or eventual incision.

Rest the patient and apply heat locally, in the form of hot-water compresses. Hot saline solution (two level teaspoonfuls of table salt to one litre of water) can be used for the compresses. The temperature of the solution should be around 43 °C. If the compresses cannot be handled comfortably by the attendant, then they are too hot for the patient.

To relieve the pain, give acetylsalicylic acid tablets, in the usual dose (see page 305).

If (a) the abscess does not appear to be ready for incision (see below), that is if you cannot detect —by gentle pressure on either side—fluctuation of pus in it, and (b) the temperature remains above 38 °C, give antibiotic treatment. For a patient not allergic to penicillin, give procaine benzylpenicillin, 600 000 units intramuscularly, and at the same time start the standard antibiotic treatment (see page 308).

As soon as you are satisfied that pus is present, open the abscess and evacuate the pus. Do not wait for the abscess to burst.

Treatment by incision

The following items are required for dealing with an abscess with pus in it:

- scalpel
- tissue forceps
- dressing forceps
  - Autoclave or boil these instruments for 20 minutes in the sterilizer. Place the sterilizer (with water drained off) on a clean towel. Allow it to cool.

- a bowl of hot (37 °C) antiseptic lotion (1% solution of cetrimide)
- cotton wool made into swabs
- a kidney dish to collect the pus
- a container for the disposal of soiled swabs and dressings
- a 30-cm strip of sterile ribbon gauze.

Clean your hands thoroughly with soap, water, and nail-brush, and get an assistant to arrange the patient comfortably and in a good light.

1. Inspect the area closely and decide exactly where to make the incision. It should be at the site of greatest fluctuation and since, as a general rule, blood vessels and nerves run in the long axis of the body, along this axis; with such an incision, there is less likelihood of damaging these structures than with a transverse incision.

2. Paint the abscess and a wide area of surrounding healthy skin with antiseptic solution (1% cetrimide).

3. Take a scalpel and make a deliberate incision at least 1.5 cm long over the most prominent fluctuant area. If the abscess is on a limb, instruct the assistant to steady it. Pus should discharge freely. If it does not, insert the closed blades of the forceps into the wound and open them up widely. Next withdraw the forceps and, taking a swab in each hand, exercise gentle pressure on each side of the abscess to help evacuation of the pus. Squeezing is unnecessary and may be dangerous, since it can spread infection.

4. Using dressing forceps, pick up a length of sterile ribbon gauze and insert it into the wound. Pack it in lightly and leave about 10 cm on the surface of the wound. The object is to keep the wound open so that it drains effectively and heals from the bottom up.

5. Clean the area with a sterile swab.

6. Apply sterile gauze, cotton wool, and bandages.

Continuation treatment

Keep the part at rest for 24 hours and then remove the gauze drain. If the discharge is very slight, the patient free from pain, and the temperature settling, put on a simple sterile gauze dressing. Put a dry dressing on daily until the wound heals.

Note. Boils or carbuncles on or around the nose, in the nostrils, or on the lips should NOT be opened. There is always a danger of the infection being extended to the brain, with serious consequences. These lesions should be allowed to discharge spontaneously. Get RADIO MEDICAL ADVICE on whether to give antibiotics in such cases.

Subsequent management

If the patient feels ill and has a temperature, he should be put to bed and given either 2 paracetamol or 2 acetylsalicylic acid tablets every 6 hours, to control the pain. If the temperature continues for more than a day, get RADIO MEDICAL ADVICE on whether to give antibiotics.

As the discharge is infected, you should dispose of the dressing carefully, sterilize any instruments or bowls you have used, and wash your hands thoroughly.

The dressings should be changed daily.

Always test the urine for glucose if any patient has an abscess, carbuncle, or bad boil. The test is best carried out on a specimen of urine passed about 2–2½ hours after a substantial meal. If glucose is found in the urine the patient should see a doctor at the next port because he may have diabetes (see page 186).

Bronchitis

Bronchitis is an inflammation of the bronchi, which are the branches of the windpipe inside the lungs. There are two forms, acute (of recent origin) and chronic (of long standing).

Acute bronchitis

This may occasionally occur as a complication of some infectious fever (for instance, measles) or other acute disease. More usually, however, it is an illness in itself. It usually commences as a severe cold or sore throat for a day or two, and then the patient develops a hard dry cough, with a feeling of soreness and tightness in the chest which is made worse by coughing. Headache and a general feeling of being unwell are usually present. In mild cases there is little fever, but in severe cases the temperature is raised to about 38–39 °C and the pulse rate to about 100, while the respiration rate is usually not more than 24.

In a day or two the cough becomes looser, phlegm (sputum) is coughed up (at first sticky, white, and difficult to bring up, later greenish-yellow, thicker, and more copious), and the temperature falls to normal. The patient is usually well in about a week to 10 days, but this period may often be shortened if antibiotic treatment is given.

Note.
- The rise in temperature is only moderate.
- The increase in the pulse and respiration rates is not very large.
- There is no sharp pain in the chest.

These symptoms distinguish bronchitis from pneumonia (see page 221), which gives rise to much greater increases in temperature and pulse rate, with obviously rapid breathing and a blue tinge to the lips and sometimes the face. The absence of pain distinguishes bronchitis from pleurisy (page 220), for in pleurisy there is severe sharp pain in the chest, which is increased on breathing deeply or on coughing.

General treatment

The patient should be put to bed and propped up with pillows, because the cough will be frequent and painful during the first few days. A container should be provided for the sputum, which should be inspected. Frequent hot drinks will be comforting. Smoking should be discouraged.

Specific treatment

Give 2 tablets of acetylsalicylic acid every 4 hours. This is sufficient treatment for milder cases with a temperature of up to 38 °C which can be expected to return to normal within 2–3 days. If the temperature is higher than 38 °C,

give phenoxymethyl penicillin potassium tablets (500 mg) at once, followed by 250 mg of the same drug every 6 hours for the next 5 days. If the patient is allergic to penicillin, sulfamethoxazole + trimethoprim tablets (400 + 80 mg), 2 tablets every 12 hours for 5 days, should be given instead.

Should there be no satisfactory response to treatment after 3 days, seek RADIO MEDICAL ADVICE.

Note. Sulfamethoxazole + trimethoprim must not be given to a woman who is pregnant or might be pregnant.

Subsequent management

The patient should remain in bed until his temperature has been normal for 48 hours.

Examination by a doctor should be arranged at the next port.

Chronic bronchitis

This is usually found in people past middle age who are aware of the diagnosis. Exposure to dust and fumes and inhalation of tobacco smoke predispose to the development of chronic bronchitis. Sufferers usually have a cough of long standing. If the cough is troublesome, give codeine sulfate, 15 mg (half a tablet), repeated after 4 hours if necessary.

Superimposed on his chronic condition, a patient may also have an attack of acute bronchitis, for which treatment (as above) should be given. If this occurs, the body temperature is usually raised and there is a sudden change from a clear, sticky or watery sputum to a thick yellow sputum. Anyone with chronic bronchitis should seek medical advice on reaching his home port.

Cellulitis

This is a septic skin condition, but is unlike an abscess in that the inflammation spreads under the skin without being localized. The skin is red and swollen and, when the infection has taken hold, the skin will pit on pressure as in oedema (page 216). The patient will usually feel unwell and shivery, and often has a headache and fever. The nearby lymph nodes will become enlarged and painful (page 211, Lymphatic inflammation).

Treatment

General treatment

All patients with fever should be put to bed. If the swelling is other than very slight, the affected part should, if possible, be elevated.

Specific treatment

Give procaine benzylpenicillin, 600 000 units intramuscularly, then the standard antibiotic treatment (page 308).

Chest pain

When the patient has been examined, the temperature, pulse, and respiration rates recorded, and the signs and symptoms noted, use Fig. 125 and Table 6 to diagnose his condition or to confirm your diagnosis.

More information about each condition and the treatments are given separately for the various illnesses.

Cholecystitis—inflammation of the gall-bladder

Cholecystitis may occur in either acute or chronic form and is nearly always associated with the presence of stones in the gall-bladder. The patient is usually middle-aged or older, overweight, and in chronic cases there is often a history of long-standing indigestion with flatulence made worse by fried or fatty foods. In a typical acute attack, there is a sudden onset of pain in the right, upper quarter of the abdomen in the gall-bladder area. The pain is usually moderately severe, constant rather than colicky, and may spread through the body towards the right shoulder-blade and sometimes to the right shoulder-tip. Fever, nausea, and vomiting are present, and the patient tends to lie still in bed rather than roll about. This stillness is an

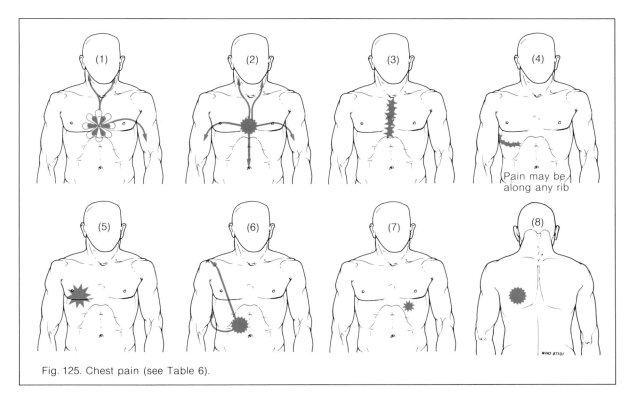

Fig. 125. Chest pain (see Table 6).

Table 6. Chest pain: associated signs

Diagram[a]	Position and type of pain	Age group	Onset	Breathless	General condition	Blue lips and ears	Pale colour
1	behind breastbone – down left arm, up into jaw or down into abdomen; constricting	middle-aged and older	sudden, usually after effort	no	looks ill and anxious	no	yes
2	behind breastbone, up into jaw, down into abdomen; down either arm, usually left; crushing	middle–aged and older; can occur in younger people	sudden, often at rest	yes (severe)	looks very ill; collapsed, restless, vomiting	often	yes
3	burning sensation up behind the whole of breastbone	any	may follow mild indigestion	no	good; may vomit	no	not usually
4	along line of ribs on one side; aching	any, but more likely in older people	slow	no	good	no	no
5	any part of rib cage; sharp stabbing, worse on breathing and coughing	any	sudden	slightly	good	no	no
5, 7, 8	any part of rib cage; sharp stabbing, worse on breathing and coughing	any	gradual or sudden; often follows a cold	yes	looks very ill; flushed	yes	no
5, 7, 8	any part of rib cage; sharp pain	any	sudden	yes	good at first	later	yes
6	pain passes from right abdomen through to shoulder–blade and to tip of right shoulder	usually middle–aged	slow	no	ill, sometimes flushed; vomiting	no	not usually
6	same distribution as for cholecystitis; agonizing colicky pain	any, often middle–aged	sudden	yes, when spasms are present	ill, restless; nausea and vomiting	no	yes
	at site of injury; sharp stabbing made worse by breathing	any	sudden	no	normally good; but may be shocked	no	yes (when shocked)
	any part, often in back; dull aching	any	slow	no	good	no	no

[a] Numbers refer to Fig. 125.

Sweating	Temperature	Pulse rate/min	Respiration rate/min	Tenderness	Additional information	Probable cause of pain
yes	normal	normal	18	none	can be brought on by effort, eating a large meal, cold, or strong emotion; passes off in two or three minutes on resting; patient does not speak during an attack	angina pectoris (page 203)
yes	normal	raised, 90–120	increased, 24 +	none	pulse may be irregular; heart may stop	coronary thrombosis (page 204)
no	normal	normal	18	none	patient may notice acid in mouth	heartburn (page 209)
no	usually normal	normal	normal	often between ribs in affected segment	small spots similar to those of chickenpox appear along affected segment; breathing will be painful; may affect other parts of the body	shingles (page 229)
no	elevated, 37.5–39.5°C	raised, 100–120	increased, 24	none	may be the first sign of pneumonia	pleurisy (page 220)
yes	elevated, 39–40.5°C	raised, 100–130	greatly increased, 30–50	none	dry persistent cough at first, then sputum becomes "rusty"	pneumonia (page 221)
no	normal	raised, 72–100	increased, 18–30	none	may be caused by penetrating wound of chest or occur spontaneously; symptoms and signs depend on the amount of air in the pleural cavity; the affected side moves less than the normal side	pneumothorax (page 221)
no	elevated up to 38°C	raised up to 110	slightly increased, 18	over gallbladder area	note that pain in the right shoulder-tip may result from other abdominal conditions causing irritation of the diaphragm	cholecystitis (page 179)
yes	usually normal	raised, 72–110	increased up to 24 or more during spasms	over gallbladder area		biliary colic (page 172)
only if shocked	normal	raised, if shocked	increased	at affected area	fractured ribs may penetrate lung; look for bright red frothy sputum and pneumothorax	fracture of the rib (page 32)
no	normal	normal	normal	at affected areas	"nodules" may be felt; common site around the upper part of the back	muscular rheumatism (page 222)

important diagnostic sign in distinguishing cholecystitis from biliary colic where the patient is extremely restless during the spasms of colic (page 172).

On feeling the abdomen, local tenderness over the gall-bladder is often found, with an associated hardness of contracted, right, upper abdominal muscles.

If the hand is slid gently under the rib margin in the gall-bladder area while the abdominal muscles are drawn in during a deep breath, it is usually possible to find a localized, very tender place.

In diagnosis, cholecystitis must not be confused with biliary colic, right-sided pneumonia, hepatitis, perforation of a peptic ulcer, or right-sided pyelitis (see Table 5, pages 162–163, and Table 6, pages 180–181).

Treatment

General treatment

The patient should be confined to bed and solid food should be withheld until the nausea subsides, but adequate fluids (except milk) should be given. Thereafter, a bland diet without fried or fatty foods should be offered. A hot-water bottle applied to the gall-bladder area will alleviate pain. The temperature, pulse, and respiration should be recorded. The white of the eye should be inspected each day for jaundice, and the urine and faeces examined for changes associated with jaundice (page 210).

Further management. All cases, even if recovered, should be seen by a doctor when convenient.

Specific treatment

Give phenoxymethyl penicillin potassium 250-mg tablets, 2 tablets to start with, then 1 tablet every 6 hours for 5 days. If the patient is allergic to penicillin, give the alternative standard antibiotic treatment (see page 308). In an uncomplicated case, the condition should improve after 2 days. If the pain and fever increase or biliary colic starts (page 172) or jaundice appears (page 210), get RADIO MEDICAL ADVICE.

Colds (common cold, coryza, rhinitis)

The symptoms of the common cold are: temperature, runny nose, red and watery eyes, malaise, aching muscles, chilliness, and often a sore scratchy throat and cough. A cold lowers a person's resistance to other diseases and permits secondary infections. Symptoms of a cold may precede many communicable diseases, so the patient should be watched carefully for other symptoms of these diseases. A septic sore throat may start as a cold. A cold may lead to bronchitis, pneumonia, and middle-ear disease.

Treatment

Unless symptoms develop that indicate a more serious disease, the treatment for a cold should be symptomatic. The patient should be kept in bed until the temperature is normal and he feels reasonably able to function. Acetylsalicylic acid, 600 mg, should be given by mouth every 3–4 hours to help relieve the symptoms. If it is not well tolerated by the patient, paracetamol, 500 mg, may be tried at the same frequency.

Antibiotics should NOT be given.

The patient should drink plenty of fluids such as water, tea, and fruit juices. He should be advised to blow his nose gently to avoid forcing infectious material into the sinuses and middle ear. When symptoms subside for 24 hours, the patient should get out of bed but restrict activities for a day or two before returning to full duty. This will also help to stop the spread of the cold to other crew members.

Warning. Anyone who is deaf or slightly deaf as the result of a cold, should not travel by air or go skin-diving.

Constipation

Constipation is a symptom, not a disease, and is rarely an acute or serious medical problem.

Treatment

Frequently changes in diet, environment, type of work, degree of physical activity, and emotional or nervous upsets may result in constipation. The patient should be advised to eat regularly, drink ample amounts of water, and take regular exercise. A gentle laxative such as magnesium hydroxide suspension may be given. Prunes or prune juice could be added to the patient's diet.

Persistent constipation of recent onset or a change in bowel habits may indicate a serious underlying bowel condition. The seaman should be advised to seek medical attention when port is reached.

As a temporary relief from constipation, magnesium hydroxide suspension may be given (1–2 15-ml tablespoonfuls daily).

Cough

Coughing is a sudden forceful expulsion of air from the lungs, usually in a series of efforts. Although annoying, a cough helps to get rid of phlegm (sputum) that builds up in air passages.

Coughs may be productive (of sputum) or non-productive (dry). The sputum may be purulent (with pus), copious or scanty, thick or thin and fluid, clear or frothy, odourless or foul-smelling, blood-streaked or manifestly bloody. A cough may be acute or chronic, occasional or persistent, slight or severe, painful or painless.

Coughing is not a disease in itself but a symptom. An acute cough is usually caused by an infection of the upper respiratory system. A productive cough that lasts for more than 3 months frequently means that the patient is suffering from chronic bronchitis, even though he does not recognize that he is ill until he becomes short of breath. Because of cigarette-smoking and air pollution, thousands of people become victims of chronic bronchitis and eventually of emphysema. Chronic cough with fever suggests a more serious condition, such as tuberculosis, pneumonia, or even carcinoma of the lung. Chronic cough without fever may indicate heart disease, bronchial asthma, or bronchiectasis (in-fection and degeneration of the air passages). In all cases of chronic cough, a doctor on shore should be consulted.

The following general observations may be helpful.

Simple bronchitis usually follows a viral infection or "cold" that is accompanied sometimes by a sore throat, a raw heavy feeling behind the breastbone, and a dry cough that changes into a productive cough.

Pleurisy is manifested by a severe pain in the chest wall that is aggravated by deep breathing.

With *pneumonia,* there is usually fever, often a productive cough with pus or sputum, and pain in the chest.

Tuberculosis of the lungs may be associated with a slight but prolonged cough.

Cancer of the lung has become alarmingly frequent in persons who have been heavy smokers. Early diagnosis of cancer is difficult but cough, spitting blood, persistent fever, and loss of weight may be early warnings.

When a cough accompanies an acute illness, especially when there is fever, a full history should be obtained from the patient. After examining the patient and his sputum, the most likely cause of the illness should be determined. Prepare a request to obtain RADIO MEDICAL ADVICE.

Treatment

Coughs due to colds and viral bronchitis are treated symptomatically with acetylsalicylic acid, as described under Bronchitis (page 177).

For persistent and severe coughing accompanying respiratory infections, give half of a 30-mg tablet of codeine, several times a day, if necessary.

Specific treatment should be directed to the cause of the illness. The patient's pulse, temperature, and rate and depth of respiration should be noted.

(See also: Asthma, page 171; Bronchitis, page 177; Pleurisy, page 220; Pneumonia, page 221; and Tuberculosis, page 145.)

Dental emergencies

The following dental first aid procedures are intended to relieve pain and discomfort until professional care is available.

Bleeding

Bleeding normally occurs following removal of a tooth. However, prolonged or profuse bleeding from a tooth socket must be treated.

Treatment

To treat bleeding, excessive blood and saliva should be cleared from the mouth. Then, a piece of gauze 5 cm × 5 cm, should be placed over the extraction site and biting pressure applied by the patient. It is important to fold the gauze to a proper size well adapted to the extraction site. The pad should be left undisturbed for 3–5 minutes, then replaced as necessary. Once bleeding has stopped, the area should be left undisturbed. If bleeding is difficult to control, a piece of gauze, 5 cm × 5 cm twisted into a thin cone shape or rolled (see Fig. 126) should be packed into the site and a second gauze pressure pack placed over it. The patient should apply biting pressure for 30 minutes to 1 hour and continue biting if necessary. The mouth should not be rinsed for 24 hours. A soft diet should be maintained for two days.

Lost fillings

Fillings may come out of teeth because of recurrent decay around them, or a fracture of the filling or tooth structure.

Treatment

If pain is absent, no treatment will be required for a lost filling and the patient should be advised to see a dentist when in port. If the tooth is sensitive to cold, a temporary dressing should be put into the cavity. First, the tooth is isolated by placing a 5 cm × 5 cm piece of gauze on each side. A cotton pellet can be used to dry the cavity. A drop of oil of cloves should be placed on cotton and gently pressed into the cavity; this will usually control the pain and may be repeated 2 or 3 times daily as necessary.

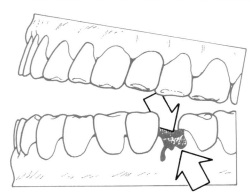

A. Press on each side to close the tooth socket.

B. Make a pad which is larger than the socket.

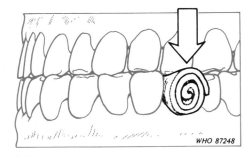

C. Place the pad over the socket and bite firmly.

Fig. 126. Control of bleeding following removal of a tooth.

Toothache without swelling

This condition is usually caused by irritation or infection of the dental pulp from a cavity, lost filling, or a recurrent problem in a tooth that has a filling in place.

Treatment

The patient who has a toothache without swelling of the gums or face should be advised to chew on the other side of his mouth. Foods should not be too hot or too cold. Pain may be relieved with acetylsalicylic acid, 600 mg by mouth. If the patient does not tolerate this drug, a 500-mg paracetamol tablet should be given. The patient with a toothache should be told to swallow the acetylsalicylic acid and never to hold the tablets in the mouth as this will burn the soft tissues. If the aching tooth has a large cavity, the instructions for placing a sedative cotton dressing, described on page 184, under Lost fillings, should be followed.

Toothache with swelling

Toothache with swollen gums or facial tissue is often the result of infection by tooth decay that involves the dental pulp and spreads into the tissues of the jaws through the root canals. The condition is also common as a result of infections associated with diseases of the gums, periodontal membrane, and the bone that supports the teeth. In all cases, there is frequently pain, swelling, and the development of an abscess with pus formation.

Treatment

The patient with mouth and facial swelling should be observed closely and the following data noted: (1) the exact area of the swelling, initially and during the illness; (2) the type of swelling, whether soft, firm, or fluctuant (movable tissue containing a pus-filled cavity); (3) degree of difficulty in opening and closing the mouth; and (4) the oral temperature, morning and night. These data are important for following the patient's progress and evaluating the effectiveness of the treatment.

The pain should be controlled with acetylsalicylic acid as described above under Toothache without swelling.

For infection, an initial dose of 500 mg of phenoxymethyl penicillin potassium should be given by mouth, followed by 250 mg every six hours. If the patient is allergic, or suspected of being allergic, to penicillin, oral erythromycin should be used in the same dosage and frequency. The patient should be kept on the antibiotic for at least 4 days after he becomes afebrile (without fever). He should be instructed to see a dentist at the earliest opportunity.

The patient should be advised to rinse the mouth with warm saline solution (a quarter teaspoonful of table salt in 200 ml of warm water) for 5 minutes of each waking hour. This will cleanse the mouth and help to localize the infection in the mouth. Also, saline solution may produce earlier drainage and relief from pain. After the pain and swelling subside, the oral rinsing should be continued until the patient is seen by a dentist.

Dental infection

Dental infection usually occurs when decay extends into the pulp of the teeth. Bacteria from the mouth will enter the tissues of the jaws via the canal in the tooth's root. The infection may remain mild or may progress to a swelling in the mouth or face, after producing fever, weakness, and loss of appetite.

Treatment

Discomfort from a dental infection may be controlled with acetylsalicylic acid, 600 mg by mouth. If the patient does not tolerate acetylsalicylic acid, a 500-mg paracetamol tablet should be given. Antibiotics are used as described in the section Toothache with swelling, but RADIO MEDICAL ADVICE should be obtained beforehand.

Painful wisdom tooth (pericoronitis)

Pericoronitis is an infection and swelling of the tissues surrounding a partially erupted tooth, usually a wisdom tooth (third molar). Often a small portion of the crown or a cusp of the offending tooth can be seen through the soft tissues. The soft tissues appear swollen and the degree of inflammation or redness may vary considerably. When the infection is severe, the patient may complain of difficulty in opening the mouth. When the area is examined carefully, pus may be found coming from underneath the soft tissues in the area of the partially erupted tooth.

Treatment

For a painful wisdom tooth, the area between the crown of the tooth and the soft tissues should be flushed with warm saline solution (a quarter teaspoonful of table salt in 200 ml of warm water). In addition, the patient should be treated as directed under Toothache with swelling (page 185).

Trench mouth (Vincent's infection)

Vincent's infection is a generalized infection of the gums. During the acute stage it is characterized by redness and bleeding of the gums. Usually there is a film of greyish tissue around the teeth. There is usually a very disagreeable odour and a foul metallic taste in the mouth. The acute stage may be accompanied by a moderately high fever. Lymph glands in the neck may be swollen.

Treatment

The patient should be advised to eat an adequate diet but avoid hot or spicy foods. The fluid intake should be increased.

For pain, 600 mg of acetylsalicylic acid should be given by mouth every 3–4 hours as needed. If it is not well tolerated by the patient, try 500 mg of paracetamol at the same frequency.

For infection, an initial dose of 500 mg of phenoxymethyl penicillin potassium should be given by mouth, followed by 250 mg every 6 hours. If the patient is allergic, or suspected of being allergic, to penicillin, oral erythromycin should be given at the same dosage. The patient should be kept on the antibiotic until at least 4 days after the fever has gone. He should be instructed to see a dentist at the earliest opportunity.

Denture irritation

Generalized inflammation in the denture area is usually due to poor oral hygiene. Inflammation in localized areas usually requires some alteration or adjustment of the denture by a dentist. These localized areas are usually located where the border of the denture rests against the tissues.

Treatment

The patient should avoid using the denture until the soft tissues have healed. The denture should be cleaned carefully with mild soap and water and stored in a water-filled container to avoid dehydration of the base material. The patient should be referred to a dentist for appropriate adjustment of the denture.

Diabetes

In diabetes, the body is unable to use or store all the sugar derived from the carbohydrates eaten in a normal diet. The excess sugar remains in the blood and passes into the urine, carrying water with it. This loss of sugar and water from the body causes increased appetite and thirst.

Diabetics do not produce enough insulin, which is a hormone (regulating the blood sugar level) secreted into the blood by the pancreas. Adjustments in the metabolism of sugar have to be made by changing the diet and/or amount of insulin. Urine sugar (glucose) determinations help to find the proper dietary adjustment and insulin needs.

Diabetes is characterized by loss of weight, weakness, excessive thirst, and the frequent passage of large quantities of urine. These symptoms may be modified according to the age of the patient.

In young people, the symptoms are present in a more severe form of the disorder, which may show itself as a rapid, acute illness. In older people, particularly if they are overweight, the disease may come on more gradually and only be suggested by the development of thirst and more frequent passage of urine. In both age groups, the disease may show itself by successive crops of boils or carbuncles. Diabetes can be made worse by infection.

If diabetes is suspected, test the urine for sugar (page 107) about 2–3 hours after a large meal. If the test is positive and if the other symptoms of diabetes are present, it should be assumed that the patient is suffering from the disease until there is proof to the contrary.

Treatment

Put the patient on a strict diet containing no starchy or sugary foods. This will normally avoid complications such as coma (see below) until full diagnosis and treatment can be carried out under medical supervision.

Two kinds of coma can occur in diabetes: diabetic coma and insulin coma.

- *Diabetic coma* can occur as the first sign of diabetes in a young person with the acute form of the disease or develop in a known diabetic when the insulin level is too low and the sugar in his blood has risen too high.
- *Insulin coma* is seen in the known diabetic who has taken too much insulin or not enough food and whose blood sugar is too low.

Table 7 describes the features that distinguish these two types of coma.

If the patient is unconscious, it may be possible to confirm the diagnosis from clues in his belongings. A known diabetic taking insulin or another diabetic drug may carry a supply of sugar or sweets. He may have an identity card or bracelet or neck chain stating he is diabetic. Give treatment as for an unconscious patient (page 104) and get RADIO MEDICAL ADVICE.

If the patient is passing into a coma but not unconscious and the problem seems to be too little insulin, ask him if he has any insulin and get his advice on how much to give. If he has none, put him to bed, and get RADIO MEDICAL ADVICE. If the problem is too much insulin and he is still conscious, then give him 4 lumps or 2 heaped teaspoonfuls of sugar dissolved in warm water at once and keep him under strict observation.

If it is difficult to distinguish between the two conditions, give a conscious patient the sugar, as it will do no harm, even if too little insulin is present.

If in doubt always obtain RADIO MEDICAL ADVICE.

Note on insulin and other drugs. There are a number of different kinds of insulin which vary in strength and length of action, and all are given by injection. There are also other drugs used to control diabetes and these are in tablet form. If you have to give insulin or other drugs to a diabetic, always check the instructions on the container very carefully. Insulin should only be given in accordance with advice from a doctor. Diabetics should not be employed at sea.

Table 7. Distinguishing features of diabetic coma and insulin coma

Feature	Diabetic coma (high blood sugar)	Insulin coma (low blood sugar)
onset	gradual	sudden
temperature	initially below normal	normal
pulse	rapid, weak	normal
respiration	laboured, deep gasping	normal or sighing
skin	blue tinge, dry	sweating common
breath	smell of acetone (sweet, like nail varnish or musty apples)	no sweet smell
tongue	dry	moist
dehydration	present	absent
mental state	no disturbances	confusion, sometimes fits
vomiting	common	rare
urine		
sugar	much present	trace or absent
ketone	present	absent

Diarrhoea and dysentery

Diarrhoea is defined as an abnormal increase in the amount, frequency, and fluidity of the evacuations from the intestine. Diarrhoea is not a disease itself but a symptom of trouble in the intestinal tract. In this respect, it is like cough, chills, and fever, which are general symptoms of many diseases.

Dysentery, characterized by griping abdominal pains and frequent stools containing blood and mucus, is caused by an inflammation of the intestines, particularly of the large bowel.

Diarrhoea and dysentery are often used interchangeably to describe a variety of conditions with loose stools. Normally, during the process of digestion, food is moved slowly through the intestines to allow for its absorption. In diarrhoea, the motion of the intestines (peristalsis) is speeded up and the stools are soft or semisolid, but they may become watery, possibly frothy, and may have a very foul odour.

There are many different causes of diarrhoea and dysentery. Generally, the symptoms are produced by an infectious organism, its toxic products, toxins, or allergens. Infection may be caused by viruses, a wide variety of bacteria, and one-celled parasites such as amoebae. The non-infectious causes include poisoning from heavy metals such as mercury, allergies to certain foods, and emotional upsets.

In most cases of diarrhoea there is no inflammation of the intestines. The loss of fluid through large watery stools may cause serious dehydration; shock, collapse, or death may occur when diarrhoea is very severe. This is due to a loss of the water and salts from the body. Severe dehydration may occur rapidly.

Signs that may be useful in determining the cause of intestinal illness and its severity include:

- *Character of stools.* Are they watery? What is the colour? Is there blood, mucus, or pus? Is it all liquid, or are there some formed pieces?
- *Frequency of stools.* How often does the patient pass stools?
- *Signs and symptoms of dehydration.* Is the mouth very dry? Is the patient very thirsty? Do the eyeballs seem sunken? If you pinch the skin, does the fold return slowly to its former position? Is there vomiting, rash, fever, abdominal pain? Is the patient alert or drowsy?
- *History.* Has the patient ever had intestinal symptoms before? If so, when? Does the patient have any idea what might be causing the symptoms?
- *Epidemiology.* Is anyone else on board the ship sick? What symptoms do the patients have in common? What have they eaten in common, on board or on shore?

Data on all these points should be reported to the doctor on shore, when he is requested by radio for advice on handling the case or an outbreak of diarrhoea among the crew.

Treatment of diarrhoea

The principle of diarrhoea treatment is to replace water and salt lost in stools and vomit; in most cases this can be done orally. Oral rehydration salts (ORS) are packed in sachets or aluminium bags (each containing 3.5 g of sodium chloride, 2.9 g of trisodium citrate (or 2.5 g of sodium bicarbonate or baking-soda), 1.5 g of potassium chloride, and 20 g of glucose, which have to be dissolved in a litre of drinking-water). If ORS are not available, a suitable drink can be made by mixing 8 level teaspoons of sugar and 1 level teaspoon of salt in a litre of water. The solution should be given first rapidly and then in small volumes, one glass (200 ml) after each bowel movement, to replace the continuing losses.

When the patient is in shock (see page 17) and unable to drink, and he continues to lose a great amount of water, get RADIO MEDICAL ADVICE on the necessity of giving him intravenous fluids, such as 0.9% (9 g/litre) sodium chloride solution, or dextran injection, 6%, and sodium chloride, 0.9%, available in the ship's medicine chest (or others, like lactated Ringer's solution). Intravenous infusions (see page 117) may be ordered only by a physician, and they are required only for very severe cases.

To relieve diarrhoea, a 30-mg codeine sulfate tablet may be given; this may be repeated after 4 hours, if necessary.

The patient should be kept in bed and made as comfortable as possible. A liquid or low-residue diet should be given that includes soft drinks and broths containing salt, as soon as the patient feels hungry. Spicy, fatty, or greasy foods should be avoided. If there is blood in the vomit or in the stools, signs of dehydration (especially a daily weight loss of 2 kg or more) or decreasing urinary output (less than 500 ml in 24 hours), RADIO MEDICAL ADVICE should be promptly obtained.

In most cases of diarrhoea, no antibiotics are required. But in severe cases with high temperature (39–40 °C) phenoxymethyl penicillin potassium tablets, 250 mg every 6 hours for 5 days, should be given (this medication should be replaced by erythromycin, in the same dosage and frequency, in patients allergic to penicillin).

In acute cases of diarrhoea, the possibility of enteric fever (see page 130), cholera (see page 128), and malaria (see page 135) should be considered and appropriate treatment given.

Every case of diarrhoea should be treated as an infectious condition, and the patient should be isolated in his (single) cabin, or in the ship's hospital (see Standard isolation, page 298).

If the condition does not settle within 48 hours or if many cases of diarrhoea occur among the crew at the same time, get RADIO MEDICAL ADVICE.

Specific causes of diarrhoea and some special treatments are outlined below.

Amoebic dysentery

This is caused by a one-cell parasite, an amoeba that infects the bowel and is particularly prevalent in the tropics. The infection, known as amoebiasis, is an intestinal disease which may appear in acute or chronic form. The patient with acute amoebiasis usually has abdominal pains, chills, and bloody and mucoid diarrhoea, with many loose stools during the day. Chronic amoebiasis will produce mild abdominal discomfort with diarrhoea containing blood and mucus alternating with periods of constipation. The diagnosis requires laboratory identification of the amoeba in the faeces.

If there is a suspected case of this infection on board ship, get RADIO MEDICAL ADVICE.

Cholera

See page 128.

Enteric fever

See page 130.

Virus infections

Infection with several viruses will cause nausea, vomiting, upper abdominal discomfort, headache, malaise, low-grade fever, and diarrhoea. The stools are watery without blood and mucus. The patient often feels well between bouts of diarrhoea and vomiting. Oral rehydration salt solution should be given for treatment (see page 188), 1–2 litres or more daily, depending on the amount of fluid lost by the patient (see Fluid balance, page 101).

Prevention of diarrhoea

See: Personal hygiene, page 299; Food hygiene, page 285; Liquid transport and potable water, page 288; Disinfection procedures, Annex 5, page 354; Enteric fever, page 130.

Drug abuse

It is a matter of great concern that some seafarers obtain and use drugs illegally.

The commonest drug used by seafarers is cannabis or pot. When it is smoked there is an odour of burnt leaves or rope. Attempts are often made to disguise this smell. Pot-smoking is more often a communal than a solitary activity.

It is very difficult to identify by inspection the various "hard" drugs, as they are supplied in various shapes, sizes, colours, and consistencies.

Prolonged use of any drug results in mental deterioration and personality changes of varying degree. It may be very difficult for a ship's officer

Table 8. Narcotics and other drugs commonly abused; guide to identification [a]

Type of drug and slang names [b]	Physical symptoms	Look for	Dangers
AMPHETAMINES AND METHAMPHETAMINE (bennies, pep pills, dexies, copilots, wake-ups, lid poppers, hearts, uppers)	aggressive behaviour, giggling, silliness, rapid speech, confused thinking, no appetite, extreme fatigue, dry mouth, bad breath, shakiness, dilated pupils, sweating; subject licks lips, rubs and scratches nose excessively; chain-smoking, extreme restlessness, irritability, violence, feeling of persecution, abscesses	pills, tablets or capsules of varying colours, chain-smoking, syringes	hallucinations, death from overdose; speeds rate of heart-beat, may cause permanent heart damage or heart attacks; loss of weight, addiction, mental derangement; suicidal depression may accompany withdrawal
BARBITURATES (barbs, blue devils, goof balls, candy, yellow jackets, phennies, peanuts, blue heavens, downers, red birds)	drowsiness, stupor, dullness, slurred speech, drunk appearance, vomiting, sluggish, gloomy, staggering, quarrelsome	tablets or capsules of varying colours, syringes	unconsciousness, coma, death from overdose, physiological addiction, convulsions or death from abrupt withdrawal
BARBITURATE-LIKE DRUGS			
chloral hydrate (knockout drops, joy juice, Peter, Micky Finn (mixed with alcohol))	similar to barbiturates	capsules (blue and white, rust, and red), and syrup	gastric distress is common; circulatory collapse may occur
benzodiazepines— chlordiazepoxide, diazepam, flurazepam, and others (downers)	similar to barbiturates	Librium capsules (green and black); Valium tablets (white 2 mg, yellow 5 mg blue 10 mg); Dalmane capsules (red and yellow); other sizes or brands may be different in appearance	
methaqualone (ludes, sopors, Qs, the love drug, quads)	similar to barbiturates; also vomiting, hypotension, pulmonary oedema	tablets (white, green, pink); capsules (light and dark blue, light and dark green)	especially dangerous in combination with alcohol
CANNABIS (pot, grass, reefers, locoweed, Mary Jane, hashish, tea, gage, joints, sticks, weed, muggles, mooters, Indian hay, mu, griffo, mohasky, gigglesmoke, jive)	sleepiness, talkativeness, hilarious mood, enlarged pupils, lack of coordination, craving for sweets, erratic behaviour, loss of memory, distortions of time and space, intellectual deterioration	strong odour of burnt leaves or rope, with characteristic sweetish odour; small seeds in pocket lining, cigarette paper, discoloured fingers, pipes	inducement to take stronger narcotics, antisocial behaviour
COCAINE (leaf, snow, speedballs, crack)	muscular twitching, convulsive movements, strong swings of mood, exhilaration, hallucinations, dilated pupils	white odourless powder	convulsions, death from overdose, feelings of persecution, psychic dependence
HALLUCINOGENS LSD (acid, sugar, Big D, cubes, trips) DMT (businessman's high) STP	severe hallucinations, feelings of detachment, incoherent speech, cold sweaty hands and feet, vomiting, laughing, crying, exhilaration or depression, suicidal or homicidal tendencies, chills, shivering, irregular breathing	cube sugar with discoloration in centre, strong odour, small tube of liquid	LSD causes suicidal tendencies, unpredictable behaviour, brain damage from chronic usage, hallucinations, panic, accidental death, persecution feelings

Table 8 *(continued)*

Type of drug and slang names[b]	Physical symptoms	Look for	Dangers
NARCOTICS			
heroin (H, horse, scat, junk, snow, stuff, harry, joy powder) morphine (white stuff, Miss Emma, M, dreamer)	stupor, drowsiness, needle marks on body, watery eyes, loss of appetite, bloodstain on shirt sleeve, «on the nod», constricted (small) pupils that do not respond to light, inattentive, slow pulse and respiration	needle or hypodermic syringe, cotton, tourniquet (string, rope or belt), burnt bottle caps or spoons, glassine[c] envelopes, traces of white powder round nostrils from sniffing or inflamed membranes in nostrils, small capsules containing white powdered substance	death from overdose, mental deterioration, damage to brain, heart, and liver, embolisms, infections from use of dirty needles and equipment
cough medicine that contains codeine sulfate or opium (schoolboy) paregoric	from large doses: drunk appearance, lack of coordination, confusion, excessive itching; small doses show little effect	empty bottles of cough medicine or paregoric	causes addiction
VOLATILE SOLVENTS model aeroplane glue, lighter fluid, gasoline, paint thinner, many aerosols, household and commercial fluids	violence, drunk appearance, dreamy or blank expression, odour of glue or other solvents on breath, excessive nasal secretion, watering of eyes, poor muscular control, delirium, hallucinations	tubes of glue, glue smears, paper or plastic bags, empty aerosol cans, lighter-fluid containers, gasoline cans	damage to lung, brain, and liver, death from suffocation or choking, anaemia

[a] Source: National Institute on Drug Abuse, United States Public Health Service.
[b] Slang names are given in parentheses.
[c] Glazed, translucent, greaseproof paper.

to differentiate between a drug user and a person suffering from some form of mental illness.

The signs and symptoms of addiction vary according to the drug, and the picture may be complicated by the user mixing two drugs to obtain maximum effect. The symptoms may be sudden in onset because of overdosage or withdrawal, or they may appear slowly during prolonged use.

The following indications may be helpful in deciding upon a diagnosis of drug abuse.

- Unexplained deterioration in work performance
- Unexplained changes in pattern of behaviour towards others
- Changes in personal habits and appearance, usually for the worse
- Loss of appetite
- Inappropriate behaviour: for example, wearing long-sleeved shirts in very hot weather to conceal needle-marks, and sunglasses to conceal large or small pupils
- Needle punctures and bruises on the skin of the arms and thighs, or septic spots that are the result of using unsterile needles
- Jaundice (hepatitis) through the use of improperly sterilized syringes and needles (page 210).

If you have suspicions, make discreet inquiries of other crew members. These may reveal alterations in behaviour patterns in the patient. There may be rumours of drug problems on board.

Do not accept the patient's word that he is not a drug-user, as lying, cheating, and concealment are all part of the picture.

In Table 8 the most commonly used narcotics are listed (by their pharmacological and slang names), and descriptions are given of the physical symptoms typical of intoxication with them and dangers connected with their abuse.

Treatment

Remove any drugs from the patient and try to identify them and their source.

Always obtain RADIO MEDICAL ADVICE.

If the patient is unconscious, give the appropriate treatment (Unconscious patient, page 104). If the symptoms are those of mental disturbance, see Mental illness, page 213.

Note. Police and Customs officials take a very strong interest in certain drugs and how they come to be on your ship. Any confiscated drug should be clearly labelled and locked away in a secure place and noted in the official logbook.

If you are returning to your country the presence of prohibited drugs on board should be reported to the Customs, which will take appropriate action.

In other countries inquiries as to the proper procedure should be made through the ship's agents.

Ear diseases

The parts of the ear

The ear is concerned with the functions of hearing and equilibrium. There are three divisions of the ear: *outer ear, middle ear,* and *inner ear.*

The outer ear is comprised of the auricle *(pinna),* a skin-covered cartilaginous framework which projects from the head, and the *external auditory canal.* This canal, lined with hairs and glands that secrete earwax *(cerumen),* is about 2.5 cm long, and extends to the middle ear.

The ear-drum *(tympanic membrane* or *typanum)* separates the external auditory canal from the middle ear. In the middle ear, three tiny movable bones (the *ossicles)* modify and conduct sound vibrations from the ear-drum to the inner ear.

The ear-drum and the ossicles are so delicate that violent vibrations of the air, like those caused by the explosion of a bomb or the firing of a heavy gun, may injure them. The three ossicles of each ear are called *malleus, incus,* and *stapes* and, in the order named, resemble a miniature hammer, anvil, and stirrup.

Air is let into or out of the middle ear through the *Eustachian tube,* which leads to the upper part of the throat. The Eustachian tube allows the air pressure in the middle ear to equal that of air entering the external ear canal. A nose or throat infection can spread to the middle ear by way of the Eustachian tube. Blowing the nose may force infected material into the middle ear. An infection of the middle ear may result in an abscess and running ears. Sometimes infection may extend from the middle ear to the *mastoid cells* in the temporal bone and cause mastoiditis. When this happens, a brain abscess or permanent deafness may result.

The *mastoid process* is the large, rounded, bony prominence behind the pinna. It contains many tiny cavities resembling a honeycomb. It is sometimes inflamed by the spread of infection from the middle ear.

Vibrations that are carried to the inner ear by the external canal, the ear-drum, and the ossicles are converted into nerve impulses and transmitted to the brain by the auditory nerve. The inner ear consists of the *osseous* (bony) labyrinth and the *membranous* labyrinth. The osseous labyrinth is composed of a series of cavities: the vestibule, three *semicircular canals,* and the *cochlea* ("snail-shell"). The membranous labyrinth is located within the osseous labyrinth and has the same general shape. The sense of hearing is transmitted to the auditory nerve through the cochlea. The semicircular canals are concerned with equilibrium. They are filled with fluid, and any movement of the head results in a corresponding movement of the fluid in the three canals. The movement of the fluid generates nerve impulses, which cause a person to make adjustments in position to maintain balance. The motion of an aeroplane or of a ship can produce dizziness and nausea. This *motion sickness* may be called "sea sickness", "air sickness", or "bus sickness", depending upon the type of vehicle in which the person is riding when he experiences the symptoms.

How to examine an ear

Compare the appearance of both ears. Look for swelling or redness of the pinna and the sur-

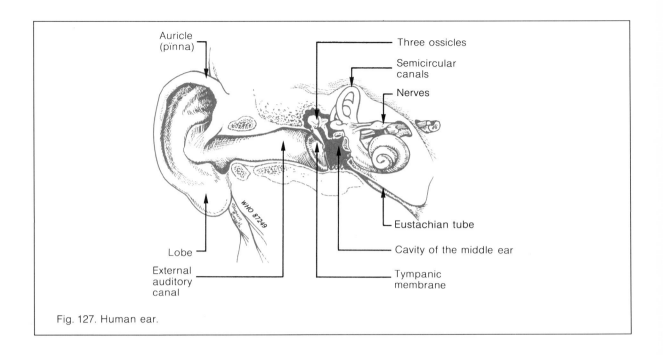

Fig. 127. Human ear.

rounding area, and for discharge from the ear passage. Feel for tender or enlarged lymph nodes around the affected area and compare them with those of the other ear (page 211).

In a good light, pull the pinna gently backwards and upwards to enable inspection further inside the ear passage.

Press firmly on both mastoid processes. Tenderness of one may indicate middle ear or mastoid infection.

Check the duration, intensity, and nature of any earache. Establish if hearing has been diminished or if there are added noises in the ear and if the sense of balance has been impaired.

Earache

An earache may be caused by infection of the middle ear; an inflammation, an abscess, or a boil of the external auditory canal; inflammation of the Eustachian tube; dental conditions; mumps; and inflammation of the mastoid bone or other structures nearby.

The ears frequently ache, feel sore, or have a feeling of fullness during a head cold or other disease in which the respiratory passages are affected. Acute infection of the middle ear causes severe earache and usually results in the formation of an abscess.

Wax in the ear

Accumulated wax may cause only slight discomfort in the ear passage but, if it has hardened and is near the ear-drum, pain may be felt when swallowing or blowing the nose. Hearing is often diminished, especially if water gets into the passage. It is often possible to see the wax plug when the entrance to the ear passage is examined in good light.

Treatment

No attempt should be made to scrape out the wax.

The patient should lie down with the affected ear uppermost.

Slightly warmed vegetable oil should be put into the ear passage and left for 5 minutes before wiping away any drops that run out when the head is tipped sideways.

Repeat this treatment twice a day for 3 days. Do not put a cotton-wool plug in the ear.

If relief of symptoms is not satisfactory, ear-syringing should be arranged at the next port.

Infection of the outer ear (otitis externa)

This is a common infection in hot weather or after swimming, especially in the tropics and subtropics. The condition frequently affects both ears, whereas boils and middle ear infection occur mainly in one ear. Pain is not a feature of the disease but the ear may be uncomfortable and itch, with a discharge from the ear passage. The skin of the ear passage is liable to bleed slightly and appears red, shiny, and abraded.

Treatment

The ear passages should be thoroughly mopped out with cotton-wool swabs until dry. Sometimes it is better for the patient to do this for himself under supervision. Next, a few aluminium acetate ear-drops should be put in one ear passage while the patient is lying on one side. After he has spent 5 minutes in that position, the ear should be dried and the other ear similarly treated. Repeat the treatment at 2-hourly intervals until the discharge has ceased. If there is no improvement after 2 days, tetracycline ear-drops should be put in the ear passage(s), 3–4 drops three times a day, until the patient sees a physician.

The patient must not swim or get water into his ears when washing until he has been seen by a doctor or his ears have been normal for 2 weeks. Under no circumstances should cotton-wool or other ear plugs be used.

Boil in the ear

A boil in the ear passage causes a throbbing pain which increases in severity over several days. When the boil is about to burst, there is a sudden stab of pain followed by a small discharge of blood-stained pus with much relief of pain. If the pinna is gently drawn upwards and backwards, it is often possible to see the boil in the ear passage. Pulling the pinna in this manner usually increases the pain and confirms the diagnosis. An inflamed middle ear causes similar pain, but pulling the pinna does not make the pain worse.

The ear passage of the affected side may be obviously narrowed and red in comparison with the other side. The lymph glands draining the infected area may be swollen and tender.

Treatment

Use aluminium acetate ear-drops every 2 hours until the pain goes. If the boil bursts, clean the ear passage, which should subsequently be kept clean and dry.

Infection of the middle ear (otitis media)

An infection of the nose or throat may spread to the middle-ear cavity via the Eustachian tube (Fig. 127, page 193).

When normal drainage of the middle ear through the Eustachian tube is impaired, pressure within the small cavity increases. Infected secretions will then burst through the ear-drum, causing a perforation.

At first there is deep-seated earache, throbbing and nagging like toothache, with some deafness and maybe noises in the ear. The patient feels ill, and his temperature rises. As the pressure increases, the pain becomes worse until the ear-drum perforates. Discharge through the perforation brings relief of both pain and fever. The lymph glands around the ear are not enlarged. The mastoid bone may be tender to pressure firmly applied. The sequence of events may be modified if the infection responds rapidly to antibiotic treatment.

General treatment

The patient should be put to bed and the temperature, pulse, and respiration rate recorded every 4 hours. Two acetylsalicylic acid tablets should be given every 4 hours until the pain disappears. *Warm* olive oil ear-drops may be comforting.

Specific treatment

Even if you only suspect that the patient may have otitis media you should give *as soon as possible,* in order to prevent perforation of the drum, either:

- procaine benzylpenicillin, 600 000 units intramuscularly, followed by the standard antibiotic treatment, or
- 500 mg of erythromycin, followed by 250 mg every 6 hours for 5 days, if the patient is allergic to penicillin.

If the patient is not better at the end of the 5 days, seek RADIO MEDICAL ADVICE.

Subsequent management

When antibiotic treatment is completely successful, the inflammation will settle, pain and fever will subside, and there will be no perforation or discharge.

If perforation does occur, the ear passage should be dried every two hours. Perforation does not imply that the antibiotic has not worked. The full 5-day course of treatment must be given.

When the patient feels better and has no fever, he can be allowed out of bed, but the ear must be kept as clean and dry as possible. All cases should be seen by a doctor when the ship is next in port; swimming and air travel are not advised until approved by a doctor.

Infection of the mastoid cells

A middle-ear infection sometimes spreads to the mastoid cells. This can happen at any time during the course of a long-standing middle-ear infection when a perforated ear-drum, together with a septic discharge, has been present for months or years.

In new middle-ear infections, mastoids should be suspected whenever a patient continues to feel unwell, complains of earache and continuing discharge, and is feverish 10–14 days after the onset. There will be extreme mastoid tenderness, even though a full course of antibiotics has been given. This is a serious complication which may require specialized treatment ashore. Get RADIO MEDICAL ADVICE.

Epilepsy (and other convulsive seizures)

Epilepsy is a chronic nervous disorder characterized by muscular convulsions with partial or complete loss of consciousness. The seizures are brief (several seconds), recur suddenly at irregular intervals, and are usually followed by several hours of confusion, stupor, or deep sleep. Epilepsy has been called "falling sickness" because the patient falls suddenly and usually makes no effort to protect himself from injury. Epilepsy may vary from mild to severe. In the mild form, there is momentary loss of consciousness or confusion and slight muscular twitching without falling. In the severe form, the patient suddenly falls as if struck by an overwhelming blow.

An epileptic may have a seizure at any time.

The patient will suddenly emit a peculiar cry and fall down. He may strike the floor or any object in his way, cut or bruise himself badly, or break a bone. His body usually becomes stiff and rigid for a short time, during which he stops breathing and becomes blue or purple in the face. This phase of the seizure is followed by generalized spasmodic convulsions of the entire body with jerking of the arms, legs, and head, contortions of the face, and foaming at the mouth. The eyes may roll back and forth, but there is no feeling in them and they can be touched without the patient flinching. He may bite or chew his tongue or cheeks so that froth in the mouth becomes blood-stained. Urination or bowel movements may occur involuntarily.

Usually, after several minutes, the convulsion subsides. The patient may regain consciousness or fall into a deep stuporous sleep that may last for several hours. When he awakes, he may be confused or very grouchy and ill-tempered. He probably will have no recollection of the attack.

It is obvious, from the suddenness and nature of the seizures, that epileptics should not be permitted to go aloft. Also, they should never be allowed to enter the engine-room, where there are moving parts of machines on which they might fall, or other potentially dangerous places. In general, a person known to be an epileptic should be advised not to accept employment at sea.

Treatment

During the convulsion

Bystanders should try to prevent the patient from hurting himself and should make him as comfortable as possible. His movements should not be restrained completely, unless he is in danger of falling from a high place or injuring himself in some unusual manner. To keep him from biting or chewing his tongue, something should be inserted carefully between his teeth, such as a twisted handkerchief or a pencil wrapped in cloth. Hard objects should never be inserted. A coat or pillow should be placed under his head, and his threshing legs and arms covered with a blanket to prevent self-injury during the convulsion. Medicines should not be given by mouth. Artificial respiration will not be needed, because the phase during which the patient ceases to breathe is usually very short. After the seizure, while dazed, exhausted, or asleep, the patient may be carried or helped to his bunk. Enough bedding should be placed over the patient to keep him comfortably warm. Usually, he will sleep for some time. However, if he is awake and restless he may be given one dose of phenobarbital, 60 mg by mouth.

Sometimes, a patient may pass from one seizure into another, without intervening recovery of consciousness. This condition, known as status epilepticus, always involves danger to life. The patient may become profoundly exhausted, lapse into coma, and die. Otherwise, an epileptic attack is seldom fatal.

In the case of status epilepticus, obtain RADIO MEDICAL ADVICE, regarding treatment. While waiting for this advice, give the patient an injection of diazepam, 10 mg intramuscularly. If the seizure is not interrupted in 5 minutes you may repeat this drug intramuscularly and in the same doses, every 10 minutes, four or five times.

Between attacks

There is little that can be done at sea to treat epilepsy, except to keep the patient from injuring himself during an attack, and to prevent recurrences by routine use of whatever medicament may have been prescribed for the patient.

The severity and frequency of attacks may be reduced by phenobarbital. RADIO MEDICAL ADVICE should be obtained on the dosage of this medicament.

Convulsions similar to epilepsy

These may occur in otherwise normal persons as the result of a severe acute illness, brain injury, meningitis, nephritis, insulin injection, high blood pressure, paralytic stroke, brain tumour, toxins, cyanide poisoning, or strychnine poisoning. The treatment of such convulsions should be the same as that outlined for epilepsy.

Eye diseases

(See also: Eye injuries, page 76.)

Anatomy of the eye

The eye is a sphere approximately 2½ cm in diameter formed by a tough outer coat called the *sclera* and the clear front portion known as the *cornea*. Six muscles attached to the sclera work in various combinations to move the eye. Ocular movements are very precise and rapid.

The cornea is the window through which light enters the eye. There are no blood vessels in the normal cornea, and it is extremely sensitive and especially susceptible to injury or infection. If scarring occurs from injury, the cornea loses its transparency at the site of the scar, which may markedly impair vision. The cornea has an extremely high concentration of nerve fibres which

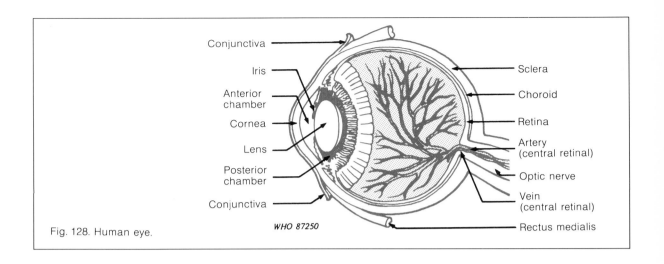

Conjunctiva

Iris

Anterior chamber

Cornea

Lens

Posterior chamber

Conjunctiva

Sclera

Choroid

Retina

Artery (central retinal)

Optic nerve

Vein (central retinal)

Rectus medialis

Fig. 128. Human eye.

WHO 87250

make it extremely sensitive to the slightest insult. A superficial scratch, abrasion, or the smallest foreign body can cause extreme pain with reflex tearing and redness (inflammation) of the eye.

The back surface of the eyelids and the exposed portion of the white part of the eye (sclera) are lined with a paper-thin covering called the *conjunctiva*; it does not cover the cornea. The conjunctiva may become infected and produce a red eye with a variable amount of pus, mucus, or water discharge. This infection is called conjunctivitis.

The internal portions of the eye are the *anterior chamber, iris, lens, vitreous body,* and *retina* (see Fig. 128). The anterior chamber, a space filled with watery fluid, lies between the cornea and the coloured portion of the eye (iris). The *iris* is a pigmented muscular structure which opens and closes the pupil to allow more or less light to enter the eye, depending on the level of illumination. This works much the same as the iris diaphragm that controls the amount of light entering a camera.

Just behind the iris is the *lens,* which can change shape to focus light rays on the back of the eye. When the lens becomes cloudy, it is called a *cataract.* Behind the lens is the *vitreous body,* a cavity filled with a clear jelly known as the *vitreous humour.*

The innermost layer of the eye is the *retina,* with specialized nerve cells which are sensitive to light and colour. The retina acts in much the same way as the film in a camera, but converts the light rays it receives into nerve impulses which are transmitted to the brain by the *optic nerve.* In the brain, the nerve impulses are interpreted as sight.

Chronic eye diseases

Cataracts

A cataract is a clouding of the lens of the eye. This usually occurs as a feature of aging in people over 60, but may occur at a much younger age.

Cataracts may develop without an obvious cause, but some are the result of severe injuries.

Persons suspected of having a cataract should visit a specialist on shore for a complete eye examination. In almost all cases, the cure for cataracts is surgical removal.

Glaucoma

Glaucoma is an eye disease in which the fluid substance in the eyeball is under higher pressure than usual.

Acute congestive glaucoma is an extremely serious condition requiring immediate treatment

197

by an eye specialist. There is a sudden increase in the eye pressure, accompanied by extreme pain, redness of the eye, and slight cloudiness of the cornea. The pupil does not react to light. In addition to severe pain, which may be accompanied by nausea and vomiting, the patient experiences somewhat decreased vision and perceives coloured haloes round bright lights.

In some cases, glaucoma develops as a result of damage due to previous injury or inflammation of the eye.

Treatment. Emergency surgery is often required to lower the pressure in the eye and prevent irreversible loss of vision. Cases of acute congestive glaucoma should always be referred to a physician, so RADIO MEDICAL ADVICE should be obtained in suspected cases. If professional treatment cannot be provided immediately, the physician giving advice by radio may direct the temporary use of pilocarpine hydrochloride eye-drops and, to relieve the pain, 600 mg of acetylsalicylic acid every 3 to 4 hours as needed or one 500-mg paracetamol tablet every 6 hours.

If pain is very severe, one 10-mg ampoule of morphine sulfate may be given intramuscularly upon RADIO MEDICAL ADVICE.

Infectious eye diseases

The most common infectious eye diseases that might be encountered aboard ship include blepharitis (infection of the eyelid margins), conjunctivitis (infection of the conjunctiva), sties (infection of the glands in the lid margins), and, more rarely, keratitis (infection of the cornea). Trachoma is also found in some areas.

Before any medicament is used in the eye the patient should be questioned about possible allergies to any of its ingredients.

Blepharitis

Blepharitis is an inflammation of the margins of the eyelids with redness and thickening, plus crusting that resembles dandruff. There is itching, burning, loss of eyelashes, watering and sensitivity to light. There may be shallow marginal ulcers.

Treatment. Anti-infective eye-drops may be used during the day and 1% tetracycline eye ointment applied, at night and on rising, directly to the lashes at the lid margins with a sterile applicator or clean fingertips.

RADIO MEDICAL ADVICE should be obtained. If the condition persists, the patient should consult an ophthalmologist on reaching shore.

Conjunctivitis

Conjunctivitis is an infection of the conjunctiva of the eye by bacteria or viruses.

The patient will have a red eye, a variable amount of pus, discharge, and watering, and at times slight pain or sensitivity to light. The eyelids often stick together in the morning, and it may be necessary to soak the eyes before they can be opened.

Viral conjunctivitis is transmitted from person to person through infected fingers, fomites (bedding, clothing, door-knobs, books etc.), or through improperly sterilized ophthalmic instruments.

The disease, once introduced, may rapidly spread among crew members. It has a sudden onset, and the typical signs are: photophobia (intolerance of light), oedema of eyelids, watering, and subconjunctival haemorrhages in the form of purplish red spots. The disease normally affects one eye first, then spreads to the other eye as well; it lasts 10–30 days.

Note on prevention. To prevent the spread of conjunctivitis, isolate the patient for the duration of his illness, and warn other crew-members to maintain scrupulous personal hygiene: to use only their own towels, or disposable towels, and to wash their hands frequently.

Treatment. The treatment of conjunctivitis consists of applying anti-infective eye-drops or tetracycline eye ointment. It may not be very effective if the conjunctivitis is of viral origin.

Warning. Corticosteroid preparations (for instance, hydrocortisone ointment) should never be used in the treatment of conjunctivitis and keratitis without proper ophthalmological supervision.

Keratitis (inflammation of the cornea)

There are several kinds of keratitis, an inflammatory condition that affects the cornea, the transparent part of the eyeball. It is more serious than conjunctivitis because scarring of the cornea may result in a serious loss of vision. Keratitis may be due to primary or secondary infections from bacteria and viruses.

Although symptoms may vary among the several types of keratitis, there is usually a scratchy pain that is moderate to severe, redness, excessive watering of the eye, a conjunctival discharge, and blurred vision.

Treatment. For suspected keratitis, RADIO MEDICAL ADVICE should be sought. For all types of confirmed keratitis, only an ophthalmologist should prescribe treatment.

For superficial abrasions of the epithelium of the cornea, local application of eye-drops is recommended.

See the warning at the end of the section on conjunctivitis above.

Trachoma

Trachoma is a form of conjunctivitis caused by a virus and is common in many parts of the world. The word itself means "roughness", and this describes the granular state of the inner surface of the eyelids. The condition is usually of long standing and may remain unsuspected until the inner surfaces of the lids are inspected. There may be a history of discharge from the eyes, often only slight. The edges of the eyelids tend to assume a purplish colour, and the inner surface, especially of the upper eyelid, is dark red and has scattered small white flecks like sago grains. New blood vessels may extend into the cornea,

usually from the upper part of the eye, and the area may become ulcerated and interfere with sight.

Treatment. A patient suspected of having trachoma should be referred to a doctor at the next port of call. In the meantime, tetracycline eye ointment should be applied locally (see Fig. 113, page 120) twice a day, until the patient sees a doctor. Normally, the above treatment will continue for 1–2 months.

Fainting

Fainting is due to a temporarily insufficient supply of blood to the brain as a result of one or more of the following conditions:

- fatigue, fright, fear, emotion, mental shock;
- lack of food, lack of fluids, heat exhaustion;
- injury, pain, loss of blood;
- lack of fresh air.

If a person looks pale and starts to sway, prevent him from fainting by making him sit down with his legs apart and his head well down between his knees, or lay him flat on his back and raise his legs. If you are sure that he can swallow, give him a little water; this will help to revive him.

Note. A myocardial infarction (see page 204) can sometimes be painless. Take this possibility into consideration, if (*a*) your patient has a history of previous chest pains, or (*b*) there was no apparent reason for fainting. In such a case, when you may suspect a heart disease (a "silent", painless, myocardial infarction), get RADIO MEDICAL ADVICE.

Food-borne diseases (food poisoning)

Food-borne diseases—some forms of which are sometimes also referred to as food poisoning—are illnesses of an infectious or toxic nature caused, or thought to be caused, by the consumption of food (including drinks) or water.

The term applies to:

- diseases caused by microorganisms that multiply in the intestine, with or without invasion of mucosa or other tissue;

- diseases caused by bacteria that produce enterotoxins (toxins that affect tissues of the intestinal mucosa) during their colonization and growth in the intestinal tract; and
- intoxications caused by the ingestion of food containing poisonous chemicals, naturally occurring toxins, or toxins produced by microorganisms (algae, moulds, bacteria).

On board ship, outbreaks of food-borne disease may occur within a short space of time among crew-members and passengers who have consumed one or more foods in common. Foods frequently incriminated in food-borne diseases include various meats, poultry, mayonnaise and mayonnaise-containing salads, rice, pastries, custards, ice cream, etc. The interval between eating contaminated food and the onset of symptoms may be as short as 2–4 hours, but some contaminants need a longer incubation period of the order of 12–24 hours.

The onset in most cases is abrupt and sometimes violent, with severe nausea, cramps, vomiting, diarrhoea, and prostration; sometimes with lower than normal temperature and blood pressure. The duration of illness in otherwise healthy individuals is usually no more than 1 or 2 days. However, in persons who are susceptible to illness (e.g., infants, the elderly, chronically ill persons) complications may arise.

Treatment

In severe cases, rest in bed for at least 24 hours, without solid foods, is indicated. Mild cases need only rehydration and a restricted diet.

Fluid should be given in as large a quantity as the dehydrated and thirsty patient demands and can tolerate. A solution of oral rehydration salts flavoured with fruit juice should be used for this purpose (see Treatment of diarrhoea, page 188).

When the diarrhoea appears to have settled, a slow return to the normal diet can be made.

Prevention

Perishable food should be kept hot (over 60 °C) or cold (0–4 °C) and covered; it should not be kept at room temperature for longer than neces-

sary. The temperature in the galley and mess refrigerators should be monitored daily and always kept in the "safe" range (0 °C–4 °C).

To prevent food-borne diseases, strict adherence to the principles of food hygiene is essential (see page 285).

Botulism

Botulism is a food-borne disease of special significance, which may occur after consuming improperly processed foods; these may include canned foods, sausages, smoked or processed meats, and others.

Symptoms usually appear 1–2 days after eating contaminated food. They start with dry mouth, visual difficulty (blurred or double vision), and drooping of upper lids, followed by paralysis; sometimes vomiting and diarrhoea also occur. The fatality rate is high.

In a suspected case of botulism, immediately obtain **RADIO MEDICAL ADVICE** on treatment.

Prevention

Never consume food from cans with bulging lids, or food that smells "off".

Gout and gouty arthritis

Gout is a disturbance of kidney function in which the excretion of a particular acid in the urine is impaired. Crystals formed from the acid are deposited in, and cause inflammation of, tissues such as cartilage and ligaments.

Gout often runs in families and affects men at or over middle age more frequently than women. The first attack usually affects the big toe, but recurrent attacks may involve any of the elbow or hand joints or those of the ankle and foot. The attack often happens during the night when the affected joint suddenly swells up and becomes severely painful, especially on movement. The overlying skin becomes very red and shiny. The patient often feels irritable and short-tempered before and during the attack. Mild fever may be present, but the general health is unimpaired. Attacks usually last for 2 or 3 days, then the joint returns to normal.

General treatment

The patient should rest in bed. The application of either heat or ice to the affected joint may be comforting.

An affected foot joint should be protected from pressure of bed clothes by the use of a bed cradle (see page 98). **Alcoholic drinks should not be allowed.**

Give acetylsalicylic acid or paracetamol tablets to relieve pain.

(See also: Acute rheumatism (Rheumatic fever), page 222.)

Haemorrhoids (piles)

Haemorrhoids are enlarged veins surrounding the last 3–5 cm of the rectum and its outlet, the anus. Not all haemorrhoids bleed, but bleeding occurs sooner or later in most untreated cases.

They may be external or internal. External haemorrhoids are found below the anal sphincter (the muscle that closes off the anus). They are covered by skin and are a brown or dusky purple colour. Internal haemorrhoids may protrude through the anal sphincter. These are covered by a mucous membrane, and are bright red or cherry-coloured.

Haemorrhoids are usually noticed because of bleeding, pain, or both after the bowels have moved. Hard faeces can scrape the haemorrhoids and will increase discomfort and bleeding. Faecal soiling of underclothes may occur if the anal sphincter is lax. Occasionally, the blood in an external haemorrhoid may clot and give rise to a bluish painful swelling about the size of a pea at the edge of the anus, a *thrombosed* external haemorrhoid.

For inspection of the anus, the patient should be instructed to lie on his left side with both knees drawn up to his chin. When he is in this position, separate the buttocks. The anus should be carefully inspected for swellings caused by external haemorrhoids or by internal haemorrhoids that have come down through the anus.

Treatment

The patient should be advised to eat wholemeal bread, breakfast cereals containing bran, vegetables, and fruit in order to keep the faeces as soft as possible. Fluid intake should be increased. After a bowel action, the patient should wash the anus with soap and water, using cotton wool. He should then thoroughly wash his hands, using a soft nail-brush to ensure cleanliness of the nails.

In the case of extremely painful external haemorrhoids, bed rest may be advisable. Taking a hot bath after defecating can be comforting. Hydrocortisone ointment 1% may give some relief, but before giving it, consult a doctor on shore. The condition usually subsides in about 7–10 days.

The patient should be told if he has internal haemorrhoids, so that he can push them back after washing his back passage. If they are painful and bleeding, an antihaemorrhoidal suppository should be inserted into the back passage after washing but before drying the area.

If the haemorrhoids cannot be pushed back (prolapsed internal haemorrhoids) the patient should be put to bed face downwards with an ice-pack over the prolapsed haemorrhoids. After some time—30 minutes to one hour or upwards—the prolapsed haemorrhoids should have shrunk and it should be possible to push them back.

Bleeding from haemorrhoids is usually small in amount. Local discomfort round the anus may be relieved by calamine lotion or zinc oxide paste. Any patient with haemorrhoids should always be seen by a doctor at the next port, both for treatment and to exclude any more serious disease of the bowel.

Hand infections

Many infections of the hands could be prevented by simple measures that are often neglected in practice. Small scratches, cuts, abrasions or pricks should never be ignored, and they should be treated by thorough washing in soap and water before being covered by a protective dressing.

Inflammation and suppuration of a hand or finger wound may lead to internal scarring which could result in some loss of hand function. It is always advisable to start a course of standard antibiotic treatment (page 308) as soon as the signs of inflammation affect a hand or finger (see also Lymphatic inflammation, page 211).

Some common finger infections are described in this section.

Pulp infection

An infection of the fleshy pulp in the top segment of a finger will cause a rapid increase of internal pressure in the segment, which can result in lasting damage unless treatment is promptly given. Infection may follow quite a trivial injury such as a needle prick or other minor puncture wound. Slight soreness of the pulp within a few hours of injury may quickly progress to a severe throbbing pain accompanied by redness and tense swelling of the whole pulp.

Treatment

When symptoms start, give procaine benzylpenicillin 600 000 units intramuscularly, and begin standard antibiotic treatment (page 308). The patient should remain at rest with the hand elevated above shoulder height. Pain should be relieved by 2 acetylsalicylic acid or paracetamol tablets every 4–6 hours.

Inflammation round the base of a nail

This is usually due to infection that has entered through a split at one corner of the nail skin-fold and spread round the nail base. The semi-circle of skin becomes shiny, red, swollen and painful.

General treatment

The arm should be kept at rest in a sling.

Specific treatment

A course of standard antibiotic treatment should be given (page 308). With treatment, the infection usually subsides without pus formation. If pus should form, it can often be seen as a small "bead" just under the skin. The pus should be released by making a tiny cut over the "bead". A paraffin gauze dressing under a dry dressing should be applied twice daily until the discharge has finished. Protective dry dressings should then be applied until healing is completed.

Headache

A headache is a symptom of an illness and not a disease in itself. Some of the more common causes of headache are listed below, and reference should be made to the relevant pages in this guide.

Common causes

- Onset of an acute illness, when headache is almost always associated with fever and feeling ill. Examples are influenza and infectious diseases such as measles, typhoid, etc.
- Common cold with associated sinusitis (page 223).
- Over-indulgence in alcohol.
- Tension caused by worry, work, or family difficulties. Headaches of this kind are not associated with fever or feeling ill; they are sometimes associated with eye-strain.

Less common causes

- Migraine, which usually occurs only on one side of the head and is associated with vomiting and visual disturbances such as flashing lights.
- Brain disease; acute as with meningitis (page 140) and less acute as with raised blood pressure (by no means a common symptom, see page 208) and stroke (page 231).

Treatment

Always take the patient's temperature and, if it is raised, put him to bed and watch for the possible development of further signs and symptoms. Otherwise, give two acetylsalicylic acid or paracetamol tablets, which may be repeated every 4 hours. For treatment of more severe pain, see the section on analgesics (page 305).

All cases of *persistent headache* should be referred to a doctor at the first convenient opportunity.

Heart pain and heart failure

When the calibre of the coronary arteries becomes narrowed by degenerative change, insufficient blood is supplied to the heart and consequently it works less efficiently. The heart may then be unable to meet demands for extra work beyond a certain level and, whenever that level is exceeded, attacks of heart pain (angina pectoris) occur. Between episodes of angina, the patient may feel well.

Any diseased coronary artery is liable to get blocked by a blood clot. If such a blockage occurs, the blood supply to a localized part of the heart muscle is shut off and a heart attack (coronary thrombosis) occurs.

Angina pectoris (pain in the chest)

Angina usually affects those of middle age and upwards. The pain varies from patient to patient in frequency of occurrence, type, and severity. It is most often brought on by physical exertion (angina of effort), although strong emotion, a large meal, or exposure to cold may also be precipitating factors. The pain appears suddenly and reaches maximum intensity rapidly before ending after 2 or 3 minutes. During an attack, the sufferer has an anxious expression, his face is pale or grey, and he may break out in a cold sweat. He is immobile and will not walk about. Bending forward with a hand pressed to the chest is a frequent posture. Breathing is constrained by pain, but there is no true shortness of breath.

When the attack ends (and never during it), the patient will describe a crushing or constricting pain or sensation felt behind the breastbone. The sensation may feel as if the chest were compressed in a vice, and it may spread to the throat, to the lower jaw, down the inside of one or both arms—usually the left one—and maybe downwards to the upper part of the abdomen (see Fig. 125 (1)).

Once the disease is established, attacks usually occur with gradually increasing frequency and severity.

General treatment

During an attack, the patient should remain in whatever position he finds most comfortable. Afterwards he should rest. He should take light meals and avoid alcohol, tobacco, and exposure to cold. He should limit physical exertion and attempt to maintain a calm state of mind.

Specific treatment

Pain can be relieved by sucking (not swallowing) a tablet of glyceryl trinitrate (0.5 mg). The tablet should be allowed to dissolve slowly under the tongue. These tablets can be used as often as necessary and are best taken when the patient gets any symptoms indicating a possible attack of angina. Tell the patient to remove any piece of the tablet that may be left when the pain has subsided, since glyceryl trinitrate can cause a throbbing headache.

If the patient is emotional or tense and anxious, give him 5 mg of diazepam at equal intervals, three times daily during waking hours, and, if he is sleepless, 10 mg at bedtime. The patient should continue to rest and take the above drugs as needed until he sees a doctor at the next port.

Warning. Sometimes angina pectoris appears abruptly and without exertion or emotion, even when the person is resting. This form of angina is often due to a threatened or very small coronary thrombosis (see next page) and should be treated as such, as should any attack of anginal pain lasting for longer than 10 minutes.

Frequent easily provoked attacks often precede a myocardial infarction. RADIO MEDICAL ADVICE should always be obtained in such cases. Evacuation of the patient should be arranged as soon as possible.

Coronary thrombosis (myocardial infarction)

A heart attack happens suddenly and while the patient is at rest more frequently than during activity. The four main features are pain of similar distribution to that in angina (page 203), shortness of breath, vomiting, and a degree of collapse that may be severe. Sweating, nausea, and a sense of impending death are often associated features.

The pain varies in degree from mild to agonizing, but it is usually severe. The patient is often very restless and tries unsuccessfully to find a position that might ease the pain. Shortness of breath may be severe, and the skin is often grey with a blue tinge, cold, and covered in sweat. Vomiting is common in the early stage and may increase the state of collapse.

In mild attacks, the only symptom may be a continuing anginal type of pain with perhaps slight nausea. It is not unusual for the patient to believe mistakenly that he is suffering from a sudden attack of severe indigestion.

General treatment

The patient must rest at once, preferably in bed, in whatever position is most comfortable until he can be taken to hospital. Exertion of any kind must be forbidden and the nursing attention for complete bed rest (page 98) provided. Restlessness, often a prominent feature, is usually manageable if adequate pain relief is given. Most patients prefer to lie back propped up by pillows, but some prefer to lean forward in a sitting position to assist breathing (see Fig. 31, page 33). An hourly record of temperature, pulse, and respiration should be kept. Smoking and alcohol should be forbidden.

Specific treatment

Whatever the severity of the attack, it is best to give all cases an initial dose of morphine, 15 mg intramuscularly, at once. If the patient is anxious or tense, give diazepam, 5 mg three times a day, until he can be placed under medical supervision. In serious or moderate attacks, give a further 15 mg of morphine, intramuscularly, 3–4 hours after the initial injection. The injection may be repeated every 4–6 hours as required for pain relief. Get RADIO MEDICAL ADVICE.

Specific problems in heart attacks

If the pulse rate is less than 60 per minute, give the patient atropine, 1 mg intramuscularly, and raise the legs. The dose should be repeated after 4 hours, if the pulse rate remains less than 60 per minute. However, should a repeat dose become necessary, get RADIO MEDICAL ADVICE.

If the heart stops beating, get the patient on to a hard flat surface and give heart compression and artificial respiration (page 6) at once.

If there is obvious breathlessness the patient should sit up. If this problem is associated with noisy, wet breathing and coughing give one 40-mg furosemide tablet, restrict fluids, start a fluid balance chart (page 102), and get RADIO MEDICAL ADVICE.

Paroxysmal tachycardia

Tachycardia is excessively rapid heart action, with a pulse rate above 100. This condition comes in bouts (paroxysms). The patient will complain of a palpitating, fluttering, or pounding feeling in the chest or throat. He may look pale and anxious, and he may feel sick, light-headed, or faint. The attack starts suddenly and passes off, after several minutes or several hours, just as suddenly. If the attack lasts for a few hours, the patient may pass large amounts of urine. The pulse will be difficult to feel because of the palpitations, so listen over the left side of the chest between the nipple and the breastbone and count the heart rate in this way. The rate may sometimes reach 160–180 beats or more per minute.

General treatment

The patient should rest in the position he finds most comfortable. Reassure him that the attack will pass. Sometimes an attack will pass if the patient takes and holds a few very deep breaths, or if he makes a few deep grunting exhalations. If this fails, give him a glass of ice-cold water to drink.

Specific treatment

If these measures do not stop an attack, give diazepam, 5 mg. Check the heart rate every quarter of an hour. If the attack is still continuing after 2 hours, get RADIO MEDICAL ADVICE.

Note. Heart rate irregularities are likely to occur when a person has consumed too much food, alcohol, or coffee; smoked to excess; or is emotionally excited. Unless they are associated with symptoms of heart disease (pain), there is usually no cause for alarm. However, the patient should be advised to consult a physician.

Congestive heart failure

Congestive heart failure occurs when the heart is unable to perform its usual functions adequately. This results in a reduced supply of blood to the tissues and in congestion of the lungs. In acute failure, the heart muscle fails quickly and the lungs become congested rapidly. In chronic failure, the heart muscle fails gradually and the body has time to compensate. However, when compensation is no longer adequate, fluid will begin to accumulate in the lower parts of the body. Swelling most often appears in the legs and feet, but it may occur in other parts of the body. Although there are many underlying causes of congestive heart failure, the most common are chronic coronary, hypertensive, and arteriosclerotic heart disease.

The signs and symptoms of the disease depend on whether the onset of failure was sudden or gradual. Generally, a gradual loss of energy and a shortness of breath (dyspnoea) occur upon exertion. In more acute cases, the patient may cough up frothy, bloodstained, or pink sputum. Later, shortness of breath may appear during periods of lesser activity, and the patient may need to sit up in bed, or sleep on several pillows at night, to breathe more easily. Ankle swelling may occur owing to the accumulation of fluid in the tissues and, as failure progresses, the swelling may involve the hands, legs, and abdomen. The liver may become enlarged owing to congestion, resulting in discomfort and tenderness. In more advanced cases, there may be blueness of the skin, especially at the lips, ears, and fingernails.

Treatment

(For acute failure, see Coronary thrombosis (myocardial infarction), page 204.)

In severe cases of chronic failure, the patient should be confined to bed in a sitting or semi-sitting position. Heavy meals should be avoided, and the food kept as salt-free as possible. Smoking should be prohibited. RADIO MEDICAL ADVICE must be obtained. **A patient with chronic heart failure should receive medicaments only upon medical advice.**

Heat exposure

(See also: Fluid balance, page 101; Preventing heat illness, page 300; Prickly heat, page 228.)

Excessive heat may affect the body in a variety of ways, resulting in several conditions: heat-stroke, heat cramps, and heat exhaustion.

Heat-stroke (sunstroke)

Heat-stroke is a medical emergency that is associated with a potentially high mortality rate. It occurs when the body's main mechanism of heat loss (evaporation of sweat) is blocked. There may be early warning symptoms of headache, malaise, and excessive warmth, or a general picture of heat exhaustion (see page 207). The onset is usually abrupt with sudden loss of consciousness, convulsions, or delirium. Sweating is absent in the typical case.

On physical examination, the skin is hot, flushed, and dry (see Fig. 129). In severe cases, tiny rounded haemorrhage spots may appear. Deep body temperature is high, frequently in excess of 41 °C. A rectal temperature above 42 °C is not uncommon, and indicates a poor outlook for the patient. The pulse will be rapid and strong and may go up to a count of 160 or more. Respiration may be rapid and deep, and the blood pressure elevated slightly. The pupils of the eyes will first contract, then dilate. Muscular twitching, cramps, convulsions, and projectile vomiting may occur and may be followed by circulatory collapse and deep shock.

Because of the extreme seriousness of heat-stroke, all members of the vessel's crew should be taught the importance of recognizing cessation of sweating, so that corrective measures can begin at an early reversible stage.

For prevention of heat-stroke and other heat exposure injuries, see page 300.

Treatment

Immediate treatment must be given to reduce the body temperature, or brain damage and death may occur. The patient should be undressed and placed in a tub of cold (around 20 °C) water; or covered with continuous cold packs such as wet blankets; or sponged with cold water until the temperature drops (see page 109). The tem-

perature should be taken every 10 minutes and not allowed to fall below 38.5 °C. The skin should be massaged during this procedure to prevent constriction of the blood vessels, to stimulate return of the cooled blood to the overheated brain and other areas, and to speed up the heat loss. After the body temperature has dropped, the patient should be placed in bed in a cool room with a fan or air-conditioner blowing towards the bed. If the body temperature starts to rise, it will be necessary to begin the cooling procedure again. Do **not** give the patient morphine sulfate, epinephrine, or stimulants. **Sedatives (phenobarbital) are given only if convulsions occur,** to control them. The patient should be kept in bed for several days and cautioned against later exposure to heat.

Heat cramps (stoker's cramps)

Heat cramps affect individuals working in high temperatures. The condition involves severe pain and spasms of the abdominal or skeletal muscles and is a result of profuse sweating and a failure to replace the salt loss. The cramps are usually more severe when the individual has been drinking large amounts of fluids without replacing the salt.

The cramps begin suddenly and occur most frequently in the muscles that bend the arms and legs. The patient may be lying down with the legs drawn up, while crying out with the severe pain. The skin may be pale and wet, the blood pressure remains normal, and the rectal temperature runs from about 36.6 to 37.7 °C. Usually there is no loss of consciousness. Although an untreated attack may last for hours, the condition is not considered dangerous.

Treatment

The patient should be moved to a cool place and given water with one teaspoonful of table salt added to each glass. Half a glass of the salt water should be given initially and then again every 15 minutes for an hour, or until the symptoms are relieved. Massage or manual pressure to the muscle may help to relieve the cramp. If a more serious problem seems to be present, RADIO MEDICAL ADVICE should be obtained.

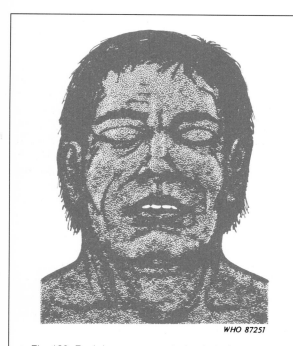

WHO 87251

Fig. 129. Facial appearance in heat stroke.

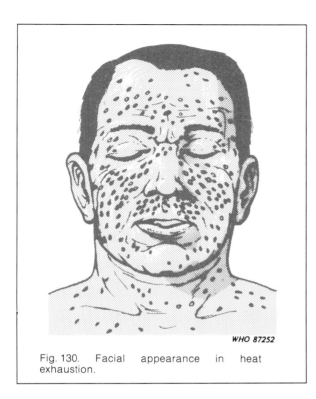

Fig. 130. Facial appearance in heat exhaustion.

Heat exhaustion (heat prostration, heat collapse)

Exhaustion or collapse in the heat is caused by excessive loss of water and salt from the body. It occurs commonly among persons working in hot environments such as furnace rooms, bakeries, and laundries, or from exposure to hot, humid heat while outdoors. The circulation to such vital organs as the heart and brain is disturbed by the pooling of blood in the capillaries of the skin in order to cool the body. The capillaries constrict to compensate for this deficient blood supply, so that the patient's skin appears pale and clammy (see Fig. 130).

Weakness, dizziness, nausea, dim or blurred vision, and mild muscular cramps may signal the attack. There is profuse sweating. The pulse will be fast and weak, the pupils dilated, and the respirations rapid and shallow.

Treatment

To improve the blood supply to the brain when fainting has occurred or seems likely to occur, the patient should be placed in a sitting position with the head lowered to the knees. Then he should be placed in a reclining position with all tight clothing loosened. Sips of cool water containing one teaspoonful of table salt per glass should be given orally; approximately half a glass should be given every 15 minutes for an hour. If the patient vomits, fluids by mouth should be stopped. If oral fluids are discontinued and the patient is in a deep state of collapse, 0.9% (9 g/litre) sodium chloride infusion should be given intravenously upon RADIO MEDICAL ADVICE.

The patient should be instructed to remain off work for several days and to avoid exposure to excessively high temperatures during that time.

Hernia (rupture)

The abdominal cavity is a large enclosed space lined by a sheet of tissue. The muscles of the abdominal wall resist the varying changes of pressure within the cavity. Increased pressure may force the protrusion of a portion of the lining tissue through a weak spot in the muscles of the abdominal wall. This forms a pouch and usually, sooner or later, some part of the abdominal contents will be pushed into the pouch. It may appear at the navel or through an operation scar, but the commonest position is in the groin. The weakness may have been present from birth, but it may be brought on by a chronic cough or strain. At first, a rupture is noticed under the skin as a soft rounded swelling which is often no larger than a walnut, but it may become very much bigger after some months. The swelling tends to disappear when the patient is lying down, but it reappears when he stands up or coughs. Normally there is no severe pain, but usually a sense of discomfort and dragging is present.

When a hernia is suspected, the patient must always be examined while standing. In the groin (inguinal hernia, Fig. 131), the swelling of a rupture must not be confused with swollen lymph

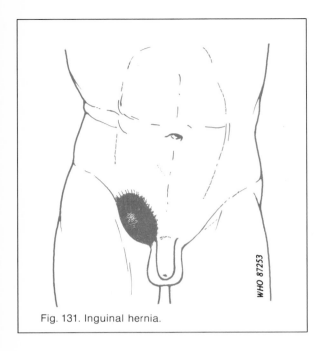
Fig. 131. Inguinal hernia.

WHO 87253

glands (page 211). Usually there are several of these swollen tender glands, and they do not disappear when the patient lies down.

It is sometimes possible to see and to feel an impulse transmitted to the hernia swelling, if the patient is asked to cough forcibly several times.

Treatment

A person who knows he is ruptured has often learned to push the swelling back for himself. He should be removed from heavy work. An operation to cure the weakness is necessary. If the hernia is painful, the patient should be put to bed. Often the swelling can be replaced into the abdomen by gentle pressure when the patient is lying on his back with his knees drawn up. He should be kept in bed until he can be seen by a doctor at the next port.

Strangulated hernia

(See also: Intestinal colic, page 210.)

Most hernias, whatever their size, manage to pass backwards and forwards through the weak-

ness in the abdominal wall without becoming trapped in the opening. However, the contents of the hernia pouch may occasionally become trapped and compressed by the opening and it may be impossible to push them back into the abdomen. The circulation of blood to the contents may be cut off and if a portion of intestine has been trapped, intestinal obstruction (page 210) may occur. This is known as strangulated hernia and, unless attempts to return the abdominal contents through the hernia weakness are successful, surgical operation will become urgently necessary.

An injection of morphine sulfate, 15 mg intramuscularly (1½ ampoules), should be given at once. The patient should then lie in bed with his legs raised at an angle of 45° and his buttocks on a pillow. In about 20 minutes, when the morphine has completely relieved the pain, try again by *gentle manipulation* to coax the hernia back into the abdomen. If you are not successful within 5 minutes, stop. In any event get RADIO MEDICAL ADVICE.

High blood pressure (hypertension)

As blood is pumped by the heart, it exerts a pressure on the walls of the arteries. This pressure—blood pressure—varies within normal limits. During activity it tends to be higher; during sleep, lower. It also shows a tendency to be slightly higher in older people.

The blood pressure is *temporarily* raised when a person is exposed to anxiety, fear, or excitement, but it reverts rapidly to normal when the causal factor is removed. It is more *permanently* raised when the artery walls are hardened or otherwise unhealthy, in kidney disease, and in long-standing overweight. In respect of the latter, an improvement in blood pressure can often be achieved by a reduction in weight.

The onset of high blood pressure is usually slow. The early symptoms may include headaches, tiredness, vague ill health, and lassitude. However, high blood pressure is more often found in people who have no symptoms, and a sure diagnosis is only possible with a sphygmomanometer (see Blood pressure, page 95). A patient with suspected high blood pressure should be referred for a medical opinion at the next port.

If the degree of hypertension grows more severe, then the symptoms of headache, tiredness, and irritation become more common and there may be nose-bleeding, visual disturbances, and anginal pain (see Angina pectoris, page 203). Occasionally, however, the first sign of hypertension is the onset of complications such as stroke (page 231), breathlessness (through fluid retention in the lungs), heart failure (page 205) or kidney failure. You should check for the latter by looking for oedema (page 216) and testing the urine for protein (page 107).

Treatment

Temporary hypertension, due to anxiety, should be treated by reducing any existing emotional or stress problems, as outlined under Mental illness (page 213). Anyone thought to be suffering from severe hypertension, or who gives a history of previous similar trouble, should be kept at rest, put on a diet without added salt, and given diazepam, 5 mg three times daily, until he can be referred for a medical opinion ashore.

Persons suffering from a degree of hypertension requiring continuous medication are not suitable for service at sea.

High temperature (hyperpyrexia)

(See also Heat exposure, page 205; Preventing heat illness, page 300; and Prickly heat, page 228.)

Hyperpyrexia is the word used to describe too high a body temperature, i.e., one of 40 °C or higher. Such temperatures can be dangerous to the survival of the individual and require careful management and nursing. The three main reasons for hyperpyrexia are heat exposure (see p. 205), infections that cause fever, and damage to the part of the brain that controls body temperature.

Treatment

Any person who has a temperature of 40 °C or more MUST be cooled rapidly until the body temperature is below 39 °C. Tepid sponging (see page 109) is usually the easiest method. In addition, ice-packs or cold wet compresses may be applied to the forehead, armpits, and groin, and iced drinks given. The air-conditioning controls should be altered, and a fan should be used to increase air movement and evaporation from the skin.

If the brain centre that controls body temperature is damaged (in head injuries, with compression of the brain), heat regulation may be upset for many days. Patients thus affected sometimes need to be surrounded by ice-packs or to have frequently changed cold-water bottles placed around them. Read the sections on fluid balance (page 101) and on giving fluids to replace loss of salt (page 102).

If possible get the patient into a bath or under a shower where the water is below normal body temperature. Otherwise, lay the patient down and proceed with a tepid sponge bath (see page 109).

Indigestion

Indigestion occurs when food fails to undergo the normal changes of digestion in the alimentary canal. It is a symptom and not a disease. Occasional indigestion may be of no consequence, but chronic indigestion may indicate such serious maladies as cancer or an ulcer.

The symptoms may include discomfort after eating, fullness in the upper stomach, bloating, belching, wind, heartburn, pain beneath the breastbone, nausea, headache, foul breath, coated tongue, constipation, or inability to sleep.

The causes of occasional attacks of acute indigestion are:

- overeating, excessive drinking or smoking, and eating irritating foods; going to bed just after having a heavy meal.
- emotional upset: the digestive secretions, intestinal peristalsis, and other functions of the digestive tract are disrupted if a person eats when angry, depressed, or emotionally upset.

Treatment

For mild attacks of indigestion, aluminium hydroxide gel with magnesium hydroxide oral suspension, 15 ml, should be given every hour until the symptoms subside. If the patient is very distressed and has not vomited, vomiting should be induced. This may be accomplished by the patient touching the back of his throat with his finger or drinking 3–4 glasses of warm salty water (a teaspoonful of table salt to a glass). If severe pain is present, a hot-water bag should be applied to the upper abdomen.

For chronic indigestion, the diet should be limited as far as possible to the foods that cause the least distress to the patient. The patient should be advised to eat slowly and chew his food thoroughly. Bowel regularity should be maintained. It is important to find the underlying cause of the indigestion because it may point to a very serious disease. The patient should be advised to consult a physician at the next port of call.

Intestinal colic

Intestinal colic causes a griping pain which comes and goes over the whole abdomen. The pain is due to strong contractions of the muscle round the bowel.

Intestinal colic is *not* a diagnosis; it is a symptom of many abdominal conditions, but commonly it is associated with food poisoning (page 199), the early stages of appendicitis (page 169), and any illness that causes diarrhoea (page 188). However, the most serious condition associated with severe intestinal colic is intestinal obstruction.

Intestinal obstruction

Intestinal obstruction may come on either slowly or suddenly; a common cause is a strangulated hernia (page 208). The bowel will always try to push intestinal contents past any obstruction, and as it does so the bowel muscle will contract strongly, causing colicky pain. The strong contractions may be seen and also heard as loud gurgling noises (page 160).

In the early stages, the patient may often complain of an attack of wind and constipation.

Later on he can pass neither wind nor faeces downwards. The patient's abdomen may distend and harden, owing to the production of gas he cannot get rid of, and the bowel sounds become louder. The patient may vomit, at first the stomach contents and later faecal matter.

General treatment

As one of the causes of obstruction is a strangulated hernia, look carefully for this condition and do everything possible to alleviate it, if present (page 208). Whatever the cause, it is essential for the patient to be removed as quickly as possible to a place where surgical treatment can be carried out to relieve the obstruction. Delay can be fatal. Get RADIO MEDICAL ADVICE.

In the meantime, put the patient to bed. Give him *nothing* by mouth except water to wash out his mouth if he vomits. Fluids may need to be given intravenously to maintain fluid balance (page 117). Get RADIO MEDICAL ADVICE.

Specific treatment

The patient may be given morphine, 10 mg intramuscularly.

Jaundice

Jaundice is a yellow discoloration of the skin and of the whites of the eyes due to an abnormally high accumulation of bile pigment in the blood.

If the patient is fair-skinned, jaundice will give the skin a yellow tinge, but tanned or dark skins may not show any obvious change of colour. In all patients, a yellow tinge can be seen in the white of the eye. It is best to look for jaundice in the corners of the eye by daylight, as some forms of artificial lighting can impart a yellow tinge.

A patient with jaundice will often complain of an itching skin and state that he had nausea and was vomiting for 2–4 days before the colour change was noticed. His urine will be the colour of strong tea, and his faeces will be light in colour and have the appearance of clay or putty. The colour and quantity of both should be recorded. On a ship the most likely causes of jaundice are viral hepatitis A (infectious hepatitis) (page 133) and gallstones (page 179). If the patient has jaundice, get RADIO MEDICAL ADVICE, providing at the same time information on the presence or absence of pain in the stomach, chills and fever, and blood in the stools.

General treatment

The patient should be put to bed and given a fat-free diet. Unless the radio medical doctor advises otherwise, it should be assumed that the patient has viral hepatitis A and this means that he should be in strict isolation (page 298). There is no specific treatment for jaundice that can be given on board ship. Any patient with jaundice should see a doctor at the next port.

(See also: Hepatitis, viral, page 133.)

Lymphatic inflammation

Lymphatic system

The human body is nourished and defended from bacterial infection by the *lymphatic system*.

All substances exchanged between blood and body cells are transported in a fluid called *lymph*. Part of blood plasma, lymph seeps through the capillary walls, constantly feeding and bathing the tissues. The lymph returns to the bloodstream through the walls of the capillaries, by way of a system of thin-walled vessels *(lymphatics)*. Lymph glands are an important barrier to the spread of infection in the body. Clusters of lymph glands *(lymph nodes)* act as traps in the lymphatics for bacteria and other tiny particles. In the lymph nodes, these particles are attacked and destroyed by white blood cells. Infected lymph glands become enlarged and can be felt as tender lumps in the neck, armpits, groin, and bend of the elbow. The *bubo* (inflammatory swelling) that may follow venereal disease is a cluster of infected lymph glands in the groin (see Fig. 132).

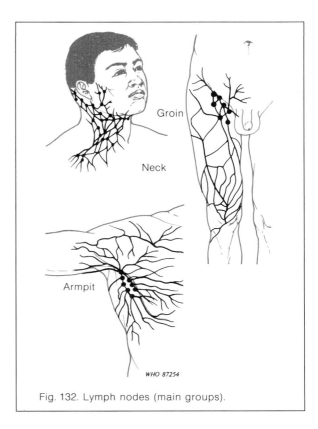

Fig. 132. Lymph nodes (main groups).

The lymphatic system includes:

1. A *system of tiny ducts* with walls one-cell thick (a capillary network).
2. *Larger vessels* which funnel lymph into the cardiovascular system.
3. *Lymph nodes* which act as filters and produce certain germ-fighting white blood cells (lymphocytes).
4. *Tonsils and adenoids:* tissues that strain out foreign particles.
5. *The spleen:* the largest lymphatic organ in the body.

When the lymphatic system is infected, lymphangitis and lymphadenitis (see next page) develop. Generalized enlargement of the lymph glands is a characteristic of glandular fever (page 132).

211

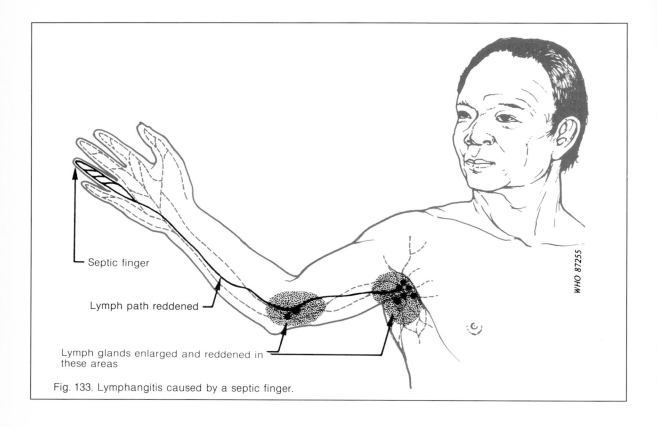

Septic finger

Lymph path reddened —

Lymph glands enlarged and reddened in these areas

WHO 87255

Fig. 133. Lymphangitis caused by a septic finger.

Lymphangitis

Lymphangitis is recognized by the presence on the skin of a red line (the course of the lymph vessel) spreading from an infected area such as a small boil on the wrist, or from an almost invisible infected cut. The red line will tend to travel towards the nearest lymph node (gland). In the case of a small boil at the wrist, for example, the line will extend to the gland at the inner side of the elbow and maybe to the glands under the armpit (Fig. 133).

General treatment

Check the patient's temperature, pulse, and respiration, and examine the related lymph nodes to see if they are tender or enlarged.

Specific treatment

If the condition is lymphangitis *without* a raised temperature and *without* lymphadenitis (see be-

low), give the standard antibiotic treatment (page 308). If the temperature is raised or if lymphadenitis is also present, or if the patient feels really unwell, give patients not allergic to penicillin one dose of procaine benzylpenicillin, 600 000 units intramuscularly, and proceed with the standard antibiotic treatment. If the condition does not begin to respond to the treatment after one day, get RADIO MEDICAL ADVICE.

Lymphadenitis

Lymphadenitis is an inflammation of the lymph nodes. It follows infection elsewhere in the body (see Lymphangitis above). It should not be confused with glandular fever (page 132).

Lymph node inflammation usually occurs a day or two after the primary infection. If the node suddenly becomes tender and swollen, this indicates a rapid spread of infection. Further signs are a rise in body temperature and the patient feeling ill.

General treatment

Search parts of the body adjacent to the glands for the source of infection. The following table may be of help:

Location of lymph nodes	Area to be searched for infection
in front of ear	scalp, ear, face, forehead
neck	shoulder, neck, mouth, teeth, throat, face, scalp
below collar bone	chest, shoulder
under armpit	hand, arm, shoulder
elbow	hand, forearm
groin	foot, leg, thigh, genitals, anus, buttock
knee	foot, leg

Even if you are treating the patient for an infection in one of the areas covered by the inflamed node you should check the other areas as well.

Specific treatment

If the patient feels generally well and does not have a raised temperature, and if the cause of the inflammation is not particularly serious, e.g., a small boil that has already discharged, no antibiotics should be given. For other cases, the treatment is as for lymphangitis. If the lymphadenitis is caused by genital ulcers, see page 149.

(See also: Glandular fever, page 132; Lymph node swelling, page 154.)

Mental illness

Many people feel low-spirited or irritable when physically ill, but this feeling gradually disappears as their physical condition improves. What we may term true mental illness occurs on its own. There is a change in behaviour, which may be just slightly unusual, or bizarre and completely abnormal. It is important to realize that the person who is mentally ill may or may not know that he is acting in an abnormal way.

The common symptoms of mental disease are an abnormal suspiciousness and irritability. It can be very hard to decide at times whether the person concerned is just a complainer or a loner, or whether he is mentally ill. The distinction is easy if he speaks about hearing voices when nobody is around or seeing people who are long dead. It is not so easy, however, if he speaks about things that could be true, such as not getting overtime because his supervisor doesn't like him, or being discriminated against because he belongs to a religious minority.

At times, the person may become unusually quiet and withdrawn for no known reason. He may move very slowly or awkwardly, seem dazed or preoccupied, and be unable to carry out instructions or reply to questions. If he speaks, what he says may not have much to do with what is going on around him. He may even sit or lie entirely motionless for long periods, although not really stuporous or in a coma. He may show no interest in food.

To diagnose mental illness in detail is a highly skilled job, and all that needs to be done at sea is to recognize the condition, handle the situation correctly, and deliver the patient into skilled hands at the earliest opportunity. This may not be an easy task with someone who may be irrational, suicidal, or even violent. A great deal of time and effort may be needed.

How to handle someone who is mentally ill

Approach the person in a quiet, calm and friendly manner, remembering to accept him *as he is,* for what he is experiencing is very real to him. Try to establish a sympathetic relationship by talking to him about his feelings and problems. Give the impression you want to understand him. Do not contradict or argue, however irrational his remarks, as this might provoke more withdrawal or even aggression. Offer comfort and help where you think it is needed. Try to inquire at some point about previous episodes of a similar nature. Above all keep the tone of the interview calm, friendly, and sympathetic.

Three types of mental illness may be seen at sea: anxiety, depression, and obvious madness.

Anxiety

A worried and anxious person is usually aware of his state of mind, but is unable to cope with the situation that is provoking the anxiety. Physically, he may not be able to sleep or may have gone off his food. By encouraging him to share his problems, you could help a great deal. Listen sympathetically to what he has to say. Your own common sense and independent opinion might give him another perspective on the matter.

Remember also that an anxious person might show depressive tendencies and that it is important to look out for this development (see below).

Treatment

For anxiety without depression, the drug of choice is diazepam. Begin by giving a 5-mg diazepam tablet three times a day. If, after 24 hours of treatment, the anxiety is not calmed, give 10 mg of diazepam three times a day. The dose of diazepam can be adjusted upwards or downwards, when you can observe the effect of a particular dose rate over a 24-hour period.

A sedative should always be given at night to any anxious person, so that he has a good night's sleep. For people who are mildly anxious, not very restless, and who are of average size or below, give 5 mg of diazepam (tablet) about half an hour before bedtime. For people who are very anxious and restless and whose body size is large, give 10 mg of diazepam. After the first night, adjust the dose of this drug in line with the effect produced by the previous dose. If the person slept well or very well, give the same dose or a reduced dose. If the person did not sleep well on 5 mg of diazepam, give 10 mg the next night.

For anxiety with *depression,* give the treatment indicated below for depression.

Depression

Two kinds of depression are usually described. The first has an *obvious cause,* such as the death of a close friend or relative. The second kind of depression occurs *without apparent cause.*

In both kinds of depression the symptoms are similar, ranging from feeling miserable to being suicidal. Every intermediate stage can be found. The person may be emotionally up one day and down the next. Sleep may be disturbed, the person waking in the early hours of the morning and then staying awake. Morose and even sullen in appearance, the person retires within himself and speaks only when spoken to. It may be difficult to get a clear story from him, because he is deep in misery and simply wants to be left alone. When he is alone, he may sit and cry, so inquire sympathetically about this, because it helps to indicate the level of depression.

A severe depression sometimes progresses into a stupor, which may be a symptom of other diseases. The patient may lie awake in bed, but do nothing of his own accord. He may respond very slowly to orders. Mentally dull, he may not know where he is or what day it is. His face will resemble a mask, and he will be able to think of little besides death and dying.

RADIO MEDICAL ADVICE should be obtained without delay when the patient is stuporous.

Very depressed people may try to commit suicide. It is essential to recognize those at risk so that correct precautionary measures can be taken. By a natural progression of questioning about the patient's general feelings, it should be possible to establish whether suicide has been contemplated.

Treatment

The drugs used to treat depression are slow-acting and generally take 2–3 weeks to produce significant benefit, so do not be discouraged if you observe little immediate effect. Make sure that the patient takes the drug by watching him swallow it on every occasion. Give 50 mg of amitriptyline about half an hour before bedtime on the first day, and the same dose twice (morning and evening) on the second and subsequent days. Amitriptyline has sedative as well as antidepressant properties, so DO NOT GIVE ANY OTHER SEDATIVE.

Treatment should begin as soon as depression is diagnosed and should continue until the person is handed over to medical care.

A common minor side-effect of amitriptyline is dryness of the mouth; this is not a reason to stop giving the drug. Alcohol adversely affects the treatment and should be prohibited. Get medical advice at the next port of call.

How to deal with a potential suicide

Anyone who appears to be deeply depressed or who talks of suicide or threatens suicide should *never* be left alone. This is not an easy thing to accomplish in practice. The person should be confined to a cabin and kept there under supervision. The deck is a dangerous place and the ship's side may be a temptation to suicide. The person must be escorted, even to the toilet, the door being left ajar. All medicines and drugs must be removed, as well as all string, rope, and sharp, or potentially sharp, objects (razors, knives, mirrors, bottles, and so on), and the person should eat only with a spoon. Details of the nursing care needed by such people are given on page 103.

Obvious madness (acute psychosis)

Any person who is obviously mad will require a good deal of looking after. In such cases it is always wise to assume that the person's behaviour is so unpredictable that he may at any time become violent or suicidal, often without provocation or warning. Anyone who shows signs of severe mental illness should at once be sedated with chlorpromazine and kept under close observation. He should in the early stages be approached by *two* people. **Failure to observe these precautions can result in injuries.** Refer to the section on nursing cases of severe mental illness (page 103) for further guidance.

Treatment

On the first day give chlorpromazine, 25 mg three times a day by mouth. On the second and subsequent days, give 50 mg three times a day; if this is not enough to control symptoms, 100 mg three times a day may be required.

If the patient is very excited and/or unwilling to take chlorpromazine by mouth, give the drug by intramuscular injection in doses of 50 mg twice or three times a day, as necessary to control symptoms.

Neuritis and neuralgia

Neuritis is a disease of a single nerve, or two or more nerves in separate areas, or of many nerves simultaneously. It causes paroxysmal pain (neuralgia) and tenderness which extend along the course of one or more nerves.

As some nerves contain both sensory and motor fibres, disease or damage will cause loss of sensation in an area of the skin with paralysis of the muscles.

There may be burning, tingling, or numbness, and the area will be sensitive to pressure. When the sciatic nerve, which extends from the buttocks down the back of the thigh to the lower leg, is affected, the condition is known as *sciatica*. Intense shooting pains on one side of the face are called facial neuralgia.

Some causes of neuritis are: poor physical condition; chronic local infections such as abscessed teeth or diseased tonsils; straining or stretching or other injury to the nerves; pressure on a nerve area from a tumour or overgrowth of bone; and inadequate diet. It may be associated with chronic diseases such as arthritis and diabetes.

Brachial neuralgia

This causes pain in the shoulder and down the arm. It often also affects the neck and spreads from the neck over the head from back to front. It is usually due to acute or chronic intervertebral disc damage and/or arthritis in the neck. If pain is severe and disabling, bed rest and analgesics will be necessary (page 305). In milder cases, appropriate analgesics will be sufficient.

(See also instructions on treatment, page 216.)

Dental neuralgia

See Toothache, page 184.

Facial neuralgia (trigeminal neuralgia)

The patient is usually *past middle age* and develops intermittent intense pain in one side of the face. The pain can be devastating. In severe cases it can be triggered by chewing, by washing the face, or even by draughts of cold air.

The patient may need to rest in a dark, draught-free room. RADIO MEDICAL ADVICE may be necessary in severe cases if the usual analgesics are ineffective.

Post-herpetic neuralgia

Following an attack of shingles (herpes zoster, page 229), some patients experience a persistent, mild to severe and disabling, neuralgic pain which will require alleviation with analgesics.

Sciatica

This is pain radiating into the buttock and/or down the back of the leg.

Treatment

All severe or recurrent cases of neuralgia should be referred to a doctor as soon as practicable. Radio advice may be required.

To determine the underlying cause of neuritis, a complete medical check-up is necessary. Emergency treatment at sea is usually confined to symptoms. The most useful emergency treatment is rest for the affected part and applications of heat. A neuritic arm can be kept at rest in a sling. In severe sciatia, the patient must stay in bed.

For severe pain, acetylsalicylic acid, 600 mg given by mouth, should be repeated every 4 hours, as necessary.

The patient should be given plenty of liquids. A substantial and varied diet of easily digested food may help to build up the patient's general health and may improve the neuritic condition, if vitamin deficiency is a contributing cause.

Oedema

Oedema is the name given to the presence of an abnormal collection of fluid in the tissues under the skin. It is not a disease in itself but a sign that there is some underlying condition that causes the fluid to gather.

Its presence can be confirmed by gently pressing the tip of one finger on the affected part for 10 seconds. When the finger is taken away, a dent will be seen in the skin.

Generalized oedema

Generalized oedema occurs in chronic heart failure (see page 205) when the heart's efficiency as a pump is grossly impaired. This condition is not often found on board ship. Oedema can also be found in long-standing disease of certain structures within the kidney. This condition is extremely rare at sea and is beyond the scope of this book.

In all cases of generalized oedema, test the urine for protein (page 107). If protein is present in the specimen, give no treatment and get RADIO MEDICAL ADVICE.

Oedema caused by heart disease

In heart disease, the swelling first appears in the feet and ankles and spreads up the legs. If the patient is in bed, the oedema will collect under the skin overlying the lower part of the spine. The swelling is worse in the evenings or after exertion. In addition, fluid will collect in the lungs, causing a cough and breathlessness.

General treatment

The patient should be put to bed and a fluid balance chart started. Fluid intake should be restricted, as advised in the section on fluid balance (page 101).

Specific treatment

If fluid restriction is insufficient to cause a decrease in the amount of oedema, give one 40-mg furosemide tablet each morning for 2 or 3 days each week, followed by a drug-free period, until the patient can be put under medical care. Get RADIO MEDICAL ADVICE on the possible cause of generalized oedema in your patient. The patient should be warned that he will pass large volumes of urine at frequent intervals, beginning soon after the tablet has been taken, and provision should be made for this.

Localized oedema

This condition is much more common on board ships. It can be found:

- in one or both legs where venous return is *sluggish* because of varicose veins (page 238)
- in one leg where venous return is *obstructed* because of inflammation of varicose veins (page 238)
- at any site in association with boils, abscesses, or carbuncles (page 176).

It can occur temporarily in the ankles and feet (*a*) as a result of standing for a long time in a hot climate or sitting in one place, as in a lifeboat; or (*b*) in females just before starting a period.

An examination will reveal the cause of the oedema. The treatment is that of the cause, and the appropriate sections of this guide should be consulted. Relief will be obtained by elevating the affected part.

Paraphimosis

This is a condition in which a naturally tight foreskin is retracted over the head of the penis and cannot be pulled forward. It can occur in some individuals following sexual intercourse. The head of the penis is constricted by the tight band of foreskin, and becomes swollen, congested, and painful.

Treatment

Put the patient to bed. The congestion should be relieved by application of ice-packs until the foreskin can be manipulated over the head of the penis again. This is done by pressing the head of the penis backwards with the thumbs and, at the same time, drawing the foreskin over and forward with the fingers (Fig. 134).

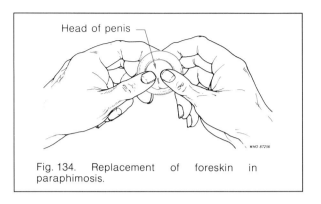

Fig. 134. Replacement of foreskin in paraphimosis.

Peptic ulcer

A peptic ulcer is an open sore, usually benign, that occurs in the mucous membrane of the inner wall of the digestive tract in or near the stomach. Peptic ulcers are of two types: (1) *gastric ulcers,* which occur in the stomach, and (2) *duodenal ulcers,* which form in the duodenum, the first section of the small intestine. Although the cause of these ulcers is obscure, excessive secretion of hydrochloric acid and gastric juice in the stomach is an important factor in their production.

In normal digestion, both the stomach and duodenum are exposed to the action of the gastric juice. Oversecretion of the acidic gastric juice is a prime factor in the production of duodenal ulcers and the reactivation of healed ulcers. Emotional strain, due to suppressed anger or other psychological problems, is a contributing factor to ulcer formation. Certain medicaments (such as acetylsalicylic acid) or excessive use of alcoholic beverages may cause ulcers.

A shallow ulcer may heal within a short time, but more often it becomes deep-seated and causes recurring bouts of indigestion (see page 209) and pain.

At first, discomfort is noticed about three hours after meals at a point half-way between the navel and the breastbone in the mid-line or slightly towards the right side. Within days or weeks, the discomfort develops into a gnawing pain associated with a feeling of hunger occurring 1–3 hours after meals. Sleep is often disturbed by similar pain in the early part of the night. The pain is relieved temporarily by taking food or indigestion medicine. Vomiting is uncommon, but acidic stomach fluid is sometimes regurgitated into the mouth ("heartburn"). The appetite is only slightly diminished, and weight loss is not marked. Bouts of indigestion lasting weeks or months alternate with symptom-free periods of variable length. With gastric ulcers, pain tends to come on sooner after a meal and vomiting is more common than with duodenal ulcers.

On examination of the abdomen, tenderness localized to the area mentioned above will be found by gentle hand pressure.

The symptoms of the peptic ulcer may be similar to those of other disorders of the digestive tract, such as indigestion (see page 209), and diseases of the liver (see Hepatitis, viral, page 133), gallbladder (see page 179), and right kidney (see Urinary problems, page 235).

Treatment

The patient should rest in bed but may be allowed up for washing and meals. Frequent small meals of bland food should be provided, with milk drinks in between. Tobacco and alcohol should not be allowed. One aluminium hydroxide tablet should be given half way between meals. Pain relief tablets are not necessary, and acetylsalicylic acid, which often irritates the gut, should never be given. The patient should be sent to a doctor at the next port for full investigation.

Complications

The ulcer may extend through the thickness of the gut wall, causing a hole (perforation), or it may erode the wall of a blood vessel, causing serious internal bleeding.

Bleeding peptic ulcers

Most peptic ulcers, gastric or duodenal, have a tendency to bleed, especially if they are long-standing. The bleeding may vary from a slight oozing to a profuse blood loss which may endanger life. The blood always appears in the faeces.

Small amounts may not be detected but larger amounts of digested blood turn the faeces, which may be solid or fluid, black and tarry. In some cases fresh, bright red blood may be vomited, but when there is partially digested blood, the vomit looks like coffee grounds.

The patient usually has a history of indigestion, and sometimes the symptoms may have increased shortly before haemorrhage takes place.

General treatment

The patient must be put to bed at once and should be kept at rest to assist clot formation (see Internal bleeding, page 40). Obtain RADIO MEDICAL ADVICE, and get the patient to hospital as soon as possible.

A pulse chart should be started, since a rising pulse rate would be an indication for urgent hospital treatment. The patient should be given nothing by mouth during the first 24 hours, except sips of iced or cold water. After the first 24 hours, small amounts of milk or milky fluids can be given with 15–30 ml of milk each hour for the first 12 hours. This amount can then be doubled, provided that the patient's condition is not getting worse.

Specific treatment

Give 15 mg of morphine (1½ 10-mg ampoules) intramuscularly at once, then give 10–15 mg every 4–6 hours, depending on the response to treatment, which aims at keeping the patient quiet, at rest, and free from worry.

If bleeding continues at a worrying rate, which will be indicated by a rising pulse rate and a deterioration in the patient's condition, all that can be done is to try to get the patient to hospital as quickly as possible and to attempt to meet fluid requirements by giving fluids intravenously (page 117). Get RADIO MEDICAL ADVICE. A fluid input/output chart (page 102) should be started.

Perforated ulcer

When perforation occurs, there is a sudden onset of agonizing abdominal pain, felt at once in the upper central part before spreading rapidly all over and accompanied by some degree of general collapse and sometimes vomiting. The patient is very pale and apprehensive and breaks out in a profuse cold sweat. The temperature usually falls, but the pulse rate is at first normal or slow, although weak. The patient lies completely still either on his back or side, with his knees drawn up, and he is afraid to make any movement which might increase his agony—even talking or breathing movements are feared, and questioning is often resented.

Large perforations produce such dramatic symptoms that the condition is unlikely to be mistaken for others causing abdominal pain, in which the patient is likely to move about in bed and cry out or complain when pain increases. The pain is most severe just after perforation has occurred, when the digestive juices have escaped from the gut into the abdominal cavity. However, after several hours, the pain may become less severe and the state of collapse be less marked but this apparent recovery is often short-lived.

On feeling the abdomen with a flat hand, the abdominal muscles will be found to be completely rigid—like feeling a board. Even light hand pressure will increase the pain and be resented by the patient, especially when the upper abdomen is felt. It will be seen that the abdomen does not take part in breathing movements. The patient *cannot* relax the abdominal muscles, which have been involuntarily contracted by pain.

As the size of a perforation can vary from a pinhole to something much larger in diameter, a *small* perforation may be confused with appendicitis (page 169) because the pain begins centrally. But:

- with a perforated ulcer, the pain is usually in the upper middle abdomen at first and not around the navel as in appendicitis;
- with a perforated ulcer, the central upper pain remains as the main source when the pain starts to be experienced elsewhere, whereas in appendicitis the pain *moves,* the central colicky pain becoming a sharp pain in the right lower quarter of the abdomen; and

- a patient with a perforation usually has a history of previous indigestion, but this does not apply to patients with appendicitis.

General treatment

It is essential that the patient should be transferred to hospital as quickly as possible. Get RADIO MEDICAL ADVICE. The patient should be strictly confined to bed. A temperature, pulse, and respiration chart should be started with readings every hour for the first 24 hours and then every 4 hours. The perforation may close naturally if nothing is given by mouth for the first 24 hours.

Specific treatment

It is essential to achieve adequate pain relief, so give 15 mg of morphine (1½ 10-mg ampoules) intramuscularly at once. In a case of severe pain not satisfactorily controlled by such an injection, a further injection may be given within the first hour. Thereafter, the injection should not be repeated more frequently than every 4 hours. Acetylsalicylic acid tablets must never be given.

All patients, unless sensitive to penicillin, should be given procaine benzylpenicillin, 600 000 units intramuscularly, at once, followed by the same dose every 12 hours until the patient is seen by a doctor. If the patient is sensitive to penicillin, wait for 24 hours before commencing standard antibiotic treatment with erythromycin (page 308).

Subsequent management

After the first 24 hours, if progress is satisfactory, a small amount of milk or of milk and water in equal proportions can be given. Start with 15–30 ml of fluid each hour for the first 12 hours. The amount can then be doubled, provided the pain does not become worse. If milk is well tolerated, increasing amounts can be given frequently. Apart from milk and water, the patient should consume nothing until he is in hospital ashore.

Peritonitis

Peritonitis is an inflammation of the thin layer of tissue (the peritoneum) that covers the intestines and lines the inside of the abdomen. It may occur as a complication of appendicitis after about 24–48 hours (page 169) or of certain other serious conditions (e.g., perforation of a peptic ulcer).

The onset of peritonitis may be assumed when there is a general worsening of the condition of a patient already seriously ill with some abdominal disease. It commences with severe pain all over the abdomen—pain which is made worse by the slightest movement. The abdomen becomes hard and extremely tender, and the patient draws up his knees to relax the abdominal muscle. Vomiting occurs and becomes progressively more frequent, large quantities of brown fluid being brought up without any effort. The temperature is raised (up to 39 °C or above) and the pulse is feeble and rapid (110–120), gradually increasing in rate. The pallid anxious face, the sunken eyes, and extreme general weakness all confirm the gravely ill state of the patient. If hiccoughs begin, this must be regarded as a very serious sign.

Treatment

Peritonitis is a very serious complication of abdominal disease, so get RADIO MEDICAL ADVICE and deliver the patient to hospital as soon as possible, Until this can be done, manage the illness as follows.

- **Treat the infection.** Give procaine benzylpenicillin, 1 200 000 units intramuscularly, and metronidazole, 200 mg, at once; then give procaine benzylpenicillin, 600 000 units intramuscularly, every 12 hours and metronidazole, 100 mg, every 8 hours. If the patient is sensitive to penicillin, give erythromycin, 500 mg, and metronidazole, 200 mg, at once, and then erythromycin, 250 mg, every 6 hours and metronidazole, 100 mg, every 8 hours. If the patient was being treated for appendicitis, this means changing to intramuscular injections of penicillin but continuing with the metronidazole.

- **Correct dehydration.** Following RADIO MEDICAL ADVICE, intravenous fluid may be given, if necessary. Keep a fluid input/output chart (page 102). If thirst continues, cautiously allow sips of water.
- **Keep regular records.** Make notes of the patient's temperature, pulse, and respiration every hour, and of any change for better or worse in his condition

Pleurisy

Pleurisy is inflammation of the pleural membranes that line the chest cavity and surround the lungs. Often it is associated with bronchitis, pneumonia, and tuberculosis.

The onset of pleurisy is usually sudden with a cough and a sharp stabbing pain in the chest. The pain is made worse by breathing or coughing and relieved by preventing movement of the affected side.

If a pleurisy occurs without the other signs of pneumonia (see page 221), get RADIO MEDICAL ADVICE. All cases of pleurisy, even if recovered, should be seen by a doctor at the first opportunity.

Shingles, severe bruising, or the fracture of a rib, or muscular rheumatism in the chest wall may cause similar pain, but the other features of pleurisy will not be present and the patient will not be generally ill.

Pleural effusion (fluid round the lung)

In a few cases of pleurisy the inflammation causes fluid to accumulate between the pleural membranes at the base of a lung. This complication should be suspected if the patient remains ill but the chest pain becomes less and chest movement is diminished on the affected side by comparison with the unaffected side.

General treatment

If pneumonia is present follow the instructions on page 221. Otherwise, confine the patient to bed. If there is difficulty in breathing, put the patient in the half sitting-up position or in the leaning forward position with elbows on a table (Fig. 31). Get RADIO MEDICAL ADVICE.

Pleurodynia

This is a form of rheumatism affecting the muscles between the ribs. In this condition, there is no history of injury and no signs of illness; pain along the affected segment of the chest is the only feature. The pain is continuous in character and may be increased by deep breathing, by other muscular movement, and by local pressure.

It should not be confused with pleurisy (page 220) or shingles (page 229). Treatment should consist of 2 tablets of acetylsalicylic acid or 2 tablets of paracetamol every 6 hours. Local heat may be helpful. Read the section on analgesics page 305), if the above treatment is ineffective.

Pneumonia—lobar pneumonia

Lobar pneumonia is an inflammation of one or more lobes of the lung. It may have a rapid onset over a period of a few hours in a previously fit person, or it may occur as a complication during the course of a severe cold or an attack of bronchitis.

The patient is seriously ill from the onset, with fever, shivering attacks, cough, and a stabbing pain in the chest made worse by breathing movements or the effort of coughing. The breathing soon becomes rapid and shallow, and there is often a grunt on breathing out. The rapidity of the shallow breathing leads to deficient oxygenation of the blood with consequent blueness of the lips. The cough is at first dry, persistent, and unproductive, but within a day or two thick, sticky sputum is coughed up; this is often tinged with blood, giving it a "rusty" appearance. The temperature is usually as high as 39–40.5 °C, the pulse rate 110–130, and the respiration rate is always increased to at least 30 and sometimes even higher.

Treatment

General treatment

Put the patient to bed at once and follow the instructions for bed patients (page 98). The patient is usually most comfortable and breathes most easily if propped up on pillows at 45°. Provide a beaker for sputum, and measure and examine the appearance of the sputum.

Encourage the patient to drink (water, tea, fruit juice) because he will be losing a lot of fluid both from breathing quickly and from sweating. Encourage him to eat whatever he fancies.

Specific treatment

RADIO MEDICAL ADVICE should be obtained on the medication suggested below.

Give two 250-mg ampicillin capsules every 6 hours for the first 2 days, and then one capsule every 6 hours for the next 5 days.

If the patient is allergic to ampicillin, give 2 tablets of sulfamethoxazole + trimethoprim every 12 hours for 5 days. Acetylsalicylic acid or paracetamol tablets can be given to relieve pain (2 tablets of either of these drugs, repeated every 6 hours, if necessary).

Subsequent management

The patient should be encouraged to breathe deeply as soon as he is able to do so and be told not to smoke. Patients who have had pneumonia should be kept in bed until they are feeling better and their temperature, pulse, and respiration are normal. Increasing activity and deep breathing exercises are helpful in getting the lungs functioning normally after the illness. Patients who have had pneumonia should not be allowed back on duty until they have seen a doctor.

Pneumothorax

A pneumothorax results when air gets between the pleura (two membranes covering the outside of the lungs and the inside of the chest). Air gets into the pleural cavity usually as a result of a penetrating chest wound (page 31) or a localized weakness in the lung. When pneumothorax

221

arises without association with an injury, it is called spontaneous pneumothorax. Sometimes, but not always, as the air escapes into the cavity a short sharp pain may be felt, followed by some discomfort in the chest. The effect of the air is to deflate the lung and thus cause breathlessness. The extent of the deflation, and the consequent breathlessness, will depend upon the amount of air in the cavity. The patient's temperature should be normal, but his pulse and respiration will reflect the extent to which he is breathless.

When any associated wound or lung weakness starts to heal, the air in the cavity will gradually be absorbed and the lung will eventually reflate.

General management

Following the emergency treatment for pneumothorax associated with an injury (page 31) and for cases of spontaneous pneumothorax, put the patient to bed in the sitting-up position used for breathlessness (page 33). He should see a doctor at the next port. If the patient suffers from more than slight breathlessness when he is resting in bed, get RADIO MEDICAL ADVICE.

Rheumatism

Acute rheumatism (rheumatic fever)

This is an acute, feverish illness affecting young persons and is quite separate from rheumatism in the popular sense (see Muscular rheumatism, below).

Rheumatic fever starts fairly suddenly, although it may be preceded by a sore throat and a general sense of illness, together with pains flitting from joint to joint. The temperature rises rapidly to between 39 °C and 40 °C and then one or more of the joints becomes hot, swollen, red, and painful, especially on movement.

The joints most commonly affected are the knees, ankles, shoulders, and wrists, but not all the joints are affected at once. The disease tends to attack first one and then another joint over a period of 2–6 weeks. The patient sweats profusely and suffers the usual symptoms associated with a high temperature.

There is a milder form of rheumatic fever, in which the general symptoms and fever are less severe although the characteristics of the disease remain unaltered. The most important aspect of rheumatic fever is that, more often than not, the inflammation affects the heart as well as the joints. In that event, heart valve disease may develop later in life.

Treatment

The main objective is to avoid undue damage to the heart, and to this end the patient must be kept at absolute rest in bed in whatever position he finds most comfortable, He must not be allowed out of bed for any purpose whatever. He should be fed and washed and he should use a bedpan and urine bottle. General nursing principles (page 91) must be followed closely. The patient should be encouraged to drink plenty of water, fruit juice, milk, or soup. The affected joints should be wrapped in cotton wool for comfort. Acetylsalicylic acid has a specific anti-rheumatic property when given in sufficient quantity. Give two 300-mg tablets of this drug every *three* hours, day and night, until the patient can be transferred to medical care (which should be as soon as possible).

Restlessness and sleeplessness should be treated with diazepam, 5 mg at intervals of either 4 or 6 hours according to the response to treatment.

Muscular rheumatism (fibrositis)

Muscular rheumatism is a general term used to describe many aches and pains of uncertain cause in the soft tissue of the trunk and limbs. There is usually muscular stiffness in the affected part associated with local tender points (nodules). The general health is unaffected.

An attack often follows a period of physical stress, and it can vary from a mild ache to a disabling pain. The shoulder region and neck or the lower back and buttocks are commonly affected.

Treatment

When discomfort is severe, the affected part must at first be rested. Two acetylsalicylic acid or paracetamol tablets should be given three times a day until the pain is eased.

The affected part should be wrapped warmly, and the application of local heat is beneficial. Gentle massage will often bring relief, especially after a hot bath. Normal activity should be encouraged as soon as the acute symptoms subside.

Chronic rheumatism (osteoarthritis)

This term is often used to describe the stiffness and pain felt in a joint and nearby muscles when degenerative change (wear and tear) has affected the joint. It is the commonest form of arthritis affecting those of middle age and upwards.

The weight-bearing joints of the lower trunk and spine are most often affected. Gradually increasing pain and stiffness with some restriction of movement are noticed in one or more joints. The symptoms are often worse after a period of inactivity. Although of gradual onset, the condition may flare up during periods of overactivity when symptoms resembling muscular rheumatism may become more troublesome. Then rest is necessary to remove strain from the joint. Local applications of heat, together with acetylsalicylic acid or paracetamol, will relieve symptoms. Medical advice on long-term treatment should be sought when convenient.

(See also: Pleurodynia, page 221.)

Seasickness (motion sickness)

Seasickness is largely attributable to the motion of the ship. Persons unused to the sea are most susceptible, but even experienced seafarers may be affected in rough conditions.

The effects of seasickness vary from a slight sense of nausea, dryness of the mouth, headache, weakness, and cold sweat to repeated vomiting, giddiness, and a greater or lesser degree of prostration. In severe cases, extensive vomiting can lead to loss of body fluid inducing dehydration and general collapse.

Prevention

One 50-mg cyclizine hydrochloride tablet should be taken an hour before embarking or in anticipation of need, followed by one tablet every 6 hours thereafter for a maximum of 48 hours. Seasickness may still develop, but the tablets are far more likely to be effective if taken before symptoms are present. Drowsiness, dry mouth, and blurred vision may arise as side-effects, and patients should be warned accordingly.

Treatment

In mild cases, the condition will gradually wear off, perhaps during sleep, and no specific treatment is necessary. The patient should be kept quiet and warm. Small amounts of dry food, such as crackers, dry bread, or toast, may settle his stomach. The attack often disappears after a few hours. The symptoms may be diminished by placing the patient in a reclining position, with his head on a pillow and eyes focused on a fixed distant point or closed.

Cracked ice may be given to check the vomiting and to relieve thirst.

More severe cases of prolonged vomiting may be treated with cyclizine hydrochloride tablets, 50 mg every 6 hours, as needed. The tablets should normally make the patient drowsy, and he should be encouraged to sleep for 4–6 hours to allow the seasickness to abate. On awakening, the patient should drink several glasses of oral rehydration salt solution in the course of 2–3 hours to replace water and salts lost during vomiting.

Sinusitis

Sinusitis is the inflammation of the accessory sinuses (hollows) of the skull. These communicate with the nose through small openings. The larger sinuses in both cheek bones (maxillary) and in the forehead (frontal) are most commonly affected (see Fig. 135).

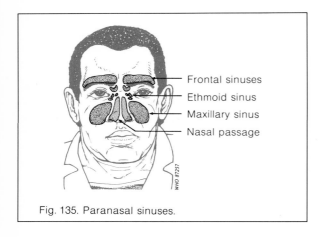

Frontal sinuses
Ethmoid sinus
Maxillary sinus
Nasal passage

Fig. 135. Paranasal sinuses.

Sinusitis usually begins suddenly, often during or just after a common cold. The small opening of one or more sinuses becomes blocked and pus will be trapped in the cavity, causing local tenderness, pain, and fever. The condition is often worse on waking and gradually diminishes throughout the day.

Maxillary sinusitis

The pain is felt in the cheek bone and is increased by pressing firmly on the bone or by tapping with a finger on the bone. The pain is usually made worse when the patient bends forward. There is often a foul-tasting and -smelling discharge into the back of the mouth and nose. Sometimes the eye on the affected side is bloodshot.

Frontal sinusitis

The pain is felt round the bony ridge which lies under the eyebrow, and firm pressure there, and sometimes inward pressure on the corner of the eye socket next to the nose, will cause tenderness. There may be an intermittent nasal discharge of pus from the infected sinus. The patient is usually feverish and feels unwell. Sometimes the eye on the affected side is bloodshot.

Treatment

The patient should be put to bed and kept there until his temperature has been normal for 24 hours. He should be told not to blow his nose but to wipe it. Apart from being painful, blowing the nose may force the infection further back and make the disease worse.

Hot, moist compresses or a hot-water bag may be applied over the forehead, nose, and cheeks to help relieve discomfort or pain.

For pain relief, see section on analgesics (page 305).

The patient should be told not to travel by air or to skin-dive until allowed to do so by a doctor.

If the sinusitis continues for more than a few days or recurs frequently, the patient should be advised to consult a doctor at the next port of call.

Skin disease

The skin may be affected in many diseases. This is especially so in infectious diseases such as chickenpox and measles. Recognition and treatment of the underlying condition will be the appropriate cure for such skin eruptions. Any patient with a skin problem should therefore be questioned on his general state of health and, if necessary, an appropriate examination made.

Some skin diseases remain localized but, as spread may be unrecognized by the patient, it is usually best to inspect the skin as a whole. The origin and later distribution of the eruption should be noted, together with its duration and nature.

Barber's rash (sycosis barbae)

This is an infection of the hair roots (follicles) of the beard area of the face and neck which is caused by shaving. The area affected is usually small at first, but is spread more widely by an infected razor, shaving-brush, or hand-towel, or by rubbing the face with the hand. At the onset, each affected hair root is surrounded by a small red spot, which soon develops into a septic blister. The blisters invariably break and form crusts.

General treatment

The patient should stop shaving at once and, if desired, facial hair should be kept short by clipping it with scissors. The razor should be replaced or sterilized in boiling water for at least 10 minutes before use after the condition has cleared. Rubbing or scratching the face should be discouraged. Disposable paper tissues or towels should be used.

Specific treatment

Give the standard antibiotic treatment (page 308). If weeping is present, the affected area should be bathed several times a day with a solution of one teaspoonful of potassium permanganate in 500 ml of water. This may cause a temporary discoloration of the skin, which will soon disappear when treatment ends.

Chaps

These are cracks on the backs of the hands, feet, lips, ears, or other parts of the body caused by exposure to cold wind or salt water, or by washing in cold weather without drying the skin properly. There is often much irritation and pain. The affected parts should be freely smeared with petroleum jelly and kept warm. Gloves should be worn.

Chilblains

See page 265.

Dermatitis

Most of the dermatitis seen on board ship is due to irritation of the skin by substances that have been handled or misused. In a much smaller number of cases, the cause is allergy (see Allergic reactions, page 167). The common irritants that cause dermatitis are detergents, cleaning powders, solvents, oil, and paraffin.

There are various types of dermatitis but, in most cases, the condition starts as a diffuse reddening of the affected skin. Soon small blisters form on the reddened area and, later, these blisters break, releasing a thin, yellowish fluid which forms crusts. There is usually considerable irritation of the skin. An attempt should be made to identify the irritant that has caused the dermatitis. The patient should then avoid contact with any known cause as far as possible. It should be borne in mind that a substance, for instance a detergent, with which the patient has been in contact for some time without any adverse effect, may suddenly become an irritant.

Specific treatment

Apply a thin smear of 1% hydrocortisone ointment to the affected part three times daily.

(See also: Contact dermatitis (curly weed rash), page 246.)

Athlete's foot

The web between the little and adjacent toe on both feet is first affected. The skin is thickened and split but later becomes white and sodden and looks dead. The condition may spread to other toe webs, and also to the tops and soles of the feet. In severe infections the affected area may be red, inflamed, and covered with small blisters which may weep or become septic. Itching is usually present and troublesome. This condition can be passed from person to person through wearing others' seaboots and sharing bathrooms. Personal hygiene to avoid the spread of infection is therefore important.

Treatment

The feet should be washed morning and night with soap and water before each treatment. Loose shreds of white sodden skin should be removed gently, using paper tissues, before applying a thin smear of benzoic and salicylic acid ointment. In severe cases, before applying the ointment, the feet should be bathed in a solution of one teaspoonful of potassium permanganate in 500 ml of water. If benzoic and salicylic acid ointment causes smarting and irritation, miconazole nitrate cream may be used instead. The patient should wear cotton socks, which can be boiled.

Dhobie[1] itch (ringworm of groin)

This form of ringworm is usually acquired by using infected clothes, socks, games-kits, or towels and it is easily picked up from wet bath-mats in hotels and swimming pools. The inner surfaces of the upper thighs are affected by intensely itchy, red, spreading patches, which often extend to the crotch and involve the scrotum. The patches have a well-defined, slightly scaly, raised margin. The armpits may be similarly affected.

Always look for the presence of athlete's foot, which may be the source of infection. If this is present, it must be treated at the same time to prevent reinfection.

Treatment

Cotton underpants, preferably boxer shorts, should be worn and changed daily. They should be boiled after use.

In acute cases, there may be considerable weeping from the lesions, so cool compresses with aluminium acetate powder solution (4 g to half a litre of water) should be applied for 15 minutes, three to four times daily. When the acute inflammation has subsided, the area should be treated three times daily with benzoic and salicylic acid ointment. Treatment should continue for 2 weeks after the condition has cleared. The ointment should not be applied to the scrotum and, if it is affected, miconazole cream should be used.

Ringworm (tinea)

(See also Dhobie itch, above.)

Ringworm is a fungus infection that produces rings on the skin. Each ring is red with a peeling and slightly swollen outer edge where the live fungus is advancing towards uninfected skin. The normal-coloured area in the centre of the ring is skin that has healed after the fungus has passed. The rings may join or overlap each other (Fig. 136).

General treatment

The fungus cannot survive on cold dry skin, but thrives on hot sweaty skin. Anything that can be done to keep the temperature down and the skin dry is beneficial. Sunlight, provided the patient does not sweat, is of help. Air-conditioning and cool breezes are always beneficial. If the affected area is normally covered, cotton clothes should be worn and boiled for 10 minutes each day after use.

Specific treatment

Apply a small amount of benzoic and salicylic acid ointment to the advancing edge of each ring twice a day until the condition clears.

Impetigo

This skin infection (caused by bacteria) usually affects exposed areas such as the face and hands.

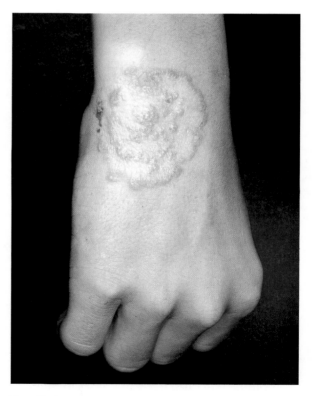

Fig. 136. Ringworm.

---

[1] "Dhobie" is Hindi for "laundryman".

It starts as a thin-walled blister, which soon breaks and becomes covered with an amber-coloured crust. This gives the impression of being "stuck on", and the surrounding skin is often not reddened. The eruption spreads rapidly, especially on the beard area of the face and neck. It sometimes affects the skin-folds around the mouth, nose, and ears, where it may cause red, sodden cracks. In severe cases the scalp may be affected. It is a highly contagious disease which is easily spread by the patient to other parts of his body, or to other persons, unless strict precautions are taken.

General management

The high risk of contagion should be explained to the patient, who should not touch the eruptions. If the face is affected, he should not shave and the beard should be clipped with scissors. Disposable paper tissues or towels should be used, and any bedding, clothing, or equipment likely to have been in contact with the eruption should be thoroughly boiled after use. The hands should be washed thoroughly after the affected area has been bathed or unintentionally touched.

Infected food-handlers in the catering department should be removed from duty until the condition has cleared.

Specific treatment

If the patient is not allergic to penicillin, systemic antibiotic treatment should be given, with oral phenoxymethyl penicillin potassium, one 250-mg tablet four times daily for a 10-day course. Patients allergic to penicillin should be given 250 mg of erythromycin by mouth four times daily for 10 days.

If there are systemic symptoms such as fever and chills, the patient should be placed on bed rest with ample fluid intake. Acetylsalicylic acid, 600 mg, should be given by mouth every 3–4 hours, as needed.

The affected area should be bathed twice a day for about 10 minutes with a solution of one teaspoonful of potassium permanganate in 500 ml of water. The skin should be dried with disposable paper tissues. Facial eruptions should be left uncovered, but those on the hands or any part covered by clothing should be protected with a dry dressing which should be changed daily.

Pediculosis (lice infestation)

Three varieties of lice live on human beings—head lice, body lice, and crab lice. They bite the skin to obtain blood for nourishment, thereby causing itching, with consequent scratching, and sometimes infection in the bite marks. Female lice lay many eggs, which hatch out within a fortnight. The eggs (nits) are pinhead-sized objects which adhere either to hair shafts (head and crab lice) or to seams of underclothes (body lice).

Head lice

The hair at the back and sides of the head is usually more heavily infested. Scratching can cause infection manifested as septic areas resembling impetigo. The adjacent lymph glands in the neck may be enlarged and tender (page 211).

Treatment for head lice. Wet the patient's hair and rub one tablespoonful of 1% lindane cream into the patient's scalp. Do not wash the head until 24 hours later. Anyone who has lain on the patient's bed should be told that he or she may have caught the infestation, and should be treated as above if there is any doubt.

Body lice

Body lice are a problem because they may transmit diseases such as typhus fever and relapsing fever. These lice are usually not seen on the body, as they live in the seams of clothing and attach themselves to the body only when they are feeding. Nits, seen as small grey or white sacs, are also found in the seams of clothing. On examination of the patient, the attendant will see scratch marks and bite marks which appear as tiny punctures with encircling redness. Lesions are located mostly on areas where the clothing comes in close contact with the skin, such as the shoulders, the chest, round the waist, and the buttocks. Persistent itching is typical.

Treatment for body lice. The skin of the affected areas should be washed thoroughly with soap and water and dried. Then 1% lindane cream should be well rubbed into the skin of the affected area and into the areas adjacent to it. The patient should not have a bath or shower for 24 hours. A single application of the cream is usually sufficient.

After this treatment, bedding should be changed and clean clothes worn. Used bedding and clothing should be suitably disinfected (boiled).

Pubic lice (crab lice)

See page 156.

Prickly heat

People commonly experience this complaint on first entering tropical areas, particularly where heat is associated with high humidity. It usually affects parts where clothing rubs or is tight, such as the waistline and neck, but skin-folds and the limbs may also be involved. The rash appears at first as scattered, small, red pimples which prick or sting rather than itch, to the extent that sleep may be disturbed. In the centre of the pimples very tiny blisters may develop, and these may be broken and infected by scratching.

Prickly heat may be associated with heat illness, in which case it may be accompanied by tiredness, loss of appetite, and headache (page 205).

Treatment

The patient should avoid vigorous exercise or any activity that leads to increased sweating. Clothing should be light, porous, and loose-fitting. Sufficient cold showers should be taken

to relieve symptoms and remove sweat, but soap should not be used on the affected part because its frequent use may remove the natural skin oils.

Afterwards, the skin should be dried by gentle patting rather than rubbing. The eruption should be dabbed with calamine lotion. The condition may be expected to disappear if the patient can move to a cooler climate or remain in air-conditioned surroundings.

If sleep is disturbed, 5 mg of diazepam may be given.

Scabies

This is an infestation of the skin by the scabies mite, which causes an intensely itchy skin rash. It is highly contagious and conveyed by close body contact.

The mites burrow into the superficial layers of the skin, preferring those parts where it is soft and thin, such as the webs of the fingers, the front of the wrists, the lower parts of the abdomen, the buttocks, the genitalia, and the breasts, although other places may also be affected. The skin of the head and neck above the collar-line is not affected, and this is an important diagnostic sign.

The mites tend to burrow at night when the patient is warm in bed. Itching is then severe and sleep is disturbed. The burrows are short, slightly raised above the surface, and there may be a small dark or red spot at one end. They may not be seen easily, even with a magnifying glass, unless they are engrained with dirt. Unfortunately, persistent scratching may have caused red pimples, septic spots, scratch marks, weals, or dermatitis and, at that stage, the diagnosis may be difficult. If more than one person is affected and an infestation with lice has been excluded, scabies is the most probable cause.

Specific treatment

The patient should scrub himself all over with soap and water and then dry himself thoroughly before applying 1% lindane cream to the whole of his body (including the soles of the feet) except the face and scalp. Missing out any area, except the face and scalp, can lead to reinfestation. The patient should not have a bath or shower during the next 24 hours. Itching and irritation usually disappear within several hours, but may persist for 1–2 weeks. A second course of treatment after 7–10 days may sometimes be necessary.

Underclothing and bed linen should be washed and boiled, but it is unnecessary to send blankets, bedding, and clothes to be disinfected. It is enough to put them aside for 2 weeks, not using them. Clothes should be thoroughly ironed with a very hot iron. Crew members who have been in close proximity to the patient should be checked for possible scabies infestation.

Shingles (herpes zoster)

Shingles is a painful disease in which whitish blisters with red margins occur on the skin along the course of a nerve—usually a single nerve in the wall of the chest, but sometimes a nerve of the face or thigh. The first symptoms of shingles are much like those of any feverish attack. The person may feel unwell for a few days, with a slight rise of temperature and vague pains all over. The pain then settles at a point on one side of the body where the skin is red and tender; on examination blisters will be discovered, varying in size from a pin's head to a pea. These increase in number and spread for a day or two until, quite often, there is a half-ring round one side of the affected part of the body, for instance the left or right side of the chest only, The blisters burst in about a week or 10 days and dry up with scabbing, but, particularly in more elderly persons, the pain may continue long after the scabs have fallen off.

The occurrence of shingles of the eye, or tissues round the eye, is a serious problem requiring early medical attention (get RADIO MEDICAL ADVICE).

Treatment

The affected skin should not be washed. A cool compress of aluminium acetate solution (4 g in ½ litre of water) may be applied for 15 minutes, four times daily. After drying, the entire area involved should be covered with calamine lotion.

For pain, acetylsalicylic acid tablets or paracetamol tablets should be given.

Urticaria (nettle-rash)

This is a sensitivity reaction of the skin (see Allergic reactions, page 167) in which itchy, raised weals similar to nettle stings appear. The cause may be apparent when the reaction is localized and is the response to an insect bite or jellyfish sting, but any part of the skin may be affected and no precipitating cause may be found. Sometimes nettle-rash appears suddenly, if a particular food (for instance, shellfish or fruit) has been eaten. The patient is usually aware of similar episodes in the past. In like manner, medicines or injections may cause skin reactions, and nettle-rash is a common manifestation. The penicillin family of antibiotics is the most common offender and, when these are given by injection, a severe reaction may occur (page 167). Other commonly used medicines that either cause nettle-rash or make it worse are acetylsalicylic acid and codeine.

Nettle-rash is usually easy to recognise as a slightly raised, reddened area with a hard white centre. Weals usually appear quickly, then subside, only to be replaced by weals in another area. This pattern may be present over a few hours or days and then cease. The patient does not usually feel ill, but is often alarmed and should be reassured that the condition is seldom dangerous.

General treatment

Always inquire from the patient if he knows of any possible cause for the rash and check on *all* drugs that the patient is taking or has been taking in the previous few weeks, and on *all* substances he has handled or touched. If the cause can be identified and removed, no further attacks will occur. Should the cause not be removed, treatment by medicines can only suppress or damp down the reaction, without curing the condition.

Specific treatment

To alleviate the rash, give a 4-mg chlorphenamine tablet every 4–6 hours (depending on the severity of the rash) for 5 days. If the patient has not seen a doctor, continue treatment until the condition subsides. Always warn the patient that the drug may sooner or later make him sleepy and that alcohol will increase the side-effects and therefore should not be taken during the course of treatment.

(See also: Erysipelas, page 131; Personal hygiene, page 299.)

Sore throat

A common complaint, sore throat may be local or it may be part of a serious illness. Tonsillitis (inflammation of the tonsils) and abscesses in the tissues of the tonsillar area are examples of localized throat conditions. Laryngitis is the inflammation of the voice box. Diphtheretic and streptococcal sore throat are conditions with marked systemic effects. Streptococcal sore throat resembles scarlet fever, but differs from it clinically in the absence of a skin rash.

Most sore throats are associated with the winter ailments of coughs and colds. Some are caused by the inhalation of irritants or the consumption of too much tobacco. Most are relatively mild, though in some the tonsils or larynx may be inflamed.

Tonsillitis

This is the inflammation of the tonsils, the fleshy lumps on either side of the back of the throat. The symptoms are soreness of the throat, difficulty and pain in swallowing, and a general feeling of being ill with headache, chilliness, and aches all over, all of which come on fairly suddenly. The patient may find it difficult to open his mouth. He also looks ill and has a flushed face. The tonsils will be swollen, red, and covered with many yellow spots or streaks containing pus. The tonsillar lymph glands become enlarged and can be felt as tender swellings behind the angles of the jaw on one or both sides.

The temperature and pulse rate are normally raised. If treatment does not appear to be helping after 2–3 days, glandular fever should be considered as an alternative diagnosis (page 132). Feel in the armpits and groin for enlarged glands indicating glandular fever.

Laryngitis

This is inflammation of the voice box, or larynx, the area that includes the Adam's apple. In addition to the more general causes mentioned for sore throat, the inflammation may be caused by overuse of the voice. There is generally a sense of soreness of the throat, pain on swallowing, and a constant dry irritating cough, while the voice is usually hoarse and may be lost altogether. Usually the temperature is found to be normal, and the patient does not feel ill. Occasionally, however, there is a slight fever, and in other cases bronchitis may be present.

General treatment for sore throats

Take the patient's temperature, and feel for tender enlarged glands in the neck.

Patients with sore throats should not smoke.

For simple tonsillitis or sore throat, gargling with warm salt water (a teaspoonful of salt to half a litre of water) every 3 hours may be all that is needed.

Give patients with only a mild sore throat, and no general symptoms of illness and fever, acetylsalicylic acid or paracetamol to relieve the pain.

Mild sore throats should NOT be treated with antibiotics.

Patients with tonsillitis, or a sore throat accompanied by fever, whose glands are swollen and who feel generally unwell should be put to bed and can be given paracetamol and a gargle as above.

Give patients not allergic to penicillin one injection of 600 000 units of procaine benzylpenicillin intramuscularly, and follow this after 12 hours with the standard antibiotic treatment (page 308).

Subsequent management

Keep a check on the general condition of the patient and keep a record of his temperature, pulse, and respiration. Recovery will usually begin within 48 hours, and the patient can be allowed up when his temperature is down and he feels better.

Peritonsillar abscess (see below) can be a complication following tonsillitis.

Peritonsillar abscess (quinsy)

This is an abscess that can follow tonsillitis. It forms normally round one tonsil, and the swelling pushes the tonsil downwards into the mouth. The patient may find it so difficult and painful to swallow that he may refuse to eat. He may have earache on the affected side. The swelling on the tonsil will be extremely tender, and a finger pressing gently inwards just below and behind the angle of the jaw will cause pain. There is usually fever, sometimes quite high (up to 40 °C). The throat will be red and a swelling will be seen above the tonsil on the affected side.

General treatment

The patient should be put to bed and his temperature, pulse, and respiration taken and recorded every 4 hours. Give a liquid diet or minced food in a sauce, as solids are usually painful to swallow. Ice-cold drinks are much appreciated as they dull the pain and thus allow some fluid and nourishment to be taken.

Specific treatment

Give the patient one intramuscular injection of 600 000 units of procaine benzylpenicillin unless the patient is allergic to penicillin, and immediately start the standard antibiotic treatment (page 308).

If the patient cannot swallow whole tablets he may be able to take them ground up in water or in a teaspoonful of honey. If swallowing is impossible and the patient is not allergic to penicillin, give procaine benzylpenicillin, 600 000 units intramuscularly, every day for 5 days.

Give 2 acetylsalicylic acid or paracetamol tablets every 6 hours to relieve the pain.

Subsequent management

A peritonsillar abscess may settle down with treatment, or it may burst. The patient should be told that the abscess will be very painful before it bursts, and that when the abscess does break there will be severe pain, followed by a discharge of pus which should be spat out. The patient should be given a mouthwash of water to gargle with after the abscess breaks. Soon after the abscess has broken, the patient will feel much better and he can be allowed up when his temperature has remained normal for 24 hours.

Stroke and paralysis (cerebrovascular accident)

Stroke

A stroke occurs when the blood supply to some part of the brain is interrupted. This is generally caused by:

- a blood clot forming in the blood vessel (cerebral thrombosis)
- a rupture of the blood vessel wall (cerebral haemorrhage)
- obstruction of a cerebral blood vessel by a clot or other material from another part of the vascular system (cerebral embolism)
- pressure on a blood vessel, e.g., by a tumour.

A stroke can be a complication of high blood pressure.

A stroke generally occurs suddenly, usually in middle-aged or old people, without warning signs. In more severe cases, there is a rapidly developing loss of consciousness and a flabby, relaxed paralysis of the affected side of the body. Headache, nausea, vomiting, and convulsions may be present. The face is usually flushed, but may become pale or ashen. The pupils of the eyes are often unequal in size. The pulse is usually full and rapid, and breathing is laboured and irregular. The mouth may be drawn to one side and often there is difficulty in speaking and swallowing.

The specific symptoms will vary with the site of the lesion and the extent of brain damage. In mild cases, there may be no loss of consciousness and paralysis may be limited to weakness on one side of the body.

In a severe stroke there is loss of consciousness, the breathing is heavy and laboured, and the patient may lapse into a coma and die.

The outcome of a stroke will depend upon the degree of brain compression or damage. When it is fatal, death usually occurs in 2–14 days and seldom at the time of the attack. Most patients with first or second attacks recover, but recurrent attacks are likely. The extent of permanent paralysis will not be determined for at least 6 months.

Treatment

Good nursing care is essential after a stroke. The patient should be undressed as gently as possible and placed in bed with the trunk of the body, shoulders, and head elevated slightly on pillows. An attendant should be assigned to stay with the patient. Extra care should be taken to prevent the patient from choking on saliva or vomit. The patient's head should be turned to one side so that fluids can flow out of the mouth. Mucus and food debris should be removed from the mouth with a piece of cloth wrapped round a finger. If there is fever, cold compresses should be applied to the forehead. If the patient is conscious and able to swallow, liquid and soft foods may be given. To prevent bedsores the patient should be kept clean and turned to a different position in bed every 3–4 hours. Bowel regularity should be maintained.

RADIO MEDICAL ADVICE must be obtained, and early evacuation to hospital should be anticipated.

Injury to spinal cord

Paralysis may also occur when the spinal cord is injured.

If the spinal injury is situated in the back, it will result in a paralysis from the waist down (paraplegia). If the spinal injury is situated in the neck, all four limbs will be paralysed (quadriplegia).

It is important to remember that in spinal injuries there will be paralysis of the bladder and bowel, and control will be lost over the excretion of urine and faeces.

There is no specific treatment for paralysed patients, other than general nursing care (page 91). Fig. 137 and 138 show how to rest the patient on the bed and support the paralysed limbs. Gentle movement of the joints should be carried out several times a day to prevent them seizing up.

Facial paralysis (Bell's palsy)

This is paralysis of one side of the face. It is usually of rapid onset, and it can be complete in a few hours. The patient cannot close the eye or blink. Food may collect in the affected cheek and there may be dribbling from the corner of the mouth, which tends to droop. In the majority of cases, the patient recovers over a period of time.

The loss of blinking may lead to dryness of the eyeball and contamination by dust. Conjunctivitis may develop and it should be treated (page 198).

Testicular pain

There are two conditions that may cause testicular pain:

- twisting of the testicle, which can follow a sudden effort, causing the testicle to twist on its cord and cut off the blood supply (this is an uncommon condition and, when it occurs, frequently affects a testicle that is suspended in an abnormal, horizontal line);
- inflammation of the testicles.

Both conditions show many similar features. The testicle becomes painful, swollen, and very tender. The scrotum also becomes inflamed, and fluid will collect inside it adding to the swelling and pain. It may be difficult to tell the difference between the two conditions, but the following facts will be of help.

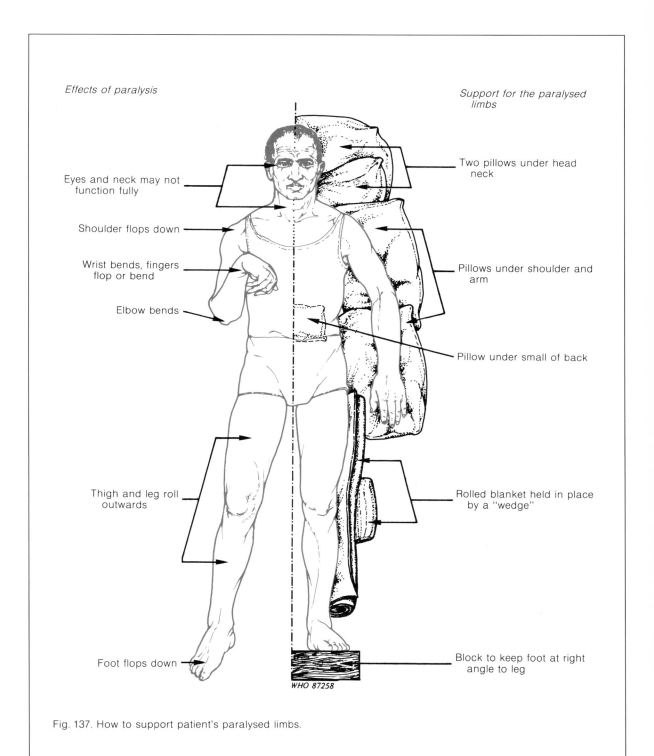

Effects of paralysis

Support for the paralysed limbs

Eyes and neck may not function fully

Shoulder flops down

Wrist bends, fingers flop or bend

Elbow bends

Thigh and leg roll outwards

Foot flops down

Two pillows under head neck

Pillows under shoulder and arm

Pillow under small of back

Rolled blanket held in place by a "wedge"

Block to keep foot at right angle to leg

WHO 87258

Fig. 137. How to support patient's paralysed limbs.

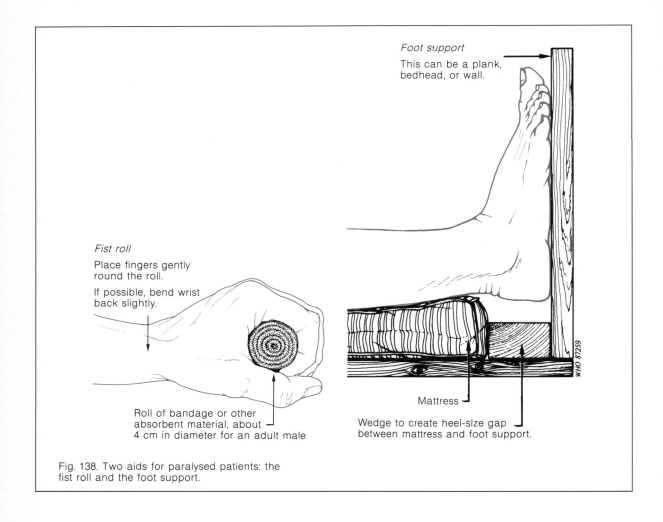

Foot support
This can be a plank, bedhead, or wall.

Fist roll
Place fingers gently round the roll.

If possible, bend wrist back slightly.

Roll of bandage or other absorbent material, about 4 cm in diameter for an adult male

Mattress

Wedge to create heel-size gap between mattress and foot support.

WHO 87259

Fig. 138. Two aids for paralysed patients: the fist roll and the foot support.

With *twisting*, the patient is usually young and, although in great discomfort, does not feel ill. There may be a history of physical effort. The onset of pain is very sudden. Check the position and lie of the other testicle. With *inflammation*, there may be a history of infection. The patient feels ill, he is feverish and the pulse rate is increased. He may pass urine frequently, experiencing a burning sensation.

A useful test is to support the testicles in a suspensory bandage for one hour. Do not give any pain-killers. If within the hour the pain is partially relieved, you are probably dealing with an inflammation; if not, or the pain is worse, the condition is a twisting of the testicle.

(See also Mumps, page 141.)

Treatment

Get RADIO MEDICAL ADVICE at once.

If inflammation is suspected, put the patient to bed and support the testicles by placing a pillow between the legs and letting the scrotum rest on it. Relieve pain by giving acetylsalicylic acid or paracetamol tablets every 6 hours. Also give two tablets of sulfamethoxazole + trimethoprim every 12 hours for 6 days.

Injury to the testicles

This not uncommon condition is usually the result of falling astride a rope under tension or a hard surface.

The testicles become very swollen and tender, and there is a great deal of pain. Depending on the severity of the injury, bruising will appear on the scrotum and can extend up the shank of the penis, up the abdominal wall and down into the thighs.

General treatment

The patient should be put to bed with the testicles supported on a pillow. He should be given 2 paracetamol or acetylsalicylic acid tablets every 6 hours. The urethra may be bruised or more severely injured. Always check that the patient can pass urine. If there is any difficulty, get RADIO MEDICAL ADVICE.

In all cases of disease or injury to the testicles, the patient should be referred to a doctor for examination at the next port, even if the condition appears to be getting better.

Other swellings of the scrotum

Two conditions should be borne in mind:

■ a large hernia which has passed down from the groin into the scrotum (see Hernia, page 207);
■ a hydrocele (see Fig. 139).

Both these swellings can become very large, but there is no great tenderness, no inflammation, no rise in temperature or pulse rate, and the patient does not feel ill.

A hydrocele is a collection of fluid in the scrotum, often caused by a minor injury which the patient may not remember. In contrast to those caused by twisting or infection, these swellings are not inflamed or tender, and the patient does not feel ill or feverish. However, the one exception to this general rule is strangulated hernia (see page 208).

A hydrocele may be distinguished from a hernia in the scrotum in the two following ways.

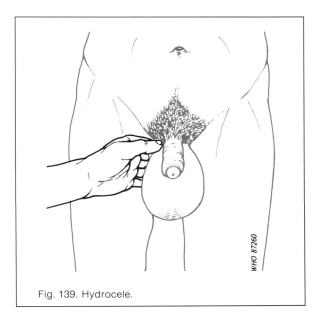

Fig. 139. Hydrocele.

WHO 87260

■ In a darkened room, place a lighted torch behind the swelling. If there is fluid present, as in the case of a hydrocele, the swelling will become translucent.
■ Grasp the top of the swelling with the thumb and forefinger and judge if it is confined to the scrotum or if it is continuous up into the groin. If it is entirely in the scrotum, suspect a hydrocele; if it is continuous with a swelling in the groin, then it is a hernia.

The treatment for both these conditions is surgical, and the patient should be seen at the next port by a doctor. In the meantime some relief may be obtained by supporting the scrotum in a suspensory bandage, particularly in the case of a hydrocele.

Urinary problems

(See also: Sexually transmitted diseases, page 147.)

Urinary system

The urinary system produces urine to rid the body of certain wastes that result from cellular action. Urine is normally composed of water

235

and salts, but in certain illnesses, sugar, albumin (a protein), cells, and cellular debris also may be present. Identifying the composition of urine is helpful in the diagnosis of some illnesses.

The urinary system includes two *kidneys* (where the urine is formed); two *ureters* (tubes to carry urine from the kidneys to the bladder); the *bladder* (a reservoir for urine until discharged); and the *urethra* (the tube that carries the urine from the bladder to the outside of the body) (see Fig. 140).

Kidneys

The kidneys, bean-shaped organs weighing about 200 g each, are on either side of the spinal column in the upper quadrants of the abdominal cavity, at about the level of the last lower rib. The kidneys are deeply embedded in fatty tissue, well protected by the heavy muscles of the back, and are seldom injured except by severe trauma.

The kidneys purify blood and maintain a proper fluid and chemical balance for the body. About 96% of urine is water. The quantity of urine excreted (over one litre daily) and the analysis of its composition (urinalysis) inform the physician whether the kidneys are working properly. When the kidneys fail, the body is poisoned by wastes that cannot be excreted. This *uraemia,* if not treated properly, may lead to death.

Bladder and urethra

The bladder is a muscular sac. When empty, it lies entirely within the pelvis, behind and beneath the pubis. Because of its vulnerable location, especially when distended, the bladder may be punctured, ruptured, or otherwise injured when the abdomen is struck heavily or the pubis is broken.

The urethra is the canal that empties the urine from the bladder. It also carries male seminal fluid (semen) on ejaculation. Through the external opening of the urethra, bacteria and other organisms may travel to the bladder, to the kidneys by way of the ureters, or to the testicles through the seminal ducts, causing infection of these organs.

Renal colic (kidney-stone colic)

Stones composed of crystals of various salts and other solid particles may form in the kidneys. A stone may remain in the kidney without causing any trouble, but often it causes a dull pain in the loin, accompanied on occasion by passing of blood in the urine. Acute pain (renal colic) does not arise until a stone enters the tube (the ureter) leading from the kidney to the bladder.

The pain, which is agonizing, comes on suddenly. It starts in the loin below the ribs then shoots down to the groin and testicle. Each bout may last up to 10 minutes with a similar interval between bouts. The patient is unable to keep still and rolls about, calling out with each paroxysm of pain. Vomiting and sweating are common. The pulse is rapid and weak but the temperature usually remains normal. An attack usually lasts for several hours before ending, often abruptly, when the stone moves downwards to the bladder.

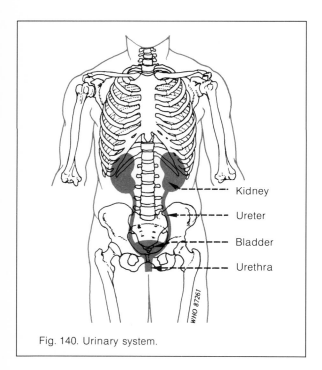

Fig. 140. Urinary system.

Kidney

Ureter

Bladder

Urethra

WHO 87261

General treatment

The patient should be put to bed.

The first objective for treatment of renal colic is relief of pain. Changes in position may help pass the stone.

Always examine a specimen of urine, when it is available, for clots or frank blood. Test also for protein (page 107).

Specific treatment

As soon as possible, mix 15 mg of morphine (1½ 10-mg ampoules) with 0.5 mg of atropine in the same syringe and inject intramuscularly. The acute pain may not recur, once relieved, but renewed paroxysms of pain are an indication to repeat the injection at intervals of not less than 4 hours.

RADIO MEDICAL ADVICE on further treatment should be obtained.

The patient should be encouraged to drink a glass of water every half hour, or hour, to increase the flow of urine. The urine may be filtered through gauze to see if the stone or stones have been passed.

When the stone is passed, the patient should continue to drink fluids freely. The diet should be liquid or soft for a day or two, or longer if the patient continues to feel ill. If chills and fever occur, indicating infection of the genitourinary tract, sulfamethoxazole + trimethoprim may be indicated (see Inflammation of the bladder and kidneys, below). RADIO MEDICAL ADVICE should be obtained again. The patient should be advised to see a doctor at the next port. The stone, if passed, should be given to the doctor.

Inflammation of the bladder and kidneys (cystitis and pyelitis)

This relatively common inflammation, which may affect the bladder alone (cystitis) or the bladder together with the kidneys (pyelitis), occurs more often in women than men. Predisposing factors are poor hygiene, co-existing disease of the urinary system or genitalia (kidney or bladder stones, urethritis, vaginal discharge), or partial obstruction of the outflow of urine (enlarged prostate gland).

The usual symptoms of cystitis are dull pain in the pit of the abdomen and in the crotch, with a frequent or constant need to pass small quantities of urine, which causes a burning sensation when passed. The temperature is moderately raised and the patient feels generally unwell.

A specimen of the infected urine may contain matter or small amounts of blood. A cloudy appearance and an unusual odour may be noticed.

In contrast to this usual pattern of disease, cystitis can occur without temperature change or general symptoms so that, apart from frequent urination, the patient may not realise that infection is present.

When the kidneys are also inflamed, there will in addition be pain in one or both loins with a high temperature (38–40 °C). The patient will feel very ill with widespread aching, shivering attacks, and even vomiting.

General treatment

In all save the mildest cases, the patient should be put to bed. The temperature, pulse, and respiration should be recorded, and the urine examined daily and tested for protein (page 107).

Two to four litres of bland fluid should be drunk each 24 hours. Hot baths and heat applied to the lower abdomen will ease the bladder discomfort.

Specific treatment

Give two tablets of sulfamethoxazole + trimethoprim every 12 hours for 7 days. If the response to treatment is unsatisfactory, get RADIO MEDICAL ADVICE.

Acute stoppage or retention of urine

A stoppage is present when a person is unable to urinate even though the bladder is full. Much pain and suffering are caused as the bladder becomes increasingly distended. It can be felt in the lower abdomen as a rounded, tender swelling above the pubic bone and, in severe cases, can extend upwards as far as the navel.

In these cases, there is always some degree of blockage somewhere in the tube (urethra) between the bladder and the external opening. Common causes include localized injury, a scar within the tube (stricture), urinary stone stuck in the tube, holding the water too long (particularly during or after heavy drinking), and, most common in men past middle age, an enlargement of the prostate gland. This enlargement may previously have caused difficulty with urination such as a poor stream, trouble in starting and stopping, dribbling, and a frequent, urgent need to urinate during both day and night.

Acute retention of urine is rare in women.

Treatment

The patient should lie in a hot bath, where he should try to relax and to pass urine. If he has severe discomfort, give 15 mg of morphine intramuscularly before he gets into the bath. Give him nothing to drink. Keep the bath water really hot. If urination has not occurred within half-an-hour, the penis and genital area should be washed thoroughly in preparation for catheterization (see Catheterization of the urinary bladder, page 110).

Nephritis (glomerulonephritis)

This inflammation or degeneration of the kidneys may occur in acute or chronic forms.

Acute nephritis

The acute inflammation interferes with the removal of waste products from the bloodstream. Suddenly the amount of urine passed may markedly decrease, there may be swelling (oedema) of the ankles, and the skin may turn pale and pasty. Also the usual symptoms of acute diseases may occur, such as malaise, pain in the small of the back, headache, fever (usually slight), shortness of breath, nausea, and vomiting.

With reasonable care, acute nephritis may clear up in a few weeks to a few months. However, the disease is always serious. Aggravated cases may

terminate fatally in a relatively short time, or they may go on to chronic nephritis despite the best treatment.

Prolonged exposure to cold temperatures (without proper clothing or other protection) or overindulgence in alcohol may also be associated with kidney damage. Other common causes of kidney damage and acute nephritis are: toxins from such focal infections as abscessed teeth or paradental purulent inflammation; toxins from acute infectious diseases, such as tonsillitis, meningitis, typhoid fever, and gastrointestinal disorders; chemical poisoning, e.g., mercury poisoning;[1] and extensive burns.

Treatment. In a suspected case of this disease on board ship, obtain RADIO MEDICAL ADVICE.

The diet should be soft and easily digested. Both salt and water intake should be kept low, especially if there is swelling of the ankles (see Oedema, page 216).

Chronic nephritis

Symptoms include swelling of the ankles, puffiness around the eyes, pale pasty skin, malaise, headache, nausea, vomiting, and a decrease in the amount of urine.

Medical assistance regarding treatment should be sought early. An accurate measure of the urine over 24-hour periods will help the doctor giving medical advice by radio.

Varicose veins

Veins have thin walls which are easily distended by increased pressure within the venous system. When pressure is sustained, a localized group of veins may become enlarged and have a knotted appearance in a winding rather than straight course. Such changes, which usually take place slowly over a period of years, commonly affect the veins of the lower leg and foot and those in

---

[1] See: *Medical first aid guide for use in accidents involving dangerous goods.* London, International Maritime Organization, 1985, pp. 33–34.

the back passage (see Haemorrhoids, page 201). The surrounding tissues often become water-logged by seepage of fluid from the blood in the engorged veins (see Oedema, page 216). Gravity encourages the fluid to gather in the tissues closest to the ground.

When the leg veins are affected, at first there are no symptoms, but aching and tiredness in the leg invariably appear later on, with some swelling (oedema) of the foot and lower leg towards evening.

General treatment

In most cases the patient is able to continue to work, provided the veins are supported by a crepe bandage during the daytime. This should be applied firmly from the foot to below the knee when the patient gets up in the morning.

After work, the swelling may be reduced by sitting with the leg straightened, resting on a cushion or pillow, and raised to at least hip level. Swelling is usually considerably reduced after the night's rest. If swelling is persistent and troublesome, bed rest may be indicated. The patient should be seen by a doctor when convenient.

Bleeding

Varicose veins are particularly liable to bleed either internally or externally if knocked or scraped accidentally. The leg should be raised, and a sterile dressing applied to the affected place and secured in position by a bandage. Varicose veins are prone to inflammation (see Phlebitis, below), so it is best for the patient to remain in bed with the leg elevated for several days.

Phlebitis

Inflammation of a vein (phlebitis) with accompanying clotting of the blood within the affected vein is a common complication of varicosity. The superficial veins or the veins deep within the leg may be affected and those of the calf more often than those of the thigh.

In superficial inflammation, the skin covering a length of vein becomes red, hot, and painful and is hard to the touch. Some localized swelling is usually present, and sometimes the leg may be generally swollen below the inflammation. A fever may be present, and the patient may feel unwell. Inflammation of a deep vein is much less frequent, but it has more serious consequences. In such cases there are no superficial signs, but the whole leg may be swollen and aching.

General treatment

In all cases of deep-vein phlebitis, the patient should be confined to bed and the affected leg should be kept completely at rest. Bed rest should continue until the patient is seen by a doctor at the next port.

Patients with mild superficial phlebitis need not be put to bed. The affected leg should be supported by an elastic bandage applied from the foot to below the knee. Swelling of the leg should be treated by sitting with the leg elevated and supported on a pillow after working hours.

Cases of more extensive superficial phlebitis may require bed rest, if the symptoms are troublesome or the patient is feverish.

Varicose ulcer

When varicose veins are present for a number of years, the skin of the lower leg is often affected by the poor circulation. It becomes thin and dry in appearance, with itchy red patches near the varicosity. Slight knocks or scratching may then lead to the development of ulceration, which invariably becomes septic.

General treatment

The patient should be nursed in bed with the leg elevated on pillows to reduce any swelling. A paraffin-gauze dressing, covered by a dry dressing thick enough to absorb the purulent discharge, should be applied under a bandage. Varicose ulcers are often slow to heal, and the patient should see a doctor at the next port.

Worms

Intestinal worms usually occur as a result of eating uncooked or undercooked infected meat or fish, or soil-contaminated fruit and vegetables. Few infestations by intestinal worms require emergency treatment. There is a specific treatment for most of them which may be postponed until port has been reached.

Infestations by threadworms and roundworms are the most common; tapeworm and trichinosis infestations can also occur among crewmembers.

The identification of worms in the faeces is dealt with on page 106.

Threadworms (pinworms)

This is the most common type of worm infestation. The gut is infested with many small worms, up to 1.2 cm in length and resembling white cotton threads. Marked irritation may be caused round the anus by the migration of the female worms, which pass through the anus to lay eggs on the surrounding skin. This irritation occurs particularly at night, when the person affected is warm in bed, and his impulse to scratch becomes almost irresistible. Worm eggs then contaminate the anal skin and are deposited on clothing and bedclothes. Failure to wash the hands each time there has been contact with the eggs can result in personal reinfestation, contamination of foodstuffs, or conveyance of the eggs to other people.

General treatment

Prevention of reinfestation is essential. The nails should be kept short, and the hands should be washed scrupulously after defecation or scratching. Underclothes, pyjamas, and bedclothes should be washed frequently.

Specific treatment

The patient should be given pyrantel orally in a single dose, calculated according to body weight in the ratio of 10 mg per kg (for instance, 500 mg for a person weighing 50 kg). The patient's bed linen and underclothes should be changed just after the treatment and boiled before laundering to avoid reinfestation.

Roundworms

Roundworms are similar in appearance to earthworms. Infestation with them is usually a result of eating contaminated salads or vegetables that have been insufficiently cleaned or cooked. The worm eggs may also contaminate drinking-water. The first sign of infestation may be the presence of a worm in the faeces, but vague abdominal pain may occur.

Specific treatment

Pyrantel should be given in a single dose, calculated according to the patient's weight: 10 mg per kg of body weight (maximum dose, 1 g).

Tapeworms

Tapeworm infestation comes from eating contaminated pork or beef that has been cooked insufficiently to kill the worm larvae. The worm usually grows to a length of 4–10 metres, and is made up of white flat segments. There may be no symptoms but, in some cases, there is increased appetite with vague abdominal pains and occasional diarrhoea.

Treatment (with niclosamide, a drug that is not available on board ship) should start as soon as possible, preferably after confirmation of the diagnosis in a laboratory.

Trichinosis

Trichinosis is contracted by eating undercooked pork contaminated with the trichinella worm. The worms reproduce in the bowel wall and, eventually, thousands of larvae reach the muscles, where they form small cysts. Usually the first symptom is swelling (oedema) of the upper eyelids, followed by muscular soreness and pain, profuse sweating, thirst, chills, weakness, fever, and collapse. A mild infection, however, may go unrecognized. Trichinosis may occur as an epidemic among the crew.

In a suspected case of trichinosis, RADIO MEDICAL ADVICE should be obtained.

Prevention

All meat or meat products supplied to the ship's kitchen must have been properly tested for trichinella and tapeworm larvae.

Special precautions should be taken by crew-members eating food on shore in countries where sanitary standards are low. Uncooked fish and meat, raw vegetables, and vegetable salads should not be consumed there. In many areas, particularly in the tropics, human excreta are used as fertilizer in gardens. Raw vegetables grown there may be a source of roundworm infestation (and also of infection with bacterial and viral communicable diseases).

Chapter 9
Diseases of fishermen

Contents

(See also: Bites and stings, page 173.)

Infections of the fingers and hands

Fishermen are particularly liable to hand and finger infections because of the very nature of the things they must handle in the course of fishing operations. They can be pricked by fish spines and bones or by broken ends of wires from the warps, and they can sustain minor cuts and abrasions which may go unnoticed at the time. Germs are carried into the wounds from fish slime and guts, inflammation soon occurs, and pus is quickly formed.

The anatomy of the hand is extremely complicated, but two features should be noted:

- Infection and the formation of pus in the tissues of the tips of the fingers cause a great deal of swelling and pain at the end of the finger (a pulp infection).
- The hand tendons (leaders) are enclosed either partially or completely in sheaths (Fig. 141). A finger infection may spread along the tendon sheath towards the communal sheath in the palm, particularly when the little finger or thumb is affected. Infection of the palm sheath causes severe pain and swelling of the whole hand.

All finger and hand infections are very painful and disabling; indeed, some can cause permanent disability. They can be prevented by:

- thorough washing of the hands at the end of each work period on deck;
- prompt treatment of all minor cuts, scratches, or abrasions;
- immediate treatment as soon as the typical throbbing pain of inflammation is noticed anywhere in the hand or fingers.

From the diagram, it will be seen that the tendons run down the midline of the fingers (Fig. 141).

Any incision to allow pus to escape from a finger infection must be made on the side of the finger to avoid cutting into the tendon sheaths and spreading the infection.

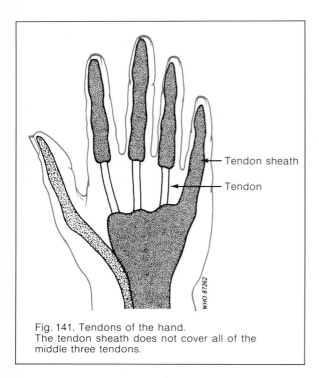

Tendon sheath

Tendon

WHO 87262

Fig. 141. Tendons of the hand.
The tendon sheath does not cover all of the
middle three tendons.

Infections of the fingertips, pulp, or nail-fold

These are usually caused by pricks from fish spines or bones or from fragments of wire. These conditions are discussed on pages 201–203, to which reference should be made.

Whitlows

These are inflammatory sores on the finger. The cause is the same as for pulp infections. The fingers soon become swollen and the pain is usually a throbbing one.

Treatment

Give the standard antibiotic treatment (page 308) as soon as the swelling or the throbbing pain is noticed. If the infection comes to a head, make a small incision over it with a scalpel to allow the pus to escape. Be careful where you make this incision (see page 243).

Infection of the deep structures of the palm (palmar space infection)

This is usually caused by an extension of a deep infection of any finger or of an infection of the tendon sheath of the little finger, by a deep prick on the palm, or by a deep stab-wound from a knife in the palm. Fortunately, since antibiotics have been carried on fishing vessels, this condition has become comparatively rare.

Usually there is a finger infection that has been ignored. The whole hand becomes swollen. Pain is severe and throbbing and is made worse by movement of the fingers. There is often a rise in body temperature.

If treatment is not undertaken quickly, permanent disability may result.

General treatment

Allow the patient to rest in his bunk. Elevate the hand. Arrange for the patient to go ashore at the nearest port.

Specific treatment

Give two 250-mg phenoxymethyl penicillin potassium tablets every 6 hours and continue to do so until the patient can be landed at the nearest port. If he is allergic to penicillin, give 500 mg of erythromycin every 6 hours.

If in doubt, seek RADIO MEDICAL ADVICE.

Lymphangitis

Although this condition is dealt with elsewhere (page 212), it is included here as it is frequently found as a complication of pricks with wire, bones, and fish spines to the fingers and hands.

Fig. 133 shows the pathways along which infection passes up the lymph channels of the arm from sepsis in the fingers. This appears as a fiery red line or lines on the skin, and the glands at the elbow and under the arm may be enlarged and tender.

There may be no obvious sign of infection in the hand. The red lines indicate that infection is present and that treatment should be started as soon as possible to prevent further spread (page 212).

Salt-water boils

The cuffs of the waterproof clothing worn by fishermen rub the sand and grit brought up in the nets into the skin of the wrists and the backs of the hands, causing minute abrasions. The cuffs are usually covered with fish slime from sorting and gutting operations, and bacteria in the slime infect these abrasions.

The sores appear as small irritating spots which soon become tiny, painful, septic blisters round the wrists and on the backs of the hands. Some become large boils, and the whole area may become inflamed, hard, and very painful.

The sores can be prevented by thoroughly washing the hands and wrists after coming off duty, and by frequently scrubbing the cuffs of waterproof garments, inside and out, with soap and fresh water. When the cuffs become cracked and worn, the garment should be replaced.

Treatment

The affected parts should be bathed frequently with hot water, then covered with a dressing soaked in ichthyol and glycerine. (See also: Boils, abscesses, and carbuncles, page 176.)

If frank boils develop, give the standard antibiotic treatment (page 308). When a boil comes to a head, it should be opened with a sterile needle and allowed to drain.

Jumbo wrist (fishermen's tenosynovitis of the wrist)

This condition arises when prolonged repetitive movements of the wrist cause inflammation of the sheaths through which the tendons glide.

It is common when fishermen are involved in prolonged gutting or when they return to sea after being ashore for a long time. Hand movements at the wrist (as in gutting) cause localized pain and a sensation of fine grating. This grating can be felt by the examiner when he lays the palm of his hand lightly over the painful place and asks the patient to carry out the appropriate movements.

Treatment

The only effective treatment is to rest the wrist for 8–10 days. Do this by immobilizing the wrist with a splint, or apply adhesive strapping from the palm of the hand to just below the elbow. If the patient continues to work with this condition, it not only becomes worse but will require a much longer period of immobilization when he returns to shore.

The condition often recurs after further prolonged gutting.

Fishermen's conjunctivitis

This is an acute inflammation of the conjunctivae (the thin lining membranes of the eye) due to contact with the juice of certain marine growths.

When these growths are trawled up, they may burst in the cod end of the net, and the juice, which contains minute sharp siliceous particles, may be squirted into a fisherman's eye, where it will quickly set up an intense irritation.

If treatment is not given as soon as possible, the conjunctivae become red and inflamed and later appear to be blistered. The eyes are extremely painful and there is marked photophobia (dislike of light). If untreated, the eyes will be closed up by the inflammation.

Treatment

Wash out the eyes to get rid of the juices (page 56). Rapid relief can be obtained by instilling tetracycline eye ointment into the eyes every 2 hours until the condition settles, and thereafter three times daily for 5 days. The eyes should be examined by a doctor on return to port.

Fish erysipeloid

This disease arises from minor pricks or skin abrasions caused by the bones or fins of fish. Particles of fish and/or infected fish slime are carried into the wounds.

Inflammation starts as a small red area, the margins of which become swollen and purple in colour, and spreads rapidly up the fingers and arms. The margin remains purple and raised, while the centre appears to be only slightly inflamed. The whole area of skin affected is swollen and tender and may itch and burn. Lymphangitis may occur (page 212).

Treatment

Fish erysipeloid can be prevented by thorough washing with soap and hot water at the end of each period of working on deck. When the disease is seen, treatment should be started at once. Give standard antibiotic treatment (page 308). If the patient is allergic to penicillin or if the condition flares up when treatment with penicillin is completed, give sulfamethoxazole + trimethoprim, 2 tablets every 12 hours for 6 days.

Contact dermatitis ("curly weed" rash)

A form of dermatitis is caused by contact with a type of seaweed known to fishermen as "curly weed", which grows in the shallow waters of the North Sea, off the north-west coast of Scotland, around Greenland, and in some Norwegian waters.

The disease occurs mainly from March to November and usually among those who fish these waters in seine-net vessels. It rarely affects deep-water fishermen, except for those who have been sensitized during previous work in the North Sea before coming into contact again with the weed in deep-sea vessels elsewhere. Not all fishermen in contact with curly weed develop the rash or become sensitized. The process of sensitization can be very gradual but, once it is established, even contact with nets used in the area can be enough to precipitate an attack.

The rash usually appears as a dermatitis on the backs of the hands, wrists, and forearms and on the inside surface of the elbows. Once the allergy is established, further contact causes the rash to spread to the face and the eyes and ultimately to the whole body. The affected parts are itchy, reddened, and swollen. The weeping and drying of the area causes painful cracks to appear in the skin. Where the face and eyes are involved, there is marked swelling especially round the eyes, together with conjunctival inflammation.

Treatment

The only effective treatment is to remove the patient from all further contact with curly weed. He should be advised to change to a deep-water ship. The rash normally clears up when the patient comes ashore, but in established cases further treatment may be required. Treat on board by giving 4 mg of chlorphenamine every 8 hours. The patient should be warned that he may feel sleepy as a side-effect of the drug. Hydrocortisone ointment 1% should be applied to the affected skin parts two or three times a day.

Conjunctival inflammation should be treated by instilling anti-infective eye drops into the eyes at 6-hourly intervals until the condition settles.

Removing a fish hook

Two methods for removing fish hooks are described below. Method 1 is best used if you can feel the barb close to the skin, while method 2 is more useful for small hooks or where there is no danger of the barb of the hook damaging blood vessels and other structures when it is moved.

Whichever method you choose to use, first clean the hook and the area of skin round the hook with 1% cetrimide solution, or with soap and water.

Study Fig. 142 and 143, so that you are familiar with the movements required.

Method 1

Put a loop of strong thin line round the shank of the hook and slide it down until it touches the skin. Press the eye of the hook down with one finger until it is flat, or nearly flat, with the skin. This will detach the barb from the tissues. Keep the hook in this position and pull on the line

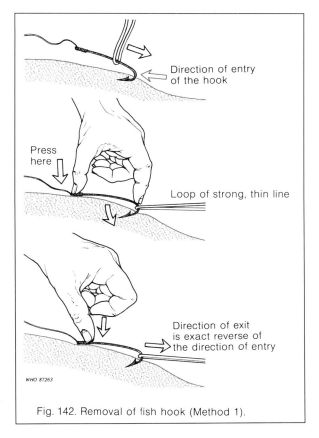

Fig. 142. Removal of fish hook (Method 1).

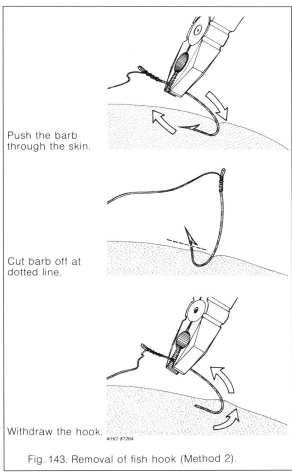

Fig. 143. Removal of fish hook (Method 2).

sharply. The hook will then pull out of the wound through the point of entry.

Method 2

Feel for the position of the barb and inject 1% lidocaine subcutaneously into the area (see Fig. 124, page 175). Wait 5 minutes for the anaesthetic to take effect.

Grasp the shank of the hook firmly in a pair of pliers (Fig. 143). Following the curve of the hook, push the barb through the skin until the barb and part of the curve of the hook are visible. Clip off the barb and withdraw the hook, again following the curve of the hook.

Treatment

General treatment

Clean the wound with 1% cetrimide solution and apply a dry dressing.

Specific treatment

Give the standard antibiotic treatment (page 308) in all cases, as the hooks will be infected from the baits.

247

Chapter 10

Pregnancy and women's medical problems

Menstruation

In most healthy women, menstrual loss lasts for 3–6 days in a regular rhythm of 28-day cycles. Small variations both in amount lost and rhythm occur even in the same individual. The loss is usually accompanied by a sense of heaviness and mild discomfort which is not incapacitating. Some younger women are prone to increased first-day pain associated with colicky spasms and sometimes nausea, vomiting, and faintness. Another common menstrual disturbance is the onset of dull, wearing pain in the groin and back about 3–4 days before the flow, which may or may not relieve the pain. Some degree of premenstrual tension is not uncommon, in which generally heightened emotions, together with difficulty in concentrating, may cause inefficiency at work. These variations should be borne in mind when dealing with abdominal pain in a woman.

Treatment of painful menstruation

Do not be persuaded to give anything stronger than acetylsalicylic acid tablets or paracetamol to relieve pain. A hot bath followed by rest in bed may be required, if the pain or other symptoms are incapacitating.

Delayed or missed menstruation

Pregnancy is the commonest cause of delayed menstruation in a healthy woman whose cycle has previously been regular. If she has been sexually active and menstruation is two weeks overdue, she should consult a doctor for pregnancy testing when convenient.

Other causes of delayed menstruation are an irregular cycle, mental or physical stress, and disease. In every case the previous menstrual history should be recorded.

Pregnancy

Pregnant women should NOT be at sea. Suspect pregnancy if the patient:

- has missed one or more periods;
- has morning sickness (nausea or vomiting);

Contents

- considers that her breasts are bigger and heavier than before;
- considers that her nipples, with the surrounding pigmentation, have darkened;
- has to urinate more frequently.

The abdominal swelling is rarely noticeable before the 16th week of pregnancy.

Bleeding during pregnancy or suspected pregnancy

Bleeding during the first 6 months indicates a threatened or inevitable miscarriage. The patient should be put to bed and kept there until the bleeding stops, as it may in threatened miscarriages. If the bleeding does not stop and it is accompanied by pain, miscarriage is inevitable. Follow the instructions given in the section on miscarriage (below).

Bleeding during the 7th to 9th month of pregnancy is likely to be the onset of labour (childbirth) (see page 253) or due to an abnormal position of the afterbirth (placenta) in the womb (uterus). In either case the woman should go to bed and stay there until she can be put ashore urgently. Get RADIO MEDICAL ADVICE.

No drug, apart from paracetamol, should be given to a pregnant woman, except on the advice of a doctor who knows she is pregnant OR if she is in danger of losing her life, when drugs may have to be given before medical advice can be obtained.

Other vaginal bleeding

By definition, this is either bleeding in a woman past the menopause or non-menstrual bleeding in a woman of child-bearing age who is not pregnant. If the bleeding is slight in amount, the patient should be put to bed and kept there until it stops. When the bleeding is more than slight and continuing, start a pulse chart (page 94) and give 15 mg of morphine intramuscularly, Get RADIO MEDICAL ADVICE. It may be necessary to get the woman to hospital as soon as possible. No attempt should be made to plug the vagina. Also see Contraceptive pill, page 252, for "breakthrough bleeding".

Ectopic pregnancy

An ectopic pregnancy occurs when a fertilized egg begins to develop outside the womb. A frequent place for this to happen is in one of the tubes (Fallopian tubes) leading from the ovaries to the womb.

The growing egg may split the tube within three weeks of a normal menstrual period or at any time up to the 8th week of pregnancy, giving the signs described below and causing an emergency. Usually one menstrual period has been missed before the appearance of pain and/or bleeding. The patient will complain of moderate to severe pain in the pit of the abdomen, accompanied by a small amount of irregular vaginal bleeding. The blood is often dark in colour like coffee-grounds.

In such a case, it is important to ask the patient for the date of her last period and also to ask her about recent sexual activity.

Always suspect ectopic pregnancy in a woman aged 15–45 years (i.e., of reproductive age) with abdominal pain and a delayed menstrual period.

As a rule of thumb, a little pain with much vaginal bleeding indicates a miscarriage (see below) from the womb, but a lot of pain with little vaginal bleeding is more likely to indicate an ectopic pregnancy. When the tube splits, a blood vessel may be damaged, causing severe internal bleeding with very severe abdominal pain and collapse (page 40). If ectopic pregnancy is suspected, look at Table 5, Part B, pages 162–163. Get RADIO MEDICAL ADVICE at once.

Miscarriage

The usual time for miscarriage is around the 12th week of pregnancy (3rd missed menstrual period).

In a threatened miscarriage, the woman notices slight vaginal bleeding and discomfort similar to normal menstrual pain. She should be put to bed and kept at rest under observation until her symptoms cease. Her temperature should be recorded and, if it is above 38 °C, she should be given standard antibiotic treatment (see page 308). Thereafter she should rest for several days and be excused all strenuous duties until she sees a doctor at the next port.

In most cases the symptoms do not settle and micarriage becomes inevitable, with increased bleeding and continuing pain. The patient should be put to bed and remain under close observation. A half-hourly pulse chart should be started. All extruded blood should be examined for clots and solid material indicating that miscarriage has occurred. Get RADIO MEDICAL ADVICE.

If the pulse rate rises either with or without severe bleeding, give 0.5 mg of ergometrine intramuscularly. Remove all pillows, and nurse the patient flat in bed. The injection may be repeated 2 hours later, if the pulse rate is still high and bleeding continues. In this case, keep the radio medical adviser informed of developments. If the treatment does not reduce the bleeding and the patient is very restless and distressed, do not give more ergometrine, but 15 mg of morphine may be given.

Salpingitis

(See also: Abdominal pain, page 160; and Table 5, Part B, pages 162–163.)

Salpingitis is an inflammation of the Fallopian tubes, which go from the womb (uterus) to the ovaries. It may be difficult to differentiate from cystitis (see page 237) or appendicitis (see page 169).

Salpingitis may be caused by various organisms, but sometimes it follows a recent abortion or an attack of a sexually transmitted disease. There is lower abdominal pain on one or both sides just above the mid-line of the groin. Local abdominal tenderness can be felt at either or both of these places. Sometimes there is a bloodstained vaginal discharge. The pain, if on the right side only, may be mistaken for appendicitis (page 169) but it does not begin over the centre of the abdomen before moving to the right. In addition, the temperature in salpingitis usually tends

to be higher than that recorded in appendicitis. Pain on passing water will indicate that cystitis rather than salpingitis is present.

Treatment

General treatment

The patient should be put to bed, and her temperature, pulse, and respiration should be recorded every 4 hours.

Specific treatment

If the patient is not allergic to drugs of the penicillin group, give phenoxymethyl penicillin potassium tablets, 500 mg every 6 hours, and metronidazole, 200 mg every 8 hours. Continue the treatment for 2 weeks. If the patient is allergic to penicillin, she should be given erythromycin, 500 mg at once and 250 mg every 6 hours, with metronidazole as above. Continue the treatment for 2 weeks. Patients should be referred to a doctor at the next port.

Pruritus vulvae (external genital itching)

The vulva is the term given to the external female genital organ.

A minor degree of itching can occur there in pregnancy, at the menopause, and on menstruation. When more persistent and troublesome itching occurs, if may affect the whole or part of the vulva and sometimes extend backwards to the anal region. In like manner, anal itching can spread to the vulva. The condition is usually worse at night when the patient is warm in bed. A vaginal discharge may or may not be present. The patient will usually be able to give a good description of any local abnormality such as a rash, swelling, redness, or discharge. If the complaint is of itching only, consider such causes as crab lice, scabies, dermatitis, diabetes, and threadworm. Always examine the urine for sugar (see Diabetes, page 186) and the faeces for threadworms (page 106). Psychological factors are often responsible for itching, in the absence of other symptoms. If an examination is necessary, and is carried out by a man, it is advisable that a chaperon, preferably a woman, should be present throughout. The examination should be restricted to visual inspection only.

If a vaginal discharge is present, it may be due to a sexually transmitted disease (page 154). Patients with a vaginal discharge should see a doctor at the next port.

Meanwhile if the patient has much discomfort, give a 200-mg metronidazole tablet every 8 hours for 7 days, and instruct the patient to insert a miconazole nitrate pessary high into her vagina each night for 14 consecutive nights (treatment must be continued throughout menstruation, if it occurs). Miconazole nitrate cream should be smeared on the affected external areas.

Warning: No alcohol should be taken during the period of treatment with metronidazole. The patient should refrain from sexual activity while under treatment.

Contraceptive pill

The so-called contraceptive pill will not with certainty prevent conception during the first month of use, or be effective thereafter unless taken precisely in accordance with instructions. Regular usage may cause side-effects too numerous to list, but rashes, headaches, increased premenstrual tension, and weight gain are a few not uncommon effects. Advice by a doctor on using a different pill is necessary, if side-effects are troublesome.

The menstrual periods are usually regular when the pill is taken correctly. However, slight vaginal bleeding may occur as "breakthrough bleeding" in mid-cycle and should be distinguished from other causes that require specific treatment. The woman should be reassured and advised to consult her doctor.

Chapter 11
Childbirth

Contents

Although pregnant women at term should not be at sea, one may sometimes be on board ship and commence labour during the voyage. If this happens, every effort must be made without delay to get her ashore to hospital before the birth. In full-term pregnancies, most births are normal, but some, without forewarning, can give rise to problems threatening the lives of both mother and child. The earlier the birth, the greater the danger to the life of the child. If, for any reason, the pregnant woman cannot be put ashore in time to be hospitalized, every effort should be made to place her under the care of a doctor or a midwife; failing this, an attempt should be made to find someone on board who is familiar with childbirth.

The following paragraphs describe what should be done if the mother gives birth before you have been able to make arrangements for medical care. Mother and child should be seen by a doctor as soon as possible after the birth.

Introduction

A child is normally born about 40 weeks after the mother becomes pregnant. Sometimes, for various reasons, the birth may come on prematurely. If a child is born 3 or more months prematurely on board ship, it may not survive (see Miscarriage, page 250). However, there are some simple things that can be done to improve the chances of survival of premature babies (see page 257).

Onset of childbirth

When a woman goes into labour, she starts having pains at intervals in the lower part of her back and abdomen. At this stage, seek RADIO MEDICAL ADVICE and keep in contact. The so-called labour pains become stronger and more frequent over a number of hours, until they occur every minute or so. About this time, there will probably be a "show", which consists of a small amount of blood and mucus trickling from the vagina. The birth process has now started to take place. Usually in a short time, but sometimes only after several hours, the bag of water in which the infant is enveloped in the

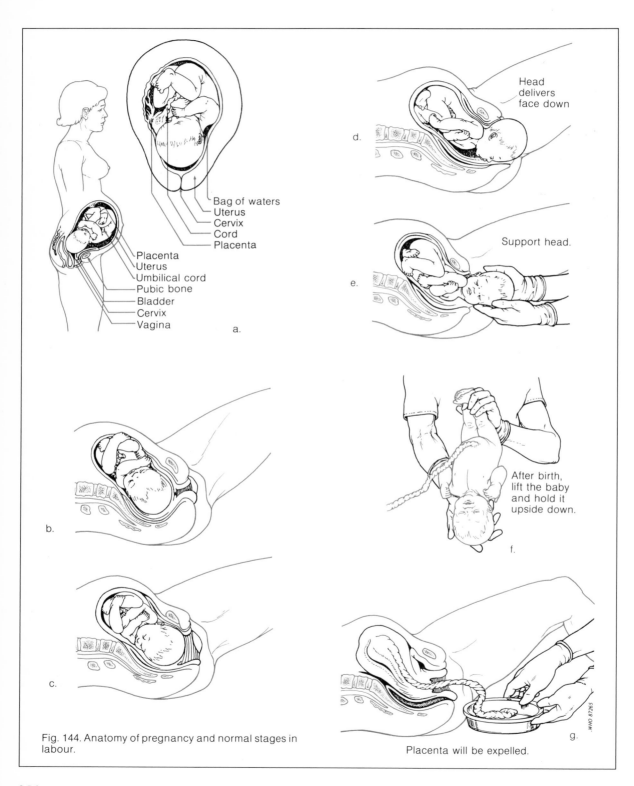

Bag of waters
Uterus
Cervix
Cord
Placenta

Placenta
Uterus
Umbilical cord
Pubic bone
Bladder
Cervix
Vagina

a.

b.

c.

Head delivers face down

d.

Support head.

e.

After birth, lift the baby and hold it upside down.

f.

Placenta will be expelled.

g.

Fig. 144. Anatomy of pregnancy and normal stages in labour.

womb bursts, and quite a large amount (250 to 500 ml) of a sticky watery fluid will escape from the vagina. The woman should be encouraged to empty her bowel and bladder at the beginning of labour. It is also important that the bladder should be kept empty throughout labour. The descent and delivery of the child may last from half an hour to several hours (see Fig. 144).

Preparation for the birth

A suitable cabin should be made ready in good time. If possible, it should be large enough to allow access from the foot and both sides of the bunk. If the ship's hospital is to be used, any other patient should be moved out to other accommodation. Alternatively, if the patient cannot be moved, or if the hospital has recently been used for a patient suffering from an infectious illness, the labour and birth should take place in another cabin, which should be made as clean and as hygienic as possible. It should be kept warm, but not too hot, at a temperature of around 21 °C. A waterproof sheet should be put across the bunk immediately under the top sheet in order to protect the mattress. A plentiful supply of hot water, soap, flannels, and towels will be required, together with a bedpan, sanitary towels (not tampons), a sterile receptacle for the afterbirth, a plastic bag in which to store the afterbirth, 4 pieces of tape each about 10 inches long, surgical scissors, cotton wool, 2 small sterile dressings, bandages, and surgical spirit. All instruments and the tape must be sterilized by boiling for at least 20 minutes. In addition, it will be necessary to have, ready for use, a clean soft blanket in which to wrap the child, a suitable box with clean sheets to act as a cot, and a clean nightdress and sheets for the mother after the birth.

The attendant(s) at the birth should be in good health and not suffering from coughs, colds, or any infectious disease, diarrhoea, or any skin disease. Before doing anything for the mother or baby, each attendant must wash and scrub his or her hands, wrists, and forearms thoroughly with soap and water and should, if possible, have freshly laundered clothes or a freshly laundered overall or gown to wear.

The birth

Once the labour pains have started, temperature, pulse, and respiration rates should be taken and recorded every hour. If the mother has had a child before, it will probably be unnecessary to give much advice, but if it is her first child, she will naturally be more apprehensive, and may need to be encouraged frequently and told that she is doing well. She may be most comfortable lying on her side, with her head supported on a pillow and her knees well drawn up. However, if she wishes to sit or lie in another position, or to walk around the cabin, she should be allowed to do so. She should be kept warm and can be given a warm drink, if necessary, but no alcohol. She should not be left alone; it is preferable for somebody she trusts (e.g., a relative or friend) to be with her the whole time to comfort and to reassure her, particularly during the later stages of labour, when the pains can be quite severe and she may become distressed. Advise her not to bear down or to push with the pains in the early stages, but rather to breathe quickly so as to lessen their effects. Premature or too rapid expulsion of the baby's head may tear the vagina.

The baby usually emerges head first, and nothing should be done at this stage other than to clear any membrane from the baby's nose and mouth so that it can breathe, and to check as the neck appears that the cord is not wrapped around it. If it is, pull it over the back of the head down to the front to free it (Fig. 145). If the cord is tight around the neck, knot the tapes tightly, about an inch apart, round the cord, cut between these with the surgical scissors, and separate the severed ends from around the baby's neck.

As soon as the baby is completely born, it should be lifted clear of the mother without pulling the cord, which is still attached to the placenta. Again, make sure that the baby's nose and mouth are not covered by anything that would stop it from breathing, then hold it firmly, but very gently, upside down (Fig. 144f) for a few seconds to allow any fluid to drain out of its throat and nose. The baby will usually start to breathe spontaneously, but if it does not, cover the baby's nose and mouth with your mouth and

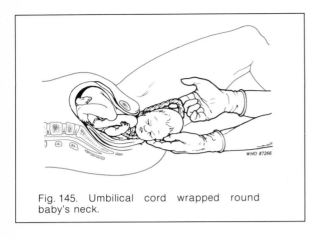

Fig. 145. Umbilical cord wrapped round baby's neck.

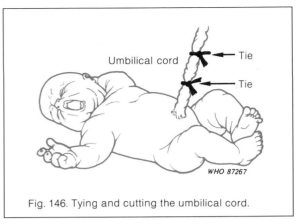

Fig. 146. Tying and cutting the umbilical cord.

give gentle artificial respiration, using very small puffs of air. When the baby is breathing, lay it down, preferably on its side, where you can watch its progress, and, with sterile swabs soaked in sterile water, clean the baby's eyes. Then, a few minutes after the cord has stopped pulsating, tie two pieces of tape tightly round the cord (do not rush this step); one piece of tape should be tied about 5 cm from the baby's abdomen, and the other piece about 2½ cm further along the cord towards the mother; then cut between the two ties (Fig. 146). Put a sterile dressing on the baby's abdomen over the stump of the cord, and wrap the child in a soft blanket. During the next 5 minutes, check whether the baby's stump is bleeding; if it is, tie a third piece of tape round the cord.

The baby should be put to the mother's breast as soon as possible, with both mother and baby covered by a blanket. The mother's body warmth will ensure that the baby is at the right temperature. The sucking of the baby on the mother's nipples can also hasten the expulsion of the afterbirth (see next section).

Actions after tying the cord

You should deal with the baby as quickly as possible, so that your attention can be directed to the mother. She should be resting quietly, and there may be a slight loss of blood mixed with the remains of the fluid from the bag of water,

which need cause no concern. If, however, bleeding is excessive, you should put one hand on the lower part of the abdomen and feel for the womb, which will be recognized as a lump, rising up from the pelvis, about the size of a small coconut. Try to keep the womb hard by gentle massage. About 15–20 minutes after the birth of the baby, the mother will probably have some more pains and the afterbirth (placenta) will be expelled naturally with some blood. The placenta is a fleshy-looking object, like a flat cake, about 15–20 cm in diameter, with the cord attached to its centre (Fig. 144g). Do not attempt to hasten the expulsion of the afterbirth by pulling on the cord.

The cord, placenta, membranes, and other material that come out of the mother should be placed in the plastic bag, sealed in, and stored in a refrigerator until they can be taken with the mother and child to a hospital or doctor for examination. After the expulsion of the placenta, prepare an intramuscular injection of 0.5 mg of ergometrine and inject it into the upper outer quadrant of the buttock (see page 116). This will make the womb contract and lessen the danger of haemorrhage.

The mother should now be washed, given a clean sanitary towel, and a clean nightdress, and the bed should be remade with clean sheets. If the birth has caused any external tears, get RADIO

MEDICAL ADVICE about the need to stitch any of them. After the mother has been made comfortable, she should be given a warm drink and if she has not already done so, should be allowed to hold the baby to the breast for a short while. She will then probably want to sleep.

Someone must stay with the mother in case she starts to haemorrhage; if she does, get RADIO MEDICAL ADVICE.

Subsequent management

The care of the mother and of the baby should be handed over to a hospital or doctor on shore as soon as possible, but in the absence of skilled help and until they can be put ashore the following regime should be adopted. The mother's temperature should be taken night and morning; if there is any rise of temperature above 37.8 °C, give 500 mg of ampicillin at once, followed by 500 mg every 6 hours to a total of 7 doses. If the mother is allergic to ampicillin or to penicillin, give erythromycin. A full course must be given. If the temperature remains normal, however, and the mother feels well, she should be encouraged to get up for a time each day after the first 24 hours. She should have a normal diet with plenty of fluids, including milk. During the first few days of convalescence, a watch should be kept on her bladder and bowels. She may have a little difficulty in passing water at first owing to the stretching of the muscles and general soreness of the area. This is usually overcome with encouragment and reassurance.

Attempting to pass water while sitting in a warm bath will often help initially. If the bowels are not open after 3 days, a mild laxative should be given.

The baby should be put to the mother's breast soon after birth, and at frequent intervals thereafter. The milk flow is usually established by the 2nd or 3rd day. Both breasts should be used at each feed, and 7–10 minutes at each breast should be allowed. For the first few days of life, a baby usually loses weight, but birth weight should have been regained by the 10th day.

The baby should be washed after 24 hours. Prepare a bowl of warm water, some toilet soap, and a clean flannel. Lay the baby on a towel and gently wash the scalp, face, and body so as to remove the white, wax-like material that covers it. Leave the area round the cord unwashed, and keep it dry by covering it with a sterile dressing. After carefully drying the baby by patting it gently with the towel, re-dress the cord with a new sterile dressing. The dressing should be renewed every 2–3 days. Normally the cord shrivels up and comes away in about 10 days.

If the baby is born dead or badly malformed, get RADIO MEDICAL ADVICE.

Premature birth

If the baby is premature or is very small (less than 5 lbs) special care must be taken. It is important that the baby is kept warm and is given breast milk. The baby should be kept close to the mother, both for warmth and for maternal stimulation. Both baby and mother should be transferred to the care of a doctor ashore as soon as possible.

Chapter 12

Medical care of castaways and rescued persons

Contents

This chapter deals with survival after the abandonment ("ditching") of a vessel at sea. It describes the medical treatment of survivors on the survival craft and aboard the rescue vessel. The need for prior training on the principles involved and continuing follow-up instruction cannot be overemphasized. During an abandonment, there will be little or no time to consult a manual.

Abandonment of vessel

Lifeboat drills must be conducted to prepare for possible disaster. Both crew and passengers must be instructed in the procedures to be followed. Reasons for such instruction should be given to all concerned, because procedures will be remembered better when the necessity for them is understood.

Forced immersion is the primary hazard to life after surviving the initial impact of hitting the water. It should be kept in mind that no ocean or lake has a temperature equal to body temperature. Thus, in all latitudes, anyone in open water will lose heat, and heat loss lowers the internal body temperature. As the internal body (core) temperature falls below normal and generalized hypothermia develops (see page 262), there is an increasing likelihood of ventricular fibrillation and cardiac arrest.

The loss of body heat is one of the greatest hazards to the survival of a person in the sea.

The extent to which generalized hypothermia threatens life is determined by the water temperature and the length of exposure. The bodily effects of subnormal temperature will vary depending on geography, season, duration and activity in the water, and body insulation (the amount of fatty tissue and clothing of the individual).

Practical hints for people forced to abandon ship have been published in a pamphlet distributed by the International Maritime Organization.[1] This pamphlet should be available on board ship, and should be used for training the crew.

---

[1] INTERNATIONAL MARITIME ORGANIZATION. *A pocket guide to cold water survival.* London, IMO, 1982.

These hints, aimed at increasing the chances of survival in cold water following disaster at sea, are reproduced below:

1. Put on as much warm clothing as possible, making sure to cover head, neck, hands, and feet.
2. If an immersion suit is available put it on over the warm clothing.
3. If the immersion suit does not have inherent flotation, put on a life-jacket and be sure to secure it correctly.
4. Anyone who knows that he is likely to be affected by seasickness should, before or immediately after boarding the survival craft, take some recommended preventive tablets or medicine in a dose recommended by the manufacturer. The incapacitating effect of seasickness interferes with your survival chances; the vomiting removes precious body fluid, while seasickness in general makes you more prone to hypothermia.
5. Avoid entering the water if possible, e.g., board davit-launched survival craft on the embarkation deck. If davit-launched survival craft are not available, use over-side ladders, or if necessary lower yourself by means of a rope or fire hose.
6. Unless it is unavoidable, do not jump from higher than 5 metres into the water. Try to minimize the shock of sudden cold immersion. A sudden plunge into the cold water can cause rapid death or an uncontrollable rise in breathing rate that may result in an intake of water into the lungs. If it is absolutely necessary to jump into the water, you should keep your elbows to your side and cover your nose and mouth with one hand, while holding the wrist or elbow firmly with the other hand. Do not jump into the water astern of the life-raft in case there is any remaining headway on the ship.
7. Once in the water, whether accidentally or as a result of abandoning ship, orientate yourself and try to locate the ship, lifeboats, life-crafts, other survivors, and other floating objects. If you were unable to prepare yourself before entering the water, button up clothing at this point. In cold water, you may experience violent shivering and great pain. These are natural body reflexes that are not dangerous. You do, however, need to take action as quickly as possible before you lose full use of your hands; button up clothing, turn on signal lights, locate whistle, etc.
8. While afloat in the water, do not attempt to swim unless it is to reach a nearby craft, a fellow survivor, or a floating object on which you can lean or climb. Unnecessary swimming will "pump" out any warm water between your body and the layers of clothing, thereby increasing the rate of body-heat loss. In addition, unnecessary movements of your arms and legs send warm blood from the inner core to the outer layer of the body. This results in a very rapid heat loss. Hence, it is most important to remain as still as possible in the water, however painful it may be. Remember, pain will not kill you, but heat loss will!
9. The position you assume in the water is also very important in conserving heat. Float as still as possible with your legs together, elbows close to your side, and arms folded across the front of your life-jacket. This position minimizes the exposure of the body surface to the cold water. Try to keep your head and neck out of the water.
10. Try to board a lifeboat, raft, or other floating platform or object as soon as possible in order to shorten the immersion time. Remember, you lose body heat many times faster in water than in air. Since the effectiveness of your insulation is seriously reduced by soaking in water, you must now try to shield yourself from wind to avoid a wind-chill effect (convective cooling). If you manage to climb aboard a lifeboat, shielding can be accomplished with the aid of a canvas cover or tarpaulin, or an unused garment. Huddling close to the other occupants of the lifeboat will also conserve body heat.

11. Keep a positive attitude of mind about your survival and rescue. This will improve your chances of extending your survival time until rescue comes. Your will to live does make a difference!

12. DO NOT DRINK ALCOHOL BEFORE ABANDONING SHIP. It is dangerous —it not only causes rapid heat loss, but also impairs judgement.

Survivor pick-up by survival craft (lifeboat or raft)

Surviving in a lifeboat or life-craft (hereafter referred to as "the survival craft") is one of the most strenuous ordeals an individual can face. It involves combat against all the elemental forces at sea, one's own physical limitations, and — most of all—fear, hysteria, and despair. Thus, before survivors are picked up, or as soon as immediate rescue operations have been completed, a firm chain of command, based on previous positions of authority, must be established aboard the vessel. The individual in command of a survival craft (referred to in this chapter as the captain) is responsible for the immediate welfare (physical safety, medical condition, and morale) of its crew, as well as its other occupants.

When injury to a survivor is suspected, the methods used in transferring him to the survival craft should be the same as those outlined in the general first aid instructions in Chapter 1 of this guide.

The captain of the survival craft must be the one to decide how long artificial respiration on unconscious victims should be continued; how food, water, and medical supplies are distributed; and when to signal for help.

Immediate medical problems aboard survival craft

Trauma

Injuries should be handled as outlined in Chapter 4. However, a prepared medical survival kit might not be available, so the rescuers will have to improvise. The following measures are suggested.

The first objective in caring for any injured person is to provide life-saving treatment. Without equipment this may be accomplished by:

- controlling haemorrhage with direct pressure;
- giving mouth-to-mouth artificial respiration when needed;
- treating absence of pulse or cardiac stoppage by heart compression (see page 9)
- treating shock by placing a survivor's head lower than the rest of his body, and keeping him warm
- treating fractures by strapping the extremity to the opposite side, if nothing is available that can be used for splinting (for example, splint one leg to the other, one arm to the chest, or one forearm to the other with hands touching elbows);
- relieving pain by simple reassurance and giving medicines, if available.

Persons rescued from drowning

Those rescued promptly from drowning usually recover spontaneously, if they have not spent too much time in cold water and their body temperature has not been abnormally lowered (see page 262).

Treatment

Treatment for persons who have almost drowned should consist of immediate mouth-to-mouth artificial respiration, and heart compression, if needed (see pages 8–12).

If the person has trouble breathing, mouth-to-mouth artificial respiration may be helpful, even though he is breathing on his own (see Basic life support, page 6). Efforts to drain water from the the lungs of those rescued from drowning are not generally indicated or helpful, and should not be attempted. However, victims tend to swallow large volumes of water and their stomachs may become distended. This distension impairs ventilation and circulation, and it should be alleviated as soon as possible.

The water may be forced out and distension relieved by turning the victim on his side and compressing the upper abdomen. Also, the victim may be turned over into a face-downwards position and lifted under the stomach with the rescuer's hands to force the water out.

Generalized hypothermia due to immersion

As already mentioned, generalized hypothermia is the leading cause of death among shipwreck survivors.

In a cold environment, body-heat production will automatically increase in an effort to balance heat loss. But, if the rate of heat loss exceeds the rate of heat production, then the body temperature must fall and hypothermia will result.

Generalized hypothermia commonly occurs in most survivors extracted from cold water. The victims are strikingly pale, frequently have generalized muscular rigidity, are shivering, and exhibit varying levels of consciousness and shock. In addition, death by drowning is a frequent consequence of weakness caused by hypothermia, supervening before death from hypothermia alone would have occurred.

Treatment

The treatment for hypothermia will depend on the condition of the survivor. Generally speaking, survivors who are rational and capable of recounting their experiences, although shivering dramatically, merely need to have all their wet clothes removed and replaced with dry clothes or blankets. However, always bear in mind that even conscious survivors can collapse and become unconscious shortly after rescue. Alcohol should be avoided at all costs.

In more serious cases, in which the survivor is not shivering and is semi-conscious, unconscious, or apparently dead, immediate first aid measures will be necessary to preserve life. The following measures are recommended for dealing with such a survivor:

- On rescue, always check the survivor's breathing.
- If the survivor is not breathing, ensure that the airway is clear and start artificial respiration immediately (mouth-to-mouth or mouth-to-nose).
- Attempts at providing basic life support should be continued for at least 30 minutes (if medical advice is not available).
- If the survivor is breathing but unconscious, lay him in the unconscious position as illustrated on page 6 (Fig. 3). This is necessary to ensure that his breathing is not obstructed by his tongue or by vomit.
- Avoid all unnecessary manhandling; do not even remove wet clothes; do not massage.
- Prevent further loss of heat through evaporation and from exposure to the wind. Wrap the patient in blankets, preferably keeping him horizontal with his head slightly down.

Emotional factors

Under ideal conditions the healthy uninjured person may be able to survive 3 days at sea in a lifeboat or raft. However, survival for more than a month is not uncommon. The single most important factor in castaway survival is the **will to live**. This has been proved time and again in sea disasters and "ditchings". Often survivors have made every mistake in the book, but were saved by their determination to live.

The actions and emotional stability of the castaways depend first upon the morale and psychological strength of both the group and the individual. A group of experienced seamen, for instance, will be psychologically stronger than a group of shocked passengers.

As time is spent on the survival craft awaiting rescue, the group's morale may weaken seriously. Keeping survivors active is important. An assignment to various tasks—nursing care, supply tally, rescue watch, among other activities —will divert and occupy the mind and may help to keep hopes high. Lone survivors should make every effort to conserve energy and resources. They may imagine that they hear voices or see things that are not really there. Keeping the mind active with mental exercises may help to prevent this development.

Mental derangement may appear at any time before or after the rescue.

It is the duty of all survivors to recognize and treat mental disturbances, but the ultimate responsibility rests with the captain of the survival craft. Anxiety is most contagious and can destroy chances of survival on the open sea.

The best treatment for anxiety is to reassure patients and other people in the lifeboat and assign small tasks to keep them occupied. Acute agitation should be treated promptly, as the situation demands. For some victims forcible restraint may need to be applied. Morphine sulfate, 10 mg intramuscularly, repeated every 4 hours as needed, may serve to calm the anxious.

Other medical problems aboard survival craft

Seasickness

Seasickness (motion sickness) is an acute illness characterized by loss of appetite, nausea, dizziness, and vomiting. Preventive measures are often effective (see page 223).

Sunburn

Sunburn is one of the principal medical hazards of survival on the open sea, regardless of latitude. It may vary from a first- to a third-degree burn, depending upon the exposure and the protection available to the victim. Initially, sunburn is generally characterized by redness, oedema, and tenderness of the skin. It may be accompanied by local pain, fever, nausea, vomiting, diarrhoea, weakness, or even prostration.

Sunburn is prevented by keeping fully clothed at all times and, if possible, staying under a canopy. Survivors should avoid looking directly into the sun or at the glare from the water. Those aboard the survival craft should wear sunglasses during all daylight hours. In addition to these obvious precautions, a sun-screening agent should be applied liberally to all exposed parts of the body during periods of exposure to strong sunlight.

Hydration and nutrition

If rescue is delayed, maintaining both hydration and nutrition aboard the survival craft will become progressively more difficult. Food supplies are less essential than water. Lifeboat stores are often limited to hard candy, which provides a small amount of energy. Its main value is in boosting the morale of hungry survivors.

Although survival craft carry a limited quantity of potable water, they may be equipped with desalting kits or a solar still which would provide additional drinking-water. Each desalting kit provides about half a litre of safe drinking-water. Although the water is likely to be acrid and discoloured, it is safe when prepared according to the instructions on the kit. The capacity of a solar still is limited; it will yield about 4 litres of water per day in temperate climates with sunlight. This distilled water looks and smells better than the water produced by desalination. Efforts should be made to store rainwater.

If it is likely that more than one day will pass before rescue, a minimal amount of water should be issued during the first 24 hours. This will allow survivors' bodies to activate water-saving mechanisms that will later reduce the need for water. Survivors who have spent some time in the water, or who have swallowed sea-water, may have a demanding thirst; this should be partially satisfied. After the first day, half a litre of water daily per person should be consumed. In tropical climates, if stores are adequate, the ration should be increased to compensate for excessive loss of water due to sweating.

Heat exposure

Special problems are created aboard survival craft by exposure to tropical heat. In certain circumstances, fluid loss by sweating alone can be extremely high. The body will adjust to exceptional heat to some extent, but full acclimatization rarely occurs.

Dehydration can be prevented by minimizing activity during the daylight hours and by making the best use of clothing as a canopy.

Treatment for dehydration consists of increasing the water ration, as supplies permit (see Hydration and nutrition, page 263).

Heat exhaustion is caused by a loss of body water and salt (for symptoms and treatment, see page 207).

Heat cramps are painful spasms of the muscles of the extremities, back, or abdomen due to salt depletion. The skin is usually moist and cool, and twitching of muscles is frequent (for other information and treatment, see page 206).

Heat-stroke (sunstroke) is a medical emergency (for discussion and treatment, see page 205).

Medical resources aboard lifeboat

Lifeboats, life-rafts, life-floats, and buoyant apparatus should be furnished with certain provisions. The equipment must be of good quality, efficient for the purpose for which it is intended, and kept in good condition. The lifeboats for ocean and coastwise, seagoing, self-propelled vessels should each be equipped with a first aid kit.

When ships travel by infrequently used waterways or in colder climates, it is advisable to have *in addition* a more comprehensive survival kit (in waterproof packaging) prepared and ready to be placed aboard lifeboats or life-rafts, when needed. Contents for such a kit are proposed in Table 9. This list of medicaments and surgical supplies is planned for a complement of 20–30 survivors for a period of one week.

The ship's master should assign the individual in charge of the sick-bay and medicine chest to prepare *medical survival kits,* or have them prepared ashore. The person designated by the master to be responsible for these kits should store them in a compartment that can be maintained at temperatures above freezing, but not above room temperature. *On abandoning ship,* it

Table 9. Medical survival kit[a] suggested for lifeboats aboard merchant vessels

Description of item	Unit	No. of units	Comments
Medicaments			
acetylsalicylic acid tablets, 300 mg, 100s	bottle	1	minor aches or pain, antipyretic
cyclizine hydrochloride tablets, 50 mg, 100s	bottle	5	seasickness, mild antihistamine
diazepam tablets, 5 mg, 100s	bottle	3	tranquillizer (controlled substance)
morphine sulfate injection, 10 mg/ml, 1 ml disposable cartridge,[b] 10s	package	1	analgesic, sedative (controlled substance)
sodium chloride tablets, 1 g, 100 s	bottle	1	heat cramps
sunscreen preparation	package	40	protection against sunburn
tetracycline hydrochloride capsules, 250 mg, 100s	bottle	2	broad-spectrum antibiotic
Surgical supplies			
bandage, elastic, 10 cm roll, 12s	box	1	
bandage, gauze, roll, sterile, 10 cm × 10 m, 12s	box	1	
bandage, absorbent, adhesive, 2 cm × 8 cm, 100s	box	1	
pad, sterile, 10 cm × 10 cm, 100s	box	2	
scissors, bandage, Lister	item	1	
soap	cake	20	
sunglasses	item	20	
syringe, hypodermic cartridge holder[b]	item	2	
tape, adhesive, surgical, 5 cm × 5 m roll, 6s	box	1	
thermometer, clinical	item	2	

[a] To be available in the event of forced abandonment of a vessel in unfrequented waterways.
[b] The disposable cartridge for the medicament and the syringe holder should be purchased from the same supplier, to make sure that the cartridge will fit the syringe.

would be this person's responsibility to see that the officer-in-charge of a lifeboat receives such a kit.

Injectable doses of morphine sulfate may be stored in these kits. However, the ship's compartment in which morphine sulfate is stored should be locked securely at all times and checked at frequent intervals by the master. The master and the officer concerned should be the only ones with the key or lock combination.

Medical problems of the rescued castaway on board the rescue vessel

The treatment of survivors will depend on the nature of the rescue facility and the number and medical condition of the survivors.

Personnel on the rescue vessel should rapidly sort all survivors, according to their physical condition, into:

(*a*) those with minor injuries whose condition will not be worsened by delay in treatment (to be treated last or as time permits);

(*b*) those who are sick or injured but potentially treatable with the facilities at hand.

The latter group includes those who urgently require medical attention. Some persons in this group may be given first aid and relegated to group (*a*). For example, a broken arm could be splinted quickly and set later, after other more critical problems have been taken care of.

Victims rescued from drowning must receive immediate treatment as discussed on page 261, and in more detail under Basic life support, page 6.

Every submersion victim, even one requiring minimal treatment, should preferably be evacuated to a hospital for follow-up care.

Cold exposure injuries (local)

Cold injuries to parts of the body (face, extremities) are caused by exposure of tissues and small surface blood vessels to abnormally low temperatures. The extent of the injury depends upon such factors as temperature, duration of exposure, wind velocity, humidity, lack of protective clothing, or presence of wet clothing. Also, the harmful effects of exposure to cold are intensified by fatigue, individual susceptibility, existing injuries, emotional stress, smoking, and drinking alcohol.

Cold injuries to parts of the body fall into three main categories: chilblains, immersion foot, and frost-bite.

Chilblains

This relatively mild form of cold injury occurs in moderately cold climates with high humidity and temperatures above freezing (0–16 °C). Chilblains usually affect ears, fingers, and the back of the hand; but they may affect the lower extremities, especially the anterior tibial surface of the legs.

They are characterized by the skin turning a bluish red and by a mild swelling often associated with an itching, burning sensation which may be aggravated by warmth. If exposure is brief, these manifestations may disappear completely with no remaining signs. However, intermittent exposure results in the development of chronic manifestations, such as increased swelling, further discoloration of the skin (which becomes a deep reddish purple), blisters, and bleeding ulcers which heal slowly to leave numerous pigmented scars.

Treatment. For skin discomfort, apply a bland soothing ointment such as petrolatum. People susceptible to chilblains should avoid the cold or wear woollen socks and gloves.

Immersion foot

This form of cold injury is caused by exposure of the lower extremities to water at above-freezing temperatures, usually below 10 °C, for more than 12 hours. It characteristically occurs among shipwrecked sailors existing on lifeboats or rafts in enforced inactivity, with a poor diet, with wet and constricting clothing, and in adverse weather conditions. Clinical manifestations include swelling of the feet and lower portions of the legs, numbness, tingling, itching, pain, cramps, and skin discoloration.

In cases of immersion foot uncomplicated by trauma, there is usually no tissue destruction.

Treatment. After rescue every effort should be made to avoid rapid rewarming of the affected limbs. Care should be taken to avoid damaging the skin or breaking blisters. *Do not* massage affected limbs.

Prevention. Every effort should be made by survivors to keep their feet warm and dry. Shoe-laces should be loosened; the feet should be raised and toe and ankle exercises encouraged several times a day. When possible, shoes should be removed and unwanted spare clothing may be wrapped round the feet to keep them warm. Smoking should be discouraged.

Frost-bite

This is the term applied to cold injuries where there is destruction of tissue by freezing. It is the most serious form of localized cold injury. Although the area of frozen tissue is usually small, frost-bite may cover a considerable area. The fingers, toes, cheeks, ears, and nose are the most commonly affected parts of the body. If exposure is prolonged, the freezing may extend up the arms and legs. Ice crystals in the skin and other tissues cause the area to appear white or greyish-yellow in colour. Pain may occur early and subside. Often, the affected part will feel only very cold and numb, and there may be a tingling, stinging, or aching sensation. The patient may not be aware of frost-bite until someone mentions it. When the damage is superficial, the surface will feel hard and the underlying tissue soft when depressed gently and firmly. In a deep, unthawed frost-bite, the area will feel hard and solid and cannot be depressed. It will be cold and numb, and blisters will appear on the surface and in the underlying tissues in 12–36 hours. The area will become red and swollen when it thaws, gangrene will occur later, and there will be a loss of tissue (necrosis). Time alone will reveal the kind of frost-bite that has been present. It is fortunate therefore that the treatment for various degrees of frost-bite is ite. identical except for superficial frost-bite. **A frost-bite of the superficial, dry, freezing type should be thawed immediately to prevent a deep-freezing injury of the part involved. However, never thaw a frozen extremity before arriving at a facility with water, heat, and equipment where the extremity can be rewarmed rapidly.**

Treatment. All freezing injuries follow the same sequence in treatment: first aid, rapid rewarming, and care after first aid.

(*a*) *First aid.* The principles of first aid in localized cold injury are relatively few. The two most important things are to get the patient to a place of permanent treatment as soon as possible and then to rewarm him. It is important to note that a patient can walk for great distances on frost-bitten feet with little danger. Once rewarming has started, it must be maintained. All patients with local cold injuries to the lower extremities become litter cases. Refreezing or walking on a partially thawed part can be very harmful. During transportation and initial treatment, the use of alcoholic drinks should not be permitted, because they affect capillary circulation and cause a loss of body heat. Ointments or creams should not be applied.

(*b*) *Rapid rewarming.* The technique of rewarming has two phases: (1) treatment of exposure; and (2) treatment of the local cold injury. Treatment of exposure consists of actively rewarming the patient. This is done in principle by the removal of cold and the addition of warmth. *Removal of cold* is accomplished by removal of all cold and wet clothing and constricting items such as shoes and socks. *Addition of warmth* is provided from external and internal sources. External warmth is added by providing the patient with prewarmed clothes and blankets. Giving a patient a cold change of clothes, a cold blanket, or a cold sleeping-bag will cause a rapid dissipation of his residual heat. If necessary, it would be better to have someone give the clothing he is wearing to the patient. Someone should warm the patient's sleeping-bag before he gets into it. A good source of warmth is the body heat of other people. In general, internal warmth is provided by hot liquids and an adequate diet.

There are two techniques of *rapid rewarming:* wet and dry.

Wet rapid rewarming, which is preferred, is accomplished by completely immersing the affected part in an adequate amount of water at a temperature of 40–42 °C. The bath should be tested frequently with a thermometer. If one is not available, the attendant should pour some of the water over the inside of his wrist to make sure the bath is not too hot. Warming should be discontinued when the affected part becomes flushed; this is usually within 20 minutes. Further rapid wet rewarming is not necessary.

The dry rapid rewarming technique takes three to four times as long as the wet technique and is best accomplished by the use of natural body warmth, for example, by putting the patient's hands in someone else's armpits or by sharing warm clothing with him. Also, the patient can be exposed to warm room air.

Do not make such a patient walk and do not massage the affected part. Do not use water hotter than 44 °C, nor recool with ice or snow, and do not expose extremities near an open flame or fire.

(*c*) *Care after first aid.* After the rewarming of a cold injury to a lower extremity, the patient is treated as a litter case. All constricting clothing items should be removed, total body warmth should be maintained, and sleep should be encouraged.

After rewarming, the affected part should be cleansed carefully with water, or soap and water, taking care to leave the blisters intact. A soft sterile dressing should be applied. Dry, sterile gauze should be placed between toes and fingers to keep them separated. The patient should be placed in bed with the affected part elevated and protected from contact with the bedding.

If available, a bed cradle can be used, or one can be improvised from boxes to keep sheets and blankets from touching the affected area. Additional heat should *not* be applied.

Morphine sulfate, 10 mg, may be given intramuscularly for pain and repeated every 4 hours as needed, but *only if* RADIO MEDICAL ADVICE *recommends it.*

Generalized immersion hypothermia aboard the rescue vessel

At environmental temperatures of less than 20–21 °C, man's survival depends upon insulation (body fat, clothing), the ratio of body surface to volume, the basal metabolic rate, and the *will to survive.*

Seawater freezes at −2 °C. It may be assumed that most polar water with ice is as cold as this. In polar water, the body temperature falls very rapidly. Consciousness lasts 5–7 minutes, the ungloved hand is useless in 1–5 minutes, and death occurs in 10–20 minutes. It has been found that severe exposure of the head and neck to cold can cause massive cerebral haemorrhage. These parts of the body should be specially protected.

The rectal temperature should be taken in people rescued from cold water. This can help in estimating the chances of survival in each individual case.

When the rectal temperature is below 35 °C, hypothermia progressively lowers the basal metabolic rate, heart rate, and blood pressure and produces uncontrollable shivering. Hallucinations, apathy, and stupor or unconsciousness occur at 27–30 °C; and death from ventricular fibrillation or cardiac arrest at 21–28 °C.

Treatment

The treatment of generalized (immersion) hypothermia begins with artificial respiration, using oxygen if available, Unheated oxygen should not be used for the hypothermia victim, because it will mean added cold; warm, moist oxygen should therefore be administered. An oral airway should be inserted. When respiration is absent or poor, or where there is *no detectable carotid pulse* (see page 3), it may be difficult to tell if the patient is dead or alive. **If there is uncertainty about the possibility of life, always try artificial respiration and heart compression.**

When life-saving measures have been carried out, the patient's wet clothing should be removed and plans made for his immediate and rapid warming. If possible, immersion in a hot bath carefully maintained at 40–42 °C is desirable. If facilities are not available for maintaining a hot bath, hot-water bottles or heating-pads with layers of blankets can be used to warm patients. Great care is needed to avoid burns, to which the cold patient is especially vulnerable. Also, an airway must be maintained if the patient is unconscious.

It is recommended that heat be applied only to the central core of the body. It is of critical importance NOT to attempt to warm the victim's arms or legs since heating of the limbs causes cold blood to flow from them to the body core, causing further detrimental cooling of the core. Such incorrect treatment of hypothermia may induce a condition known as "after-drop".

The patient should be placed in the controlled temperature bath, or other methods of warming should be applied, until the rectal temperature is above 35 °C and he has stopped shivering.

Where there is a large number of cases, first treat those not breathing (but alive) and those who are unconscious. The continuous pouring of water heated to 40–42 °C over those waiting for treatment will increase the number of survivors.

The patient with hypothermia must be observed closely. Depression of breathing and cough reflexes may occur, and secretions may be retained. If a suction unit is available, catheter suction of the airway should be carried out frequently to remove secretions.

Nothing should be given by mouth because the patient may inhale liquid into the lungs, or he may vomit owing to a lack of bowel motility. Alcoholic drinks should not be given until 24 hours after recovery.

It may be necessary to administer intravenous fluids, but this should be done only after getting RADIO MEDICAL ADVICE. If breathing becomes shallow or slow, mouth-to-mouth artificial respiration should be given to support the patient's respiration (see page 8).

In the unconscious patient with hypothermia, the pulse and blood pressure should be checked every 15 minutes and the rectal temperature every half hour. If the patient is comatose or appears to be in shock (see page 17), RADIO MEDICAL ADVICE should be obtained.

When the patient has been conscious for approximately 12–24 hours, 500 mg of tetracycline hydrochloride should be given by mouth every 6 hours for the next 5 days.

Plans should be made to evacuate the patient from the vessel to the nearest medical facility as soon as possible.

Contamination with oil

Do not clean oil off the skin (except round the mouth and eyes) until the person is warm and comfortable. Survivors who have recovered from hypothermia (see page 267) can be taken to a warm shower or bathroom and should have all their clothes taken off. Then their skin should be wiped with soft cloth and strong paper towels to remove as much of the oil as possible. Injured or burned areas should be wiped with care or not at all. Next, if a strong warm shower is available, it can be used to remove much of the oil. Hair-shampoo will remove oil from the hair and can be used to help remove oil from the body. Then, with time, patience, help, and wiping, and using good toilet soap to clean the skin, the rest of the oil can be washed away. Solvents, scouring compounds, kerosene, and other cleaners not designed for skin-cleaning *must not* be used. It is, however, permissible to use jellied cleansing agents designed for the purpose. But the main cleaning-up is best accomplished by being patient and gentle, by mechanical removal of the oil by wiping and by a strong shower, and by using hair-shampoo and toilet soap.

Dehydration and malnutrition

Survivors who have been adrift for several days may be suffering from dehydration. If they have been adrift for several weeks, malnutrition may also be a problem. Caution should be exercised in trying to reverse either dehydration or malnutrition rapidly. Give oral rehydration salt solution or sweetened fluids in quantities that will produce a urinary output of one litre per day initially. In temperate climatic conditions (or air-conditioned accommodation), this will usually mean an input of about 2 litres a day. If the weather is warm and the skin is moist or sweaty, higher intakes may be permitted. Initially, a diet of nourishing liquids (sugar and water or milk or soup) will satisfy nutritional requirements and should be given for the first 2 days. Then small amounts of normal food can be given additionally. RADIO MEDICAL ADVICE should be sought. This diet should continue until either the survivor can be transferred to care ashore or medical assistance is given on board.

Chapter 13
Death at sea

Contents

Care of the dying

There is never a stage when nothing can be done to help a patient. One may be quite unable to prevent him from dying, but there remains the task of ensuring that he is preserved from suffering and pain, that he has people around him to care for him, and that his dignity as a human being is preserved and respected. If the patient is obviously dying, make sure that he remains tranquil in mind and body during the period of dying. Comfort, companionship, compassion, and the complete relief both of mental and physical suffering, should be the aims. If slight pain is present, it must be relieved by giving acetylsalicylic acid tablets or paracetamol in doses of 2 tablets every 3–4 hours. If the patient is suffering from severe pain, read page 305. In the event of mental distress, confusion, or behavioural problems, consult pages 103 and 213.

Signs of death

Never consider anyone to be dead until you *and others* agree that the following signs are present.

- *The heart has stopped.* No pulse will be felt and no heart sounds will be heard. Put your ear on the left side of the chest near the nipple and listen carefully. If you are not sure what to listen for, listen to the left side of the chest of a live person first. To test that the circulation has stopped, tie a piece of string tightly round a finger. In life the finger becomes bluish, but in death it remains white. Slight pressure on the finger-nail or lip in life will cause the area to become pale, and when the pressure is released the colour is regained. In death, this will not occur.
- *Breathing has stopped.* Listen with your ear right over the nose and mouth. You should feel no air coming out and should see no chest and abdominal movement. A mirror held in front of the nose and mouth will be clouded by the moisture in the outgoing breath in life, but no clouding will occur in death.
- *The person looks dead.* The eyes become dull and the skin pale. The pupils are large. Shining a bright light into the eye does not make the pupil smaller.

These are the immediate signs of death. Later signs are as follows.

- *Rigor mortis.* This is a stiffness of the body that usually comes on about 3–4 hours after death. The timing will depend to some extent on the ambient temperature. The stiffness lasts for 2–3 days. It is most easily felt in places like the jaw, the elbow, and the knee.
- *Post-mortem lividity or staining.* Blood in a dead body will tend to gravitate. So, if the body was left lying on its back after death, there will be reddish or purplish patches resembling bruises over the back and over the back of the limbs that were downwards. This is called "post-mortem lividity or staining". It is possible to deduce from this staining what position the body was in after death.
- *The cornea goes milky.* The cornea is the clear window at the front of the eye. It goes milky about 15 hours after death.
- *Decomposition.* Changes due to decomposition can be seen 2–3 days after death and will usually appear first in the abdomen where a greenish colour may be observed. This is a certain sign of death.

While none of the signs described above is infallible in itself, there is usually little difficulty in coming to a decision when they are taken together.

Mistaken death: a warning

A person who has taken *large doses of certain drugs,* usually sedatives or tranquillizers, or who is suffering from hypothermia (page 262), may look dead, but may be alive. Mistakes have been made in this respect. Check carefully for shallow breathing, for a pulse, for heart sounds, and so on, as described above. If you are aware of the possibilities for error, you are less likely to make a mistake. All the circumstances surrounding the death may help you decide whether drug overdose and hypothermia are possibilities.

Cause of death

It is important to try to establish the reasons for death. Causes of death can be ascribed to two main groups:

- natural causes such as illnesses;
- injuries, which may be accidental or non-accidental.

If the person has been ill on board, records of the nature and progress of the illness and of the treatment given will have been made. These records should be carefully preserved in case any further inquiries are necessary. Similarly, in the case of injuries, the circumstances of the incident that led to the injury or injuries should be investigated and recorded. The record of the investigations, together with the medical records, should be carefully preserved. It must always be remembered that medico-legal inquiries may subsequently be necessary even when there are, at the time, no apparent criminal or suspicious circumstances surrounding a death. If the circumstances of death are unusual, sudden, or unknown, or if there is any suspicion of criminal intent, there should if possible be a post-mortem examination by a pathologist (page 274).

Identification of a dead body[1]

If the ship is near port it may be possible to put the body in a bath with plenty of ice all round —remember to put some ice in the bath first. It might even be possible, if the ship is not near port, to keep the body in a refrigerator or cold-store set aside for the purpose and to arrange for its examination by a pathologist. If, however, the body cannot be kept and burial at sea is necessary, it is essential to examine the body thoroughly and to note down every observation that can possibly assist in subsequent identification. This is a task that must be undertaken by at least two people.

Clothing

Strip the body of all clothing. Clothing should be removed without tearing or cutting. List each item briefly, and note any initials or names on

---

[1] These observations relate mainly to the identification of a dead body recovered from the sea or the body of a passenger. Usually, there will be no difficulty in identifying the body of a crew-member known to many people on board.

the garments. Any papers, wallet, money, etc. should be included in the list. Any articles that are wet should be dried and should then be put into a plastic bag, sealed, labelled, and kept in a safe place for handing over to the police or to other authorities at the next port. Clothing must be dried and afterwards suitably wrapped and labelled for handing over. When handing over clothing and other articles, check each item against the list and get a receipt from the person to whom they are delivered.

Examination of the body

Examine the body carefully and record the following data:

- race;
- skin colour;
- approximate age;
- height.

To measure height, straighten out the body with the legs fully extended. Make two marks on the deck, one in line with the heels, the other in line with the top of the head. Measure and record the distance between the lines.

Next note the development of the body (whether fat, thin, wasted, muscular, etc.).

Inspect the head and face: record the length and colour of the hair; note the eyebrows, and describe any facial hair. The complexion should be described (for example: sunburnt, pale, florid, sallow). Record the colour of the eyes and the shape of the nose. Open the mouth and examine the teeth, noting whether they are sound, decayed, or missing. Dentures should be removed, cleaned, and placed with the other articles kept for future examination.

Inspect the rest of the body: record all birthmarks, moles, scars, or deformities from injuries. Note the exact position of all scars and describe their length and width. A diagram may help. Note whether circumcised or not. Vaccination scars should be noted. Tattoos should be described, and any words or letters noted. Record the size, position, general appearance, and colour of such tattoos. Wounds and bruises

should be noted; try to decide whether they could explain the death. Note the exact position, depth, and dimensions of all wounds, Describe the character of the wounds: clean cuts as from a knife, or ragged tears, or bullet-wounds. Note any skin blackening or singeing of clothing around the entrance bullet-wound. Look for the exit wound showing where the bullet left the body (this is always bigger than the entry wound). Feel under the skin for a bullet that may be lodged there and, if there is one, note the position. Look carefully for signs of bruising round wounds or if there has been any escape of blood from wounds, as shown by blood clots, blood-staining of the surrounding skin, blood on the clothing, or blood in the area where the body was found. This will help to distinguish injuries caused during life (which bleed) from those caused after death (which do not bleed). Note also any broken bones. External signs of disease such as boils, ulcers, varicose veins, or skin rashes, should be recorded.

Use of a camera

If the circumstances of death are other than straightforward, photograph the body where it was found and from several angles. When the body is moved, take more pictures of the scene to show any blood on the deck or other evidence. Take general pictures of the unclothed body and special views of any wounds, scars, and injuries. Try to record all observations you think may be of help in identification or of interest with regard to the cause of death. Note why you took each picture and what you intend it to show. Remember to have all your observational notes countersigned, and to make all appropriate entries in the official log book.

The time of death

A note of the time of examination and a record of any of the following phenomena may help in later estimation of the time of death.

Feel the surface of the body. Is the body warmer under the clothing than in exposed areas? Tem-

273

perature is best felt using the back of the fingers and hand. If possible, take the temperature of the body with an ordinary (not a clinical) thermometer 5 cm inside the rectum. Look for rigor mortis (page 272).

Look for putrefaction. The earliest change is green or greyish discoloration over the lower part of the abdomen. This discoloration spreads to the rest of the abdomen, to the trunk, up the neck to the head, and into the limbs. Note the extent of discoloration. Late signs of putrefaction show as swelling due to gas in the tissues. The appearance is bloated, and the abdomen is swollen. The skin becomes moist and peels. Bags of reddish or greenish fluid may form on the surface. The odour is very offensive. The pressure of gas may force froth or fluid out of the nose, mouth, and anus. The tongue may protrude. When putrefaction has advanced to this extent, some of the data required for identification cannot be obtained. The features will be much altered by swelling and discoloration, the eyeballs will be bulging or collapsed, and the hair, teeth, and nails will be loose or easily detached.

Disposal of the body

Retention for burial ashore or post-mortem examination

Wherever possible, a body should be retained for post-mortem examination or for burial ashore. For the sake of the deceased person's relatives and to preserve the body in the best possible condition, thoroughly wash and dry the body all over. Comb out and part the hair, and give attention to the fingernails. Straighten the arms and legs, and interlock the fingers over the thighs. Tie the ankles together to keep the feet perpendicular. With forceps, place a good plug of cotton wool well up in the rectum. Pass a catheter tube into the bladder and empty it completely; if this is impracticable, make a firm tie around the root of the penis. A plug of cotton wool may be passed into each nostril. The body should then be put in a body bag and kept in a refrigerator or cold store set aside for the pur-

pose. Packing in ice in a bath is an alternative, if near port.

Burial at sea

If there is no suspicion of foul play, if for any reason it is not possible to retain the body, or if so requested by next-of-kin, the body may be buried at sea. In this case, it is not necessary to do more than to lay the body on a flat surface, straighten the legs and arms, and interlock the fingers over the thighs. The hair should be brushed off the forehead, the face washed, and the jaw secured by passing a bandage under the chin and over the top of the head, where it may be tied or clipped.

For burial at sea, the body has traditionally been sewn into a length of canvas of standard width and about 4.5 metres in length, weighted by fire bars sewn to the canvas on either side of the legs below the knees. It is probable that these items may not be available on a modern ship. In seeking substitutes, bear in mind that the shroud needs to be made of a very strong material and the weights sufficiently heavy to ensure rapid sinking and permanent submersion of the body. There should be three or four slits or openings in the material to allow the gases of decomposition to escape and prevent flotation due to trapped air. Burial should not take place in soundings in any part of the world.

After preparation, the body should be placed upon an improvised platform resting on the ship's side-rail and a suitable trestle or other support, covered by a ship's flag, secured to the inboard edge of the platform. Wooden blocks screwed under the platform and resting against the ship's side-rail will prevent the platform sliding outboard when the inboard end is raised to allow the body to slide from under the flag into the sea. It is very important to ensure that the whole operation proceeds smoothly and respectfully without unseemly mishaps. If the ship is small and there is a heavy sea, precautions must be taken to ensure that the body will not be prematurely lost and will not fail to drop cleanly into the sea at the right moment. This may warrant fastening guide-rails on the platform. The seamen allocated to perform the disposal must be carefully briefed. On receipt of a discreet signal, they must raise the inboard end of the platform to allow the body to slide from under the flag into the sea.

When the family is notified that the remains were committed to the deep, the ship's master should indicate the longitude and latitude where this took place. Also, the master should find out if the next-of-kin wants the flag sent to the family with the personal effects of the deceased.

Chapter 14
External assistance

Contents

Radio Medical Advice

Radio Medical Advice is available, by radio telegraphy or by direct radio-telephonic contact with the doctor, from a number of ports in all parts of the world. It may, on occasion, be obtained from another ship in the vicinity which has a doctor on board. In either instance, it is better if the exchange of information is in a language common to both parties. Coded messages are a frequent source of misunderstanding and should be avoided as far as possible.

It is very important that *all* the information possible should be passed on to the doctor and that *all* his advice and directives should be clearly understood and fully recorded. A comprehensive set of notes should be ready to be passed on to the doctor, preferably based on the format given on pages 278–279 — part (*a*) is for cases of illness, part (*b*) for cases of injury. Have a pencil and paper available to make notes, and remember to transcribe these notes on to the patient's and ship's records after receiving them. It is a good idea to record the exchange of information by means of a tape-recorder, if one is available. This may then be played back to clarify written notes. The doctor may not be aware of the contents of your ship's medical chest, and it will save time and bother if you have a list of the drugs and appliances available.

It may be necessary, under certain circumstances, to withhold the name of the patient when obtaining medical advice, in order to preserve confidentiality. In such cases the patient's name and rank may be submitted later in writing to complete the doctor's records.

Information to have ready when requesting Radio Medical Advice

Complete the appropriate form or notes *before* asking for assistance. Give the relevant information to your radio adviser. Write down any advice you are given as you receive it, and repeat it back to the adviser to avoid misunderstanding.

(a) In the case of illness

1 *Routine particulars about the ship*

   1.1   Name of ship
   1.2   Call sign
   1.3   Date and time (GMT)
   1.4   Course, speed, position
   1.5.1 Port of destination is ... and is ... hours/days away
   1.5.2 Nearest port is ... and is ... hours/days away
   1.5.3 Other possible port is ... and is ... hours/days away
   1.6   Local weather (if relevant)

2 *Routine particulars about the patient*

   2.1   Surname of casualty
   2.2   Other names of casualty
   2.3   Rank
   2.4   Job on board (occupation)
   2.5   Age and sex

3 *Particulars of the illness*

   3.1   When did the illness first begin?
   3.2   How did the illness begin (suddenly, slowly, etc.)?
   3.3   What did the patient *first* complain of?
   3.4   List *all* his complaints and symptoms.
   3.5   Describe the course of his *present* illness from the beginning to the present time.
   3.6   Give any important *past* illnesses/injuries/operations.
   3.7   Give particulars of known illnesses that run in the family (family history).
   3.8   Describe any social pursuits or occupations that may be important (social and occupational history).
   3.9   List *all* medicines/tablets/drugs that the patient was taking *before* the present illness began and indicate the dose(s) and how often taken (see 6.1)

3.10 Has the patient been taking any alcohol or do you think he is taking non-medicinal drugs?

4 *Results of examination of the ill person*

   4.1   Temperature, pulse, and respiration
   4.2   Describe the general appearance of the patient.
   4.3   Describe the appearance of the affected parts.
   4.4   What do you find on examination of the affected parts (swelling, tenderness, lack of movement, etc.)?
   4.5   What tests have you done and with what result (urine, other)?

5 *Diagnosis*

   5.1   What do you think is the diagnosis?
   5.2   What other illnesses have you considered (differential diagnosis)?

6 *Treatment*

   6.1   List ALL the medicines/tablets/drugs that the patient has taken or been given *since the illness began* and indicate the dose(s) and the times given or how often given (see 3.9). Do not use the term "standard antibiotic treatment". Name the antibiotic given.
   6.2   How has the patient responded to the treatment given?

7 *Problems*

   7.1   What problems are worrying you now?
   7.2   What do you think you need to be advised on?

8 *Other comments*

9 *Comments by the radio doctor*

(b) In the case of injury

1   *Routine particulars about the ship*

1.1   Name of ship
1.2   Call sign
1.3   Date and time (GMT)
1.4   Course, speed, position
1.5.1   Port of destination is ... and is ... hours/days away
1.5.2   Nearest port is ... and is ... hours/days away
1.5.3   Other possible port is ... and is ... hours/days away
1.6   Local weather (if relevant)

2   *Routine particulars about the patient*

2.1   Surname of casualty
2.2   Other names of casualty
2.3   Rank
2.4   Job on board (occupation)
2.5   Age and sex

3   *History of the injuries*

3.1   *Exactly* how did the injuries arise?
3.2   When did the injuries occur?
3.3   What does the patient complain of? (List the complaints in order of importance or severity.)
3.4   Give important past illnesses/injuries/operations.
3.5   List ALL medicines/tablets/drugs that the patient was taking *before* the present injury (injuries) and indicate doses and how often taken.
3.6   Has the patient been taking any alcohol or do you think he is taking non-medicinal drugs?
3.7   Does the patient remember everything that happened, or did he lose consciousness even for a very short time?
3.8   If he lost consciousness, describe when, for how long, and the degree of unconsciousness (page 97).

4   *Results of examination*

4.1   Temperature, pulse, and respiration
4.2   Describe the general condition of the patient.
4.3   List what you believe to be the patient's injuries in order of importance and severity.
4.4   Did the patient lose any blood? If so, how much?
4.5   What tests have you done and with what result (urine, other)?

5   *Treatment*

5.1   Describe the first aid and other treatment you have carried out since the injuries occurred.
5.2   List ALL the medicines/tablets/drugs that the patient has taken or been given, and indicate the dose(s) and the times given or how often given. Do not use the term "standard antibiotic treatment". Name the antibiotic given.
5.3   How has the patient responded to the treatment?

6   *Problems*

6.1   What problems are worrying you now?
6.2   What do you think you need to be advised on?

7   *Other comments*

8   *Comments by the radio doctor*

Evacuation by helicopter

Do not ask for a helicopter unless the patient is in a serious situation and certainly never in the case of a trivial illness or for your own convenience. Remember that, apart from the expense of helicopter evacuation, the pilot and crew often risk their lives to render assistance to ships at sea and their services should be used only in an emergency.

The normal procedure is as follows.

Contact the shore radio station and ask for medical advice; your call will normally be transferred to a doctor. Give the doctor all the information you can so that he can assess the seriousness of the situation. He will normally give advice on the immediate care of the patient. After the link call is over, the doctor will advise the coastguard service on the best method of evacuation and, should helicopter evacuation be thought desirable, the coastguard will make the necessary arrangements and will keep in touch with the ship.

Do not expect a helicopter to appear right away. There are certain operational matters to consider and, although the service is always manned, apparent delay may ensue. Remember that the range of a helicopter is limited, depending on the type in service, and you may be asked to rendezvous nearer land. In bad weather and at extreme ranges it may be necessary to arrange for another aircraft to overfly and escort the helicopter for safety reasons, and this aircraft may have to be brought from another base. Arrangements may have to be made for a refuelling stop to be made at, say, an oil rig, so that the helicopter can make the pick-up and then fly back without further stops.

All this takes time and, as it is done with the utmost efficiency, please do not keep calling to ask where the helicopter is.

When helicopter evacuation is decided upon, the following measures should be taken.

1. It is essential that the ship's position should be given as accurately as possible. The bearing (magnetic or true) and distance from a fixed object, like a headland or lighthouse, should be given if possible. The type of ship and colour of hull should be included, if time allows.
2. Give details of your patient's condition, and advise immediately if there is any change in it. Details of his mobility are especially important, as he may have to be lifted by stretcher.
3. Inform the bridge and engine-room watches. A person should be nominated to communicate with the helicopter.
4. Helicopters in many countries are fitted with a VHF and/or UHF radio transmitter. They cannot normally work on the MF frequencies, although certain large helicopters can communicate on 2182 kHz MF. If direct communication between the ship and the assisting helicopter cannot be effected on either VHF or 2182 kHz, it may be possible to communicate via a lifeboat if there is one is in the vicinity. Alternatively a message may be passed via a Coast Radio Station or Coastguard Station on 2182 kHz, or on VHF.
5. The ship must be on a steady course giving minimum ship motion.
6. An indication of relative wind direction should be given. Flags and pennants are suitable for this purpose. Smoke from a galley funnel may also give an indication of the wind, but, in all cases where any funnel is producing exhaust, the wind must be at least two points off the port bow.
7. Clear as large an area of deck (or covered hatchway) as possible and mark the area with a large letter "H" in white. Whip or wire aerials in and around the area should, if at all possible, be taken down.
8. All loose articles must be securely tied down or removed from the transfer area. The downwash from the helicopter's rotor will easily lift unsecured covers, tarpaulins, hoses, rope, rubbish, etc., thereby presenting a serious flying hazard. If ingested by the engine, even small pieces of paper can cause a helicopter to crash.
9. From the air, especially if there is a lot of shipping in the area, it is difficult for the pilot of a helicopter to pick out the particular ship he is looking for from the many in sight, unless that ship uses a distinctive distress signal that can be clearly seen by him. One such signal is the orange-coloured smoke signal carried in lifeboats.

This is very distinct from the air. An Aldis lamp can also be seen, except in very bright sunlight when the lifeboat heliograph could be used. The display of these signals will save the helicopter pilot valuable time in locating the casualty and may mean all the difference between success and failure.

10. Never hook the hoist cable of the helicopter to any part of the ship.

11. The winch wire should be handled only by personnel wearing rubber gloves. A helicopter can build up a charge of static electricity which, if discharged through a person handling the winch wire, can kill or cause severe injury. The helicopter crew will normally discharge the static electricity before commencing the operation, by dipping the winch wire in the sea or allowing the hook to touch the ship's deck. However, under some conditions, sufficient static electricity can build up during the operation to give unprotected personnel a severe shock.

12. When cooperating with helicopters in rescue operations, ships should not attempt to provide a lee while helicopters are engaged in winching operations, as this tends to create turbulence.

13. The survivor is placed in the stretcher, strapped in such a manner that it is impossible for him to slip or fall out, and both stretcher and crewman are winched up into the helicopter. If the patient is already in a Neil-Robertson type stretcher, this can either be lifted straight into the aircraft or placed in the rigid frame stretcher.

14. At all times, obey the instructions of the helicopter crew. They have the expertise to do this job quickly and efficiently.

15. If the hoist is being carried out at night, point searchlights vertically to aid in locating the ship. Light the pick-up area as well as possible. Be sure you do NOT shine any lights on the helicopter, so that the pilot is not blinded. If there are any obstructions in the vicinity, put lights on them so that the pilot will be aware of them.

Preparation of the patient for evacuation

Place in a plastic envelope the patient's medical records (if any), together with any necessary papers (including passport), so that they can be sent with him.

Add notes of any treatment given, and see that he has a tag attached to him if morphine has been given.

If possible, ensure that your patient is wearing a life-jacket, before he is moved to the stretcher.

Ship-to-ship transfer of doctor or patient

This is a seamanship problem that demands high standards of competence for its safe and efficient performance. There should be no need to advise professional seamen concerning this operation, but this guide may occasionally be in the hands of yachtsmen or operators of small craft, to whom a few reminders may be helpful.

A very large tanker or other ship under way at sea may require 30 minutes or an hour to bring her main propulsion machinery to standby, so use your daylight signalling apparatus or VHF as soon as possible. Loaded, large tankers require several miles to lose headway and are difficult to manoeuvre close to small craft.

Light (unloaded) ships of any type and high-sided passenger ships will make considerable leeway when stopped and must be approached with caution. Some ships may have to turn their propellers very slowly during the operation.

Keep clear of the overhang of bows or stern, especially if there is any sea running. Also beware of any permanent fendering fitted at ships' sides. The general rule is that the ship with the higher freeboard will provide illumination and facilities for boarding and will indicate the best position.

Do not linger alongside for any reason; as soon as the operation is completed, use full power to get your craft clear. There may be a suction effect that will hold you alongside, and this may be dangerous if you do not use full power. For your own safety, make sure you are seen and that your actions are communicated to the master of the larger ship, and act promptly on his instructions.

Communicating with doctors

As a matter of courtesy as well as of information, a letter or form should always be sent with any patient who is going to see a doctor. The crew member will be a stranger to the doctor, and there might even be a language difficulty. A clearly written communication in a foreign language is often easier to understand than a spoken one. The letter should include routine particulars about the crew member (name, date of birth) and about the ship (name of ship, port, name of agent, owner). The medical content of the letter should be set out in a systematic way, providing the doctor with a synopsis of everything known about the patient that may be relevant, including *copies* of any information from doctors in previous ports. The use of a form for this purpose along the lines of that in Annex 4 (page 352) is particularly valuable, since the doctor is requested to write back to the master on the form.

Chapter 15

Environmental control on board ship

Contents

Environmental controls are concerned with the complex of climatic, physical, and biological factors that act on an individual, his community, and his natural or man-made surroundings. These controls ultimately determine his health and survival.

The seaman's health and survival depend mainly on three related controls:

- his own efforts to maintain his physical and mental efficiency at an optimum level;
- the organization of the physical facilities and the supplies necessary to maintain him in a state of maximum efficiency; and
- the efforts of other personnel, ashore and afloat, to create and maintain conditions conducive to his health.

The seaman should expect and find certain facilities, supplies, and conditions in his shipboard environment. In turn, he and his fellow crew members have a major responsibility for the state of that environment. Individual and group health are totally dependent on a proper give-and-take attitude among the crew, as well as good medical services on board.

A give-and-take attitude is particularly important in maintaining good environmental sanitation on board ship. Proper sanitation is impossible unless each crew member cooperates. At the same time, the ship's master should ensure good sanitary conditions on board through periodic inspections by himself or suitable persons to whom he delegates this responsibility.

Proper ventilation, lighting, food hygiene, liquid transport, waste disposal, ship inspection, and the control of disease vectors (carriers) are discussed in this chapter.

Ventilation

For effective ventilation, there must be an adequate flow of clean air with sufficient oxygen content; controlled humidity to prevent "sweating", mould, and allergic reactions; and controlled temperatures to make the atmosphere comfortable.

Modern vessels use ventilation and forced air to create the conditions most suitable for working in the compartments of ships.

There are still some old ships in service that are not fitted with a modern air-conditioning system. They may have cowl ventilators, but these are not very effective in the tropics. However, with the judicious use of all openings and the aid of efficient electric fans, some measure of comfort may be achieved in these ships, too.

Ships built particularly for service in temperate climates need an improved air supply, if they are used for tropical runs.

With any ventilation system, and particularly when electric fans are used, the air flow should not be aimed directly at the bare body, since this may promote chills and colds.

Adequate ventilation in living spaces and food stores is important for the health of all on board ship. This is often arranged by means of a recirculating air-conditioning system. As it is obviously undesirable that the air from a room occupied by an infectious person should be recirculated, purpose-built ships' hospitals have separate ventilation systems. However, when a person with an infectious disease has to occupy a cabin, all possible steps should be taken to prevent contaminated air from recirculating. For example, a porthole or external door not subject to an inflow of air should be opened, wherever possible, to exhaust the contaminated air.

Besides bacterial contamination of air, a common hazard aboard ship is the accumulation of gases in holds, bunkers, paint lockers, tanks, and other confined areas. Such gases may be toxic (poisonous) or they may displace oxygen. Crew members entering such an enclosed space may become ill or die of asphyxia (see Suffocation, page 43).

Among commonly found toxic gases are carbon monoxide, carbon dioxide, ammonia, chlorine, nitrogen, and petroleum gases. These gases and others are found in varying combinations in shipboard fires; in empty oil, chemical, and storage tanks; and in bilges, skin tanks, and certain cargo holds. Certain classes of cargo absorb oxygen or give off toxic gases. This is particularly true of products of plant origin such as linseed cakes, resin, and tobacco.

Poisonous gases or fumes may be formed in chemical, petroleum, or whale-oil tanks as a result of the decomposition of residues remaining after the tanks are emptied. Fumes can develop from cargoes of hides that have become moist and have fermented. Enclosed freshly painted compartments can be lethal, if not properly ventilated. Also dangerous are ships' tanks that have been painted.

Information on these and other toxic substances carried by ships, and on the health hazards connected with their transport, may be found in the IMO publication *Medical first aid guide for use in accidents involving dangerous goods*[1] which is the Chemicals Supplement to this volume.

Mechanical refrigeration systems are potentially dangerous owing to the risk of a leakage of ammonia, Freon, or other refrigerants into enclosed spaces. Cyanide or other gases used to fumigate ships present a serious hazard during fumigation and afterwards until the areas affected have been properly aired.

In every case, safety depends on proper ventilation and proper individual precautions. It is the responsibility of the deck officer and/or chief engineer to ensure that, when compartments or tanks must be entered or cleaned, the area has been ventilated thoroughly, that all explosive gases have been vented, and that the oxygen supply is adequate. In addition, the responsible officer should make sure that the first person entering the area wears a lifeline so that he can be retrieved if he becomes faint or ill. The work crew should be checked continuously during the first half-hour of work. Proper oxygen canister-type gas masks and someone who knows how to use them should be available, if a rescue becomes necessary.

---

[1] *Medical first aid guide for use in accidents involving dangerous goods.* London, International Maritime Organization, 1985.

These precautions should be reinforced by frequent training demonstrations and emergency drills for all ship's personnel in the use of rescue and mask equipment.

Lighting

Adequate lighting on board ship is essential for efficiency and safety. Fatigue and eyestrain develop rapidly in poor illumination. Work performance is reduced, accidents increase, and consciously or unconsciously the individual's morale deteriorates.

Good lighting is important, especially in the engine room, galley, chartroom, and companion-ways. In the engine-room, high-level illumination free from glare is desirable. Lights should be located so that crew-members will cast the fewest possible body shadows upon their work, and equipment will not create pools of darkness.

The relationship of lighting to safety in the engine-room, companion-ways, and ladder-wells is obvious. Good visibility is also necessary in the galley, pantry, scullery, and head. Adequate illumination in the areas where food is served and prepared is essential to proper food-handling and to the maintenance of adequate standards of sanitation.

Food hygiene

The procurement, preparation, and serving of food aboard most vessels are the primary responsibility of the steward's department. The galley crew and others in the department are responsible for the cleanliness of the food preparation and storage areas, and for ensuring that food is served in the mess areas and dining saloons with due regard to hygiene.

It is the responsibility of the ship's master and the chief steward to monitor the health of those handling food and to make regular and unscheduled inspections of areas used for the storage, preparation, and service of food, as well as the self-dispensing food service units aboard the ship.

The proper care of a ship's food services and supplies involves the food-handlers; the conditions of purchase; the surroundings in which the food is stored, prepared, and served; the care of the utensils and utilities; the disposal of food wastes; and the control of vectors of disease such as insects and rodents.

Food-handlers

Aboard a merchant vessel, food-handlers should be members of the steward's department and directly responsible to the chief steward for overall direction.

Persons who either are suffering from a disease capable of being transmitted by food or water or are carriers of such a disease should not be employed in food preparation or food-handling.

Food-handlers should be kept under regular surveillance. Staff who have infected wounds or sores, who are suffering from gastrointestinal illness or any other condition likely to cause the contamination of food or of surfaces coming into contact with food, or who have been in contact with a person suffering from a food- or waterborne disease should report immediately to the management. They should be excluded from food-handling until given medical clearance to return to work.

All persons applying for jobs as food-handlers should undergo a pre-recruitment medical examination, and a professional assessment should be made of their clinical history. Only those who are free from infection and are proved not to be carriers should be engaged. While this will ensure that the food-handler is healthy at the time of recruitment, it is important to impress on employees their obligation to report any of the above-mentioned conditions should they occur during employment.

Physical examinations for food service personnel are carried out in major ports by the medical department of the shipping company, the city health department, or some other facility designated by the company, the union, or the country.

It is the responsibility of the purser, chief steward, and chief cook to ensure that any food-handler aboard has proper health certification.

All food-handlers should receive basic instruction in hygiene, its application to the work they do, company regulations and procedures, health requirements, use of equipment, use of protective clothing, code of practice in handling food, reporting of sickness, personal hygiene, and general hygienic standards in working areas.

The food-handler must pay scrupulous attention to the cleanliness of himself and his clothing. He must wear clothing designed for food service areas, and this clothing should be laundered regularly and worn only during working hours.

To encourage high standards of personal hygiene among food service workers, toilet and lavatory facilities must be readily accessible from the food preparation area. Hand-washing facilities, with sanitary soap-dispensers and individual towels should be available in the food preparation area (see page 288).

Food service facilities

In general, the surfaces of all decks, bulkheads, and deckheads in the areas where food is processed, served, and stored should be corrosion-free, smooth, and easy to clean. All surfaces coming into contact with foods should be of material that is corrosion-resistant, non-toxic, non-absorbent, smooth, durable, and easy to clean.

Cooking utensils and equipment must be made of materials that are non-toxic; that is, they should not be made of metals such as cadmium, lead, zinc, or antimony. The positioning of the equipment and storage of the utensils should be planned with a view to their safe, efficient use.

Proper plumbing equipment in the food service areas is mandatory. Potable water only[1] should be piped into such areas, except that non-potable water may be piped to garbage-grinder

---

[1] See: *Guidelines for drinking-water quality. Vol. I. Recommendations.* Geneva, World Health Organization, 1984.

eductors. Food service equipment and areas should be adequately drained, and the drains should be protected from any backflow of wastes.

The chief steward and the chief engineer must ensure that the foregoing recommendations are implemented, and make regular sanitary inspections to see that no health hazards develop.

Food storage

Non-refrigerated items

The non-refrigerated foods can be divided into *bulk items* and *broken or lot items*. The bulk items are boxed, bagged, or canned. While each has specific storage needs, all have certain common requirements such as a storage area that can be locked and separated from non-food items. Bulk items must be kept away from dampness, condensation, or waste waters, and free of poisons and contaminants. They should be stored in a protected, cool, dry area, rotated regularly, and protected from rodent and insect contamination. If such food becomes infected or outdated, it must be destroyed.

Once foods are removed from the dry storage room and dispensed to the day stores, they must be protected from contamination after the original protective packaging is removed.

Bulk foods must be stored with access for inspection, and at the same time they must be readily accessible for use. They must be kept clear of all cleansing or chemical agents. Supplies should not be stored directly on the deck, but raised at least 15 cm above it to facilitate cleaning and reduce harbourage of insects and rodents.

After being loaded aboard ship, *boxed foods* should be utilized quickly to minimize vermin infestation. They must be dated for proper utilization and, once opened, should never be left in storage.

Non-refrigerated *bulk items* such as cereals, beans, and sugar, as well as vegetables such as potatoes and onions, are extremely susceptible to external contamination, insect and rodent infestation, and rupture. They must be protected by storage in easily cleaned vermin-proof containers or bins.

Non-refrigerated *canned or bottled items* are usually stored in boxes or crates. They are best protected by maintaining a rotating inventory, keeping the units dry and preferably cool, and eliminating damaged or distorted cans or tins. Corrugated paper boxes should be emptied and removed from the ship as soon as possible, as they are apt to harbour insects.

Refrigerated items

The same basic requirements apply to the storage of refrigerated items. However, refrigerated storage is more confined, and specified temperatures must be maintained.

Refrigerated foods fall into two general groups — *frozen foods* and *cooled foods*.

Frozen foods must be kept at between −18 and −23 °C from time of freezing until time of preparation. Under these conditions, food retains its normal taste and appearance and has a shelf-life of 1–6 months. Once thawed, however, such food must be used immediately and not refrozen under any circumstances. Once food is thawed, it rapidly deteriorates and may become toxic as a result of bacterial action. To facilitate utilization, frozen food is stored in packaged units. Once a package is opened, the contents must be wrapped, kept frozen in the day stores, and used at the earliest opportunity.

The *cooled food items* kept in storage most often are fresh fruits and vegetables, processed and cooked meat products, and foods prepared for rapid utilization. These, as well as leftovers, should be kept covered and stored at between 0 °C and 7 °C depending on the product.

Both the freezer and cooler compartments should have highly accurate, adjustable thermostats for temperature control. Thermometers should be easily visible to persons working in passageways serving the refrigerated spaces and on the engineer's control panel.

In storage areas for cooled foods, the humidity ranges from moderate to high. Cooled foods, properly handled, have a storage life of from 1 day to 4 months, depending on the item. Leftover food should be assumed to have a shelf-life of not more than 48 hours because of the possibility of contamination. At 4 °C and below, this danger is minimized.

Both frozen and cooled foods keep better when the refrigeration unit is properly drained, kept clean, and free of ice, frost, food spillage or residue, fungus, and slime. To maintain freezer efficiency, remove frost or ice before it reaches 5 mm in thickness.

When defrosting, wash the freezer with steam or heavily chlorinated, warm, soapy water to remove slime, dirt, grease, and fungus. Shelves, hooks, and grids should be removed and washed with a warm detergent solution, then steamed down, rinsed in hot water, and, if possible, sun dried or heat dried. The refrigerator decks should be cleaned and scrubbed with a hot detergent solution and then rinsed.

After cleaning, the refrigerator should be loaded so that stores are placed neatly, with no physical overloading, and separated to allow free circulation of air. Foods to be refrigerated should be stored in shallow metal pans or plastic containers covered with wax paper, plastic, or aluminium foil.

The chief steward must ensure the cleanliness of the storage areas and food storage equipment; and the chief engineer must ensure the effective functioning of these units.

See also the section on Food-borne diseases, page 199.

The galley (ship's kitchen)

The galley should be equipped, illuminated, and maintained in such a way as to ensure good sanitation. The equipment should be made of corrosion-resistant, non-toxic materials that are easy to clean. All galley areas, especially the cooking areas, should be protected against fire, easy to clean, and capable of being rapidly emptied of smoke, steam, odours, and gases.

Waste, particularly food scraps, should be kept in sturdy, tightly covered garbage-cans.

Where possible, all galley equipment and utensils should be fixed in place. Non-fixed utensils should be hung or stored to avoid loss, damage, or injury to seamen when the ship rolls.

Foodstuffs, supplies, cookware, crockery, and utensils should be thoroughly cleaned after each use and stored in containers that can be secured when the items in question are not in use.

Toilet and washing facilities

Adequate toilet facilities for food-handlers should be readily available near food preparation areas. On smaller vessels, these facilities may be shared by the crew. They should be accessible at all times.

Preferably, toilets should not open directly into spaces where food is prepared, stored, or served. Where they do, the doors should be tight-fitting and self-closing. Wherever possible, there should be a ventilated space between the toilets and areas where there is food.

Adequate hand-washing facilities should be provided within or adjacent to toilets and should include hot and cold running water from a single mixing outlet, a single-service paper or cloth towel dispenser or drying device, suitable soap or detergent or other acceptable cleansing agent, and signs over the basin reading WASH HANDS AFTER USING TOILET – WASH BASIN BEFORE AND AFTER USE. Signs warning personnel to wash their hands after using the toilet should also be conspicuously posted on the bulkhead adjacent to the door of the toilet.

Where a common wash-basin serves both a food-handling space and a toilet for food-handlers, a sign reading WASH HANDS OFTEN – WASH BASIN BEFORE AND AFTER USE should be posted above it.

On ships where hand-washing facilities exist in a stateroom for food service employees, easily accessible from the food-handling areas, additional facilities are not required in the food-handling areas. In such cases, individual cloth towels for food-handlers are acceptable.

Scullery sinks, slop sinks, laundry tubs, dish-washing sinks, and similar facilities should not be used for hand-washing.

Non-potable wash-water (see below) may be used for wash-basins, provided that it is heated to a temperature of 77 °C. Only potable water should be used for the cold water supply to wash-basins.

Liquid transport and potable water

Ship's liquid transport systems

Specialized piping systems on ships include the *bilge system* which collects drainage that must be pumped overboard; the *clean ballast system* which maintains the proper trim, stability, and immersion of the vessel; and the *fuel oil and oily ballast system* which stores and transfers clean oil to the ship's fuel system, and secondarily replaces the used oil with sea-water as part of the ballast system.

Other specialized piping systems are the *fire system,* which supplies water under pressure to the ship's fire stations and to the deck and anchor wash areas; the *sanitary system,* which supplies water to the heads and other sanitary fixtures; and the *wash-water system,* which supplies fresh water from skin and/or peak tanks. **The wash-water system must be independent of all other piping systems and outlets should be labelled:** NOT FIT TO DRINK.

An important specialized piping system is the *drinking-water system,* which supplies potable water to drinking-fountains and to washing and culinary units. The drinking-water system must be protected, and isolated from all other systems.

Potable water sources

"Potable water" covers water used for drinking, cooking, and the washing of cooking and eating utensils, as well as the water used in the ship's hospital.

To be potable, water should be free from pathogenic organisms and harmful chemicals. Its quality should comply with the WHO *Guidelines for drinking-water quality,*[1] especially as concerns microbiological requirements.

The handling of water must be rigidly controlled from source to consumer to avoid contamination.

Potable water on board ship is derived either from distillation or from natural sources. Distilled water is either fresh or salt water that has been converted to steam and back to water. It is relatively free from impurities but has a flat taste. Natural water, or "shore water", is usually obtained from wells, springs, or freshwater bodies ashore. It usually has to be treated, either ashore or afloat, to protect the health of the crew.

Potable water transport system

The water system of a port city is the usual source of potable water. It is made available to the ship either through watering-points at dockside or from water-boats.

Each vessel should carry sufficient special hose to load its potable water. This hose should be kept in a storage cabinet labelled "Potable Water Hose Only" and should not be used for any other purpose.

A deck officer should be responsible for the cleanliness and safety of a ship's filling hose and its ends, as well as the connections of dockside, water-boat, or shipside filling lines. These connections — outlet and inlet — must be at least 40 cm above the dock, water-boat deck, and ship's deck, and housed with a proper fitting. Each such watering-point connection must be labelled "Potable Water Filling".

Potable water should be transported from the storage areas to dispensing units through iden-

tified (i.e., colour-coded, non-cross-connected pipes made of safe metals or plastic). All potable water outlets must be protected from back-siphonage by an air-gap or approved vacuum-breaker.

Potable water storage

To avoid contamination, potable water tanks should have no common partition with tanks containing non-potable liquids – including skin tanks. The tank should be labelled "Potable water" and be accessible through a watertight, preferably side-mounted, manhole. It must have an overflow and relief valve or vent, be completely drainable from a bottom drain, able to withstand pressure, and have water-level gauges or petcocks.

The tanks should be emptied periodically for inspection and maintenance, after which they should be thoroughly scrubbed and flushed out, and the whole potable water system disinfected with chlorine, as described in Annex 5.

Anyone entering any potable water tanks should wear clean clothing and footwear, and should not be suffering from skin infections, diarrhoea, or any communicable disease.

Taking water on board

If you are taking water for drinking purposes from a source that is new to you, or about which you have doubts, you should ask your agents for advice as to whether the water is likely to contain germs or harmful minerals. Remember that bright, clear, sparkling water may easily contain disease organisms such as the cholera vibrio or harmful minerals such as lead.

If you believe that the water is acceptable, ensure that the potable water storage tanks on your ship are in order. Check that the delivery cocks on the shore and the receiving point on the ship are properly cleaned. Examine the hose to ensure that it is clean, in good working order, and free from leaks (germs can get in through leaks in the hose). Then ensure that the ends of the hose do not drag across the quay, fall into the sea, or drag across your deck.

---

[1] *Guidelines for drinking-water quality. Vol. I. Recommendations.* Geneva, World Health Organization, 1984.

You may, however, be compelled to take on board water which, while free of harmful minerals, may be contaminated with disease organisms. In case of any doubt you should disinfect the water in the way described in Annex 5.

Disinfection of potable water

According to the *Guidelines for drinking-water quality*[1] published by WHO, the following conditions should be met to ensure effective disinfection with chlorine:

- turbidity should preferably be less than 1 nephelometric turbidity unit
- the contact time should be greater than 30 minutes and the pH preferably less than 8.0, resulting in a free chlorine residual of 0.2–0.5 mg/litre.

It should be noted that the above conditions will not ensure that the water is free from pathogenic protozoa and helminths, since these organisms are considerably more resistant to chlorine disinfection than bacteria or viruses. In such a case, careful filtration followed by chlorination may be necessary to ensure the absence of these pathogenic organisms. It is of course preferable to obtain water from a source that is free from them to start with.

The procedure for the disinfection of potable water with chlorine is described in Annex 5.

Distillation units

A chlorination unit in tandem with a distillation unit will ensure that drinking-water is of acceptable hygienic quality. The whole system will require chlorination after the tanks have been opened up and cleaned, or after possible contamination of the water.

Disposal of liquid and solid wastes

Liquid wastes are organic materials that can be moved in a liquid. These include body excretions

such as faeces, urine, sputum, and vomit; sink, laundry, and washroom wastes; food, tank, bilge, and engine-room wastes; and other degradable materials. Aided by flushing from the sanitary water system, these wastes are mixed with water and carried out of the vessel by its waste pipes.

Solid wastes are any discarded materials that are not readily degradable without heat or pressure. Aboard ship, these include discarded items such as surgical dressings, disposable containers, and refuse.

Both liquid and solid wastes are health hazards. Contamination by these wastes can cause outbreaks of typhoid fever, paratyphoid fever, cholera, or dysentery. Rats, flies, and other vectors of disease thrive on solid wastes. Consequently, in disposing of waste from the vessel, care must be taken not to endanger the health of persons aboard the vessel or in off-ship areas.

Control of disease vectors

In the chapter on communicable diseases (see page 123), reference is made to a number of infections transmitted by insects such as mosquitos (malaria, yellow fever), fleas (plague), lice (typhus fever), ticks, flies, and cockroaches. Animals and birds (rats, mice, parrots, dogs, etc.) may also be disease carriers.

Thanks to the development of effective control measures, the spread of vector-borne diseases and their vectors from country to country by ships is less of a problem nowadays than it was in the past. Still, the control of disease vectors is an important part of disease prevention on board ship. This control is the responsibility of the ship's master and other persons designated by him. The shipping company, through the master, also has a major responsibility for the cleanliness of the ship.

Control of rodents

Rats on a ship are a menace to health and a nuisance. They cause extensive damage to cargo and food, and rat-droppings contain organisms that produce intestinal diseases. Because rats

---

[1] *Guidelines for drinking-water quality. Vol. I. Recommendations.* Geneva, World Health Organization, 1984, p. 18.

usually attempt to forage in the galley and food storage areas, these organisms are likely to be introduced into the food supplies. Rats also carry fleas which may transmit plague and typhus fever. Because of these dangers, ships heavily infested with rats must be fumigated. Fumigation is a laborious, expensive, and dangerous procedure; it can, however, be avoided through adequate rat-control measures.

Despite reasonable precautions by the ship's personnel and port authorities, some rats may be on board. However, infestation can be avoided by ensuring that they do not have access to food and there are no suitable nesting-places for them, and by trapping or otherwise destroying them before they breed and develop colonies.

The frequent inspection of a ship for signs of rat life (trails or runs marked by dirt or droppings) will indicate the kind of measures that should be taken to prevent rat infestation.

There are four general measures available:

- preventing the rats from getting aboard;
- rat-proofing the ship, thus "building out" the rats by eliminating their living-places or harbourages;
- keeping all food protected and avoiding the accumulation of food scraps, thus "starving out" the rodents; and
- killing them by trapping, poisoning, or fumigation by experts from authorized agencies.

To prevent rats from coming aboard, every available precaution should be taken, including the proper placement and maintenance of rat-guards on all mooring lines and illumination of the gangplank.

Rat-proof construction is built into most modern ships.

Rat-proofing includes the elimination of hidden spaces and dead spaces conducive to rat harbourage. If such spaces cannot be eliminated, they should be constructed in such a manner that it is impossible for rats to get in. The ship must be kept in good repair if rat-proofing is to be continuously effective. Lockers, boxes, dunnage, or other movable equipment not part of the ship's original structure should not be permitted to provide temporary shelters for rodents.

Starving of the rats must accompany rat-proofing. All food and garbage should be stored in metal containers with tightly fitting metal covers. Nothing edible should be left exposed. Food or edible waste spilled accidently in any part of the ship should be cleaned up promptly. These measures will help to control flies and cockroaches as well as rats and mice.

Trapping is a good method of keeping down the rat population. Snap traps, which are more effective and practicable than the cage type, should be set along ledges, bulkheads, and other places used as rat runs. Meat, bacon rind, or cheese may be used as bait for the traps, if the rats cannot get at these foods in any other place. Apples, pears, dates, potatoes, and turnips also make good bait. The bait trigger should be pointed toward the bulkhead or rat run. The rat should be given the chance to nibble at the bait for the first few days before the trap is set. After a rat is caught, the trap should *not* be flamed or scalded; the odour of the rat will help in catching others. The kind of bait should be varied. Precautions should be taken to avoid touching dead rats because of the danger of infected fleas.

The anticoagulants are the rodenticides (rat poisons) generally recommended by health authorities. These rodenticides are available commercially.

The anticoagulant rodenticides, such as warfarin and diphenadione, kill in a radically different manner from the older acute (single dose) poisons such as zinc phosphide. They must be ingested for several consecutive days before they become effective.

Warning. Most rodenticides are poisonous to man. Therefore, all chemicals (rodenticides and insecticides) that are used to control vectors should be kept in their original containers, which should be properly labelled and securely stored away from food (stores and cargo).

Although it is a costly operation, a badly infested ship may be treated best by fumigation. The decision to fumigate a ship will depend upon the estimated number of rats aboard, the type of cargo, and the itinerary. For example, fumigation may be necessary if a ship has recently called at a plague port.

The gases most commonly used for ship fumigation are hydrogen cyanide and methyl bromide. **These are extremely poisonous to human beings as well as to insects and rodents.** Fumigation must therefore be carried out by experts.

Before fumigation is begun, the ship must be tied up at a distance from other vessels. It is absolutely necessary to make sure there is *no one on board* except those authorized to do the fumigating.

After fumigation, the holds and superstructures must be aired. Tests must be made for the gas, after about an hour of airing. Beds and clothing must be thoroughly aired on deck for at least two hours because the gas has a strong tendency to remain in clothing and bedding. **Men have died as a result of returning too soon to compartments not completely aired and free of gas. A fumigated ship should not be boarded until released by the fumigating officer.** Also, any food that has been exposed to the gaseous fumigant must be destroyed.

Control of insects

Even with present control measures, it is impossible to keep a ship completely free of insects. This is because of the variety of insects, their many methods of gaining access to the ship, and their ability to survive despite efforts to destroy them. Flies and mosquitos may board the vessel at wharves or in harbours. Bedbugs, fleas, lice, and ticks may be brought aboard on the bodies, clothing, or personal gear of crew or passengers. Fleas may also be carried aboard by rats. Cockroaches may be present in provisions or cargo brought aboard the ship.

Insects transmit disease when germs on their bodies come in contact with food or other articles. Insects may also pick up and pass on disease by biting. For example, *Anopheles* mosquitos transmit malaria, lice transmit typhus fever, and fleas transmit plague.

The suppression of insect infestation on board ship demands coordination by ship and shore personnel. Unless control is continued at sea, the most thorough campaign to destroy insects and rodents on a ship in port will not pay off. It is easier and less costly to maintain controls constantly, than to apply sporadic intensive measures only in port. Furthermore, it will make living and working conditions better at all times.

To fight insects successfully, one must first know the habits of each type and apply this knowledge. For example, *body lice* live on the human body and clothing; personal cleanliness will therefore go a long way towards preventing louse infestation. *Bedbugs* are most likely to seek shelter in mattresses and cracks around beds; thus cleanliness and frequent inspection are valuable control measures. *Cockroaches* breed prolifically in areas where food is available; therefore, strict cleanliness in areas where food is stored, prepared, or eaten is of great importance. *Flies* are attracted by unprotected food and refuse; hence, they can be curbed if exposure of food is kept to a minimum, and if refuse is placed in clean, tightly covered cans for prompt disposal.

Personal and environmental cleanliness are the most satisfactory components of long-range insect control. Insecticides are useful in providing immediate, although temporary, relief from a heavy insect infestation. The sporadic or casual use of insecticides is of little value if the underlying unsanitary conditions persist, because the insecticide's effects wear off, and the surviving insects, new generations of insects, and newly introduced insects rapidly recreate the infestation. For the best results, insecticides should be used only as a supplement to cleanliness and other permanent control measures.

Insect control operations present hazards to crew members in the form of contact with poisons, machinery, and flammable materials. The safest effective pesticide should be used, and personnel should be constantly aware of the special hazards. Only properly trained, responsible personnel should be allowed to do insect control work. **Personnel should work in pairs, never alone.** Bystanders should be kept away, and chemicals and equipment should be under constant control to prevent their being stolen or picked up by accident. Regular maintenance and careful use of equipment are imperative.

It should be appreciated that insects can become resistant to insecticides and that failure to control them may be due to this factor and not to inefficient application of insecticide. If insecticide resistance is suspected, a change to a different type of insecticide is indicated and specialist advice may be necessary.

Warning. Care must be taken to avoid the contamination of drink, food, or surfaces used for food preparation with insecticides.

Some characteristics of the insects most commonly found aboard ship are given below, together with suggestions for their control.

Flies

Domestic flies, some of which bite, may transmit enteric (intestinal) diseases to man. Their larvae and eggs may infest human flesh and intestines as well as stored foods.

Environmental control. Store all refuse in durable cans with tight lids and maintain insect-screening.

Chemical control. Insecticides may be applied as residual sprays (water-dispersible powders or aqueous emulsions) to leave a toxic deposit on surfaces where flies rest or breed. Space sprays are released as a fog or fine mist and kill on contact. Use residual and space sprays indoors and residual sprays outdoors. DDT and related compounds should not be used, as houseflies have developed resistance to them. Bromophos, fenchlorphos, fenitrothion, jodfenphos (iodofenphos), or pirimiphos-methyl applied at 1.0–2.0 g of active ingredient (a.i.) per m^2 or permethrin applied at 0.025–0.05 g of a.i./m^2 are suitable for residual applications on board. Deodorized kerosene formulations of dichlorvos, 5 g/litre (0.5%), fenchlorphos, 20 g/litre (2%), malathion, 50 g/litre (5%), pirimiphos-methyl

20 g/litre (2%), permethrin 0.5 g/litre (0.05%), or synergized natural pyrethrins 1–4 g/litre (0.1–0.4%) may be used for space treatment in most circumstances. Where there is a fire hazard, space spraying can be carried out by aerosol dispensers containing insecticide and non-flammable propellants.

Mosquitos

Several species of mosquito suck blood and may transmit malaria, yellow fever, encephalitis, filariasis, and other diseases.

Environmental control. Eliminate standing water and maintain insect screening.

Chemical control. The widespread mosquito vector of yellow fever and dengue fever, associated with tropical seaports, is almost universally DDT-resistant in port areas. Suitable insecticides, applied as residual sprays, include bendiocarb at 0.4 g of a.i./m^2, malathion, fenitrothion, and pirimiphos-methyl at 1–2 g of a.i./m^2 and permethrin at 0.5 g of a.i./m^2. Space-spray measures may be used as indicated above for flies.

Cockroaches

Cockroaches produce unpleasant odours, transmit diarrhoea and dysentery, and damage stocks of food.

Environmental control. Eliminate cracks, crevices, and dead spaces; store food and garbage properly; keep entire area scrupulously clean; watch for, and destroy, all cockroaches and their egg cases, particularly those introduced with luggage, food stores, and furniture; remove corrugated cardboard boxes and cartons from provision storerooms as soon as feasible.

Chemical control. Suitable sprays include bendiocarb 2.4–4.8 g/litre (0.24–0.48%), chlorpyrifos 5 g/litre (0.5%), diazinon 5 g/litre (0.5%), dichlorvos 5 g/litre (0.5%), jodfenphos (iodofenphos) 10 g/litre (1%), malathion 30 g/litre (3%), pirimiphos-methyl 25 g/litre (2.5%) and permethrin 1.25–2.5 g/litre (0.125–0.25%). Dusts include bendiocarb 10 g/kg (1%), malathion 50 g/kg (5%), pirimiphos-methyl 20 g/kg (2%), and permethrin 5 g/kg (0.5%). Propetamphos 20 g/litre (2%) formulated with dichlorvos 5 g/litre (0.5%) has been used as an aerosol for the control of household pests, including cockroaches.

Lice, bedbugs, and fleas

These ectoparasites, which live on the outside of the body, cause discomfort and may transmit disease.

Environmental control. Maintain personal hygiene by bathing and by laundering clothing and bedding frequently; keep cabins clean by vacuuming floors, rugs, and upholstered furniture weekly; watch for, and eliminate, ectoparasites introduced with luggage, clothing, bedding, or furniture; eliminate cracks and crevices where they hide.

Chemical control. The most satisfactory types of formulation for eliminating *body lice* are powders and dusts, which can be applied easily and rapidly. About 30 g per person should be applied evenly from sifter-top cans over the inner surface of the underwear, with special attention to seams. The seams and folds of other garments should also be treated. If the body lice are susceptible to DDT, dust containing 10% DDT (100 g/kg) is the insecticide of choice. Where there are DDT-resistant lice, the following insecticides may be applied as dusts: carbaryl 50 g/kg (5%), jodfenphos (iodofenphos) 50 g/kg (5%), lindane 10 g/kg (1%), malathion 10 g/kg (1%), permethrin 5 g/kg (0.5%), propoxur 10 g/kg (1%), and temephos 20 g/kg (2%).

For control of occasional infestations, the easiest method is to heat the clothing to 70 °C or higher for 1 hour.

For *head-louse* infestations, liquid formulations are more acceptable than powders or dust. An aqueous suspension containing 10 g/litre (1%) lindane or a lotion containing 5 g/litre (0.5%) deodorized malathion in isopropyl alcohol can be used, or 20 g/litre (2%) temephos in an appropriate solvent. Bioallethrin is used in lotion and shampoo preparations (3–4 g/litre; 0.3–0.4%) and in aerosols (6 g/litre; 0.6%). The

liquid formulations are applied by spraying or other means so that the hair is thoroughly wet. Treated persons should not bathe or shampoo for at least 24 hours. The amount applied is 10–20 ml of emulsion or 5–10 ml of solution per head. Care should be taken to avoid getting insecticide into the eyes.

Bedbugs are controlled by means of interior residual sprays designed to ensure that the insecticides penetrate their hiding-places. Bedsprings, slats, mattresses, cracks and crevices in the walls and floors, and furniture should be treated. Infested bedclothes should be washed or dry-cleaned. DDT 50 g/litre (5%) emulsion or solution is the insecticide of choice where bedbugs are still susceptible. For DDT-resistant bugs, diazinon 5 g/litre (0.5%), fenchlorphos 10 g/litre (1%), jodfenphos (iodofenphos) 10 g/litre (1%), lindane 5 g/litre (0.5%), malathion 20 g/litre (2%) or pirimiphos-methyl 10 g/litre (1%) can be used. The addition of natural pyrethrins 1–2 g/litre (0.1–0.2%) to the residual insecticide formulations will increase the effectiveness of the treatment by irritating the bedbugs and causing them to leave their hiding-places, thereby increasing their contact with the fresh insecticide deposits. For bedbugs resistant to DDT and organophosphorus compounds, 10 g/litre (1%) carbaryl, dioxacarb, or propoxur may be used. Deltamethrin, as a 0.05 g/litre spray or 0.05 g/kg dust (0.005%), is effective for flushing out and killing bedbugs, or bendiocarb as a 2.4 g/litre (0.24%) spray or 10 g/kg (1%) dust may be used. Infants' bedding, including cribs, should not be treated with residual insecticides. Treated mattresses should be dried completely before being covered with sheets for reuse. Residual spraying should be undertaken early in the day so that the room will dry before it is used again for sleeping.

In the case of *fleas,* insecticides are applied mainly to sleeping areas and beds. Emulsions, solutions, or suspensions of bendiocarb 2.4 g/litre (0.24%), DDT 50 g/litre (5%), deltamethrin 0.05 g/litre (0.005%), jodfenphos (iodofenphos) 10 g/litre (1%), lindane 10 g/litre (1%), malathion 20 g/litre (2%), natural pyrethrins 2 g/litre

(0.2%), permethrin 1.25 g/litre (0.125%), and pirimiphos-methyl 10 g/litre (1%) can be used for spraying. Dust formulations, too, are often suitable and are commonly used for the treatment of dogs and cats.

Pests in stored products

These pests (cockroaches, beetles, moths, ants, mites, silverfish, springtails) damage clothing and rugs and ruin stocks of foods.

Environmental control. Store food and other products in an orderly, sanitary manner in a cool, dry room on racks up off the floor; use old stocks first; inspect stocks regularly and dispose of any found to be infested.

Chemical control. Spray storerooms with an insecticide approved for use in food service areas, making sure that none gets in or on stored food.

Sanitary inspection

Regular inspections are necessary to maintain a vessel in good sanitary condition. The persons making the inspections should be on the alert for signs of vermin and rodent infestation and should check general order and cleanliness. Areas which should be inspected thoroughly include:

forepeak	sewage disposal
provision store-room	washroom and head
galley	cold storage space
pantry	refrigeration space
issue room	mess space
sickbay	living spaces
scullery	shelter deck
garbage disposal	holds
brig spaces	

Frequent monitoring by the ship's master and senior officers will also help to keep the crew aware of the need to maintain scrupulous cleanliness.

Chapter 16
Disease prevention

Contents

Many diseases are more easily prevented than cured. The prevention of disease plays a very important part in the practice of medicine, and in no place is it more important than on board ship.

Conditions at sea may not be as conducive to health as those ashore. Opportunities for recreation, exercise, and a hygienic lifestyle are necessarily restricted; living quarters may be less commodious, and there are fewer opportunities of obtaining fresh food. For long periods of time, seafarers are separated from their families; they spend months in the restricted area of their ship, with a small number of fellow crew-members around them. Such conditions create boredom and stress, which may contribute to some of the ailments and diseases that occur among seafarers.

Ships' masters should therefore pay particular attention to the health and welfare of their crews, ensuring that appropriate preventive measures are taken.

Prevention of communicable diseases

(See also: Food-borne diseases, page 199; Prevention of sexually transmitted disease, page 158; Suppression of malaria, page 135.)

Measures for the prevention or control of communicable diseases are intended to break the chain of infection at its weakest link. In general, control measures attempt to prevent exposure to infection. These measures are strengthened by increasing the resistance of the susceptible host. This can be achieved by active or passive immunization or by the prophylactic use of drugs.

Isolation

The isolation of an ill patient will prevent the spread of disease to other persons on board. It is convenient to categorize isolation into two types:

- strict
- standard

Strict isolation

The patient is confined to the ship's hospital or to a cabin that is set aside for his sole use in a quiet part of the ship and has been stripped of all unnecessary furnishings and carpets to facilitate cleaning and disinfection.

The patient must be seen only by the person who nurses him and this person should be instructed to carry out the appropriate nursing procedures (see Chapter 5).

If disposable eating and drinking utensils are available, these should be used and later destroyed. Should ship's dishes and cutlery have to be used, they should be washed and sterilized (by boiling for 20 minutes) after use and kept in the cabin or hospital. They should never be washed up with utensils used by other members of the crew.

All used bed-linen and towels should be boiled or disinfected. Faeces and urine should be passed into bedpans or urine bottles and, at sea, disposed of in a flushing water-closet set aside for the purpose. The attendants should wear disposable gloves when handling these items, and care should be taken not to splash the contents about. The pans and bottles should be boiled after use. In port, faeces and urine should not be flushed away but should be disinfected and disposed of after consultation with the port health authority. It is important to dispose of any used syringes and needles in the correct way. Place the needle-container back on the needle while it is still attached to the syringe. Enclose the syringe and needle in a plastic bag and seal the neck. Place this in another plastic bag and seal the neck. At sea, it can then be weighted and thrown overboard. In coastal or shallow waters, the bags should be kept in the isolation room until arrival in port when they should be handed to the port health authority for disposal. The attendant's gloves should be disposed of in the same way.

Note. The attendant should wash his hands each time the gloves are removed.

(See also: Ventilation, page 283.)

Standard isolation

The patient is isolated in the ship's hospital or in a cabin set aside for his use. There is no need to observe the stringent rules for strict isolation. While the patient is ill, visitors should be discouraged. When he shows signs of recovery, this ban can be lifted but visitors should be instructed to stay only for short periods. While he is convalescing, visiting should be encouraged to relieve boredom.

Immunization

Every seagoing person, if only for self-protection and convenience, should be immunized against diphtheria, tetanus, and poliomyelitis. Booster immunizations for diphtheria and tetanus at 5-year intervals should be kept up to date. Protection against tetanus (lockjaw) by the injection of a toxoid vaccine is universally recommended as part of good preventive medical practice. Tetanus is common on land throughout the world. At sea, exposure to tetanus is especially high on ships carrying cattle, horses, hides, or similar cargoes.

The need for seafarers to be immunized against yellow fever, cholera, and typhoid fever depends on the route and destination of the vessel. The medical services of the shipping company or the health authorities of the home port can provide the necessary advice on the subject. Yellow fever vaccination at *10-year intervals* is required for disembarkation in many tropical American and African countries. Cholera vaccination may be required at *6-month* intervals for travel to certain parts of the world.[1]

Environmental sanitation

Environmental sanitation, which is very important in the control of communicable diseases, is intended to prevent the spread of pathogens by eliminating both sources and modes of transmission. Examples include: the sanitary treat-

---

[1] For up-to-date information on vaccination requirements, consult: *Vaccination certificate requirements and health advice for international travel.* Geneva, World Health Organization, published annually.

ment, handling, distribution, and dispensing of water, milk, and food; the treatment and disposal of sewage to avoid contamination of water and food supplies; and the control of vectors of disease.

These subjects were dealt with in the previous chapter.

Port health clearance

Measures for the prevention and control of the spread of epidemic diseases by international transport are governed by the International Health Regulations,[1] which have been agreed to by practically all the maritime countries of the world. The Regulations are applied in most countries by port health officers.

In any of the circumstances indicated below, it is advisable to seek advice and to give information by radio, preferably within 4–12 hours of the estimated time of arrival at the port.

- The occurrence on board during the voyage of: death other than by accident; illnesses where the person concerned had a temperature of 38 °C or greater, accompanied by a rash, glandular swelling, or jaundice, or persisting for more than 48 hours; diarrhoea severe enough to interfere with work or normal activities.
- The presence on board of a person suffering from an infectious disease or who has had symptoms that may indicate the presence of infectious disease.
- The occurrence on board, during the voyage, of abnormal mortality among rats, suggesting the possibility of an outbreak of plague among them (see Plague, page 141).

Prevention of other diseases

(See also: Ventilation, page 283, regarding dangers of entering tanks; and Chapter 12, Medical care of castaways and rescued persons, page 259, regarding prevention of injuries due to exposure.)

---

[1] *International Health Regulations (1969),* 3rd annotated ed. Geneva, World Health Organization, 1983.

Balanced diet

A balanced diet, containing the correct proportions of protein, carbohydrate, fats, vitamins, and essential minerals such as iron, is vital to the maintenance of good health.

Protein is derived from foods such as meat, fish, and beans; carbohydrates from cereals and bread; and vitamins and essential minerals from all of these and from fruit and vegetables. In the seafarer's diet, a correct balance of different foodstuffs should be sought. Fresh vegetables and fruit should always be provided in the necessary quantities.

It is also important that the ship's cook should prepare meals that are suitable for the crew, bearing in mind that food requirements in cold, mild, and tropical climates vary.

Nowadays, there is practically no risk of deficiency diseases occurring among crews of ships. However, overeating may present a health risk for individual seafarers, particularly those whose duty on board ship does not involve much physical exercise. The resultant obesity could be the first step to various diseases. Also, moderation in alcohol consumption and smoking will help maintain seafarers in good condition and reduce the risk of disease among them.

Personal hygiene

Hygienic living protects the health of the individual. The health of a seaman depends in part on his own efforts to maintain standards of cleanliness and neatness.

Personal cleanliness includes good care of the skin, hair, nails, mouth, and teeth, and proper maintenance of clothing, towels, and other personal gear. A daily bath or shower, particularly in hot weather or after working in hot compartments, is conducive to good health and lessens the possibility of cuts or scratches becoming infected. Brisk rubbing with a rough towel after a bath or shower stimulates circulation, promotes good skin tone, and gives a feeling of well-being. Clean clothing should be put on following a bath or shower.

Care of the mouth and teeth by regular use of a toothbrush after meals is an essential factor in the prevention of gum disease, infection, and tooth decay. Before brushing natural teeth, any partial dentures should be removed and carefully cleaned with a brush and mild soap or special denture cleanser. Unclean removable dentures are particularly harmful to the remaining natural teeth. Full artificial dentures should be cleaned regularly after meals, and particularly at bedtime, to remove food residues which can cause mouth odour and encourage infection.

The importance of washing hands at appropriate times cannot be overemphasized. Crew-members should wash their hands before eating. It is also of vital importance, if cleanliness is to be maintained and the spread of infection reduced, that hands should be washed immediately after urinating or defecating.

Adequate sleep is necessary for health, well-being, and efficiency. Sleep requirements may vary considerably, and the sleeping habits of crew-members may be quite dissimilar. However, unbroken periods of rest for everyone are desirable.

Hair should be shampooed frequently, cut at regular intervals, and preferably kept short.

Cleanliness aboard ship can be encouraged by providing sufficient hot water in convenient wash-places. A laundry and drying-room for washing clothes also help to maintain a high standard of cleanliness.

Each member of the crew should use only his own towels and be responsible for their cleanliness. Wet towels should not be folded and stowed away, dirty towels should be laundered as soon as possible and not allowed to accumulate.

Preventing heat illness

In very hot conditions, the minimum of clothing should be worn to allow the largest possible surface for free evaporation of sweat. If there is much direct heat from the sun (radiant heat), light white cotton clothing will reflect the heat and keep the body temperature below danger limits. Fair-skinned people should remember that they burn more easily and should take precautions. Also, they should be warned that very long exposure (i.e., over a period of years) to sun, and therefore to ultraviolet radiation, increases the risk of skin cancer.

Perspiration is the body's best heat control mechanism, but the sweat consists mainly of salt and water which must be replaced. The salt is best taken with food and supplemented by salt-containing drinks to prevent heat cramps. A person requires at least 4 litres of fluid per day in conditions of moderate heat. For work in high temperatures, the requirement may rise to 6–7 litres.

When the ambient temperature is above 32 °C in very humid climates, or above 43 °C in dry air, there will be a risk of heat illness, especially when work has to be carried out. This applies particularly to work in engine-rooms and other enclosed spaces.

Air temperature, movement of air, humidity, and radiant heat all combine to cause heat exhaustion, heat cramps, or heat stroke (see pages 205–207). Extreme caution should therefore be exercised in allowing work in conditions of excessive heat.

In emergency situations where the work has got to be done, short spells of work (say 10 minutes) may be permitted, but people must be allowed to cool off completely before being allowed back into the hot environment.

More information on the prevention of heat illness may be found in the *Encyclopaedia of occupational health and safety*.[1]

Exposure

Sunburn, frostbite, heat illness, and hypothermia may occur in the course of routine duty and must be guarded against. Sunburn, although often only a minor discomfort, can be dangerous. A person drowsy after drinking alcohol

---

[1] *Encyclopaedia of occupational health and safety*. Geneva, International Labour Office, 1983, vol. I, pp. 1015–1022.

who decides to sleep in the sun may very well wake up suffering from serious burns. Special care should also be taken against frostbite and hypothermia (lowering of the body temperature). Hypothermia will most frequently be present in persons who have fallen overboard. Normal body temperature cannot be maintained in water at temperatures below 20 °C. Removal of clothing and swimming movements accelerate heat loss. The treatment of heat illnesses and other conditions due to exposure is dealt with on pages 205–207 and in Chapter 12.

Lifting heavy weights

Backache, sciatica, lumbago, and slipped disc are frequently caused by attempting to lift heavy weights or by lifting weights incorrectly. If the legs are not bent and the object is lifted by straightening a bent back, there will always be a risk of damage to the spinal column. The leg and thigh muscles are the most powerful in the body and they should be used when lifting, the torso and head being kept straight to avoid bending stresses. Everyone should be properly instructed in the correct technique for lifting and carrying, and should not be allowed to attempt to lift excessively heavy objects.

Exercise and boredom

Very few seamen aboard ship exercise hard enough to cause them to become breathless or to increase the rate of their heart-beat. Unused muscles and organs tend to atrophy. On long, tedious voyages, people are also likely to suffer from boredom and lack of interest, which can also be detrimental to health.

Drug abuse, various ailments, and neuroses frequently stem from boredom and lack of absorbing leisure-time activities on board ship. The ship's master should therefore initiate and encourage various recreational and learning activities to occupy his crew during off-duty hours at sea.

A good ship's library, arts and crafts, language lessons, games, contests, hobbies, discussions, etc. can contribute towards creating a more lively and involving climate aboard ship.

Chapter 17
Advice on medicines

Contents

Ship's medicine chest

In the sick-bay (ship's hospital), there should be cabinets and drawers to provide separate storage space for different groups of medicines, such as *internal* medicines, *external* drug preparations, *poisons,* and *controlled substances* (requiring greater security). Also, a refrigerator should be available, not necessarily in the sick-bay, for medicines that require storage in a cool or cold place. To avoid confusion, the equipment, instruments, and surgical supplies should be stored in spaces separate from those holding pharmaceuticals.

Cabinets should be large enough to hold a "working quantity" of the recommended medicines (pages 310–312) and surgical equipment, instruments, and supplies (pages 334–338). They should permit orderly and convenient storage. All stand-up medicine containers should preferably be arranged alphabetically, by generic name, with the labels clearly visible. Adequate lighting should be provided.

Immediately after use, medicaments and surgical supplies should be returned to their proper places. Medicines should never be put into the medicine cabinet in an open unlabelled glass, cup, or other container. If the content of a container is not known for certain, it should be destroyed.

Generally the shipping company will delegate the immediate responsibility for the ship's sick-bay and the medicine chest to a deck or staff officer who is trained in fundamental medical techniques. This officer should be the only person (other than the ship's master) to have the keys of the sick-bay, the medicine chest, and the locker where controlled medicines are stored. This officer should be responsible solely to the master for the sick-bay and medical supplies. A duplicate set of sick-bay keys should be in the master's safe, or some other secure place.

Narcotics, stimulants, sedatives, and other controlled substances should be kept in a locked compartment.

The shelves of the medicine cabinet should be equipped with guard-rails, dividers, or other devices; and drawers should have catches to prevent bottles and other items from falling or moving when the ship rolls and pitches.

It is important that the contents of the ship's medicine chest should be inspected annually by a pharmacist. Changes may occur in medicaments which are predictable to a pharmacist, even though not physically apparent.

Also the expiry date of medicines should be checked periodically, and expired drugs should be replaced by fresh supplies.

Procurement and storage

The following rules should be observed to help ensure that the medicines will meet the proper standards at the time of use.

- Purchase medicines in the manufacturer's package, whenever possible.
- If the local brand or trade name of the drug does not correspond with the generic name, as given in the list of medicines in this guide, an additional label with the generic name should be put on each package. The dose in milligrams per tablet or per vial/ampoule should be clearly indicated on the package, as well as the expiry date, the lot or control number, and the name and address of the manufacturer.
- Procure medicines in the smallest practicable size, such as acetylsalicylic acid tablets, 300 mg, in containers of 100s, rather than 500s. In addition, capsules, tablets, and other dosage forms should be obtained in individually packaged and labelled doses when available.
- Date all medicine containers upon receipt.
- Place the new stock behind the old stock on the shelf for proper rotation of supplies.
- When medicines are first received, carefully read all labels on containers to ensure that the vendor has not made an error and has supplied the kind and strength of medicament requested.
- Note the recommended storage temperature (Table 10). When none is specified, the drugs should be stored at a room temperature of 15–25 °C. Some of the drugs should be kept

under refrigeration (2–5 °C), but care must be taken not to freeze them, otherwise they will lose their potency, or the ampoules will be broken.

- Medicines must be protected against excessive humidity, and light. Powders, tablets, etc. should be kept in tightly closed metal boxes, or in bottles with glass stoppers.
- Controlled substances, such as narcotics, depressants, and stimulants, should have special labels reading CONTROLLED DRUG. Other warning labels should also be used where appropriate, e.g., POISON, or FOR EXTERNAL USE.

Medicines obtained by individuals

If a seaman goes to a doctor ashore, he should be asked to obtain from the doctor a written note indicating both the pharmaceutical name of any medicine prescribed and when and how it is to be taken. If the seaman returns with a medicine, check that the written instructions tally with the description, etc. on the bottle, ampoule, or box of medicine. It may be necessary to check the prescription with the radio medical doctor.

Controlled drugs

Controlled drugs are those preparations that, in most countries, are subject to prescription requirements limiting their distribution and use. Some of the drugs (such as morphine) are subject to very strict controls.

A ship must not carry quantities of these drugs greater than those specified in the list of medicines in this guide (see Table 10, page 310), unless required to do so by a doctor, for valid reasons.

Controlled drugs should be obtained only from a retail pharmacist or other person licensed to supply drugs, and he will require an order worded along the lines shown opposite. The order must be signed by either the vessel's owner or its master.

Requisition of controlled drugs

To: [name and address of authorized supplier]
From: [name of ship, and of master or shipowner]
Address: [address of ship or shipowner]
Please supply [name, strength, and quantity of drugs].
The above drugs are required for the medical stores of [name of vessel].
Signature:
Name in capital letters:
Occupation:
Date:

Regulations in some countries require that a record of any treatment given to anybody on board, including the type and quantity of any medicines and drugs supplied, must be entered in the log book. Additionally, for controlled drugs, the master of the vessel is required to maintain, in a bound book, a "two-section" register. The two sections of the register should detail why, when, and in what quantity the master purchased, impounded, dispensed, or disposed of the drugs. The register must be kept for two years after the date of the last entry in it.

Use of analgesics (pain-killing drugs)

The selection of pain-killers carried aboard will deal with every variety of pain likely to be met. Individual patients will vary in their response to treatment, so it will be necessary to exercise some judgement in deciding the dose and the preparation or combination of preparations that is necessary in each case. It is always best not to discuss the choice of medicine with the patient, or within his hearing. It is also important to prescribe with confidence and to assure the patient that the medicine will bring relief. The pain-killers carried are:

- for mild to moderate pain:
  acetylsalicylic acid tablets, 300 mg
  paracetamol tablets, 500 mg
- for severe pain:
  morphine sulfate, 10-mg injections.

Acetylsalicylic acid (aspirin)

The usual dose given to relieve pain is 2 tablets, repeated if necessary every 6 hours.

This drug will act rapidly to relieve most forms of mild to moderate pain, particularly those affecting muscles and joints. It will also help to reduce a high temperature, a property that makes it particularly useful in dealing with the aches and pains experienced in feverish conditions. The side-effects of treatment are usually mild and of infrequent occurrence (see page 313).

Paracetamol

Usual dose: 2 tablets, repeated if necessary every 6 hours.

This drug is effective in reducing pain. It is a suitable alternative treatment for patients who do not tolerate acetylsalicylic acid.

Morphine sulfate

Usual dose: 10–15 mg (1–1½ ampoules).

This is a powerful pain killer, which should be used only where specifically mentioned in this guide, or when advised by a doctor.

Morphine is given either by subcutaneous injection, when it will act within 10–15 minutes, or by intramuscular injection to obtain slightly quicker pain relief.

When very severe pain is present, it may be necessary to repeat doses (as described on page 324). In all cases, after three injections have been given, RADIO MEDICAL ADVICE should be sought on the advisability and frequency of further morphine injections.

See also the indications of the action of morphine and the caution and warning on its use, on page 324.

Dispensing medicines

When a diagnosis has been made, note from the relevant section of the guide the name and strength of the medicine prescribed and the method of giving it. Medicines prescribed in the guide should be taken by mouth unless the guide states that they should be given some other way. Note too the amount to be given at any one time, the interval between doses, and the number of days during which the medicine should be given. Then obtain from the medical cabinet the medicine with the same name and strength.

Take great care to give the dose the guide advises, as expressed in grams (g) or milligrams (mg). For some drugs (as for instance chloroquine), the recommended dosage may be specified in relation to the patient's weight, for instance, 5 milligrams of chloroquine base per kg of body weight. For a patient who weighs 60 kg, for example, the following simple calculation gives the dose: 60 kg × 5 mg = 300 mg of base. Since one 250-mg chloroquine phosphate tablet contains only 150 mg of base, 2 tablets of this drug will be needed.

With many drugs, particularly antibiotics such as penicillin or erythromycin, it is necessary to maintain a constant concentration of the drug in the bloodstream. This is best achieved by administering it at uniform intervals, such as every 6 hours around the clock.

It is advisable to avoid taking certain drugs at mealtimes. Others should be taken along with a lot of fluid (for example, sulfamethoxazole + trimethoprim). Such recommendations should be followed as closely as possible to obtain the best results.

When administering the standard antibiotic treatment, ensure that all the medicine is taken, even if the patient seems cured by the third day. To terminate the course prematurely, because the patient feels better, may lead to a resurgence of infection.

One person, other than the patient, should be made responsible for giving him his medicine and recording the amount and time of each dose. The patient should not normally be told to treat himself, nor should medicines be left at the bedside. In malarial areas one officer should be responsible for giving each crew-member the preventive drug; the drug should not be left on the mess table for crew-members to take if they remember to do so.

If the treatment prescribed is completed, and the patient is not fully recovered, do not simply give more of the same treatment but get RADIO MEDICAL ADVICE.

Used with knowledge and care, medicaments can be lifesaving, but, used irrationally, they may do much harm. NO medicament should be taken indiscriminately.

Side-effects and interactions of drugs

Many drugs produce side-effects, hypersensitivity, or allergy. Before giving a medicine, first read the **Caution** note relating to each of the drugs contained in the ship's medicine chest, in Chapter 18 (pages 313–330). Allergic reactions and their treatment are described on page 167.

Another possible problem may be the interaction of medicaments. An example of a particularly serious interaction between drugs is the dangerous (and even occasionally fatal) combination of two or more central nervous system (CNS) depressants. A tranquillizer such as chlorpromazine in combination with a sedative such as phenobarbital may produce coma and cardiac and/or respiratory arrest, and cause death.

It is important to remember that ethyl alcohol is a central nervous system depressant and that, if it is taken in conjunction with other CNS depressants, even a moderate amount of alcohol can be fatal. It is best to advise any patient taking drugs to exercise moderation in the consumption of alcoholic beverages or, ideally, to abstain from them.

With most of the drugs listed, a patient will not notice any side-effects. Even when he does, it will often be of little importance — for instance slight nausea or diarrhoea, or a slight rash. This should not be a deterrent to the use of the prescribed medicines, **strictly in accordance with the instructions given by the guide, or by a doctor.**

Occasionally the side-effects will be pronounced, and in this case they should not be ignored. A decision on continuation or change of treatment will then be needed. The guide offers some advice on alternative treatment.

If a side-effect is pronounced, it will usually be necessary to seek RADIO MEDICAL ADVICE.

Dispensing for children

If at all possible, get RADIO MEDICAL ADVICE before giving medicines to children under 16 years. If you cannot get that advice in the time available, you should use the advice given below. In either event, during the hour following any medication, note the child's general condition and take the pulse and respiration rates from time to time. If the child seems faint, or the pulse or respiration rate becomes either rapid or slow, get RADIO MEDICAL ADVICE before giving another dose.

Tablets and capsules

In giving tablets and capsules to small children, it will probably be easier if the tablet for adults is crushed and the required amount abstracted and given mixed with honey, jam, a little orange juice, or milk.

Morphine

Do not give morphine to children under 10 years of age.

For children aged 10–15 years, do not give more than 10 mg (in exceptional cases more than that may be given, on the advice of the radio medical doctor).

Erythromycin tablets, 250 mg

- Under 2 years: ½ tablet every 6 hours
- 2–8 years: 1 tablet every 6 hours
- 8 years and over: adult dose

Tetracycline hydrochloride capsules, 250 mg

Do not give tetracycline to children under 12 years. For children 12 years and over, the adult dose may be prescribed.

Phenoxymethylpenicillin potassium tablets, 250 mg

- Under 2 years:
  ¼ tablet every 6 hours, when the adult dosage is 1 tablet every 6 hours
  ½ tablet every 6 hours, when the adult dosage is 2 tablets every 6 hours
- 2–13 years:
  ½ tablet every 6 hours, when the adult dosage is 1 tablet every 6 hours
  1 tablet every 6 hours, when the adult dosage is 2 tablets every 6 hours
- 13 years and over: adult dosage

Procaine benzylpenicillin injection, 600 000 units/ml

- Under 2 years: 150 000 units (¼ ml) every 12 hours
- 2–8 years: 300 000 units (½ ml) every 12 hours
- 8 years and over: adult dose

Cyclizine hydrochloride tablets, 50 mg

- Under 6 years: ¼ tablet
- 6–13 years: ½ tablet
- 13–16 years: ¾ tablet

Sulfamethoxazole + trimethoprim tablets, 480 mg

Do not give these tablets to infants aged less than 6 months.

- 6 months to under 6 years: 240 mg (½ tablet) every 12 hours
- 6–13 years: 1 tablet every 12 hours
- 13 years and over: adult dose

Lotions, creams, ointments, and drops

Follow any instructions on the container, otherwise treat the child as an adult; do not be lavish with any application, especially to children under 4 years.

Other medicines

Give the dose, if any, recommended on the container, or:

- up to and including 1 year: ¹⁄₁₀ of the adult dose
- 1–4 years: ⅓ of the adult dose
- 4–10 years: ½ of the adult dose
- 10–15 years: ¾ of the adult dose

Standard antibiotic treatment

Reference has been made to the following treatment for a number of complaints, using the words "give the standard antibiotic treatment" for the sake of brevity.

For patients not allergic to penicillin

(see: Note on the use of penicillin, this page)

If able to take tablets by mouth:

- phenoxymethylpenicillin potassium (250-mg tablets) 2 tablets, followed by 1 tablet every 6 hours for 5 days

If unable to take tablets by mouth:

- procaine benzylpenicillin, 600 000 units intramuscularly once a day for 5 days

For patients allergic to penicillin

If able to take tablets by mouth:

- erythromycin, 500 mg, followed by erythromycin, 250 mg, every 6 hours for 5 days

If vomiting:

- 30 minutes before a dose of erythromycin is taken, give one 50-mg cyclizine hydrochloride tablet (to a child aged 1–10 years, give half a tablet; those over 10 years can be given one tablet)

Note on the use of penicillin

Penicillin is a powerful drug, capable of destroying the germs causing many diseases, but it should not be used lightly since people may become sensitive to it. Mild sensitivity may cause a general disturbance, with transient itching rashes, weals, and swelling of the skin; severe sensitivity may cause fainting, collapse, and even death. Severe cases (see Anaphylactic shock, page 167) are rare, but if collapse occurs after the administration of penicillin, give a subcutaneous injection of epinephrine, 1 ml ampoule, immediately. Whenever a penicillin injection is given, a sterile syringe and an ampoule of epinephrine should be kept within reach.

In view of the danger of sensitivity, it is important always to question a patient about to receive penicillin on whether he has ever had any reactions to penicillin. If he has had such reactions, or may possibly have had them, do not give penicillin, either by mouth or by injection, but give erythromycin instead.

Provide any patient who has been given penicillin and is going to a hospital ashore with a note stating how much penicillin he has had and how and when it has been given.

Penicillin is usually most effective in acute inflammation. Some of the more common causes of acute inflammation at sea are: boils, abscesses, carbuncles, cellulitis, erysipelas; infected wounds and burns; infected ears; tonsillitis and quinsy (peritonsillar abscess); and pneumonia.

Chapter 18

List of medicines

Medicines recommended for the ship's medicine chest

It is assumed that the officer who has the responsibility for the care and treatment of seamen aboard a merchant vessel in either the A or B categories (described below) will have had training in the administration and use of the recommended medicines.

Column A of Table 10 shows the minimum number of packaged items (figures in Unit column) recommended for ocean-going merchant vessels without a doctor aboard. The quantities of medicaments are based on an estimated 6-month inventory for a crew complement of 25–40 persons.

Column B of Table 10 gives the minimum number of packaged items recommended to be carried aboard merchant vessels engaged in coastal trade or going to nearby foreign ports, and not more than 24 hours away from a port of call. The quantities of medicaments are based on an estimated 6-month inventory for a crew complement of approximately 25 persons.

Column C of Table 10 gives the minimum number of packaged items recommended for fishing boats or private craft which normally do not carry more than 15 persons and are never more than a few days from the home port, or only a few hours from a port of call.

If a doctor is assigned to a ship, the lists of medicines, surgical equipment, instruments, and supplies may be expanded.

Contents

Table 10. List of medicines recommended for the ship's medicine chest

Item no.	Description of item	Unit	Quantities A	B	C	Notes
1.	Acetylsalicylic acid, 300 mg tablets, 100s	bottle	6	3	2	also known as aspirin
2.	Alcohol, rubbing (70% ethyl alcohol), 500 ml	bottle	6	2	1	
3.	Aluminium acetate, ear drops, 13% solution in 20-ml bottle with dropper	bottle	6	2	2	
4.	Aluminium acetate powder, 2-g packets, for making equivalent aluminium acetate solution (Burrow's), 12s	box	2	–	–	for external use only
5.	Aluminium hydroxide gel, with magnesium hydroxide or magnesium trisilicate, oral suspension, 360 ml	bottle	6	–	–	
6.	Aluminium hydroxide, with magnesium hydroxide or magnesium trisilicate, 1-g tablets, 100s	bottle	10	3	3	
7.	Aminophylline suppository, rectal, 500 mg, 12s	box	2	1	–	refrigerate
8.	Amitriptyline tablets, 25 mg, 100s	bottle	1	1	–	
9.	Ampicillin capsules, 250 mg, 100s	bottle	3	1	–	
10.	Antihaemorrhoidal suppositories, 12s	box	6	1	–	refrigeration preferable
11.	Ascorbic acid tablets (vitamin C), 50 mg, 100s	bottle	3	1	–	
12.	Atropine sulfate injection, 0.5 mg/ml, 1-ml ampoules, 10s	box	6	1	–	
13.	Benzathine benzylpenicillin, injection, 2.4 million units per 5-ml vial	item	20	–	–	
14.	Benzoic and salicylic acid ointment, 30-g tube	item	2	1	–	
15.	Calamine lotion, plain, 120 ml	bottle	8	1	1	
16.	Calcium gluconate, effervescent tablets, 1 g, 30s	box	1	–	–	
17.	Cetrimide 40% solution, 500 ml (disinfectant)	bottle	3	1	1	this is a concentrated (stock) solution; when 1% cetrimide is mentioned in the guide, the stock solution should be diluted (see page 316)
18.	Charcoal, activated, powder, 120 g	bottle	1	1	1	
19.	Chloroquine phosphate tablets, 250 mg, 100s	bottle	1	1	1	for the suppression and treatment of malaria
20.	Chlorphenamine maleate tablets, 4 mg, 20s	bottle	3	1	–	
21.	Chlorphenamine maleate injection, 10 mg, 1-ml ampoules, 10s	box	2	1	–	
22.	Chlorpromazine hydrochloride tablets, 25 mg, 20s	bottle	4	2	1	
23.	Chlorpromazine hydrochloride injection, 25 mg in 1-ml ampoules, 10s	box	2	1	–	
24.	Clove oil, 20 ml	bottle	2	1	1	
25.	Codeine sulfate tablets, 30 mg, 100s	bottle	1	1	–	controlled substance
26.	Cyclizine hydrochloride tablets, 50 mg, 100s	bottle	4	1	1	
27.	Dextran injection, 6%, and sodium chloride, 0.9%, 500 ml, with administration set	bottle	6	–	–	
28.	Diazepam injection, 5 mg/ml, 2-ml ampoule	item	20	–	–	controlled substance
29.	Diazepam tablets, 5 mg, 100s	bottle	2	1	–	controlled substance

Table 10 *(continued)*

Item no.	Description of item	Unit	Quantities A	B	C	Notes
30.	Dimercaprol injection, 100 mg in 2-ml ampoules, 10s	box	6	2	1	antidote in metal poisoning
31.	Doxycycline hydrochloride tablets, 100 mg, 100s	bottle	2	–	–	
32.	Ephedrine sulfate tablets, 25 mg, 100s	bottle	1	–	–	
33.	Epinephrine hydrochloride injection, 1:1000, 1-ml ampoules, 10s	box	2	1	1	
34.	Ergometrine maleate injection, 0.2 mg in 1-ml ampoules, 10s	box	1	–	–	
35.	Erythromycin (stearate or ethylsuccinate) tablets, 250 mg, 100s	bottle	3	1	–	
36.	Eye anaesthetic drops, 0.5% solution of tetracaine hydrochloride, in dropper bottles, 10 ml	bottle	2	1	–	should be marked: "For external use"
37.	Eye antiinfective drops, 1% solution of chloramphenicol in dropper bottles, 10 ml	bottle	3	2	1	
38.	Eye ointment, 1% tetracycline hydrochloride, 4-g tube	item	6	3	1	
39.	Eyewash or eye-irrigating solution, isotonic, sterile, in plastic squeeze bottle, 120 ml	bottle	6	1	1	
40.	Fluorescein sodium ophthalmic strip, sterile (1%, on paper applicators), 200s	package	1	–	–	
41.	Furosemide tablets, 40 mg, 100s	bottle	1	–	–	
42.	Glyceryl trinitrate tablets, 0.5 mg, 20s	bottle	2	1	1	keep bottle tightly closed; store at temperature of 0–25 °C
43.	Hydrocortisone sodium succinate, 100-mg vial, for injection, intravenous, or intramuscular	vial	5	–	–	
44.	Hydrocortisone ointment 1%, 30-g tube with rectal tip	item	6	2	2	
45.	Ichthyol and glycerine ointment (ichthammol 10%, glycerine, soft paraffin, wool fat 90%), in 100-g container	item	3	2	1	more containers are needed on fishing vessels with a crew of over 30 people
46.	Insect repellent (diethyltoluamide solution), 50-ml	bottle	12	6	2	
47.	Iodine, 2.5% solution, in 100-ml bottles with glass stoppers	bottle	4	2	1	bottles should be marked: "POISON, for external use only"
48.	Lidocaine hydrochloride injection 1%, 2-ml ampoule	item	12	–	–	
49.	Lindane cream, 1%, 60-g tube	item	12	2	–	for external use
50.	Magnesium hydroxide suspension, 550 mg/10 ml, 500 ml	bottle	8	2	2	
51.	Metronidazole tablets, 200 mg, 100s	bottle	5	2	–	
52.	Miconazole nitrate, 2%, vaginal cream, with applicator, in 80-g container	item	5	2	–	
53.	Miconazole nitrate, 100-mg, pessary and inserter	item	20	10	–	
54.	Mineral oil (liquid petrolatum), 500 ml	bottle	1	1	–	
55.	Morphine sulfate injection, 10 mg/ml, 1-ml ampoules, 10s	box	2	1	–	controlled substance
56.	Naloxone hydrochloride injection, 0.4 mg/ml, 1-ml ampoule	item	6	–	–	

Table 10 *(continued)*

Item no.	Description of item	Unit	Quantities A	B	C	Notes
57.	Neomycin + bacitracin ointment (5 mg neomycin + 500 IU bacitracin zinc per g), 30-g tube	item	20	10	5	keep at temperature of 2–20 °C
58.	Oral rehydration salts (sodium chloride 3.5 g, sodium bicarbonate 2.5 g (or trisodium citrate 2.9 g), potassium chloride 1.5 g, glucose 20 g) in water-proof bags/sachets	item	50	20	5	one bag/sachet should be dissolved in 1 litre of boiled cooled water
59.	Oxygen, size E tank	item	2	1	–	the tank should always be full of oxygen
60.	Paracetamol, 500-mg tablet	item	300	150	100	
61.	Petrolatum, white, 60-g tube	item	6	2	2	
62.	Phenobarbital tablets, 30 mg, 100s	bottle	3	1	–	controlled substance
63.	Phenoxymethylpenicillin potassium tablets 250 mg, 100s	bottle	3	1	–	
64.	Pilocarpine hydrochloride eye-drops, 2%, 15-ml dropper bottle	bottle	2	1	–	
65.	Potassium permanganate, 100 g	bottle	2	1	–	for external use
66.	Probenecid tablets, 500 mg, 100s	bottle	2	1	–	
67.	Procaine benzylpenicillin, sterile suspension, injection, 600 000 units/ml, 1-ml vials, 10s	box	2	1	–	refrigerate
68.	Proguanil tablets, 100 mg, 100s	bottle	1	1	1	
69.	Pyrantel tablets, 250 mg, 50s	bottle	1	–	–	
70.	Quinine sulfate tablets, 300 mg, 100s	bottle	2	–	–	
71.	Quinine dihydrochloride, injection, 300 mg/ml, 2-ml ampoule, 10s	box	2	–	–	
72.	Salbutamol aerosol inhaler unit	item	2	1	–	
73.	Sodium chloride injection, 0.9%, 1000 ml	bottle	6	2	–	administration sets should be obtained from the manufacturer of the intravenous solution
74.	Sodium chloride tablets, 1 g, 1000s	bottle	2	1	1	
75.	Spectinomycin hydrochloride, injection, 2 g per 5-ml vial	item	20	–	–	
76.	Sulfamethoxazole + trimethoprim (400 mg + 80 mg) tablets, 20s	bottle	10	5	–	
77.	Talc (talcum powder), 120 g	can	6	3	3	
78.	Tetanus immune human globulin, 250 units, vial or ampoule	item	5	–	–	refrigerate, do not freeze. Note: this drug should be carried only on ships that carry cattle, horses, or hides
79.	Tetanus toxoid adsorbed, single dose , ampoule	item	10	–	–	refrigerate, do not freeze
80.	Tetracycline ear-drops, 1% tetracycline solution in dropper bottle, 10 ml	bottle	10	5	1	
81.	Tetracycline hydrochloride capsules, 250 mg, 100s	bottle	3	1	–	
82.	Water, sterile, 5-ml ampoules, 10s	box	3	2	–	
83.	Zinc oxide paste, 30-g tube	item	12	3	3	

Medicines: uses, adult dosages, and cautions

1. Acetylsalicylic acid (aspirin) tablets, 300 mg

Use: (1) To relieve aches and pains in diseases such as influenza, the common cold, and sinusitis. (2) To relieve headache, neuralgia, muscular aches, joint pains, and fever.

Adult dosage: For headache, 1–3 300-mg tablets, repeated in 6 hours, if necessary. For pains and aches in joints and pains associated with neuralgia, colds, and other ailments, 2 tablets repeated every 6 hours, as needed. For severe pain not relieved by acetylsalicylic acid alone, 2 tablets administered with a 30-mg tablet of codeine sulfate may be indicated.

Caution: Some individuals are sensitive to this drug. Small doses may cause swelling of the eyelids, nose, lips, tongue, or the entire face; they may also cause a hive-like rash, dizziness, and nausea. In some persons this sensitivity is very severe. These individuals usually know that aspirin can cause them to have a reaction and that they should not take the drug. Individuals sensitive to this drug are frequently subject to hay fever, asthma, or hives. In such individuals, paracetamol should be considered as an alternative for the treatment of mild pain.

Gastrointestinal disturbances (dyspepsia, nausea, vomiting, and concealed bleeding) sometimes occur, especially with prolonged administration of acetylsalicylic acid. These effects can be diminished by taking the drug with milk or food.

Acetylsalicylic acid should not be given to patients with a past history of peptic ulceration or those prone to regular indigestion. Specific inquiries should always be made on this point before prescribing.

2. Alcohol, rubbing (70% ethyl alcohol)

Use: As an antiseptic for "degerming" the skin prior to injections and other surgical procedures. For disinfecting the hands, rub the skin gently but thoroughly for 3 minutes with gauze or cloth soaked with the alcohol.

3. Aluminium acetate, 13% solution, ear-drops

Use: For treating a boil in the ear.

Adult dosage: Instil 3–5 drops (see Ear medication, page 120) every 2–3 hours during the day, for several days.

4. Aluminium acetate powder, 2-g packets, for making equivalent aluminium acetate solution (Burrow's solution)

Use: For external use only. A solution/mixture, prepared from a powder pack as indicated on the carton, is used as a soothing, astringent wet dressing for inflamed or "weeping" areas of the skin. It is an effective, simple remedy for inflammation of areas of the skin due to insect bites, poison ivy, or certain fungal infections such as athlete's foot (acute dermatophytosis).

Adult dosage: Mix 1 or 2 packets in 500 ml of water, as directed on the package for specific conditions, or as directed by a physician. Do *not* strain or filter. The solution is applied in the form of wet compresses to the affected areas; this should be repeated several times a day, each time for at least an hour. Also, it may be used as a soak for hands or feet in acute infections such as contact eczema or athlete's foot.

Caution: *Keep away* from the eyes. DO NOT GIVE INTERNALLY. If irritation or sensitivity develops, treatment should be discontinued.

5. Aluminium hydroxide gel, with magnesium hydroxide or magnesium trisilicate, oral suspension

Use: In treating gastric hyperacidity and peptic ulcer, acid indigestion, or sour stomach. Generally promotes healing and relieves pain. Neutralizes hydrochloric acid in the stomach without producing an alkaline reaction. The liquid form of the drug is more effective than the tablet form.

Adult dosage: 10 ml (about 2 teaspoonfuls) 2 hours after meals and at bedtime. Dose and frequency depend on severity of symptoms and relief obtained. The dose range is 5–30 ml per administration. In severe gastritis it can be given every 2 hours, possibly with half a glass of milk.

Caution: Moderate constipation or diarrhoea may occur. This drug should *not* be administered simultaneously with others, such as tetracycline hydrochloride and barbiturates, because it might interfere with their absorption. After prolonged high-dosage use, nausea, vomiting, and intestinal obstruction have been noted.

6. Aluminium hydroxide, with magnesium hydroxide or magnesium trisilicate, tablets

Use: Same as for the oral suspension; however, somewhat less effective.

Adult dosage: 1 or 2 tablets, chewed thoroughly before swallowing, 2–4 hours after meals, as needed, and at bedtime.

Caution: Same as for the oral suspension.

7. Aminophylline suppository, rectal, 500 mg

Use: To facilitate breathing in patients who have bronchial asthma, asthmatic bronchitis, pulmonary emphysema, and certain types of heart failure. Wheezing is usually an indication for use. The drug also has diuretic activity (increases urination). Give only on RADIO MEDICAL ADVICE.

Adult dosage: Insert one 500-mg suppository rectally. This dose may be repeated in 8–12 hours. The total dose should not exceed 1 g (2 suppositories) in 24 hours.

Caution: Store in a refrigerator at 2–8 °C to prevent deterioration. Remove any wrapping before inserting the suppository. Rectal irritation may occur with continued use.

8. Amitryptiline tablets, 25 mg

Use: A psychotherapeutic drug used in the treatment of depression and anxiety. It is a slow-acting drug, and should be used only after obtaining RADIO MEDICAL ADVICE. Amitryptiline has sedative as well as antidepressive properties, so do not give any other sedative along with it.

Adult dosage: 50 mg orally the first day before bedtime, and the same dose morning and evening on the second and consecutive days.

Caution: Do not give this drug to people with a history of seizures, of urinary retention, of glaucoma (see page 197), or of chronic liver diseases, or to patients with cardiovascular complications. A minor side-effect is dryness of the mouth. The patient taking amitryptiline should not drink alcohol.

9. Ampicillin capsules, 250 mg

Use: For chest infections, urinary and gastrointestinal infections, and infections of the tonsils and throat. **Give only on RADIO MEDICAL ADVICE from a physician.**

Adult dosage: Recommended for susceptible infections. The usual dosage is 1–2 250-mg capsules or tablets four times a day, up to the total dosage of 3.5 g (14 × 250-mg capsules) for one course of treatment.

The daily dose of ampicillin should be administered simultaneously with 2–4 500-mg tablets of probenecid (see page 326) to prolong the effective blood concentrations of ampicillin.

Caution: Ampicillin, chemically quite similar to penicillin, can cause the same types of allergic reaction, such as anaphylactic reaction and skin rash. **Persons allergic to penicillin should be assumed to be allergic to ampicillin.** Before administering, determine from the patient, if possible, whether he is allergic to either penicillin or ampicillin. Allergic (anaphylactic) reactions can be severe or even fatal. If the patient is allergic to the drug, RADIO MEDICAL ADVICE should be obtained for an alternative anti-infective treatment. If a reaction occurs, discontinue ampicillin, and give emergency treatment (see Allergic reactions, page 167).

Ampicillin may produce other side-effects such as nausea, vomiting, or diarrhoea.

10. Antihaemorrhoidal suppositories

Use: For temporary relief of itching, burning, and soreness from haemorrhoids (piles). Soothes inflamed haemorrhoids. The patient should try to avoid straining on the stool, heavy lifting, coughing, and excessive sneezing. Control constipation (so that straining should not be necessary) with *mild* laxatives. Warm baths may help.

Adult dosage: Remove the wrapper and insert one suppository as deeply as possible into the rectum in the morning, at bedtime, and immediately after each bowel movement.

Caution: Keep suppositories refrigerated. If a suppository is soft, hold it under cold water before insertion.

11. Ascorbic acid (vitamin C) tablets, 50 mg

Use: Febrile states, chronic illness, and infection may increase the need for this vitamin. Deficiency of this vitamin causes scurvy. Symptoms of mild deficiency include bleeding gums and loosened teeth.

12. Atropine sulfate injection, 0.5 mg/ml

Use: Injectable atropine sulfate is included for use as an antidote in the treatment of poisoning by insecticides containing organophosphate or carbamate chemicals as part of their formulation. Get RADIO MEDICAL ADVICE in the event of such poisoning.

Adult dosage: If it is determined that one of the above-mentioned poisons is involved, atropine sulfate should be administered at once to prevent coma, cyanosis, or convulsions. In organophosphate or carbamate poisoning, 2–3 mg should be given subcutaneously at once, followed by 1 mg every 15 minutes, until the skin is flushed and dry, or the pulse is mild and rapid. **If cyanosis (bluish discoloration of skin) occurs, oxygen should also be administered.**

Caution: The above doses, which are needed to counteract the poison, result in dry, flushed, or warm skin, dryness of the mouth, rapid pulse, and rapid breathing. These symptoms may lead to restlessness, hallucinations, and disorientation, followed by depression, medullary paralysis, and death. Do not administer this drug before obtaining RADIO MEDICAL ADVICE.

13. Benzathine benzylpenicillin injection, 2.4 million units per 5 ml

Use: As an antibiotic, particularly for treatment of syphilis.

Adult dosage: The customary therapeutic dose is 2.4 million units administered intramuscularly in a single dose. The preferred injection site is in the inner aspect of the upper outer quadrant of the buttock (see Fig. 106, page 116).

Caution: Penicillin preparations should not be used in patients with known hypersensitivity to the drug. If they are administered to such patients, a severe allergic (anaphylactic) reaction (see page 167) may occur rapidly and could result in death. **Before administering any penicillin preparation, determine, if possible, whether the patient is allergic to penicillin.** Should the patient be allergic to the drug. RADIO MEDICAL ADVICE should be obtained concerning an alternative anti-infective treatment.

Whenever an injection with a penicillin preparation is given, epinephrine hydrochloride injection, 1:1000, and also hydrocortisone sodium succinate, 100 mg, should be at hand, ready for immediate administration in case of a severe anaphylactic reaction (see treatment for anaphylactic reaction, page 168).

When treated with penicillin patients with primary or secondary syphilis may develop a Jarisch-Herxheimer reaction, which usually appears 6–12 hours after the injection. This reaction is characterized by fever, chills, joint aches, increased swelling of the primary lesion, or increased prominence of the secondary rash. It is caused by the sudden destruction of a great number of the organisms that cause the disease and should not give rise to alarm. Analgesics such as acetylsalicylic acid may help to alleviate the symptoms.

14. Benzoic and salicylic acid ointment

Use: This ointment is used in treating fungal infections of the skin. When applied to skin, it causes the upper layers of the skin to peel off (keratolysis). This action, along with a mild anti-fungal effect, helps in the treatment of the infection.

Adult dosage: The ointment should be applied once or twice daily to the area involved.

Caution: *External use only.* Use should be discontinued if irritation or redness occurs.

15. Calamine lotion, plain

Use: For relieving itching or irritated skin, heat rash, and hives. Shake the bottle well. Wet a pad of cotton with the lotion and pat it on the affected area.

Caution: Do *not* use on open or "weeping" sores.

16. Calcium gluconate, effervescent tablets, 1 g

Use: This medicament is intended to be used primarily in cases of poisoning by oxalic acid or sodium fluoride.[1] This sort of poisoning may cause a depletion of the calcium content of the blood, resulting in convulsions. Calcium gluconate acts by restoring needed calcium to the blood.

Adult dosage: Dissolve 5 tablets in 250 ml of water, to be drunk immediately.

17. Cetrimide, 40% solution (this stock solution should be diluted before use)

Use: Disinfectant, for external use only. For cleansing the skin before an operation, in abscess incision, and for disinfecting wounds and burns. Also used for cleansing some contaminated glass and metal utensils (see page 121).

Polyethylene tubing, catheters, and other plastic articles may also be disinfected in 1% cetrimide

solution, but the time of immersion should not exceed half an hour.

Dilution: To obtain the 1% solution, take 5 ml of the stock (40%) solution and add it to 195 ml of freshly boiled and cooled water. The diluted solution should be used within 7 days; afterwards it should be discarded.

Caution: Some patients may become allergic to cetrimide after repeated applications; this is shown by excessive dryness of the skin.

18. Charcoal, activated, powder

Use: In the initial treatment of most poisonings (because of its property to adsorb many poisons).

Adult dosage: 10 g (2 tablespoonfuls). Mix the powder with water prior to administration. Repeat if the patient vomits.

Note: Activated charcoal is a general antidote. It should not be used in place of the specific antidote for a poison when that antidote is available (see Chapter 2, page 53). It should not be used on unconscious patients, because of the danger of aspiration of the powder.

19. Chloroquine phosphate tablets, 250 mg (a tablet contains 150 mg of chloroquine base)

Use: To prevent and treat malaria. When a ship is in a known malarial area, obtain medical advice from a physician on the prophylactic measures effective in that region.

Adult dosage: For details (including dosage for children), see Malaria, page 135.

Caution: Although chloroquine is generally safe and well tolerated, even in pregnant women, poisoning accidents have occurred following the ingestion of doses of 1.5–2.0 g. In children, half this amount may be fatal, so drug supplies should be carefully supervised.

Minor side-effects may occur in association with the usual prophylactic and therapeutic doses, and include nausea and vomiting (especially if the drug is taken on an empty stomach), and

[1] INTERNATIONAL MARITIME ORGANIZATION. *Medical first aid guide for use in accidents involving dangerous goods.* London, IMO, 1985.

occasionally itching of the palms, soles, and scalp. These symptoms disappear when the drug is discontinued.

20. Chlorphenamine maleate tablets, 4 mg

Use: For treating allergic reactions, such as hay fever, urticaria, and anaphylactic shock (in addition to other measures).

Adult dosage: 1 tablet, one to three times daily.

Caution: Side-effects including drowsiness, dryness of mouth, blurred vision, nausea, and sweating, may occur in people taking this medicament.

The patient's ability to work may be impaired. Alcoholic drinks increase the likelihood of side-effects.

Do not give to patients with a history of glaucoma, asthma, or peptic ulcer; consult the doctor before giving it to pregnant women or to children.

21. Chlorphenamine maleate injection, 10 mg in 1 ml

Use: See previous item. May be given subcutaneously or intramuscularly.

Adult dosage: 1 to 2 injections a day.

Caution: As for chlorphenamine maleate tablets, above.

22. Chlorpromazine hydrochloride tablets, 25 mg

Use: For treating anxiety, tension, and agitation; also to control nausea and vomiting.

Adult dosage: 25 mg for the control of vomiting; for cases of obvious madness (see page 215), give 1 tablet three times a day and consult the doctor, who may advise increasing this dosage.

Caution: Side-effects include drowsiness, allergic reactions, dry mouth. Do not give to comatose patients. Alcohol is likely to make side-effects worse. Stopping treatment may cause problems —get RADIO MEDICAL ADVICE.

23. Chlorpromazine hydrochloride injection, 25 mg in 1 ml

Use: Same as for chlorpromazine tablets. For intramuscular injection.

Adult dosage: 50 mg (2 ampoules) should be given to patients with delirium tremens (see page 165); this dose may be repeated after 6 hours. In other cases, 1 or 2 25-mg injections daily.

Caution: Intramuscular injections may be painful and may cause a lump at the injection site; patients should lie down for half an hour afterwards. See also caution for chlorpromazine tablets.

24. Clove oil

Use: For the relief of toothache when there is a cavity in the tooth. If possible, dry the cavity with cotton wrapped on a toothpick and then pack it with a piece of cotton that has been dipped in oil of cloves. This procedure may be repeated as often as necessary. Because clove oil has an irritating effect on tissues, use extra care to avoid contact with surrounding gum or other mouth areas.

25. Codeine sulfate tablets, 30 mg

Use: (1) To relieve coughing; (2) in diarrhoea.

Adult dosage: For the persistent and severe coughing accompanying severe respiratory infections, give half a 30-mg tablet as often as every 2 hours, if necessary. This time-interval should be lengthened as soon as the cough is controlled. Codeine sulfate should be discontinued as soon as the cough is relieved.

In diarrhoea, 30 mg may be given, repeated after 4 hours if necessary.

Caution: Codeine sulfate is an addiction-producing drug, but has less addiction liability than morphine. It may produce nausea, vomiting, constipation, and dizziness.

Warning: A controlled substance. An exact record of its use must be kept.

317

26. Cyclizine hydrochloride tablets, 50 mg

Use: For relief of nausea, vomiting, and dizziness associated with motion sickness (seasickness). To prevent seasickness.

Adult dosage: Give one 50-mg tablet 30 minutes before sailing or before rough weather, if seasickness is expected. Continue giving 1 tablet three times a day before meals during periods of actual or potential seasickness.

Caution: May cause some drowsiness and dryness of the mouth. Patients exhibiting drowsiness while receiving cyclizine hydrochloride should *not* be allowed to operate complicated machinery or stand watch, because the drug may cause inability to concentrate. Alcohol tends to aggravate side-effects.

27. Dextran injection, 6%, and sodium chloride, 0.9%, 500 ml

Use: To expand plasma volume and maintain blood pressure in the emergency treatment of shock caused by a loss of blood. Also used in the treatment of burns. Dextran should be purchased in a package that includes an administration set.

Note: Give only on RADIO MEDICAL ADVICE from a physician. Only trained people can administer this drug intravenously (see page 117).

Adult dosage: 500 ml infused intravenously at the rate of 20 ml per minute, so that the entire amount is given over a period of about 30 minutes. Repeated infusions may be given when necessary, should blood or its derivatives not be available. The total amount administered should not exceed 20 ml per kilogram of body weight during the first 24 hours.

Caution: In order to prevent air from entering the patient's vein, do not allow the bottle to drain completely of fluid. Blood is preferred over plasma or dextran in the treatment of shock associated with bleeding and severe burns. Hypersensitivity reactions (itching, rash, nasal congestion, difficult breathing, tightness of the chest, and mild hypotension) are the primary side-effects observed. However, the incidence is low and the reactions are generally mild. Patients should be observed closely for symptoms of anaphylaxis (see Anaphylactic shock, page 167) during the first 30 minutes of dextran infusion. If vomiting, difficulty in breathing, tightness of the chest, or urticaria occur, the infusion should be discontinued immediately and RADIO MEDICAL ADVICE should be obtained on the possible administration of other drugs.

28. Diazepam injection, 5 mg/ml, 2 ml

Use: (1) For treatment of severe agitation, including acute alcohol withdrawal states and convulsions (epilepsy); (2) may be useful for shivering due to generalized hypothermia, see page 262.

Adult dosage: The usual dosage is 2–10 mg (intramuscularly, deep into the muscle), which may be repeated once in 1–4 hours, depending upon the response and the severity of the condition.

Caution: The injection should be given only on medical advice. Overdosage leads to fatigue, drowsiness, diminished reflexes, dizziness, mental confusion, and coma. It should not be given with sedative preparations or narcotics, as it may intensify sedation. Side-effects with normal dosages may include dryness of the mouth, subnormal body temperature, fever, slurred speech, or visual disturbances in a very few persons. The dosage should be adjusted or the medicament discontinued, if these symptoms occur.

The drug should be given with extreme caution to persons prone to drug abuse.

Warning: A controlled substance. Keep an exact record of its use. Store in a locked cabinet.

29. Diazepam tablets, 5 mg

Use: (1) For treatment of common anxiety and tension, and (2) for the management of agitation during alcohol withdrawal.

Adult dosage: Varies from 2 to 10 mg, 2–4 times a day, depending upon the condition being treated.

Caution: Overdosage leads to fatigue, drowsiness, light-headedness, diminished reflexes, dizziness, mental confusion, and coma. Patients exhibiting drowsiness should *not* be allowed to work complicated machinery or stand watch.

Other precautions as for diazepam injections, see previous item.

Warning: The same as for diazepam injections, see previous item.

30. Dimercaprol injections, 50 mg/ml, 2-ml (= 100-mg) ampoules

Use: The drug is used as an antidote in poisoning. Indicated in the treatment of arsenic (pesticides), gold, and mercury poisonings; also in acute lead poisoning, in combination with calcium disodium edetate. Always obtain RADIO MEDICAL ADVICE in the event of such poisoning.

Recommended dosage (in adults): If general symptoms of poisoning occur, give dimercaprol, 200 mg intramuscularly every 6 hours for the first day, every 8 hours on the second day, and then twice a day for 3 days. Injections should be deep into the muscle; the site of injection should be changed at each administration.

Caution: Adverse reactions to this medicament include: headache, nausea, vomiting, abdominal pain; pain and sterile abscesses at injection sites; raised blood pressure and excessively rapid heart action (the blood pressure and pulse rate will return to normal within 2 hours).

31. Doxycycline hydrochloride tablets, 100 mg

Use: Antibacterial agent used in the treatment of urinary infections. It is given in cases of both gonococcal and nongonococcal urethritis after spectinomycin hydrochloride or sulfamethoxazole/trimethropin has been used. See text for dosage when this regime is used.

Adult dosage: The usual dose for adults is 200 mg on the first day of treatment, given as 100 mg every 12 hours, followed by a maintenance dose of 100 mg daily. In severe infections, e.g., chronic infection of the urinary tract, 100 mg every 12 hours is recommended.

Caution: Should not be given to pregnant women and nursing mothers. Untoward and toxic effects may occur, the most frequent being gastrointestinal symptoms (nausea, vomitting, diarrhoea, etc.) and allergic reactions. In the event of an allergic reaction, treatment must be stopped.

32. Ephedrine sulfate capsules, 25 mg

Use: (1) To relieve difficult breathing in asthma; (2) to prevent asthmatic attacks in chronic cases (effects appear 30–60 minutes after administration); and (3) to relieve nasal congestion in hay fever and severe head colds. Obtain RADIO MEDICAL ADVICE before using this drug.

Adult dosage: One 25-mg capsule four times a day. If ephedrine is used for several days, phenobarbital may be indicated to overcome its stimulant effects (one 30-mg phenobarbital tablet up to three times a day).

Caution: Adverse effects include tremors, heart palpitation, mental anxiety, insomnia, and headache. The drug should *not* be given to patients with chronic heart disease, high blood pressure, glaucoma, diabetes, or hyperthyroidism. It may cause urinary retention in older men.

33. Epinephrine hydrochloride injection, 1:1000, 1 ml

Use: (1) For acute asthma attacks and for severe allergic reactions to penicillin and other drugs, and to insect bites; (2) for cardiac or circulatory failure.

Adult dosage: By subcutaneous or intramuscular injection, 0.3 ml of 1:1000 solution, every 2 hours as necessary. The usual dosage range is 0.1–0.5 ml in asthma, and up to 1 ml in other conditions.

Caution: Epinephrine may cause anxiety, heart palpitation, and headache. Excessive doses can cause acute hypertension and irregular heartbeat. *Except in life-threatening situations,* it should *not* be administered to patients with hypertension, diabetes, hyperthyroidism, or heart disease.

34. Ergometrine maleate injection, 0.2 mg in 1-ml ampoules

Use and dosage: This medicament (intramuscular injection) administered to the mother after delivery of an infant, will make the womb contract and lessen the danger of haemorrhage. One ampoule only may be given, after obtaining RADIO MEDICAL ADVICE, just after the expulsion of the placenta.

Caution: Ergometrine should not be given to persons with hypertension. DO NOT give it before the complete expulsion of the placenta. Possible side-effects: nausea and vomiting, dizziness, headache, palpitation, and allergic reactions.

35. Erythromycin tablets, 250 mg

Use: For a variety of infections of the upper and lower respiratory tract; infections of the mouth, gums, and teeth; infections of the nose, ears and sinuses. Give this antibiotic only when RADIO MEDICAL ADVICE has been received from a physician. It may be useful for patients allergic to penicillin, and for some infections resistant to penicillin.

Adult dosage: One 250-mg tablet, four times a day (for serious infections, dosage may be increased to two 250-mg tablets, four times a day) —to be continued for 48 hours or more *after* symptoms have subsided.

Caution: Occasionally, a skin rash may develop that will require discontinuation of the drug. If the drug is discontinued because of a sensitivity reaction, RADIO MEDICAL ADVICE on alternative therapy should be obtained. Sometimes abdominal discomfort, cramping, or nausea and vomiting may occur; these complaints usually diminish as therapy continues. The drug should not be given to people known to be sensitive to it.

36. Eye anaesthetic drops (0.5% solution of tetracaine hydrochloride)

Use: For local anaesthesia of the eye, before removing foreign bodies. Put 3 drops inside the eyelids, repeat this three times at 2-minute intervals.

Caution: Careful use is advised in patients with known allergies. After receiving these drops, the eye should be protected by a pad.

37. Eye anti-infective drops (1% solution of chloramphenicol)

Use: For treating infectious eye diseases (blepharitis, conjunctivitis). Apply 3–4 drops to each eye, three to four times a day, in the manner described in Eye medication (page 118).

38. Eye ointment (1% tetracycline hydrochloride)

Use: (1) For superficial eye infections, trachoma, inflammation of the eyelids and tear sacs, and (2) for the prevention of eye infection when an injury renders the eye or an adjacent area vulnerable to infection.

If the eye infection does not improve in 24 hours, RADIO MEDICAL ADVICE should be obtained.

Adult dosage: Apply the ointment on the inside of the lower eyelid (see Fig. 113, page 120) every 3–4 hours.

Caution: Do not let the tip of the eye-ointment tube touch the eyelid (thus aviding contamination of the medicament).

Persons known to be allergic to tetracycline should not be treated with this ointment.

The ointment should be used for a limited period of time only (about a week), if it is given without doctor's control.

39. Eyewash or eye-irrigating solution, isotonic, sterile

Use: For irrigating or flushing the eye to wash away foreign particles, mucous secretions, and fluorescein dye used in diagnosis. Before use, warm the bottle with the solution to body temperature.

Directions: Point the tip of the applicator downwards towards the eye and gently squeeze the plastic bottle to irrigate the eye. Use generously.

Caution: Keep the container tightly closed. Do not let the dispensing tip touch the eye or any surface, because this may contaminate the solution.

40. Fluorescein sodium ophthalmic strip, sterile

Use: This is an ophthalmic diagnostic agent, used for the detection of lesions or small foreign bodies embedded in the cornea of the eyeball. Damaged—abraded or ulcerated—corneal tissue absorbs the dye, and the lesion appears greenish or yellowish. Foreign bodies are surrounded by a green ring.

Dosage and aministration: Anaesthetize the eye with one drop of 0.5% tetracaine hydrochloride eye-drops. Remove the fluorescein strip from the sterile wrapper without touching the dyed end. Moisten the dyed end with sterile eye-irrigating solution. Lift the upper eyelid and touch the dyed tip of the strip to the outside corner of the eye; allow the dye to flow across the eye. The patient should close the eyelid tightly after application, to distribute the stain.

Caution: Before using the strip, if the eye is dry, instil a drop of sterile eyewash solution.

41. Furosemide tablets, 40 mg

Use: Furosemide is a potent short-acting diuretic, which causes the production of urine by affecting the kidneys. It is indicated in the treatment of excess body fluid (oedema) associated with congestive heart failure, cirrhosis of the liver, or certain kidney diseases.

Dosage: The usual oral dosage for adults is 20–80 mg in a single dose in the morning, for 2–4 consecutive days each week, followed by a drug-free period. However, the dosage will vary, depending on the disease and the patient's response.

Caution: This drug should be used only after getting RADIO MEDICAL ADVICE. The doctor will advise on the dosage and on possible side-effects. If excessive doses are administered, there is a rapid loss of sodium, potassium, and calcium electrolytes, in addition to water. The drug is contraindicated in women of child-bearing age.

42. Glyceryl trinitrate, 0.5-mg tablet

Use: For an acute attack of angina pectoris.

Adult dosage: One tablet dissolved under the tongue (sublingually) at the onset of chest pain usually provides complete relief in 1–3 minutes. Flushing of the face or a throbbing headache may occur. The drug may be given hourly up to several times a day without harm. The patient should sit when taking the drug.

Caution: Do not give the drug if the patient has a history of glaucoma. A volatile substance. Tablets lose potency upon exposure to air, excessive heat, or moisture. Keep bottle tightly capped and in a relatively cool place. Store tablets in original glass bottle only; do not transfer to another container. If the container is opened during a voyage, replace it on returning to the home port.

43. Hydrocortisone sodium succinate for injection, 100 mg

Use: USE ON MEDICAL ADVICE ONLY: (1) for severe shock—large doses, combined with standard methods of combating shock, help restore blood pressure and circulation; (2) for acute allergic reactions—after epinephrine (or other substances that elevate blood pressure)—to combat severe asthma, drug reactions, and anaphylactic reactions (for example, to penicillin); and (3) for the control of life-threatening inflammation of the lungs after a patient has inhaled vomit (aspiration pneumonitis). Exceptionally, in a case of anaphylactic shock, when there is no time to obtain **RADIO MEDICAL ADVICE**, 100 mg of this drug may be given intramuscularly.

Adult dosage and administration: Dosage depends on the type and severity of the condition. The dose may be as low as 20 mg per day to suppress inflammation, or as high as 2.5 g or more in severe shock. Administer intramuscularly or intravenously, strictly following the doctor's instructions.

Caution: *Not* for patients with ulcerated corneas, acute psychoses, or a history of active or inactive tuberculosis, except in special life-threatening situations. **Use with caution** in patients with a history of stomach ulcers, in patients suffering from infections, and in the presence of diabetes, hypertension, glaucoma, convulsive disorders, and chronic renal diseases.

44. Hydrocortisone ointment, 1%

Use: For temporary relief of certain skin disorders, common rashes, inflamed skin, and disorders causing itching and discomfort. It may be used for temporary relief of itching, burning, and soreness from haemorrhoids (piles).

Adult dosage: Apply a thin film to the affected skin 2–4 times a day. Apply sparingly and with gentle rubbing. Clean the skin before each use.

Warning: Do not apply to the eyes. Do not use for extended periods of time without a physician's order. Discontinue use, if the condition gets worse. This ointment should not be administered to patients with chickenpox, or to people suffering from general infections.

45. Ichthyol and glycerine ointment

Use: For treatment of boils, fishermen's hand infections, salt-water boils, etc.

Dosage: Apply once a day to the affected area.

46. Insect repellent (diethyltoluamide) solution

Use: External use only. To repel mosquitos, chiggers, flies, and other biting insects. It can be used on clothing or the skin, protecting for up to 8 hours. Shake several drops into the palm of one hand and, after rubbing the hands together, apply to the exposed skin and to clothes at points where insects are likely to bite through, e.g., over the shoulder blades, ankles, knees, and hips.

Caution: Do not apply near eyes, nose, or mouth.

47. Iodine, 2.5% solution

Use: For external use only. For disinfecting the skin round wounds, and for the treatment of small cuts and skin bruises to prevent infection.

Caution: Bottles containing iodine should be marked: "POISON. For external use only."

48. Lidocaine hydrochloride injection, 1%

Use: As a local anaesthetic in minor surgical procedures.

Dosage: Up to several ampoules may be used for local anaesthesia. It is important not to exceed the smallest dose necessary to produce the desired result. Inject slowly (subcutaneously, as in Fig. 124, page 175) and with frequent aspirations, to guard against accidental intravenous injection.

Caution: Lidocaine should not be given to patients with a known history of allergy (hypersensitivity) to any local anaesthetic. In such people, dangerous side-effects may develop: drowsiness, unconsciousness, and respiratory arrest.

Epinephrine, hydrocortisone sodium succinate, and syringes should be immediately available when any local anaesthetic is used. The ampoule with the unused contents should be discarded.

49. Lindane cream, 1%

Use: For infestations of scabies and lice. A single application usually eliminates the parasites, but a second application is sometimes necessary. Only for external use.

Adult dosage: After a bath or shower, apply a thin layer directly to the involved skin and hair (but not to the face). Keep it on the skin for 12–24 hours, depending on the infestation. Then the patient should bathe or shower thoroughly and put on clean clothes. The bed-linen should be changed. If the first application is not successful, a second application may be made after 4 days. Clothing and bed-linen should be boiled to prevent reinfection.

Caution: This cream is irritating to mucous membranes and should *not* come into contact with the eyes. If there is accidental contact, flush the eyes with sterile irrigating solution.

Prolonged and repeated applications should be avoided, as there may be absorption through the skin.

50. Magnesium hydroxide suspension, 550 mg/10 ml

Use: As a laxative.

Adult dosage: For constipation, give 1–2 15-ml tablespoonfuls daily as needed.

Caution: *Never* give magnesium hydroxide suspension to a patient with abdominal pain, without first consulting a doctor. The patient may have appendicitis which can be aggravated by a laxative.

51. Metronidazole, 200-mg tablets

Use: (1) For the treatment of salpingitis and other diseases of women (see Chapter 10), and (2) for the treatment of amoebic dysentery (see page 189).

Adult dosage: (1) For diseases of women, usually 1 tablet every 8 hours for 2 weeks. (2) For the dosage in amoebic dysentery, get RADIO MEDICAL ADVICE.

Caution: This drug should be given to pregnant women only after obtaining RADIO MEDICAL ADVICE.

Patients should be advised not to take alcoholic beverages while on medication, because abdominal cramps, nausea, vomiting, and headache may occur.

Women patients with salpingitis should refrain from sexual activity while under treatment with metronidazole.

52. Miconazole nitrate, 2% vaginal cream

Use and dosage: In the treatment of external vaginal itching (see page 251). The cream should be smeared on the affected external areas twice a day.

Caution: Discontinue treatment if any symptoms suggesting sensitivity or irritation occur (if the condition deteriorates instead of improving).

53. Miconazole nitrate, 100-mg pessary and inserter

Use and dosage: Like miconazole vaginal cream, in genital itching. Instruct the patient to insert the pessary high into her vagina each night for 14 consecutive nights (treatment should continue throughout menstruation if it occurs).

Caution: Avoid contact of this drug with the eyes. Do not give to patients who have had allergic reactions to this drug before. Discontinue if a burning sensation or skin rash occurs.

54. Mineral oil (liquid petrolatum)

Use: Mineral oil (liquid petrolatum) is used as a skin emollient or protective agent. It may also be used to help remove ointments or creams from treated skin areas.

Its administration by mouth may be indicated after the ingestion of certain poisons, including alkalis.

Adult dosage: Apply liberally over areas of the skin.

55. Morphine sulfate injection, 10 mg/ml, 1 ml

Use: For severe pain not relieved by other analgesics. **Obtain RADIO MEDICAL ADVICE prior to use.** Discontinue as soon as the pain can be relieved by other drugs that can be given orally and are less addictive.

Action of morphine:
- relieves pain, calms the mind, reduces restlessness
- depresses breathing and coughing
- slows the heart rate
- slows normal gut movements
- may initially cause vomiting.

Adult dosage: For the relief of severe pain following injuries or burns, and severe pain of sudden origin in the abdomen or chest, give 10–15 mg intramuscularly. If the pain is unrelieved, or if it recurs soon after the first dose, a second dose of 10 mg intramuscularly may be given 1 hour or more later. Give further doses, *if necessary,* at intervals of at least 4 hours—not sooner. If the patient is to be transferred within 4 hours of receiving morphine, note the time and dosage on a tag securely tied to the front part of the patient's clothing.

Caution: An addiction-producing drug. Do not repeat the injection unless ordered to do so by a physician. Unless the radio medical doctor has instructed you to do so, NEVER GIVE MORPHINE:

(1) when the respiratory rate has slowed to less than 12 breaths per minute;
(2) when breathing is difficult (reduced) and the lips and skin are blue, or when the patient has a chest infection or asthma;
(3) when mental dullness, unconsciousness, or coma are present, especially after head injury; and
(4) for any uses other than those recommended in this guide, except on the order of a physician.

Warning: Morphine sulfate is a controlled substance. Keep an exact record of its use. Keep stock locked away.

56. Naloxone hydrochloride injection, 0.4 mg/ml, 1 ml

Use: For the *emergency treatment* of respiratory depression resulting from the administration of narcotics, such as morphine. Also indicated for the detection of suspected acute narcotic overdose.

Adult dosage: May be given by subcutaneous, intramuscular, or intravenous injection. The intravenous route of administration is recommended only for emergency situations. The usual dose is 0.4 mg, repeated every 2 or 3 minutes until a favourable response is achieved. If *no* improvement is noted after 2 or 3 doses, another cause of the depression should be suspected.

Obtain RADIO MEDICAL ADVICE on whether the use of naloxone is indicated.

Caution: The use of naloxone does not preclude that of other resuscitative measures when indicated, such as the maintenance of an adequate airway, artificial respiration, and heart compression. Naloxone is *not* effective in the treatment of respiratory depression caused by non-narcotic drugs, such as alcoholic beverages, and hypnotics such as phenobarbital.

57. Neomycin + bacitracin ointment (5 mg neomycin + 500 international units bacitracin zinc per gram)

Use: In treatment and prevention of infection, in second- and third-degree burns.

Adult dosage: The cream or ointment should be applied to cleansed burnt areas once or twice daily to a thickness of 1–2 mm. Continue as long as there is a possibility of infection, unless a significant adverse reaction occurs.

Caution: Local adverse reactions may occur, such as pain, burning, or itching. RADIO MEDICAL ADVICE should be sought to determine whether the drug should be discontinued.

58. Oral rehydration salts, in aluminium bag, sealed (contents of each bag to be dissolved in 1 litre of boiled cooled water)

Use: For the treatment of diarrhoea and other diseases causing dehydration.

Dosage: Give the solution to the patient to drink rapidly, for instance, 1 glass every 5–10 minutes, until the signs of dehydration disappear (see Diarrhoea page 188, and Cholera, page 128). Then give 1 glass after each bowel movement, to replace the continuing loss of water and salts.

59. Oxygen

Oxygen is a gas that constitutes about 20% of ordinary air; it is necessary for the maintenance of life.

Use: To make up for lack of oxygen in blood and tissues, the signs and symptoms of which are cyanosis (bluish colour to skin and nail-beds), dyspnoea (rapid, shallow breathing), rapid, thready pulse, and restlessness. Oxygen may be indicated for respiratory diseases, cardiac diseases, poisoning from gases, massive haemorrhage, and shock.

Adult dosage: The usual adult dose is 6–8 litres per minute by mask; or 5–6 litres per minute by nasal catheter.

Caution: Only trained personnel should administer oxygen. **The use of oxygen presents an explosion hazard.** In the immediate area, do not allow any smoking, open flames, electrical devices, flammable liquids (such as alcohol and ether), or any device that may cause a spark or is combustible. Compressed oxygen is marketed in metal cylinders; these must be handled carefully to prevent their falling or bumping into each other.

60. Paracetamol tablets, 500 mg

Use: (1) To relieve pain, and (2) to relieve fever.

This pain-killer is of similar strength to acetylsalicylic acid and is effective in reducing fever. It provides a suitable alternative treatment for patients suffering from mild or moderate pain who are unable to tolerate acetylsalicylic acid.

The tablets are large and should be broken or powdered, if they prove difficult to swallow.

Adult dosage: 2 tablets, repeated if necessary every 6 hours.

Caution: Be careful not to exceed the dose indicated, because this may be dangerous to the patient.

61. Petrolatum (white petroleum jelly)

Use: As a bland and neutral protective dressing. Apply to minor burns, abrasions, or dry skin.

62. Phenobarbital tablets, 30 mg

Use: (1) For insomnia; (2) for relatively prolonged sedation, as in some anxiety and tension states and in hypertension; and (3) for treatment of epilepsy.

Adult dosage: To induce sleep, 90 mg at bedtime. As a sedative, one 30-mg tablet, 1–4 times daily. In epilepsy, the dose should be adjusted to the individual; consult the doctor in each case. The average range for an adult is 50–120 mg daily, although much higher doses may be required for short periods of time.

Caution: Phenobarbital may slow down the patient's physical and mental reflexes; therefore, he must be extremely careful when operating machinery. Excessive doses of this long-acting barbiturate may lead to drowsiness and lethargy. It may alter the effectiveness of other drugs. Patients taking this drug SHOULD NOT TAKE ALCOHOL.

Warning: Long-term use may cause addiction. A controlled substance. Keep locked in a cabinet in the sick-bay. Keep an exact record of its use.

63. Phenoxymethylpenicillin potassium tablets, 250 mg

Use: For susceptible infections. Give on RADIO MEDICAL ADVICE.

Adult dosage: Usually, an initial dose of two 250-mg tablets should be given by mouth, followed by one 250-mg tablet every 6 hours. Sometimes larger doses are necessary, if recommended by a doctor.

Caution: Penicillin preparations should *not* be used in patients with known hypersensitivity to the drug. If they are administered to such patients, a severe allergic (anaphylactic) reaction may occur rapidly and could result in death. **Before administering any penicillin preparation, determine, if possible, whether the patient is allergic to penicillin.** Should the patient have a history of sensitivity to any penicillin or have other known or suspected allergies, obtain RADIO MEDICAL ADVICE for an alternative anti-infective treatment.

If an anaphylactic reaction does occur, prompt treatment is needed (see treatment for anaphylactic reaction, page 168).

64. Pilocarpine hydrochloride eye-drops, 2%

Use: For the management of glaucoma (see page 197). Pilocarpine hydrochloride eye-drops constrict the pupil. It is anticipated that this medicament will be needed aboard ship only for patients who have run out of their own supply.

Adult dosage: For glaucoma, 2 drops in the eye every 6 hours daily, or as prescribed.

Caution: To prevent contamination of the medicament during administration, keep the tip of the eye-dropper or its container from touching any part of the eye or surrounding areas.

65. Potassium permanganate (crystals), 100 g

Use: Diluted in water (1 g of crystals to 0.5–1 litre of water). This substance is used for the disinfection of the skin and mucous membranes and for the treatment of some skin diseases.

Caution: The substance (or any highly concentrated dilution of it) is very toxic if ingested.

66. Probenecid tablets, 500 mg

Use: As an adjunct to intensive therapy with benzylpenicillin, with ampicillin, and a number of other penicillins, for prolonging the effective blood concentration of these drugs.

Adult dosage: Generally, one 500-mg tablet four times a day, as long as penicillin is taken.

Caution: Probenecid is well tolerated, but some patients may experience nausea. In rare instances, sensitivity may result in a skin rash.

67. Procaine benzylpenicillin, sterile suspension, injection, 600 000 units/ml, 1 ml

To be given ONLY on RADIO MEDICAL ADVICE from a physician.

Use and adult dosage: For susceptible infections. For general information on the indications for the use of this antibiotic preparation, see the package insert. The dosage varies with the disease being treated.

Administration: By deep intramuscular injection, which will yield adequate blood levels for 12–24 hours to deal with most susceptible microorganisms. The preferred injection site is in the inner aspect of the upper outer quadrant of the buttock (see Fig. 106, page 116). Repeated injections should be in alternate buttocks. Before injecting, pull back on the syringe plunger to make sure that the point of the needle does not lie within a blood vessel. If blood appears, remove the needle and discard the syringe and needle. Prepare a new dose and repeat the procedure at another site.

Caution: Penicillin preparations should not be used in patients with known hypersensitivity to the drug. If they are administered to such patients, a severe allergic (anaphylactic) reaction (see page 167) may occur rapidly and could result in death. **Before administering any penicillin preparation, determine, if possible, whether the patient is allergic to penicillin.** Should the patient be allergic to the drug, RADIO MEDI-CAL ADVICE should be obtained concerning an alternative anti-infective treatment.

Whenever an injection with a penicillin preparation is given, epinephrine hydrochloride injection, 1:1000, and also hydrocortisone sodium succinate, 100 mg, should be at hand, ready for immediate administration in case of a severe anaphylactic reaction (see treatment for anaphylactic reaction, page 168).

68. Proguanil tablets, 100 mg

Use: For prevention of malaria, given either alone or in association with chloroquine. When a ship is in a known malarial area, obtain medical advice on the prophylactic measures effective in that area. See pages 136–137 for details of dosages.

Note: Proguanil is a very safe drug, and very few side-effects have been reported. However, malaria parasites in many parts of the world may be resistant to this drug, and the appearance of fever following exposure to malaria transmission, even when the patient has been taking proguanil (alone or in combination with chloroquine) may be the result of a malarial infection.

69. Pyrantel tablets, 250 mg

Use: For the treatment of (1) pinworm infections and (2) roundworm infections, in adults and children.

Dosage: Orally, in a single dose of 10 mg per kg of body weight (2 tablets for a patient weighing 50 kg). The highest single dose should not exceed 4 tablets (1 g). May be administered without regard to ingestion of food or time of day. May be taken with either milk or fruit juice.

Caution: There may be some adverse reactions to this drug, such as lack of appetite, nausea, vomiting, diarrhoea, headache, drowsiness, and skin rashes.

Note: RADIO MEDICAL ADVICE should be obtained before administering this drug to pregnant women or to children less than 2 years old.

70. Quinine sulfate tablets, 300 mg

Use: In the treatment of acute attacks of malaria contracted in certain areas (see Malaria, page 135). Quinine sulfate is *not* administered to prevent or suppress infection.

Adult dosage: For acute malaria attacks, give 2 tablets every 8 hours, until the patient sees a doctor. If the treatment has to be continued for more than 10 days, get RADIO MEDICAL ADVICE. This medicine should be taken after meals to lessen the possibility of stomach upsets.

Caution: Quinine sulfate may produce toxic symptoms, such as ringing in the ears or a sensation of fullness in the head. Larger doses may cause hearing difficulty or deafness. There may be severe headache, flushed skin, disturbed vision, profuse sweating, abdominal pain, nausea, vomiting, diarrhoea, delirium, convulsions, and collapse.

71. Quinine dihydrochloride injection, 600 mg per 2 ml

Use: In the treatment of acute attacks of malaria when the patient is unable to tolerate oral medication because of repeated vomiting or impairment of consciousness (see Malaria, page 135).

Adult dosage: For acute malaria attacks in adult patients unable to take oral drugs, give 600 mg intramuscularly (in the upper outer quadrant of the buttock, see p. 116) every 8 hours until the patient can take oral medication. At that time, stop the injections and give quinine sulfate tablets.

Caution: The injection must be given with care, since occasionally sterile abscesses may be produced. Toxic side-effects are as for quinine sulfate tablets, and include ringing in the ears, dizziness and nausea.

72. Salbutamol, aerosol

Use: In bronchial asthma, as inhaled spray. The medicament dilates the bronchi and brings quick relief (within several minutes) in an asthmatic attack.

Adult dosage: Usually 0.1–0.5 ml (2 puffs) of solution of salbutamol, given as a spray. Closely follow manufacturer's instructions on how to use the spray.

73. Sodium chloride injection, 0.9%, 500 ml

Use: Intravenously (1) to replace water, chloride, and sodium lost in extensive vomiting or diarrhoea, (2) in dehydration due to excessive sweating, and (3) in mild haemorrhage. **Obtain RADIO MEDICAL ADVICE before administering** (see page 117).

Adult dosage: Depends on patient's condition. Generally, 1500–3000 ml may be given over 24 hours. Do not give intravenous solutions at a faster rate than 500 ml per hour, except on RADIO MEDICAL ADVICE.

Caution: As with any injection, sterile procedures should be observed. Do not administer any intravenous solution unless it is clear and free of particles. Watch the solution carefully while it is being administered. In order to keep air from entering the patient's vein, do *not* allow the bottle to drain completely of fluid.

74. Sodium chloride tablets, 1 g

Use: To help avoid heat exhaustion, heat stroke, or heat cramps by replenishing body salts lost through excessive perspiration.

Adult dosage: Depends on the amount of perspiration. For profuse sweating, give 1 tablet with a full glass of water, every 4 hours during working hours. If weather is hot but perspiration is not excessive, give 1 tablet with a full glass of water, every 8 waking hours.

75. Spectinomycin hydrochloride, injection, 2 g per 5 ml

Use: This broad spectrum antibiotic is used for the treatment of acute, uncomplicated gonorrhoeal urethritis and proctitis in men and acute,

uncomplicated gonorrhoeal cervicitis and proctitis in women.

Adult dosage: For primary treatment of acute, uncomplicated gonorrheal urethritis, cervicitis and proctitis, the dose is a single intramuscular injection of 2 g (5 ml).

Caution: Spectinomycin should not be given to pregnant women or to children since its safety in these groups has not been established. It has no effect against syphilis, and blood tests for syphilis should performed on anyone who has been treated for sexually transmitted disease with spectinomycin alone.

76. Sulfamethoxazole + trimethoprim (400 mg + 80 mg) tablets

Use: For the treatment of urinary infections, after obtaining RADIO MEDICAL ADVICE.

Adult dosage: 1–2 tablets every 12 hours, for 7 days. Give each dose with a full glass of water. See Chapter 7 for dosage to be given in the case of a sexually transmitted disease.

Caution: Do not give this drug to infants under 6 months of age, to pregnant women, or to patients with a history of chronic renal or liver disease, asthma, or allergy. The patient should take adequate fluids to prevent crystals of this drug forming in the urine, and stone formation. Possible adverse reactions include: nausea, headache, skin conditions. In the event of appearance of a skin rash or allergic reaction, treatment should be stopped. Avoid prolonged exposure to sunlight while taking this drug, as severe reactions are possible.

77. Talc (talcum powder)

Use: As a skin lubricant and protector, and as a dusting powder for such skin irritations as chafing and prickly heat.

Caution: Do not use as a lubricant for hands or gloves when surgery is called for. If talc should get into surgical incisions, wounds, or certain body cavities, the result could be granuloma formation.

78. Tetanus immune human globulin, 250 units, vial or ampoule

Use: To provide passive immunity to tetanus in a patient who is not protected through vaccination with adsorbed tetanus toxoid and has sustained a potentially contaminated wound.

Adult dosage: For passive immunization, 250 units by *intramuscular* injection only.

If it is not certain whether the patient has previously been immunized with adsorbed tetanus toxoid, give a dose of *tetanus immune human globulin* and at the same time, a reinforcing (booster) dose of 0.5 ml of *adsorbed tetanus toxoid* in a different extremity with a separate syringe.

If the patient has received a booster dose or full basic series of the toxoid vaccination within the past 5 years, do not give either the toxoid or the tetanus immune human globulin.

Check the expiry date on the vial before administration.

Caution: Side-effects following intramuscular administration are infrequent, mild, and usually confined to the injection area. Although systemic reactions are rare, epinephrine hydrochloride injection, 1:1000, should be available for immediate use if needed.

Store at 2–8 °C and avoid freezing (freezing will cause the medicament to lose potency).

Note: This drug should be carried only on ships transporting horses, cattle, and hides.

79. Tetanus toxoid, adsorbed

Use: For active immunization against tetanus.

Adult dosage: For primary immunization of adults and children over 6 years of age, 3 doses are required (see package insert for amount of each dose—usually 0.5 or 1.0 ml). The toxoid is injected intramuscularly into the lateral aspect of the upper arm. The second dose is given 4–6 weeks after the first, and the third dose 6 months to 1 year after the second. Thereafter, the recommended dose is administered every 5 years.

It is not necessary to give booster injections more often than every 5 years. If a dose is given as a part of wound management, the next regular dose to maintain ability to react promptly to a booster injection of tetanus toxoid will not be needed for another 5 years.

Caution: Store the toxoid in the refrigerator (at 2–8 °C), but avoid freezing (freezing will cause it to lose potency). Severe reactions to the toxoid are rare; some local soreness and redness may persist for 2 or 3 days. Epinephrine hydrochloride injection, 1:1000, should always be available for use in case of an anaphylactic reaction following the administration of tetanus toxoid.

80. Tetracycline ear-drops, 1% tetracycline solution in 10-ml dropper bottle

Use: In the treatment of ear infections (see page 192).

Adult dosage: Instil 3–5 drops, three to four times a day for 3–5 days. If the treatment is not effective, consult a physician about the case.

81. Tetracycline hydrochloride capsules (or tablets), 250 mg

Use: For susceptible infections; **to be given after receiving RADIO MEDICAL ADVICE.** Do not give to children under 12 years of age.

Adult dosage: Usually, one 250-mg capsule every 6 hours. In severe illness, increase to two 250-mg capsules every 6 hours.

Because food interferes with the absorption of tetracycline, the drug should not be given orally less than 1 hour before a meal, or sooner than 2 hours after a meal. Tetracycline should not be administered with milk or with foods containing calcium. Antacids containing aluminium, magnesium, or calcium will also impair the absorption of tetracycline from the gastrointestinal tract and should not be given.

Caution: Prolonged therapy may result in superinfection of the colon with nonsusceptible bacteria and yeast. The drug may produce loss of appetite, nausea, vomiting, bulky loose stools, and diarrhoea in some patients.

Special information. Do not administer this drug after the expiry date on the label. The decomposition of tetracycline produces a highly toxic substance, which can cause serious kidney damage.

82. Water, sterile, in 5-ml ampoules

Use: To dissolve penicillin in powder form.

83. Zinc oxide paste (Lassar's plain zinc paste)

Use: A nontoxic, protective, water-insoluble, mildly astringent, and antiseptic paste employed in a large variety of diseases and irritations of the skin. Zinc oxide paste differs from zinc oxide ointment in that it is somewhat more protective.

Dosage: Apply as needed in a thin layer to skin areas to be treated or protected from sunlight or weather.

Table 11. Groups of medicines according to the site and nature of their action

Note. It is important that all medicines listed below should be given strictly in accordance with the instructions given in the text of this guide.

A. For external use

Dermatological medicines	benzoic and salicylic acid ointment	*Antidotes*	atropine sulfate injection
	calamine lotion		charcoal, activated, powder
	hydrocortisone 1% ointment		dimercaprol injection
	ichthyol and glycerine ointment		naloxone hydrochloride injection
	lindane cream (for scabies)	*Antiepileptics*	diazepam tablets
	miconazole nitrate vaginal cream		diazepam injection
	mineral oil		phenobarbital tablets
	petrolatum, white	*Anti-infective drugs*	
	talc (talcum powder)	amoebicides	metronidazole tablets
	zinc oxide paste	anthelminthic drugs (to treat worm infestation)	piperazine tablets
Surgical disinfectants	alcohol, rubbing, 70%	antibacterial drugs	ampicillin capsules
	cetrimide 1% solution		benzathine benzylpenicillin injection
	iodine 2.5% solution		doxycycline tablets
Other medicines	aluminium acetate powder (for making Burrow's solution)		erythromycin tablets
	insect repellent		phenoxymethylpenicillin potassium tablets
	potassium permanganate		procaine benzylpenicillin injection
			spectinomycin hydrochloride injection
			sulfamethoxazole + trimethoprim tablets
B. For internal use			tetracycline hydrochloride capsules
Anaesthetics, local	lidocaine 1% injection	antimalarial drugs	chloroquine tablets
Analgesics (pain-killing drugs)	acetylsalicylic acid tablets		proguanil tablets
	morphine sulfate injection		quinine dihydrochloride injection
	paracetamol tablets		quinine sulfate tablets
Antiallergics	chlorphenamine maleate tablets		
	chlorphenamine maleate injection	*Blood substitutes*	dextran and sodium chloride injection

Table 11 (*continued*)

Cardiovascular drugs (for treating heart diseases and blood circulation problems)	glyceryl trinitrate tablets epinephrine injection furosemide tablets	*Immunologicals* (immunoglobulins and vaccines)	tetanus immune human globulin injection tetanus toxoid injection
Childbirth, drug used in	ergometrine maleate injection	*Psychotherapeutic drugs* (for mental illness)	amitriptyline tablets chlorpromazine hydrochloride tablets chlorpromazine hydrochloride injection diazepam tablets diazepam injection
Diagnostic agents	fluorescein sodium ophthalmic strips		
Diuretics (drugs increasing the secretion of urine)	furosemide tablets		
Ear medicaments	aluminium acetate ear-drops tetracycline ear-drops	*Respiratory tract, drugs acting on the*	
		anti-asthmatic drugs	aminophylline suppositories ephedrine sulfate capsules epinephrine injection salbutamol oral inhalation
Eye medicaments	eye anaesthetic drops eye anti-infective drops eye tetracycline ointment eyewash or eye-irrigation solution Fluorescein sodium ophthalmic strip (for diagnosis) pilocarpine hydrochloride eye-drops	cough-controlling drug	codeine sulfate tablets
		Sedatives	phenobarbital tablets
		Solutions correcting water and electrolyte disturbances	oral rehydration salts solution sodium chloride injection
		Urinary infections, drugs for	sulfamethoxazole + trimethoprim tablets
Gastrointestinal drugs	aluminium hydroxide gel with magnesium hydroxide oral suspension aluminium hydroxide with magnesium hydroxide tablets anti-haemorrhoidal suppositories codeine tablets cyclizine hydrochloride tablets magnesium hydroxide suspension oral rehydration salts	*Vitamins*	ascorbic acid tablets
		Women's diseases, drugs for	metronidazole tablets miconazole nitrate pessaries miconazole nitrate vaginal cream
		Other medicines	clove oil (for the relief of toothache) hydrocortisone injections oxygen probenecid tablets (used with penicillin) pyrantel (for worms)

Ships carrying dangerous goods

Ships carrying dangerous goods may need to have on board extra medicines for treatment of people accidentally exposed to toxic substances. The *Medical first aid guide for use in accidents involving dangerous goods (MFAG)*[1] describes general and specific treatment of exposure to a wide range of chemicals, and includes a list of necessary medicines. This list is reproduced in Table 12. Note that many of these medicaments are also recommended for inclusion in the basic ship's medicine chest (Table 10). However, on ships carrying dangerous goods, larger quantities will generally be needed. The quantities recommended in Table 12 are based on an estimate of risk and should generally be sufficient to treat the following numbers of people.

---

[1] Published by the International Maritime Organization, London, 1985.

In case of inhalation:

- a complete crew of about 24 in the event of a major emergency (e.g., an explosion) for a period of 24 hours, by which time evacuation can be expected to have been completed or additional supplies of medicines to have been brought in by the rescue services;
- a few persons exposed in a lesser emergency until the ship reaches the next port or the casualties are cured.

In case of ingestion or eye contact: one or two people until landed or cured.

In case of skin contact (leakage or spillage): four people until landed or cured.

Reference should be made to the *MFAG* for detailed descriptions of the use and dosages of the medicaments.

Table 12. Medicines recommended to be carried on board ships for treatment of people exposed to toxic substances

Name	Recommended standard unit	Format	Quantity
Aluminium hydroxide, with magnesium hydroxide or magnesium trisilicate[1]	1 g	tablet	100
Aminophylline[1]	360 mg	suppository	60
Ampicillin[1]	500 mg	capsule	100
Ampicillin	500 mg	ampoule	100
Amyl nitrite	0.17 mg in 0.2 ml	ampoule	96
Ascorbic acid (Vitamin C)[1]	1 g	tablet	120
Ascorbic acid (Vitamin C)	500 mg in 5 ml	ampoule	20
Atropine sulfate[1]	1 mg in 1 ml	ampoule	200
Calcium gluconate 2%	25 g	tube	6
Calcium gluconate effervescent[1]	1 g	tablet	10
Charcoal, activated[1]	5 g	sachet or powder	10
Chlorphenamine[1]	10 mg in 1 ml	ampoule	20
Chlorpromazine[1]	25 mg in 1 ml	ampoule	80
Diazepam[1]	10 mg in 2 ml	ampoule	60
Dimercaprol[1]	100 mg in 2 ml	ampoule	160
Ethyl alcohol 10% solution	500 ml	bottle	4
Fluorescein sodium 1% or 2%[1]		eye test strip	100
Furosemide	20 mg in 2 ml	ampoule	40
Furosemide[1]	40 mg	tablet	80
Glucose	500 g	powder	1
Macrogol 300	1 litre	bottle	2
Methylene blue 1%	10 ml	ampoule	40
Metoclopramide hydrochloride	10 mg in 2 ml	ampoule	60
Morphine sulfate[1]	15 mg in 1 ml	ampoule	30
Naloxone hydrochloride[1]	0.4 mg in 1 ml	ampoule	30
Paracetamol[1]	500 mg	tablet	120
Phytomenadione (Vitamin K_1)	10 mg in 1 ml	ampoule	4
Salbutamol aerosol inhaler unit[1]	0.1 mg per dose	200 dose container	4
Sulfamethoxazole + trimethoprim[1]	400 + 80 mg	tablet	50
Tetracycline hydrochloride, 1%, eye ointment[1]	4 g	tube	10

[1] This drug is also recommended for inclusion in the basic ship's medicine chest (Table 10). However, recommended quantities may be different.

Chapter 19

Surgical equipment, instruments, and supplies

Equipment and supplies recommended for the ship's medicine chest

The kinds of surgical equipment, instruments, and supplies that are recommended to be maintained on board vessels, and the quantities needed, are shown in Table 13.

It is assumed that the officer aboard a merchant vessel, in either the A or B categories described below, who has the responsibility for the care and treatment of seamen, will have had training in the administration and use of the recommended items.

Column A of Table 13 shows the minimum number of items (figures in Unit column) recommended for ocean-going merchant vessels without a doctor aboard. The quantities are based on an estimated 6-month inventory for a crew complement of 25–40 persons.

Column B of Table 13 gives the minimum number of items recommended to be carried aboard merchant vessels engaged in coastal trade or going to nearby foreign ports, and not more than 24 hours away from a port of call. The quantities are based on an estimated 6-month inventory for a crew complement of approximately 25 persons.

Column C of Table 13 presents the minimum number of items recommended for fishing boats or private craft which normally do not carry more than 15 persons and are never more than a few days from the home port, or a few hours from a port of call.

Contents

Table 13. Surgical equipment, instruments, and supplies recommended for the ship's medicine chest

Item no.	Description of item	Unit	Quantities A	B	C	Notes
Equipment						
1.	Basin, emesis, kidney shape	item	1	1	–	
2.	Basin, wash, with rim	item	1	1	–	
3.	Bedpan	item	1	1	–	
4.	Cane, with rubber tip	item	1	1	–	
5.	Crutch, adjustable, wood, with rubber tip	pair	1	–	–	
6.	Eye cup, for eye irrigation	item	2	1	1	made of glass or plastic that is not affected by boiling
7.	Funnel, metal 12-cm diameter	item	1	1	1	
8.	Glass cylinder, 50 cm³, graduated	item	1	1	1	for measuring liquids
9.	Glass cylinder, 500 cm³, graduated	item	1	1	1	for measuring liquids (to prepare 1% cetrimide solution from stock solution)
10.	Heating-pad, electric, waterproof, AC/DC	item	1	1	–	
11.	Hot-water/ice bag, rubber, stopperless type	item	1	1	–	
12.	Litter, Stokes	item	1	1	1	
13.	Magnifying glass (×8 loupe)	item	1	1	–	
14.	Neil-Robertson stretcher	item	1	1	–	
15.	Oxygen unit, portable, with size E oxygen cylinder, adult face mask, regulator, tubing, wrench, instruction books (all in self-contained carrying case)	item	1	1	1	more than one unit may be necessary, depending on the type of ship and the cargo carried
16.	Spare oxygen cylinder, size E, for item 15 (filled with oxygen)	item	1	1	–	
17.	Refrigerator, about 60-litre capacity, with inside thermometer, cyclamatic automatic defrosting, to operate on a ship's electrical current, and fitted with a lock	item	1	1	–	
18–20 Restraining equipment						
18.	Cuffs, leather or cloth	item	2	1	–	restraints may be improvised from bedsheets
19.	Mummy restraint (whole-body restraint)	item	1	1	–	
20.	Side-board	item	2	2	–	
21.	Resuscitator, hand-operated, with excess pressure relief device, inlet check valve with nipple for optional connection to low-pressure oxygen line	item	1	1	1	consists of a compressible bag with a check valve, storage bag, grommets, adult face mask, and a non-rebreathing valve
22.	Rubber inflatable ring-pad	item	1	–	–	
23.	Scales, adult, weighing, clinical, capacity 150 kg	item	1	–	–	
24.	Sphygmomanometer, aneroid, 300-mm Hg scale, hand type, complete in case	item	1	1	1	instrument for taking blood pressure

Table 13 *(continued)*

Item no.	Description of item	Unit	Quantities A	B	C	Notes
25.	Splints, inflatable, arm, for above/below elbow, assorted sizes, 6s	package	1	1	1	
26.	Splints, inflatable, leg, for above/below knee, assorted sizes, 6s	package	1	1	1	
27.	Splints, finger, aluminium, padded, assorted sizes, 6s	package	1	1	1	
28.	Sterilizer, steam pressure type, for dressings and instruments	item	1	–	–	should be of a type with a drying phase
29.	Sterilizer, water type, 3-litre capacity, electric (chamber approximately 28 × 14 × 10 cm)	item	1	1	–	preferably with automatic cut-off, when there is insufficient water
30.	Stethoscope, disc-diaphragm type	item	1	1	1	
31.	Thermometer, bath	item	2	1	–	
32.	Tray, with cover, for sterilization of small instruments	item	1	–	–	to be a component of the sterilizer; must fit inside sterilizer compartment
33.	Urinal, male	item	2	1	–	
34.	Receptacle, with pedal-operated lid, 12-litre capacity	item	1	–	–	
Publications						
35.	International medical guide for ships (newest edition)	item	1	1	1	
36.	Medical first aid guide for use in accidents involving dangerous goods (newest edition)	item	1	1	1	
37.	International Health Regulations (newest edition)	item	1	1	1	
38.	Vaccination certificate requirements and health advice for international travel	item	1	–	–	
Instruments						
39.	Airway, pharyngeal, plastic, adult and child sizes	item	2	1	1	
40.	Blade, surgical knife, detachable small tang, sterile					
	(a) No. 10	package	1	1	–	
	(b) No. 15	package	1	1	–	
41.	Forceps, dressing, bayonet-shaped, Adson, 18 cm	item	1	1	1	
42.	Forceps, haemostat, curved, Halstead, mosquito, 15 cm	item	2	–	–	
43.	Forceps, haemostat, straight, Spencer-Wells, 15 cm	item	2	–	–	
44.	Forceps, haemostat, curved, Kelly, 15 cm	item	2	–	–	
45.	Forceps, splinter, tweezers, 10 cm	item	1	1	1	
46.	Forceps, tissue, 2–3 dents					
	(a) 13 cm	item	1	1	1	
	(b) 18 cm	item	1	1	1	
47.	Handle, knife (scalpel), No. 3	item	2	1	–	for detachable surgical knife blades
48.	Scissors, bandage, Lister, angular, one point sharp, one point blunt, 20 cm	item	3	1	1	
49.	Scissors, surgical straight, 15 cm	item	2	1	1	
50.	Hammer, reflex-testing, 20 cm	item	1	–	–	
51.	Needle-holder, suture, Hegar-Mayo, 14 cm	item	2	1	–	for suturing wounds

Table 13 *(continued)*

Item no.	Description of item	Unit	Quantities A	B	C	Notes

Supplies

Item no.	Description of item	Unit	A	B	C	Notes
52.	Adhesive tape, surgical					
	(*a*) 5 cm × 5 m	roll	6	3	1	
	(*b*) 2 cm × 5 m	roll	6	3	1	
53.	Administration set, intravenous, with butterfly hub needle, 1 mm × 40 mm, sterile, disposable	item	6	1	–	procure from the manufacturer that supplies the intra-venous fluids
54.	Applicators, wood, cotton-tipped ends, sterile, 2 mm × 15 cm, 50s	package	3	2	1	
55.	Bandage, cotton, elastic, rubberless, 12s					
	(*a*) 10 cm × 5 m roll	box	1	–	–	
	(*b*) 8 cm × 5 m roll	box	1	1/2	1/2	
	(*c*) 5 cm × 5 m roll	box	1	1/2	1/2	
56.	Bandage, gauze, roller, sterile 3 cm × 10 m, two-ply, clinging, 2 safety-pins, 12s	package	1	1	1	elastic gauze bandage
57.	Bandage, absorbent, adhesive, 5 cm × 5 m, 100s	box	2	1	1	absorbent bandage with adhesive
58.	Bandage, gauze, roller, sterile					
	(*a*) 10 cm by 5 m	item	60	30	30	individually wrapped
	(*b*) 12 cm by 5 m	item	40	20	10	individually wrapped
59.	Casualty dressing, adhesive, individually wrapped, sterile					
	(*a*) 9 cm × 6 cm	item	30	15	10	
	(*b*) 18 cm × 9 cm	item	20	10	5	
60.	Bandage, muslin, triangular, folded, with 2 safety-pins, 90 × 130 cm	item	4	2	1	
61.	Tube-gauze-type bandage for finger	item	10	5	2	
62.	Spray dressing, 120 ml	bottle	4	2	1	
63.	Petrolatum-gauze burn-and-wound dressing, various sizes, individually packed, sterile	item	20	10	5	
64.	First aid emergency dressing					
	(*a*) small size	item	10	10	5	additional information on first aid dress-ings below[1]
	(*b*) medium size	item	20	10	10	
	(*c*) large size	item	20	10	5	
65.	Bottle, vial, amber, 50 ml, glass or plastic, for cap-sules or tablets	item	50	20	–	self-sticking labels should be procured and kept with these bottles
66.	Catheter, double-eye, pointed, Robinson, sterile, dis-posable:					
	(*a*) 6 French (2 mm)	item	1	1	–	for urinary catheterization.
	(*b*) 8 French (3 mm)	item	1	1	–	6 French and 8
	(*c*) 12 French (4 mm)	item	1	1	–	French catheters
	(*d*) 14 French (5 mm)	item	1	1	–	can be used for
	(*e*) 16 French (5.5 mm)	item	1	1	–	pharyngeal suction

[1] Pad: cotton wool enclosed in absorbent gauze. Bandage: open-weave gauze with pad stitched to it 30 cm from one end. Pad to be folded lengthwise with the surface of the dressing on the inside and the rolled end of the bandage on the outside. Free end of bandage to be wound round the rolled end and the pad. Sterilized in separate sealed wrappers. Label with size of pad and following instruction: "Unwind short length of bandage, straighten pad by pulling on ends of bandage. Apply pad to wound without touching it. Bandage firmly."

Table 13 (continued)

Item no.	Description of item	Unit	Quantities A	B	C	Notes
67.	Catheterization tray, sterile, disposable, regular type: a 14 French straight catheter, sterile gloves, small forceps, cotton balls, lubricant, antiseptic solution, underpad and drape, specimen container and label	item	3	1	—	
68.	Clinical record chart	item	50	10	—	
69.	Temperature/pulse chart	item	50	10	—	
70.	Medical report form for seafarers	item	100	50	50	see Annex 4
71.	Clinical record chart	pad	1	1	—	
72.	Collar, cervical, with strap	item	1	—	—	
73.	Cotton, absorbent, sterile, 100 g	package	3	1	1	
74.	Cotton absorbent,					
	(a) 50-g roll	item	20	10	5	
	(b) 200-g roll	item	10	5	5	
75.	Finger cots, rubber, assorted sizes, 12s	box	1	1	1	
76.	Flashlight (penlight type), with replacement batteries	item	1	1	1	
77.	Gauze bandage, tubular, 2 cm by 5 m, rolled, with applicator	item	5	2	1	covering bandage for fingers and toes
78.	Gloves, surgical, sterile, disposable, large size (7½ or 8), 12s (pairs)	box	1	—	—	
79.	Gowns, surgical	item	5	—	—	
80.	Mask, face, disposable	item	50	20	—	
81.	Medicine cup (waxed paper or plastic), 30 ml, graduated, disposable, 100s	box	1	1	1	
82.	Microscope slide	item	100	50	—	
83.	Mortuary transfer bag, leakproof	item	2	1	—	
84.	Needle, hypodermic, 0.5 mm × 16 mm, sterile, 6s	package	6	1	—	needles to fit into the type of syringes carried on board
85.	Needle, intramuscular injection, 1 mm, 5 cm, 6s	package	3	1		
86.	Needle, intravenous injection, 1.1 mm, 3 cm, 6s	package	2	1		
87.	Occult blood detection tablet, with 60 filter papers, 60s	package	1	—	—	for detection of occult blood in faeces or sputum; follow instructions for use given by the manufacturer
88.	Pad, abdominal, sterile combined dressing, gauze, 20 cm × 20 cm, individually sealed	item	6	3	3	
89.	Pad, cotton, eye, sterile, individually sealed, 12s	package	1	1	1	
90.	Pad, non-adherent sterile dressing, non-woven cotton and rayon fabric with perforated plastic cover, individually sealed, 8 cm × 10 cm	item	100	50	20	dry dressing material for wounds
91.	Safety-pin, rustless,	item	100	50	20	assorted sizes
92.	Scrubbing-brush, hand	item	2	2	1	
93.	Sheath, rubber (condom), 3s	package	a sufficient quantity			
94.	Sheet, waterproof, 110 cm × 180 cm	item	2	1	1	
95.	Skin closure, adhesive, surgical, sterile (butterfly closure), 6 mm, 25s	package	2	1	1	to close wounds in place of sutures when feasible

Table 13 *(continued)*

Item no.	Description of item	Unit	Quantities A	B	C	Notes
96.	Skin closure, adhesive, sutureless, sterile, 10 cm × 8 cm	item	10	5	–	
97.	Suture, tapered, 1/2 circle, non-traumatic needle, 28 mm, absorbable, non-boilable, 70 cm long, size 00, sterile, individually sealed, 12s	package	1	–	–	
98.	Suture, armed, 1/2 circle, 25-mm, non-traumatic needle, non-absorbable, silk, braided, 45 cm long, size 000, sterile, individually sealed, 12s	package	2	1	–	
99.	Suture, armed, 3/8 circle, 20-mm needle, size 000, sterile, absorbable, individually sealed, 12s	package	1	–	–	
100.	Suture, armed, non-absorbable, polyester, 3/8 circle, 13-mm needle with non-traumatic point, size 5–0, sterile, sealed, 12s	package	1	–	–	
101.	Suture removal kit, containing: suture-removing forceps, sterile, and suture removal scissors, sterile	kit	1	–	–	
102.	Syringe, glass					injection needles should fit the type of syringes carried; glass syringes may be used, when disposable syringes are not available, (see Table 3, Disinfection and sterilization, page 121)
	(a) 2 ml	item	4	2		
	(b) 5 ml	item	4	2		
	(c) 20 ml	item	2	1		
103.	Syringe, plastic, disposable, sterile, individually sealed, with injection needle:					once used they should be discarded
	(a) 2 ml, with hypodermic needle, 1/2 mm, 16 mm	item	50	25	10	
	(b) 2 ml, with intramuscular needle, 1 mm, 5 cm	item	50	25	10	
	(c) 5 ml, with intramuscular needle, 1 mm, 5 cm	item	30	25	10	
104.	Test strip and colour chart, combined (urinary blood, glucose, ketone, protein, bilirubin, and pH), 100s	bottle	1	1		
105.	Test tablets, kit, glucose (reducing sugar) in urine, individually sealed, 36s	package	3	–	–	
106.	Tissues, facial	box	6	3	1	
107.	Thermometer, clinical, fever	item	6	2	2	supplied with oral and rectal type of bulbs
108.	Tourniquet, non-pneumatic, blood-taking type, composed of gum rubber with Velcro-type fastener	item	1	1	1	
109.	Tongue-depressor, wooden	item	100	50	20	
110.	Towels, paper, sterile, disposable, individually wrapped, 12s	package	2	1	–	
111.	Towels, surgical, cotton, 12s	package	1	–	–	
112.	Wrapping material	package	1	–	–	for wrapping instruments and dressings for sterilization

Table 14. Disinfectants

Description of item	Unit	Quantities		
		A	B	C
1. Chlorinated lime, 250-g	can	10	5	2
Use: As a disinfectant and deodorant for faeces, urine, glass, and earthenware. (*Not* for disinfecting metal instruments or rubber articles.) It is sprinkled liberally over the substance to be disinfected, mixed thoroughly (if indicated) by stirring with a wooden tongue-depressor or suitable implement, and allowed to stand for at least 1 hour. A small amount of water may be added to facilitate mixing, if necessary.				
Caution: Open container cautiously, away from face and eyes. Replace lid immediately after use to prevent loss of chlorine. Chlorinated lime loses much of its activity, even with careful storage, in a year. *Keep separate from internal medicines.*				
2. High-test calcium hypochlorite, 1-litre, in granular form, containing about 70% available chlorine	bottle	10	5	5
Use: (1) For disinfecting water (see page 290), and (2) for the disinfection of smooth, hard-surfaced objects in the dietary area, and cutlery. For this purpose a solution with 100 parts per million available chlorine should be used (take 1.5 g of granules of calcium hypochlorite to 10 litres of water).				
Caution: Same as for chlorinated lime.				
Note: 70 g of high-test calcium hypochlorite will disinfect 1000 litres (1 tonne) of potable water.				
3. Sodium hypochlorite 10% solution, 1-litre	bottle	10	5	5
Use: For disinfecting smooth, hard surfaces and objects (tables, dishes, cutlery, etc.) in dietary area. Dissolve 40 ml of the solution in 10 litres of potable water.				
Caution: Keep separate from internal medicines. Label the bottles "DISINFECTANT".				
4. Aqueous phenolic 30% solution, 1-litre	bottle	1	1	–
Use: As a disinfectant, for smooth, hard-surfaced objects, in non-dietary area; walls, floors etc. Before use, dilute with water 1:10 to obtain the 3% solution used for disinfection.				
Caution: Open bottles cautiously, away from eyes and face. Avoid contamination of skin. Phenol is a highly toxic substance. Keep separate from internal medicines. Label the bottles "POISON".				

Procurement and storage

Where commercially available, packaged sterile disposable supplies and equipment should be procured, especially disposable needles, syringes, medicine cups, dressing and suture trays, catheter trays, enema preparations, and surgical gloves. When items are processed and sterilized aboard ship, there is always the danger that they will be inadequately sterilized, and their use could possibly result in adding an infection to an already ill patient.

Commercially packaged and pre-sterilized disposable items are protected by inner and outer envelopes, which are mechanically sealed. This type of packaging prevents biological contaminants from gaining access to the interior so sterility will be maintained for as long as the package remains intact.

The contents of intact sterile disposable packages should remain sterile until the package is opened. However, to ensure that the contents will not have deteriorated, *they should be replaced at least every 5 years, or on the expiry date marked on the package, whichever occurs first.*

Sterilizing reusable items

Should it be necessary to process and sterilize reusable (non-disposable) supplies, equipment, or instruments, only persons who have been fully trained in sterilization techniques and procedures should be assigned to this activity.

When it is necessary to pre-package and sterilize reusable items for future use, the following factors should be kept in mind. Under normal conditions of clean storage, items enclosed in wrapping material suitable for sterilization by steam under pressure, and sterilized correctly, will remain sterile for at least 30 days. This also applies to articles placed in autoclavable plastic coverings with effective closures. Deterioration of the wrapping material and rough handling of the packages are contributory factors to possible contamination.

Insecticides

Use: For the control of flies, mosquitos, cockroaches, lice, bedbugs, fleas, and pests in stored products. Residual sprays, space sprays, deodorized kerosene formulations, aerosols, and powders of suitable insecticides (see Control of insects, page 292) should be carried, according to needs. In using insecticides, the instructions of the manufacturer should be strictly followed.

Caution: Care must be taken to avoid contaminating drink, food, or surfaces used for preparing food with these substances.

Rodenticides (rat poisons)

Use: For the control of rodents aboard ship. Anticoagulant rodenticides, such as warfarin and diphenadione, are available commercially under various names. In using them, follow the instructions of the manufacturer closely.

Caution: Most rodenticides are poisonous to man (see Control of rodents, page 290).

Annex 1

Anatomy and physiology

Treatment of illness on board ship requires some understanding of the anatomy and physiology of the human body.

The principal bones and muscles of the body are shown in Fig. 147 and Fig. 148, the position of the main arteries and veins in Fig. 149, and the contents of the chest and abdomen in Fig. 150 and Fig. 151.

The skeletal system

The skull forms a case that contains and protects the brain. It consists of many bones, firmly joined to one another except for the lower jaw, which moves at joints just in front of the ears. The skull rests on the upper end of the backbone, which is made up of a series of small bones placed on top of each other. These bones are called vertebrae and collectively compose the spinal column, within which is housed the spinal cord; nerves emerge from the cord at the level of each vertebra. At the lower end of the backbone is the pelvis, formed by the hip-bones, one on either side, which together form a basin to support the contents of the abdomen. On the outer side of either hip is a cup-shaped socket into which the rounded head of the femur (or thigh bone) fits, forming a ball-and-socket joint. The femur ends at the knee, where it forms a hinge-like joint with the strong tibia (shin-bone) which can easily be felt under the skin. On the outer

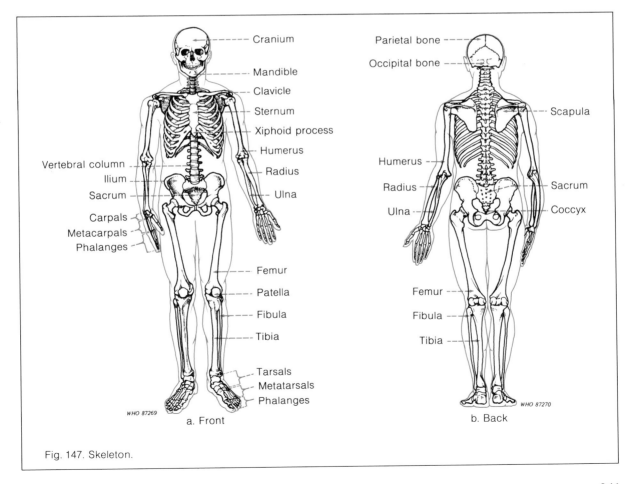

Cranium
Mandible
Clavicle
Sternum
Xiphoid process
Humerus
Radius
Ulna
Vertebral column
Ilium
Sacrum
Carpals
Metacarpals
Phalanges
Femur
Patella
Fibula
Tibia
Tarsals
Metatarsals
Phalanges

WHO 87269

a. Front

Parietal bone
Occipital bone
Scapula
Humerus
Radius
Sacrum
Ulna
Coccyx
Femur
Fibula
Tibia

WHO 87270

b. Back

Fig. 147. Skeleton.

side of the shin-bone is attached the slender fibula. In front of the knee-joint lies the patella (kneecap), the shape of which can be easily felt. At the ankle the foot is joined to the lower ends of both the tibia and fibula by another hinged joint. The foot is made up of many small bones of different shapes. There are two bones in the great toe and three in each of the other toes.

Twelve ribs are attached to the backbone on either side. Each rib, with the exception of the two lowermost on either side, curves round the chest from the backbone to the sternum (breast-bone) in front. As can be seen from Fig. 147, the lowermost ribs have no attachment to the ster-num in front. The ribs form the chest and protect the lungs, heart, and other internal or-gans. When you take a deep breath, your ribs move slightly upwards and outwards so as to expand your chest. The sternum, flat and dag-ger-shaped, lies just under the skin of the front of the chest, and to its upper end is attached the clavicle (collar-bone). On either side this bone goes out horizontally to the point of the shoul-der and acts like an outrigger in keeping the shoulder in position. The outer end of the collar-bone joins with the scapula (shoulder-blade), which is a triangular bone lying at the upper and outer part of the back on either side. Each scapula has a shallow socket into which fits the rounded upper end of the humerus (arm bone). At the elbow the arm bone forms another hinge-like joint with the radius and ulna (the forearm bones), and these join with the hand at the wrist. The wrist and hand, like the foot, are made up of many small bones. There are two bones in the thumb and three in each finger.

The muscular system

Voluntary muscles are found in the head, neck, limbs, back, and walls of the abdomen (Fig. 148). They are attached to bones by fibrous tissue which is frequently in the form of a cord and is then called a tendon or leader. When a muscle contracts in response to an impulse sent to it through a nerve, it becomes shorter and thicker and draws the bones to which it is at-

tached nearer to one another. The brain controls such movements.

Involuntary muscles are found in the stomach and intestines, heart, blood vessels, and other internal organs of the body. As the name indi-cates, they are not under the influence of the will, but function on their own, day and night.

The circulatory system (heart and blood vessels)

The body contains about five litres of blood, which circulates to all the tissues of the body (Fig. 149). It is kept moving round the body by the heart, a muscular pump about the size of a clenched fist situated in the chest behind the breastbone, lying between the lungs, rather more on the left than on the right. The heart has two sides; the right side receives the venous blood coming back to it from the body in general and pumps it through the lungs, where it passes through minute tubes, gives up carbon dioxide, and takes up a supply of oxygen. The oxygenated blood now passes to the left side of the heart, which pumps it to all parts of the body through the arteries. This blood carries oxygen, food, water, and salts to the tissues; it is bright red in colour. It also conveys heat to all parts of the body and contains various substances to coun-teract infections in the tissues. The arteries are like thick-walled tubes and decrease in diameter away from the heart. In the tissues the smallest blood vessels are very minute and are called capillaries. The blood, having supplied the tis-sues with oxygen and other substances and re-moved the carbon dioxide that has accumulated, becomes darker in colour. The capillaries take it into the veins, thin-walled tubes that carry the blood back to the right side of the heart.

Some of the blood passes to the stomach and intestines and, having taken up food products, carries them away to be stored in the liver. Blood is also taken by arteries to the kidneys and there gets rid of waste products, which are passed in the urine.

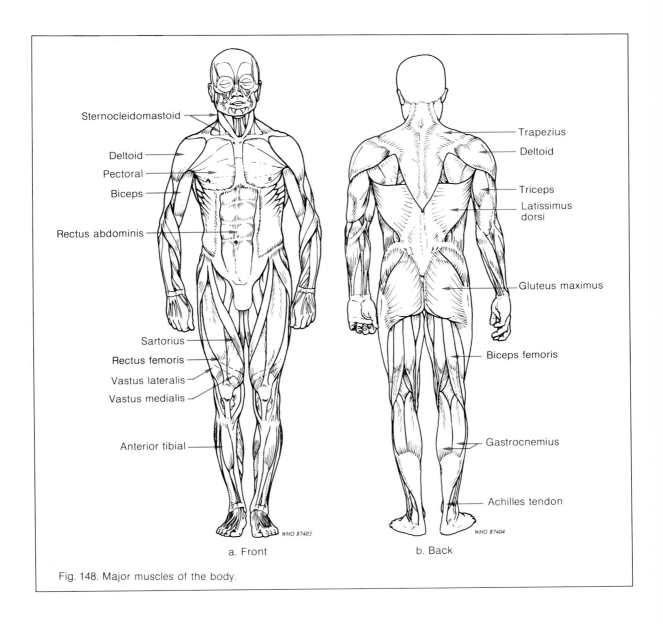

Sternocleidomastoid

Deltoid

Pectoral

Biceps

Rectus abdominis

Sartorius

Rectus femoris

Vastus lateralis

Vastus medialis

Anterior tibial

Trapezius

Deltoid

Triceps

Latissimus dorsi

Gluteus maximus

Biceps femoris

Gastrocnemius

Achilles tendon

WHO 87403

WHO 87404

a. Front

b. Back

Fig. 148. Major muscles of the body.

As the blood passes along the arteries, they pulsate at the same rate as the heart is pumping. The average normal pulse rate is about 70 per minute, but it increases with exercise, nervousness, fear, fever, and various illnesses. The pulse is usually counted by feeling the artery at the front of the wrist just above the ball of the thumb.

The respiratory system

Every time a breath is taken, the air (containing oxygen) passes through the nose or mouth and past the larynx or voice-box into the windpipe. The windpipe divides into two main tubes called bronchi, each of which then divides up into

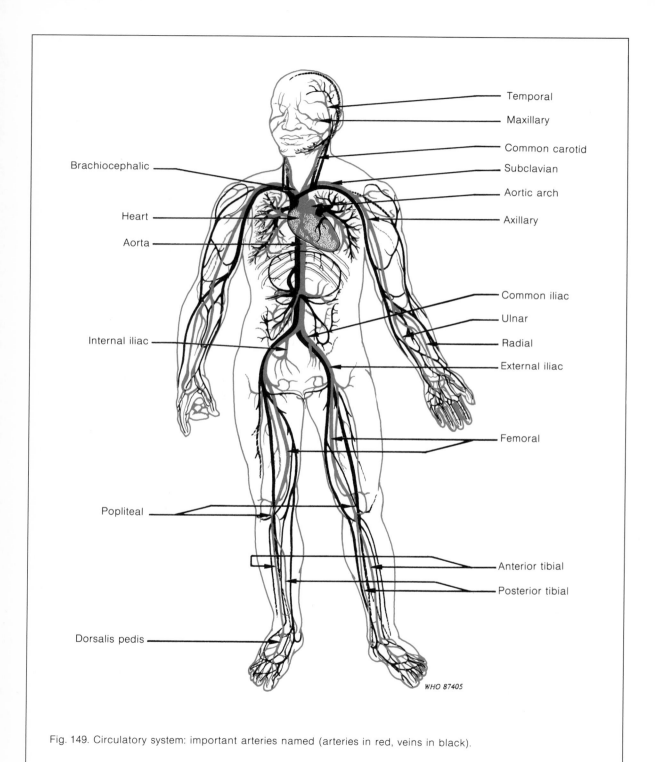

Fig. 149. Circulatory system: important arteries named (arteries in red, veins in black).

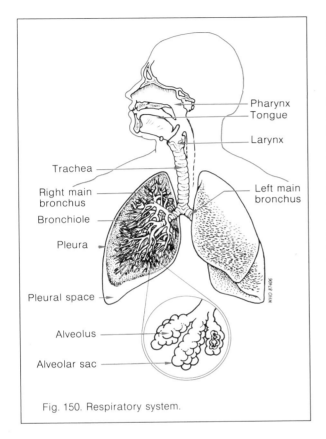

Fig. 150. Respiratory system.

people think that it is the ribs moving in and out that produce the act of breathing. Rib movement does in fact play quite a big part, but the main work is done by the diaphragm moving up and down. The diaphragm is a large dome-shaped muscle which separates the chest from the abdominal cavity. When the diaphragm muscle contracts, its dome becomes flattened and draws down the lungs, causing air to enter them; when it relaxes, the lungs become smaller and the air in them is expelled. The muscles of the abdomen also help in breathing. When they tighten, they press the abdominal contents against the diaphragm and help in expelling air from the lungs, and when they relax, they assist the diaphragm in drawing down the lungs in breathing in.

The normal rate of breathing at rest is 16 to 18 times a minute, but it increases considerably with exertion and also with certain diseases, especially those affecting the heart and lungs.

The digestive system and abdomen

Food in the mouth is broken up by chewing and tongue movements and mixed with saliva (spittle), which lubricates it and starts the digestive processes. When it is in a suitable state it passes to the back of the throat, where muscular action forces it down the oesophagus, or gullet, a muscular tube in the neck behind the windpipe. The gullet runs down the back of the chest between the two lungs, then passes through the diaphragm into the stomach.

As may be seen in Fig. 151, the stomach lies mainly in the left upper part of the abdominal cavity, partly behind the lower left rib cartilages and just under the heart. When food enters the stomach, various digestive juices act upon it, and the stomach muscles contract and relax, mixing it thoroughly. The capacity of the adult stomach is about one litre.

Still only partly digested, the food passes into the small intestine, where more digestive juices, especially those from the liver and pancreas, mix with it. Nourishment and fluids are absorbed from this coiled-up tube, which is about six

many smaller bronchial tubes that pass into the lung tissue. The air breathed in passes through these small tubes into minute air cells called alveoli, each of which is surrounded by capillaries. The blood in the capillaries gives up carbon dioxide and takes up oxygen. In breathing out, the air passes back along the same respiratory passages and is breathed out through the nose or mouth.

Each lung is covered by a lubricated membrane called the pleura. The inner side of the chest wall is lined with the same kind of membrane. These two layers of pleura are in contact and slide smoothly over one another during breathing.

The lungs are rather like elastic sponges, and the many air cells in them expand with breathing in and are compressed with breathing out. Most

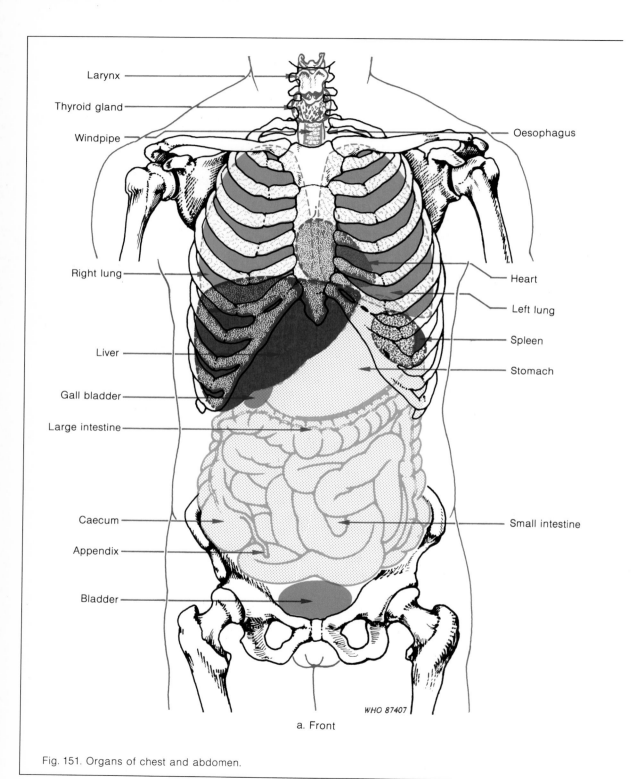

Larynx

Thyroid gland

Windpipe

Oesophagus

Right lung

Heart

Left lung

Liver

Spleen

Gall bladder

Stomach

Large intestine

Caecum

Small intestine

Appendix

Bladder

WHO 87407

a. Front

Fig. 151. Organs of chest and abdomen.

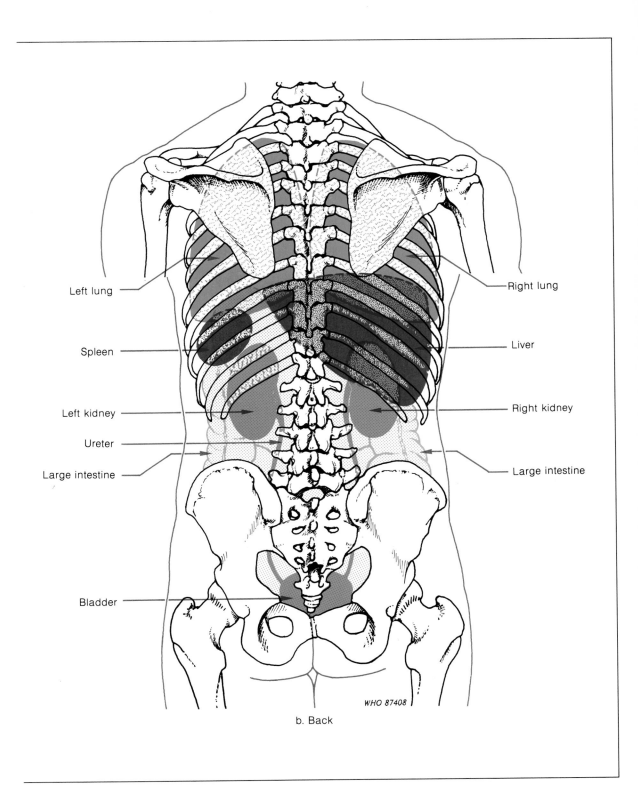

Left lung

Right lung

Spleen

Liver

Left kidney

Right kidney

Ureter

Large intestine

Large intestine

Bladder

WHO 87408

b. Back

metres long, and the residue of the food passes into the large intestine, or colon, at a point in the lower part of the right side of the abdomen, close to where the appendix is situated. In the large intestine more moisture is extracted from the food residue. At its far end, the large intestine joins the rectum, and here the unwanted. food residue collects and is passed out of the body by the back passage or anus.

The liver secretes the important digestive juice called bile (a greenish/brownish fluid) and, on its surface, has a small reservoir called the gall-bladder, where a supply of bile is kept available. The liver also deals with, and stores, digested food materials.

The spleen (Fig. 151) is a solid oval-shaped organ in the upper part of the left side of the abdominal cavity at the back of the stomach, just above the kidney. Its functions are largely connected with the blood and it may be enlarged in certain diseases.

The urinary system

(See Fig. 140, page 236)

The kidneys are at the back of the upper part of the abdominal cavity, one on either side of the spine. They remove water and certain waste products from the blood and produce urine. Urine leaves each kidney by a small tube called the ureter, the two ureters entering the back of the bladder, which is a muscular bag situated in the front part of the cavity of the pelvis. Urine collects in the bladder and is expelled from it through a tube leaving its under-surface. This tube is called the urethra and in the male is contained in the penis.

The nervous system

The nervous system consists of the brain, the spinal cord, and the nerves that issue from them. The brain, in the cavity of the skull, is a mass of nervous tissue. The coordinating centre of the body, it acts like a computer, receiving messages through the incoming (sensory) nerves and the special nerves connected with sight, smell, hearing, etc., deciding on the action necessary, then sending out orders to the various parts of the body by the outgoing (motor) nerves.

The spinal cord is composed of similar tissue; it leaves the under-surface of the brain through an opening in the base of the skull and passes down a canal in the vertebral column. To pursue the analogy with a computer, it contains the trunk lines running between the brain and the various parts of the body and also a number of local nerve centres. At intervals down the spinal column, nerve trunks issue from the spinal cord containing both motor and sensory fibres; these nerves make contact with the muscles, which they cause to contract, and with the skin and other organs, where the sensory messages to the brain and spinal column start.

Autonomic nervous system

This is a fine network of nerves which help control the functions of various organs in the body. It, too, has local nerve centres, such as the solar plexus, which is situated in the upper part of the abdomen behind the stomach. Although connected with certain parts of the brain, it is not controlled by the will but functions automatically day and night. It regulates the rate at which the heart pumps, in accordance with the demands of the various bodily systems at any particular time. It also helps control the muscles of the stomach and intestine and the rate and depth of breathing.

Skin

The skin covers and protects the body. It consists of two layers. The outer layer is hard, contains no blood vessels or nerves, and protects the inner layer, where the very sensitive nerve-endings lie. The skin contains numerous sweat glands, the roots of the hair, and special glands that lubricate the skin and the hair.

Sweat consists of water, salt, and other substances. Sweating cools the body and helps to regulate its temperature.

Regions of the body

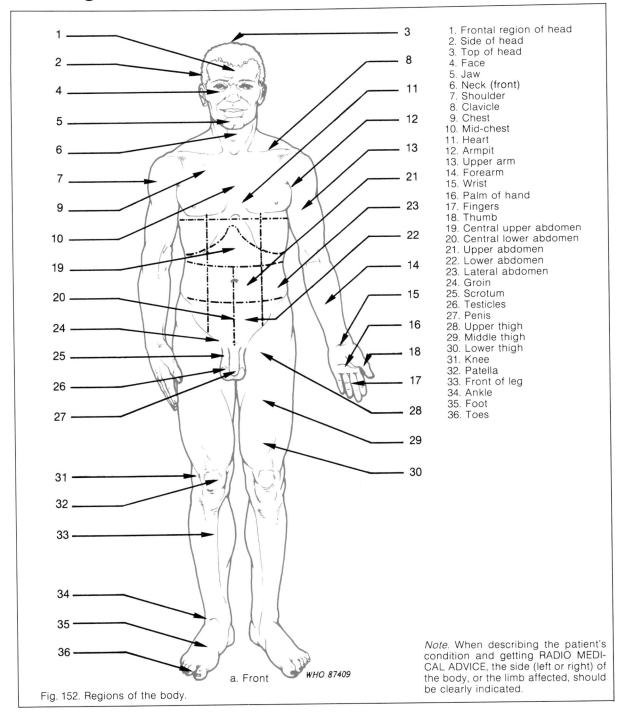

1. Frontal region of head
2. Side of head
3. Top of head
4. Face
5. Jaw
6. Neck (front)
7. Shoulder
8. Clavicle
9. Chest
10. Mid-chest
11. Heart
12. Armpit
13. Upper arm
14. Forearm
15. Wrist
16. Palm of hand
17. Fingers
18. Thumb
19. Central upper abdomen
20. Central lower abdomen
21. Upper abdomen
22. Lower abdomen
23. Lateral abdomen
24. Groin
25. Scrotum
26. Testicles
27. Penis
28. Upper thigh
29. Middle thigh
30. Lower thigh
31. Knee
32. Patella
33. Front of leg
34. Ankle
35. Foot
36. Toes

a. Front   WHO 87409

Fig. 152. Regions of the body.

Note. When describing the patient's condition and getting RADIO MEDICAL ADVICE, the side (left or right) of the body, or the limb affected, should be clearly indicated.

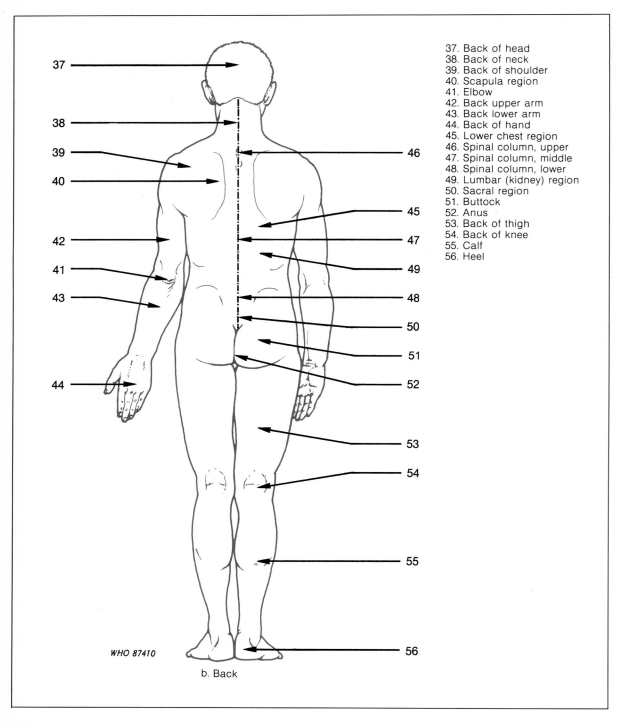

37. Back of head
38. Back of neck
39. Back of shoulder
40. Scapula region
41. Elbow
42. Back upper arm
43. Back lower arm
44. Back of hand
45. Lower chest region
46. Spinal column, upper
47. Spinal column, middle
48. Spinal column, lower
49. Lumbar (kidney) region
50. Sacral region
51. Buttock
52. Anus
53. Back of thigh
54. Back of knee
55. Calf
56. Heel

WHO 87410

b. Back

Weights and measures and their approximate equivalents

Weights

1 kilogram (kg)	= 1000 grams (g)
	≃ 2.2 pounds (1b)
1 g	= 1000 milligrams (mg)
	≃ 15 grains (gr)
453 g	≃ 1 lb
28 g	≃ 1 ounce (oz)
1 oz	≃ 480 grains
1 gr	= 60 mg

Note. Care must be taken not to confuse 1 gram (abbreviated g) with 1 grain (abbreviated gr): 1 gram of a medicament would be 15 times stronger than 1 grain.

Liquid capacity

1 litre (l)	= 1000 millilitres (ml)
	≃ 35.2 fluid ounces (UK) (fl oz (UK))
	≃ 33.8 fl oz (US)
1 decilitre (dl)	= 0.1 litre
	≃ 3.5 fl oz (UK)
	≃ 3.4 fl oz (US)
568 ml	= 1 pint (UK)
	= 20 fl oz (UK)
473 ml	= 1 pint (US)
	= 16 fl oz (US)
28 ml	= 1 fl oz (UK)
30 ml	= 1 fl oz (US)
5 ml	= 1 teaspoonful

Note the difference between measures of liquid capacity in the UK and US systems:

1 pint (US)	≃ 0.8 pint (UK).

Annex 4

Medical report form
for seafarers

For completion by ship's doctor or master, and hospital or doctor ashore, in cases of illness or injury affecting seafarers.

Note. Copies of this form should be provided for the seafarers' medical records, ship's master (or his representatives), and hospital/doctor ashore.

For completion by ship's master:

Date _____

Surname of patient, other names _____

Date of birth _____   Name of ship _____

Nationality _____   Shipowner _____

Seafarer's registration no. _____   Name of ship's representative/agent on shore _____

Shipboard position held _____   Address and telephone no. of ship's representative on shore _____

Details of illness or injury. Treatment received on board ship (enclose attachments if necessary) _____

_____

_____

_____

Date of onset of illness _____   Date injury occured _____

Date work ceased on board _____

For completion by hospital or examining doctor on shore [a]

Diagnosis _____

_____

_____

Date when patient first examined _____

[a] Full medical documentation should be attached, as necessary.

Details of
specialized examinations _____

_____

_____

_____

_____

_____

_____

Treatment given (generic names
of drugs, dosage, route of
administration) _____

_____

Further treatment to be
given on board ship _____

_____

Precautions to be
taken on board ship _____

_____

Other observations of hospital or examining doctor _____

YES   NO

Should see another doctor? [ ] [ ]   When? Specify speciality,
                                          if necessary _____

Is the illness contagious   [ ] [ ]   Estimated duration
or infectious?   of illness _____

Fit for normal work now   [ ] [ ]

Fit for normal work from   _____ (indicate date)

Fit for restricted work   [ ]   Specify _____

Unfit for work   [ ]   For how many days? _____

Bed rest necessary   [ ]   For how many days? _____

Recommended to be

– repatriated   [ ]   YES   NO   YES   NO
                                         Air transport [ ] [ ]   Should be   [ ] [ ]
– hospitalized   [ ]   recommended?   accompanied?

Name of doctor (in capital letters, written or
stamped), position held, address, telephone number _____

_____

Place and date _____ Signature of doctor _____

_____

Annex 5

Disinfection procedures

Procedure for disinfection of water systems with chlorine[1]

The chlorine compounds that may be used for disinfecting water systems are chlorinated lime, high-test calcium hypochlorite, or commercially prepared sodium hypochlorite solution. Chlorinated lime and sodium hypochlorite solution can be readily purchased. As these compounds deteriorate on exposure to air, they should be purchased in small containers, which should be tightly closed after use. All such products should be kept in a cool, dark place. The following instructions should be followed in the disinfection of potable-water systems by means of chlorine compounds:

(a) Thoroughly scrub the storage tanks and flush the tanks and distribution system with potable water.

(b) Determine the volume of water necessary to fill the tanks and distribution system completely; the amount of disinfecting agent required can then be determined from Table A1. When chlorine compounds or solutions other than those mentioned in the table are used, the dosages should be adjusted accordingly.

(c) Prepare the chlorine solution as follows.

Chlorinated lime. Place the appropriate amount of chlorine compound in a clean, dry bucket. Add a small amount of water, and mix to a thick paste. Dilute the paste by adding water gradually and stirring constantly until 4–8 litres of solution are ob-

Table A1. Amount of chlorine compound required for a 50-ppm (50 mg/litre) solution

Capacity of system (including tanks and piping) (litres)	Amount of chlorine coumpound required			
	Chlorinated lime 25% (kg)	High-test calcium hypochlorite 70% (kg)	Sodium hypochlorite solution	
			5% (litres)	10% (litres)
1 000	0.2	0.07	1	0.5
5 000	1	0.4	5	2.5
10 000	2	0.7	10	5

tained (warm water is better than cold for this purpose). Allow the solution to stand for 30 minutes, so that the undissolved particles may settle to the bottom. Pour off the clear liquid (the chlorine solution), if necessary filtering it through muslin or cheesecloth.

High-test calcium hypochlorite. Place the required amount in a bucket, fill with water to within a few inches of the top, and stir until the powder is dissolved (disregard any slight turbidity).

Sodium hypochlorite solution. No preparation required.

(d) Introduce the chlorine solution into the potable-water tanks.

(e) Immediately after the introduction of the chlorine solution, the tanks should be completely filled with potable water. The turbulence of the incoming water will generally ensure adequate mixing.

(f) Open the taps and outlets of the distribution system nearest the storage tanks, and allow the water to flow until chlorinated water appears. Working outwards from the tanks, open successively the other taps and outlets until all have been flushed with chlorinated water. Care should be taken to ensure that the pressure tank is filled with chlorinated water. Since a certain amount of the chlorinated water will have been drawn from the storage tanks, they should be refilled to overflowing, and chlorine solution should be added, if necessary, to make up the concentration in the tanks to 50 ppm (50 mg/l).

---

[1] This procedure has been chosen for inclusion here because of the relative ease with which chlorine compounds can be procured and used for the required purpose. There are various alternative methods; disinfection with agents other than chlorine may be preferred, or the national health administration may prefer to issue its own instructions.

(g) The chlorinated water should be allowed to remain in the storage tanks and the piping system for at least 4 hours before it is discharged. In an emergency, the contact time may be shortened to 1 hour by increasing the dosage to 100 ppm (100 mg/l).

(h) After this contact period, the tanks and distribution system should be drained and flushed with potable water until the water no longer has an objectionable taste of chlorine.

(i) Fill the storage tanks with potable water.

Procedure for disinfection of potable water with chlorine

Disinfection of the water, whether regular or intermittent, should be accomplished by methods approved by the national health administration. When chlorine is the accepted disinfectant, the following procedure should be used.

The chlorine should preferably be applied in the form of a hypochlorite solution, using a commercial hypochlorinator designed for the purpose. It is desirable to apply the chlorine in direct proportion to the flow rate of the water being treated. Therefore, an automatic, proportional control hypochlorinator should be used. It should be constructed or equipped so that the flow of the hypochlorite solution may be observed. Its capacity should be determined on the basis of the maximum flow rate of the water and the treatment required to produce a satisfactory chlorine residual (not less than 0.2 ppm (0.2 mg/litre) of free chlorine). A sampling cock should be provided at an appropriate place in the system for taking test samples to check the residual chlorine and the operating efficiency of the feeder. A commercial testing kit for determining the residual chlorine should be obtained with the hypochlorinator.

When water is treated regularly by chlorination, provision should be made for a baffled holding-tank of sufficient capacity to provide a suitable contact period for the chlorine and water. This period of contact should end before any water is delivered to the next treatment unit or the distribution system, and should be computed on the basis of maximum rate of flow through the contact tank. The contact period should be at least 30 minutes, with a free chlorine residual of at least 0.2–0.5 ppm (0.2–0.5 mg/litre).

For checking the effectiveness of water chlorination, the residual chlorine present in water samples can be estimated by a chlorimetric test. Commercial equipment is available for this purpose, and an appropriate kit can be carried on board ship. The manufacturer's instructions provided with the kit should be closely followed.

The use of liquid chlorine presents the hazard of escaping gas, and the space requirements for the acceptable installation and operation of equipment and the storage of reserve cylinders are considerable.

Joint ILO/WHO Committee on the Health of Seafarers

Geneva, 15–21 September 1981

Members

Dr Chew Pin Kee, Occupational Health Physician and Consultant, Singapore Industrial Health Service, Singapore

Dr B. Marschall, Medical Director, Institute for Occupational and Social Hygiene, Karlsruhe, Federal Republic of Germany *(Chairman)*

Mr E. Raeng, Counsellor, Norwegian Shipping Federation, Oslo, Norway

Mr D. Seaman, Director, Professional and Welfare Services, Merchant Navy and Airline Officers' Association, London, England

Dr E. Shani, ZIM Israel Navigation Co. Ltd, Haifa, Israel

Mr M. Sorensen, General Secretary, Danish Merchant Navy Officers' Association, Copenhagen, Denmark *(Vice-Chairman)*

Mr F.J. Whitworth, International Shipping Federation, London, England *(Vice-Chairman)*

Representatives of the Inter-Governmental Maritime Consultative Organization[1]

Dr H. Ebert, Medical Director, Transportation Medical Service of the German Democratic Republic, Rostock, German Democratic Republic

Mr L.M. Goll, Head, Cargoes Section, Maritime Safety Division, IMCO, London, England

Mr J.E. Hand, Department of Trade, Marine Division, London, England *(Co-Rapporteur)*

Dr S.M. Raper, Guy's Health District, Poisons Unit, New Cross Hospital, London, England

Observers invited by ILO

Seafarers

Mr M. Condiotti, International Organization of Masters, Mates, and Pilots, New York, NY, USA

Mr B.E. Lanpher, International Organization of Masters, Mates, and Pilots, New York, NY, USA

Mr J. Luciani, President, Argentine Engineering Officers' Union, Buenos Aires, Argentina

Mr A. Selander, Assistant General Secretary, International Transport Workers' Federation, London, England

Dr A. Turnbull, Honorary Medical Adviser, Merchant Navy Airline Officers' Association, London, England

Shipowners

Dr S.S. Larsen, Danish Shipowners' Association, Copenhagen, Denmark

Dr R.F. Russell, Professor of Ship's Medicine, Maine Maritime Academy, Castine, ME, USA

Dr O.W. Tenfjord, Medical Superintendent, Wilhelmsen Shipping, Oslo, Norway

Dr E.N. Watson, International Shipping Federation Limited, London, England

Observers invited by WHO

Dr B.R. Blais, Fleet Surgeon, Department of the Navy, Washington, DC, USA

Dr G.I. Kurenkov, Deputy Director, Institute of Hygiene of Water Transport, Moscow, USSR

Dr T.L. McCasland, Director, Public Health Service Hospital, San Francisco, CA, USA

---

[1] Since the meeting, the name of this organization has been changed to the International Maritime Organization (IMO).

Mr J. Stuer, World Confederation of Labour, Brussels, Belgium

Secretariat

Mr T. Braida, Maritime Branch, ILO, Geneva, Switzerland

Dr B. Bedrikow, Occupational Safety and Health Branch, ILO, Geneva, Switzerland

Dr M. A. El-Batawi, Chief Medical Officer, Office of Occupational Health, WHO, Geneva, Switzerland

Mr B. K. Nilssen, Chief, Maritime Branch, ILO, Geneva, Switzerland *(Joint Secretary)*

Dr S. Tomaszunas, Medical Officer, WHO Regional Office for South-East Asia, New Delhi, India *(Co-Rapporteur)*[1]

Dr C. Xintaras, Scientist, Office of Occupational Health, WHO, Geneva, Switzerland *(Joint Secretary)*

---

[1] Dr S. Tomaszunas continued as a consultant to the Office of Occupational Health, WHO, during the period 1982–83, to assist in the implementation of the recommendations of the Joint ILO/WHO Committee on the Health of Seafarers.

Index